Media Resources Featured in

MYLITERATURELAB.COM

FICTION

Toni Cade Bambara *The Lesson*: About the Author, Longman Lecture, Comprehension Quiz, Essay Questions

Raymond Carver About the Author, Bibliography

Kate Chopin *The Story of an Hour*: About the Author, Critical Overview, Bibliography, Longman Lecture, Comprehension Quiz, Essay Questions

Louise Erdrich *The Red Convertible*: About the Author, Comprehension Quiz, Essay Questions

William Faulkner *A Rose for Emily*: About the Author, Critical Overview, Bibliography, Critical Essay and Questions, Comprehension Quiz, Essay Questions

Nathanial Hawthorne *The Birthmark*: About the Author, Critical Overview, Bibliography, Comprehension Quiz, Essay Questions

Ernest Hemingway About the Author, Bibliography

Shirley Jackson *The Lottery*: About the Author, Critical Essay, Comprehension Quiz, Essay Questions

James Joyce About the Author, Bibliography

D. H. Lawrence About the Author

Bharati Mukherjee *A Father*: About the Author, Comprehension Quiz, Essay Questions

Joyce Carol Oates *Where Are You Going, Where Have You Been?*: About the Author, Critical Overview, Bibliography, Longman Lecture, Comprehension Quiz, Essay Questions

Tim O'Brien *The Things They Carried*: About the Author, Longman Lecture, Comprehension Quiz, Essay Questions

Flannery O'Connor About the Author

John Steinbeck *The Chrysanthemums*: About the Author, Comprehension Quiz, Essay Questions

John Updike *A & P*: About the Author, Critical Overview, Bibliography, Interactive Reading, Evaluation Questions, Student Essay, Critical Essay, Writing Prompts, Comprehension Quiz, Essay Questions

Alice Walker *Everyday Use*: About the Author, Critical Overview, Longman Lecture, Bibliography, Student Essay, Comprehension Quiz, Essay Questions

Eudora Welty *Why I Live at the P.O.*: About the Author, Longman Lecture, Lecture Questions

POETRY

Matthew Arnold "Dover Beach": Audio

Elizabeth Bishop "One Art": About the Author, Critical Overview, Bibliography, Longman Lecture, Critical Essay and Questions

Gwendolyn Brooks "We Real Cool": About the Author, Critical Overview, Bibliography, Interactive Reading, Critical Essay and Questions, Comprehension Quiz, Essay Questions

Robert Browning "My Last Duchess": About the Author, Longman Lecture, Audio Essay, Video, Critical Essay, Student Essay

Billy Collins "Introduction to Poetry": About the Author, Critical Overview, Bibliography, Evaluation Questions, Writing Prompts

E. E. Cummings "anyone lived in a pretty how town": About the Author, Critical Overview, Bibliography, Audio, Critical Essay, Comprehension Quiz, Essay Questions

Emily Dickinson "Because I Could Not Stop for Death": About the Author, Critical Overview, Bibliography, Longman Lecture, Lecture Questions, Comprehension Quiz, Essay Questions

"Wild Nights-Wild Nights!": Critical Overview, Audio

John Donne "Death Be Not Proud": About the Author, Critical Overview, Bibliography, Audio

"A Valediction: Forbidding Mourning": Critical Overview, Evaluation Questions, Writing Prompts

(continued)

LITERATURE
and the
WRITING PROCESS

Backpack Edition

Elizabeth McMahan
Illinois State University

Susan X Day
University of Houston

Robert Funk
Eastern Illinois University

Linda S. Coleman
Eastern Illinois University

Longman
Boston Columbus Indianapolis New York San Francisco
Upper Saddle River Amsterdam Cape Town Dubai London Madrid
Milan Munich Paris Montréal Toronto Delhi Mexico City
São Paulo Sydney Hong Kong Seoul Singapore Taipei Tokyo

Senior Editor: Vivian Garcia
Senior Supplements Editor: Donna Campion
Executive Marketing Manager: Joyce Nilsen
Production Manager: Jacqueline A. Martin
Project Coordination and Electronic Page Makeup: Elm Street Publishing Services/
Integra Software Services Pvt. Ltd.
Senior Cover Design Manager: Nancy Danahy
Cover Designer: Nancy Sacks
Cover Image: Lake Moraine, Banff, Alberta, Canada © AlphaDoug/Alamy
Photo Researcher: Pearson Image Resource Center/Kathy Ringrose
Image Permission Coordinator: Joanne Dippel
Senior Manufacturing Buyer: Roy L. Pickering, Jr.
Printer and Binder: R. R. Donnelley, Crawfordsville
Cover Printer: R. R. Donnelley, Crawfordsville

For permission to use copyrighted material, grateful acknowledgment is made to the
copyright holders on pp. 753–756, which are hereby made part of this copyright page.

Library of Congress Cataloging-in-Publication Data

Literature and the writing process:backpack edition/Elizabeth
McMahan...[et al.].—1st ed., Backpack ed.
  p. cm.
Includes bibliographical references and index.
ISBN-13: 978-0-205-73072-8 (alk. paper)
ISBN-10: 0-205-73072-8 (alk. paper)
1. College readers.   2. English language—Rhetoric—Problems, exercises, etc.
3. Report writing—Problems, exercises, etc.   4. Literature—Collections.
PE1417.M453 2010
808'.0427—dc22

                                                                        2010030261

6 7 8 9 10—DOH—16 15 14

Longman
is an imprint of

PEARSON

www.pearsonhighered.com

ISBN-13: 978-0-205-73072-8
ISBN-10: 0-205-73072-8

Contents

Contents by Genre

Drama

Thematic Table of Contents

Preface

This book grew out of our long-standing interest in the possibilities of integrating the study of literature with the practice of composition. Many of our students have learned to write perceptively and well using literature as their subject matter. Great literature is always thought-provoking, always new. Why not utilize it to sharpen critical thinking and improve writing skills? Toward that end, we have combined an introduction to literature anthology with detailed instruction in the writing process.

Our Purpose

This backpack version of *Literature and the Writing Process* contains almost all of the writing instruction from the full-length edition. The primary difference is that the backpack version includes fewer literary selections for students to read, analyze, and write about. The backpack version supplements the seven stories, seventeen poems, and two plays within the writing-instruction chapters with collections of seventeen short stories, sixty-four poems, and five plays. But the main goal is the same for both versions: to guide students through the allied processes of analytical reading and argumentative writing. To accomplish this goal, the rhetorical instruction is carefully integrated with the critical study of literature. As our book's title indicates, *Literature and the Writing Process* shows students how to write essays about the elements involved in interpreting short stories, poems, and plays.

Our Organization

The book is divided into four main parts:

- **Part I, Composing: An Overview,** provides a thorough introduction to the composing process as it applies to writing about literature. This part contains individual chapters on prewriting, writing (drafting), and rewriting. A separate chapter, "Writing a Convincing Argument," provides detailed instruction and numerous examples on the most effective ways to argue an interpretation of a literary selection. Part I also includes a chapter on researched writing, which offers instruction in planning, researching, and documenting a paper with secondary sources, along with an updated description of the MLA Style for citing and crediting these sources.
- **Part II, Writing About Short Fiction,** begins with a brief introduction on how to read short stories, followed by five chapters on writing about the individual elements of fiction: structure, imagery and symbolism, point of view, setting and atmosphere, and theme. Each chapter focuses

on a story that clearly illustrates the literary technique to be studied. This part also contains an anthology of seventeen short stories.

- **Part III, Writing About Poetry,** begins with a brief chapter on reading poetry, followed by three chapters on writing about key elements in poetry: persona and tone, poetic language, and poetic form. These chapters focus on poems that illustrate the literary concepts under discussion. This part also contains an anthology of fifty-one poems; a group of six paired poems for comparison; and a thematic portfolio of seven poems about war.

- **Part IV, Writing About Drama,** begins with an introductory chapter on how to read a play, followed by two chapters on writing about structure and character in drama with each chapter focusing on a particular play. This part also contains an anthology of five plays.

These four parts are supplemented by a concise discussion of Critical Approaches for Interpreting Literature. We also include a Thematic Table of Contents for instructors who favor a thematic approach to literary study.

Student Writing Samples

These eight examples of critical writing model how to analyze and interpret literature:

- The complete composing protocol that a student followed in developing her interpretation of James Joyce's "Eveline," including samples of prewriting, drafting, post-draft outlining, revising, editing, and the final draft (Chapters 1, 2, and 4).
- A paper illustrating the use of claims, evidence, and reasoning in arguing an interpretation of Dagoberto Gilb's "Love in L.A." (Chapter 3).
- An expanded and documented version of the paper on "Eveline" (Chapter 5).
- The second and final drafts of a paper on symbolism in Shirley Jackson's "The Lottery" (Chapter 7).
- A response paper on persona and tone in A. E. Housman's "To an Athlete Dying Young" (Chapter 13).
- The second and final drafts of a paper on imagery in John Donne's "A Valediction: Forbidding Mourning" (Chapter 14).
- A paper on form and meaning in Robert Frost's "The Silken Tent" (Chapter 15).
- A paper on the gender conflict in Sophocles's *Antigone* (Chapter 17)

Our Appreciation

We are grateful to the reviewers whose comments and suggestions helped us craft this backpack edition: Booker T. Anthony, Fayetteville State University; Consuella Bennett, Morehouse College; Melanie R. Benson, University of Hartford; Bethany Blankenship, University of Montana Western; Jeana DelRosso, College of Notre Dame of Maryland;

Dr. Deborah De Vries, Oxnard College; Bonnie Dowd, Montclair State University; Mary Dutterer, Howard Community College; Kimberly Fangman, Southeast Community College; Gayle Gaskill, St. Catherine University; Sally Jayne Gilpin, Collin County Community College; Dwonna N. Goldstone, Austin Peay State University; Catherine Keohane, Montclair State University; James Knippling, University of Cincinnati; Deborah Miller, University of Georgia; Chivas Sandage, Westfield State College; Linda E. Smith, Fort Hays State University; Frederick Smock, Bellarmine University; Ronald J. Tulley, The University of Findlay; Susan Vervaet, Montclair State University; and Jessica Walker, University of Georgia.

Thanks also to the Pearson staff who assisted us in producing the backpack edition: our editor, Vivian Garcia; her editorial assistant, Heather Vomero; and Jacqueline A. Martin, production manager. We would also like to thank Sue Nodine, our incomparable project editor at Elm Street Publishing Services.

To Dan LeSeure, Brian Carter, Bill Weber, and Casey Sutherland: our undying appreciation for their continued inspiration, support, and comfort.

Elizabeth McMahan
Susan X Day
Robert Funk
Linda S. Coleman

PART I

Composing: An Overview

This text serves a dual purpose: to enable you to enjoy, under-stand, and learn from imaginative literature; and to help you to write clearly, intelligently, and correctly about what you have learned. Our instruction is designed to guide you through the interrelated processes of analytical reading and critical writing. Part I begins with the prewriting process and then shows you how to follow through to the completion of a finished essay about a literary work. In this section we also offer a sepa-rate chapter on how to use the elements of argument in writing about literature, and we conclude with detailed instruction on how to incorporate secondary sources into your writing.

1

The Prewriting Process

Your study of writing, as we approach it in this book, will focus on the composing process: prewriting, writing, rewriting, and editing. The first part of the text takes you through each stage, explaining one way of putting together a paper on James Joyce's "Eveline." The following parts, which include more short stories, plus poems and plays, offer further advice for understanding and writing about these various kinds of literature.

We realize, of course, that our chronological, linear (step-by-step) explanations of the writing process are not entirely true to experience; most of us juggle at least two of the steps at a time when we write. We put down half a sentence, go back and revise it, make notes of some details to include later in the essay, and then finish the sentence, perhaps crossing out and correcting a misspelled word—a combination of prewriting, writing, rewriting, and editing. We have adopted the linear, step-by-step presentation because it allows us to explain this complicated process.

Reading for Writing

To prepare for your study of the stages of writing an essay about a literary topic, find a comfortable spot and read the following short story.

 James Joyce   1882–1941

James Joyce rejected his Irish Catholic heritage and left his homeland at age twenty. Though an expatriate most of his adult life, Joyce wrote almost exclusively about his native Dublin. His first book, *Dubliners* (1914), was a series of sharply drawn vignettes based on his experiences in Ireland, the homeland he later described as "a sow that eats its own farrow." His novel *Ulysses* (1933) was banned for a time in the United States because of its coarse language and frank treatment of sexuality; it is now often ranked as the greatest novel of the twentieth century.

Eveline

She sat at the window watching the evening invade the avenue. Her head was leaned against the window curtains and in her nostrils was the odour of dusty cretonne. She was tired.

Few people passed. The man out of the last house passed on his way home; she heard his footsteps clacking along the concrete pavement and afterwards crunching on the cinder path before the new red houses. One time there used to be a field there in which they used to play every evening with other people's children. Then a man from Belfast bought the field and built houses in it—not like their little brown houses but bright brick houses with shining roofs. The children of the avenue used to play together in that field—the Devines, the Waters, the Dunns, little Keogh the cripple, she and her brothers and sisters. Ernest, however, never played: he was too grown up. Her father used often to hunt them in out of the field with his blackthorn stick; but usually little Keogh used to keep nix and call out when he saw her father coming. Still they seemed to have been rather happy then. Her father was not so bad then; and besides, her mother was alive. That was a long time ago; she and her brothers and sisters were all grown up; her mother was dead. Tizzie Dunn was dead, too, and the Waters had gone back to England. Everything changes. Now she was going to go away like the others, to leave her home.

Home! She looked round the room, reviewing all its familiar objects which she had dusted once a week for so many years, wondering where on earth all the dust came from. Perhaps she would never see again those familiar objects from which she had never dreamed of being divided. And yet during all those years she had never found out the name of the priest whose yellowing photograph hung on the wall above the broken harmonium beside the coloured print of the promises made to Blessed Margaret Mary Alacoque. He had been a school friend of her father. Whenever he showed the photograph to a visitor her father used to pass it with a casual word:

"He is in Melbourne now."

She had consented to go away, to leave her home. Was that wise? She tried to weigh each side of the question. In her home anyway she had shelter and food; she had those whom she had known all her life about her. Of course she had to work hard, both in the house and at business. What would they say of her in the Stores when they found out that she had run away with a fellow? Say she was a fool, perhaps; and her place would be filled up by advertisement. Miss Gavan would be glad. She had always had an edge on her, especially whenever there were people listening.

"Miss Hill, don't you see these ladies are waiting?"

"Look lively, Miss Hill, please."

She would not cry many tears at leaving the Stores.

But in her new home, in a distant unknown country, it would not be like that. Then she would be married—she, Eveline. People would treat her with respect then. She would not be treated as her mother had been. Even now, though she was over nineteen, she sometimes felt herself in danger of her father's violence. She knew it was that that had given her the palpitations. When they were grow-ing up he had never gone for her, like he used to go for Harry and Ernest, be-cause she was a girl; but latterly he had begun to threaten her and say what he would do to her only for her dead mother's sake. And now she had nobody to

A late nineteenth-century photo of Fade Street in Dublin, which conveys a sense of the neighborhood where Eveline grew up.

protect her. Ernest was dead and Harry, who was in the church decorating business, was nearly always down somewhere in the country. Besides, the invariable squabble for money on Saturday nights had begun to weary her unspeakably. She always gave her entire wages—seven shillings—and Harry always sent up what he could but the trouble was to get any money from her father. He said she used to squander the money, that she had no head, that he wasn't going to give her his hard-earned money to throw about the streets, and much more, for he was usually fairly bad on Saturday night. In the end he would give her the money and ask her had she any intention of buying Sunday's dinner. Then she had to rush out as quickly as she could and do her marketing, holding her black leather purse tightly in her hand as she elbowed her way through the crowds and returning home late under her load of provisions. She had hard work to keep the house together and to see that the two young children who had been left to her charge went to school regularly and got their meals regularly. It was hard work— a hard life—but now that she was about to leave it she did not find it a wholly undesirable life.

She was about to explore another life with Frank. Frank was very kind, manly, open-hearted. She was to go away with him by the night-boat to be his wife and to live with him in Buenos Ayres where he had a home waiting for her. How well she remembered the first time she had seen him; he was lodging in a house on the main road where she used to visit. It seemed a few weeks ago. He was standing at the gate, his peaked cap pushed back on his head and his hair tumbled forward over a face of bronze. Then they had come to know each other. He used to

10

meet her outside the Stores every evening and see her home. He took her to see
The Bohemian Girl and she felt elated as she sat in an unaccustomed part of the
theatre with him. He was awfully fond of music and sang a little. People knew
that they were courting and, when he sang about the lass that loves a sailor, she
always felt pleasantly confused. He used to call her Poppens out of fun. First of
all it had been an excitement for her to have a fellow and then she had begun to
like him. He had tales of distant countries. He had started as a deck boy at a
pound a month on a ship of the Allan Line going out to Canada. He told her
the names of the ships he had been on and the names of the different services. He
had sailed through the Straits of Magellan and he told her stories of the terrible
Patagonians. He had fallen on his feet in Buenos Ayres, he said, and had come
over to the old country just for a holiday. Of course, her father had found out
the affair and had forbidden her to have anything to say to him.

"I know these sailor chaps," he said.

One day he had quarrelled with Frank and after that she had to meet her
lover secretly.

The evening deepened in the avenue. The white of two letters in her lap
grew indistinct. One was to Harry; the other was to her father. Ernest had been
her favourite but she liked Harry too. Her father was becoming old lately, she
noticed; he would miss her. Sometimes he could be very nice. Not long before,
when she had been laid up for a day, he had read her out a ghost story and made
toast for her at the fire. Another day, when their mother was alive, they had all
gone for a picnic to the Hill of Howth. She remembered her father putting on
her mother's bonnet to make the children laugh.

Her time was running out but she continued to sit by the window, leaning
her head against the window curtain, inhaling the odour of dusty cretonne.
Down far in the avenue she could hear a street organ playing. She knew the air.
Strange that it should come that very night to remind her of the promise to her
mother, her promise to keep the home together as long as she could. She remembered the last night of her mother's illness; she was again in the close dark
room at the other side of the hall and outside she heard a melancholy air of Italy.
The organ-player had been ordered to go away and given sixpence. She remembered her father strutting back into the sickroom saying:

"Damned Italians! coming over here!"

15

As she mused the pitiful vision of her mother's life laid its spell on the very
quick of her being—that life of commonplace sacrifices closing in final crazi-
ness. She trembled as she heard again her mother's voice saying constantly with
foolish insistence:

"Derevaun Seraun! Derevaun Seraun!"[1]

She stood up in a sudden impulse of terror. Escape! She must escape! Frank
would save her. He would give her life, perhaps love, too. But she wanted to live.
Why should she be unhappy? She had a right to happiness. Frank would take
her in his arms, fold her in his arms. He would save her.

She stood among the swaying crowd in the station at the North Wall. He held
her hand and she knew that he was speaking to her, saying something about the
passage over and over again. The station was full of soldiers with brown bag-
gages. Through the wide doors of the sheds she caught a glimpse of the black

---

[1]"The end of pleasure is pain!"

mass of the boat, lying in beside the quay wall, with illumined portholes. She answered nothing. She felt her cheek pale and cold and, out of a maze of distress, she prayed to God to direct her, to show her what was her duty. The boat blew a long mournful whistle into the mist. If she went, tomorrow she would be on the sea with Frank, steaming towards Buenos Ayres. This passage had been booked. Could she still draw back after all he had done for her? Her distress awoke a nausea in her body and she kept moving her lips in silent fervent prayer.

A bell clanged upon her heart. She felt him seize her hand: 20
"Come!"
All the seas of the world tumbled about her heart. He was drawing her into them: he would drown her. She gripped with both hands at the iron railing.
"Come!"
No! No! No! It was impossible. Her hands clutched the iron in frenzy. Amid the seas she sent a cry of anguish.
"Eveline! Evvy!"   25
He rushed beyond the barrier and called to her to follow. He was shouted at to go on but he still called to her. She set her white face to him, passive, like a helpless animal. Her eyes gave him no sign of love or farewell or recognition.

(1914)

Now that your reading of Joyce's story has given you material to mull over, you should consider some questions that good writers think about as they prepare to write. Granted, experienced writers might go over some of these *prewriting* matters almost unconsciously—and perhaps *as* they write instead of before. But in order to explain how to get the process going for you, we will present these considerations one by one.

Who Are My Readers?

Unless you are writing a journal or a diary for your own satisfaction, your writing always has an *audience*—the person or group of people who will read it. You need to keep this audience in mind as you plan what to say and as you choose the best way to express your ideas.

Analyze the Audience

No doubt you already have considerable audience awareness. You would never write a job application letter using the latest in-group slang, nor would you normally correspond with your dear Aunt Minnie in impersonal formal English. Writing for diverse groups about whom you know little is more difficult than writing for a specific audience whom you know well. In this class, for instance, you will be writing for your fellow students and for your instructor, a mixed group sorted together by a computer registration system. Although they are diverse, they do share some characteristics. For one thing, when you begin to write a paper about "Eveline," you know that your audience has read the story; thus, you need not summarize the plot. Also, the people in your audience are college-educated (or becoming so); therefore, you need not avoid difficult words like *epitome*, *eclectic*, or *protean* if they are the appropriate choices. Other shared qualities will become apparent as you get to know your classmates and your instructor.

Prewriting Exercise

Compose a brief letter persuading Eveline that she should (or should not) leave Frank. Your argumentative tactics, your attitude, and even your word choice must be affected by what you know about Eveline from reading the story—her essential timidity, her insecurity, her self-doubt, her capacity for self-deception. Take all this into account as you present your argument for or against leaving Frank.

Then, write briefly to her bullying father explaining to him why his dutiful daughter has deserted him (assuming she has gone).

Finally, write Frank a short letter explaining why Eveline will not be going away with him (assuming she stays in Dublin).

Be prepared to discuss with the class specific ways in which your letters are different when you change your audience. Read at least one other student's letters to see how another writer handled the tasks.

Why Am I Writing?

Every kind of writing, even a grocery list, has a purpose. You seldom sit down to write without some aim in mind, and this purpose affects your whole approach to writing. The immediate response to the question "Why am I writing?" may be that your teacher or your employer asked you to. But that answer will not help you understand the reasons that make writing worth doing—and worth reading.

Reasons for Writing

Sometimes you may write in order *to express* your own feelings, as in a diary or a love letter. More frequently, though, you will be writing for several other people, and the response you want from these prospective readers will determine your purpose. If, for instance, you want your audience to be amused by your writing (as in an informal essay or friendly letter), your purpose is *to entertain*. If you want your readers to gain some knowledge from your writing (say, how to get to your house from the airport), then you are writing *to inform*. If you want your readers to agree with an opinion or to accept an idea (as in a letter to the editor or an advertisement), then you are writing *to persuade*. Of course, these aims overlap—as do most things in the writing process—but usually one purpose predominates.

Most of your writing in this course, as in real life, will be an argument one way or another. Your purpose is often to convince your reader to agree with the points you are making. Logical ideas set down in clear, interesting writing should prove convincing and keep your readers reading.

Prewriting Exercise

In writing the three letters to various characters, you have already noticed how audience and purpose can change the way you think and write about "Eveline." After studying the four writing suggestions that follow, reread the story. You may discover that you have more ideas and feelings about it than you first imagined. Thinking about prospective readers and determining your purpose will help you understand your own views and reactions better.

1. If your purpose is *to express* your personal response:
   Write down your feelings about Eveline in a journal entry or in a brief note to a close friend. Do you sympathize with Eveline? Pity her? Does she irritate you or make you angry? Be as forthright as you can.

2. If your purpose is *to inform* someone else:
   Write a brief summary (less than one hundred words) of "Eveline" for a fellow student who wants to know if the story is worth reading.
   Write a slightly longer summary for your instructor (or someone else who has read the story) who wants to know if you have grasped its important points.
   Which summary was easier to write? What purposes besides providing information were involved in each summary?

3. If your purpose is *to entertain* yourself or your readers:
   How would you rewrite the ending of "Eveline" to make it more positive or romantic—to make it appeal to a wider audience? Would such an ending be consistent with the earlier parts of the story? Would it be true to human experience?

4. If your purpose is *to persuade* your readers:
   The author tells us that Eveline held two letters in her lap, but we do not know their contents. Write your version of one of them. Try to construe from evidence in the story what Eveline would have said to convince her father or her brother that she had good reasons for going away with Frank. How would she persuade them to forgive her? Consider also what other purposes Eveline would try to achieve in each of these letters.

What Ideas Should I Use?

Understanding literature involves learning what questions to ask yourself as you read. To deepen your comprehension and develop ideas for writing, you need to examine the work carefully and think critically about its component parts.

Reading and Thinking Critically

Critical reading and thinking involves several overlapping procedures: analysis, inference, synthesis, and evaluation. The word *critical* does not mean "disapproving" or "faultfinding" in this context; it means thorough, thoughtful, inquisitive, and logically demanding. As a critical reader you want to discover meanings and relationships that you might otherwise miss in uncritical, superficial reading.

- *Analysis* involves examining the parts or elements of a work, the better to understand it.
- *Inference* entails drawing conclusions about a work based on your analysis. When you infer, you explore the implications of various elements (such as plot, characterization, structure, tone) and interpret their meaning.
- *Synthesis* is the process of putting your analysis and inferences together into a new, more informed understanding of the work. You create this new understanding by making connections, identifying patterns, and drawing conclusions.
- *Evaluation* means defending the judgments you have made about a work's meaning, significance, or quality.

Chapters 6, 12, and 16—"How Do I Read Short Fiction?" "How Do I Read Poetry?" and "How Do I Read a Play?"—provide specific suggestions and questions to guide you in analyzing, making inferences, synthesizing, and evaluating literary works. Here are some suggestions and questions from those chapters, along with their critical reading basis.

Example of Questions Inviting Analysis

What is the central conflict of the play? Does the play contain any secondary conflicts (subplots)? How do they relate to the main conflict?

Example of Questions That Require Inferences

Who is the main character? Does this person's character change during the course of the story? Do you feel sympathetic toward the main character? What sort of person is she or he?

Example of Questions Involving Synthesis

What is the theme (the central idea) of this poem? Can you state it in a single sentence?

Example of Evaluation Questions

Which of the poems conveys the horrors of war most effectively? Why?

Discovering and Developing Ideas

You read critically to derive meaning from a work, and you continue to think critically as you go about discovering ideas to write about. This discovery process, called **invention**, is more effective if you employ one of the following techniques designed to help you analyze literary works and generate ideas about them.

Self-Questioning

These are the kinds of questions you might ask yourself when studying a work of literature: questions about characters, their circumstances, their motives and conflicts, their fears and expectations, their relations with other characters; questions about the setting in which the story takes place; questions about any repeated details that seem significant; questions about the meaning and value of actions and events. Write out your responses to these questions about "Eveline" and keep them handy as you formulate your essay.

1. What is Eveline's home life like?
2. How does she expect her new life to be different?
3. Do you think this expectation is realistic?
4. Why is the word *dust* mentioned so often?
5. List all the concrete details you can find that describe Eveline's home.
6. How old is Eveline? Is her age important for any reason?
7. What sort of person is her father? What kind of "bad way" is he in on Saturday nights?
8. How does Eveline feel about her father?
9. What sort of person was Eveline's mother? What happened to her? Does Eveline identify with her mother in any way?
10. How does Eveline feel about her dead mother?
11. What do you think her mother meant when she kept repeating "the end of pleasure is pain"? Why would she say this? Was she really crazy—or only worn down?
12. What does Eveline's father mean when he tells her, "I know these sailor chaps"? What possible reasons could he have for trying to break up Eveline's romance?
13. What sort of person is Frank? What does Eveline actually know about him?
14. Has Eveline romanticized Frank in any way? Is her father's objection to him perhaps justified?
15. What is Eveline's duty to her father? What promise did she make to her dying mother?
16. What is her duty to herself? Does she really believe she has a "right to happiness"? Why or why not?
17. How does Eveline feel about leaving her brother?
18. In what ways is Eveline "like a helpless animal"? What is she afraid of?
19. Why do you think her eyes give Frank "no sign of love or farewell or recognition"?
20. Do you think Eveline made the right decision? Why or why not?

During the invention stage, you want to turn up as many ideas as possible. Later, after choosing a focus for your paper, such as characterization or theme, you will select those story details that you will be discussing when developing your argument. Even though you narrow your focus, you still need to consider other elements of the story—imagery, symbolism, setting, point of view—as these elements serve to reveal character or theme.

Directed Freewriting

Many people find that they can best bring ideas to the surface by writing freely, with no restrictions about correctness. When you engage in *freewriting* in order to "free" ideas from your subconscious mind, you should think of a pertinent question and just start writing.

Consider this question: "Why does Eveline stay with her abusive father?" As you think, start writing. Set down everything that comes to mind; do not concern yourself with spelling, word choice, or punctuation. You are writing for your own benefit, attempting to discover everything about Eveline's decision that you have in mind after reading and thinking about the story.

After writing for ten minutes (or after you run out of ideas), stop and read over what you have said. Underline any idea that might serve as the focus for a paper. Put stars or asterisks in the margin beside any ideas that sound useful as support for your interpretation. Figure 1-1 provides an example of freewriting turned out by a student on this same question.

If you find freewriting a good method for generating ideas, you may want to go through the process again. This time write down a statement that you underlined in your first freewriting as a possible approach for your paper. Let's say you decide to focus (as our student did) on the idea that Eveline's sense of insecurity causes her to remain with her father. Put that sentence at the top of a fresh sheet of paper and begin writing. Continue recording your thoughts until you either run out of ideas or run out of time (fifteen minutes is usually enough). Then read over your freewriting, underlining or putting stars by any ideas that you think would be good support to include in your paper.

Problem Solving

Another method of generating material for a paper involves *problem solving*. Consider some part of the work that you feel you need to understand better and pose yourself a problem, like the following:

Explain the ending of the story so that it is understandable and believable.

As you seek a solution, ask yourself more questions.

- Why does Eveline refuse to leave her pinched, narrow life with her father and the younger children?
- Is there anything about the way she was brought up that makes this action seem reasonable, perhaps inevitable?
- Would her life have been different if she had been born male instead of female? What happened to her brothers, for instance?
- Does her religion have any bearing on her decision?

Write down all the reasons you can find to help explain why Eveline does not leave home. Do any of these reasons shed light on the overall meaning of the story? Do you now perhaps see a meaningful point you could develop into an essay?

Clustering

Another useful way of getting ideas out of your head and down on paper involves *clustering*. Begin with a blank sheet of paper. In the center, write a crucial question about the story that you want to investigate, and circle the words. Then, draw a line out from that circle, write an idea or a question related to the central idea, and circle that.

Why does Eveline stay? She feels a sense of duty - to her mother (dying wish/promise) ✦ Father old, lonely, needs her to keep house. She needs to be <u>loved</u>, feel she belongs. ✦ Naturally she's afraid to leave home for the first time - and go so far away. She's ✦ <u>insecure</u>. But she's 19 - must want to test her wings, have a better life than her poor mother's. She's suffocating there in all that dust! Frank offers freedom + romance - and <u>fun</u>. She thinks she likes him, may even love him - but not sure. Her father has warned her about Frank. And how ✦ much does she actually know about him? What if he's all promises, promises - and then deserts her halfway around the world? Maybe her father's right! How does she ✦ feel about her parents? She knows her mother's life was miserable + she died a pitiful death. She fears her father (who ✦ must have caused a lot of her mom's misery + hardship) But E. <u>has a strong sense of duty.</u> And does love her father, despite his faults.

Figure 1-1   Directed Freewriting

Spiraling out from that circle, add and circle any further associations that you can make. Continue drawing lines from the center, like spokes radiating from a wheel, and record any other ideas or questions that are related. When you finish, you will have a cluster of related

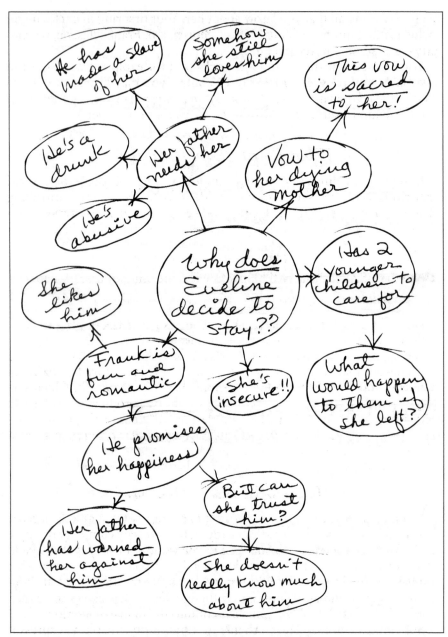

Figure 1-2 Clustering

ideas resembling Figure 1-2, which explores the question "Why does Eveline decide to stay with her father?"

Clustering works just fine with statements, as well as with questions. If you think you might want to write a paper focusing on the characterization of Eveline, you could just write her name in the center of the page and begin recording all that you know about her. Your first ring of circles might include father, mother, siblings, house, church, job, Frank, lifestyle, personality—and spiral out from there.

You can see that this technique works well for exploring any aspect of a work. As you progress through this course, you may decide to write in the middle of the page *point of view*, *setting*, *imagery*, or whatever element you think might serve as a meaningful focus for your paper.

What Point Should I Make?

Besides providing a thorough understanding of the story, these prewriting activities serve to stir up ideas for a *thesis*—the controlling idea for your paper—and to help you discover evidence to support convincingly the observations you will make in developing that thesis.

Relate a Part to the Whole

One bit of advice that will help you write meaningful literary papers is the following:

> Devise a thesis that makes its point by relating some aspect of the work to the meaning of the whole—that is, to its theme.

Our questions so far have led you to approach Joyce's story by analyzing character and plot. But writing a simple character sketch (in which you discuss what sort of person Eveline is) would not produce a satisfactory critical paper. You need to go beyond that one-dimensional approach and make your essay say something about the story itself. In short, you must argue that your analysis of her character relates to the theme.

How Do I Find the Theme?

You may have learned that the *theme* of a work is the moral. In a sense that is true, but a moral suggests a neatly stated, preachy comment on some vice or virtue, whereas a literary theme will seldom be so pat and should never sound preachy. In order to discover theme you need to decide what you have learned from reading the story. What did the author reveal about the behavior of human beings, about the conduct of society? Rather than looking for a moral, look for some insight into the human condition.

Sometimes you may have a theme in mind but be unable to express it except in a cliché. You could, for instance, see the theme of "Eveline" as an acceptance of the old adage "Better the devil you know than the devil you don't." Although this idea is acceptable as a theme, a clearer statement would relate the concept more closely to the story, as follows:

> In "Eveline," Joyce focuses on the painful choices a young woman faces concerning her desire for a better life, her duty to her family, and her fear of leaving home.

Certainly her character—the kind of person she is—relates directly to this theme. If, for instance, Eveline had been a willful, disobedient child who grew up into a rebellious, irresponsible young woman, the outcome of the story would surely be different.

The problem is thus to find a thesis that will allow you to argue that Eveline's upbringing has conditioned her for the inevitable failure of nerve, the return to servitude and security, the relinquishing of hopes and dreams.

Stating the Thesis

A good thesis statement should be a *complete sentence* that clearly conveys the point you plan to support in your argument. Notice the difference between a *topic*, which is not a complete sentence, and a ***thesis***, which is.

Topic   A characterization of Eveline

Thesis   Joyce's characterization of Eveline as a dutiful daughter enables us to discover why she makes her strange decision at the end.

Topic   The role of the church in "Eveline"

Thesis   The role of the Catholic church is crucial in shaping Eveline's personality and in helping us understand why she sacrifices herself for her family.

Topic   Dust as a symbol in "Eveline"

Thesis   Joyce's use of dust as a controlling symbol in "Eveline" reinforces our understanding of this young woman's dreary, suffocating, arid life.

Your thesis sentence should be broad enough to include all the ideas that are necessary as evidence but narrow enough to make a precise statement of your main point and focus your thoughts. If your thesis is too broad—as, for example, "Joyce's characterization of Eveline is extremely well drawn"—you may end up skimming the surface, never providing a meaningful interpretation of the work. A thesis evaluating the excellence of Joyce's character development needs to connect this point with the whole story. Notice that the previous overly broad thesis is unsatisfactory for another reason: it fails to make a real point.

A better thesis for a paper on "Eveline" might be stated in any of the following ways:

Eveline's Catholic upbringing as a dutiful daughter makes impossible her hopes for a happier life.

If Eveline had been born male instead of female, she might have escaped her unhappy home life, as her brother did.

Eveline, "trapped like a helpless animal" by her promise to her dying mother, is morally unable to break her vow and flee her miserable home to seek a new life for herself.

Having been thoroughly beaten down by her brutal, domineering father, Eveline lacks the self-confidence to flee in search of her own life.

Most of the ideas and details you need to support any of these thesis statements will appear in the freewriting or clustering that you have already completed. In the next chapter, we will suggest some ways in which you might arrange this material in the paper itself.

2

The Writing Process

Now that you have examined your reactions to "Eveline," collected your ideas, and formulated a thesis sentence, you are ready to organize this material into a workable arrangement for writing.

How Should I Organize My Ideas?

A traditional but effective format includes three parts: the beginning (the introduction), the middle (the body), and the end (the conclusion). This simple plan will serve for almost any piece of writing.

The *beginning* of the paper has two main functions: to engage your readers' interest and to let them know what point you expect to make. The *middle* portion of your paper develops and supports the main point with details, examples, reasons, and explanations that make the general thesis more specific and more understandable. The *end* of the paper returns your readers to the main point by spotlighting the general idea you want them to accept after reading your essay. Later in the chapter, we will offer you more specific suggestions about how to begin and end a paper effectively. For now, we want to wrestle with the problem of organizing the body—or the middle part—of your paper about "Eveline."

Arguing Your Interpretation

If you want your readers to accept your interpretation of "Eveline," you have to convince them that your point of view is valid. In other words, an interpretation is an argument, and you can organize your essay according to the standard features of argumentative writing.

The Elements of Good Argument

Claims, evidence, reasoning, and *refutation* are the building blocks of effective **argument**; you need to understand and use them in order to write persuasively. Knowing how these elements work together will also help you organize your thoughts more effectively.

Claims   The "engine" that propels any argument is its *claim*. In various kinds of writing, claims are also called propositions, premises, conclusions, hypotheses, or recommendations. In literary criticism, a claim is usually called a *thesis*, the term we use in this book. The sample thesis "Eveline lacks courage to flee from her domineering father and to seek her own happiness" makes a claim about the title character; it also implies that explaining her behavior is a meaningful way to interpret the story as a whole. The primary claim is usually broken down into several secondary claims, or *topic sentences*, that justify and explain the main thesis.

Evidence   Evidence tells your readers how you arrived at your interpretation and shows them what your claims are based on. Most of the evidence in literary argument will come from within the reading—details and examples from the work itself. In some cases, evidence can come from your own experience; for example, your observation that people often fear the unknown might support an analysis of Eveline's motivation. Some of your evidence may also come from outside the text; for example, you might use information about the situation of Catholic working-class women in Ireland in the early 1900s and connect it to Eveline's decisions.

Reasoning   The thinking process you use to connect the evidence to your claims is called *reasoning*. Sometimes the point or validity of the evidence is obvious, but more often than not you need to explain how you arrived at your interpretation. For example, you can identify words and phrases from the story that indicate Eveline is afraid of her father, but you probably should explain how you arrived at that conclusion and why you think this fear could extend to all men, including Frank. This way, your reader can share your line of reasoning.

Refutation   Arguments always assume that other points of view are possible. In literary criticism, the case for your interpretation will be strengthened if you treat other possible readings with respect and understanding. Acknowledging and responding to these other views is called *refutation*. There is no best place to refute opposing opinions. Sometimes you will want to bring up other interpretations early and deal with them right away. Another approach is to anticipate objections as you argue your own interpretation point by point. Many writers add a refutation section after they have presented the evidence and reasoning on their own side. Wherever you include the refutation, your goal is to show why other interpretations are faulty or inaccurate or limited. Often, you will be able to present contrasting evidence or alternate reasoning to reveal both the weakness of another view and the strength of your own position.

Building an Effective Argument

Presenting a conventional argument involves five tasks.

1. Introduce the subject you are going to write about—for example, Eveline's decision not to go with Frank—and supply some context for your approach.
2. State your main point or thesis. This is your *claim.*
3. Provide *evidence* and *reasoning* to support your claims. This will be the longest part of your argument; each secondary claim will probably take a paragraph or more to develop.
4. Respond to opposing viewpoints. This is called the *refutation.*
5. Sum up your argument by reminding your readers of your thesis and the strength of your evidence.

Writers often alter this conventional order of tasks, especially steps 3 and 4. For example, in the sample student essay at the end of Chapter 4, the author considers several possible answers to her thesis question before presenting her main claim in the last two paragraphs. In other words, the writer rejects, or refutes, other interpretations before advancing her own.

Following are two brief plans for a literary argument based on one of our sample thesis statements. The first plan states the thesis, or claim, and indicates the subpoints that will become topic sentences for several paragraphs of development and support.

1. *Beginning:* Eveline lacks courage to flee from her domineering father and to seek her own happiness.
2. *Middle:* Evidence of Eveline's lack of courage can be seen in the following:
   —her passivity as a female who lacks the resources and imagination to challenge her traditional role
   —her physical fear of her father, perhaps generalized to all men
   —her reverence for her mother's memory and the promise she made to keep the family together
3. *End:* Eveline exemplifies how a woman may be trapped by passivity, fear, and obligations.

The second plan organizes the middle of an argument on the same thesis by stating the topic sentences as fears that contribute to Eveline's lack of courage. These topic sentences act as secondary claims that support and explain the main interpretation.

2. *Middle:* Eveline's lack of courage is illustrated in these ways:
   —She is afraid to go against her religious beliefs.
   —She is afraid something will happen to her father if she leaves him.
   —She is afraid her mother's memory will continue to haunt her.
   —She is afraid Frank will treat her as her father treated her mother.

By writing out the subpoints, you provide yourself with a plan to follow in writing the paragraphs that will make up the main part (the body) of your essay. Chart 2-1 offers a checklist for arguing an interpretation.

Arranging the Ideas

As you write the middle section of your argument, you will have to decide which point to take up first and which ones to use later in the development of your main claim. Ordinarily, you can arrange your secondary claims in two ways: logical order or chronological order.

Logical order involves arranging ideas in a way that will appeal to your readers' intelligence and good sense. Many writers begin with a less crucial idea and work up to their most important one. The logic behind this arrangement is based on the assumption that since your final point is the one your readers are most likely to remember, it should also be your strongest point.

In the second plan for writing just presented to you for a paper on "Eveline," the topic sentences about fears are arranged according to the increasing strength of Eveline's feelings. The plan starts with a general point about religion, moves to more specific fears about leaving her father and remembering her mother, and concludes with an insight into what could happen in her life with Frank. The last idea is particularly appropriate, because it sums up the previous two points by relating Eveline's anxiety about Frank to her feelings about her parents' relationship.

Chronological order, which is based on time, involves writing about events in the order in which they occur. Most narratives, such as short stories and novels, use a chronological approach. Because you will be

---

Chart 2-1   Checklist for Arguing an Interpretation

1. Make sure your interpretation is reasonable and consistent.
2. Express your interpretation in a clear thesis statement.
3. Write an introduction that states your thesis and indicates briefly how you intend to support it.
4. Place the key claims of your argument in topic sentences.
5. Present your claims in a clearly defined, logical order.
6. Provide plenty of specific evidence to back up your interpretive claims.
7. Make explicit the links between your interpretation and the evidence you provide.
8. Avoid getting bogged down in mere summary.
9. Anticipate objections to your interpretation and address them in your paper.
10. Write a conclusion that recaps your argument and highlights the significance of your interpretation.

writing about literature, your organization for a paper could simply follow the chronology of the work under consideration. If you do this, be sure that your essay clearly reflects a critical thinking process, or your paper will seem like a mere plot summary.

Developing with Details

The balance between your interpretive points and the details you use to support them is critical. If your argument goes too far in the interpretive direction, it sounds too abstract, personal, and unconvincing. If it goes too far in listing details, it seems as though you are summarizing the work rather than analyzing it. Let us look further into maintaining an effective balance.

Within your argument, you will make several critical generalizations relating to your main point. These are the topic sentences that bolster the thesis. Remember to state each generalization clearly and to support each one with enough specific references to the story to be convincing. Sort through the observations that you made in your prewriting, and select those that relate to the topic sentences in your plan. The following example shows how a writer uses specific details and brief quotations from the story to develop the idea stated in the topic sentence:

> Eveline lacks courage to seek a life of her own because she fears that her father will not be able to cope if she leaves him. Her anxiety is heightened as she recalls that she and her brothers and sisters are grown up and that her mother is dead. If she leaves, her father will be all alone. She realizes that he is "usually fairly bad on a Saturday night" and recognizes that his drinking problem will not get any better after she leaves. Also she has noticed that "Her father was becoming old lately" and she assumes that "he would miss her." As a dutiful daughter, Eveline seems to feel that going away with Frank means abandoning her aging father, and that may be why she has written a letter to him—to ease the blow of her departure and to soothe her own conscience.

Questions for Consideration

In the preceding example, is there adequate support for the topic sentence? What story details has the writer cited to develop the main point? What other details could be used? Where does the writer bring in personal opinion or interpretation? Do you think the interpretation is reasonable?

Maintaining a Critical Focus

The placement of your analytical content affects how a reader perceives your argument. Even with a solid interpretation, your paper could still sound like a plot summary if you imbed your critical insights in the middle of paragraphs. In order to achieve a sharp critical focus, the topic sentences (usually the first one of each paragraph in the body of the paper) should be critical observations supporting or relating to your thesis. In academic writing, placing the topic sentences at the beginnings of paragraphs helps your instructor to follow your thinking. You should, in each paragraph, use the plot details to support or prove the critical generalization in the topic sentence.

Distinguishing Critical Comments from Plot Details

The difference between a critical comment and a plot detail or poetry detail is illustrated in these sample sentences:

Plot detail	Jackson's story opens on a balmy summer day.
Critical comment	By setting her story on a balmy summer day, Jackson creates a false sense of well-being.
Plot detail	"Seventeen Syllables" begins with a communication problem between the teenager Rosie and her mother.
Critical comment	The first scene, a communication breakdown between the teenager Rosie and her mother, introduces the conflict between first- and second-generation immigrants to the United States.
Poetry detail	In Brooks's poem "Sadie and Maud," Sadie's life is described more fully than Maud's.
Critical comment	Brooks describes Sadie's life more fully than Maud's, suggesting that Sadie lived more fully.

(Notice that authors can be referred to by their last names: "Jackson" is Shirley Jackson and "Brooks" is Gwendolyn Brooks.)

Plot detail	Larry eventually identifies with his father in "My Oedipus Complex."
Critical comment	Larry provides a humorous model of Freud's developmental theory.
Combined	Larry's final identification with his father resolves his Oedipus complex in a humorous rendering of Freud's developmental theory.

How Should I Begin?

Your introduction is crucial to the effectiveness of your essay—and often proves to be the most difficult to write. Try to think of this part as challenging (rather than merely hard to do), and you may find yourself rising to new heights of accomplishment.

Postpone If Nothing Comes

Remember that you do not have to write your introduction first just because it appears first in the finished essay. As long as you have your thesis clearly in mind (or clearly written out on your planning sheet), you can start right in on the body of the paper. Once you begin generating material, you may suddenly perceive an idea that will serve nicely as a beginning. Or if you postpone your introduction until the next day, your subconscious mind may provide you with the perfect opening. You may find that some of your best ideas come to you in the shower.

Write an Appealing Opening

Work especially hard on your opening sentence. You want to engage the interest of your readers immediately. If you begin like this,

> "Eveline" is a very interesting short story by James Joyce.

no one other than your loving mother is likely to read any further unless paid to. You should mention the author and title somewhere in your introduction (even though both may appear in your title). But try also to incorporate something specific in that first sentence. You might want to focus your readers' attention on an incident that you consider significant.

> In his short story "Eveline," James Joyce portrays a young woman paralyzed by the need to make a decision that will change the course of her life.

Or you could start this way:

> In James Joyce's "Eveline," we see a tired young woman accustomed to the "odour of dusty cretonne" trying to muster courage to exchange her dreary existence for the unknown excitements of life with a "sailor chap" in exotic Buenos Ayres.

Or you might try this:

> In the closing lines of James Joyce's "Eveline," the young woman of the title stands "passive, like a helpless animal," watching her dreams of romance and excitement fade into the mist.

State the Thesis

Even more important than an arresting opening sentence is the need to let your readers know somewhere in the introductory paragraph what the paper is going to be about. But try to avoid stating your main point too bluntly.

> I am going to show that Eveline stays home with her domineering father because she lacks courage to go with Frank.

Beginning the thesis with "I am going to show" is stylistically ineffective because that part is understood—any thesis at all could begin with those words. They waste the first few words of the sentence, words that should be full of meaning. Instead, describe the direction of your thought, the case that you will present within your essay, using vivid language. Your thesis should sound more like this:

> Having been thoroughly beaten down by her brutal, domineering father, Eveline lacks the courage to go with Frank in search of her own happiness.

That sentence includes some psychologically powerful words—*beaten down, brutal, domineering, courage,* and *happiness*—which invite a reader to continue.

If you combine your thesis with a general statement about the story, you should produce a worthwhile introduction for a short paper.

> In James Joyce's "Eveline," we see a tired young woman accustomed to the "odour of dusty cretonne" trying to muster courage to exchange her dreary existence for the unknown excitements of life with a "sailor chap" in exotic Buenos Ayres. But having been thoroughly beaten down by her brutal father, Eveline lacks the courage to go with Frank in search of her own happiness.

How Should I End?

Your conclusion is just as important as your introduction—perhaps even more so. You want to leave your readers feeling satisfied that you have written something worth reading, that their time has not been wasted. Do not give them a chance to ask, "Well, so what?" at the end.

Relate the Discussion to Theme

Impress your readers with the value of your discussion by reinforcing in the conclusion how your analysis illuminates the theme, or meaning, of the work. This process may involve echoing your thesis statement from the introduction. But take care to avoid simply repeating what you said at the beginning. Your conclusion should offer a clear expression of how your discussion relates to the theme of the story.

Postpone or Write Ahead

Conclusions, like introductions, do not necessarily have to be written when you come to them. If you should get some additional insight concerning the theme as you work on composing the main part of the paper, take a minute to jot down the idea so that you can later incorporate this insight into your ending. Or you could stop right then, write the final paragraph, and put it aside until you come to it. Chances are that you may change this conclusion later, but having something to work with is an enormous help—especially if you are getting tired.

Write an Emphatic Final Sentence

No matter how exhausted you are when you compose your final paragraph, do not risk ruining the effect of your entire essay by letting your conclusion trail off at the end with a limp last sentence. Regardless of the brilliance of your argument, your readers are going to feel let down if you end like this:

> All in all, I think "Eveline" was a fine story, and I think anyone would enjoy reading it and maybe even learn something from it.

One student's final paper on "Eveline" (which you will read in its entirety later) closes briefly, yet effectively:

> Afraid of failing on her own, Eveline retreats into the familiar, telling herself that life with father cannot be as frightening as a risky, unknown life with Frank. So strong is her fear of failure that it overrides her fear of her father. She seems to decide that a predictable—if dreary and abused—life is better than a life without security or pattern.

Composing the First Draft

At this point you should be ready to compose the first draft of your essay on "Eveline." You have completed the prewriting activities, devised a working thesis statement, arranged your main supporting points, and selected plenty of details to use for development. You may even have written some of your introduction and conclusion. Now is the time to move beyond these preliminary stages and write a complete draft of your paper.

Pausing to Rescan

You may have been told to get your first draft down on paper as quickly as possible and then, once it is completed, to revise it. This is probably not bad advice if you suffer from writer's block, but recent studies show that most skilled writers go about it in a different way. Experienced writers tend to pause frequently as they compose—to scan and perhaps reword what they have just written; to think about what to say next; to make additions, substitutions, or deletions; to be sure a sentence says what they want it to say.

If you tend to write headlong without pausing once you begin, perhaps you should try to slow down. Mina Shaughnessy, a noted composition expert, speaks of "the messy process that leads to clarity" in writing. This messy process involves pausing and thinking and reviewing in order to write well.

Quoting from Your Sources

The Modern Language Association (MLA) has set a standard way to credit a source when you quote material in an essay. If you are using only a single *primary* source—the work of literature under discussion—you cite in parentheses after the quotation the page (or pages) on which you found that material.

> Eveline admits that hers is "a hard life," yet decides "now that she was about to leave it she did not find it a wholly undesirable life" (5).

If you are using more than one primary source, you need to include the author's last name in the parentheses—with only a single blank space separating it from the page number—unless you mention the author's name in the text of your paper.

> At the end of the story Eveline is "like a helpless animal" (Joyce 7), and Hulga at the end is similarly helpless, "left sitting on the straw in the dusty sunlight" (O'Connor 130).

(*Note:* If you are using library sources, the situation becomes more complicated. Consult Chapter 5 for complete instruction in writing researched papers.)

The Source Citation Even if you are citing only your primary source, let your readers know what it is. If you use direct quotations, you will include page numbers in your paper, and readers need to know which book those page numbers come from. On a separate page at the end of your essay, center the title (Work Cited or Works Cited) at the top. Using double spacing, provide complete publication information for your source or sources. The Work Cited entry for a paper on "Eveline" using the current edition of this text would look like this:

> Joyce, James. "Eveline." *Literature and the Writing Process Compact Edition.* Ed. Elizabeth McMahan et al. Boston: Pearson/Longman, 2010. 3–7. Print.

Notice the *hanging* indention. Indent all lines after the first line five spaces. Use an abbreviated form of the publisher's name—just *Pearson*, not *Pearson Education, Inc.* If you are using more than one source, alphabetize the entries by their authors' last names.

Sample Student Paper: First Draft

The paper that follows is the first draft of an essay on "Eveline" written by Wendy Dennison, a student at Illinois State University. The directed freewriting for this paper appears in Figure 1-1. The comments, suggestions, and questions in the margin were made by Wendy's instructor.

Sample Student Paper: First Draft

1

Wendy Dennison

English 102   *Are there too many*
                                     rhetorical questions?
January 23, 2005

For Fear of Failing Alone

Mention   Eveline, the title character of Joyce's short story,
title of
story here ——→ is given that once-in-a-lifetime chance—to leave her

                 old life to begin a new one. But she rejects the offer
Isn't it
Frank?   Fate—or God—makes, preferring instead to settle

                 back down into the dusty, abusive life she has led.

                 Why does she not go away with Frank? The obvious

                 responses—duty to her mother's dying wish, the love

                 of her father, the love of her home—do not quite ring

                 true, for Eveline owes little or nothing to her parents   *Do you*
                                                                                  want to
                 or her home. In fact, leaving seems a much more logi-   *give away*
                                                                                  your con-
                 cal choice. So why does Eveline really stay behind?   *clusion?*

                 She is afraid of failure. ◄——————————————————————

                     What does Eveline really owe her mother? Her

Does this ¶   "promise . . . that she keep the home together as long
need more
details?   as she could" (6) was unfairly given. It was unfair of

                 her mother to ask such a thing of her, as it prevents

                 her from having a life of her own. It is very likely that

                 Eveline will never marry and leave her father as long

                 as he is alive, for she will always recall that promise.

                 Why stay for this?

                     Why should we be surprised that Eveline might

                 wish to leave her father? An abusive drunk, he has

                 taken advantage of her promise to her mother. She is

                 forced to keep house for him, yet must beg from him

good   money with which to do so. He practically accuses her
intro of
quotation   of stealing, claiming, "she used to squander the money,

                 that she had no head, that he wasn't going to give her

Dennison 2

his hard-earned money to throw about the streets . . ."
(5). A bully, he has scared her with threats of beatings,
giving her "palpitations" (4). Eveline realizes that with
her brothers gone, there is "nobody to protect her" (4)
from her father's rage. Why would she ever want to
stay with a man of whom she is terribly afraid? She did
remember happy moments with him when the family
went on picnics and he was jolly and played with the
children.

Does this detail fit?

    Eveline's home life is so unhealthy that she would
be wise to leave it all behind. For all that she does, she
still does not feel quite a part of everything. For example, she knows nothing about the picture of the priest,
not even his name. The dustiness of the house, of
which Joyce reminds us periodically, is suggestive of
the pervading dirtiness and squalor of her daily life. It
is significant also that she often thinks about her
unpleasant, unhappy job. Her home is clearly not
conducive to happiness. So why does she stay there?

Why is this im- portant?

best word?

Does this fit?

Combine sentences?

    The only real reason why Eveline would stay in
Irelnad is the fact that she is desperately afraid of
failing on her own. If she leaves the familiar, no matter
how unpleasant, she risks failure. "She was about to
explore another life with Frank" (5). The word
"explore" is significant here, as it brings to mind
uncertainty and risk, two factors that Eveline is not
prepared to deal with. She admits that hers "was a
hard life," yet thinks, "now that she was about to
leave it she did not find it a wholly undesirable life"
(5). When she sits in the growing darkness—the threat
of her father returning from work—with the letters in
her lap, Eveline calls up a couple of good memories
to calm her fears, effectively helping to convince
herself to stay home.

Check whole paper for typos

good!

tense shift?

sentence OK?

Dennison 3

Afraid of failing on her own, Eveline retreats into

Is this a good detail to use here?

the familiar, convincing herself that life with father cannot be as frightening as a risky life with Frank. "Why should she be unhappy? She had a right to happiness" (6) Indeed, Eveline decides that a predictable—if abusive and unhealthy—life is better than one without direction or pattern.

Well done, Wendy! But please outline this draft to be sure the material is tightly unified.

Dennison 4

Not
accurate!
Check the
MLA style!

Work Cited

Joyce, James. "Eveline," in <u>Literature and the</u>
<u>Writing Process</u>. By Elizabeth McMahan, Susan X
Day, and Robert Funk. NJ: Prentice Hall, 2005.
Pages 3–7.

3

Writing a Convincing Argument

Y ou can write about literary works in several ways. You can record your reactions and explore how the work affects you personally; you can describe the work for others who might want to read it; you can evaluate the work and tell why you liked or disliked it. But the customary way to write about a literary work is to *interpret* it. Interpreting is also one of the most challenging ways to write about literature. The goal of this chapter is to show you how to develop your opinions about literature and shape them into clear, convincing essays that explain what a literary work means.

Interpreting and Arguing

When you interpret a story or poem or play, you say to other readers, "This is how I read this work; this is what I think it means." Because literary texts are often complex and seldom obvious, you can assume that other readers will not necessarily interpret a work in the same way you do. So, in addition to explaining the meaning, you will also have to convince your audience that your reading is reasonable and well founded. In other words, you will be *arguing* for your interpretation.

Presenting your interpretation as an argument will focus your writing and require you to look more carefully and closely at the literary selection. An effective way to mount an argument for your interpretation is to begin with these two steps:

- Identify an *issue* about the work that you want to discuss.
- Formulate a *claim* that takes a position on the issue.

Identifying Issues

An issue is a subject or problem that people argue about. Many issues about a literary work relate to its *theme*. When you interpret a story or play or poem, you are actually explaining its theme—and arguing for your understanding of that theme. You'll remember in Chapter 1 we offered this advice: "Devise a thesis that makes its point by relating some aspect of the work to the meaning of the whole—that is, to its theme." This strategy of identifying an issue and making a claim about it will help you to write a meaningful literary paper.

A good way to identify an issue is to see it as a question with no obvious or clear answer. In Chapter 1, we recommended that you ask yourself questions as you are reading. This self-questioning will not only generate material to consider using as evidence, but it will also help you to locate the issues in a literary work. For her essay on "Fear of Failure in Joyce's 'Eveline'" (pages 67–70), Wendy Dennison identified this key issue:

> Why does Eveline not go away with Frank when the opportunity seems so attractive?

The issue that Wendy identified is a *major issue*, a question asked by most readers of the story and one that has a number of answers.

There are, of course, other questions that readers ask about "Eveline." Several came out in our prewriting exercises in Chapter 1:

- What is the significance of Eveline's promise to her mother?
- Would Eveline's life have been different if she had been born male?
- What role does religion play in Eveline's decision?
- How realistic is Eveline's romance with Frank?
- Why does the author mention "dust" so often in the story?

These issues are interesting and important, but individually they are *minor issues* that relate to just one part of the story. Identifying a broader issue, however, would make it possible to include some of them as part of a more complete interpretation of the story's themes:

> How did social custom and her religious upbringing condition Eveline to abandon her hopes and dreams for a better life?

The specific issues of gender, religion, and Eveline's promise to her mother could then be used to answer this larger question.

The issues, of course, are quite different in various works of literature, but in working toward a claim, the process remains the same. In preparing to write about Dagoberto Gilb's short story "Love in L. A.," for instance, Brian Carter used the self-questioning approach to identify a couple of issues that he thought would direct him to a convincing interpretation:

- What is the nature of the "love" referred to in the title?
- Who is fooled by Jake's lies?
- What purpose does fantasy serve for Jake?

Making Claims

Once you have identified the issue that will be the center of your interpretation, you are ready to make a claim about that issue. If you stated the issue as a question, then your claim will be an answer to that question. Wendy Dennison answered her issue question with this claim:

> Afraid of failing on her own, Eveline retreats into the familiar, telling herself that life with her father cannot be as frightening as a risky, unknown life with Frank.

Working out an answer to your issue question may require several drafts, and you will probably refine and revise your claim as you are putting your interpretation together.

An effective claim will make a clear, significant assertion about the way you interpret the work's theme. It can also provide a concise preview of the way you are going to develop your case. For example, the issue question about the influence of custom and religion might be answered with this claim:

> Religious and social traditions have trapped Eveline: her Catholic upbringing, her responsibilities as a dutiful daughter, and her promise to her dying mother make it impossible for her to imagine leaving home and seeking a new life for herself.

The answers to issue questions about "Love in L. A." might produce these claims:

> The "love" that exists in L. A., according to this story, is superficial, materialistic, and self-centered.
>
> Jake consciously adapts his performance to fool and manipulate his audience, but he doesn't succeed with Mariana.
>
> Jake's fantasies allow him to avoid the truth: he isn't going anywhere.

If you think a claim is the same as a thesis statement, you're right. The term *claim* makes it clear that you are taking a stand about the meaning of a work and that you will back up your interpretation with ***evidence*** and ***reasoning***.

Using Evidence

As we pointed out in Chapter 2, the evidence in a literary argument tells your audience where you got the ideas for your interpretation. The most important evidence will come from the literary work itself: facts, details, descriptions, incidents, key terms, and phrases. Direct quotations provide clear evidence that your claims are grounded in the text, but you'll want to be smart about quoting from the literary work.

Presumably, your audience has already read the story or poem or play; you need only remind them of passages that support your interpretation. You also have to think about when to summarize and how to use a brief summary to advance your claims. You can summarize an incident or scene to help establish a point or observation—and then explain or interpret that point—but long summaries will detract from your argument. The following example uses material from the story to support a claim that religion plays a role in Eveline's decision. The supporting evidence is highlighted and labeled:

> Eveline's Catholic upbringing is established early in the story. As **she looks around the room, surveying the "familiar objects from which she had never dreamed of being divided" (4),** Eveline takes special note of two items: **an old photograph of the priest who had been a friend of her father's** and **a colored print of the promises made to Blessed Margaret Mary Alacoque.** Then, in the story's final scene, as **she stands in the station, waiting to board the boat,** Eveline **"prayed to God to direct her, to show her what was her duty"** and **"kept moving her lips in silent fervent prayer" (7).**

summary and quotation

specific details

summary

quotations

Brian Carter supported his claim about the "web of falsehoods" Jake weaves for Mariana by listing examples:

> His car has **fake license plates;** he has **no insurance;** he has no intention of paying for his mistake. He claims to have **glamorous occupations,** despite driving **a decrepit '58 Buick.**

specific details

You may also be asked to use evidence from outside the literary work. You might wonder, for instance, why James Joyce mentioned the promises made to Blessed Margaret Mary Alacoque. Information about those promises might be useful in developing and supporting a claim about Eveline's religious upbringing. The process of finding and using evidence in sources outside a literary work is covered in detail in Chapter 5.

Obviously, the more evidence you have, the more convincing your interpretation will be. But facts, details, and quotations by themselves do not make an argument. You have to explain how you are using this evidence to support your interpretation.

Using Reasoning

As we pointed out in Chapter 2, "the thinking process you use to connect the evidence to your claims is called *reasoning*." You'll want to give the *reasons* for drawing your conclusions about a work's meaning. In this excerpt from her essay, Wendy Dennison explained the reasoning behind her claim that Eveline's main problem is fear of the unknown (the explanations are highlighted in bold type):

> **If she leaves the familiar, no matter how unpleasant, she risks failure.** "She was about to explore another life with Frank" (5), we are told, in faraway Beunos Ayres. **The word** *explore* **is significant, as it brings to mind uncertainty and risk, two factors that Eveline is not prepared to deal with.** She admits that hers is "a hard life," yet she thinks that "now that she was about to leave it she did not find it a wholly undesirable life" (5). When she sits in the growing darkness with the letters in her lap, Eveline calls up a couple of good memories—of her father being jolly once on a picnic, of his kindness once when she was sick. **We see her trying to calm her fears, trying to convince herself that her home life is more bearable than it is.**

You can see a clear pattern in the six sentences of this paragraph:

—Make a claim (sentence 1).
—Quote some evidence from the story (sentence 2).
—Interpret the meaning of the evidence (sentence 3).
—Bring up some more evidence (sentences 4 and 5).
—Explain how the evidence supports the claim in the first sentence (sentence 6).

This pattern of stating claims, citing evidence, explaining the evidence, making another (related) claim, and citing more evidence is used time and again in developing an interpretation.

Here's another example that combines evidence and interpretive explanations to support a claim about Eveline's decision. The explanations are highlighted in bold type:

> **Religion plays an important role in shaping Eveline's decision not to leave with Frank.** As she sits by the window, looking at the "familiar objects" that she "had dusted once a week for so many years" (4), she notices a faded photograph of a priest who had once been a school friend of her father. But the priest is in Melbourne now, **having left Eveline's father just as she is planning to do.** Next to the photo is "a coloured print of the promises made to Blessed Margaret Mary Alacoque," **a symbol of devotion to home and family in the Catholic Church.** Margaret Mary Alacoque had a vision in which Jesus promised to bless any home where Alacoque's picture is exhibited, **a promise that parallels the one that Eveline made to her dying mother to "keep the home together as long as she could" (6). The photo and the print indicate how Eveline is tied to her parents; they also remind her of the traditional obligations of a good Catholic daughter. Their religious associations only increase the guilt she feels about trying to make a life for herself.**

In his final paragraph, Brian Carter used reasoning to explain why Jake's character is so transparently foolish:

> We all laugh at such a clown, and it makes us comfortable to know that *we* aren't like Jake. Perhaps, though, while we are off guard, Gilb intends to plant a nagging thought that we *are*—just a little.

Answering Opposing Views

As we explained in Chapter 2, your interpretation will be strengthened if you anticipate and respond to other readings of the work, a process sometimes referred to as *refutation* or *rebuttal*. By definition, your claims are arguable, so you can expect that other readers will not always agree with the way you interpret the evidence. As you plan and draft your interpretation, make a list of all the opposing views you can think of. You can get help from friends and classmates who have also read the literary work. Anticipating other possible readings should cause you to reexamine why and how you arrived at your own point of view. Such a reconsideration will almost certainly help you to refine and deepen your interpretation.

Some writers answer opposing views in a separate section, sometimes immediately after the introduction as a bridge to rest of the essay. Other writers save their refutations until after they have presented their own case. A particularly effective strategy is to handle opposing views point by point as you argue at the same time for your claims, as Wendy Dennison did when weighing the importance of Eveline's promise to her dying mother:

> But surely her promise to "keep the home together as long as she could" (6) was given under extreme circumstances. It was unjust of her mother to ask such a sacrifice of her, and Eveline is aware of the unfairness. . . . Surely that promise cannot be the only reason she stays.

Brian Carter led into his main claim by including an opposing interpretation of Jake:

> Some readers might find Jake too obvious and predictable to be interesting. But his character is drawn large and clueless to make a point.

Wherever you place your response to different readings, your goal is to explain why these views are faulty or incomplete. At the very least you want to show that your reading is just as valid and compelling.

Organizing Your Argument

The conventional structure for arguing your interpretation should include five elements, usually presented in this order:

1. The issue (subject)
2. Your claim about the issue (thesis)
3. The evidence that supports your claim (facts, details, quotations)
4. The reasoning that connects the evidence to your claim (explanations)
5. Your refutation of opposing views (explanations and counterevidence)

As you saw in the examples in this chapter, writers frequently combine elements 3, 4, and 5 (evidence, reasoning, and refutation).

In Chapter 2, we showed you how to arrange the steps for arguing the claim that "Eveline lacks courage to flee from her domineering father and to seek her own happiness" (see page 20). The approach we illustrated in Chapter 2 is called *inductive reasoning*. It is perhaps the most common way of arguing an interpretation. But you can also arrange your arguments in other ways; two common ones are the *counterargument* and the *comparative argument*.

Using the Inductive Approach

An inductive argument moves from specific examples and observations to a general conclusion. It parallels the process you go through when reading a piece of literature: you notice details and points, words and phrases, comments and actions, which add up to your understanding of what the work means. When you reread in order to write about the work, you look even more closely for specifics to confirm your initial reactions, raise possible questions, and build an interpretation. With this accumulation of specific evidence, you can then identify the issues you want to write about and the claims you want to make about those issues.

In planning an inductive argument, you start with your major claim (thesis) and then list the minor claims that support your interpretation. You can see a sample outline for this method on page 20. Here is another example:

Major claim: Eveline doesn't leave with Frank because she subconsciously suspects that he will not really "save her" and "give her life."

Minor claims:

1. Eveline doesn't really know much about Frank.
2. She may recognize that what he has told her is more fiction than fact.
3. She has firsthand knowledge of the duplicity men are capable of.
4. The ending seems to confirm her suspicions.

If you were to flesh out these claims with specific details and explanations, you would be prepared to write a draft.

Major claim: Eveline doesn't leave with Frank because she subconsciously suspects that he will not really "save her" and "give her life." Her doubts and suspicions make it impossible for her to overcome the power of family and religion.

Minor claims:

1. Eveline doesn't really know much about Frank.
   —met only "a few weeks ago"
   —"They had come to know each other"—vague and unclear
   —no last name
2. She may recognize that what he has told her is more fiction than fact, too good to be true.
   —exotic "tales of distant countries" and "terrible Patagonians"
   —why the "pleasantly confused" feeling when he sang "about the lass that loves a sailor"?
   —claims he "had fallen on his feet" in Buenos Aries: vague and without specific content
   —romantic promise of a "home he has waiting for her"
   —father's suspicions: "I know these sailor chaps"
3. She has firsthand knowledge of the duplicity of men.
   —father sometimes nice and thoughtful
   —but also a violent drunk who abused his wife and threatens Eveline
   —would Frank treat her the same way?
4. The ending seems to confirm her suspicions.
   —thought he "would take her in his arms, fold her in his arms"
   —instead he "seize[ed]" her hand and called to her
   —he "rushed beyond the barrier and called to her to follow"—but he did not come back

The inductive plan of Brian Carter's essay would look like this:

Major claim: Through presenting a clownishly self-glorifying character, "Love in L. A." leads the reader to think about the illusions of personal glory in his or her own life.

Minor claims:

1. The metaphor of the cars going nowhere is central: Jake is stuck, with no destination in life, though the situation might appear otherwise.
2. Jake tells plenty of lies about the quality of his life, but doesn't fool Mariana.
3. Jake's failure with Mariana gives him only the slightest self-doubt, and then he returns to his fantasy world.
4. While we are amused at the situation and ridiculing Jake's excesses, our defenses are down, and we remember our own self-inflating fantasies.

Making a Counterargument

You can anticipate how other readers might interpret a work and organize your own interpretation as a point-by-point refutation of those other possible views. This approach is effective for tackling especially complex or controversial selections and for clearing up common misunderstandings. Wendy Dennison, for example, defines her major claim by suggesting how other people might answer the issue (Why does Eveline fail to leave with Frank?) and by talking back to them. After dealing with several other readings of Eveline's motives, Wendy is ready to make the case for her own interpretation.

Arguing through Comparison

Another way to argue an interpretation is to use comparisons. Setting two works or two interpretations side-by-side permits you to use one of them to throw light on the other. Comparison involves looking at similarities; contrast directs attention to differences. But you can combine the two by showing how things that seem to be alike are really different, or vice versa.

The comparison/contrast method follows the notion that we can find out what something *is* by discovering what it is *not*. You can begin by establishing the basis for the comparison (the similarities) and then move on to the features that set the two works apart (the differences). For example, in comparing Dagoberto Gilb's "Love in L. A." (page 45) with John Updike's "A & P" (page 285), you might start by noting that both stories feature a brash, disaffected young man who unsuccessfully tries to impress an attractive young woman. You could then argue that the endings reveal a significant contrast: Jake remains pretty much unenlightened and unchanged, while Sammy realizes he has perhaps made a life-altering decision.

You could also develop an interpretation that shows how two seemingly different characters are alike in several key ways. For example, you could contrast Eveline with Elisa, the main character in John Steinbeck's "The Chrysanthemums" (page 244), pointing out the differences in their age, marital status, personality, attitude toward work, and interaction with the men in their families. After describing their differences, you could then point out two surprising and significant similarities: each woman gets a glimpse of an attractive new life from a charming stranger, but neither one has the courage to break away from her domestic trap.

Organizing a Comparison/Contrast   There are two standard ways of arranging the material in a comparison/contrast. One way is to make all your points about one work first and then to do the same for the second work. You could group all the pertinent details about Eveline in one block, followed by the contrasting points about Elisa in a second block.

This method is relatively easy to handle and works perfectly for showing how things have changed—or, in the case of Eveline and Elisa, have *not* changed. The two stories were written twenty-five years apart and deal with women of very different means and temperament, yet both end up defeated in their effort to find happiness and fulfillment. Eveline is paralyzed "like a helpless animal," and Elisa is "crying weakly—like an old woman."

A second approach involves subdividing your major claim into specific points and explaining how each point relates to one work (or character) and then to the other. The method allows you to emphasize the primary points of comparison (or contrast). But the point-by-point organization can disintegrate into little more than a list of similarities and differences if you fail to relate the points to a unifying claim. Here is a sample plan for an interlocking comparison of the stories "A & P" and "Love in L. A.," focusing on the main characters, Jake and Sammy. The comparison supports the claim that both young men are slackers but that only Sammy appears ready to grow up and move on.

1. Life/work situation
   —Jake: unemployed; main accomplishment is keeping his old car clean and running
   —Sammy: stuck in a dead-end job, taking orders from a boss he doesn't like and being careful not to upset his parents

2. Character and personality
   —Jake: fantasizes mainly about cars; concerned only with showiness and appearances, not with honesty and ethics
   —Sammy: lively, frustrated, judgmental; builds up his low self-esteem by denigrating and stereotyping customers and co-workers

3. Interaction with women
   —Jake: tries to charm and impress Mariana, who is way out of his league; gets her phone number (which may be phony), but can tell that she really doesn't buy his act
   —Sammy: critical and sexist, but very taken with Queenie, mainly because she's aloof and clearly unattainable; quits his job to impress her, but she takes no notice

4. Final realization
   —Jake: unfazed and carefree; resumes driving and fantasizing about his dream car
   —Sammy: sticks to his decision to quit, but realizes "how hard the world was going to be to me hereafter"

Sample Student Essay

In the following essay, student Brian Carter argues for his interpretation of the story "Love in L. A." by Dagoberto Gilb. You can read the story at the end of this chapter on pages 45–47. The main character, Jake, dominates the story and provides the focus for Brian's major claim, which argues for a carefully designed effect on the story's readers. The marginal notes identify key features and strategies in building this argument.

Carter 1

Brian Carter

Professor Day

English 102A

14 October 2008

Lying in L. A.

Dagoberto Gilb's misleading title "Love in L. A."
sets the stage for this short, humorous story
involving a fender bender on a crowded Los Angeles
freeway. This story is not about love, certainly not in
the traditional sense of the word, nor is it about a
minor car accident; it is about something more
profound: our highly prized illusion of personal good
fortune and the fantasies and lies we use to maintain
that illusion. The story establishes its central
metaphor in the first sentence with the phrase
"motionless traffic" (432). The automobile is
supposed to be one of our main keys to personal
freedom, providing the means to a destination—but
not in this case. We are introduced to the main
character, Jake, while he is mentally creating a
detailed fantasy about his quest for the ultimate
lifestyle, achieved through upgrading his automobile.
An FM radio, a velvet interior, heating and cooling
systems—such luxuries would, of course, lead him
to the promised land of "necklaced ladies in satin
gowns, misty and sexy like a tequila ad" (432).

Reality snaps Jake out of his fantasy world when
he hits the car in front of him. Unfortunately, Jake's capacity for self-delusion thrusts him into another equally
ridiculous fantasyland, this time played out in the real
world. In his interactions with Mariana, the victim of
his carelessness, we learn that Jake's
self-concept is built on lies, presumably distilled from
endless practice at imagining what his life should be

Major claim

Minor claim

Evidence: details, quotation

Minor claim

Carter 2

at this stage of development. He clumsily tries to woo Mariana with a web of falsehoods. His car has fake license plates; he has no insurance; he has no intention of paying for his mistake. He claims to have glamorous occupations, despite driving a decrepit '58 Buick. | *Evidence: details*

Mariana is young, lives with her immigrant parents, drives the car her dad bought her, but nonetheless is more worldly-wise than Jake and views him with suspicion. Although Jake interprets her polite smiles as promising, Mariana isn't buying any of his lines, clearly wanting to get the whole accident information exchange over with as soon as possible. Her skepticism about Jake is revealed when she pulls up behind him and writes down the license plate numbers on his car before leaving (434). | *Evidence: reasoning*

Gilb draws the character of Jake quite broadly as a self-deluded fool, although Jake does seem to have a fleeting moment of awareness when he takes "a moment or two to feel both proud and sad" about his interaction with Mariana (434). | *Minor claim*

Perhaps his repeatedly failing efforts to set up a date crack his fantasy shell. However, he immediately repairs it: "His sense of freedom swelled as he drove into the now moving street traffic" (434). | *Evidence: quotation*

Some readers might find Jake too obvious and predictable to be interesting. But his character is drawn large and clueless to make a point. We all laugh at such a clown, and it makes us comfortable to know that *we* aren't like Jake. | *Refutation*

Perhaps, though, while we are off guard, Gilb intends to plant a nagging thought that we *are*—just a little. Haven't most of us been stuck in a traffic jam, imagining some unearned luxuries that would change our lives, oblivious to the fact that we aren't going anywhere? | *Major claim: conclusion*

Carter 3

Work Cited

Gilb, Dagoberto. "Love in L. A." *Literature and the Writing Process.* Ed. Elizabeth McMahan, Susan X Day, and Robert Funk. 8th ed. Upper Saddle River: Prentice, 2007. 432-34. Print.

Dagoberto Gilb 1950–

Dagoberto Gilb was born in Los Angeles, the son of an undocumented immigrant Mexican mother and a Spanish-speaking Anglo father from East Los Angeles. He put himself through college, earning a B.A. and an M.A. in philosophy. He then spent sixteen years as a construction worker, taking time off every few months to write. His collection of stories, *The Magic of Blood* (1993), made him, according to one critic, "the voice of labor and unionism, once even as a headliner alongside legendary folk singer Pete Seegar." He now lives in Austin, Texas, and is a professor in the creative writing program at Southwest Texas State University, in San Marcos.

Love in L. A.

Jake slouched in a clot of near motionless traffic, in the peculiar gray of concrete, smog, and early morning beneath the overpass of the Hollywood Freeway on Alvarado Street. He didn't really mind because he knew how much worse it could be trying to make a left onto the onramp. He certainly didn't do that every day of his life, and he'd assure anyone who'd ask that he never would either. A steady occupation had its advantages and he couldn't deny thinking about that too. He needed an FM radio in something better than this '58 Buick he drove. It would have crushed velvet interior with electric controls for the L. A. summer, a nice warm heater and defroster for the winter drives at the beach, a cruise control for those longer trips, mellow speakers front and rear of course, windows that hum closed, snuffing out that nasty exterior noise of freeways. The fact was that he'd probably have to change his whole style. Exotic colognes, plush, dark nightclubs, mai tais and daiquiris, necklaced ladies in satin gowns, misty and sexy like in a tequila ad. Jake could imagine lots of possibilities when he let himself, but none that ended up with him pressed onto a stalled freeway.

Jake was thinking about this freedom of his so much that when he glimpsed its green light he just went ahead and stared bye-bye to the steadily employed. When he turned his head the same direction his windshield faced, it was maybe one second too late. He pounced the brake pedal and steered the front wheels away from the tiny brake lights but the smack was unavoidable. Just one second sooner and it would only have been close. One second more and he'd be crawling up the Toyota's trunk. As it was, it seemed like only a harmless smack, much less solid than the one against his back bumper.

Jake considered driving past the Toyota but was afraid the traffic ahead would make it too difficult. As he pulled up against the curb a few car lengths ahead, it occurred to him that the traffic might have helped him get away too. He slammed the car door twice to make sure it was closed fully and to give himself another second more, then toured front and rear of his Buick for damage on or near the bumpers. Not an impressionable scratch even in the chrome. He perked up. Though the car's beauty was secondary to its ability to start and move, the body and paint were clean except for a few minor dings. This stood out as one of his few clearcut accomplishments over the years.

Before he spoke to the driver of the Toyota, whose looks he could see might present him with an added complication, he signaled to the driver of the car that hit him, still in his car and stopped behind the Toyota, and waved his hands and shook his head to let the man know there was no problem as far as he was concerned. The driver waved back and started his engine.

"It didn't even scratch my paint," Jake told her in that way of his. "So how   5
you doin'? Any damage to the car? I'm kinda hoping so, just so it takes a little more time and we can talk some. Or else you can give me your phone number now and I won't have to lay my regular b. s. on you to get it later."

He took her smile as a good sign and relaxed. He inhaled her scent like it was clean air and straightened out his less than new but not unhip clothes.

"You've got Florida plates. You look like you must be Cuban."

"My parents are from Venezuela."

"My name's Jake." He held out his hand.

"Mariana."   10

They shook hands like she'd never done it before in her life.

"I really am sorry about hitting you like that." He sounded genuine. He fondled the wide dimple near the cracked taillight. "It's amazing how easy it is to put a dent in these new cars. They're so soft they might replace waterbeds soon." Jake was confused about how to proceed with this. So much seemed so unlikely, but there was always possibility. "So maybe we should go out to breakfast somewhere and talk it over."

"I don't eat breakfast."

"Some coffee then."

"Thanks, but I really can't."   15

"You're not married, are you? Not that that would matter that much to me. I'm an open-minded kinda guy."

She was smiling. "I have to get to work."

"That sounds boring."

"I better get your driver's license," she said.

Jake nodded, disappointed. "One little problem," he said. "I didn't bring it. I   20
just forgot it this morning. I'm a musician," he exaggerated greatly, "and, well, I dunno, I left my wallet in the pants I was wearing last night. If you have some paper and a pen I'll give you my address and all that."

He followed her to the glove compartment side of her car.

"What if we don't report it to the insurance companies? I'll just get it fixed for you."

"I don't think my dad would let me do that."

"Your dad? It's not your car?"

"He bought it for me. And I live at home."   25

"Right." She was slipping away from him. He went back around to the back of her new Toyota and looked over the damage again. There was the trunk lid, the bumper, a rear panel, a taillight.

"You do have insurance?" she asked, suspicious, as she came around the back of the car.

"Oh yeah," he lied.

"I guess you better write the name of that down too."

He made up a last name and address and wrote down the name of an insur-   30
ance company an old girlfriend once belonged to. He considered giving a real phone number but went against that idea and made one up.

"I act too," he lied to enhance the effect more. "Been in a couple of movies."
She smiled like a fan.

"So how about your phone number?" He was rebounding maturely.

She gave it to him.

"Mariana, you are beautiful," he said in his most sincere voice.

"Call me," she said timidly.

Jake beamed. "We'll see you, Mariana," he said holding out his hand. Her hand felt so warm and soft he felt like he'd been kissed.

Back in his car he took a moment or two to feel both proud and sad about his performance. Then he watched the rear view mirror as Mariana pulled up behind him. She was writing down the license plate numbers on his Buick, ones that he'd taken off a junk because the ones that belonged to his had expired so long ago. He turned the ignition key and revved the big engine and clicked into drive. His sense of freedom swelled as he drove into the now moving street traffic, though he couldn't stop the thought about that FM stereo radio and crushed velvet interior and the new car smell that would even make it better.

(1993)

The Rewriting Process

You are probably relieved and pleased that you have completed the first draft of your essay. A large portion of your work is finished. But do not be in a rush to print out the final version yet. You need first to do a careful revision of your paper.

⟹•⟸

What Is Revision?

Revision involves more than just tidying your prose. The process of correcting your spelling, punctuation, and mechanics is called *editing*, but your paper is not ready for that yet. First you need *re-vision*, seeing again, to discover ways to make your writing better. Schedule your time so that you are able to lay the rough draft aside at least overnight before attempting to revise. While a draft is still warm from the writing, you cannot look at it objectively. And looking at it objectively is the basis of revision.

As you examine your cooled-down essay, you may even see that while you were writing, your main claim shifted somewhat. Sometimes writers discover what they actually want to say while trying to write something different. For example, one student argued the point in the first draft of a paper on Flannery O'Connor's short story "Good Country People" that the main characters are all self-deceived. As she reread her draft, she noticed that she had focused almost entirely on Hulga Joy and her mother but had said almost nothing about the young Bible salesman. After some reflection—and another reading of the story—she decided to change her claim to emphasize the point that the Bible salesman, who makes his living through willful deception, is the only character who is not self-deceived. By shifting her focus to a consideration of this insight, the student discovered a number of related ideas that she had previously overlooked and thus was able to strengthen the content of her interpretation.

That student was able to get some distance from her own writing, to look at it as another reader might. In revising, *look at your paper from the reader's point of view*. What questions might a reader want to ask you? These must be anticipated in the paper, because you will not be around

48

to answer them. One of the best ways to get another reader's perspective is to enlist the help of peer reviewers.

Getting Feedback: Peer Review

Writers routinely seek the help of potential readers to find out what is working and what is not working in their drafts. Even professional writers ask for suggestions from editors, reviewers, teachers, and friends. Someone else can often see places where you *thought* you were being clear but were actually filling in details only in your head, not on the page.

The ideal people to help you evaluate your first draft are the members of your own writing class. They will be familiar with the assignment and will understand why you are writing the paper and for whom. Here are some guidelines to follow when asking for help with your revision.

1. *Specify the kind of help you want.* If you already know that the spelling needs to be checked, ask your readers to ignore those errors and focus on other elements in the draft. If you want suggestions about the thesis or the introduction or the tone or the organization or the examples, then ask questions about those features.
2. *Ask productive questions.* Be sure to pose questions that require more than a yes or no answer. Ask readers to tell you in detail what *they* see. You can use the questions in the Peer Evaluation Checklist (Chart 4-1, page 50) to help you solicit feedback.
3. *Don't get defensive.* Listen carefully to what your reviewers say; don't argue with them. If something confused them, it confused them. You want to see the writing through their eyes, not browbeat them into seeing it the way you do.
4. *Make your own decisions.* Remember that this is your paper; you are responsible for accepting or rejecting the feedback you get. If you don't agree with the suggestions, then don't follow them. But also keep in mind that your peer reviewers are likely to be more objective about your writing than you are.

Revising in Peer Groups

In many writing classes, students work together on their papers. Meeting in small groups, they read photocopies of each other's drafts and respond to them. Sometimes, students post their drafts on a classroom management system or by e-mail. If your instructor doesn't arrange for peer review, try to get several readers' reactions to your drafts. You can meet together outside of class or use Internet communication.

Working in peer review groups gives you a chance to write for readers other than the teacher. You increase your audience awareness, get immediate feedback on your drafts, and have a chance to discuss them with someone who doesn't have the power of a grade over you.

Chart 4-1   Peer Evaluation Checklist for Revision

The following questions are designed to address the typical concerns in arguing a literary interpretation. They will help you evaluate your own or another student's first draft.

1. Does the paper meet the assignment? What is the major claim? Does the whole paper relate to this claim? Is the claim interesting or too predictable?
2. Is the interpretation argued clearly and consistently? Make a note of any sentences or paragraphs that you had to reread. Make a note of any words or phrases that you found confusing.
3. Is the argument well organized? Is it logical? Is there perhaps a better order for the major points of the argument? Are there any paragraphs or points that do not seem to belong?
4. Is there enough material to make the interpretation clear and convincing? Does it need further details or examples? Make a note of places you would like to see more details or examples. Write questions to help the writer add details. For example, if the essay says, "Eveline did not much like her father," you could ask, "Exactly how did she feel about him?"
5. Are all the quotations from the story accurate? Do they appear within quotation marks?
6. Does the opening capture the reader's attention and make the major claim of the paper clear? Does the conclusion provide an intelligent, satisfactory ending for the argument?

But it takes skill to be an honest and critical reader of someone else's writing. When giving feedback, whether in groups or one-on-one, you should observe certain ground rules to ensure that your responses are productive and helpful.

- Remember that drafts are works in progress which writers intend to develop and improve. You are acting as an informed, interested reader who has questions and suggestions for improvement.
- Pay attention to *what* the other writers are saying, just as you hope they'll pay attention to what you are saying. In other words, focus on content first.
- Avoid the extremes of saying that everything is wonderful or finding fault with every detail. Instead, give thoughtful, sympathetic responses— the kind of feedback that you would like to receive.
- Talk about the writing, not about the writer. If you notice errors, feel free to mention them, but concentrate on responding and suggesting rather than correcting the writer.

Once you have gathered reactions and suggestions from your peer reviewers—and perhaps from your instructor, too—you are ready to begin rewriting. The rest of this chapter will guide you through the specifics of revising and editing.

What Should I Add or Take Out?

Revising is hard work, and you may wonder just where and how to start. If you have not been following a plan carefully worked out before you began writing, you should begin the revising process by outlining your first draft.

Outlining After the First Draft

To be sure that your discussion is unified and complete—that is, to discover whether anything needs to be taken out or added—you should briefly outline your rough draft. It may seem odd to make an outline *after* you have written the paper, but listing your main ideas and supporting details will enable you to review your essay quickly and easily. You can examine its skeleton and decide whether everything fits together properly. This step in the revising process is *essential* if you have written the first draft without an outline or a detailed plan.

Making the Outline

An outline, whether done before or after the first draft, allows you to check for sufficient and logical development of ideas as well as for unity throughout the essay. Your introductory paragraph should contain your thesis, perhaps stated in a general way but stated clearly enough to let your readers know what your focus is. Here is one way to construct an after-writing outline:

1. Take a separate sheet of paper and write your thesis statement at the top.
2. Add the topic sentences stating the main ideas of your paragraphs, along with the supporting points in each one.

Your final paragraph should draw a conclusion concerning the thesis—a conclusion that relates the material in the body of the paper to the theme or purpose of the literary work.

Checking the Outline

Check your outline this way:

1. Make sure that the idea in every topic sentence is a significant critical observation relating directly to your thesis.
2. If not, revise the topic sentence until it clearly supports your thesis—or else delete the whole paragraph.

Just as the topic sentence of each paragraph should relate to the thesis of the paper, every piece of supporting evidence in the paragraph should relate to its topic sentence. So, next check the organization within each paragraph this way:

3. In each body paragraph, examine your supporting details to be sure that each relates directly to the topic sentence.

4. Make sure that none of your points repeats an idea included elsewhere (unless you are repeating for emphasis). Eliminate any careless repetition.

5. Decide whether your support is adequate. Think about whether you have included the most convincing details and whether you have enough of them.

6. If you decide you do not have sufficient support for a topic sentence, you need to rethink the point in order to expand it, or consider omitting the paragraph if the ideas are not essential. Sometimes you can combine the material from two paragraphs into a single new one having a broader topic sentence.

Sample After-Writing Outline

Because one peer reader of Wendy Dennison's paper on "Eveline" noticed that a couple of examples might be out of place, Wendy outlined her first draft. Here is her after-writing outline. (Her draft appeared in Chapter 2.)

1. Introduction
   —Eveline refuses to leave with Frank because she fears failure (thesis)

2. Her deathbed promise to her mother was unfair.
   —unfair to ask Eveline to give up her own life

3. She has good reasons to want to leave her father.
   —he's a drunk, takes advantage of the promise
   —he's stingy
   —he abuses her verbally
   —he's a bully, might actually beat her
   —he was sometimes fun in past, played at picnics

4. Her home life is so unhealthy she should leave.
   —doesn't feel a part of everything (picture of priest)
   —dust in house = dirtiness, squalor of her life
   —thinks of leaving and remembers her dreary job

5. Her only reason for staying is that she's afraid.
   —leaving the familiar could mean failure
   —quotation: "about to explore" suggests uncertainty
   —life is hard, so she thinks of good memories to convince herself
      to stay

6. She retreats into the familiar to avoid risk.
    —feels she has a right to happiness
    —decides a predictable life is better than one without direction and pattern (conclusion)

Examining the Sample Outline

If you examine Wendy's outline carefully, you can see a few problems.

Paragraph 2   Wendy needs more material about why the promise to her dying mother was unfair.

Paragraph 3   The last point, about "fun in past," does not relate to the topic sentence for the paragraph, which focuses on "good reasons to want to leave."

Paragraph 4   The last point, about Eveline's job, does not relate to the topic sentence for the paragraph, which focuses on Eveline's "unhealthy" home life.

Paragraph 5   The last point, about Eveline's "good memories," provides a good place to move the example about "fun in past" from paragraph 3.

Paragraph 6   The first point, about Eveline's "right to happiness," does not relate to the topic sentence, which focuses on Eveline's retreat "into the familiar," but could well be moved to paragraph 2 to support the topic sentence idea that her death bed promise was unfair.

In the final draft of Wendy's paper, which appears on pages 67–70, you will see how she took care of the problems revealed by her outline.

Outlining Exercise

For practice in checking the relevance and organization of ideas, outline the following paragraph in the way we just described, putting the topic sentence at the top of the page, and then listing each supporting idea.

Eveline lacks courage to seek a life of her own because she fears that her father will not be able to cope if she leaves him. Her anxiety is heightened as she recalls that she and her brothers and sisters are grown up and that her mother is dead. If she leaves, her father will soon be all alone. She realizes that he is "usually fairly bad on a Saturday night" (5) and recognizes that his drinking problem will not get any better after she leaves. Also she has noticed that "Her father was becoming old lately" and assumes that "he would miss her" (6). As a dutiful daughter, Eveline seems to feel that going away with Frank means abandoning her aging father, and that may be why she has written a letter to him—to ease the blow of her departure and to soothe her own conscience.

Next, examine your outline. Do you see any irrelevant points? Can you think of any important ideas or details that have been omitted from the paragraph? Are the points arranged in an effective order? Would another arrangement be better?

Now look at the following outline and see whether it matches yours.

Topic sentence: Eveline fears her father will not be able to manage if she leaves him.

1. Eveline thinks about his loneliness—children grown, wife dead.
2. She fears his drinking problem worsening.
3. She worries that he is becoming old lately.
4. She assumes "he would miss her."
5. She writes letter to ease the blow.

Your outline may not come out exactly like this one, but the main idea is to be sure you have included all of the supporting details.

Here are some observations to consider for a revision of the sample paragraph, based on the outline of its major points:

1. Point 1 could be expanded to include details about the neighbors who have died (Tizzie Dunn) and moved away (the Waters family).
2. An earlier draft of the paragraph included the point about Eveline's promise to her mother, but it was dropped as being irrelevant to the topic sentence. Do you agree?
3. The paragraph's supporting points appear in the same order as they do in the story. Is this chronological organization effective? Would some logical order be better?

What Should I Rearrange?

A crucial part of revision involves giving some thought to the order of your paragraphs and the order of the supporting details within them. The order in which they came to your mind is not necessarily the best. Luckily, rearranging is fairly easy once you have an after-writing outline.

Many writers use cutting and pasting on the computer to experiment with various arrangements of their ideas, reading different versions and deciding which order is most effective. They rearrange paragraphs and even sentences. For instance, sometimes the last sentence you write in a paragraph turns out to be a good topic sentence and should be moved to the beginning. Sometimes the paragraph you write at the essay's end would work better as the introduction to the paper.

If you experiment this way, save each version under a different file name (eve1, eve2, eve3, for example), so that your computer retains all the choices you have created. Otherwise, each new version may overwrite the old one, and you will lose pieces you may want later.

The two principles you need to use in considering how well your points are arranged are *logic* and *emphasis*. Both principles allow you to arrange ideas in a certain sequence. The following questions will help you devise an appropriate arrangement.

1. Should I arrange the paragraphs and details in my essay in the same order in which they appear in the work I am analyzing?

If you are writing a paragraph supporting the topic that Eveline is timid, you might collect details from throughout the story. You could then put those details in the same order as they appear in the story.

2. Should I organize the descriptions in terms of space?

In a paper examining the significance of the objects in Eveline's home, you might take up these objects as though presented in a tour around the room. Other descriptions may be arranged from near to far, from outside to inside, from small to large.

3. Should I arrange my main points along a scale of value, of power, of weight, or of forcefulness? Could I use an arrangement of
   —negative to positive?
   —universal to individual?
   —most influential to least influential?
   —general to specific?
   —least impressive to most impressive?

You can arrange your ideas in either direction along any of these scales— negative to positive or positive to negative, for instance. It is usually effective to place the most emphatic point last in any essay. If you are writing about several of Eveline's reasons for not going with Frank, and you believe that the most influential reason is her promise to her dying mother, you would include that idea in the last paragraph of the body of your paper, opening with a transition like this:

> Though her timidity in general and her fear of her father in particular affect Eveline's final decision, her promise to her mother is the most powerful influence.

The strongest-point rule is just a guideline, of course. Try to arrange your ideas in a way your readers will find effective.

Does It Flow?

The best way to examine the flow (the **coherence**) of your prose is to read it aloud. Recording your essays on tape and playing them back enables you to hear with some objectivity how your writing sounds. You might also entice a friend to read your paper aloud to you. Whatever method you use, listen for choppiness or abruptness. Your ideas should be arranged in a clear sequence that is easy to follow. Will your readers experience any confusion when a new idea comes up? If so, you need stronger connections between sentences or between paragraphs—*transitions* that indicate how one idea is related to the next.

For example, when you see the words *for example*, you know what to expect. When you see *furthermore* opening a paragraph, your mind gets ready for some addition to the previous point. By contrast, when you see phrases like *on the other hand* or *by contrast*, you are prepared for something different from the previous point.

These clearly transitional phrases can be supplemented by more subtle echo transitions (in this paragraph, the words *transitional phrases* echo the main idea of the preceding paragraph), and by pronoun reference (in this paragraph, the word *these* refers to the examples in the preceding paragraph). Another technique that increases coherence in writing is the repetition of key terms and structures. In the paragraph you are reading, the key terms are forms of the words *transition*, *echo*, *refer*, and *repeat*. In the paragraph preceding this one, notice the repetition of the phrase *when you see* and, in this paragraph, the repetition of *in this paragraph* and *the word(s)*. Parallel ideas are presented in parallel ways.

In short, here are the techniques for achieving coherence.

1. A clearly sequenced flow of ideas
2. Transitional terms (see Chart 4-2 on page 57 for a handy list)
3. Echo transitions that link the opening of a paragraph to the topic of the previous paragraph
4. Repetition of key terms
5. Repetition of parallel sentence structures

A Revising Checklist to help you review all the important aspects of the revising process appears in Chart 4-3 on page 57.

What Is Editing?

During revision, you focused on making your paper organized, well developed, and coherent. In the editing stage, you should concentrate on improving your sentences and refining your use of language.

Which Sentences Should I Combine?

Once you are satisfied that your ideas proceed smoothly, consider the possibility of combining sentences to avoid needless repetition of words and to eliminate choppiness. You may also decide to combine sentences to achieve emphasis and variety. Probably you can discover many ways to improve your sentences.

Chart 4-2   Transitional Terms for All Occasions

To Continue to a New Point

next, second, third, besides, further, finally

To Make an Addition to a Point

too, moreover, in addition, for example, such as, that is, as an illustration, for instance, furthermore

To Show Cause and Effect

therefore, consequently, as a result, accordingly, then, thus, so, hence

To Show Contrast

but, still, on the other hand, nevertheless, however, conversely, notwithstanding, yet

To Show Similarity

too, similarly, in the same way, likewise, also

To Emphasize or Restate

again, namely, in other words, finally, especially, without doubt, indeed, in short, in brief, primarily, chiefly, as a matter of fact, no doubt

To Conclude a Point

finally, in conclusion, to summarize, to sum up, in sum

Chart 4-3   Revising Checklist

1. Is my thesis idea intelligent and clearly stated?
2. Is my argument logically and effectively organized? Does the main idea of every paragraph relate directly to the thesis?
3. Are the paragraphs fully developed, with plenty of specific examples or illustrations to support the topic sentences?
4. Do the ideas flow coherently? Are the transitions easy to follow?
5. Have I accomplished my purpose? Does the paper make the point I set out to prove?

Combining for Conciseness

If you find that you are sometimes repeating the same word without meaning to, you may eliminate the problem by combining sentences. For instance, you might have written something like this:

Twain savagely attacks conformity in the scene where the villagers stone the woman. The woman is suspected of being a witch.

Because the repetition of *the woman* serves no useful purpose, the two statements can be more effectively phrased in a single sentence.

> In a scene showing the villagers stoning a woman suspected of being a witch, Twain savagely attacks conformity.

When you combine sentences in this way, you take the main idea from one sentence and tuck it, usually as a modifier of some sort, within another sentence. We can illustrate the process in reverse to help you see more clearly what the technique involves. Notice that the following sentence contains two simple statements:

> Theodore, who did not wish to throw a stone, was horrified by the cruelty.

The two main ideas in that sentence are these:

> Theodore was horrified by the cruelty.
> Theodore did not wish to throw a stone.

You can recombine those sentences in various ways, depending on which idea you choose to emphasize.

> Horrified by the cruelty, Theodore did not wish to throw a stone.
> Not wishing to throw a stone, Theodore was horrified by the cruelty.

Sentence combining not only eliminates wordiness but also adds variety and focus. The various combinations provide numerous stylistic choices.

Sentence-Combining Exercise

The following sentences, all written by students, include needless repetition and wordiness that can be eliminated by sentence combining. Decide which idea in each pair of sentences should be emphasized, and put that idea in the main (independent) clause. You will, of course, need to change, add, or omit words as you work to improve these sentences, but try not to leave out any significant ideas.

1. The second common stereotype is the dark lady. Usually the dark lady stereotype symbolizes sexual temptation.
2. Kate Chopin wrote a short story called "The Storm." As the title of the story suggests, it is about a rainstorm and shows how people respond to the storm.
3. Emily Dickinson's poetry is sometimes elliptical. It is thus sometimes difficult for readers to get even the literal meaning of her poems.
4. There are three major things to consider in understanding Goodman Brown's character. These things include what the author tells us about

Brown, what Brown himself says and does, and how other people respond to him.

5. Most of the incidents that inspire Walter Mitty's fantasies have humorous connotations associated with them. These can be broken down into basically two groups, the first one being his desire to be in charge of a situation.

Rearranging for Emphasis and Variety

When you rewrite to gain emphasis and variety, you will probably restructure sentences as well as combine them. In fact, you may find yourself occasionally dividing a sentence for easier reading or to produce a short, emphatic sentence. The following are some techniques to help you in polishing your sentence structure.

Varying the Pattern

The usual way of forming sentences in English is to begin with the subject, follow with the verb, and add a complement (something that completes the verb), like this:

Walter Mitty is not a brave person.

Any time you depart from this expected pattern, you gain variety and some degree of emphasis. Notice the difference.

A brave person Walter Mitty is not.

Here are other variations that you may want to try.

A Dash at the End: Twain found constant fault with humanity—with what he called "the damned human race."

An Interrupter Set Off by Dashes or Commas: Twain considered humanity in general—"the damned human race"—inferior to the so-called lower animals.

A Modifier at the Beginning: Although he loved individual human beings, Twain professed to loathe what he called "the damned human race."

A Short-Short Sentence Because most of the sentences you will write are moderately long, you gain considerable emphasis when you follow a sentence of normal length with an extremely short one.

Plagiarizing, which means borrowing the words or ideas of another writer without giving proper credit, is a serious infraction. Do not do it.

Deliberate Repetition   Just a few pages ago, we cautioned you to combine sentences rather than to repeat words needlessly. That caution still holds. But repeating words for emphasis is a different matter. Purposeful repetition can produce effective and emphatic sentences.

> Twain believed that organized religion was folly, a folly to be ridiculed discreetly.
>
> One cannot talk well, study well, or write well if one cannot think well.

That last sentence (modeled after one written by Virginia Woolf) repeats the same grammatical structure as well as the same words to achieve a powerful effect.

Exercise on Style

Rewrite the following ordinary sentences to achieve greater emphasis, variety, and conciseness.

1. Edith Wharton was born into a rich, upper-class family, but she was not even allowed to have paper on which to write when she was a child.
2. Her governesses never taught her how to organize ideas in writing, so when she decided to write a book on the decoration of houses, she had to ask her friend Walter Berry to help her write it.
3. She married Teddy Wharton when she was twenty-three years old, and he always carried a one-thousand-dollar bill in case she wanted anything.
4. Her good friend Henry James gave her advice to help her improve her novels, yet her novels invariably sold far more copies than James's did.
5. She was awarded the Legion of Honor, which is the highest award given by the French government, following World War I for her refugee relief activities.

Which Words Should I Change?

You may have a good thesis and convincing, detailed support for it—but your writing *style* can make the difference between a dull, boring presentation and a rich, engaging one.

Check Your Verbs

After examining the construction of your sentences, look at the specific language you have used. Read through the rough draft and underline the verbs. Look for forms of these useful but well-worn words:

is (are, was, were, etc.)	go	has
get	come	move
do	make	use

Consider substituting a different verb, one that presents a type of image—visual or otherwise—to your readers. For example, this sentence is grammatically correct but dull:

Eveline does her work with reluctance.

Searching for a more precise verb than *does*, you might write

Eveline reluctantly plods through her work.

Plods suggests a picture of poor Eveline with slumped shoulders and slow steps, dragging through the day.

Occasionally you can pick up a lively word from somewhere else in a limp sentence and convert it into the main verb.

Eveline is unable to leave her home because she is trapped by a promise to her dead mother.

Trapped is an arresting word in that sentence, and you could shift it to an earlier position to good effect.

A promise to her dead mother traps Eveline in her miserable home.

This revision also cuts unnecessary words out of the first version.

Use Active Voice Most of the Time

Although the passive voice sometimes offers the best way to construct a sentence, the habitual use of the passive sprinkles your prose with colorless helping verbs, like *is* and *was*. If a sentence is in passive voice, the subject does *not* perform the action implied by the verb.

The paper was written by Janet, Jo's roommate.
The assignment was given poorly.
Her roommate's efforts were hindered by a lack of understanding.

The paper, the assignment, and the roommate's efforts did *not* carry out the writing, the giving, or the hindering. In active voice, the subjects of the sentences are the doers or the causes of the action.

Jo's roommate, Janet, wrote the paper.
The teacher gave the assignment poorly.
Lack of understanding hindered her roommate's efforts.

Use Passive Voice If Appropriate

Sometimes, of course, you may have a good reason for writing in the passive voice. For example, you may want to give a certain word the important position of subject even though it is not the agent of the action. In the sentence

Sensory details are emphasized in this paragraph.

the *details* are the key point. The writer of the paragraph (the agent of the action) is not important enough even to be included. In active voice, the key term would be pushed to the middle of the sentence, a much weaker position.

The writer emphasizes sensory details in this paragraph.

Clearly, you need not shun the passive, but if any of your sentences sound stilted or awkward, check to see if the passive voice may be the culprit.

Exercise on Passive Voice

Change passive voice to active in the following sentences. Feel free to add, delete, or change words.

1. Antigone is treated brutally by Creon because of her struggle to achieve justice.
2. Creon was not convinced by her tirade against his unbending authority.
3. Conflict between male and female was portrayed in the play by the author.
4. If even a small point is won against a tyrant by society, considerable benefit may be experienced.
5. The tragedy is caused by the ironbound authority exercised by Creon.

Feel the Words

Words have emotional meanings (**connotations**) as well as direct dictionary meanings (**denotations**). You may be invited to a get-together, a soiree, a social gathering, a blowout, a blast, a reception, a bash, or a do, and although all are words for parties, the connotations tell you whether to wear jeans or feathers, whether to bring a case of cheap beer or a bottle of expensive wine.

In writing, take into account the emotional content of the words you use. One of our favorite essays, "The Discus Thrower," opens with this sentence:

I spy on my patients.

The word *spy* immediately captures the imagination with its connotations of intrigue and mystery and its slight flavor of deception. "I watch my patients when they don't know it" is still an interesting sentence because of its denotative content, but essayist Richard Selzer's version commands emotional as well as intellectual engagement.

We are not encouraging you to puff up your prose with strings of adverbs and adjectives; indeed, a single emotionally charged word in a simple sentence can be quite powerful.

Exercise on Word Choice

Rewrite the following sentences using livelier words and cutting unnecessary words.

1. The first sentence of "A Good Man Is Hard to Find" is a foreshadowing of what happens to the grandmother at the end of the story.
2. The conversations between members of the family show that they are not the idealized American family on vacation but are self-absorbed and ignorant.
3. There are many instances of lying, untruths, and self-deception in the story.
4. Three men come up to the family after their car accident, but they are strange in their clothing and actions, and they are not there to help.
5. Each character has his or her own way of saying things, a manner of speech which is often amusing in a dark kind of way.

Attend to Tone

Tone—the reflection of a writer's attitude—is usually described in terms of emotion: serious, solemn, satirical, humorous, sly, mournful, expectant, and so on. Although most writing about literature calls for a plain, direct tone, other attitudes can be conveyed. Negative book reviews, for instance, sometimes have a sarcastic tone. A writer unsympathetic to Eveline might describe her as "a spineless drudge who enjoys her oppression," whereas a sympathetic reader might state that Eveline is "a pitiful victim of a brutal home life." Someone who wants to remain neutral could describe Eveline as "a young woman trapped by duty and her own fears." These variations in tone, conveyed by word choice, reflect the writers' differing attitudes toward what is being discussed.

Once you establish a tone, you should stick with it. A humorous or sarcastic section set unexpectedly in a straightforward, direct essay will distract or disconcert your readers. Be sure to set your tone in the first paragraph; then your readers will unconsciously adjust their expectations about the rest of the paper.

Use Formal Language

The nature of your audience will also determine the level of usage for your writing. Essays for college classes usually require *formal language*, a style that takes a serious or neutral tone and avoids such ***informal*** *usage* as most contractions, slang, and sentence fragments, even intentional ones.

Even one shift from formal usage to informal usage can distract your readers:

> Eveline fully intends to leave with Frank, but she gets hung up at the point of departure.

The words *hung up* are surprisingly slangy in the context of a literary essay. An alternative that stays at the same usage level might read this way:

> Eveline fully intends to leave with Frank, but she becomes paralyzed at the point of departure

Formal writing often involves a third-person approach.

> One can sympathize with Eveline, at the same time regretting her weakness.
> The reader sympathizes with Eveline, ...

Most people today consider the use of first-person plural (*we, us, our, ours*) quite acceptable in formal papers.

> We sympathize with Eveline, ...
> Eveline gains our sympathy, ...

A growing number of people think the use of the first-person singular (*I, me, my, mine*) is also acceptable in formal writing.

> I sympathize with Eveline, ...
> Eveline gains my sympathy, ...

But avoid the informal second person, *you*. Do *not* write, "You can see that Eveline is caught in a terrible bind."

What Is Proofreading?

Proofreading is the last step in preparing your final draft. After you have improved your sentences and refined your word choices, you must force yourself to read the paper one last time to pick up any careless mistakes or typographical errors. Jessica Mitford rightly says that "failure to proofread is like preparing a magnificent dinner and forgetting to set the table."

Try Reading It Backward

To avoid getting so interested in what you have written that you don't see your errors, read your sentences from the last one on the page to the first, that is, from the bottom to the top. Because your ideas will lack continuity in reverse order, you stand a better chance of keeping your attention focused on each sentence *as* a sentence. Be sure that every word is correctly spelled, that each sentence is complete and correctly punctuated. Be sure to run your spelling checker and to think over its suggestions, which may be imperfect. Don't automatically accept whatever appears, or you may end up using *slyly* when you meant *slightly*!

Look for Your Typical Errors

If you know that you often have problems with certain elements of punctuation or **diction,** be on guard for these particular errors as you examine each sentence.

1. Make sure that each sentence really is a sentence, not some fragment— especially those beginning with *because, since, which, that, although, as, when*, or *what*, and those beginning with words ending in *ing*.
2. Make sure that independent clauses joined by *indeed, moreover, however, nevertheless, thus*, and *hence* have a semicolon before those words, not just a comma.
3. Make sure that every modifying phrase or clause is close to the word it modifies.
4. If you know you have a problem with spelling, check every word and look up all questionable ones. Run your spelling checker, and verify that its suggestions are really the words you want.
5. Be alert for words that you know you consistently get wrong. If you are aware that you sometimes confuse words that sound alike (*it's/its, your/you're, there/their/they're, effect/affect*), check the accuracy of your usage. Remember that your spelling checker will not help you here.

If you are not sure how to correct the errors just mentioned, you will find a handy Proofreading Checklist in Chart 4-4 on page 66.

Read the Paper Aloud

In an earlier section, we recommended reading your paper aloud as a means of checking coherence. It's a good idea to read it aloud again to catch words left out or carelessly repeated.

Find a Friend to Help

If you have a literate friend who will help you proofread your paper, you are in luck. Ask this kind person to point out errors and to let you know whether your thesis is made plain at the beginning, whether every

---

Chart 4-4 Proofreading Checklist

1. Have I mixed up any of these easily confused words?

its/it's	their/they're/there	lie/lay
effect/affect	suppose/supposed	our/are
your/you're	woman/women	use/used
to/too/two	prejudice/prejudiced	then/than
who's/whose	accept/except	cite/site

2. Have I put an apostrophe appropriately in each of my possessive nouns?
3. Have I carelessly repeated any word?
4. Have I carelessly left any words out?
5. Have I omitted the first or final letter from any words?
6. Have I used the proper punctuation at the end of every sentence?
7. Have I spelled every word correctly?

---

sentence is clear, and whether the paper as a whole makes sense. You risk having to do further revising if any of your friend's responses prove negative, but try to be grateful for the help. You want to turn in a paper you can be proud of.

Relying on someone else to do your proofreading, though, is unwise. There will be writing situations in college that preclude your bringing a friend to help (e.g., essay examinations and in-class essays). Learn to find and correct your own errors so you will not risk failure when you go it alone.

Sample Student Paper: Final Draft

The following is the final draft of Wendy Dennison's paper on "Eveline." This finished version reflects the changes she made in organization to correct the problems revealed by her after-writing outline. The paper also includes editing changes she made to achieve precision in word choice and to increase the effectiveness of each individual sentence.

Sample Student Paper: Final Draft

Wendy Dennison

Professor McMahan

English 102

6 February 2005

Fear of Failure in Joyce's "Eveline"

In his short story "Eveline," James Joyce gives the protagonist an exciting chance to leave her old life and begin a new one. But she rejects this offer that Frank—or Fate—makes, preferring instead to settle back into the dreary life she has known all along. Why does she not go away with Frank when the opportunity seems so attractive? We need to examine Eveline's timid personality in order to discover the answer.

Since Eveline has been raised a Catholic, we know she would not take her promise to her dying mother lightly. But surely her promise to "keep the home together as long as she could" (6) was given under extreme circumstances. It was unjust of her mother to ask such a sacrifice of her, and Eveline is aware of the unfairness: "Why should she be unhappy? She had a right to happiness" (6). We know that Eveline will always be haunted by that promise, but we do not expect her to give up her chance for a life of her own in order to be a dutiful daughter. Surely that promise cannot be the only reason she stays.

We certainly should not be surprised that Eveline might wish to leave her abusive father. A hot-tempered heavy drinker, he has taken advantage of his daughter's promise to her mother. She is forced to keep house for him, yet must beg for money to feed the family.

He practically accuses her of stealing, claiming that "she used to squander the money, that she had no head, that he wasn't going to give her his hard-earned money to throw about the streets" (4-5). He has so frightened her with threats of beatings that she has "palpitations" (4). Eveline realizes that with her brothers gone, there is "nobody to protect her" (4) from her father's rage. Her father has treated Eveline badly and may abuse her even worse in the future. To leave him would obviously be in her best interest, yet something keeps her there.

Eveline's home life is so unhealthy that we feel she would be wise to leave. Despite all the chores she performs, she still does not feel entirely at home in her father's house. For example, she knows nothing about the picture of the priest (4), not even his name, yet the portrait seems quite important to her father. The dustiness of the house, of which Joyce reminds us periodically, suggests the pervasive dreariness of her daily life as she looks around "wondering where on earth all the dust came from" (4). Since her home is clearly not conducive to happiness, why does she stay there?

The main reason Eveline would remain in Ireland is that she is desperately afraid of the unknown. If she leaves the familiar, no matter how unpleasant, she risks failure. "She was about to explore another life with Frank" (5), we are told, in faraway Buenos Ayres. The word *explore* is significant, as it brings to mind uncertainty and risk, two factors that Eveline is not prepared to deal with. She admits that hers is "a hard life," yet thinks that "now that she was about to leave it she did not find it a wholly undesirable life"

(5). When she sits in the growing darkness with the letters in her lap, Eveline calls up a couple of good memories—of her father being jolly once on a picnic, of his kindness once when she was sick. We see her trying to calm her fears, trying to convince herself that her home life is more bearable than it is.

Afraid of failing on her own, Eveline retreats into the familiar, telling herself that life with father cannot be as frightening as a risky, unknown life with Frank. So strong is her fear of failure that it overrides her fear of her father. She seems to decide that a predictable—if dreary and abused—life is better than a life without security or pattern.

Dennison 4

Work Cited

Joyce, James. "Eveline." *Literature and the Writing Process*. Ed. Elizabeth McMahan, Susan X Day, and Robert Funk. 7th ed. Upper Saddle River: Prentice, 2005. 3–7. Print.

5

Researched Writing

At some point you may be asked to write a literary paper that doesn't draw entirely on your own understanding and judgments. In other words, you will have to do some *research*. When writing a researched paper about literature, you begin, as always, with a *primary source*—the story, poem, or play the paper is about—but you expand the range of your coverage to include *secondary sources*—critical, biographical, historical, and cultural documents that support your interpretation of the primary work (or works).

Using Library Sources in Your Writing

Most student writers consult secondary sources to help them explain, develop, and strengthen their ideas and opinions. That's what Wendy Dennison did with her essay "Fear of Failure in Joyce's 'Eveline'" (see pages 67–70 in the previous chapter). Although Wendy had worked out her own arguments for why Eveline did not go away with Frank, she and her instructor thought it would be enlightening to see what other readers thought. So Wendy went to the library to find material by critics who had published their interpretations of "Eveline," especially about the ending of the story. After reading and taking notes from a number of books and articles, Wendy revised her paper by incorporating comments from several critics into her discussion. The revised, documented version of her essay appears on pages 88–92.

Although not everyone produces a finished paper before doing research, some writers do prepare a first draft before looking at secondary sources. Others consult secondary materials to help them decide on a topic. Another common strategy is to use the ideas of others as a platform for an interpretation, first summarizing several views and then presenting a different interpretation, a synthesizing conclusion, or an analysis of their conflicting points of view.

Secondary sources can help you in a number of different ways to develop an essay about literature:

- *Analyzing the features of a single work.* Why does E. E. Cummings disregard traditional form and punctuation in his poetry? How does the chorus function in *Antigone*?
- *Exploring connections between a work and the author's life.* How might Dorothy Parker's attitudes toward romance in her life illuminate her poem "One Perfect Rose"? How autobiographical is Anne Sexton's "You All Know the Story of the Other Woman"?
- *Assessing the impact of social, historical, or cultural backgrounds on a work.* What is the role of the blues tradition in *Fences* by August Wilson? How do psychological theories of family systems illuminate "The Rocking-Horse Winner"?
- *Understanding the political or artistic objectives of a work.* In what ways can Luis Valdez's play *Los Vendidos* be seen as a drama of social protest? How well does *Antigone* illustrate Aristotle's theory of tragedy?
- *Comparing themes or characters in several works.* How do the mother-daughter relationships in stories by Tillie Olsen, Hisaye Yamamoto, Flannery O'Connor, and Joyce Carol Oates illustrate different kinds of maternal-filial bonding? What attitudes toward sports are expressed in Housman's "To an Athlete Dying Young," Updike's "Ex-Basketball Player," and Hirsch's "Execution"?

You will find ideas for researched writing in the questions that follow most of the literary selections in this book.

Conducting Your Research

The prewriting you do for a documented paper is similar to the prewriting you would do for any literary essay. You still need to consider your audience, determine your purpose, discover and develop your ideas, and decide what point you want to make. The techniques and advice presented in Chapter 1 will help you with these tasks. But the next steps will be different, perhaps even new to you. First and foremost, you have to track down relevant secondary sources, a challenging procedure that involves libraries, computer terminals, and stacks of papers and index cards. The following sections will guide you through this process.

Locating Sources

More than likely you will conduct your search for sources on a computer. Most college libraries offer workshops to help students locate materials, conduct computer searches, use online databases, and navigate the Internet. If these courses are not required, take them anyway—you could save yourself hours of aimless wandering. Your library's information desk will provide you with schedules of these valuable sessions.

Using the Online Catalog

Most libraries today list their holdings in a computerized *online public access catalog* (OPAC). The opening screen of the OPAC at the library Wendy Dennison used shows that she can search for books, journals and magazines, and other items owned by her library and by other libraries in the state. In electronic databases, such as InfoTrac and EBSCO, you can usually search for sources by author, title, and publication year and also by subject or *keywords*.

Subject searches focus only on the source's contents and yield more limited, precise results. They work best when the *descriptors* (subject headings) conform to a database's directory of terms. For your library's catalog, the directory is the *Library of Congress Subject Headings (LCSH)*, which is available in printed form in the reference room. *Keyword searches* look through the entire database and are not dependent on pre-set subject headings. If you know your exact subject, you will want to begin with a subject search. A keyword search, on the other hand, is a good place to limit and refine your subject and discover specific descriptors. Remember that computers are unforgiving about spelling and typing errors. When your results are not what you expected, check the accuracy of the search terms you used.

To begin her search of the online catalog, Wendy typed in the LSCH heading "Joyce, James, 1882–1941" and selected "subject" in the "search by" menu. The results showed more than seventy entries, most of which contained sublistings for specific titles. In other words, her library owns hundreds of books and other materials about James Joyce. Wendy refined her search by adding "Dubliners" (the title of the collection that contains "Eveline") to her descriptor; she found that her library had eight books on this topic. She saw which ones were available and where they were located in the library. Wendy also browsed a number of items under the subheading "criticism and interpretation" and took down information about books that appeared to deal with Joyce's early works. She felt she had plenty of material to begin her review of critical opinions about the motivations of Eveline.

Using Indexes and Databases

Even though you might find valuable material in books to use in documenting your ideas and critical judgments, your paper will not be well researched unless you also find articles and reviews relevant to your topic. These sources are now available electronically through online databases and text archives that your library subscribes to. The library homepage that Wendy was using allowed her to move from the online catalog to a list of more than a hundred searchable indexes, bibliographies, and other electronic reference tools.

The reference librarian recommended that Wendy look first at two computerized indexes to find publication information on articles about "Eveline": the *MLA International Bibliography* and the *Humanities International Index*. Other databases, like *Academic Search Elite* and *Expanded Academic Index ASAP*, also provide citations for journal articles, but they cover a wide range of academic subjects. These may be suitable for gathering background information, but the *MLA International Bibliography* is the best choice for finding authoritative, scholarly sources about literature. Journals, like magazines and newspapers, are published periodically, but are written by and for academics or expert scholars. Journals rarely have advertising, eye-catching artistic touches, or slick covers. Each journal is devoted to a specific academic subject, often a very narrow one.

When Wendy typed "Eveline" in the "find" box of the MLA search screen, she got 132 hits. The display also prompted her to narrow her results by subject and gave her several words and phrases to add to her search term. Wendy selected "Joyce, James," which reduced the list to forty-one entries. She could view these entries one at a time or print out the entire list. Each citation included the article title, the name of the periodical, and the volume, date, and page number; it also supplied the call number for any publications in her library. Many of the entries contained a brief summary of the article's content, and several included the full text of the article for her to read or print. She could also send the data to her home computer by e-mail.

Wendy browsed through these findings and printed the citations for several articles that looked promising. Because the library did not own several of the periodicals, the librarian suggested requesting copies of the articles through an interlibrary loan, but that would take several days. Another option was to consult a full-text database, such as *JSTOR* (*Journal Storage Project*) or *ProjectMUSE*, to see if the articles were available there. Wendy discovered two promising articles in *JSTOR* and printed them out.

These were just some of the electronic tools that Wendy used to search for possible sources. Other generally available indexes and abstracts for researching literary topics include *Gale's Literary Index, Humanities International Index, Periodical Abstracts,* and *Readers' Guide to Periodical Literature.* Popular and relevant full-text databases include *Annual Bibliography of English Language and Literature, EBSCO Academic Search Premier, Humanities Full Text, InfoTrac Expanded Academic Index ASAP, LexisNexis Academic Universe, WilsonSelect Plus, Book Review Digest Plus, Literature Online,* and *Literature Resource Center.*

Your library may subscribe to many of the same indexes and databases, but you need to find out what's available and how to use them. You may also be able to access these resources from your home or other location through a proxy service that verifies your status as a library card holder.

Using the Internet

A number of useful online databases and text archives are accessible over the Internet. Chart 5-1 presents selected Internet sources for doing literary research; this listing focuses on well-established popular and scholarly sites that feature useful links and other resources that may be valuable during the initial stages of your research. You can locate additional resources using any one of several different search engines—such as Netscape, Safari, Firefox, Google, Yahoo!, Ask.com, and Microsoft Explorer—that catalog Web sites in directories and allow you to conduct keyword searches.

You can also join electronic communities called *newsgroups*, through which members exchange information about a common interest or affiliation by posting questions and answers to online sites. Or you can

---

Chart 5-1   Internet Sources for Literature

Directories for Finding Sites

Voice of the Shuttle   http://vos.ucsb.edu
  An annotated guide to literary resources online, with more than seventy pages of links.

Literary Resources on the Net   http://andromeda.rutgers.edu/~jlynch/Lit
  A collection of links dealing primarily with English and American literature.

IPL Literary Criticism Collection   http://www.ipl.org/div/litcrit
  From the Internet Public Library, a collection of critical and biographical Web sites about authors and their works.

Virtual Reference Works

Bartleby.com   http://www.bartleby.com
  Bills itself as the "preeminent Internet publisher of literature, reference, and verse, providing students, researchers, and the intellectually curious with unlimited access to books and information on the Web, free of charge."

Encyclopedia Mythica   http://www.pantheon.org
  Online encyclopedia covering mythology, folklore, and legends.

Reviews and Criticism

Arts & Letters Daily   http://aldaily.com
  A service of the *Chronicle of Higher Education*; includes daily links to essays, book reviews, interviews, and news in a wide range of online publications; coverage of literary topics is substantial.

become a member of an Internet discussion group, frequently called a *listserv*, whose subscribers use e-mail to converse on a particular subject. You will find e-mail discussion groups to join at Google Groups (http://groups.google.com), Yahoo! Groups (http://groups.yahoo.com), and Tile.net (www.tile.net/lists).

If you need additional information, you can visit one of these helpful reference sites:

Librarians' Internet Index	http://lii.org/search/file/netsearch
Matisse's Glossary of Internet Terms	http://www.matisse.net/files/glossary.html

Evaluating Online Sources

Although many online sources are informative and valuable, determining their credibility can be challenging. With scholarly books and journal articles, you can consider the information credible because it has been reviewed and edited; the authors are often recognized authorities, and their claims are documented. But anyone can create and publish a Web site or join a newsgroup. So when you use information from an electronic source, you want to be confident that it is reliable and that it comes from someone with the appropriate authority. Here are some guidelines for evaluating online materials:

- *Look for credentials.* What do you know about the people supplying the information? What's the basis of their expertise? Is the source also available in an established, conventional printed form?

- *Track down affiliations.* Who sponsors the online site? Is it a reputable group that you can easily identify? Is the information influenced by commercial or political sponsorship? Does the site include links to other resources?

- *Analyze motives.* What purpose does the site serve? Many online postings are trying to buy or sell something; others are promoting a favorite cause. These don't usually make good sources for research.

- *Consider currency and stability.* Is the material updated regularly? Is there an archive for older information?

- *Confirm your information.* Can you find other sources to verify what you've found online? Ideally, you want to have several different kinds of sources to achieve a credible balance of research material.

For more details about evaluating online sources, you can visit one of these sites:

- *Evaluating Web Sites*, a comprehensive and instructive guide to judging information resources for reliability and accuracy, at http://www.lesley.edu/library/guides/research/evaluating_web.html

- *Evaluating Web Pages: Techniques to Apply & Questions to Ask,* an online tutorial from the UC Berkeley Library, at http://www.lib.berkeley.edu/TeachingLib/Guides/Internet/Evaluate.html

Finally, check with your instructor to determine the types of resources considered appropriate for your specific assignment.

Using Reference Works in Print

As you can see, the library's computers provide an overwhelming number of sources and service options. You will have to spend some time with these data systems to find out how they work and how useful they are for your research. Most libraries still hold much of this and additional useful reference material in print. The *MLA International Bibliography*, for example, continues to be issued in book form. Your library probably has print versions of many indexes and guides to articles on literature. So if the computer terminals are crowded or not working, or if you simply want some peace and quiet while researching, the reference librarian can tell you where on the shelves these books are kept. You are likely to run across valuable material on shelves near the books you seek, an advantage to this often neglected ambulatory research system.

Working with Sources

Once you have located the books and articles you want to read and assimilate, you can begin reading, taking notes, and synthesizing the material.

Taking Notes

Many researchers use note cards for keeping track of the facts and opinions they find. If you decide to use cards, work out some system for recording information. Here are some suggestions:

1. Fill out a bibliography card every time you consult a new source, and record all the details necessary for citing this source in your paper, including where to find the source again. Then put the author's last name, an abbreviated title, and the page number or numbers on all the note cards you use for this source.
2. Write only one idea or point on each card. This allows you to shuffle the cards as you figure out the precise organization of your paper.
3. Put subject headings on the cards—one or two words in the upper right-hand corner to tell you what each note is about.
4. Summarize the ideas in your own words. If you think you might want to quote directly from the source, copy the author's exact words and enclose them in quotation marks.

Computers now come with a note card program, or you can purchase software for a note card system. You can use the computer note cards just as you would use index cards: title each card by topic, and then type your notes onto the card provided by the computer.

Using a Research Notebook

Another option is a double-entry research notebook where you summarize and analyze readings all in one location.

1. Divide a notebook or computer page vertically down the middle.
2. On the left side of the page, summarize your reading of the source material, and write down the complete bibliographic data and any URLs. Any exact words or phrases need to be placed within quotation marks.
3. On the right side of the page, comment on your sources, noting their importance to your topic and their relationship to other sources.

The response side of the divided notebook shows the evolution of your thinking, lets you articulate questions that arise as you read and process information, and guides you toward a thesis for your paper. The system also helps you to avoid the cut-and-paste style of research writing because it encourages synthesis and analysis throughout the process. Finally, this record of your thoughts helps to identify which ideas are your own and which you picked up along the way—a key distinction that safeguards against inadvertent plagiarism and allows you to claim your own thoughts with confidence.

Figure 5-1 provides an example of a student's notes on the article "Eveline and the Blessed Margaret Mary Alacoque" by Donald Torchiana. In the left column, the student summarizes the key points in his own words and includes a couple of direct quotations from the article. In the right column, the student records his thoughts and reactions to the article.

Using the Printout/Photocopy Option

If the time you can spend in the library is limited, you might want to print out an online article or photocopy portions of books in order to have these materials available to study at your convenience. In fact, you might find it easier to take notes from a printout than from a computer screen. You can underline or highlight key ideas, even color-coding these highlighted passages to fit different subtopics in your paper. You can also write comments or cross-references to other sources in the margins. It's a good idea to put the information from printouts and photocopies on note cards or into your research notebook. This procedure forces you to summarize the material in your own words and makes it much easier to sort the separate items into categories.

Notes	Responses
Source: Torchiana, p. 70	
Torchiana says about Margaret Mary Alacoque that: —as a child she lost a parent and was treated like a servant by relatives who raised her. —at age 10, refused an offer of marriage	Parallels with Eveline seem clear, but what do they mean? What's Joyce suggesting? The influence of Eveline's Catholic upbringing, for sure. Her destiny to be some kind of martyr?
—entered convent at age 24 —met hostility from the rest of sisters —performed menial tasks, took care of young children —Quotation: "Virtually addicted to suffering, she was corrected more than once for her singular notions or her clumsiness and slowness." —had a vision of Christ at age 26	The first vision could be like her first glimpse of Frank. How old was Eveline when she met Frank? If he's her savior, then why not go with him? Or does she think she needs to stay and be a "sacrificial victim"? To whom? Surely not her father.
p. 71 —told she had been chosen to be the instrument by which Christ's love would be made known —The Lord took her heart and put it within His own, then returned it to her breast	Is Eveline "addicted to suffering"? Could be. Is she comfortable with this role? This idea seems similar to Brandabur's view of Eveline.
—had a number of visions; in one she was told she would be a "sacrificial victim for the lack of charity among her sister communicants."	Her promise to her dying mother seems related to this role. But it's a warning to Eveline, one she seems to recognize.
—but her vision of the Sacred Heart spread	Do the critics read too much into this? Margaret Mary is mentioned only once in the story.

Figure 5-1 Sample Entry from a Divided-Page Research Notebook

Summarizing, Paraphrasing, and Quoting

In most of your notes, you will be summarizing or paraphrasing your source materials, rather than quoting the author's exact words. In a *summary* you condense the main point of an argument or passage in your own words. A summary is useful when you want to capture the gist of an idea without including the background or supporting details. Compare these sentences from an article about "Eveline" with the summary that follows it.

> **Original** "Joyce indicates why Eveline will not, in fact, be able to escape. Paralysis will win because she is not worthy to defeat it. Her inertia is revealed by the excessive value she places on the routine satisfactions of her present existence, and on the pathetically small indications of affection which her father has been prepared to give" (Hart 50).

> **Summary** Eveline won't be able to leave because she's too attached to her father and to the familiarity of her everyday life, according to Clive Hart (50).

In a *paraphrase* you restate comments and ideas from a source, using approximately the same number of words as the original. Although written in your own words and style, a good paraphrase will reflect the author's idea, tone, and point of view more clearly than a summary does. Here's a paraphrase of the passage from Clive Hart's article:

> Hart argues that Joyce shows us that Eveline is incapable of leaving home. That she doesn't have the strength of character to break away can be seen in her desperate attachment to the comforts of a familiar life, as well as to her father's meager expressions of love (50).

You will also find comments and observations that are so well expressed that you want to use the original wording rather than summarize or paraphrase it. Be sure to record the exact words of the original quotation, as well as the numbers of the pages on which they appear. Here is an example:

> Critic Clive Hart observes that Eveline's father "used to hunt Eveline and her companions in from their play" by "wielding his blackthorn stick like an angry god" (49).

Devising a Working Outline

As you are reading and taking notes, you should also be thinking about the organization of your points and ideas. Chances are the best arrangement won't emerge until you are fairly well along with your research—possibly not until you have finished it. But as you collect more and more notes, leaf through your cards or printouts occasionally to see if you can arrange them into three or four main categories to form the major claims in your argument or analysis. The sooner you can get a plan worked out, the more efficient your research becomes. You can see exactly what you are looking for and avoid wasting time on sources that would prove irrelevant or redundant.

Writing a First Draft

As we pointed out at the beginning of this chapter, some people write a preliminary draft before beginning their research, especially if they are eager to get their arguments written down before they forget them. If you use this method, you should devise a thesis, assemble your evidence from the primary source, order your ideas, and write a first draft, following the procedures discussed in Chapter 2. Then you can go to the library, as Wendy did, to locate and read a number of pertinent secondary sources and incorporate ideas from this reading into your paper at appropriate places.

On the other hand, if you are not sure about your topic or your approach, you can go to the library, locate some relevant secondary sources, and study them carefully. Then return to the primary source and begin the discovery process again, using freewriting or questioning or problem solving to refine your topic, devise a major claim, and generate ideas. You may have to do further research as you work through your interpretation, but that's all part of the recursive nature of writing.

Organizing Your Notes

Once you have a clearly focused thesis, go back and read through your note cards. Using the headings that you put on the cards, group the ones with similar ideas together in stacks. If you photocopied most or all of your sources, write headings on the first page of each photocopy and sort the articles that way. Then consult your working plan or rough outline, and arrange the stacks in the order that the headings appear there. As you write, the necessary information will be in front of you, ready to be incorporated into the first draft of your paper.

If your stacks of cards don't follow the outline but lie there in a confused, overlapping mess, all is not lost. You can still bring order out of chaos. Here are a few methods:

1. *Tinker with your outline.* It may seem like a step backward, but now that you have new information from your research, the whole topic may look different. Look at the main headings and change any that don't seem to fit; add others that you have good material for but overlooked when you made the working outline.

2. *Put your note cards into different groupings.* This process may suggest an organizing strategy that you wouldn't think of any other way.

3. *Set your notes aside and begin writing* —even if you begin in the middle of a thought. Force yourself, as in freewriting, to keep going, even if

your paper seems repetitive, disorganized, and sketchy. Eventually, the writing will begin to take shape, giving you an idea about where to start your first draft.

4. *Find a key article on the topic, and examine its structure.* You may be able to find an organizational scheme that will work for your paper.

5. *Explain your ideas to a friend who agrees to ask questions along the way.* Tape-record your discussion, and see whether it suggests a sensible order of exposition.

Using Quotations and Paraphrases

You want to be judicious in using the material you have gathered from secondary sources. In general, depend most upon your own interpretations of the primary material, use paraphrasing to introduce ideas gleaned through research, and turn to direct quotations of secondary sources only when the wording is especially original or powerful, saving that technique for special effect. Your main goal is to argue *your* thesis or advance *your* interpretation, not simply to paste together other people's thoughts and words. Don't just sprinkle your discussion with quotations and paraphrases; work them into your analysis and explain how they support your claims. Take a look at this example from a paper about "The Lottery":

> The author reveals the savagery that is hidden just beneath the surface of seemingly civilized exteriors. This duality of human nature is exhibited through the characterization and actions of the villagers. As Cleanth Brooks and Robert Penn Warren point out, "The cruel stoning is carried out by 'decent' citizens who in many other respects show themselves kind and thoughtful" (130). When it was time for the scapegoat to be murdered, Mrs. Delacroix, who earlier had made neighborly conversation with the victim, was one of the first to pick up a stone.

As you can see, the student writer backed up her observation about the duality of human nature with a direct quotation from a secondary source. She then used a detail from the primary source to nail down the point.

Integrating Sources

Whether you are quoting directly or simply paraphrasing someone else's ideas and observations, you should always give credit in the text of your paper to the person from whom you are borrowing. The MLA documentation style requires you to cite all sources *within* the paper. These in-text citations contain three important parts:

1. an introduction of the source, telling your reader that material from some authority is coming up, who or what the source is, and what the person's credentials are, if you know them;

2. the material from the source, quoted or paraphrased; and

3. the parenthetical documentation, which tells your reader that your use of the source is over and gives the page number for the source of that particular material.

More details about in-text citations are given in the explanation of the MLA documentation style at the end of this chapter (pages 93–94).

If you want your paper to read smoothly, pay particular attention to the way you introduce quotations and paraphrases. You need a ready supply of introductory phrases to slide the source material in gracefully—phrases like "As LeSeure discovered," "Professor Weber notes," and "According to Dr. Carter." These attributions help your readers to evaluate the source material as they read it and to distinguish source material from your remarks about it. Here are some more models for you to go by:

> As critic Lawrence Stone explains, daughters in Shakespeare's England were "often unwanted and might be regarded as no more than a tiresome drain on the economic resources of the family" (112).

> According to biographer Joan Givner, the failure of Porter's personal relationship with Josephson caused a temporary inability to write (221).

> D. G. Gillham remarks that the "male 'worm' " and "female 'rose' " in "The Sick Rose" have Freudian significance and "give rise in the speaker to half-hidden feelings of indecency, guilt, and fear so easily associated with sexual experience" (11).

> Prospero's suite in "The Masque of the Red Death" has been described by Kermit Vanderbilt as "a metaphor of nature and mortality" (382).

> "A beautiful virgin walled off from an imperfect world," Rachel Brownstein points out, "is the central figure in romance" (35).

Quoting from Primary Sources

The advice for handling quotations from secondary sources also applies to quoted material from primary sources: keep quoted passages brief; use them as support for your own observations, and don't rely on a quotation to make a point for you; integrate quotations smoothly and grammatically into your own sentences; vary the way you introduce the quotations. In her essay on "Eveline," Wendy Dennison provided these models:

> Eveline realizes that with her brothers gone, there is "nobody to protect her" (5).

> "She was about to explore another life with Frank" (Joyce 4), we are told, in faraway Buenos Ayres.

You will also need to cite the work you are quoting from so that your readers know exactly which passage you are referring to and where it is located. For short stories and novels, give the author's last name and the page number in the parenthetical citation. The author's name may be omitted if you mention it in your paper or if authorship is clear from context.

> We are told that Jake "took a moment or two to feel both proud and sad about his performance" (Gilb 56).
>
> The narrator of Gilb's story tells us that Jake "took a moment or two to feel both proud and sad about his performance" (56).

For poems, line numbers alone are usually sufficient to identify the source—provided that the author and title are given in your essay.

> The speaker's assertion that "Something there is that doesn't love a wall, / That wants it down" (35–36) represents one side of Frost's theme.

You do not need to include the word *line* or *lines* or its abbreviation in the parenthetical citation. When citing a play, give the act and scene numbers (without abbreviations), plus the line numbers if the work is in verse.

> In *Othello*, Iago's striking comment, "What you know, you know. / From this time forth I will never speak a word" (5.2.299–300), serves as a philosophic closure.

The numbers separated by periods mean "act 5, scene 2, lines 299 through 300." In plays that are not written in verse, you may simply cite page numbers, as you would with a quotation from a short story.

> Bono, Troy's friend and coworker, understands why Rose keeps after her husband to build a fence around their yard. "Some people build fences to keep people out," says Bono, "and other people build fences to keep people in. Rose wants to hold on to you all" (561).

You can get additional guidance for quoting primary sources on pages 26–27 (short stories), pages 351–53 (poetry), and pages 582–83 (drama).

Avoiding Plagiarism

Research is a kind of conversation among writers, their sources, and others interested in the topic. One of the challenges for writers, then, is to clearly define their part in this broader conversation both accurately and ethically. The core principle here is *respect*: for the person whose ideas you are employing, for your own voice and credibility, and for your readers.

The failure to give proper credit to your sources is called *plagiarism*. It usually involves carelessly—or, far worse, deliberately—presenting the words or ideas of another writer as your own. Most universities have strict policies on academic dishonesty that require sanctions ranging from failing a paper, to assigning a failing grade for the course, to dismissal from the university.

You can avoid this dishonesty by using a moderate amount of care in taking notes. Put quotation marks around any passages, even brief phrases, that you copy word for word. Circle the quotation marks in red or highlight the quoted material in some way, as a reminder to give credit to the source.

You must also avoid the original wording if you decide to *paraphrase* your sources, rather than quoting directly. Changing a few words or rearranging the phrases is not enough: such close paraphrasing is still considered plagiarism. The following examples may help you to see the difference between plagiarism and paraphrasing:

Original Passage: "The interest of the story lies not in the events, but in the reasons for Eveline's failure to accept the offer of salvation" (Hart 48).

Plagiarism: One critic notes that the story's main interest is not in its events but in the reasons why Eveline fails to accept Frank's offer of salvation.

Plagiarism: Most readers are interested not in the events of "Eveline" but in the reasons for the protagonist's failure to accept her salvation.

Paraphrase: As Clive Hart notes, we are interested not in what happens in the story but in why Eveline doesn't take the chance to save herself (48).

Combined Paraphrase and Direct Quotation: Hart notes that the main interest for the reader "lies not in the events" but in "Eveline's failure to accept the offer of salvation" (48).

Direct Quotation: "The interest of the story lies not in the events," critic Clive Hart claims, "but in the reasons for Eveline's failure to accept the offer of salvation" (48).

As you use your secondary sources, remember that no one wants to do the hard work of creating ideas and shaping an appropriate language only to have someone else take credit for it.

Rewriting and Editing

Many people who do researched writing make no attempt to work in direct quotations or provide complete citations in the first draft because pausing to do so interrupts the flow of their ideas. They just jot down the name of the person who has provided the information or idea; they go back later to fill in page numbers and integrate exact quotations as they revise their first draft. Putting self-stick notes on pages of sources you intend to use will help you find the precise material later.

Documenting Your Sources

Various academic disciplines use different documentation styles. Because you are writing about literature, the appropriate one for you to follow is the Modern Language Association style. Sample entries illustrating the MLA format appear at the end of this chapter. You may also use as a model the documentation included in the sample research paper that follows on pages 88–97.

Revising the Draft

Because a research paper entails the extra demands of incorporating other people's ideas and acknowledging these sources, you will want to take special care in rewriting your early drafts. The checklist for revising and editing researched writing, Chart 5-2 (page 87), will help you to turn your draft into a successful essay.

Formatting Your Paper

The document format recommended by the *MLA Handbook* is fairly simple. But individual course requirements may vary from the MLA design, so check with your instructor before you begin preparing your final copy. Here are some features to examine:

Margins. Provide margins of at least one inch at the top, bottom, and both sides of the page.

Spacing and indentions. Double-space throughout, including quotations and the Works Cited page. Indent paragraphs one-half inch or five spaces. Long prose quotations (five or more typed lines) and quotations of more than three lines of poetry should be double-spaced and indented one inch or ten spaces from the left margin.

Page numbers. Number all pages, beginning on the first page. Put the numbers in the upper-right-hand corner about one-half inch from the top. Place your last name before the page number in case the pages later become separated. Note the correct page numbering on the sample student paper, which follows.

Heading. The MLA does not require a separate title page. If your instructor asks you to use one, follow the format he or she provides. Otherwise, give your name and the date, plus any other information requested by your instructor (such as the title and number of the course), on the first page of your text. Place this heading an inch from the top of the page, aligned with the left margin. Note the heading on the sample student paper.

Title. Double-space after the heading and center the title of your paper. Do *not* underline or place your title in quotation marks, and do not set it in large type or capitalize all the letters. Do capitalize the first and last

Chart 5-2 Checklist for Revising and Editing Researched Writing

Check the Usual Things

1. Be sure the introduction states your thesis (see pages 15–17, 24–25).
2. Be sure each paragraph is unified, coherent, and directly related to your thesis (see pages 51–52, 55–56).
3. Be sure that the transitions between paragraphs are clear and effective (see page 57).
4. Be sure your conclusion reinforces your main argument (see page 26).

Check the Special Things

1. Be sure that you have introduced direct quotations gracefully, using the name and, if appropriate, the title or occupation of the person quoted.
2. Be sure each citation is accurate.
3. Be sure that paraphrases are in your own words and that sources are clearly acknowledged.
4. Be sure that you have not relied too heavily on a single source.
5. Be sure that you have written most of the paper yourself; you need to examine, analyze, or explain the material, not just splice together a lot of quotations and paraphrases.
6. Be sure to separate quotations with some comment of your own.
7. Be sure to underline or italicize the titles of books and magazines; put quotation marks around the titles of articles, stories, poems, and chapters in books.

words and all other words *except* articles (*a, an, the*), prepositions, coordinating conjunctions, and the *to* in infinitives. Double-space between your title and the first line of text.

Textual headings. If you use headings within your paper to guide readers through the discussion, keep them as short as possible and make them specific to the material that follows. Do not boldface, italicize, or use bigger type or all capitals for these headings.

Sample Documented Student Paper

The following is the documented version of the essay that Wendy Dennison wrote about "Eveline." See pages 67–70 for the undocumented version.

Wendy Dennison

Professor McMahan

English 102

11 March 2005

Fear of Failure in Joyce's "Eveline"

In his short story "Eveline," James Joyce gives
the protagonist an exciting chance to leave her old life
and begin a new one. But she rejects this offer that
Frank—or Fate—makes, preferring instead to settle
back into the dreary life she has known all along. Why
does she not go away with Frank when the opportunity seems so attractive? One critic, Magda de
Tolentino, says "Nothing but family bonds hold her
back" (74). Another critic thinks Eveline is "imprisoned" in her passive, feminine role of housekeeper
(Ingersoll 4), while another calls her "a meaningless
sacrificial victim for a religious community lacking
charity" (Torchiana 75). Some commentators think
she's afraid of marrying Frank. Professor Edward
Brandabur, for example, claims Eveline "is ever conscious of the effects on her mother of a brutal
marriage" (63), and Professor Thomas Dilworth maintains that "her mother's marriage to her father must
subconsciously condition her anticipation of married
life" (458).

Obviously many factors affect Eveline and influence her decision not to go with Frank. But in the last
analysis, I think, we need to examine Eveline's own
character, especially her timid personality, to discover
the answer to our question. For, as Professor Warren
Beck, has pointed out, "Eveline is not simply timid;
she is racked by inner conflict, finally to the point of
distraction" (113).

Since Eveline has been raised a Catholic, we know she would not take her promise to her dying mother lightly. But surely her promise to "keep the home together as long as she could" (Joyce 6) was given under extreme circumstances. It was unjust of her mother to ask such a sacrifice of her, and Eveline is aware of the unfairness: "Why should she be unhappy? She had a right to happiness" (6). We know that Eveline will always be haunted by that promise, but we do not expect her to give up her chance for a life of her own in order to be a dutiful daughter. Surely that promise cannot be the only reason she stays.

We certainly should not be surprised that Eveline might wish to leave her abusive father. A hot-tempered heavy drinker, he has taken advantage of his daughter's promise to her mother. She is forced to keep house for him, yet must beg for money to feed the family. He practically accuses her of stealing, claiming that "she used to squander the money, that she had no head, that he wasn't going to give her his hard-earned money to throw about the streets" (5). He has so frightened her with threats of beatings that she has "palpitations" (4). Eveline realizes that with her brothers gone, there is "nobody to protect her" (5) from her father's rage. Her father has treated Eveline badly and may abuse her even worse in the future. On the other hand, as Professor Ingersoll points out, Eveline's father offers "the comfort and security of the familiar" and as he grows older will probably be "less likely to have the strength to abuse her, as he did her mother" (3). Yes, getting away from her father would be in her best interests, but something keeps her there.

Eveline's home life is so unhealthy that we feel she would be wise to leave. Despite all the chores she performs, she still does not feel entirely at home in her father's house. For example, she knows nothing about the picture of the priest (Joyce 4), not even his name, yet the portrait seems quite important to her father. The dustiness of the house, of which Joyce reminds us periodically, suggests the pervasive dreariness of her daily life as she looks around "wondering where on earth all the dust came from" (4). Critic Clive Hart sums up her condition this way:

> Eveline has memories of a happier, freer past which contrasts both with the tedium of the present and with the uncertainty of the future.... The evenings, which used to be a time for play, are now one of drudgery, and even in childhood it was evident that happiness was something transient. (49).

Since her home is clearly not conducive to happiness, why does she stay there?

The main reason Eveline would remain in Ireland is that she is desperately afraid of the unknown. If she leaves the familiar, no matter how unpleasant, she risks failure. "She was about to explore another life with Frank" (Joyce 5), we are told, in faraway Buenos Ayres. The word *explore* is significant, as it brings to mind uncertainty and risk, two factors that Eveline is not prepared to deal with. She admits that hers is "a hard life," yet thinks that "now that she was about to leave it she did not find it a wholly undesirable life" (5). According to Professor Hart, Eveline is psychologically incapable of breaking away, and it shows in "the excessive value she places on the routine satisfactions of her present existence, and on the pathetically small indications of affection which her father has been prepared to give" (50). When she sits in the growing darkness with the letters in her lap, Eveline calls up a couple of good memories—of her father being jolly once on a picnic, of his kindness once when she was sick (Joyce 6). We see her trying to calm her fears, trying to convince herself that her home life is more bearable than it is. But, as Martin Dolch points out, "Change is already beyond her capacity and fills her with a crazy fear which mistakes salvation for destruction" (99).

Afraid of failing on her own, Eveline retreats into the familiar, telling herself that life with father cannot be as frightening as a risky, unknown life with Frank. In Professor Warren Beck's view, Eveline doesn't doubt Frank: "What she doubts is herself" (116). Eveline's doubts and her fear of failure override her fear of her father. She seems to decide that a predictable—if dreary and abused—life is better than a life without security or pattern. As William York Tindall puts it, "The end [of this story] is not a coming of awareness but an animal experience of inability" (15).

Works Cited

Beck, Warren. *Joyce's* Dubliners: *Substance, Vision, and Art.* Durham: Duke UP, 1969. Print.

Brandabur, Edward. *A Scrupulous Meanness: A Study of Joyce's Early Work.* Urbana: U of Illinois P, 1971. Print.

de Tolentino, Magda. "Family Bonds and Bondage within the Family: A Study of Family Ties in Clarice Lipsector and James Joyce." *Modern Language Studies* 18.2 (1988): 73–78. *JSTOR.* Web. 28 Feb. 2005.

Dilworth, Thomas. "The Numina of Joyce's 'Eveline.'" *Studies in Short Fiction* 15.4 (1978): 456–58. *Academic Search Premier.* Web. 28 Feb. 2005.

Dolch, Martin. "Eveline." *James Joyce's* Dubliners: *A Critical Handbook.* Ed. James R. Baker and Thomas F. Staley. Belmont: Wadsworth, 1969. 96–101. Print.

Hart, Clive. "Eveline." *James Joyce's* Dubliners: *Critical Essays.* Ed. Clive Hart. New York: Viking, 1969. 48–52. Print.

Ingersoll, Earl G. "The Stigma of Femininity in James Joyce's 'Eveline' and 'The Boarding House.' " *Studies in Short Fiction* 30.4 (1993): 501–10. *Academic Search Premier.* Web. 29 Feb. 2005.

Joyce, James. "Eveline." *Literature and the Writing Process.* Ed. Elizabeth McMahan, Susan X Day, and Robert Funk. 8th ed. Upper Saddle River: Prentice, 2007. 3–7. Print.

Tindall, William York. *A Reader's Guide to James Joyce.* New York: Noonday, 1959. Print.

Torchiana, Donald T. *Backgrounds for Joyce's* Dubliners. Boston: Allen, 1986. Print.

EXPLANATION OF THE MLA DOCUMENTATION STYLE

The documentation style of the Modern Language Association (MLA)—used in English, foreign languages and some other humanities—requires that source citations be given in the text of the paper rather than in footnotes or endnotes. This in-text style of documentation involves parenthetical references.

Throughout this section, all titles of independently published works—books, plays, magazines, journals, Web sites, online databases, television and radio programs, films, and works of art—are italicized. Titles of stories, articles, songs, and other shorter works included in larger publications are punctuated with quotation marks and not italicized.

In-Text Citations

A. You will usually introduce the cited material, whether quoted or paraphrased, by mentioning the name of the author in your lead-in and giving the page number (or numbers) in parentheses. Put the parenthetical reference near the cited material, but preserve the flow of your writing by placing the citation where a pause would naturally occur, preferably at the end of the sentence, as in this example:

> Edmund Wilson tells us that the author of *Uncle Tom's Cabin* felt "the book had been written by God" (5).

B. Your readers can identify this source by consulting your Works Cited at the end of your paper. The entry for the source cited above would appear like this one:

> Wilson, Edmund. *Patriotic Gore: Studies in the Literature of the American Civil War.* New York: Oxford UP, 1966. Print.

C. If you do not mention the author in your lead-in, include his or her last name in parentheses along with the page number, without an intervening comma, like this:

> One of the great all-time best-sellers, *Uncle Tom's Cabin* sold over 300,000 copies in America and more than 2 million copies world wide (Wilson 3).

D. If you refer to one of two or more works by the same author, put a comma after the author's last name and include a shortened title in the parenthetical reference.

> (Pinker, *Stuff* 95).

E. If you are using a source written or edited by more than three people, use only the name of the first person listed, followed by "et al." (meaning "and others") in your lead-in.

> Blair et al. observe that the fine arts were almost ignored by colonial writers (21).

Because *et* means "and," it isn't an abbreviation and therefore doesn't need a period.

F.   If you have to quote indirectly—something from another source not available to you—use "qtd. in" (for "quoted in") in your parenthetical reference. This example refers to a book written by Donald Johanson and Maitland Edey:

> Richard Leakey's wife, Maeve, told the paleoanthropologist David Johanson, "We heard all about your bones on the radio last night" (qtd. in Johanson and Edey 162).

Note: It is always best to track down the original source, in case it has not been quoted precisely. You may also find even better material for your purposes in the original.

Preparing the List of Works Cited

On a separate page at the end of the paper, alphabetize your Works Cited list for all sources mentioned in your paper. Format the list according to the these rules:

- Center Works Cited at the top of the page.
- Arrange your sources in alphabetical order by the last name of the author. If the author is not given in the source, alphabetize the source by the first main word in the title (excluding *A, An,* or *The*).
- Double-space the entire list, both within and between entries.
- Use hanging indention: put the first line of each entry flush with the left margin, and indent any subsequent lines in the entry one-half inch.
- In both titles and subtitles, capitalize the first and last words and all other words *except* articles (*a, an, the*), prepositions, coordinating conjunctions, and the *to* in infinitives.
- Omit any use of the words *page* or *pages* or *line* or *lines.* Do not even include abbreviations for these terms. Use numbers alone:

  Kinsley, Michael. "Continental Divide" *Time* 7 July 1997: 89–91.

- Shorten publishers' names: for example, use Pearson instead of Pearson Education or Norton instead of W. W. Norton and Co. or Oxford UP instead of Oxford University Press or U of Illinois P instead of University of Illinois Press. See sample entries 1 through 12.
- For books, include the city of publication, usually given on the title page of the work cited. If you find two or more cities, use only the first. It is not necessary to identify a state, province, or country after the city name.
- Use lowercase roman numerals (ii, xiv) for citing page numbers from a preface, introduction, or table of contents; use uppercase roman numerals in names of monarchs (Elizabeth II).

- Abbreviate months and titles of magazines as shown in the sample entries.
- Leave one space after all concluding punctuation marks.

Sample Entries for a List of Works Cited

The following models will help you write Works Cited entries for most of the sources you will use. If you use a source not illustrated in these examples, consult the more extensive list of sample entries found in the *MLA Style Manual and Guide to Scholarly Publishing*, 3rd ed. or the *MLA Handbook for Writers of Research Papers*, 7th ed., or ask your instructor for guidance.

The MLA now recommends including the medium of publication for all entries. Sources are divided into three categories: print, Web, and other common sources. Use *Print* for books, periodicals (magazine, journals, newspapers), and other printed materials. Use *Web* for any material you retrieved online. Other common sources include *Film, CD, DVD,* and *Radio* or *Television program.* The medium of publication will usually be the last item in the citation. But when *Web* is the medium, the last item should be the date of access. The sample entries on the following pages provide plenty of examples.

Citing Print Publications

Books

1. Book by one author

> Mizejewski, Linda. *Divine Decadence: Fascism, Female Spectacle, and the Makings of Sally Bowles.* Princeton: Princeton UP, 1992. Print.

2. Two or more books by the same author

> Pinker, Steven. *The Language Instinct: How the Mind Creates Language.* New York: Morrow, 1994. Print.
>
> ---. *The Stuff of Thought: Language as a Window into Human Nature.* New York: Viking, 2007. Print.

[Give the author's name in the first entry only. Thereafter, use three hyphens in place of the author's name, followed by a period and the title.]

3. Book by two or three authors

> Anderson, Terry, and Donald Leal. *Free Market Environmentalism.* Boulder: Westview, 1991. Print.

McCrum, William, William Cran, and Robert MacNeil. *The Story of English*. New York: Viking, 1986. Print.

[Notice that only the first author's name is in reversed order.]

4. Book by more than three authors

Medhurst, Martin J., et al. *Cold War Rhetoric: Strategy, Metaphor, and Ideology*. New York: Greenwood, 1990. Print.

[The phrase *et al.* is an abbreviation for *et alii*, meaning "and others." Because *et* is the whole Latin word for *and*, don't put a period after it.]

5. Book with an editor

Gallegos, Bee, ed. *English: Our Official Language?* New York: Wilson, 1994. Print.

[When the entry begins with the editor's name, put a comma and the abbreviation "ed." for "editor" after the person's name. For a book with two or more editors, use "eds."]

6. Book with an author and an editor

Vidal, Gore. *The Selected Essays of Gore Vidal*. Ed. Jay Parini. New York: Doubleday, 2008. Print.

["Ed." in front of a name means "Edited by."]

7. Essay or article in a collection, casebook, or critical edition.

Geist, Stanley. "Portraits from a Family Album: *Daisy Miller*." *Hudson Review* 5 (Summer 1952): 203–6. Rpt. in *James's* Daisy Miller. Ed. William T. Stafford. New York: Scribner's, 1963. 131–33. Print.

[If an italicized title contains another title that should be italicized, leave the inner title without italics.]

Matthews, James H. "Frank O'Connor." Lewisburg: Bucknell UP, 1976. Rpt. in *Contemporary Literary Criticism*. Ed. Dedria Bryfonski and Laurie Harris. Vol. 14. Detroit: Gale, 1983. 399–402. Print.

["Rpt." means "reprinted."]

8. Introduction, preface, or forward

Alexie, Sherman. Introduction. *Smoke Signals: A*
   Screenplay. By Sherman Alexie. New York:
   Hyperion, 1998. vii–xi. Print.

9. Work in an anthology

Butler, Octavia. "Bloodchild." *The Norton Anthology of*
   African American Literature. Ed. Henry Louis Gates
   Jr. and Nellie Y. McKay. New York: Norton, 1997.
   2480–94. Print.

10. Article in a reference book (unsigned and signed)

"Vietnam War." *The Columbia Encyclopedia.* 6th ed.
   2007. Print.
Van Doren, Carl. "Samuel Langhorne Clemens."
   The Dictionary of American Biography. 1958 ed.
   Print.

[For widely used reference books, do not give full publication
information. List only the edition, the year of publication, and the
medium of publication.]

11. Later (second or subsequent) edition

Harmon, William, and Hugh Holman. *A Handbook to*
   Literature. 11th ed. Upper Saddle River: Prentice,
   2008. Print.

12. A translated book

Cirlot, J. E. *A Dictionary of Symbols.* Trans.
   Jack Sage. 2nd ed. New York: Philosophical Lib.,
   1976. Print.

Periodicals

13. Article in a scholarly journal

Mason, John B. "Whitman's Catalogues: Rhetorical
   Means for Two Journeys in 'Song of
   Myself.'" *American Literature* 45 (1973):
   34–49. Print.

> Treuer, David. "Smartberries: Interpreting Erdrich's *Love*
>
> *Medicine.*" *American Indian Culture & Research*
>
> *Journal* 29.1 (2005): 21–36. Print.

[Give the volume number and the issue number, when available, for all journals. Add a period and the issue number directly after the volume number: 29.1 means volume 29, issue 1.]

14. Article from a monthly or bimonthly magazine

> Tocalino, Rob. "The 20-Century American Short Story:
>
> Three Authors, Three Generations." *Bookmarks*
>
> May/June 2006: 26–31. Print.

15. Article from a weekly or biweekly magazine

> Lahr, John. "Land of Lost Souls: David Rabe's
>
> America." *New Yorker* 24 Nov. 2008: 114–20.
>
> Print.

16. Newspaper article

> Weiner, Jon. "Vendetta: The Government's Secret War
>
> against John Lennon." *Chicago Tribune* 5 Aug.
>
> 1984, sec 3:1. Print.

17. Review of a book or movie

> Grice, Helena. Rev. of *Image and Power: Women in*
>
> *Fiction in the Twentieth Century*, ed. Sarah
>
> Sceats and Gail Cunningham. *English* 46 (1997):
>
> 175–78. Print.
>
> Stack, Peter. "'Smoke' Causes Tears of Sadness,
>
> Joy." Rev. of *Smoke Signals*, dir. Chris Eyre.
>
> *San Francisco Chronicle* 3 July 1998:C7. Print.

Citing Online Publications

You are no longer required to include uniform resource locators (URLs, also called Web addresses) when citing online sources—unless you think your readers will not be able to locate the source without the URL. Conclude all entries with *Web* as the medium of publication, followed by the date of access.

Online Periodicals

18. Articles from online databases

If you retrieve source material from a full-text database, you need to indicate that you read it in electronic form. You will probably use a service to which your library subscribes, such as Academic Search Premier, JSTOR, Expanded Academic ASAP, ProQuest, Project Muse, Galenet, LexisNexis. Most of the items in these databases were previously published in print. Give the print information first. If possible, give the inclusive page numbers or, when pagination is not continuous, the first page number and a plus sign; if page numbers are not available, use *n. pag.* Do *not* include the database URL or information about the library. Complete the citation by giving the name of the database (italicized), medium of publication (Web), and the date of access. Here are examples of entries for periodical publications retrieved from online databases:

Hammer, Langdon. "Confluences of Sound and Sense: Kay Ryan's Idiosyncratic Approach to the Commonplace." *American Scholar* 77.2 (Summer 2008): 58–59. *Academic Search Premier.* Web. 14 Dec. 2008.

Kennedy, J. Gerald, and Robert Beuka. "Imperilled Communities in Edward P. Jones's *Lost in the City* and Dagoberto Gilb's *The Magic of Blood.*" *The Yearbook of English Studies* 31 (2001): 10–23. *JSTOR.* Web. 6 Oct. 2008.

Parascandola, Louis J. "Love and Sex in a Totalitarian Society: An Exploration of Ha Jin and George Orwell." *Studies in the Humanities* 33.1 (June 2005): 38+. *Expanded Academic ASAP.* Web. 22 Nov. 2008.

Welty, Eudora. Rev. of *Pilgrim at Tinker Creek* by Annie Dillard. *New York Times Book Review* 24 Mar. 1974: 36–37. *ProQuest.* Web. 14 Sept. 2007.

19. Articles published independently on the Web

For articles that are available on independent Web sites—as opposed to articles accessed from an aggregate database—cite the author, title, and publication data for the printed version as usual; then give the number of pages, paragraphs, or other sections of the electronic version, if provided on the site. Conclude with the medium of publication (*Web*) and the date of access. Here are sample entries for articles on the Web:

Borroff, Marie. "Another Look at Robert Frost's
    'Birches.'" *Literary Imagination Online* 7 (2005):
    69–80. Web. 8 Jan. 2009.

Yeoman, Barry. "Into the Closet: Can Therapy Make Gay
    People Straight?" *Salon.com* 22 May 2000: n. pag.
    Web. 23 May 2000.

"Vietnam War Memorial." *Encyclopaedia Britannica*
    Online. Encyclopaedia Britannica, 2008. Web.
    14 June 2008.

Keller, Julia. "New Hope for Do-Nothing Nobodies:
    A Guy Named Sam Johnson." *ChicagoTribune.*
    com. Chicago Tribune, 19 Oct. 2008. Web.
    23 Nov. 2008.

Other Web Sources

20. An entire Web site

Celestial TimePiece: A Joyce Carol Oates Home Page.
    Ed. Randy Souther. Gleeson Library, U of San
    Francisco, 1995. Web. 27 Nov. 2008.

21. Part of a Web site

Nelson, Cary. "Japanese American Concentration Camp
    Haiku." *Modern American Poetry.* Dept. of English,
    U of Illinois, Urbana-Champaign, 2002. Web.
    18 Nov. 2008.

Citing Other Common Sources

For other sources, include enough information to permit an interested reader to locate your original source. Be sure to arrange this information in a logical fashion, following as much as possible the order and punctuation of the entries provided earlier. To be safe, consult your instructor for suggestions about documenting unusual material.

23. A television or radio broadcast

Sedaris, David. Interview by Terry Gross. *Fresh Air.* NPR. WHYY, Philadelphia. 9 June 2008. Radio.

24. Sound recording

Welty, Eudora. "Why I Live at the P. O." Read by the author. *Essential Welty.* Rec. 1956. Dir. Ward Botsford. Caedmon, 2006. CD.

25. Film or video recording

Brokeback Mountain. Dir. Ang Lee. Perf. Heath Ledger, Jake Gyllenhaal, Michelle Williams. Screenplay by Larry McMurtry and Diana Ossana. Universal, 2005. Focus Features, 2006. DVD.

[Begin with the title (italicized) and include the director, distributor, and year of release. Include any other details that seem pertinent—names of performers, screenwriters, and producer—between the title and the distributor. For video recordings, include the release date and the medium.]

PART II

Writing About Short Fiction

This section, focusing on the short story, covers the literary and rhetorical elements that you need to understand in order to write effectively about short fiction.

6

How Do I Read Short Fiction?

As noted author Joyce Carol Oates has observed, short fiction can be difficult to understand "because it demands compression; each sentence must contribute to the effect of the whole. Its strategy is not to include an excess of detail but to exclude, to select, to focus as sharply as possible." In order to grasp the full meaning of a story, you need to read it at least twice. Preferably, let some time elapse between readings so that you can mull the story over in your mind. Your initial reading can be purely for pleasure, but the second reading should involve careful and deliberate study of all the elements that combine to produce a unified whole. You should gain both pleasure and knowledge from reading short fiction. The knowledge frequently stems from understanding the *theme*, which usually provides some insight into the human condition, although sometimes contemporary short stories simply raise moral or ethical questions and make no pretense of providing answers.

Notice the Structure

During the second reading, notice the way the story is structured. The action (that is, what happens) is called the *plot* and is usually spurred by some *conflict* involving the main character (the *protagonist*). Except in some modern works, most short stories have a clear beginning, middle, and end during which the conflict producing the action becomes increasingly intense, building to a *climax* that sometimes resolves the conflict and sometimes simply concludes it—often in catastrophe. Do not expect many happy endings in serious fiction. A somber conclusion is more likely.

Usually stories proceed in regular chronological order following a time sequence similar to that in real life. But occasionally an author employs *flashbacks*—stopping the forward action to recount an episode that happened in the past—in order to supply necessary background material or to maintain suspense. By closely following the shifts in time in Louise Erdrich's "The Red Convertible," readers discover what the narrator means when he says, "Now Henry owns the whole car, and...Lyman walks everywhere he goes." And if William Faulkner had written "A Rose for Emily" chronologically, without the distorted time sequence, the stunning impact of the conclusion would have been lost.

Consider Point of View and Setting

Sometimes the *point of view*—the position from which an author chooses to relate a story—can be crucial to the effectiveness, even to the understanding, of short fiction. In Alice Walker's "Everyday Use," we are given the mother's views and feelings about her two quite different daughters. In other stories, the point of view provides access to the thoughts and feelings of more than one character. In Nathaniel Hawthorne's "Birthmark," for example, an all-seeing, all-knowing or *omniscient* narrator provides access to the thoughts and feelings of all the major characters in the story. Ernest Hemingway, in "Hills like White Elephants," chooses to let his characters tell the story themselves through conversation. This *objective* (sometimes called *dramatic*) point of view is revealed by a glance at the pages, which consist primarily of dialogue. Some authors select one character to tell the story firsthand, but these first-person narrators can play quite different roles. In "I Stand Here Ironing," Tillie Olsen creates a strong sense of believability by presenting the reflections running through a mother's mind as she recalls her difficulties in raising a daughter with too little money and no husband to help. In Raymond Carver's "What We Talk About When We Talk About Love," the first-person narrator is essentially an observer, a peripheral character who reports the conversation between Mel and Terry but is not himself the focus of it. The narrator of "The Lesson" by Toni Cade Bambara acts as a "hostile witness" to the scenes and events she encounters, resisting the hard truths about class and oppression that she, and the reader, must finally acknowledge.

The *setting* of a story, like the point of view, is sometimes important, sometimes not. In many of the stories included in this anthology, setting plays a role of some consequence. For instance, John Steinbeck opens "The Chrysanthemums" with this description:

> The high gray-flannel fog of winter closed off the Salinas Valley from the sky and from all the rest of the world. On every side it sat like a lid on the mountains and made of the great valley a closed pot.

The isolation of the valley by the fog suggests the isolation of Elisa Allen, whose energies and experiences are restricted by her living on the ranch. As you study a short story, give some thought to the setting. Could the events just as well take place somewhere else? Or does the setting seem to play an integral part? How does its time period affect the story? Does the setting in some way add to the meaning of the work?

Study the Characters

Focusing on *characterization* often proves a fruitful approach to analyzing and writing about a short story or a play. Wendy Dennison adopts this strategy in her paper on "Eveline" (pages 67–70). You'll notice, if you look again at Wendy's paper, that she examines several other key elements to gain a thorough understanding of the title character. She discusses the setting because Eveline's dreary life is influenced by the drabness of her surroundings. She considers the plot and finds Eveline's paralysis at the end tied directly to her characterization as a timid, duty-bound daughter. She examines the imagery and finds that the religious images underscore Eveline's devout nature while, at the same time, the pervasive dust shrouds her barren existence. All of these elements combine to reveal Joyce's theme of a young woman's life sadly circumscribed by her submission to duty, family, and church.

As you reread a story, pay special attention to those passages in quotation marks that characters speak to each other. You can begin to determine characterization from these exchanges, just as you come to know real people partly by what they say. As you form an understanding of a character, notice what other people in the story say about that person and how they respond to that person, as well as what the author reveals of that person's thoughts and past behavior. Because fiction often allows us access to what the characters are thinking (as well as doing), we can sometimes know fictional persons better than we do our closest friends and family members. Sometimes, we can be certain of a character's motivation for behaving in a certain way; at other times, motivation becomes one of the elements to be determined before we can fully appreciate the work.

In Hawthorne's "The Birthmark," in order to understand why Dr. Aylmer is willing to risk his young wife's life, we need to examine his motives and behavior. In doing so, we discover that his faith in science leads to his overweening desire to create perfection—to establish (without success, of course) that science can control and improve on nature. And in Tim O'Brien's "The Things They Carried," we see that the author uses the details of what the men carried with them to take us into their minds—to reveal their motivations and define their personalities.

Foils

A *foil* is a minor character whose role sharpens our understanding of a major character by providing a contrast. Although far more common in drama than in the short story, foils can also prove useful in the analysis of works of fiction.

In Flannery O'Connor's "Good Country People," Mrs. Freeman's placid, uncultivated, but contented daughters serve to point up the discontent of the well-educated but neurotic main character, Joy/Hulga. In

"A & P," John Updike uses two minor characters to highlight why the story's narrator, Sammy, decides to quit his job. Stoksie, the fellow checker, prefigures what Sammy might become if he stays at the A & P; and Lengel, the store manager, represents the authority figure Sammy is rebelling against.

After you have read a fictional work, ask yourself why the author included the minor characters. What role do they serve in the work as a whole? Often the role of a minor character will provide an appropriate focus for writing an analysis of a short story, a novel, or a play.

Look for Specialized Literary Techniques

As you study a story on second reading, you may notice irony and foreshadowing that you missed the first time through. Since *irony* involves an upsetting of expectations—having the opposite happen from what would be usual—you sometimes need to know the outcome of an action in order to detect the full extent of the irony. *Foreshadowing* works the same way: you may not be aware of these hints of future happenings until the happenings finally occur. But when you go through a story again, both irony and foreshadowing become easily apparent and contribute to the meaning and effectiveness.

Be alert also for *images*—for words and phrases that put a picture in your mind. These images increase the enjoyment of reading fiction and, if deliberately repeated, can become *motifs* that emphasize some important element in the story and thus convey meaning. The numerous images of the protagonist's active hands and fluttering fingers in Sherwood Anderson's "Hands" establish an impression of Wing Biddlebaum's fragile, panicky nature. If a repeated image gathers significant meaning, it then becomes a *symbol*—to be clearly related to the theme or central argument of the story. Biddlebaum's nervous hands symbolize the fear and repression that restrict his existence, just as the repeated images of dust and decay in Faulkner's "A Rose for Emily" symbolize the deterioration of Miss Emily's mind and the fortunes of her once revered family.

Examine the Title

The title may in some way point toward or be related to the meaning. Richard Wright's title "The Man Who Was Almost a Man" evokes his theme: the difficulty that black males encounter in achieving manhood in America. Sometimes, the title identifies the controlling symbol, as in John Steinbeck's "The Chrysanthemums" and Sherwood Anderson's "Hands." Joseph Conrad's title "Heart of Darkness" directs us straight to his subject: the evil that lurks at the core of human nature.

Investigate the Author's Life and Times

Sometimes biographical and background information can be illuminating. For instance, knowing Hawthorne's attitude toward original sin enriches a reading of "The Birthmark," just as some knowledge of the Catholic faith can explain the circumstances that influence the young woman's decision in Joyce's "Eveline." Knowing what life was like for poor Americans during the Great Depression of the 1930s helps to clarify the forces that drive the protagonists in Wright's "The Man Who Was Almost a Man" and Olsen's "I Stand Here Ironing."

Continue Questioning to Discover Theme

Your entire study of these various elements of fiction should lead to an understanding of the meaning, or *theme*, of the story. You need to ponder everything about a short story in order to discover its theme. Keep asking yourself questions until you come up with some meaningful observation about human behavior or the conduct of society. The questions in Chart 6-1 on page 110 will guide you in exploring any story and perhaps spark that essential insight that leads to understanding.

Chart 6-1   Critical Questions for Reading the Short Story

Before planning an analysis of any of the selections in the anthology of short stories, write out the answers to the following questions to be sure you understand the piece and to help you generate material for your paper.

1. Who is the main character? Does this person's character change during the course of the story? Do you feel sympathetic toward the main character? What sort of person is she or he? Does this character have a foil?

2. What pattern or structure is there to the development of the plot? Can you describe the way the events are organized? Is the structure significant to the meaning?

3. Does surprise play an important role in the plot? Is there foreshadowing? Does the author use flashbacks?

4. Is anything about the story ironic?

5. Is there any symbolism in the story? How does the author make you aware of symbolic actions, people, or objects?

6. What is the setting—the time and location? How important are these elements in the story? Could it be set in another time or place just as well? Is the setting significant to the meaning?

7. Describe the atmosphere of the story, if it is important. How does the author create this atmosphere?

8. Who narrates the story? Is the narrator reliable? What effect does the point of view have on your understanding of the story? What would be gained or lost if the story were told from a different point of view (for example, by another character)?

9. How does the title relate to the other elements in the story and to the overall meaning?

10. What is the theme of the story? Can you state it in a single sentence? How is this theme carried out?

11. Does the author's style of writing affect your interpretation of the story? If so, how would you describe the style? For example, is it conversational or formal? Familiar or unfamiliar? Simple or ornate? Ironic or satiric?

7

Writing About Structure

When you focus on structure in discussing a literary work, you are examining the way the parts fit together to form a unified whole. Examining the structure often proves an excellent means of understanding a short story, novel, poem, or play and also provides a good way to approach a written literary analysis.

What Is Structure?

Most works of literature have an underlying pattern that serves as a framework or **structure**. You are familiar with the way plays are divided into acts and scenes, identified with numerals in the script, and marked in a stage production by the opening and closing of the curtain. The structure of television drama is often marked by commercial breaks. (For a discussion of dramatic structure, see Chapter 17, "Writing About Dramatic Structure.") Poems also have a visible structure, being divided into lines and stanzas. Sometimes poetic structure is complex and arbitrary, involving a certain number of lines, an established meter, and a fixed rhyme scheme. (See Chapter 15, "Writing About Poetic Form.") Novels, as you know, are divided into chapters, usually numbered and often titled, but sometimes not. Some short stories have no visible structure at all, but many do: they have space breaks indicating the divisions. Occasionally in stories (like Faulkner's "A Rose for Emily") and often in novellas, these sections are numbered.

In **narrative** works like novels and short stories, the plot itself is the main structural element, but these works also contain underlying structural features. Although not visible like chapter divisions or space breaks, the underlying structure serves an integral function just as a skeleton does in providing support for the body. Discovering, examining, and understanding these underlying structures will involve delving beneath the surface to discover the meaning of the work.

How Do I Discover Structure?

First, consider the *plot.* What is the central conflict and how is it re-solved? Do the events in the story move in a straight line from the beginning of the conflict to its resolution? Or are there interruptions and digressions? Are there flashbacks? Is time manipulated in any other way? If so, why? For instance, without the time shifts in the plot of Faulkner's "A Rose for Emily," there would be no suspense, and we would lose the impact of the final revelation.

If the story has any visible structural features, such as space between sections, try to figure out why they are there. Do they divide scenes? Do they indicate time shifts?

Look next for patterns, especially for contrasts and for repetitions. In "The Things They Carried," the story included in this chapter, Tim O'Brien alternates descriptions of the physical burdens of the soldiers with descriptions of the inner, psychological burdens they carry with them. The story also involves repetitions of key events told from different vantage points and with different amounts of detail.

Look always at beginnings and endings. "The Things They Carried" begins with the romantic fantasies of the main character, Jimmy Cross, which contrast sharply with the same character's fantasies of leadership at the end of the story. How did this change in character happen?

When analyzing any work of literature, don't forget to consider the title. Does it have any relationship to the plot? Sometimes the title touches on the central conflict or an important idea, thus focusing our attention on the structure of the story and reinforcing our understanding of the theme.

Looking at Structure

With our discussion of structure in mind, read Tim O'Brien's "The Things They Carried," which follows, and try to determine how the parts work together to convey the meaning of the story.

Tim O'Brien   1946–

Tim O'Brien was born in Austin, Minnesota. After graduating *summa cum laude* from Macalester College and doing graduate work at Harvard, he was drafted into the army and served in Vietnam, where he was promoted to sergeant and received the Purple Heart. "Good stories," he told an interviewer, "deal with our moral struggles, our uncertainties, our dreams, our blunders, our contradictions, our endless quest for understanding. Good stories do not resolve the mysteries of the human spirit but rather describe and expand upon those mysteries."

The Things They Carried

First Lieutenant Jimmy Cross carried letters from a girl named Martha, a junior at Mount Sebastian College in New Jersey. They were not love letters, but Lieutenant Cross was hoping, so he kept them folded in plastic at the bottom of his rucksack. In the late afternoon, after a day's march, he would dig his foxhole, wash his hands under a canteen, unwrap the letters, hold them with the tips of his fingers, and spend the last hour of light pretending. He would imagine romantic camping trips into the White Mountains in New Hampshire. He would sometimes taste the envelope flaps, knowing her tongue had been there. More than anything, he wanted Martha to love him as he loved her, but the letters were mostly chatty, elusive on the matter of love. She was a virgin, he was almost sure. She was an English major at Mount Sebastian, and she wrote beautifully about her professors and roommates and midterm exams, about her respect for Chaucer and her great affection for Virginia Woolf. She often quoted lines of poetry; she never mentioned the war, except to say, Jimmy, take care of yourself. The letters weighed ten ounces. They were signed "Love, Martha," but Lieutenant Cross understood that "Love" was only a way of signing and did not mean what he sometimes pretended it meant. At dusk, he would carefully return the letters to his rucksack. Slowly, a bit distracted, he would get up and move among his men, checking the perimeter, then at full dark he would return to his hole and watch the night and wonder if Martha was a virgin.

The things they carried were largely determined by necessity. Among the necessities or near necessities were P-38 can openers, pocket knives, heat tabs, wrist watches, dog tags, mosquito repellant, chewing gum, candy, cigarettes, salt tablets, packets of Kool-Aid, lighters, matches, sewing kits, Military Payment Certificates, C rations, and two or three canteens of water. Together, these items weighed between fifteen and twenty pounds, depending upon a man's habits or rate of metabolism. Henry Dobbins, who was a big man, carried extra rations; he was especially fond of canned peaches in heavy syrup over pound cake. Dave Jensen, who practiced field hygiene, carried a toothbrush, dental floss, and several hotel-size bars of soap he'd stolen on R & R in Sydney, Australia. Ted Lavender, who was scared, carried tranquilizers until he was shot in the head outside the village of Than Khe in mid-April. By necessity, and because it was SOP,[1] they all carried steel helmets that weighed five pounds including the liner and camouflage cover. They carried the standard fatigue jackets and trousers. Very few carried underwear. On their feet they carried jungle boots—2.1 pounds—and Dave Jensen carried three pairs of socks and a can of Dr. Scholl's foot powder as a precaution against trench foot. Until he was shot, Ted Lavender carried six or seven ounces of premium dope, which for him was a necessity. Mitchell Sanders, the RTO,[2] carried condoms. Norman Bowker carried a diary. Rat Kiley carried comic books. Kiowa, a devout Baptist, carried an illustrated New Testament that had been presented to him by his father, who taught Sunday school in Oklahoma City, Oklahoma. As a hedge against bad times, however, Kiowa also carried his grandmother's distrust of the white man, his grandfather's old hunting hatchet. Necessity dictated. Because the land was mined and booby-trapped, it was SOP

---

[1]Standard operating procedure.
[2]Radiotelephone operator.

for each man to carry a steel-centered, nylon-covered flak jacket, which weighed 6.7 pounds, but which on hot days seemed much heavier. Because you could die so quickly, each man carried at least one large compress bandage, usually in the helmet band for easy access. Because the nights were cold, and because the monsoons were wet, each carried a green plastic poncho that could be used as a raincoat or ground sheet or makeshift tent. With its quilted liner, the poncho weighed almost two pounds, but it was worth every ounce. In April, for instance, when Ted Lavender was shot, they used his poncho to wrap him up, then to carry him across the paddy, then to lift him into the chopper that took him away.

They were called legs or grunts.

To carry something was to "hump" it, as when Lieutenant Jimmy Cross humped his love for Martha up the hills and through the swamps. In its intransitive form, "to hump" meant "to walk," or "to march," but it implied burdens far beyond the intransitive.

Almost everyone humped photographs. In his wallet, Lieutenant Cross   5 carried two photographs of Martha. The first was a Kodachrome snapshot signed "Love," though he knew better. She stood against a brick wall. Her eyes were gray and neutral, her lips slightly open as she stared straight-on at the camera. At night, sometimes, Lieutenant Cross wondered who had taken the picture, because he knew she had boyfriends, because he loved her so much, and because he could see the shadow of the picture taker spreading out against the brick wall. The second photograph had been clipped from the 1968 Mount Sebastian yearbook. It was an action shot—women's volleyball—and Martha was bent horizontal to the floor, reaching, the palms of her hands in sharp focus, the tongue taut, the expression frank and competitive. There was no visible sweat. She wore white gym shorts. Her legs, he thought, were almost certainly the legs of a virgin, dry and without hair, the left knee cocked and carrying her entire weight, which was just over one hundred pounds. Lieutenant Cross remembered touching that left knee. A dark theater, he remembered, and the movie was *Bonnie and Clyde*, and Martha wore a tweed skirt, and during the final scene, when he touched her knee, she turned and looked at him in a sad, sober way that made him pull his hand back, but he would always remember the feel of the tweed skirt and the knee beneath it and the sound of the gunfire that killed Bonnie and Clyde, how embarrassing it was, how slow and oppressive. He remembered kissing her good night at the dorm door. Right then, he thought, he should've done something brave. He should've carried her up the stairs to her room and tied her to the bed and touched that left knee all night long. He should've risked it. Whenever he looked at the photographs, he thought of new things he should've done.

What they carried was partly a function of rank, partly of field specialty.

As a first lieutenant and platoon leader, Jimmy Cross carried a compass, maps, code books, binoculars, and a .45-caliber pistol that weighed 2.9 pounds fully loaded. He carried a strobe light and the responsibility for the lives of his men.

As an RTO, Mitchell Sanders carried the PRC-25 radio, a killer, twenty-six pounds with its battery.

As a medic, Rat Kiley carried a canvas satchel filled with morphine and plasma and malaria tablets and surgical tape and comic books and all the things a medic must carry, including M & M's for especially bad wounds, for a total weight of nearly twenty pounds.

As a big man, therefore a machine gunner, Henry Dobbins carried the M-60,   10 which weighed twenty-three pounds unloaded, but which was almost always loaded. In addition, Dobbins carried between ten and fifteen pounds of ammunition draped in belts across his chest and shoulders.

As PFCs or Spec 4s, most of them were common grunts and carried the standard M-16 gas-operated assault rifle. The weapon weighed 7.5 pounds unloaded, 8.2 pounds with its full twenty-round magazine. Depending on numerous factors, such as topography and psychology, the rifleman carried anywhere from twelve to twenty magazines, usually in cloth bandoliers, adding on another 8.4 pounds at minimum, fourteen pounds at maximum. When it was available, they also carried M-16 maintenance gear—rods and steel brushes and swabs and tubes of LSA oil—all of which weighed about a pound. Among the grunts, some carried the M-79 grenade launcher, 5.9 pounds unloaded, a reasonably light weapon except for the ammunition, which was heavy. A single round weighed ten ounces. The typical load was twenty-five rounds. But Ted Lavender, who was scared, carried thirty-four rounds when he was shot and killed outside Than Khe, and he went down under an exceptional burden, more than twenty pounds of ammunition, plus the flak jacket and helmet and rations and water and toilet paper and tranquilizers and all the rest, plus the unweighed fear. He was dead weight. There was no twitching or flopping. Kiowa, who saw it happen, said it was like watching a rock fall, or a big sandbag or something— just boom, then down—not like the movies where the dead guy rolls around and does fancy spins and goes ass over teakettle—not like that, Kiowa said, the poor bastard just flat-fuck fell. Boom. Down. Nothing else. It was a bright morning in mid-April. Lieutenant Cross felt the pain. He blamed himself. They stripped off Lavender's canteens and ammo, all the heavy things, and Rat Kiley said the obvious, the guy's dead, and Mitchell Sanders used his radio to report one U.S. KIA[3] and to request a chopper. Then they wrapped Lavender in his poncho. They carried him out to a dry paddy, established security, and sat smoking the dead man's dope until the chopper came. Lieutenant Cross kept to himself. He pictured Martha's smooth young face, thinking he loved her more than anything, more than his men, and now Ted Lavender was dead because he loved her so much and could not stop thinking about her. When the dust-off[4] arrived, they carried Lavender aboard. Afterward they burned Than Khe. They marched until dusk, then dug their holes, and that night Kiowa kept explaining how you had to be there, how fast it was, how the poor guy just dropped like so much concrete. Boom-down, he said. Like cement.

In addition to the three standard weapons—the M-60, M-16, and M-79—they carried whatever presented itself, or whatever seemed appropriate as a means of killing or staying alive. They carried catch-as-catch-can. At various times, in various situations, they carried M-14s and CAR-15s and Swedish Ks and grease guns and captured AK-47s and Chi-Coms and RPGs and Simonov carbines and black-market Uzis and .38-caliber Smith & Wesson handguns and 66 mm LAWs

---

[3]Killed in action.
[4]Helicopter.

and shotguns and silencers and blackjacks and bayonets and C-4 plastic explosives. Lee Strunk carried a slingshot; a weapon of last resort, he called it. Mitchell Sanders carried brass knuckles. Kiowa carried his grandfather's feathered hatchet. Every third or fourth man carried a Claymore antipersonnel mine—3.5 pounds with its firing device. They all carried fragmentation grenades—fourteen ounces each. They all carried at least one M-18 colored smoke grenade—twenty-four ounces. Some carried CS or tear-gas grenades. Some carried white-phosphorus grenades. They carried all they could bear, and then some, including a silent awe for the terrible power of the things they carried.

In the first week of April, before Lavender died, Lieutenant Jimmy Cross received a good-luck charm from Martha. It was a simple pebble, an ounce at most. Smooth to the touch, it was a milky-white color with flecks of orange and violet, oval-shaped, like a miniature egg. In the accompanying letter, Martha wrote that she had found the pebble on the Jersey shoreline, precisely where the land touched water at high tide, where things came together but also separated. It was this separate-but-together quality, she wrote, that had inspired her to pick up the pebble and to carry it in her breast pocket for several days, where it seemed weightless, and then to send it through the mail, by air, as a token of her truest feelings for him. Lieutenant Cross found this romantic. But he wondered what her truest feelings were, exactly, and what she meant by separate-but-together. He wondered how the tides and waves had come into play on that afternoon along the Jersey shoreline when Martha saw the pebble and bent down to rescue it from geology. He imagined bare feet. Martha was a poet, with the poet's sensibilities, and her feet would be brown and bare, the toenails unpainted, the eyes chilly and somber like the ocean in March, and though it was painful, he wondered who had been with her that afternoon. He imagined a pair of shadows moving along the strip of sand where things came together but also separated. It was phantom jealousy, he knew, but he couldn't help himself. He loved her so much. On the march, through the hot days of early April, he carried the pebble in his mouth, turning it with his tongue, tasting sea salts and moisture. His mind wandered. He had difficulty keeping his attention on the war. On occasion he would yell at his men to spread out the column, to keep their eyes open, but then he would slip away into daydreams, just pretending, walking barefoot along the Jersey shore, with Martha, carrying nothing. He would feel himself rising. Sun and waves and gentle winds, all love and lightness.

What they carried varied by mission.

When a mission took them to the mountains, they carried mosquito netting, machetes, canvas tarps, and extra bug juice.   15

If a mission seemed especially hazardous, or if it involved a place they knew to be bad, they carried everything they could. In certain heavily mined AOs,[5] where the land was dense with Toe Poppers and Bouncing Betties, they took turns humping a twenty-eight-pound mine detector. With its headphones and big sensing plate, the equipment was a stress on the lower back and shoulders, awkward to handle, often useless because of the shrapnel in the earth, but they carried it anyway, partly for safety, partly for the illusion of safety.

---

[5]Areas of operations.

On ambush, or other night missions, they carried peculiar little odds and ends. Kiowa always took along his New Testament and a pair of moccasins for silence. Dave Jensen carried night-sight vitamins high in carotin. Lee Strunk carried his slingshot; ammo, he claimed, would never be a problem. Rat Kiley carried brandy and M & M's. Until he was shot, Ted Lavender carried the star-light scope, which weighed 6.3 pounds with its aluminum carrying case. Henry Dobbins carried his girlfriend's pantyhose wrapped around his neck as a comforter. They all carried ghosts. When dark came, they would move out single file across the meadows and paddies to their ambush coordinates, where they would quietly set up the Claymores and lie down and spend the night waiting.

Other missions were more complicated and required special equipment. In mid-April, it was their mission to search out and destroy the elaborate tunnel complexes in the Than Khe area south of Chu Lai. To blow the tunnels, they carried one-pound blocks of pentrite high explosives, four blocks to a man, sixty-eight pounds in all. They carried wiring, detonators, and battery-powered clackers. Dave Jensen carried earplugs. Most often, before blowing the tunnels, they were ordered by higher command to search them, which was considered bad news, but by and large they just shrugged and carried out orders. Because he was a big man, Henry Dobbins was excused from tunnel duty. The others would draw numbers. Before Lavender died there were seventeen men in the platoon, and whoever drew the number seventeen would strip off his gear and crawl in head first with a flashlight and Lieutenant Cross's .45-caliber pistol. The rest of them would fan out as security. They would sit down or kneel, not facing the hole, listening to the ground beneath them, imagining cobwebs and ghosts, whatever was down there—the tunnel walls squeezing in—how the flashlight seemed impossibly heavy in the hand and how it was tunnel vision in the very strictest sense, compression in all ways, even time, and how you had to wiggle in—ass and elbows—a swallowed-up feeling—and how you found yourself worrying about odd things—will your flashlight go dead? Do rats carry rabies? If you screamed, how far would the sound carry? Would your buddies hear it? Would they have the courage to drag you out? In some respects, though not many, the waiting was worse than the tunnel itself. Imagination was a killer.

On April 16, when Lee Strunk drew the number seventeen, he laughed and muttered something and went down quickly. The morning was hot and very still. Not good, Kiowa said. He looked at the tunnel opening, then out across a dry paddy toward the village of Than Khe. Nothing moved. No clouds or birds or people. As they waited, the men smoked and drank Kool-Aid, not talking much, feeling sympathy for Lee Strunk but also feeling the luck of the draw. You win some, you lose some, said Mitchell Sanders, and sometimes you settle for a rain check. It was a tired line and no one laughed.

Henry Dobbins ate a tropical chocolate bar. Ted Lavender popped a tranquilizer and went off to pee.   20

After five minutes, Lieutenant Jimmy Cross moved to the tunnel, leaned down, and examined the darkness. Trouble, he thought—a cave-in maybe. And then suddenly, without willing it, he was thinking about Martha. The stresses and fractures, the quick collapse, the two of them buried alive under all that weight. Dense, crushing love. Kneeling, watching the hole, he tried to concentrate on Lee Strunk and the war, all the dangers, but his love was too much for him, he felt paralyzed, he wanted to sleep inside her lungs and breathe her blood and be smothered. He wanted her to be a virgin and not a virgin, all at once. He wanted to know her. Intimate secrets—why poetry? Why so sad? Why the grayness in her eyes? Why so alone? Not lonely, just alone—riding her bike across campus or sitting off by herself in the cafeteria. Even dancing, she danced alone—and it was the aloneness that filled him with love. He remembered telling her that one evening. How she nodded and looked away. And how, later, when he kissed her, she received the kiss without returning it, her eyes wide open, not afraid, not a virgin's eyes, just flat and uninvolved.

Lieutenant Cross gazed at the tunnel. But he was not there. He was buried with Martha under the white sand at the Jersey shore. They were pressed together, and the pebble in his mouth was her tongue. He was smiling. Vaguely, he was aware of how quiet the day was, the sullen paddies, yet he could not bring himself to worry about matters of security. He was beyond that. He was just a kid at war, in love. He was twenty-two years old. He couldn't help it.

A few moments later Lee Strunk crawled out of the tunnel. He came up grinning, filthy but alive. Lieutenant Cross nodded and closed his eyes while the others clapped Strunk on the back and made jokes about rising from the dead.

Worms, Rat Kiley said. Right out of the grave. Fuckin' zombie.

The men laughed. They all felt great relief.   25

Spook City, said Mitchell Sanders.

Lee Strunk made a funny ghost sound, a kind of moaning, yet very happy and right then, when Strunk made that high happy moaning sound, when he went *Ahhooooo*, right then Ted Lavender was shot in the head on his way back from peeing. He lay with his mouth open. The teeth were broken. There was a swollen black bruise under his left eye. The cheekbone was gone. Oh shit, Rat Kiley said, the guy's dead. The guy's dead, he kept saying, which seemed profound—the guy's dead. I mean really.

The things they carried were determined to some extent by superstition. Lieutenant Cross carried his good-luck pebble. Dave Jensen carried a rabbit's foot. Norman Bowker, otherwise a very gentle person, carried a thumb that had been presented to him as a gift by Mitchell Sanders. The thumb was dark brown, rubbery to the touch, and weighed four ounces at most. It had been cut from a VC[6] corpse, a boy of fifteen or sixteen. They'd found him at the bottom of an irrigation ditch, badly burned, flies in his mouth and eyes. The boy wore black shorts and sandals. At the time of his death he had been carrying a pouch of rice, a rifle, and three magazines of ammunition.

You want my opinion, Mitchell Sanders said, there's a definite moral here.

He put his hand on the dead boy's wrist. He was quiet for a time, as if counting   30
a pulse, then he patted the stomach, almost affectionately, and used Kiowa's hunting hatchet to remove the thumb.

Henry Dobbins asked what the moral was.

Moral?

You know. *Moral.*

Sanders wrapped the thumb in toilet paper and handed it across to Norman Bowker. There was no blood. Smiling, he kicked the boy's head, watched the flies scatter, and said, It's like with that old TV show—Paladin. Have gun, will travel.

---

[6]Vietcong, the North Vietnam army.

Soldiers in Vietnam on patrol.

Henry Dobbins thought about it.   35
Yeah, well, he finally said. I don't see no moral.
There it *is*, man.
Fuck off.
They carried USO stationery and pencils and pens. They carried Sterno, safety
pins, trip flares, signal flares, spools of wire, razor blades, chewing tobacco, liberated
joss sticks and statuettes of the smiling Buddha, candles, grease pencils, *The Stars
and Stripes*,[7] fingernail clippers, Psy Ops[8] leaflets, bush hats, bolos, and much more.
Twice a week, when the resupply choppers came in, they carried hot chow in green
Mermite cans and large canvas bags filled with iced beer and soda pop. They carried
plastic water containers, each with a two-gallon capacity. Mitchell Sanders carried a
set of starched tiger fatigues for special occasions. Henry Dobbins carried Black
Flag insecticide. Dave Jensen carried empty sandbags that could be filled at night
for added protection. Lee Strunk carried tanning lotion. Some things they carried
in common. Taking turns, they carried the big PRC-77 scrambler radio, which
weighed thirty pounds with its battery. They shared the weight of memory. They
took up what others could no longer bear. Often, they carried each other, the
wounded or weak. They carried infections. They carried chess sets, basketballs,
Vietnamese-English dictionaries, insignia of rank, Bronze Stars and Purple Hearts,
plastic cards imprinted with the Code of Conduct. They carried diseases, among
them malaria and dysentery. They carried lice and ringworm and leeches and paddy
algae and various rots and molds. They carried the land itself—Vietnam, the place,
the soil—a powdery orange-red dust that covered their boots and fatigues and faces.

---

[7] Official overseas military newspaper.
[8] Psychological operations.

They carried the sky. The whole atmosphere, they carried it, the humidity, the monsoons, the stink of fungus and decay, all of it, they carried gravity. They moved like mules. By daylight they took sniper fire, at night they were mortared, but it was not battle, it was just the endless march, village to village, without purpose, nothing won or lost. They marched for the sake of the march. They plodded along slowly, dumbly, leaning forward against the heat, unthinking, all blood and bone, simple grunts, soldiering with their legs, toiling up the hills and down into the paddies and across the rivers and up again and down, just humping, one step and then the next and then another, but no volition, no will, because it was automatic, it was anatomy, and the war was entirely a matter of posture and carriage, the hump was everything, a kind of inertia, a kind of emptiness, a dullness of desire and intellect and conscience and hope and human sensibility. Their principles were in their feet. Their calculations were biological. They had no sense of strategy or mission. They searched the villages without knowing what to look for, not caring, kicking over jars of rice, frisking children and old men, blowing tunnels, sometimes setting fires and sometimes not, then forming up and moving on to the next village, then other villages, where it would always be the same. They carried their own lives. The pressures were enormous. In the heat of early afternoon, they would remove their helmets and flak jackets, walking bare, which was dangerous but which helped ease the strain. They would often discard things along the route of march. Purely for comfort, they would throw away rations, blow their Claymores and grenades, no matter, because by nightfall the resupply choppers would arrive with more of the same, then a day or two later still more, fresh watermelons and crates of ammunition and sunglasses and woolen sweaters—the resources were stunning—sparklers for the Fourth of July, colored eggs for Easter. It was the great American war chest— the fruits of science, the smokestacks, the canneries, the arsenals at Hartford, the Minnesota forests, the machine shops, the vast fields of corn and wheat—they carried like freight trains; they carried it on their backs and shoulders—and for all the ambiguities of Vietnam, all the mysteries and unknowns, there was at least the single abiding certainty that they would never be at a loss for things to carry.

After the chopper took Lavender away, Lieutenant Jimmy Cross led his men into the village of Than Khe. They burned everything. They shot chickens and dogs, they trashed the village well, they called in artillery and watched the wreckage, then they marched for several hours through the hot afternoon, and then at dusk, while Kiowa explained how Lavender died, Lieutenant Cross found himself trembling.

He tried not to cry. With his entrenching tool, which weighed five pounds, he began digging a hole in the earth.

He felt shame. He hated himself. He had loved Martha more than his men, and as a consequence Lavender was now dead, and this was something he would have to carry like a stone in his stomach for the rest of the war.

All he could do was dig. He used his entrenching tool like an ax, slashing, feeling both love and hate, and then later, when it was full dark, he sat at the bottom of his foxhole and wept. It went on for a long while. In part, he was grieving for Ted Lavender, but mostly it was for Martha, and for himself, because she belonged to another world, which was not quite real, and because she was a junior at Mount Sebastian College in New Jersey, a poet and a virgin and uninvolved, and because he realized she did not love him and never would.

Like cement, Kiowa whispered in the dark. I swear to God—boom-down. Not a word.

I've heard this, said Norman Bowker.   45

A pisser, you know? Still zipping himself up. Zapped while zipping.

All right, fine. That's enough.

Yeah, but you had to see it, the guy just—

I *heard*, man. Cement. So why not shut the fuck *up?*

Kiowa shook his head sadly and glanced over at the hole where Lieutenant   50 Jimmy Cross sat watching the night. The air was thick and wet. A warm, dense fog had settled over the paddies and there was the stillness that precedes rain.

After a time Kiowa sighed.

One thing for sure, he said. The Lieutenant's in some deep hurt. I mean that crying jag—the way he was carrying on—it wasn't fake or anything, it was real heavy-duty hurt. The man cares.

Sure, Norman Bowker said.

Say what you want, the man does care.

We all got problems.   55

Not Lavender.

No, I guess not, Bowker said. Do me a favor, though.

Shut up?

That's a smart Indian. Shut up.

Shrugging, Kiowa pulled off his boots. He wanted to say more, just to lighten   60 up his sleep, but instead he opened his New Testament and arranged it beneath his head as a pillow. The fog made things seem hollow and unattached. He tried not to think about Ted Lavender, but then he was thinking how fast it was, no drama, down and dead, and how it was hard to feel anything except surprise. It seemed un-Christian. He wished he could find some great sadness, or even anger, but the emotion wasn't there and he couldn't make it happen. Mostly he felt pleased to be alive. He liked the smell of the New Testament under his cheek, the leather and ink and paper and glue, whatever the chemicals were. He liked hearing the sounds of night. Even his fatigue, it felt fine, the stiff muscles and the prickly awareness of his own body, a floating feeling. He enjoyed not being dead. Lying there, Kiowa admired Lieutenant Jimmy Cross's capacity for grief. He wanted to share the man's pain, he wanted to care as Jimmy Cross cared. And yet when he closed his eyes, all he could think was Boom-down, and all he could feel was the pleasure of having his boots off and the fog curling in around him and the damp soil and the Bible smells and the plush comfort of night.

After a moment Norman Bowker sat up in the dark.

What the hell, he said. You want to talk, *talk.* Tell it to me.

Forget it.

No, man, go on. One thing I hate, it's a silent Indian.

For the most part they carried themselves with poise, a kind of dignity. Now   65 and then, however, there were times of panic, when they squealed or wanted to squeal but couldn't, when they twitched and made moaning sounds and covered their heads and said Dear Jesus and flopped around on the earth and fired their weapons blindly and cringed and sobbed and begged for the noise to stop and went wild and made stupid promises to themselves and to God and to their mothers and fathers, hoping not to die. In different ways, it happened to all of them. Afterward, when the firing ended, they would blink and peek up. They would touch their bodies, feeling shame, then quickly hiding it. They would force themselves to stand. As if in slow motion, frame by frame, the world would take on the old logic—absolute silence, then the wind, then sunlight, then voices. It was the burden of being alive. Awkwardly, the men would reassemble themselves, first in private, then in groups, becoming soldiers again. They would repair the leaks in their eyes. They would check for casualties, call in dust-offs, light cigarettes, try to smile, clear their throats and spit and begin cleaning their weapons. After a time someone would shake his head and say, No lie, I almost shit my pants, and someone else would laugh, which meant it was bad, yes, but the guy had obviously not shit his pants, it wasn't that bad, and in any case nobody would ever do such a thing and then go ahead and talk about it. They would squint into the dense, oppressive sunlight. For a few moments, perhaps, they would fall silent, lighting a joint and tracking its passage from man to man, inhaling, holding in the humiliation. Scary stuff, one of them might say. But then someone else would grin or flick his eyebrows and say, Roger-dodger, almost cut me a new asshole, *almost.*

There were numerous such poses. Some carried themselves with a sort of wistful resignation, others with pride or stiff soldierly discipline or good humor or macho zeal. They were afraid of dying but they were even more afraid to show it.

They found jokes to tell.

They used a hard vocabulary to contain the terrible softness. *Greased,* they'd say. *Offed, lit up, zapped while zipping.* It wasn't cruelty, just stage presence. They were actors and the war came at them in 3-D. When someone died, it wasn't quite dying, because in a curious way it seemed scripted, and because they had their lines mostly memorized, irony mixed with tragedy, and because they called it by other names, as if to encyst and destroy the reality of death itself. They kicked corpses. They cut off thumbs. They talked grunt lingo. They told stories about Ted Lavender's supply of tranquilizers, how the poor guy didn't feel a thing, how incredibly tranquil he was.

There's a moral here, said Mitchell Sanders.

They were waiting for Lavender's chopper, smoking the dead man's dope. 70

The moral's pretty obvious, Sanders said, and winked. Stay away from drugs. No joke, they'll ruin your day every time.

Cute, said Henry Dobbins.

Mind-blower, get it? Talk about wiggy—nothing left, just blood and brains.

They made themselves laugh.

There it is, they'd say, over and over, as if the repetition itself were an act of 75
poise, a balance between crazy and almost crazy, knowing without going. There it is, which meant be cool, let it ride, because oh yeah, man, you can't change what can't be changed, there it is, there it absolutely and positively and fucking well *is.*

They were tough.

They carried all the emotional baggage of men who might die. Grief, terror, love, longing—these were intangibles, but the intangibles had their own mass and specific gravity, they had tangible weight. They carried shameful memories. They carried the common secret of cowardice barely restrained, the instinct to run or freeze or hide, and in many respects this was the heaviest burden of all, for it could never be put down, it required perfect balance and perfect posture. They carried their reputations. They carried the soldier's greatest fear, which was the fear of blushing. Men killed, and died, because they were embarrassed not to. It was what had brought them to the war in the first place, nothing positive, no dreams of glory or honor, just to avoid the blush of dishonor. They died so as not to die of embarrassment. They crawled into tunnels and walked point and advanced under fire. Each morning, despite the unknowns, they made their legs move. They endured. They kept humping. They did not submit to the obvious alternative, which was simply to close the eyes and fall. So easy, really. Go limp and tumble to the ground and let the muscles unwind and not speak and not budge until your buddies picked you up and lifted you into the chopper that would roar and dip its nose and carry you off to the world. A mere matter of falling, yet no one ever fell. It was not courage, exactly; the object was not valor. Rather, they were too frightened to be cowards.

By and large they carried these things inside, maintaining the masks of composure. They sneered at sick call. They spoke bitterly about guys who had found release by shooting off their own toes or fingers. Pussies, they'd say. Candyasses. It was fierce, mocking talk, with only a trace of envy or awe, but even so, the image played itself out behind their eyes.

They imagined the muzzle against flesh. They imagined the quick, sweet pain, then the evacuation to Japan, then a hospital with warm beds and cute geisha nurses.

They dreamed of freedom birds.   80

At night, on guard, staring into the dark, they were carried away by jumbo jets. They felt the rush of takeoff. *Gone!* they yelled. And then velocity, wings and engines, a smiling stewardess—but it was more than a plane, it was a real bird, a big sleek silver bird with feathers and talons and high screeching. They were flying. The weights fell off, there was nothing to bear. They laughed and held on tight, feeling the cold slap of wind and altitude, soaring, thinking *It's over, I'm gone!*—they were naked, they were light and free—it was all lightness, bright and fast and buoyant, light as light, a helium buzz in the brain, a giddy bubbling in the lungs as they were taken up over the clouds and the war, beyond duty, beyond gravity and mortification and global entanglements—*Sin loi!*[9] they yelled, *I'm sorry, motherfuckers, but I'm out of it, I'm goofed, I'm on a space cruise, I'm gone!*—and it was a restful, disencumbered sensation, just riding the light waves, sailing that big silver freedom bird over the mountains and oceans, over America, over the farms and great sleeping cities and cemeteries and highways and the golden arches of McDonald's. It was flight, a kind of fleeing, a kind of falling, falling higher and higher, spinning off the edge of the earth and beyond the sun and through the vast, silent vacuum where there were no burdens and where everything weighed exactly nothing. *Gone!* they screamed, *I'm sorry but I'm gone!* And so at night, not quite dreaming, they gave themselves over to lightness, they were carried, they were purely borne.

On the morning after Ted Lavender died, First Lieutenant Jimmy Cross crouched at the bottom of his foxhole and burned Martha's letters. Then he burned the two photographs. There was a steady rain falling, which made it difficult, but he used heat tabs and Sterno to build a small fire, screening it with his body, holding the photographs over the tight blue flame with the tips of his fingers.

---

[9]"Sorry about that!"

He realized it was only a gesture. Stupid, he thought. Sentimental, too, but mostly just stupid.

Lavender was dead. You couldn't burn the blame.

Besides, the letters were in his head. And even now, without photographs, Lieutenant Cross could see Martha playing volleyball in her white gym shorts and yellow T-shirt. He could see her moving in the rain.

When the fire died out, Lieutenant Cross pulled his poncho over his shoulders and ate breakfast from a can.

There was no great mystery, he decided.

In those burned letters Martha had never mentioned the war, except to say, Jimmy, take care of yourself. She wasn't involved. She signed the letters "Love," but it wasn't love, and all the fine lines and technicalities did not matter.

The morning came up wet and blurry. Everything seemed part of everything else, the fog and Martha and the deepening rain.

It was a war, after all.

Half smiling, Lieutenant Jimmy Cross took out his maps. He shook his head hard, as if to clear it, then bent forward and began planning the day's march. In ten minutes, or maybe twenty, he would rouse the men and they would pack up and head west, where the maps showed the country to be green and inviting. They would do what they had always done. The rain might add some weight, but otherwise it would be one more day layered upon all the other days.

He was realistic about it. There was that new hardness in his stomach.

No more fantasies, he told himself.

Henceforth, when he thought about Martha, it would be only to think that she belonged elsewhere. He would shut down the daydreams. This was not Mount Sebastian, it was another world, where there were no pretty poems or midterm exams, a place where men died because of carelessness and gross stupidity. Kiowa was right. Boom-down, and you were dead, never partly dead.

Briefly, in the rain, Lieutenant Cross saw Martha's gray eyes gazing back at him.

He understood.

It was very sad, he thought. The things men carried inside. The things men did or felt they had to do.

He almost nodded at her, but didn't.

Instead he went back to his maps. He was now determined to perform his duties firmly and without negligence. It wouldn't help Lavender, he knew that, but from this point on he would comport himself as a soldier. He would dispose of his good-luck pebble. Swallow it, maybe, or use Lee Strunk's slingshot, or just drop it along the trail. On the march he would impose strict field discipline. He would be careful to send out flank security, to prevent straggling or bunching up, to keep his troops moving at the proper pace and at the proper interval. He would insist on clean weapons. He would confiscate the remainder of Lavender's dope. Later in the day, perhaps, he would call the men together and speak to them plainly. He would accept the blame for what had happened to Ted Lavender. He would be a man about it. He would look them in the eyes, keeping his chin level, and he would issue the new SOPs in a calm, impersonal tone of voice, an officer's voice, leaving no room for argument or discussion. Commencing immediately, he'd tell them, they would no longer abandon equipment along the route of march. They would police up their acts. They would get their shit together, and keep it together, and maintain it neatly and in good working order.

He would not tolerate laxity. He would show strength, distancing himself.   100

Among the men there would be grumbling, of course, and maybe worse, because their days would seem longer and their loads heavier, but Lieutenant Cross reminded himself that his obligation was not to be loved but to lead. He would dispense with love; it was not now a factor. And if anyone quarreled or complained, he would simply tighten his lips and arrange his shoulders in the correct command posture. He might give a curt little nod. Or he might not. He might just shrug and say Carry on, then they would saddle up and form into a column and move out toward the villages of Than Khe.

(1986)

PREWRITING

Before you can begin to write about structure, you must first determine the underlying patterns that serve as a framework for the story.

Finding Patterns

Read the following questions; then carefully reread the story. Write down your answers to the questions.

1. How does each part of the story relate to the title, "The Things They Carried"?
2. What visible structure is evident, separating the parts of the story? Give each part a title that fits it. If possible, compare your titles with a classmate's and discuss your choices. If you want, create a diagram or chart that illustrates the story's structure.
3. How many different time periods are described in the story? Make a list of the main events that are described. Then organize the list according to time order.
4. Trace the Martha story line that is woven through the tale. What is the reality of the relationship between Jimmy Cross and Martha? What evidence are you looking at when you guess at this reality?
5. What do we know about each soldier in the story? How do we accumulate knowledge about each one? On the other hand, what is left out of our knowledge about each soldier, information that you might have expected? If O'Brien had written some scenes from each soldier's past as a civilian, how would that change the story? Why do you think he generally avoids these scenes?
6. Why is the death of Ted Lavender important to your understanding of the story? How many times is Lavender's death retold? How is it different in the various retellings?

WRITING

Once you understand some of the structural elements of the story, you need to choose a framework within which you can effectively present your observations—that is, a structure for your own paper.

Grouping Details

Write a sentence that explains something about the author's selection of scenes, themes, or events to include repeatedly through the story. Next, discuss which details in the story support your explanations. For example, if you mentioned that the scenes involving Martha relate to the crucial change undergone by Jimmy Cross, supporting details would include the following:

- the content of the letters from Martha
- the photographs of Martha
- the lucky pebble
- descriptions of his encounters with Martha at home
- his fantasies of what might have happened or what might happen in the future with Martha
- episodes of daydreaming about Martha
- the burning of the letters and photographs

Relating Details to Theme

An accurate description of a pattern in the story and a convincing list of supporting details will be crucial to any essay about structure. But you also need to work out a thesis—a major claim that relates the structure to the overall impact or meaning of the work. For example, an essay about the structure of "The Things They Carried" might make this claim:

> Jimmy Cross's recurring thoughts about Martha throughout the story create a picture of him as a romantic, self-deceiving, sensitive young man, a character he himself rejects in the end with the symbolic burning of her letters and photographs.

IDEAS FOR WRITING

Ideas for Responsive Writing

1. In "The Things They Carried," physical objects take on extra significance as part of each soldier's kit. Are there any items in your life that

have extra significance because they are associated with a certain period of time? What do you carry with you almost every day? What could we tell about you by looking through your backpack, handbag, wallet, or pockets? Write about how certain objects in your life could be interpreted.

2. In this story, Jimmy Cross builds an elaborate fantasy surrounding Martha, and sometimes he is quite aware that it's a fantasy. Have you ever built a fantasy on a small amount of evidence or information? How aware were you that you were out of touch with reality? Write about a daydream or fantasy that you have created with some small grounding in real life.

Ideas for Critical Writing

The following claims relate structure to meaning. Adopt one of them, revise one, or create your own for arguing an interpretation of "The Things They Carried."

1. The soldiers' situation is illuminated in "The Things They Carried" by words and details referring to different kinds of weight and lightness.

2. CRITICAL APPROACHES: For this topic, review the summary of "formalism" in the Critical Approaches for Interpreting Literature (page 748), and use a close-reading approach. Once an event or topic is introduced in "The Things They Carried," it accumulates more meaning each time it reoccurs. This process involves the reader in the construction of a coherent story about each event.

3. "The Things They Carried" is organized to mirror how people think as they go about their business in daily life, giving readers the feeling that they have entered the minds of the characters.

4. The narrator of "The Things They Carried" continually slips out of his concrete cataloguing of physical objects and wanders into the realm of psychological burdens, suggesting that Jimmy Cross will not be able to live up to his resolves at the end of the story.

Ideas for Researched Writing

1. "The Things They Carried" is the first story in a collection by Tim O'Brien, also titled *The Things They Carried*. Find out more about the whole book and how the story you have read fits into it. What is interesting about the structure of this collection of Vietnam stories? You can enter the title into your Internet search engine or start from O'Brien's home page at www.illyria.com/tobhp.html.

2. What kind of critical reception did O'Brien's story receive? Find a number of reviews and analyses of the story, and write an essay summarizing the reactions and interpretations.

REWRITING

Our advice in this section focuses on problems involved in quoting when writing about a literary work.

Integrating Quotations Gracefully

In any literary essay you will need quotations from the text of the work you are examining. In fact, when you revise your essay, always consider adding more specific evidence straight from the text. This evidence will help your readers understand the general points you make and will show what inspired your thoughts. Quoting directly also serves as a self-check; by finding specific support in the work, you confirm that your ideas are, indeed, grounded in the text and not in your fancy.

Be sure that you enclose these borrowings in quotation marks as you gracefully introduce them into your own sentences. And be sure that your own language leads grammatically into the language you are quoting. For example:

> O'Brien describes the soldiers' inner experience as "a dullness of desire and intellect and conscience and hope and human sensibility."

> At the close of the story, Cross imagines himself giving "a curt little nod" in his new role as a man in command.

> Although the narrator claims that "the things they [the soldiers] carried were largely determined by necessity," for some men these necessities included such items as a diary, comic books, and marijuana.

That last example shows how you may add your own words to explain a possibly confusing word in a quotation: use brackets. Most of the time, however, you can devise a way to avoid this awkwardness by rewriting the sentence.

> The soldiers carried objects "largely determined by necessity," according to the narrator, but for some these necessities included such items as a diary, comic books, and marijuana.

Exercise on Integrating Quotations

Here, we reprint a passage from "The Things They Carried." To practice integrating quotations, try your hand at using parts of the passage in sentences of your own.

1. Write a sentence that uses a phrase you quote directly as an example of a general point you make about the characters, events, or setting of the story.

2. Write a sentence that relates a detail to a theme of the story, using some exact quotation from the passage.

They used a hard vocabulary to contain the terrible softness. *Greased,* they'd say. *Offed, lit up, zapped while zipping.* It wasn't cruelty, just stage presence. They were actors and the war came at them in 3-D. When someone died, it wasn't quite dying, because in a curious way it seemed scripted, and because they had their lines mostly memorized, irony mixed with tragedy, and because they called it by other names, as if to encyst and destroy the reality of death itself.

8

Writing About Imagery
and Symbolism

Imagery and symbolism, two of the most important elements of
serious imaginative literature, provide rich sources of insight. The
interpretive skill necessary to detect and understand them can be developed with practice. Because the meaning or theme of a literary work
is often reinforced through imagery and symbolism, you can effectively
devote an entire paper to an examination of a key symbol or a pattern of
imagery.

What Are Images?

Images are words, sometimes phrases, that appeal to the senses and
often put a picture in your mind. Literary critics classify images roughly
into several categories.

Visual	images of sight
	("future days strung together like pearls in a rosary"—Mary E. Wilkins Freeman)
Auditory	images of sound
	("the loud, iron clanking of the lift machinery"—John Cheever)
Gustatory	images of taste
	("the acrid, metallic taste of gunfire"—Alberto Moravia)
Kinetic	images of motion
	(a thought "bumping like a helium balloon at the ceiling of the brain"—Sandra Cisneros)
Thermal	images of temperature
	("the blueblack cold" of early morning—Robert Hayden)
Tactile	images of feeling
	("the ache of marriage throbs in the teeth"—Denise Levertov)

Such images enrich our pleasure in reading and, if deliberately repeated, can become *motifs*, or patterns of imagery, that illuminate some element of the story. The images of illness and physical deformity in Flannery O'Connor's "Good Country People" form a significant motif that reflects the spiritual condition of the story's characters. In Faulkner's "A Rose for Emily," the images of progress—garages, gasoline pumps, new construction, paved sidewalks—serve to reinforce the story's conflict between the Old South and the forces of change.

What Are Symbols?

If a repeated image gathers significant meaning and seems to stand for something more than itself, it then becomes a *symbol*. In Louise Erdrich's "The Red Convertible," the old Oldsmobile symbolizes the changing relationship between the narrator and his brother. The repeated mention of dust in Joyce's "Eveline" settles into our consciousness as symbolizing the dreariness of the title character's daily life, just as dust settles on all surfaces in an unkempt house. In Kate Chopin's "The Story of an Hour," Mrs. Mallard gazes out her window at "the tops of trees that were all aquiver with the new spring life. The delicious breath of rain was in the air." Those images of spring and rain represent the prospect of a vibrant new life that is awakening in Mrs. Mallard's subconscious mind.

Because spring rains literally bring renewed life to the earth, water is used in the baptismal service in church to signify rebirth. Thus, in literature, we associate water with a vigorous, living spirit and its opposite—dryness, dust, aridity—with the death of the human spirit or the decay of moral values.

Archetypal Symbols

Some symbols, like the water and dust, are considered *archetypal* or universal—supposedly conveying a similar meaning in all cultures from the time of earliest civilizations. The circle, for instance, is an ancient symbol of wholeness or perfection; the sea has for centuries symbolized the voyage through life. Colors are often symbolic, like the crimson of the mark on Georgiana's cheek in Hawthorne's "The Birthmark." Occasionally a symbol can convey diametrically opposing meanings, depending on its context. For instance, white in our culture often stands for purity, as in bridal gowns; but Herman Melville makes the white whale in *Moby Dick* a symbol of evil incarnate, as Frost does with the "dimpled spider, fat and white" in his poem "Design." Both of those images also convey the often hidden, deceptive nature of evil. And black, frequently linked with death and evil, has many positive associations, such as a Black Belt in Judo; a cup of strong coffee; or the robes of a priest, judge, or graduate.

Phallic and Yonic Symbols

Two important and commonly employed symbols are associated with human sexuality. A *phallic symbol* suggests the potency of the male (as does the gun in Richard Wright's "The Man Who Was Almost a Man") or the force of male dominance in a patriarchal society (as does the rolling pin in Bharati Mukherjee's "A Father").

A *yonic symbol* suggests the fecundity of the female and the allure of female sexuality. Common yonic symbols are caves, pots, rooms, full-blown roses—round or concave objects resembling the shape of the primary sex organs of women. If you think fruit, then bananas are phallic and apples are yonic. Remember, though, that these objects will not always be charged with sexual significance. You must be sure that context supports a reasonable association with sexuality. Even Freud supposedly said that sometimes a cigar is just a cigar.

How Will I Recognize Symbols?

"How am I supposed to know the significance of all these things?" you may well ask. Many symbols you already understand through knowledge gathered from experience and observation. You just have to make the association. Spring signifying rebirth, for example, is a connection anyone can make who has seen the earth come alive at winter's end. Pay attention to the way objects and colors gather associations: white for brides, black for funerals, blue for sadness, red for passion or anger. Just keep making associations until you come up with a meaning that seems to fit the symbol in its context.

Reference Works on Symbols

If you draw an absolute blank, you can consult several handy volumes that allow you to look up words to discover their symbolic implications. Your library should have copies of the following works in the humanities reference section:

- Cirlot, J. E. *A Dictionary of Symbols*
- Cooper, J. C. *An Illustrated Encyclopaedia of Traditional Symbols*
- Frazer, Sir James. *The Golden Bough*
- Olderr, Stephen. *Symbolism: A Comprehensive Dictionary*
- Walker, Barbara. *The Woman's Encyclopedia of Myths and Secrets*

Looking at Images and Symbols

Recognizing images and symbols and responding to them sensitively are requirements for an informed reading of serious fiction. Read the following story by Shirley Jackson and see if you are aware, on first reading, of her use of symbolic imagery.

Shirley Jackson   *1919–1965*

Shirley Jackson did not receive attention as a writer until 1948, when the *New Yorker* published "The Lottery," a story that she wrote in just two hours. The magazine was flooded with letters, almost all of them wanting to know what the story meant. While Jackson is best known for her tales of supernatural terror, she also wrote about "the perpetual pandemonium and the constant crises" of her family life. "I can't persuade myself that writing is honest work," she once remarked. "It's great fun and I love it. For one thing, it's the only way I can get to sit down."

The Lottery

The morning of June 27th was clear and sunny, with the fresh warmth of a full-summer day; the flowers were blossoming profusely and the grass was richly green. The people of the village began to gather in the square, between the post office and the bank, around ten o'clock; in some towns there were so many people that the lottery took two days and had to be started on June 26th, but in this village, where there were only about three hundred people, the whole lottery took less than two hours, so it could begin at ten o'clock in the morning and still be through in time to allow the villagers to get home for noon dinner.

The children assembled first, of course. School was recently over for the summer, and the feeling of liberty sat uneasily on most of them; they tended to gather together quietly for a while before they broke into boisterous play, and their talk was still of the classroom and the teacher, of books and reprimands. Bobby Martin had already stuffed his pockets full of stones, and the other boys soon followed his example, selecting the smoothest and roundest stones; Bobby and Harry Jones and Dickie Delacroix—the villagers pronounced his name "Dellacroy"—eventually made a great pile of stones in one corner of the square and guarded it against the raids of the other boys. The girls stood aside, talking among themselves, looking over their shoulders at the boys, and the very small children rolled in the dust or clung to the hands of their older brothers or sisters.

Soon the men began to gather, surveying their own children, speaking of planting and rain, tractors and taxes. They stood together, away from the pile of stones in the corner, and their jokes were quiet and they smiled rather than laughed. The women, wearing faded house dresses and sweaters, came shortly after their menfolk. They greeted one another and exchanged bits of gossip as they went to join their husbands. Soon the women, standing by their husbands, began to call to their children, and the children came reluctantly, having to be called four or five times. Bobby Martin ducked under his mother's grasping hand and ran, laughing, back to the pile of stones. His father spoke up sharply, and Bobby came quickly and took his place between his father and his oldest brother.

The lottery was conducted—as were the square dances, the teen-age club, the Halloween program—by Mr. Summers, who had time and energy to devote to civic activities. He was a round-faced, jovial man and he ran the coal business, and people were sorry for him, because he had no children and his wife was a scold. When he arrived in the square, carrying the black wooden box, there was a murmur of conversation among the villagers, and he waved and called, "Little late today, folks." The postmaster, Mr. Graves, followed him, carrying a three-legged stool, and the stool was put in the center of the square and Mr. Summers set the black box down on it. The villagers kept their distance, leaving a space between themselves and the stool, and when Mr. Summers said, "Some of you fellows want to give me a hand?" there was a hesitation before two men, Mr. Martin and his oldest son, Baxter, came forward to hold the box steady on the stool while Mr. Summers stirred up the paper inside it.

The original paraphernalia for the lottery had been lost long ago, and the   5
black box now resting on the stool had been put into use even before Old Man Warner, the oldest man in town, was born. Mr. Summers spoke frequently to the villagers about making a new box, but no one liked to upset even as much tradition as was represented by the black box. There was a story that the present box had been made with some pieces of the box that had preceded it, the one that had been constructed when the first people settled down to make a village here. Every year, after the lottery, Mr. Summers began talking again about a new box, but every year the subject was allowed to fade off without anything's being done. The black box grew shabbier each year; by now it was no longer completely black but splintered badly along one side to show the original wood color, and in some places faded or stained.

Mr. Martin and his oldest son, Baxter, held the black box securely on the stool until Mr. Summers had stirred the papers thoroughly with his hand. Because so much of the ritual had been forgotten or discarded, Mr. Summers had been successful in having slips of paper substituted for the chips of wood that had been used for generations. Chips of wood, Mr. Summers had argued, had been all very well when the village was tiny, but now that the population was more than three hundred and likely to keep on growing, it was necessary to use something that would fit more easily into the black box. The night before the lottery, Mr. Summers and Mr. Graves made up the slips of paper and put them in the box, and it was then taken to the safe of Mr. Summers's coal company and locked up until Mr. Summers was ready to take it to the square next morning. The rest of the year, the box was put away, sometimes one place, sometimes another; it had spent one year in Mr. Graves's barn and another year underfoot in the post office, and sometimes it was set on a shelf in the Martin grocery and left there.

There was a great deal of fussing to be done before Mr. Summers declared the lottery open. There were the lists to make up—of heads of families, heads of households in each family, members of each household in each family. There was the proper swearing-in of Mr. Summers by the postmaster, as the official of the lottery; at one time, some people remembered, there had been a recital of some sort, performed by the official of the lottery, a perfunctory, tuneless chant that had been rattled off duly each year; some people believed that the official of the lottery used to stand just so when he said or sang it, others believed that he was supposed to walk among the people, but years and years ago this part of the ritual had been allowed to lapse. There had been, also, a ritual salute, which the official of the lottery had had to use in addressing each person who came up to draw from the box, but this also had changed with time, until now it was felt necessary only for the official to speak to each person approaching. Mr. Summers was very good at all this; in his clean white shirt and blue jeans, with one hand resting carelessly on the black box, he seemed very proper and important as he talked interminably to Mr. Graves and the Martins.

Just as Mr. Summers finally left off talking and turned to the assembled villagers, Mrs. Hutchinson came hurriedly along the path to the square, her sweater thrown over her shoulders, and slid into place in the back of the crowd. "Clean forgot what day it was," she said to Mrs. Delacroix, who stood next to her, and they both laughed softly. "Thought my old man was out back stacking wood," Mrs. Hutchinson went on, "and then I looked out the window and the kids were gone, and then I remembered it was the twenty-seventh and came a-running." She dried her hands on her apron, and Mrs. Delacroix said, "You're in time, though. They're still talking away up there."

Mrs. Hutchinson craned her neck to see through the crowd and found her husband and children standing near the front. She tapped Mrs. Delacroix on the arm as a farewell and began to make her way through the crowd. The people separated good-humoredly to let her through; two or three people said, in voices just loud enough to be heard across the crowd, "Here comes your Missus, Hutchinson," and "Bill, she made it after all." Mrs. Hutchinson reached her husband, and Mr. Summers, who had been waiting, said cheerfully, "Thought we were going to have to get on without you, Tessie." Mrs. Hutchinson said, grinning, "Wouldn't have me leave m'dishes in the sink, now, would you, Joe?," and soft laughter ran through the crowd as the people stirred back into position after Mrs. Hutchinson's arrival.

"Well, now," Mr. Summers said soberly, "guess we better get started, get this 10 over with, so's we can go back to work. Anybody ain't here?"

"Dunbar," several people said. "Dunbar, Dunbar."

Mr. Summers consulted his list. "Clyde Dunbar," he said. "That's right. He's broke his leg, hasn't he? Who's drawing for him?"

"Me, I guess," a woman said, and Mr. Summers turned to look at her. "Wife draws for her husband," Mr. Summers said. "Don't you have a grown boy to do it for you, Janey?" Although Mr. Summers and everyone else in the village knew the answer perfectly well, it was the business of the official of the lottery to ask such questions formally. Mr. Summers waited with an expression of polite interest while Mrs. Dunbar answered.

"Horace's not but sixteen yet," Mrs. Dunbar said regretfully. "Guess I gotta fill in for the old man this year."

"Right," Mr. Summers said. He made a note on the list he was holding. Then 15 he asked, "Watson boy drawing this year?"

A tall boy in the crowd raised his hand. "Here," he said. "I'm drawing for m' mother and me." He blinked his eyes nervously and ducked his head as several voices in the crowd said things like "Good fellow, Jack," and "Glad to see your mother's got a man to do it."

"Well," Mr. Summers said, "guess that's everyone. Old Man Warner make it?"

"Here," a voice said, and Mr. Summers nodded.

A sudden hush fell on the crowd as Mr. Summers cleared his throat and looked at the list. "All ready?" he called. "Now, I'll read the names—heads of families first—and the men come up and take a paper out of the box. Keep the paper folded in your hand without looking at it until everyone has had a turn. Everything clear?"

The people had done it so many times that they only half listened to the direc- 20 tions; most of them were quiet, wetting their lips, not looking around. Then

Mr. Summers raised one hand high and said, "Adams." A man disengaged himself from the crowd and came forward. "Hi, Steve," Mr. Summers said, and Mr. Adams said, "Hi, Joe." They grinned at one another humorlessly and nervously. Then Mr. Adams reached into the black box and took out a folded paper. He held it firmly by one corner as he turned and went hastily back to his place in the crowd, where he stood a little apart from his family, not looking down at his hand.

"Allen." Mr. Summers said. "Anderson.... Bentham."

"Seems like there's no time at all between lotteries any more," Mrs. Delacroix said to Mrs. Graves in the back row. "Seems like we got through with the last one only last week."

"Time sure goes fast," Mrs. Graves said.

"Clark.... Delacroix."

"There goes my old man," Mrs. Delacroix said. She held her breath while   25
her husband went forward.

"Dunbar," Mr. Summers said, and Mrs. Dunbar went steadily to the box while one of the women said, "Go on, Janey," and another said, "There she goes."

"We're next," Mrs. Graves said. She watched while Mr. Graves came around from the side of the box, greeted Mr. Summers gravely, and selected a slip of paper from the box. By now, all through the crowd there were men holding the small folded papers in their large hands, turning them over and over nervously. Mrs. Dunbar and her two sons stood together, Mrs. Dunbar holding the slip of paper.

"Harburt.... Hutchinson."

"Get up there, Bill," Mrs. Hutchinson said, and the people near her laughed. "Jones."   30

"They do say," Mr. Adams said to Old Man Warner, who stood next to him, "that over in the north village they're talking of giving up the lottery."

Old Man Warner snorted. "Pack of crazy fools," he said. "Listening to the young folks, nothing's good enough for *them.* Next thing you know, they'll be wanting to go back to living in caves, nobody work any more, live *that* way for a while. Used to be a saying about 'Lottery in June, corn be heavy soon.' First thing you know, we'd all be eating stewed chickweed and acorns. There's *always* been a lottery," he added petulantly. "Bad enough to see young Joe Summers up there joking with everybody."

"Some places have already quit lotteries," Mrs. Adams said.

"Nothing but trouble in *that,*" Old Man Warner said stoutly. "Pack of young fools."

"Martin." And Bobby Martin watched his father go forward. "Overdyke....   35
Percy."

"I wish they'd hurry," Mrs. Dunbar said to her oldest son. "I wish they'd hurry."

"They're almost through," her son said.

"You get ready to run tell Dad," Mrs. Dunbar said.

Mr. Summers called his own name and then stepped forward precisely and selected a slip from the box. Then he called, "Warner."

"Seventy-seventh year I been in the lottery," Old Man Warner said as he   40
went through the crowd. "Seventy-seventh time."

"Watson." The tall boy came awkwardly through the crowd. Someone said, "Don't be nervous, Jack," and Mr. Summers said, "Take your time, son."

"Zanini."

After that, there was a long pause, a breathless pause, until Mr. Summers, holding his slip of paper in the air, said, "All right, fellows." For a minute, no one moved, and then all the slips of paper were opened. Suddenly, all the women began to speak at once, saying, "Who is it?," "Who's got it?," "Is it the Dunbars?," "Is it the Watsons?" Then the voices began to say, "It's Hutchinson. It's Bill," "Bill Hutchinson's got it."

"Go tell your father," Mrs. Dunbar said to her older son.

People began to look around to see the Hutchinsons. Bill Hutchinson was   45
standing quiet, staring down at the paper in his hand. Suddenly, Tessie Hutchinson shouted to Mr. Summers, "You didn't give him time enough to take any paper he wanted. I saw you. It wasn't fair!"

"Be a good sport, Tessie," Mrs. Delacroix called, and Mrs. Graves said, "All of us took the same chance."

"Shut up, Tessie," Bill Hutchinson said.

"Well, everyone," Mr. Summers said, "that was done pretty fast, and now we've got to be hurrying a little more to get it done in time." He consulted his next list. "Bill," he said, "you draw for the Hutchinson family. You got any other households in the Hutchinsons?"

"There's Don and Eva," Mrs. Hutchinson yelled. "Make *them* take their chance!"

"Daughters draw with their husbands' families, Tessie," Mr. Summers said   50
gently. "You know that as well as anyone else."

"It wasn't *fair*," Tessie said.

"I guess not, Joe," Bill Hutchinson said regretfully. "My daughter draws with her husband's family, that's only fair. And I've got no other family except the kids."

"Then, as far as drawing for families is concerned, it's you," Mr. Summers said in explanation, "and as far as drawing for households is concerned, that's you, too. Right?"

"Right," Bill Hutchinson said.

"How many kids, Bill?" Mr. Summers asked formally.   55

"Three," Bill Hutchinson said. "There's Bill, Jr., and Nancy, and little Dave. And Tessie and me."

"All right, then," Mr. Summers said. "Harry, you got their tickets back?"

Mr. Graves nodded and held up the slips of paper. "Put them in the box, then," Mr. Summers directed. "Take Bill's and put it in."

"I think we ought to start over," Mrs. Hutchinson said, as quietly as she could. "I tell you it wasn't *fair*. You didn't give him time enough to choose. *Every*body saw that."

Mr. Graves had selected the five slips and put them in the box, and he   60
dropped all the papers but those onto the ground, where the breeze caught them and lifted them off.

"Listen, everybody," Mrs. Hutchinson was saying to the people around her.

"Ready, Bill?" Mr. Summers asked, and Bill Hutchinson, with one quick glance around at his wife and children, nodded.

"Remember," Mr. Summers said, "take the slips and keep them folded until each person has taken one. Harry, you help little Dave." Mr. Graves took the hand of the little boy, who came willingly with him up to the box. "Take a paper out of the box, Davy," Mr. Summers said. Davy put his hand into the box and laughed. "Take just *one* paper," Mr. Summers said. "Harry, you hold it for him." Mr. Graves took the child's hand and removed the folded paper from the tight fist and held it while little Dave stood next to him and looked up at him wonderingly.

"Nancy, next," Mr. Summers said. Nancy was twelve, and her school friends breathed heavily as she went forward, switching her skirt, and took a slip daintily from the box. "Bill, Jr.," Mr. Summers said, and Billy, his face red and his feet over-large, nearly knocked the box over as he got a paper out. "Tessie," Mr. Summers said. She hesitated for a minute, looking around defiantly, and then set her lips and went up to the box. She snatched a paper out and held it behind her.

"Bill," Mr. Summers said, and Bill Hutchinson reached into the box and felt   65
around, bringing his hand out at last with the slip of paper in it.

The crowd was quiet. A girl whispered, "I hope it's not Nancy," and the sound of the whisper reached the edges of the crowd.

"It's not the way it used to be," Old Man Warner said clearly. "People ain't the way they used to be."

"All right," Mr. Summers said. "Open the papers. Harry, you open little Dave's."

Mr. Graves opened the slip of paper and there was a general sigh through the crowd as he held it up and everyone could see that it was blank. Nancy and Bill, Jr., opened theirs at the same time, and both beamed and laughed, turning around to the crowd and holding their slips of paper above their heads.

"Tessie," Mr. Summers said. There was a pause, and then Mr. Summers looked   70
at Bill Hutchinson, and Bill unfolded his paper and showed it. It was blank.

"It's Tessie," Mr. Summers said, and his voice was hushed. "Show us her paper, Bill."

Bill Hutchinson went over to his wife and forced the slip of paper out of her hand. It had a black spot on it, the black spot Mr. Summers had made the night before with the heavy pencil in the coal-company office. Bill Hutchinson held it up, and there was a stir in the crowd.

"All right, folks," Mr. Summers said. "Let's finish quickly."

Although the villagers had forgotten the ritual and lost the original black box, they still remembered to use stones. The pile of stones the boys had made earlier was ready; there were stones on the ground with the blowing scraps of paper that had come out of the box. Mrs. Delacroix selected a stone so large she had to pick it up with both hands and turned to Mrs. Dunbar. "Come on," she said. "Hurry up."

Mrs. Dunbar had small stones in both hands, and she said, gasping for   75
breath, "I can't run at all. You'll have to go ahead and I'll catch up with you."

The children had stones already, and someone gave little Davy Hutchinson a few pebbles.

Tessie Hutchinson was in the center of a cleared space by now, and she held her hands out desperately as the villagers moved in on her. "It isn't fair," she said. A stone hit her on the side of the head.

Old Man Warner was saying, "Come on, come on, everyone." Steve Adams was in the front of the crowd of villagers, with Mrs. Graves beside him.

"It isn't fair, it isn't right," Mrs. Hutchinson screamed, and then they were upon her.

                                                                    (1948)

PREWRITING

Since much of the imagery in "The Lottery" carries symbolic significance, we will focus on symbolism as the topic for writing here. Symbols in fiction are not difficult to recognize. Usually an author will give a symbol particular emphasis by mentioning it repeatedly (like the dust in "Eveline"). A crucial symbol will sometimes be placed in the story's opening or ending.

Interpreting Symbols

Shirley Jackson directs our attention to the lottery by making it the title of her story. She also gives us abundant detail about this traditional ritual. We know the exact date and time, how the lottery is conducted, who draws and in what order, what the box and the slips of paper look like, and so forth. Clearly the lottery is the story's central symbol as well as its title. The meaning of the lottery is the meaning of "The Lottery."

Here are some points and questions to consider as you read the story a second time and try to work out your interpretation of its symbolism. Write out your answers, and if possible, share your responses with a small group of classmates.

1. Social psychologists observe that every group develops its own outcast or misfit, who is blamed for all sorts of group malfunctions and woes. Have you observed this dynamic in your own work, school, church, or family groups?
2. We are told a lot about the lottery, but not its exact purpose. Do the townspeople know? Is this omission significant? Intentional?
3. Why is much of the history of the lottery and the black box uncertain and vague? Why does Mr. Summers have to ask a question that he and everybody else already know the answer to?
4. The box used in the lottery is mentioned almost thirty times in the story—more than ten times in the phrase *the black box*. Why does the author emphasize this object and its color so strongly?
5. The stones are mentioned five times near the beginning of the story and then five or six times more at the end. Why is their presence so important? What are the historical/biblical associations of a "stoning"? Do they apply in this situation?
6. Which characters seem to stand for particular ideas or views? What about Old Man Warner? Look at his speeches and comments throughout the story. Tessie Hutchinson also gets a lot of attention, of course. What is ironic about her being the chosen

victim? Does her last name have any significance for you? If not, look up *Hutchinson* in a good encyclopedia.

WRITING

The key to a successful essay is a good *thesis*—the *claim* (or *premise* or *hypothesis* or *recommendation*) that you will argue in your interpretation. Before you get too far in your writing, try to state your thesis in a single sentence.

Producing a Workable Thesis

A useful thesis should narrow the topic to an idea you can cover within your word limit. It should indicate the direction of your thinking—what you intend to say about that idea. Be sure to state your thesis in a complete sentence that indicates how you will successfully argue your claim. The following exercise provides examples.

Exercise on Thesis Statements

The numbered thesis statements lack a clear claim. Figure out how each one can be revised to include an argument for an interpretation of the story; then write an improved version. Here is an example of the kind of revisions we hope you will produce.

No claim   Shirley Jackson's "The Lottery" contains a number of significant symbols.

Improved   In "The Lottery" Shirley Jackson uses simple objects—a box, some stones, some slips of paper—to symbolize the narrow-mindedness and brutality that result from superstitious thinking.

1. Shirley Jackson's "The Lottery" is a compelling story about scapegoats.
2. The ritual of the lottery itself serves as a symbol in Shirley Jackson's story.
3. The setting of Shirley Jackson's "The Lottery" is an important element in contributing to the effectiveness of the story.
4. The characters function symbolically in Shirley Jackson's "The Lottery."
5. Shirley Jackson's "The Lottery" reveals a great deal about society and human nature.

IDEAS FOR WRITING

Ideas for Responsive Writing

1. What is Shirley Jackson saying about traditional rituals in "The Lottery"? Think of some ritual in our present society that you think ought to be dropped—or at least reconsidered and modified—and write an essay arguing your viewpoint. Consider, for example, proms, weddings, Christmas gift exchanges, dating conventions, beauty pageants, boxing matches, funeral services, graduation ceremonies, or fraternity/sorority pledging.
2. Many readers have remarked on the hypnotic power and emotional impact of this story. Did you experience a similar reaction? Do you think the author manipulated your feelings in any way?

Ideas for Critical Writing

1. Look up the word *scapegoat* in a desk-sized or online dictionary; then look at the entry in the print or online version of *Encyclopaedia Britannica*, which will give you some historical examples of the use of scapegoats. Formulate a claim that relates the symbolism of "The Lottery" to the practice of scapegoating.
2. Write an essay focusing on the symbolism of the characters in "The Lottery," especially Tessie Hutchinson, Old Man Warner, Bill Hutchinson, Mr. Graves, and Mr. Summers. Or consider the role of the children in the story. What do they symbolize? Conclude your argument by relating your observations to the story's theme.
3. CRITICAL APPROACHES: Review the reader response approach to literary interpretation (page 751). Write an essay arguing that the symbolism in "The Lottery" can be interpreted in several different ways. Before you begin, you might ask several people to read the story and tell you what the symbols mean to them. Also read the student paper on "The Lottery" starting on page 144 as you gather material for your essay.

Ideas for Researched Writing

1. When "The Lottery" first appeared in the *New Yorker* on June 28, 1948, it was greeted with great consternation. So many subscribers wrote in seeking enlightenment or expressing outrage that Jackson responded to the deluge of mail with an essay entitled "Biography of a Story." Find out more about the initial reactions to "The Lottery," and read Jackson's response. Then write an essay arguing why you think the story generated such anger and was so widely misinterpreted.
2. Do some research on scapegoats. Write an essay claiming that scapegoats play a useful role in society, using examples from history, current events, novels, films, and your own experience. Or, if you prefer, argue the opposite—that scapegoating is so cruel and senseless that it must be condemned and eliminated.

REWRITING

As you revise your first draft, try to improve it in every way possible. Our advice at this point involves ideas for improving your introduction.

Sharpening the Introduction

Look at your introductory paragraph. Does it give your readers a clear idea of the topic and purpose? Will it arouse curiosity and interest, as well as lead into your subject?

One strategy for catching the attention of your readers involves using a pertinent quotation.

> "The less there is to justify a traditional custom," wrote Mark Twain, "the harder it is to get rid of it." This comment accurately describes the situation that Shirley Jackson presents in "The Lottery." Her story illustrates how ignorance and superstition become instilled in human society and lead to unnecessary violence.

Another relevant quotation for this introduction might be Gathorne Cranbrook's observation that "The tradition of preserving traditions became a tradition." Useful quotations like these are available in library and online sources such as *Bartlett's Familiar Quotations.*

You can also take an arresting or tantalizing quotation from the story itself. Tessie Hutchinson's final scream, "It isn't fair, it isn't right," or Old Man Warner's "There's *always* been a lottery" might serve as an effective opening for an essay on this story.

Another strategy is to pose a startling question, like this:

> Why would the people in a quiet, peaceful village publicly murder one of their neighbors every summer? This is the shocking question that Shirley Jackson forces us to consider in her symbolic story "The Lottery."

Or you can combine some suspense with a *brief* overview of the story.

> The weather is sunny and clear. The residents of a peaceful village have gathered for an important annual event. They smile and chat with one another, while the children scurry about in play. Then someone brings out a black box, and the ordinary people of this ordinary town begin the process of choosing which one of their neighbors they are going to stone to death this summer. This shocking turn of events is the premise for Shirley Jackson's story about the fear and violence that lie beneath the placid surface of human societies. The story is called "The Lottery."

Another way to introduce a critical essay is to use interesting details about the author or the story's background that relate to the focus of your essay.

In June 1948 the *New Yorker* magazine published "The Lottery," a story by Shirley Jackson. Within days the magazine began to receive a flood of telephone calls and letters, more than for any other piece of fiction it had ever published. Almost all of those who wrote were outraged or bewildered—sometimes both. Why did this story prompt such reactions? Why does it still shock readers? The answer may lie in the story's strong symbolic representation of the pointless violence and casual inhumanity that exist in all our lives.

Whatever approach you choose, keep the reader in mind. Think about reading an essay yourself. What do you expect from the introduction? Remember that the reader forms an important first impression from your opening paragraph.

Sample Student Paper on Symbolism: Second and Final Drafts

On the following left-hand pages appears the uncorrected second draft of an essay written by Todd Hageman, a student at Eastern Illinois University. On the right-hand pages you will see Todd's finished version. The questions in the margins of the final version ask you to consider the changes Todd made when he revised the paper.

Sample Student Paper: Second Draft

Todd Hageman

English 102

March 2, 2005

Symbollism in The Lottery

Shirley Jackson's "The Lottery" uses subtle symbollism along with inconngruities to exemplify the loss of significance of some rituals & traditions, and supersitions and flaws of human nature. The first incongruity used is the day the story takes place, June 27th. Jackson paints a picture of a nice, sunny summer day in a small "Anytown, USA." While Jackson paints this picture, though, the reader feels an uneasy mood and senses something is going to happen. Jackson does this by using the words "hesitant" and "reluctant" to describe the crowd while they "smile at jokes instead of laugh" (78).

The next, and one of the biggest symbols used in the story, is the box—the black box to be more exact. The box is mentioned repeatedly to bring significance to it, although the reader isn't sure why until toward the end of the story. As the lottery symbolizes tradition, the box symbolizes the lottery.

Mr. Summers, the lottery official, tells about getting a new box every year, but the talk seems to "fade off." The box was described as "faded," "splintered," and "grew shabbyier each year" (79).

Sample Student Paper: Final Draft

Hageman 1

Todd Hageman

Professor Funk

English102

9 March 2005

Symbolism in "The Lottery"

In "The Lottery" Shirley Jackson uses subtle symbolism to exemplify the emptiness of some rituals and traditions, as well as to illustrate several flaws of human nature. She begins with an incongruity in the setting on the day the story takes place, June 27. Jackson paints a picture of a sunny summer day in a small "Anytown, USA." While Jackson introduces this pleasant setting, though, the reader feels uneasy and senses that something bad is going to happen. Jackson creates this tension by using the words "hesitant" and "reluctant" to describe the crowd and by mentioning that they "smiled rather than laughed" at jokes (78).

The controlling symbol in the story is the box—the black box suggestive of death. The box is mentioned repeatedly to increase its significance, although the reader is not sure why the author stresses its importance until toward the end of the story. As the lottery symbolizes empty tradition, the box symbolizes the lottery itself.

Mr. Summers, the lottery official, speaks about getting a new box every year, but his talk seems to "fade off." The box is described as "faded," "splintered," and growing "shabbier

Why did Todd make the changes that he did in this opening sentence?

Why did he change the quotation?

How did he improve the opening sentence of this paragraph?

Why did Todd change this quotation from "grew shabbier each year"?

Why did Todd delete the second part of his thesis statement (regarding "incongruities")?

Why did he change "Jackson does this..." to "Jackson creates this tension..."?

Second Draft

The condition of the box symbolize the tradition of
the lottery, and the need for a new box symbolizes
the need for a new tradition.

There is a need for a new tradition because the
lottery itself had lost its significance. Parts of the
original lottery ritual had been allowed to lapse, and
other parts, such as the salute of the official had
"changed with the times" (79). The lottery had lapsed
and changed so much from the original lottery that
the people really didn't know why they were going
through it any more. Probably the only reason they
were going through it was the intellectual argument
used by Old Man Warner, who said, "There's always
been a lottery" (81). When Mr. Warner is informed
that some places have stopped the lottery, he comes
back with such wit as "Nothing but trouble in that,"
and "pack of young fools." (81). The latter idea
expressed brings out the idea that all change is bad
and the young are the ones who make changes.

It is generally aknowledged that the preceeding
statement is false, leaving Mr. Warner on thin ice
from which to argue. I think the author shows the
uselessness of the lottery through Mr. Warner's
ignorance.

Human nature is shown very clearliy through
Tessie in the story. Tessie shows up late at the lottery
very lackadaisical and in a joking mood before she
was picked. She even gave her husband an extra

Final Draft

Hageman 2

each year" (79). The worn-out condition of the box symbolizes the tradition of the lottery, while the need for a new box symbolizes the need for a new tradition, but the townspeople fail to see the need for change.

Why did Todd add this last comment?

There is a need for a new tradition because the lottery itself has lost its significance. Parts of the original lottery ritual have been allowed to lapse, and other parts, such as the salute of the official, have "changed with time" (79). The lottery has lapsed and changed so much from the original that the people really do not know why they are going through it anymore. Probably the only reason they continue is solemnly stated by Old Man Warner: "There's *always* been a lottery" (81). When Mr. Warner is informed that some places have stopped the lottery, he comes back with such meaningless arguments as "Nothing but trouble in *that*" and "Pack of young fools" (81). He simply believes that all change is bad and that the young are the ones who make changes.

Why did he eliminate the sarcasm directed at Old Man Warner?

Can you think of another way to revise the stilted, wordy language of Todd's original statement, "It is generally acknowledged that the preceding statement is false…"?

Most people would disagree, for Mr. Warner has little evidence to support his ideas. I think the author emphasizes the uselessness of the lottery through Mr. Warner's ignorant defense of it.

The selfishness in human nature is shown clearly in the story through Tessie. She shows up late at the lottery, lackadaisically joking with her neighbors before she is picked. She even

How does the addition of the word "selfishness" in the opening sentence improve this whole paragraph?

Second Draft

nudge as he went to draw. When Tessie found out
one of her family would be chosen, her mood
changed rather quickly, screaming "unfair!" She even
wanted her two daughters to take their chances;
which she knew was wrong. Her "friends" around
her showed their flaws by saying, "Be a good sport,"
and "We all took the same chance," and not showing
a bit of pity (82). Tessie's kids also showed no pity,
as they opened their blank pieces of paper, they were
described as "beaming and laughing" (83) with the
crowd, even though they knew it was going to be
Mom or Dad picked. The final part of human nature
exemplified was when Tessie drew the black dot.
Every time she said, "It isn't fair," the following sentence was always her getting hit with a stone, almost
as punishment for saying it. The stones seem to be
saying, "You thought it was fair until you were
picked; now take your medicine."

    The story has one key sentence which puts the
whole theme in a nutshell: "Although the villagers had
forgotten the ritual and lost the original box, they still
remembered to use stones"(83). Through the symbollism being used, the sentence can be translated into
a theme for the story. The ritual had changed with
the times and lost the original purpose, but people
still remember to look out for themselves. Every time
a villager threw a stone, he was probably thinking,
"Better you than me."

    A final thought could be about the slips of paper
and what they symbolized. Jackson mentioned

Final Draft

Hageman 3

gives her husband an encouraging nudge as he goes to draw. When Tessie finds out one of her family will be chosen, her mood changes quickly, and she screams, "It wasn't fair!" (82). She even wants her married daughter and son-in-law to take their chances along with her, which hardly suggests mother love. Her "friends" around her show their lack of pity by saying, "Be a good sport" and "All of us took the same chance!" (82). Tessie's children also show no sympathy. As they open their blank pieces of paper, they are described as beaming and laughing with the crowd, even though they know one of their parents is going to be picked. Human cruelty is also exemplified after Tessie draws the black dot. Both times she cries, "It isn't fair" (83), she gets hit with a stone, almost as punishment for objecting.

Would you have used a period in revising the comma splice, as he did? Or would you have used a semicolon? Why or why not?

The slips of paper also serve a symbolic purpose. Jackson mentions that the unused papers dropped to the ground "where the breeze caught them and lifted them off" (82). The papers could symbolize the people who have been sacrificed through the lottery. The village people make use of both the papers and the sacrificed people, then discard them as trash.

Why did Todd move his final paragraph to this position?

The story has one key sentence which captures the whole theme: "Although the villagers had forgotten the ritual and lost the original black box, they still remembered to use stones" (83).

Why did Todd replace the phrase "in a nutshell"?

Second Draft

that the unused papers were dropped to the ground
"where the breeze caught them and lifted them off"
(82). The papers could be meant to symbolize the
people who had been sacrificed through the lottery.
The village people had used both the papers and the
sacrificed people and had discarded them as trash.

Final Draft

Hageman 4

Considering the symbolism in the story, the sentence can be translated into a theme. Although the ritual had changed with the times and lost the original purpose, people still remember to look out for themselves. Every time the villagers threw a stone, they were probably thinking, "Better you than me." Jackson dramatizes for us the harm done by ignorance which causes people to cling to outworn rituals. She also shows the selfishness and cruelty that lie just beneath the civilized surface of human behavior.

How do these last two sentences that he added improve the paper?

Second Draft

Work Cited

Shirley Jackson, "The Lottery," in <u>Literature</u> and the
   <u>Writing Process</u>, New Jersey: Prentice Hall, Inc.:
   2005. 78–83.

Final Draft

Hageman 5

Work Cited

Jackson, Shirley. "The Lottery." *Literature and the Writing Process*. Ed. Elizabeth McMahan, Susan X Day, and Robert Funk. 7th ed. Upper Saddle River: Prentice, 2005. 83–89. Print.

What corrections did Todd make in his Work Cited entry?

9

Writing About Point of View

Learning about point of view in fiction will help you to understand how the author has shaped what you know and how you feel about the events in a story. When the point of view is unusual, you may want to focus your written analysis on the narrator or on the significance of the writer's choice of narrative focus.

<hr />

What Is Point of View?

In identifying *point of view*, you decide who tells the story—that is, whose thoughts and feelings the reader has access to. The storyteller, called the *narrator*, is a creation of the author and should not be confused with the author. In the following passage from "Everyday Use," Alice Walker takes the reader into the private world of her narrator's fantasy:

> Sometimes I dream a dream in which Dee and I are suddenly brought together on a TV program of this sort. Out of a dark and soft-seated limousine I am ushered into a bright room filled with many people.

In John Updike's story "A & P," the narrator's distinctive voice is established in the opening lines:

> In walks these three girls in nothing but bathing suits. I'm in the third checkout slot, with my back to the door, so I don't see them until they're over by the bread.

But in the opening of "The Lottery," we are not conscious of a narrator at all:

> The morning of June 27th was clear and sunny, with the fresh warmth of a full-summer day; the flowers were blossoming profusely and the grass was richly green.

Describing Point of View

There are several systems for labeling the point of view in a work of literature. They classify the stance and the identity of the person who reports the action—that is, the person whose eyes and mind become ours as we read the story.

In actuality, a great many points of view are possible, and you may find some overlapping among the categories we provide here, but the following should allow you to describe all of the works included in this text.

- *Omniscient:* An all-knowing narrator, who is not a character in the story or involved in the action, freely relates many or all of the character's thoughts, feelings, and actions. In this example from Sherwood Anderson's "Hands," the omniscient narrator gives us considerable information about the main character's life and personality in a single sentence:

  > Wing Biddlebaum, forever frightened and beset by a ghostly band of doubts, did not think of himself as in any way a part of the life of the town where he had lived for twenty years.

- *Limited omniscience:* The narration is limited to the thoughts and observations of a single character. In detective fiction, for instance, we often see the plot unfold strictly from the main character's (the detective's) point of view. Sometimes our perceptions are limited to those of a minor character. In the Sherlock Holmes stories, for instance, the events are reported from the point of view of Dr. Watson, the great detective's sidekick, whose admiration and awe for Holmes's skills become ours. Raymond Carver's "What We Talk About When We Talk About Love" is another example of limited omniscience in which a minor character narrates the entire story.

- *First-Person:* The narrator recounts events in which he or she has been involved as a major participant. The narrator, identified as "I" in the story, speaks directly to us. First-person narrators often present only their side of the story. Sammy, the first-person narrator in John Updike's "A & P," gives an obviously subjective account of why he quit his job. The narrator of Tillie Olsen's "I Stand Here Ironing" appears to tell her story quite honestly and with little self-deception:

  > We were poor and could not afford for her the soil of easy growth. I was a young mother, I was a distracted mother. There were other children pushing, demanding.

- *Unreliable:* If the storyteller misrepresents the facts, the narrator is considered unreliable. An emotionally disturbed person like the murderous narrator of "The Cask of Amontillado," for instance, is not interested in giving a truthful account of his motives and actions. Poe intensifies the shock and horror of the story by letting us see into the inner workings of a sinister mind.

Writers often use an unreliable narrator to emphasize the subjectivity of experience or to reveal the shallowness or self-absorption of the main character. In Eudora Welty's "Why I Live at the P.O.," the narrator, Sister, gives us her perception of the conflicts in the household—colored by her hurt feelings, her desire to be loved by everyone, and her need to be always in the right. As the narrator, however, Sister inadvertently reveals that others in the household see matters quite differently, leaving us to sort out what's really going on in the story.

- *Objective:* Here the narrator disappears and the story seems to tell itself through action and dialogue. An objective narrative does not get into the minds of the characters; it gives us only what could be recorded by a camera and a microphone.

In reading this kind of story, we have to make judgments and draw conclusions on our own. The objective narrator may edit the tape and direct the camera, but we have to figure out why the characters behave as they do. Shirley Jackson's "The Lottery" illustrates an objective point of view: the narrator presents the events without comment; we have to determine why the actions occur and what they mean.

Sometimes a story with an objective point of view is easily identified because it consists largely of conversation, like Hemingway's "Hills Like White Elephants." In this story no author comments appear, only a few actions and brief scenic details. Our understanding of the characters is based entirely on the conclusions we are able to infer from reading their conversation. Because of its similarity to the script of a play, this type of story can also be called a *dramatic* point of view.

Looking at Point of View

As you read Alice Walker's "Everyday Use," think about the implications of our getting only Mama's perception of the events surrounding her daughter Dee's visit.

Alice Walker   1944–

Alice Walker was born in Eatonton, Georgia, the daughter of poor sharecroppers. When playing with her brothers at age eight, she was blinded in her right eye by a BB gun pellet. After attending Spellman and Sarah Lawrence colleges, she became a civil rights activist. In 1965, she married Mel Leventhal, a Jewish civil rights lawyer; they became the first legally married interracial couple in Mississippi. She later coined the term "womanist," meaning a feminist of color. Her novel *The Color Purple* won the 1983 Pulitzer Prize and was made into a popular film.

Everyday Use

For Your Grandmama

I will wait for her in the yard that Maggie and I made so clean and wavy yesterday afternoon. A yard like this is more comfortable than most people know. It is not just a yard. It is like an extended living room. When the hard clay is swept clean as a floor and the fine sand around the edges lined with tiny, irregular grooves, anyone can come and sit and look up into the elm tree and wait for the breezes that never come inside the house.

Maggie will be nervous until after her sister goes: she will stand hopelessly in corners, homely and ashamed of the burn scars down her arms and legs, eying her sister with a mixture of envy and awe. She thinks her sister has held life always in the palm of one hand, that "no" is a word the world never learned to say to her.

You've no doubt seen those TV shows where the child who has "made it" is confronted, as a surprise, by her own mother and father, tottering in weakly from backstage. (A pleasant surprise, of course: What would they do if parent and child came on the show only to curse out and insult each other?) On TV mother and child embrace and smile into each other's faces. Sometimes the mother and father weep, the child wraps them in her arms and leans across the table to tell how she would not have made it without their help. I have seen these programs.

Sometimes I dream a dream in which Dee and I are suddenly brought together on a TV program of this sort. Out of a dark and soft-seated limousine I am ushered into a bright room filled with many people. There I meet a smiling, gray, sporty man like Johnny Carson who shakes my hand and tells me what a fine girl I have. Then we are on the stage and Dee is embracing me with tears in her eyes. She pins on my dress a large orchid, even though she has told me once that she thinks orchids are tacky flowers.

In real life I am a large, big-boned woman with rough, man-working hands.   5
In the winter I wear flannel nightgowns to bed and overalls during the day. I can kill and clean a hog as mercilessly as a man. My fat keeps me hot in zero weather. I can work outside all day, breaking ice to get water for washing; I can eat pork liver cooked over the open fire minutes after it comes steaming from the hog. One winter I knocked a bull calf straight in the brain between the eyes with a sledge hammer and had the meat hung up to chill before nightfall. But of course all this does not show on television. I am the way my daughter would want me to be: a hundred pounds lighter, my skin like an uncooked barley pancake. My hair glistens in the hot bright lights. Johnny Carson has much to do to keep up with my quick and witty tongue.

But that is a mistake. I know even before I wake up. Who ever knew a Johnson with a quick tongue? Who can even imagine me looking a strange white man in the eye? It seems to me I have talked to them always with one foot raised in flight, with my head turned in whichever way is farthest from them. Dee, though. She would always look anyone in the eye. Hesitation was no part of her nature.

"How do I look, Mama?" Maggie says, showing just enough of her thin body enveloped in pink skirt and red blouse for me to know she's there, almost hidden by the door.

"Come out into the yard," I say.

Have you ever seen a lame animal, perhaps a dog run over by some careless person rich enough to own a car, sidle up to someone who is ignorant enough to be kind to him? That is the way my Maggie walks. She has been like this, chin on chest, eyes on ground, feet in shuffle, ever since the fire that burned the other house to the ground.

Dee is lighter than Maggie, with nicer hair and a fuller figure. She's a woman 10 now, though sometimes I forget. How long ago was it that the other house burned? Ten, twelve years? Sometimes I can still hear the flames and feel Maggie's arms sticking to me, her hair smoking and her dress falling off her in little black papery flakes. Her eyes seemed stretched open, blazed open by the flames reflected in them. And Dee. I see her standing off under the sweet gum tree she used to dig gum out of; a look of concentration on her face as she watched the last dingy gray board of the house fall in toward the red-hot brick chimney. Why don't you do a dance around the ashes? I'd wanted to ask her. She had hated the house that much.

I used to think she hated Maggie, too. But that was before we raised the money, the church and me, to send her to Augusta to school. She used to read to us without pity; forcing words, lies, other folks' habits, whole lives upon us two, sitting trapped and ignorant underneath her voice. She washed us in a river of make-believe, burned us with a lot of knowledge we didn't necessarily need to know. Pressed us to her with the serious way she read, to shove us away at just the moment, like dimwits, we seemed about to understand.

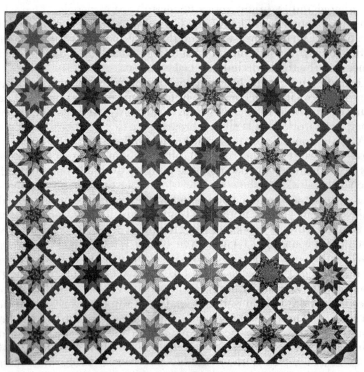

A quilt in the traditional Lone Star pattern (The Newark Museum/Art Resource, NY)

Dee wanted nice things. A yellow organdy dress to wear to her graduation from high school; black pumps to match a green suit she'd made from an old suit somebody gave me. She was determined to stare down any disaster in her efforts. Her eyelids would not flicker for minutes at a time. Often I fought off the temptation to shake her. At sixteen she had a style of her own: and knew what style was.

I never had an education myself. After second grade the school was closed down. Don't ask me why: in 1927 colored asked fewer questions than they do now. Sometimes Maggie reads to me. She stumbles along good-naturedly but can't see well. She knows she is not bright. Like good looks and money, quickness passed her by. She will marry John Thomas (who has mossy teeth in an earnest face) and then I'll be free to sit here and I guess just sing church songs to myself. Although I never was a good singer. Never could carry a tune. I was always better at a man's job. I used to love to milk till I was hooked in the side in '49. Cows are soothing and slow and don't bother you, unless you try to milk them the wrong way.

I have deliberately turned my back on the house. It is three rooms, just like the one that burned, except the roof is tin; they don't make shingle roofs any more. There are no real windows, just some holes cut in the sides, like the portholes in a ship, but not round and not square, with rawhide holding the shutters up on the outside. This house is in a pasture, too, like the other one. No doubt when Dee sees it she will want to tear it down. She wrote me once that no matter where we "choose" to live, she will manage to come see us. But she will never bring her friends. Maggie and I thought about this and Maggie asked me, "Mama, when did Dee ever *have* any friends?"

She had a few. Furtive boys in pink shirts hanging about on washday after   15
school. Nervous girls who never laughed. Impressed with her they worshipped the well-turned phrase, the cute shape, the scalding humor that erupted like bubbles in lye. She read to them.

When she was courting Jimmy T she didn't have much time to pay to us, but turned all her faultfinding power on him. He *flew* to marry a cheap city girl from a family of ignorant flashy people. She hardly had time to recompose herself.

When she comes I will meet—but there they are!
Maggie attempts to make a dash for the house, in her shuffling way, but I stay her with my hand. "Come back here," I say. And she stops and tries to dig a well in the sand with her toe.

It is hard to see them clearly through the strong sun. But even the first glimpse of leg out of the car tells me it is Dee. Her feet were always neat-looking, as if God himself had shaped them with a certain style. From the other side of the car comes a short, stocky man. Hair is all over his head a foot long and hanging from his chin like a kinky mule tail. I hear Maggie suck in her breath. "Uhnnnh," is what it sounds like. Like when you see the wriggling end of a snake just in front of your foot on the road. "Uhnnnh."

Dee next. A dress down to the ground, in this hot weather. A dress so loud it   20
hurts my eyes. There are yellows and oranges enough to throw back the light of the sun. I feel my whole face warming from the heat waves it throws out. Earrings gold, too, and hanging down to her shoulders. Bracelets dangling and making noises when she moves her arm up to shake the folds of the dress out of her armpits. The dress is loose and flows, and as she walks closer, I like it. I hear

Maggie go "Uhnnnh" again. It is her sister's hair. It stands straight up like the wool on a sheep. It is black as night and around the edges are two long pigtails that rope about like small lizards disappearing behind her ears.

"Wa-su-zo-Tean-o!" she says, coming on in that gliding way the dress makes her move. The short stocky fellow with the hair to his navel is all grinning and he follows up with "Asalamalakim, my mother and sister!" He moves to hug Maggie but she falls back, right up against the back of my chair. I feel her trembling there and when I look up I see the perspiration falling off her chin.

"Don't get up," says Dee. Since I am stout it takes something of a push. You can see me trying to move a second or two before I make it. She turns, showing white heels through her sandals, and goes back to the car. Out she peeks next with a Polaroid. She stoops down quickly and lines up picture after picture of me sitting there in front of the house with Maggie cowering behind me. She never takes a shot without making sure the house is included. When a cow comes nibbling around the edge of the yard she snaps it and me and Maggie *and* the house. Then she puts the Polaroid in the back seat of the car, and comes up and kisses me on the forehead.

Meanwhile Asalamalakim is going through motions with Maggie's hand. Maggie's hand is as limp as a fish, and probably as cold, despite the sweat, and she keeps trying to pull it back. It looks like Asalamalakim wants to shake hands but wants to do it fancy. Or maybe he don't know how people shake hands. Anyhow, he soon gives up on Maggie.

"Well," I say. "Dee."

"No, Mama," she says. "Not 'Dee,' Wangero Leewanika Kemanjo!"   25

"What happened to 'Dee'?" I wanted to know.

"She's dead," Wangero said. "I couldn't bear it any longer, being named after the people who oppress me."

"You know as well as me you was named after your aunt Dicie," I said. Dicie is my sister. She named Dee. We called her "Big Dee" after Dee was born.

"But who was *she* named after?" asked Wangero.

"I guess after Grandma Dee," I said.   30

"And who was she named after?" asked Wangero.

"Her mother," I said, and saw Wangero was getting tired. "That's about as far back as I can trace it," I said. Though, in fact, I probably could have carried it back beyond the Civil War through the branches.

"Well," said Asalamalakim, "there you are."

"Uhnnnh," I heard Maggie say.

"There I was not," I said, "before 'Dicie' cropped up in our family, so why   35 should I try to trace it that far back?"

He just stood there grinning, looking down on me like somebody inspecting a Model A car. Every once in a while he and Wangero sent eye signals over my head.

"How do you pronounce this name?" I asked.

"You don't have to call me by it if you don't want to," said Wangero.

"Why shouldn't I?" I asked. "If that's what you want us to call you, we'll call you."

"I know it might sound awkward at first," said Wangero.   40

"I'll get used to it," I said. "Ream it out again."

Well, soon we got the name out of the way. Asalamalakim had a name twice as long and three times as hard. After I tripped over it two or three times he told me to just call him Hakim-a-barber. I wanted to ask him was he a barber, but I didn't really think he was, so I didn't ask.

"You must belong to those beef-cattle peoples down the road," I said. They said "Asalamalakim" when they met you, too, but they didn't shake hands. Always too busy: feeding the cattle, fixing the fences, putting up salt-lick shelters, throwing down hay. When the white folks poisoned some of the herd the men stayed up all night with rifles in their hands. I walked a mile and a half just to see the sight.

Hakim-a-barber said, "I accept some of their doctrines, but farming and raising cattle is not my style." (They didn't tell me, and I didn't ask, whether Wangero (Dee) had really gone and married him.)

We sat down to eat and right away he said he didn't eat collards and pork was   45
unclean. Wangero, though, went on through the chitlins and corn bread, the greens and everything else. She talked a blue streak over the sweet potatoes. Everything delighted her. Even the fact that we still used the benches her daddy made for the table when we couldn't afford to buy chairs.

"Oh, Mama!" she cried. Then turned to Hakim-a-barber. "I never knew how lovely these benches are. You can feel the rump prints," she said, running her hands underneath her and along the bench. Then she gave a sigh and her hand closed over Grandma Dee's butter dish. "That's it!" she said. "I knew there was something I wanted to ask you if I could have." She jumped up from the table and went over in the corner where the churn stood, the milk in it clabber by now. She looked at the churn and looked at it.

"This churn top is what I need," she said. "Didn't Uncle Buddy whittle it out of a tree you all used to have?"

"Yes," I said.

"Uh huh," she said happily. "And I want the dasher, too."

"Uncle Buddy whittle that, too?" asked the barber.   50

Dee (Wangero) looked up at me.

"Aunt Dee's first husband whittled the dash," said Maggie so low you almost couldn't hear her. "His name was Henry, but they called him Stash."

"Maggie's brain is like an elephant's," Wangero said, laughing. "I can use the churn top as a centerpiece for the alcove table," she said, sliding a plate over the churn, "and I'll think of something artistic to do with the dasher."

When she finished wrapping the dasher the handle stuck out. I took it for a moment in my hands. You didn't even have to look close to see where hands pushing the dasher up and down to make butter had left a kind of sink in the wood. In fact, there were a lot of small sinks; you could see where thumbs and fingers had sunk into the wood. It was beautiful light yellow wood, from a tree that grew in the yard where Big Dee and Stash had lived.

After dinner Dee (Wangero) went to the trunk at the foot of my bed and   55
started rifling through it. Maggie hung back in the kitchen over the dishpan. Out came Wangero with two quilts. They had been pieced by Grandma Dee and then Big Dee and me had hung them on the quilt frames on the front porch and quilted them. One was in the Lone Star pattern. The other was Walk Around the Mountain. In both of them were scraps of dresses Grandma Dee had worn fifty and more years ago. Bits and pieces of Grandpa Jarrell's Paisley shirts. And one teeny faded blue piece, about the size of a penny matchbox, that was from Great Grandpa Ezra's uniform that he wore in the Civil War.

"Mama," Wangero said sweet as a bird. "Can I have these old quilts?"

I heard something fall in the kitchen, and a minute later the kitchen door slammed.

"Why don't you take one or two of the others?" I asked. "These old things was just done by me and Big Dee from some tops your grandma pieced before she died."

"No," said Wangero. "I don't want those. They are stitched around the borders by machine."

"That'll make them last better," I said.   60

"That's not the point," said Wangero. "These are all pieces of dresses Grandma used to wear. She did all this stitching by hand. Imagine!" She held the quilts securely in her arms, stroking them.

"Some of the pieces, like those lavender ones, come from old clothes her mother handed down to her," I said, moving up to touch the quilts. Dee (Wangero) moved back just enough so that I couldn't reach the quilts. They already belonged to her.

"Imagine!" she breathed again, clutching them closely to her bosom.

"The truth is," I said, "I promised to give them quilts to Maggie, for when she marries John Thomas."

She gasped like a bee had stung her.   65

"Maggie can't appreciate these quilts!" she said. "She'd probably be backward enough to put them to everyday use."

"I reckon she would," I said. "God knows I been saving 'em for long enough with nobody using 'em. I hope she will!" I didn't want to bring up how I had offered Dee (Wangero) a quilt when she went away to college. Then she had told me they were old-fashioned, out of style.

"But they're *priceless*!" she was saying now, furiously; for she has a temper. "Maggie would put them on the bed and in five years they'd be in rags. Less than that!"

"She can always make some more," I said. "Maggie knows how to quilt."

Dee (Wangero) looked at me with hatred. "You just will not understand. The   70
point is these quilts, *these* quilts!"

"Well," I said, stumped. "What would *you* do with them?"

"Hang them," she said. As if that was the only thing you *could* do with quilts.

Maggie by now was standing in the door. I could almost hear the sound her feet made as they scraped over each other.

"She can have them, Mama," she said, like somebody used to never winning anything, or having anything reserved for her. "I can 'member Grandma Dee without the quilts."

I looked at her hard. She had filled her bottom lip with checkerberry snuff   75
and it gave her face a kind of dopey, hangdog look. It was Grandma Dee and Big Dee who taught her how to quilt herself. She stood there with her scarred hands hidden in the folds of her skirt. She looked at her sister with something like fear but she wasn't mad at her. This was Maggie's portion. This was the way she knew God to work.

When I looked at her like that something hit me in the top of my head and ran down to the soles of my feet. Just like when I'm in church and the spirit of God touches me and I get happy and shout. I did something I never had done before: hugged Maggie to me, then dragged her on into the room, snatched the quilts out of Miss Wangero's hands and dumped them into Maggie's lap. Maggie just sat there on my bed with her mouth open.

"Take one or two of the others," I said to Dee.

But she turned without a word and went out to Hakim-a-barber.

"You just don't understand," she said, as Maggie and I came out to the car.

"What don't I understand?" I wanted to know.

80

"Your heritage," she said. And then she turned to Maggie, kissed her, and said, "You ought to try to make something of yourself, too, Maggie. It's really a new day for us. But from the way you and Mama still live you'd never know it."

She put on some sunglasses that hid everything above the tip of her nose and her chin.

Maggie smiled; maybe at the sunglasses. But a real smile, not scared. After we watched the car dust settle I asked Maggie to bring me a dip of snuff. And then the two of us sat there just enjoying, until it was time to go in the house and go to bed.

(1973)

PREWRITING

To help you examine the point of view of "Everyday Use" and see how it affects other elements of the story, write out answers to the following questions.

Analyzing Point of View

1. Who is telling this story? What kind of person is she? Describe her character traits, her strengths and weaknesses, and explain how you feel about her. Is it significant that she is not given a first name but is called only Mama throughout?

2. Why do you think Walker chose Mama as the narrator instead of Maggie or Dee/Wangero? How would the story be different if told from the point of view of one of the daughters?

3. Describe the character traits of Maggie and Dee/Wangero. How do you respond to them? Do you admire them, feel sorry for them, dislike them? Explain why.

4. Why does Mama include the account of the fire in her narration? Do we know how the house caught fire? Is it important to know? Does this past tragedy shed light on the characters' actions in the story?

5. What is the significance of the African names, dress, and hair styles? Why do you think Asalamalakim appears in the story?

6. Why does Dee/Wangero want the quilts? Why does Mama give them to Maggie?

7. What is the major conflict in the story? Who best understands the family's heritage? How do you know this?

8. Imagine the conversation that Maggie and Mama have after Dee/Wangero has left. Write a page or two of dialogue in which Maggie and Mama talk to each other about Dee.

WRITING

Before you decide to focus your paper on point of view, you need to determine its importance in the story. An analysis of point of view may not always merit a full-length paper. For instance, an omniscient point of view, while a conventional and often effective choice for narrating a story, may not prove a fruitful subject for an essay. But an analysis of point of view will sometimes, as in "Everyday Use," reveal rich insights into the meaning of the story.

Relating Point of View to Theme

After analyzing a story from the vantage of point of view, you need to think about how all your discoveries relate to its theme—its main point, its impact, its insight into human behavior. Your essay will explain why this particular point of view is effective for this particular story.

IDEAS FOR WRITING

Ideas for Responsive Writing

1. Write a description of Mama from the point of view of either Maggie or Dee/Wangero.
2. Have you ever known someone like Mama? Write a character sketch of this person, pointing out similarities to Mama.
3. In "Everyday Use," objects take on more importance than their simple functions—the quilts and the churn, for example. Are there any items like this in your life? Which of your belongings do you think your grandchildren will value? Why? Write about how objects acquire special significance.
4. Have you ever changed your name? Have you asked people to call you by a new name—for example, changing from Billy to Bill? Do you know anyone who has? Why do people change their names? Write an essay about what our names mean to us.

Ideas for Critical Writing

Here are some possible major claims that focus on point of view. Choose one of these claims, revise one, or make up your own to develop an interpretation of "Everyday Use."

1. Each memory recorded in "Everyday Use" serves to strengthen the foil relationship between Dee/Wangero and the narrator, a contrast that flares into a clash between two notions of heritage.

2. Alice Walker uses explanatory flashbacks to Dee/Wangero's early life but excludes any depiction of her current life (even such details as whether she is married or where she lives); this character appears from nowhere, ironically suggesting her own lack of heritage or cultural tradition, a lack she is quick to perceive in others.

3. By telling the story through the eyes of Mama, Walker subtly encourages us to agree with Mama's side of the underlying argument about cultural heritage.

4. Because we as readers have access to Mama's unspoken thoughts about her daughters and Hakim-a-barber, we realize that, despite the seriousness of the story, she is a great comic narrator.

Ideas for Researched Writing

1. Look up and study the topic "black nationalism" in a reference work, such as *The African-American Encyclopedia* or *Encyclopedia of African-American Culture* (the latter is available online). Then write an essay explaining how you think this social movement from the 1960s has influenced the appearance, behavior, and attitudes of Dee/Wangero.

2. "Everyday Use" is a story about many different themes and issues. Research the various critical readings of this story, and prepare a report for your classmates that summarizes and evaluates the interpretations you found.

REWRITING

When you revise, do not neglect your conclusion just because it comes last. It has a psychologically important place in your paper. Ask yourself, "Does my closing restate the main idea in an obvious, repetitive way? Will readers feel let down, dropped off, cut short?" If so, consider these ways to make your ending more lively.

Sharpening the Conclusion

1. *Description.* In concluding a discussion of the conflicts between Mama and her distasteful daughter, you might write the following:

> Thus Dee/Wangero, with her new name, her African dress, her dangling bracelets, and her braided hair, rejects the rural simplicity of her childhood culture. Sliding on her fashionable sunglasses, she leaves Mama and Maggie sitting on their porch "just enjoying" their dip of snuff, the pleasant evening, and the comfortable everydayness of their lives.

2. *A quotation from the story.* Remember that a quotation must be integrated into your own sentence, perhaps like this:

> When Maggie says, quietly, "I can 'member Grandma Dee without the quilts," we see that heritage can have a deeper meaning than

co-opting churn tops as centerpieces and hand-stitched quilts as wall hangings.

3. *An echo from your introduction.* If you wrote in your opening of the clash between two black cultures in the story, you could conclude with this echo:

Mama, pushed too far, finally proves herself a match for her sophisticated daughter, who ignores her own family heritage as she shows off her newly adopted African roots.

4. *A thought-provoking question, suggestion, or statement.*

Were Mama and Maggie right in rejecting the unfamiliar African heritage that Dee/Wangero introduces?

Perhaps society would generate fewer conflicts if people paid less attention to their individual ethnic and cultural background.

10

Writing About Setting and Atmosphere

S etting and atmosphere contribute to the effectiveness of short stories in various ways. Sometimes these elements assume enough importance to become the focus of a literary analysis.

What Are Setting and Atmosphere?

You know, of course, the meaning of *setting* in reference to a work of literature: the setting includes the location and time of the action in a story, novel, play, or poem. Sometimes setting conveys an *atmosphere*—the emotional effect of the setting and events—that contributes to the impact or to the meaning of the work. Atmosphere (or *mood*) is that feeling of chill foreboding that Poe creates by setting his tale of "The Fall of the House of Usher" in a remote, moldering mansion on the edge of a black, stagnant pool and then having eerie things happen. Atmosphere can also serve to increase irony, as Shirley Jackson does in "The Lottery" by conveying the deceptive feeling of carefree summer festivity just before turning her tale abruptly toward ritual murder. Usually, though, setting and atmosphere reflect the dominant tone and theme of a work.

In deciding whether to focus on setting or atmosphere in writing a literary paper, you need to ask yourself not only how much the effect of the work would be changed if these elements were different, but also how much you have to say about them—especially what they contribute to the power of the narrative. For instance, the stalled freeway where Dagoberto Gilb's "Love in L.A." takes place seems the perfect setting for that story. We can scarcely imagine its being set as effectively anywhere else. Los Angeles, the home of Hollywood and all the fantasies of movieland, clearly molded the main character's imaginative life and inspired the false surfaces of his identity. Sweaty, noisy traffic jams pervade this L.A. dweller's life, shape his aspirations, and stick him with plenty of downtime in which to embellish his daydreams. A freeway collision is a completely believable site for Jake to bump into his version of love. Concerning any story, if you ask yourself, "In what other surroundings and time could this story happen?" and find it difficult to imagine an answer, probably the setting is a worthwhile focus for a paper.

Looking at Setting and Atmosphere

As you read the following story by Tobias Wolff, consider how crucial setting and atmosphere are in contributing to the story's effect.

Tobias Wolff 1945–

Tobias Wolff, a Stanford University graduate, served four years as an army paratrooper, including a year in Vietnam, and now teaches creative writing at Stanford. "The disaster of television," he says, "has created a tremendous vacuum in our culture. I really regard it as a catastrophe. The monster in our house devours the imagination; it's a completely passive entertainment. And reading has been the first casualty, because reading is active, demanding." His memoir, *This Boy's Life* (1989), a painful reminiscence of growing up in his stepfather's home, was made into a popular film starring Robert De Niro and Leonardo DiCaprio.

Hunters in the Snow

Tub had been waiting for an hour in the falling snow. He paced the sidewalk to keep warm and stuck his head out over the curb whenever he saw lights approaching. One driver stopped for him but before Tub could wave the man on he saw the rifle on Tub's back and hit the gas. The tires spun on the ice.

The fall of snow thickened. Tub stood below the overhang of a building. Across the road the clouds whitened just above the rooftops, and the street lights went out. He shifted the rifle strap to his other shoulder. The whiteness seeped up the sky.

A truck slid around the corner, horn blaring, rear end sashaying. Tub moved to the sidewalk and held up his hand. The truck jumped the curb and kept coming, half on the street and half on the sidewalk. It wasn't slowing down at all. Tub stood for a moment, still holding up his hand, then jumped back. His rifle slipped off his shoulder and clattered on the ice, a sandwich fell out of his pocket. He ran for the steps of the building. Another sandwich and a package of cookies tumbled onto the new snow. He made the steps and looked back.

The truck had stopped several feet beyond where Tub had been standing. He picked up his sandwiches and his cookies and slung the rifle and went up to the driver's window. The driver was bent against the steering wheel, slapping his knees and drumming his feet on the floorboards. He looked like a cartoon of a person laughing, except that his eyes watched the man on the seat beside him.

"You ought to see yourself," the driver said. "He looks just like a beach ball with a hat on, doesn't he? Doesn't he, Frank?"

The man beside him smiled and looked off.   5

"You almost ran me down," Tub said. "You could've killed me."

"Come on, Tub," said the man beside the driver. "Be mellow. Kenny was just messing around." He opened the door and slid over to the middle of the seat.

Tub took the bolt out of his rifle and climbed in beside him. "I waited an hour," he said. "If you meant ten o'clock why didn't you say ten o'clock?"

"Tub, you haven't done anything but complain since we got here," said the man in the middle. "If you want to piss and moan all day you might as well go home and bitch at your kids. Take your pick." When Tub didn't say anything he turned to the driver. "Okay, Kenny, let's hit the road."

Some juvenile delinquents had heaved a brick through the windshield on the   10
driver's side, so the cold and snow tunneled right into the cab. The heater didn't work. They covered themselves with a couple of blankets Kenny had brought along and pulled down the muffs on their caps. Tub tried to keep his hands warm by rubbing them under the blanket but Frank made him stop.

They left Spokane and drove deep into the country, running along black lines of fences. The snow let up, but still there was no edge to the land where it met the sky. Nothing moved in the chalky fields. The cold bleached their faces and made the stubble stand out on their cheeks and along their upper lips. They stopped twice for coffee before they got to the woods where Kenny wanted to hunt.

Tub was for trying someplace different; two years in a row they'd been up and down this land and hadn't seen a thing. Frank didn't care one way or the other, he just wanted to get out of the goddamned truck. "Feel that," Frank said, slamming the door. He spread his feet and closed his eyes and leaned his head way back and breathed deeply. "Tune in on that energy."

"Another thing," Kenny said. "This is open land. Most of the land around here is posted."

"I'm cold," Tub said.

Frank breathed out. "Stop bitching, Tub. Get centered."   15

"I wasn't bitching."

"Centered," Kenny said. "Next thing you'll be wearing a nightgown, Frank. Selling flowers out at the airport."

"Kenny," Frank said, "you talk too much."

"Okay," Kenny said. "I won't say a word. Like I won't say anything about a certain babysitter."

"What babysitter?" Tub asked.   20

"That's between us," Frank said, looking at Kenny. "That's confidential. You keep your mouth shut."

Kenny laughed.

"You're asking for it," Frank said.

"Asking for what?"

"You'll see."   25

"Hey," Tub said, "are we hunting or what?"

They started off across the field. Tub had trouble getting through the fences. Frank and Kenny could have helped him; they could have lifted up on the top wire and stepped on the bottom wire, but they didn't. They stood and watched him. There were a lot of fences and Tub was puffing when they reached the woods.

They hunted for over two hours and saw no deer, no tracks, no sign. Finally they stopped by the creek to eat. Kenny had several slices of pizza and a couple of candy bars; Frank had a sandwich, an apple, two carrots, and a square of chocolate; Tub ate one hard-boiled egg and a stick of celery.

"You ask me how I want to die today," Kenny said, "I'll tell you burn me at the stake." He turned to Tub. "You still on that diet?" He winked at Frank.

"What do you think? You think I like hard-boiled eggs?" 30

"All I can say is, it's the first diet I ever heard of where you gained weight from it."

"Who said I gained weight?"

"Oh, pardon me. I take it back. You're just wasting away before my very eyes. Isn't he, Frank?"

Frank had his fingers fanned out, tips against the bark of the stump where he'd laid his food. His knuckles were hairy. He wore a heavy wedding band and on his right pinky another gold ring with a flat face and an "F" in what looked like diamonds. He turned the ring this way and that. "Tub," he said, "you haven't seen your own balls in ten years."

Kenny doubled over laughing. He took off his hat and slapped his leg with it. 35

"What am I supposed to do?" Tub said. "It's my glands."

They left the woods and hunted along the creek. Frank and Kenny worked one bank and Tub worked the other, moving upstream. The snow was light but the drifts were deep and hard to move through. Wherever Tub looked the surface was smooth, undisturbed, and after a time he lost interest. He stopped looking for tracks and just tried to keep up with Frank and Kenny on the other side. A moment came when he realized he hadn't seen them in a long time. The breeze was moving from him to them; when it stilled he could sometimes hear Kenny laughing but that was all. He quickened his pace, breasting hard into the drifts, fighting away the snow with his knees and elbows. He heard his heart and felt the flush on his face but he never once stopped.

Tub caught up with Frank and Kenny at a bend of the creek. They were standing on a log that stretched from their bank to his. Ice had backed up behind the log. Frozen reeds stuck out, barely nodding when the air moved.

"See anything?" Frank asked.

Tub shook his head. 40

There wasn't much daylight left and they decided to head back toward the road. Frank and Kenny crossed the log and they started downstream, using the trail Tub had broken. Before they had gone very far Kenny stopped. "Look at that," he said, and pointed to some tracks going from the creek back into the woods. Tub's footprints crossed right over them. There on the bank, plain as day, were several mounds of deer sign. "What do you think that is, Tub?" Kenny kicked at it. "Walnuts on vanilla icing?"

"I guess I didn't notice."

Kenny looked at Frank.

"I was lost."

"You were lost. Big deal." 45

They followed the tracks into the woods. The deer had gone over a fence half buried in drifting snow. A no hunting sign was nailed to the top of one of the posts. Frank laughed and said the son of a bitch could read. Kenny wanted to go after him but Frank said no way, the people out here didn't mess around. He thought maybe the farmer who owned the land would let them use it if they asked. Kenny wasn't so sure. Anyway, he figured that by the time they walked to the truck and drove up the road and doubled back it would be almost dark.

"Relax," Frank said. "You can't hurry nature. If we're meant to get that deer, we'll get it. If we're not, we won't."

They started back toward the truck. This part of the woods was mainly pine. The snow was shaded and had a glaze on it. It held up Kenny and Frank but Tub kept falling through. As he kicked forward, the edge of the crust bruised his shins. Kenny and Frank pulled ahead of him, to where he couldn't even hear their voices any more. He sat down on a stump and wiped his face. He ate both the sandwiches and half the cookies, taking his own sweet time. It was dead quiet.

When Tub crossed the last fence into the road the truck started moving. Tub had to run for it and just managed to grab hold of the tailgate and hoist himself into the bed. He lay there, panting. Kenny looked out the rear window and grinned. Tub crawled into the lee of the cab to get out of the freezing wind. He pulled his earflaps low and pushed his chin into the collar of his coat. Someone rapped on the window but Tub would not turn around.

He and Frank waited outside while Kenny went into the farmhouse to ask   50
permission. The house was old and paint was curling off the sides. The smoke streamed westward off the top of the chimney, fanning away into a thin gray plume. Above the ridge of the hills another ridge of blue clouds was rising.

"You've got a short memory," Tub said.

"What?" Frank said. He had been staring off.

"I used to stick up for you."

"Okay, so you used to stick up for me. What's eating you?"

"You shouldn't have just left me back there like that."   55

"You're a grown-up, Tub. You can take care of yourself. Anyway, if you think you're the only person with problems I can tell you that you're not."

"Is something bothering you, Frank?"

Frank kicked at a branch poking out of the snow. "Never mind," he said.

"What did Kenny mean about the babysitter?"

"Kenny talks too much," Frank said. "You just mind your own business."   60

Kenny came out of the farmhouse and gave the thumbs-up and they began walking back toward the woods. As they passed the barn a large black hound with a grizzled snout ran out and barked at them. Every time he barked he slid backwards a bit, like a cannon recoiling. Kenny got down on all fours and snarled and barked back at him, and the dog slunk away into the barn, looking over his shoulder and peeing a little as he went.

"That's an old-timer," Frank said. "A real graybeard. Fifteen years if he's a day."

"Too old," Kenny said.

Past the barn they cut off through the fields. The land was unfenced and the crust was freezing up thick and they made good time. They kept to the edge of the field until they picked up the tracks again and followed them into the woods, farther and farther back toward the hills. The trees started to blur with the shadows and the wind rose and needled their faces with the crystals it swept off the glaze. Finally they lost the tracks.

Kenny swore and threw down his hat. "This is the worst day of hunting I 65 ever had, bar none." He picked up his hat and brushed off the snow. "This will be the first season since I was fifteen I haven't got my deer."

"It isn't the deer," Frank said. "It's the hunting. There are all these forces out here and you just have to go with them."

"You go with them," Kenny said. "I came out here to get me a deer, not listen to a bunch of hippie bullshit. And if it hadn't been for dimples here I would have, too."

"That's enough," Frank said.

"And you—you're so busy thinking about that little jailbait of yours you wouldn't know a deer if you saw one."

"Drop dead," Frank said, and turned away. 70

Kenny and Tub followed him back across the fields. When they were coming up to the barn Kenny stopped and pointed. "I hate that post," he said. He raised his rifle and fired. It sounded like a dry branch cracking. The post splintered along its right side, up towards the top. "There," Kenny said. "It's dead."

"Knock it off," Frank said, walking ahead.

Kenny looked at Tub. He smiled. "I hate that tree," he said, and fired again. Tub hurried to catch up with Frank. He started to speak but just then the dog ran out of the barn and barked at them. "Easy, boy," Frank said.

"I hate that dog." Kenny was behind them.

"That's enough," Frank said. "You put that gun down." 75

Kenny fired. The bullet went in between the dog's eyes. He sank right down into the snow, his legs splayed out on each side, his yellow eyes open and staring. Except for the blood he looked like a small bearskin rug. The blood ran down the dog's muzzle into the snow.

They all looked at the dog lying there.

"What did he ever do to you?" Tub asked. "He was just barking."

Kenny turned to Tub. "I hate you."

Tub shot from the waist. Kenny jerked backward against the fence and buckled 80 to his knees. He folded his hands across his stomach. "Look," he said. His hands were covered with blood. In the dusk his blood was more blue than red. It seemed to belong to the shadows. It didn't seem out of place. Kenny eased himself onto his back. He sighed several times, deeply. "You shot me," he said.

"I had to," Tub said. He knelt beside Kenny. "Oh God," he said. "Frank. Frank."

Frank hadn't moved since Kenny killed the dog.

"Frank!" Tub shouted.

"I was just kidding around," Kenny said. "It was a joke. Oh!" he said, and arched his back suddenly. "Oh!" he said again, and dug his heels into the snow and pushed himself along on his head for several feet. Then he stopped and lay there, rocking back and forth on his heels and head like a wrestler doing warm-up exercises.

Frank roused himself. "Kenny," he said. He bent down and put his gloved 85 hand on Kenny's brow. "You shot him," he said to Tub.

"He made me," Tub said.

"No no no," Kenny said.

Tub was weeping from the eyes and nostrils. His whole face was wet. Frank closed his eyes, then looked down at Kenny again. "Where does it hurt?"

"Everywhere," Kenny said, "just everywhere."

"Oh God," Tub said.   90

"I mean where did it go in?" Frank said.

"Here." Kenny pointed at the wound in his stomach. It was welling slowly with blood.

"You're lucky," Frank said. "It's on the left side. It missed your appendix. If it had hit your appendix you'd really be in the soup." He turned and threw up onto the snow, holding his sides as if to keep warm.

"Are you all right?" Tub said.

"There's some aspirin in the truck," Kenny said.   95

"I'm all right," Frank said.

"We'd better call an ambulance," Tub said.

"Jesus," Frank said. "What are we going to say?"

"Exactly what happened," Tub said. "He was going to shoot me but I shot him first."

"No sir!" Kenny said. "I wasn't either!"   100

Frank patted Kenny on the arm. "Easy does it, partner." He stood. "Let's go."

Tub picked up Kenny's rifle as they walked down toward the farmhouse. "No sense leaving this around," he said. "Kenny might get ideas."

"I can tell you one thing," Frank said. "You've really done it this time. This definitely takes the cake."

They had to knock on the door twice before it was opened by a thin man with lank hair. The room behind him was filled with smoke. He squinted at them. "You get anything?" he asked.

"No," Frank said.   105

"I knew you wouldn't. That's what I told the other fellow."

"We've had an accident."

The man looked past Frank and Tub into the gloom. "Shoot your friend, did you?"

Frank nodded.

"I did," Tub said.   110

"I suppose you want to use the phone."

"If it's okay."

The man in the door looked behind him, then stepped back. Frank and Tub followed him into the house. There was a woman sitting by the stove in the middle of the room. The stove was smoking badly. She looked up and then down again at the child asleep in her lap. Her face was white and damp; strands of hair were pasted across her forehead. Tub warmed his hands over the stove while Frank went into the kitchen to call. The man who had let them in stood at the window, his hands in his pockets.

"My friend shot your dog," Tub said.

The man nodded without turning around. "I should have done it myself.   115
I just couldn't."

"He loved that dog so much," the woman said. The child squirmed and she rocked it.

"You asked him to?" Tub said. "You asked him to shoot your dog?"

"He was old and sick. Couldn't chew his food any more. I would have done it myself but I don't have a gun."

"You couldn't have anyway," the woman said. "Never in a million years."

The man shrugged.   120

Frank came out of the kitchen. "We'll have to take him ourselves. The nearest hospital is fifty miles from here and all their ambulances are out anyway."

The woman knew a shortcut but the directions were complicated and Tub had to write them down. The man told them where they could find some boards to carry Kenny on. He didn't have a flashlight but he said he would leave the porch light on.

It was dark outside. The clouds were low and heavy-looking and the wind blew in shrill gusts. There was a screen loose on the house and it banged slowly and then quickly as the wind rose again. They could hear it all the way to the barn. Frank went for the boards while Tub looked for Kenny, who was not where they had left him. Tub found him farther up the drive, lying on his stomach. "You okay?" Tub said.

"It hurts."

"Frank says it missed your appendix." 125

"I already had my appendix out."

"All right," Frank said, coming up to them. "We'll have you in a nice warm bed before you can say Jack Robinson." He put the two boards on Kenny's right side.

"Just as long as I don't have one of those male nurses," Kenny said.

"Ha ha," Frank said. "That's the spirit. Get ready, set, *over you go*," and he rolled Kenny onto the boards. Kenny screamed and kicked his legs in the air. When he quieted down Frank and Tub lifted the boards and carried him down the drive. Tub had the back end, and with the snow blowing into his face he had trouble with his footing. Also he was tired and the man inside had forgotten to turn the porch light on. Just past the house Tub slipped and threw out his hands to catch himself. The boards fell and Kenny tumbled out and rolled to the bottom of the drive, yelling all the way. He came to rest against the right front wheel of the truck.

"You fat moron," Frank said. "You aren't good for diddly." 130

Tub grabbed Frank by the collar and backed him hard up against the fence. Frank tried to pull his hands away but Tub shook him and snapped his head back and forth and finally Frank gave up.

"What do you know about fat," Tub said. "What do you know about glands." As he spoke he kept shaking Frank. "What do you know about me."

"All right," Frank said.

"No more," Tub said.

"All right." 135

"No more talking to me like that. No more watching. No more laughing."

"Okay, Tub. I promise."

Tub let go of Frank and leaned his forehead against the fence. His arms hung straight at his sides.

"I'm sorry, Tub." Frank touched him on the shoulder. "I'll be down at the truck."

Tub stood by the fence for a while and then got the rifles off the porch. Frank 140 had rolled Kenny back onto the boards and they lifted him into the bed of the truck. Frank spread the seat blankets over him. "Warm enough?" he asked.

Kenny nodded.

"Okay. Now how does reverse work on this thing?"

"All the way to the left and up." Kenny sat up as Frank started forward to the cab. "Frank!"

"What?"

"If it sticks don't force it."   145

The truck started right away. "One thing," Frank said, "you've got to hand it to the Japanese. A very ancient, very spiritual culture and they can still make a hell of a truck." He glanced over at Tub. "Look, I'm sorry. I didn't know you felt that way, honest to God I didn't. You should have said something."

"I did."

"When? Name one time."

"A couple of hours ago."

"I guess I wasn't paying attention."   150

"That's true, Frank," Tub said. "You don't pay attention very much."

"Tub," Frank said, "what happened back there, I should have been more sympathetic. I realize that. You were going through a lot. I just want you to know it wasn't your fault. He was asking for it."

"You think so?"

"Absolutely. It was him or you. I would have done the same thing in your shoes, no question."

The wind was blowing into their faces. The snow was a moving white wall in 155 front of their lights; it swirled into the cab through the hole in the windshield and settled on them. Tub clapped his hands and shifted around to stay warm, but it didn't work.

"I'm going to have to stop," Frank said. "I can't feel my fingers."

Up ahead they saw some lights off the road. It was a tavern. Outside in the parking lot there were several jeeps and trucks. A couple of them had deer strapped across their hoods. Frank parked and they went back to Kenny. "How you doing, partner," Frank said.

"I'm cold."

"Well, don't feel like the Lone Ranger. It's worse inside, take my word for it. You should get that windshield fixed."

"Look," Tub said, "he threw the blankets off." They were lying in a heap 160 against the tailgate.

"Now look, Kenny," Frank said, "it's no use whining about being cold if you're not going to try and keep warm. You've got to do your share." He spread the blankets over Kenny and tucked them in at the corners.

"They blew off."

"Hold on to them then."

"Why are we stopping, Frank?"

"Because if me and Tub don't get warmed up we're going to freeze solid and 165 then where will you be?" He punched Kenny lightly in the arm. "So just hold your horses."

The bar was full of men in colored jackets, mostly orange. The waitress brought coffee. "Just what the doctor ordered," Frank said, cradling the steaming cup in his hand. His skin was bone white. "Tub, I've been thinking. What you said about me not paying attention, that's true."

"It's okay."

"No. I really had that coming. I guess I've just been a little too interested in old number one. I've had a lot on my mind. Not that that's any excuse."

"Forget it, Frank. I sort of lost my temper back there. I guess we're all a little on edge."

Frank shook his head. "It isn't just that."   170

"You want to talk about it?"

"Just between us, Tub?"

"Sure, Frank. Just between us."

"Tub, I think I'm going to be leaving Nancy."

"Oh, Frank. Oh, Frank." Tub sat back and shook his head.   175

Frank reached out and laid his hand on Tub's arm. "Tub, have you ever been really in love?"

"Well—"

"I mean *really* in love." He squeezed Tub's wrist. "With your whole being."

"I don't know. When you put it like that, I don't know."

"You haven't then. Nothing against you, but you'd know it if you had." Frank   180
let go of Tub's arm. "This isn't just some bit of fluff I'm talking about."

"Who is she, Frank?"

Frank paused. He looked into his empty cup. "Roxanne Brewer."

"Cliff Brewer's kid? The babysitter?"

"You can't just put people into categories like that, Tub. That's why the whole system is wrong. And that's why this country is going to hell in a rowboat."

"But she can't be more than—" Tub shook his head.   185

"Fifteen. She'll be sixteen in May." Frank smiled. "May fourth, three twenty-seven p.m. Hell, Tub, a hundred years ago she'd have been an old maid by that age. Juliet was only thirteen."

"Juliet? Juliet Miller? Jesus, Frank, she doesn't even have breasts. She doesn't even wear a top to her bathing suit. She's still collecting frogs."

"Not Juliet Miller. The real Juliet. Tub, don't you see how you're dividing people up into categories? He's an executive, she's a secretary, he's a truck driver, she's fifteen years old. Tub, this so-called babysitter, this so-called fifteen-year-old has more in her little finger than most of us have in our entire bodies. I can tell you this little lady is something special."

Tub nodded. "I know the kids like her."

"She's opened up whole worlds to me that I never knew were there."   190

"What does Nancy think about all of this?"

"She doesn't know."

"You haven't told her?"

"Not yet. It's not so easy. She's been damned good to me all these years. Then there's the kids to consider." The brightness in Frank's eyes trembled and he wiped quickly at them with the back of his hand. "I guess you think I'm a complete bastard."

"No, Frank. I don't think that."   195

"Well, you *ought* to."

"Frank, when you've got a friend it means you've always got someone on your side, no matter what. That's the way I feel about it, anyway."

"You mean that, Tub?"

"Sure I do."

Frank smiled. "You don't know how good it feels to hear you say that."   200

Kenny had tried to get out of the truck but he hadn't made it. He was jack-knifed over the tailgate, his head hanging above the bumper. They lifted him back into the bed and covered him again. He was sweating and his teeth chattered. "It hurts, Frank."

"It wouldn't hurt so much if you just stayed put. Now we're going to the hospital. Got that? Say it—I'm going to the hospital."

"I'm going to the hospital."

"Again."

"I'm going to the hospital."   205

"Now just keep saying that to yourself and before you know it we'll be there."

After they had gone a few miles Tub turned to Frank. "I just pulled a real boner," he said.

"What's that?"

"I left the directions on the table back there."

"That's okay. I remember them pretty well."   210

The snowfall lightened and the clouds began to roll back off the fields, but it was no warmer and after a time both Frank and Tub were bitten through and shaking. Frank almost didn't make it around a curve, and they decided to stop at the next roadhouse.

There was an automatic hand-dryer in the bathroom and they took turns standing in front of it, opening their jackets and shirts and letting the jet of hot air breathe across their faces and chests.

"You know," Tub said, "what you told me back there, I appreciate it. Trusting me."

Frank opened and closed his fingers in front of the nozzle. "The way I look at it, Tub, no man is an island. You've got to trust someone."

"Frank—"   215

Frank waited.

"When I said that about my glands, that wasn't true. The truth is I just shovel it in."

"Well, Tub—"

"Day and night, Frank. In the shower. On the freeway." He turned and let the air play over his back. "I've even got stuff in the paper towel machine at work."

"There's nothing wrong with your glands at all?" Frank had taken his boots   220
and socks off. He held first his right, then his left foot up to the nozzle.

"No. There never was."

"Does Alice know?" The machine went off and Frank started lacing up his boots.

"Nobody knows. That's the worst of it, Frank. Not the being fat, I never got any big kick out of being thin, but the lying. Having to lead a double life like a spy or a hit man. This sounds strange but I feel sorry for those guys, I really do. I know what they go through. Always having to think about what you say and do. Always feeling like people are watching you, trying to catch you at something. Never able to just be yourself. Like when I make a big deal about only having an orange for breakfast and then scarf all the way to work. Oreos, Mars Bars, Twinkies. Sugar Babies. Snickers." Tub glanced at Frank and looked quickly away. "Pretty disgusting, isn't it?"

"Tub. Tub." Frank shook his head. "Come on." He took Tub's arm and led him into the restaurant half of the bar. "My friend is hungry," he told the waitress. "Bring four orders of pancakes, plenty of butter and syrup."

"Frank—"   225

"Sit down."

When the dishes came Frank carved out slabs of butter and just laid them on the pancakes. Then he emptied the bottle of syrup, moving it back and forth over the plates. He leaned forward on his elbows and rested his chin in one hand. "Go on, Tub."

Tub ate several mouthfuls, then started to wipe his lips. Frank took the napkin away from him. "No wiping," he said. Tub kept at it. The syrup covered his chin; it dripped to a point like a goatee. "Weigh in, Tub," Frank said, pushing another fork across the table. "Get down to business." Tub took the fork in his left hand and lowered his head and started really chowing down. "Clean your plate," Frank said when the pancakes were gone, and Tub lifted each of the four plates and licked it clean. He sat back, trying to catch his breath.

"Beautiful," Frank said. "Are you full?"

"I'm full," Tub said. "I've never been so full."   230

Kenny's blankets were bunched up against the tailgate again.

"They must have blown off," Tub said.

"They're not doing him any good," Frank said. "We might as well get some use out of them."

Kenny mumbled. Tub bent over him. "What? Speak up."

"I'm going to the hospital," Kenny said.   235

"Attaboy," Frank said.

The blankets helped. The wind still got their faces and Frank's hands but it was much better. The fresh snow on the road and the trees sparkled under the beam of the headlight. Squares of light from farmhouse windows fell onto the blue snow in the fields.

"Frank," Tub said after a time, "you know that farmer? He told Kenny to kill the dog."

"You're kidding!" Frank leaned forward, considering. "That Kenny. What a card." He laughed and so did Tub. Tub smiled out the back window. Kenny lay with his arms folded over his stomach, moving his lips at the stars. Right overhead was the Big Dipper, and behind, hanging between Kenny's toes in the direction of the hospital, was the North Star, Pole Star, Help to Sailors. As the truck twisted through the gentle hills the star went back and forth between Kenny's boots, staying always in his sight. "I'm going to the hospital," Kenny said. But he was wrong. They had taken a different turn a long way back.

(1980)

PREWRITING

As you read the story carefully a second time, pay particular attention to the descriptive passages that appeal to the senses—especially, in this story, images of snow, cold, and ice. Underline any specific words or phrases that you think contribute to the atmosphere.

Prewriting Exercise

1. Write one or two paragraphs that describe Frank, Kenny, and Tub going fishing on a hundred-degree summer day. What elements of "Hunters in the Snow" would stay the same, and what would change in this altered setting?

2. Examine the first ten paragraphs of the story, when Frank and Kenny come to pick up Tub to go hunting. What do these paragraphs reveal about the three men? What can you say about their relationship after reading only the opening of the tale?

3. What features of the setting seem essential to the way "Hunters in the Snow" unfolds? In other words, how do the snow and cold determine what happens in important ways?

4. Before planning your paper, write your responses to the following questions:

   a. When you think of men going on a hunting trip, what associations come forth? Are any of these associations reflected in the story? Are any of them contradicted or undermined?

   b. How soon in the story can you distinguish among the three characters? What are some of the ways they are distinct from one another?

   c. List the indoor scenes in this basically outdoor story. What critical events or revelations happen in each of the indoor scenes?

   d. What do you make of Frank's ordering the pancakes for Tub at the roadhouse? Is it an act of acceptance, friendship, cruelty, humor, vicarious satisfaction, or what?

   e. Although women are generally off the scene, in what ways do they influence the characters?

   f. At several points in the story, you may have been shocked by what happens. What are some of these points? Why were they shocking?

WRITING

Now that you have become familiar with the story, ask yourself still more questions: How can I make a statement about the function of setting in relation to theme? What, indeed, does the setting contribute to the overall effectiveness of the story? What does the atmosphere contribute? How do both relate to the meaning of the story? Do they *heighten* the theme, do they provide a unique opportunity for the events, or do they help the reader to understand what the story is about? Would a different setting change the story in important ways? As you think about answers to these questions, review your prewriting material and continue consulting the story for clues.

Discovering an Organization

As you are trying to solve the problems posed by the questions in the preceding paragraph, write down all the likely ideas that strike you. Do not trust your memory, or some of your best inspirations may slip away. Then try to think of some point you can make about the story that will allow you to use this information. Such a point will usually make a link between the setting and something else about the story: the characters, action, plot, motivation, meaning, or emotional impact. Once you have discovered an interesting point to pursue, write out this idea in a single, clear sentence. This idea will be your thesis. Then sort through the details related to setting in the story and ask yourself: How can I organize these details in support of my thesis? You might, for instance, group your material chronologically, arranging details according to the episodes in the story as they occur from morning till night. Or you might consider a logical arrangement, emphasizing each of the main characters in turn or focusing first on everything that happens outdoors and then on everything that happens indoors.

IDEAS FOR WRITING

Ideas for Responsive Writing

1. "Hunters in the Snow" takes place in a traditionally all-male setting, a hunting trip. In your experience, do people in small same-sex groups behave differently than they would in mixed-sex groups? If so, do they behave better or worse? Outside of hunting trips, what other occasions usually bring together small same-sex groups? Write a description of a same-sex occasion you have encountered. Emphasize the influence of the setting on people's behavior.

2. It would appear that Kenny, Frank, and Tub are a group of friends. What is the evidence? On the other hand, how do they behave as though they are not friends? What philosophies of friendship are spoken out loud? What philosophies are acted out among the three characters? Do you think that these philosophies are unusual or common?

Ideas for Critical Writing

1. Examine each reference to the snow and cold. What attitude toward nature is suggested by the way it is described? How is this attitude related to the view of human nature suggested by the story?

2. The weather conditions in "Hunters in the Snow" are portrayed as obscuring the true state of things and blurring perceptions such as vision and hearing. Relate this feature of the setting to the blurring and obscuring of truth in the human arena. What lie is pivotal to each character?

3. What effect does being cold for long periods have on people? Argue for an interpretation of the story that explains how the freezing cold drives much of the action of the story.

Ideas for Researched Writing

1. CRITICAL APPROACHES: Review the historical approaches to literary interpretation (pages 748–49). Do some research on Tobias Wolff's life, and use a biographical approach to explain his choice of setting, character, and theme in "Hunters in the Snow."

2. Using the PsychLIT database or your Internet search engine, investigate contemporary thought about male friendships. Find two or three sources that give theoretical or experimental support to the depiction of male friendship in "Hunters in the Snow." How are such friendships described and explained by experts in human behavior? Write a paper that makes a claim about the characters' relationships.

REWRITING

Once you have written out your ideas, you will try to improve every element of that draft—from the overall organization to the individual sentences.

Checking Your Organization

Each paragraph should have a topic, a main point that you can summarize in a sentence. On a separate sheet of paper, list the topics of your paragraphs. When you see the bare bones of your essay this way, you can ask yourself questions about your organization.

1. Do any of the topics repeat each other? If so, think about combining them or placing them close together. If there is a fine distinction between them, go back to the essay and express the distinction clearly.
2. Is each topic fully supported? Compare the topic as stated on your outline with the paragraph in your essay. Make sure that you can see how each sentence in the paragraph relates to the topic. Weed out sentences that only repeat the topic. Add specific details from the literary work instead.
3. Does the order of topics make sense? You might have originally written your paragraphs in the order the topics occurred to you, but that may not be the most reasonable organization for the final essay. Group similar topics together—for example, all the topics that relate setting to character should be close to each other, and so should all the topics that relate setting to theme. At the beginning of each paragraph, write a word, phrase, clause, or sentence that shows that paragraph's relationship to the paragraph before it. These transitions will help your readers know what to expect and prepare them for what comes next.

Improving the Style: Balanced Sentences

Sound organization is vital to the success of your essay; graceful style is an added gift to your reader. One stylistic plus is the balanced or parallel sentence, which puts similar ideas into similar grammatical structures, like this:

> Wolff's stories are known for their *sudden, profound,* and *powerful* endings.
>
> Good writers acknowledge the necessity of *thinking, planning, writing, revising, resting,* and then *thinking* and *revising* still further.

In the following sentence, though, the third item in the italicized series does not match. Compare it to the corrected version.

Unbalanced   The main character would not willingly give up the *carefree, extravagant,* and *drinking and staying out late* as he did when a bachelor.

Balanced   The main character would not willingly give up the *carefree, extravagant, carousing* ways of his bachelorhood.

Probably you can already handle such balancing in ordinary sentences. But pay attention during revising to make sure that all items in series are indeed balanced.

If you need an emphatic sentence for your introduction or conclusion, a good way to learn to write impressive balanced sentences is through *sentence modeling.* Many expert writers—Robert Louis Stevenson, Abraham Lincoln, Winston Churchill, Somerset Maugham—attest that they perfected their writing by studiously copying and imitating the sentences of stylists whom they admired.

Sentence Modeling Exercise

Examine the model sentence shown below to discover its structure. How is it formed? Does it use balanced phrases, clauses, or single words? Does it include any deliberate repetition of words as well as structures? Does it build to a climax at the end? If so, how? By adding ideas of increasing importance? By establishing a pattern that gathers momentum?

Once you have discovered the structure of the model sentence, write one as nearly like it as possible *using your own words and subject matter.* Then repeat this process of imitation four more times, changing your ideas with each new sentence, like this:

Model   Until the young are informed as much about the courage of pacifists as about the obedience of soldiers, they aren't educated.

—Coleman McCarthy

Imitation   Until Americans become as interested in the speeches of candidates as in the performance of athletes, they aren't ideal citizens.

Imitation   Until men are interested as much by the minds of women as by the bodies of women, they will be seen as sexist.

First copy each of the numbered sentences carefully—including the exact punctuation. Then imitate each one at least five times.

1. He sees no seams or joints or points of intersection—only irrevocable wholes.

   —*Mina Shaughnessy*

2. We made meals and changed diapers and took out the garbage and paid bills—while other people died.

   —*Ellen Goodman*

3. The refrigerator was full of sulfurous scraps, dark crusts, furry oddments.

   —*Alice Munro*

4. It is sober without being dull; massive without being oppressive.

   —*Sir Kenneth Clark*

5. Joint by joint, line by line, pill by pill, the use of illegal drugs has become a crisis for American business.

   —*Newsweek*

11

Writing About Theme

A story's theme or meaning grows out of all the elements of imaginative fiction: character, structure, symbolism, point of view, and setting. The theme is usually not an obvious moral or message, and it may be difficult to sum up succinctly. But thinking about the theme of a story and trying to state it in your own words will help you to focus your scattered reactions and to make your understanding of the author's purpose more certain. One of the pleasures of reading a good story comes from deciding what it means and why it captures your interest.

What Is Theme?

Theme has been defined in many ways: the central idea or thesis; the central thought; the underlying meaning, either implied or directly stated; the general insight revealed by the entire story; the central truth; the dominating idea; the abstract concept that is made concrete through representation in person, action, and image.

Because the theme involves ideas and insights, we usually state it in general terms. "Eveline," for instance, concerns the conflicts of a specific character, but the story's main idea—its theme—relates to abstract qualities like *duty* and *fear*. If someone asks what "Eveline" is *about*, we might respond with a summary of the plot, with details about the title character's encounter with Frank and her failure to go away with him. But if someone asks for the story's *theme*, we would answer with a general statement of ideas or values: "Eveline" shows how people can be trapped by fear and obligation.

It is easy to confuse *subject* with *theme*. The subject is the topic or material the story examines—love, death, war, identity, prejudice, power, human relations, growing up, and so forth. The theme is the direct or implied statement that the story makes *about* the subject. For example, the *subject* of "Everyday Use" is mother–daughter relationships, but the *theme* emerges from what the story says about Mama, Maggie, and Dee—and from an understanding of why these characters behave and interact as they do. The theme, then, is the insight that we gain from thinking about what we have read.

Looking at Theme

As you read "Good Country People" by Flannery O'Connor, think about how this story of a mother and a daughter and their encounter with a Bible salesman relates to other areas of human experience.

Flannery O'Connor   1925–1964

Afflicted with lupus, Flannery O'Connor spent most of her short life in Milledgeville, Georgia. After earning an M.F.A. from the University of Iowa, she returned to the family farm to raise peacocks and write about contemporary Southern life. She once observed, "Anything that comes out of the South is going to be called grotesque by the northern reader, unless it is grotesque, in which case it is going to be called realistic." A deeply religious person, O'Connor often explored the violence symbolized by physical deformity and produced by spiritual malaise.

Good Country People

Besides the neutral expression that she wore when she was alone, Mrs. Freeman had two others, forward and reverse, that she used for all her human dealings. Her forward expression was steady and driving like the advance of a heavy truck. Her eyes never swerved to left or right but turned as the story turned as if they followed a yellow line down the center of it. She seldom used the other expression because it was not often necessary for her to retract a statement, but when she did, her face came to a complete stop, there was an almost imperceptible movement of her black eyes, during which they seemed to be receding, and then the observer would see that Mrs. Freeman, though she might stand there as real as several grain sacks thrown on top of each other, was no longer there in spirit. As for getting anything across to her when this was the case, Mrs. Hopewell had given it up. She might talk her head off. Mrs. Freeman could never be brought to admit herself wrong on any point. She would stand there and if she could be brought to say anything, it was something like, "Well, I wouldn't of said it was and I wouldn't of said it wasn't," or letting her gaze range over the top kitchen shelf where there was an assortment of dusty bottles, she might remark, "I see you ain't ate many of them figs you put up last summer."

They carried on their most important business in the kitchen at breakfast. Every morning Mrs. Hopewell got up at seven o'clock and lit her gas heater and Joy's. Joy was her daughter, a large blonde girl who had an artificial leg. Mrs. Hopewell thought of her as a child though she was thirty-two years old and highly educated. Joy would get up while her mother was eating and lumber into the bathroom and slam the door, and before long, Mrs. Freeman would arrive at the back door. Joy would hear her mother call, "Come on in," and then they would talk for a while in low voices that were indistinguishable in the bathroom. By the time Joy came in, they had usually finished the weather

report and were on one or the other of Mrs. Freeman's daughters, Glynese or
Carramae. Joy called them Glycerin and Caramel. Glynese, a redhead, was
eighteen and had many admirers; Carramae, a blonde, was only fifteen but
already married and pregnant. She could not keep anything on her stomach.
Every morning Mrs. Freeman told Mrs. Hopewell how many times she had
vomited since the last report.

Mrs. Hopewell liked to tell people that Glynese and Carramae were two of the
finest girls she knew and that Mrs. Freeman was a *lady* and that she was never
ashamed to take her anywhere or introduce her to anybody they might meet. Then
she would tell how she had happened to hire the Freemans in the first place and
how they were a godsend to her and how she had had them four years. The reason
for her keeping them so long was that they were not trash. They were good
country people. She had telephoned the man whose name they had given as
reference and he had told her that Mr. Freeman was a good farmer but that his wife
was the nosiest woman ever to walk the earth. "She's got to be into everything," the
man said. "If she don't get there before the dust settles, you can bet she's dead,
that's all. She'll want to know all your business. I can stand him real good," he had
said, "but me nor my wife neither could have stood that woman one more minute
on this place." That had put Mrs. Hopewell off for a few days.

She had hired them in the end because there were no other applicants but she
had made up her mind beforehand exactly how she would handle the woman.
Since she was the type who had to be into everything, then, Mrs. Hopewell had
decided, she would not only let her be into everything, she would *see to it* that she
was into everything—she would give her the responsibility of everything,
she would put her in charge. Mrs. Hopewell had no bad qualities of her own
but she was able to use other people's in such a constructive way that she never
felt the lack. She had hired the Freemans and she had kept them four years.

Nothing is perfect. This was one of Mrs. Hopewell's favorite sayings.   5
Another was: that is life! And still another, the most important, was: well, other
people have their opinions too. She would make these statements, usually at the
table, in a tone of gentle insistence as if no one held them but her, and the large
hulking Joy, whose constant outrage had obliterated every expression from her
face, would stare just a little to the side of her, her eyes icy blue, with the look of
someone who had achieved blindness by an act of will and means to keep it.

When Mrs. Hopewell said to Mrs. Freeman that life was like that, Mrs. Freeman
would say, "I always said so myself." Nothing had been arrived at by anyone that
had not first been arrived at by her. She was quicker than Mr. Freeman. When
Mrs. Hopewell said to her after they had been on the place for a while, "You know,
you're the wheel behind the wheel," and winked, Mrs. Freeman had said, "I know it.
I've always been quick. It's some that are quicker than others."

"Everybody is different," Mrs. Hopewell said.

"Yes, most people is," Mrs. Freeman said.

"It takes all kinds to make the world."

"I always said it did myself."   10

The girl was used to this kind of dialogue for breakfast and more of it for
dinner; sometimes they had it for supper too. When they had no guest they ate
in the kitchen because that was easier. Mrs. Freeman always managed to arrive
at some point during the meal and to watch them finish it. She would stand in
the doorway if it were summer but in the winter she would stand with one elbow
on top of the refrigerator and look down at them, or she would stand by the gas

heater, lifting the back of her skirt slightly. Occasionally she would stand against the wall and roll her head from side to side. At no time was she in any hurry to leave. All this was very trying on Mrs. Hopewell but she was a woman of great patience. She realized that nothing is perfect and that in the Freemans she had good country people and that if, in this day and age, you get good country people, you had better hang onto them.

She had had plenty of experience with trash. Before the Freemans she had averaged one tenant family a year. The wives of these farmers were not the kind you would want to be around you for very long. Mrs. Hopewell, who had divorced her husband long ago, needed someone to walk over the fields with her; and when Joy had to be impressed for these services, her remarks were usually so ugly and her face so glum that Mrs. Hopewell would say, "If you can't come pleasantly, I don't want you at all," to which the girl, standing square and rigid-shouldered with her neck thrust slightly forward, would reply, "If you want me, here I am—LIKE I AM."

Mrs. Hopewell excused this attitude because of the leg (which had been shot off in a hunting accident when Joy was ten). It was hard for Mrs. Hopewell to realize that her child was thirty-two now and that for more than twenty years she had had only one leg. She thought of her still as a child because it tore her heart to think instead of the poor stout girl in her thirties who had never danced a step or had any *normal* good times. Her name was really Joy but as soon as she was twenty-one and away from home, she had had it legally changed. Mrs. Hopewell was certain that she had thought and thought until she had hit upon the ugliest name in any language. Then she had gone and had the beautiful name, Joy, changed without telling her mother until after she had done it. Her legal name was Hulga.

When Mrs. Hopewell thought the name, Hulga, she thought of the broad blank hull of a battleship. She would not use it. She continued to call her Joy to which the girl responded but in a purely mechanical way.

Hulga had learned to tolerate Mrs. Freeman who saved her from taking walks with her mother. Even Glynese and Carramae were useful when they occupied attention that might otherwise have been directed at her. At first she had thought she could not stand Mrs. Freeman for she had found it was not possible to be rude to her. Mrs. Freeman would take on strange resentments and for days together she would be sullen but the source of her displeasure was always obscure; a direct attack, a positive leer, blatant ugliness to her face—these never touched her. And without warning one day, she began calling her Hulga.

She did not call her that in front of Mrs. Hopewell who would have been incensed but when she and the girl happened to be out of the house together, she would say something and add the name Hulga to the end of it, and the big spectacled Joy-Hulga would scowl and redden as if her privacy had been intruded upon. She considered the name her personal affair. She had arrived at it first purely on the basis of its ugly sound and then the full genius of its fitness had struck her. She had a vision of the name working like the ugly sweating Vulcan who stayed in the furnace and to whom, presumably, the goddess had to come when called. She saw it as the name of her highest creative act. One of her major triumphs was that her mother had not been able to turn her dust into Joy, but the greater one was that she had been able to turn it herself into Hulga. However, Mrs. Freeman's relish for using the name only irritated her. It was as if Mrs. Freeman's beady steel-pointed eyes had penetrated far enough behind her face to reach some secret fact.

15

Something about her seemed to fascinate Mrs. Freeman and then one day Hulga realized that it was the artificial leg. Mrs. Freeman had a special fondness for the details of secret infections, hidden deformities, assaults upon children. Of diseases, she preferred the lingering or incurable. Hulga had heard Mrs. Hopewell give her the details of the hunting accident, how the leg had been literally blasted off, how she had never lost consciousness. Mrs. Freeman could listen to it any time as if it had happened an hour ago.

When Hulga stumped into the kitchen in the morning (she could walk without making the awful noise but she made it—Mrs. Hopewell was certain—because it was ugly-sounding), she glanced at them and did not speak. Mrs. Hopewell would be in her red kimono with her hair tied around her head in rags. She would be sitting at the table, finishing her breakfast and Mrs. Freeman would be hanging by her elbow outward from the refrigerator, looking down at the table. Hulga always put her eggs on the stove to boil and then stood over them with her arms folded, and Mrs. Hopewell would look at her—a kind of indirect gaze divided between her and Mrs. Freeman—and would think that if she would only keep herself up a little, she wouldn't be so bad looking. There was nothing wrong with her face that a pleasant expression wouldn't help. Mrs. Hopewell said that people who looked on the bright side of things would be beautiful even if they were not.

Whenever she looked at Joy this way, she could not help but feel that it would have been better if the child had not taken the Ph.D. It had certainly not brought her out any and now that she had it, there was no more excuse for her to go to school again. Mrs. Hopewell thought it was nice for girls to go to school to have a good time but Joy had "gone through." Anyhow, she would not have been strong enough to go again. The doctors had told Mrs. Hopewell that with the best of care, Joy might see forty-five. She had a weak heart. Joy had made it plain that if it had not been for this condition, she would be far from these red hills and good country people. She would be in a university lecturing to people who knew what she was talking about. And Mrs. Hopewell could very well picture her there, looking like a scarecrow and lecturing to more of the same. Here she went about all day in a six-year-old skirt and a yellow sweat shirt with a faded cowboy on a horse embossed on it. She thought this was funny; Mrs. Hopewell thought it was idiotic and showed simply that she was still a child. She was brilliant but she didn't have a grain of sense. It seemed to Mrs. Hopewell that every year she grew less like other people and more like herself—bloated, rude, and squint-eyed. And she said such strange things! To her own mother she had said—without warning, without excuse, standing up in the middle of a meal with her face purple and her mouth half full—"Woman! do you ever look inside? Do you ever look inside and see what you are *not*? God!" she had cried sinking down again and staring at her plate, "Malebranche[1] was right: we are not our own light. We are not our own light!" Mrs. Hopewell had no idea to this day what brought that on. She had only made the remark, hoping Joy would take it in, that a smile never hurt anyone.

The girl had taken the Ph.D. in philosophy and this left Mrs. Hopewell at a complete loss. You could say, "My daughter is a nurse," or "My daughter is a school teacher," or even, "My daughter is a chemical engineer." You could not say, "My daughter is a philosopher." That was something that had ended with the Greeks

---

[1]Nicolas Malebranche (1638–1715), French philosopher.

and Romans. All day Joy sat on her neck in a deep chair, reading. Sometimes she went for walks but she didn't like dogs or cats or birds or flowers or nature or nice young men. She looked at nice young men as if she could smell their stupidity.

One day Mrs. Hopewell had picked up one of the books the girl had just put   20
down and opening it at random, she read, "Science, on the other hand, has to assert its soberness and seriousness afresh and declare that it is concerned solely with what-is. Nothing—how can it be for science anything but a horror and a phantasm? If science is right, then one thing stands firm: science wishes to know nothing of nothing. Such is after all the strictly scientific approach to Nothing. We know it by wishing to know nothing of Nothing." These words had been underlined with a blue pencil and they worked on Mrs. Hopewell like some evil incantation in gibberish. She shut the book quickly and went out of the room as if she were having a chill.

This morning when the girl came in, Mrs. Freeman was on Carramae. "She thrown up four times after supper," she said, "and was up twict in the night after three o'clock. Yesterday she didn't do nothing but ramble in the bureau drawer. All she did. Stand up there and see what she could run up on."

"She's got to eat," Mrs. Hopewell muttered, sipping her coffee, while she watched Joy's back at the stove. She was wondering what the child had said to the Bible salesman. She could not imagine what kind of a conversation she could possibly have had with him.

He was a tall gaunt hatless youth who had called yesterday to sell them a Bible. He had appeared at the door, carrying a large black suitcase that weighted him so heavily on one side that he had to brace himself against the door facing. He seemed on the point of collapse but he said in a cheerful voice, "Good morning, Mrs. Cedars!" and set the suitcase down on the mat. He was not a bad-looking young man though he had on a bright blue suit and yellow socks that were not pulled up far enough. He had prominent face bones and a streak of sticky-looking brown hair falling across his forehead.

"I'm Mrs. Hopewell," she said.

"Oh!" he said, pretending to look puzzled but with his eyes sparkling, "I saw it   25
said 'The Cedars' on the mailbox so I thought you was Mrs. Cedars!" and he burst out in a pleasant laugh. He picked up the satchel and under cover of a pant, he fell forward into her hall. It was rather as if the suitcase had moved first, jerking him after it. "Mrs. Hopewell!" he said and grabbed her hand. "I hope you are well!" and he laughed again and then all at once his face sobered completely. He paused and gave her a straight earnest look and said, "Lady, I've come to speak of serious things."

"Well, come in," she muttered, none too pleased because her dinner was almost ready. He came into the parlor and sat down on the edge of a straight chair and put the suitcase between his feet and glanced around the room as if he were sizing her up by it. Her silver gleamed on the two sideboards; she decided he had never been in a room as elegant as this.

"Mrs. Hopewell," he began, using her name in a way that sounded almost intimate, "I know you believe in Chrustian service."

"Well, yes," she murmured.

"I know," he said and paused, looking very wise with his head cocked on one side, "that you're a good woman. Friends have told me."

Mrs. Hopewell never liked to be taken for a fool. "What are you selling?" she   30
asked.

"Bibles," the young man said and his eye raced around the room before he added, "I see you have no family Bible in your parlor, I see that is the one lack you got!"

Mrs. Hopewell could not say, "My daughter is an atheist and won't let me keep the Bible in the parlor." She said, stiffening slightly, "I keep my Bible by my bedside." This was not the truth. It was in the attic somewhere.

"Lady," he said, "the word of God ought to be in the parlor."

"Well, I think that's a matter of taste," she began, "I think..."

"Lady," he said, "for a Christian, the word of God ought to be in every room   35
in the house besides in his heart. I know you're a Chrustian because I can see it in every line of your face."

She stood up and said, "Well, young man, I don't want to buy a Bible and I smell my dinner burning."

He didn't get up. He began to twist his hands and looking down at them, he said softly, "Well lady, I'll tell you the truth—not many people want to buy one nowadays and besides, I know I'm real simple. I don't know how to say a thing but to say it. I'm just a country boy." He glanced up into her unfriendly face. "People like you don't like to fool with country people like me!"

"Why!" she cried, "good country people are the salt of the earth! Besides, we all have different ways of doing, it takes all kinds to make the world go 'round. That's life!"

"You said a mouthful," he said.

"Why, I think there aren't enough good country people in the world!" she   40
said, stirred. "I think that's what's wrong with it!"

His face had brightened. "I didn't inraduce myself," he said. "I'm Manley Pointer from out in the country around Willohobie, not even from a place, just from near a place."

"You wait a minute," she said. "I have to see about my dinner." She went out to the kitchen and found Joy standing near the door where she had been listening.

"Get rid of the salt of the earth," she said, "and let's eat."

Mrs. Hopewell gave her a pained look and turned the heat down under the vegetables. "*I* can't be rude to anybody," she murmured and went back into the parlor.

He had opened the suitcase and was sitting with a Bible on each knee.   45

"You might as well put those up," she told him. "I don't want one."

"I appreciate your honesty," he said. "You don't see any more real honest people unless you go way out in the country."

"I know," she said, "real genuine folks!" Through the crack in the door she heard a groan.

"I guess a lot of boys come telling you they're working their way through college," he said, "but I'm not going to tell you that. Somehow," he said, "I don't want to go to college. I want to devote my life to Christian service. See," he said, lowering his voice, "I got this heart condition. I may not live long. When you know it's something wrong with you and you may not live long, well then, lady...." He paused, with his mouth open, and stared at her.

He and Joy had the same condition! She knew that her eyes were filling   50
with tears but she collected herself quickly and murmured, "Won't you stay for dinner? We'd love to have you!" and was sorry the instant she heard herself say it.

"Yes mam," he said in an abashed voice, "I would sher love to do that!"

Joy had given him one look on being introduced to him and then throughout the meal had not glanced at him again. He had addressed several remarks to her, which she had pretended not to hear. Mrs. Hopewell could not understand deliberate rudeness, although she lived with it, and she felt she had always to overflow with hospitality to make up for Joy's lack of courtesy. She urged him to talk about himself and he did. He said he was the seventh child of twelve and that his father had been crushed under a tree when he himself was eight years old. He had been crushed very badly, in fact, almost cut in two and was practically not recognizable. His mother had got along the best she could by hard working and she had always seen that her children went to Sunday School and that they read the Bible every evening. He was now nineteen years old and he had been selling Bibles for four months. In that time he had sold seventy-seven Bibles and had the promise of two more sales. He wanted to become a missionary because he thought that was the way you could do most for people. "He who losest his life shall find it," he said simply and he was so sincere, so genuine and earnest that Mrs. Hopewell would not for the world have smiled. He prevented his peas from sliding onto the table by blocking them with a piece of bread which he later cleaned his plate with. She could see Joy observing sidewise how he handled his knife and fork and she saw too that every few minutes, the boy would dart a keen appraising glance at the girl as if he were trying to attract her attention.

After dinner Joy cleared the dishes off the table and disappeared and Mrs. Hopewell was left to talk with him. He told her again about his childhood and his father's accident and about various things that had happened to him. Every five minutes or so she would stifle a yawn. He sat for two hours until finally she told him she must go because she had an appointment in town. He packed his Bibles and thanked her and prepared to leave, but in the doorway he stopped and wrung her hand and said that not on any of his trips had he met a lady as nice as her and he asked if he could come again. She had said she would always be happy to see him.

Joy had been standing in the road, apparently looking at something in the distance, when he came down the steps toward her, bent to the side with his heavy valise. He stopped where she was standing and confronted her directly. Mrs. Hopewell could not hear what he said but she trembled to think what Joy would say to him. She could see that after a minute Joy said something and that then the boy began to speak again, making an excited gesture with his free hand. After a minute Joy said something else at which the boy began to speak once more. Then to her amazement, Mrs. Hopewell saw the two of them walk off together, toward the gate. Joy had walked all the way to the gate with him and Mrs. Hopewell could not imagine what they had said to each other, and she had not yet dared to ask.

Mrs. Freeman was insisting upon her attention. She had moved from the refrigerator to the heater so that Mrs. Hopewell had to turn and face her in order to seem to be listening. "Glynese gone out with Harvey Hill again last night," she said. "She had this sty."

"Hill," Mrs. Hopewell said absently, "is that the one who works in the garage?"

"Nome, he's the one that goes to chiropracter school," Mrs. Freeman said. "She had this sty. Been had it two days. So she says when he brought her in the other night he says, 'Lemme get rid of that sty for you,' and she says, 'How?' and he says, 'You just lay yourself down across the seat of that car and I'll show you.' So she done it and he popped her neck. Kept on a-popping it several times until she made him quit. This morning," Mrs. Freeman said, "she ain't got no sty. She ain't got no traces of a sty."

"I never heard of that before," Mrs. Hopewell said.

"He ast her to marry him before the Ordinary,"[2] Mrs. Freeman went on, "and she told him she wasn't going to be married in no *office*."

"Well, Glynese is a fine girl," Mrs. Hopewell said. "Glynese and Carramae   60
are both fine girls."

"Carramae said when her and Lyman was married Lyman said it sure felt sacred to him. She said he said he wouldn't take five hundred dollars for being married by a preacher."

"How much would he take?" the girl asked from the stove.

"He said he wouldn't take five hundred dollars," Mrs. Freeman repeated.

"Well we all have work to do," Mrs. Hopewell said.

"Lyman said it just felt more sacred to him," Mrs. Freeman said. "The doctor   65
wants Carramae to eat prunes. Says instead of medicine. Says them cramps is coming from pressure. You know where I think it is?"

"She'll be better in a few weeks," Mrs. Hopewell said.

"In the tube," Mrs. Freeman said. "Else she wouldn't be as sick as she is."

Hulga had cracked her two eggs into a saucer and was bringing them to the table along with a cup of coffee that she had filled too full. She sat down carefully and began to eat, meaning to keep Mrs. Freeman there by questions if for any reason she showed an inclination to leave. She could perceive her mother's eye on her. The first round-about question would be about the Bible salesman and she did not wish to bring it on. "How did he pop her neck?" she asked.

Mrs. Freeman went into a description of how he had popped her neck. She said he owned a '55 Mercury but that Glynese said she would rather marry a man with only a '36 Plymouth who would be married by a preacher. The girl asked what if he had a '32 Plymouth and Mrs. Freeman said what Glynese had said was a '36 Plymouth.

Mrs. Hopewell said there were not many girls with Glynese's common sense.   70
She said what she admired in those girls was their common sense. She said that reminded her that they had had a nice visitor yesterday, a young man selling Bibles. "Lord," she said, "he bored me to death but he was so sincere and genuine I couldn't be rude to him. He was just good country people, you know," she said, "—just the salt of the earth."

"I seen him walk up," Mrs. Freeman said, "and then later—I seen him walk off," and Hulga could feel the slight shift in her voice, the slight insinuation, that he had not walked off alone, had he? Her face remained expressionless but the color rose into her neck and she seemed to swallow it down with the next spoonful of egg. Mrs. Freeman was looking at her as if they had a secret together.

"Well, it takes all kinds of people to make the world go 'round," Mrs. Hopewell said. "It's very good we aren't all alike."

"Some people are more alike than others," Mrs. Freeman said.

Hulga got up and stumped, with about twice the noise that was necessary, into her room and locked the door. She was to meet the Bible salesman at ten o'clock at the gate. She had thought about it half the night. She had started

---

[2]Judge of probate court.

thinking of it as a great joke and then she had begun to see profound implications in it. She had lain in bed imagining dialogues for them that were insane on the surface but that reached below to depths that no Bible salesman would be aware of. Their conversation yesterday had been of this kind.

He had stopped in front of her and had simply stood there. His face was bony 75 and sweaty and bright, with a little pointed nose in the center of it, and his look was different from what it had been at the dinner table. He was gazing at her with open curiosity, with fascination, like a child watching a new fantastic animal at the zoo, and he was breathing as if he had run a great distance to reach her. His gaze seemed somehow familiar but she could not think where she had been regarded with it before. For almost a minute he didn't say anything. Then on what seemed an insuck of breath, he whispered, "You ever ate a chicken that was two days old?"

The girl looked at him stonily. He might have just put this question up for consideration at the meeting of a philosophical association. "Yes," she presently replied as if she had considered it from all angles.

"It must have been mighty small!" he said triumphantly and shook all over with little nervous giggles, getting very red in the face, and subsiding finally into his gaze of complete admiration, while the girl's expression remained exactly the same.

"How old are you?" he asked softly.

She waited some time before she answered. Then in a flat voice she said, "Seventeen."

His smiles came in succession like waves breaking on the surface of a little 80 lake. "I see you got a wooden leg," he said. "I think you're brave. I think you're real sweet."

The girl stood blank and solid and silent.

"Walk to the gate with me," he said. "You're a brave sweet little thing and I liked you the minute I seen you walk in the door."

Hulga began to move forward.

"What's your name?" he asked, smiling down on the top of her head.

"Hulga," she said. 85

"Hulga," he murmured, "Hulga. Hulga. I never heard of anybody name Hulga before. You're shy, aren't you, Hulga?" he asked.

She nodded, watching his large red hand on the handle of the giant valise.

"I like girls that wear glasses," he said. "I think a lot. I'm not like these people that a serious thought don't ever enter their heads. It's because I may die."

"I may die too," she said suddenly and looked up at him. His eyes were very small and brown, glittering feverishly.

"Listen," he said, "don't you think some people was meant to meet on account 90 of what all they got in common and all? Like they both think serious thoughts and all?" He shifted the valise to his other hand so that the hand nearest her was free. He caught hold of her elbow and shook it a little. "I don't work on Saturday," he said. "I like to walk in the woods and see what Mother Nature is wearing. O'er the hills and far away. Picnics and things. Couldn't we go on a picnic tomorrow? Say yes, Hulga," he said and gave her a dying look as if he felt his insides about to drop out of him. He had even seemed to sway slightly toward her.

During the night she had imagined that she seduced him. She imagined that the two of them walked on the place until they came to the storage barn beyond the two back fields and there, she imagined, that things came to such a pass that she very easily seduced him and that then, of course, she had to reckon with his remorse. True genius can get an idea across even to an inferior mind. She imagined that she took his remorse in hand and changed it into a deeper understanding of life. She took all his shame away and turned it into something useful.

She set off for the gate at exactly ten o'clock, escaping without drawing Mrs. Hopewell's attention. She didn't take anything to eat, forgetting that food is usually taken on a picnic. She wore a pair of slacks and a dirty white shirt, and as an afterthought, she had put some Vapex[3] on the collar of it since she did not own any perfume. When she reached the gate no one was there.

She looked up and down the empty highway and had the furious feeling that she had been tricked, that he had only meant to make her walk to the gate after the idea of him. Then suddenly he stood up, very tall, from behind a bush on the opposite embankment. Smiling, he lifted his hat which was new and wide-brimmed. He had not worn it yesterday and she wondered if he had bought it for the occasion. It was toast-colored with a red and white band around it and was slightly too large for him. He stepped from behind the bush still carrying the black valise. He had on the same suit and the same yellow socks sucked down in his shoes from walking. He crossed the highway and said, "I knew you'd come!"

The girl wondered acidly how he had known this. She pointed to the valise and asked, "Why did you bring your Bibles?"

He took her elbow, smiling down on her as if he could not stop. "You can   95 never tell when you'll need the word of God, Hulga," he said. She had a moment in which she doubted that this was actually happening and then they began to climb the embankment. They went down into the pasture toward the woods. The boy walked lightly by her side, bouncing on his toes. The valise did not seem to be heavy today; he even swung it. They crossed half the pasture without saying anything and then, putting his hand easily on the small of her back, he asked softly, "Where does your wooden leg join on?"

She turned an ugly red and glared at him and for an instant the boy looked abashed. "I didn't mean you no harm," he said. "I only meant you're so brave and all. I guess God takes care of you."

"No," she said, looking forward and walking fast, "I don't even believe in God."

At this he stopped and whistled. "No!" he exclaimed as if he were too astonished to say anything else.

She walked on and in a second he was bouncing at her side, fanning with his hat. "That's very unusual for a girl," he remarked, watching her out of the corner of his eye. When they reached the edge of the wood, he put his hand on her back again and drew her against him without a word and kissed her heavily.

The kiss, which had more pressure than feeling behind it, produced that extra   100 surge of adrenalin in the girl that enables one to carry a packed trunk out of a burning house, but in her, the power went at once to the brain. Even before he released her, her mind, clear and detached and ironic anyway, was regarding him from a great distance, with amusement but with pity. She had never been kissed before and she was pleased to discover that it was an unexceptional experience and all a matter of the mind's control. Some people might enjoy drain water if they were told it was vodka. When the boy, looking expectant but uncertain, pushed her gently away, she turned and walked on, saying nothing as if such business, for her, were common enough.

---

[3]Brand name for nasal spray.

He came along panting at her side, trying to help her when he saw a root that she might trip over. He caught and held back the long swaying blades of thorn vine until she had passed beyond them. She led the way and he came breathing heavily behind her. Then they came out on a sunlit hillside, sloping softly into another one a little smaller. Beyond, they could see the rusted top of the old barn where the extra hay was stored.

The hill was sprinkled with small pink weeds. "Then you ain't saved?" he asked suddenly, stopping.

The girl smiled. It was the first time she had smiled at him at all. "In my economy," she said, "I'm saved and you are damned but I told you I didn't believe in God."

Nothing seemed to destroy the boy's look of admiration. He gazed at her now as if the fantastic animal at the zoo had put its paw through the bars and given him a loving poke. She thought he looked as if he wanted to kiss her again and she walked on before he had the chance.

"Ain't there somewheres we can sit down sometime?" he murmured, his voice softening toward the end of the sentence.   105

"In that barn," she said.

They made for it rapidly as if it might slide away like a train. It was a large two-story barn, cool and dark inside. The boy pointed up the ladder that led into the loft and said, "It's too bad we can't go up there."

"Why can't we?" she asked.

"Yer leg," he said reverently.

The girl gave him a contemptuous look and putting both hands on the ladder,   110 she climbed it while he stood below, apparently awestruck. She pulled herself expertly through the opening and then looked down at him and said, "Well, come on if you're coming," and he began to climb the ladder, awkwardly bringing the suitcase with him.

"We won't need the Bible," she observed.

"You never can tell," he said, panting. After he had got into the loft, he was a few seconds catching his breath. She had sat down in a pile of straw. A wide sheath of sunlight, filled with dust particles, slanted over her. She lay back against a bale, her face turned away, looking out the front opening of the barn where hay was thrown from a wagon into the loft. The two pink-speckled hillsides lay back against a dark ridge of woods. The sky was cloudless and cold blue. The boy dropped down by her side and put one arm under her and the other over her and began methodically kissing her face, making little noises like a fish. He did not remove his hat but it was pushed far enough back not to interfere. When her glasses got in his way, he took them off of her and slipped them into his pocket.

The girl at first did not return any of the kisses but presently she began to and after she had put several on his cheek, she reached his lips and remained there, kissing him again and again as if she were trying to draw all the breath out of him. His breath was clear and sweet like a child's and the kisses were sticky like a child's. He mumbled about loving her and about knowing when he first seen her that he loved her, but the mumbling was like the sleepy fretting of a child being put to sleep by his mother. Her mind, throughout this, never stopped or lost itself for a second to her feelings. "You ain't said you loved me none," he whispered finally, pulling back from her. "You got to say that."

She looked away from him off into the hollow sky and then down at a black ridge and then down farther into what appeared to be two green swelling lakes.

She didn't realize he had taken her glasses but this landscape could not seem exceptional to her for she seldom paid any close attention to her surroundings.

"You got to say it," he repeated. "You got to say you love me." 115

She was always careful how she committed herself. "In a sense," she began, "if you use the word loosely, you might say that. But it's not a word I use. I don't have illusions. I'm one of those people who see *through* to nothing."

The boy was frowning. "You got to say it. I said it and you got to say it," he said.

The girl looked at him almost tenderly. "You poor baby," she murmured. "It's just as well you don't understand," and she pulled him by the neck, face-down, against her. "We are all damned," she said, "but some of us have taken off our blindfolds and see that there's nothing to see. It's a kind of salvation."

The boy's astonished eyes looked blankly through the ends of her hair. "Okay," he almost whined, "but do you love me or don'tcher?"

"Yes," she said and added, "in a sense. But I must tell you something. There 120 mustn't be anything dishonest between us." She lifted his head and looked him in the eye. "I am thirty years old," she said. "I have a number of degrees."

The boy's look was irritated but dogged. "I don't care," he said. "I don't care a thing about what all you done. I just want to know if you love me or don'tcher?" and he caught her to him and wildly planted her face with kisses until she said, "Yes, yes."

"Okay then," he said, letting her go. "Prove it."

She smiled, looking dreamily out on the shifty landscape. She had seduced him without even making up her mind to try. "How?" she asked, feeling that he should be delayed a little.

He leaned over and put his lips to her ear. "Show me where your wooden leg joins on," he whispered.

The girl uttered a sharp little cry and her face instantly drained of color. The 125 obscenity of the suggestion was not what shocked her. As a child she had sometimes been subject to feelings of shame but education had removed the last traces of that as a good surgeon scrapes for cancer; she would no more have felt it over what he was asking than she would have believed in his Bible. But she was as sensitive about the artificial leg as a peacock about his tail. No one ever touched it but her. She took care of it as someone else would his soul, in private and almost with her own eyes turned away. "No," she said.

"I known it," he muttered, sitting up. "You're just playing me for a sucker."

"Oh no no!" she cried. "It joins on at the knee. Only at the knee. Why do you want to see it?"

The boy gave her a long penetrating look. "Because," he said, "it's what makes you different. You ain't like anybody else."

She sat staring at him. There was nothing about her face or her round freezing-blue eyes to indicate that this had moved her; but she felt as if her heart had stopped and left her mind to pump her blood. She decided that for the first time in her life she was face to face with real innocence. This boy, with an instinct that came from beyond wisdom, had touched the truth about her. When after a minute, she said in a hoarse high voice, "All right," it was like surrendering to him completely. It was like losing her own life and finding it again, miraculously, in his.

Very gently, he began to roll the slack leg up. The artificial limb, in a white 130 sock and brown flat shoe, was bound in a heavy material like canvas and ended in an ugly jointure where it was attached to the stump. The boy's face and his voice were entirely reverent as he uncovered it and said, "Now show me how to take it off and on."

She took it off for him and put it back on again and then he took it off himself, handling it as tenderly as if it were a real one. "See!" he said with a delighted child's face. "Now I can do it myself!"

"Put it back on," she said. She was thinking that she would run away with him and that every night he would take the leg off and every morning put it back on again. "Put it back on," she said.

"Not yet," he murmured, setting it on its foot out of her reach. "Leave it off for awhile. You got me instead."

She gave a little cry of alarm but he pushed her down and began to kiss her again. Without the leg she felt entirely dependent on him. Her brain seemed to have stopped thinking altogether and to be about some other function that it was not very good at. Different expressions raced back and forth over her face. Every now and then the boy, his eyes like two steel spikes, would glance behind him where the leg stood. Finally she pushed him off and said, "Put it back on me now."

"Wait," he said. He leaned the other way and pulled the valise toward him and   135
opened it. It had a pale blue spotted lining and there were only two Bibles in it. He took one of these out and opened the cover of it. It was hollow and contained a pocket flask of whiskey, a pack of cards, and a small blue box with printing on it. He laid these out in front of her one at a time in an evenly-spaced row, like one presenting offerings at the shrine of a goddess. He put the blue box in her hand. THIS PRODUCT TO BE USED ONLY FOR THE PREVENTION OF DISEASE, she read, and dropped it. The boy was unscrewing the top of the flask. He stopped and pointed, with a smile, to the deck of cards. It was not an ordinary deck but one with an obscene picture on the back of each card. "Take a swig," he said, offering her the bottle first. He held it in front of her, but like one mesmerized, she did not move.

Her voice when she spoke had an almost pleading sound. "Aren't you," she murmured, "aren't you just good country people?"

The boy cocked his head. He looked as if he were just beginning to understand that she might be trying to insult him. "Yeah," he said, curling his lip slightly, "but it ain't held me back none. I'm as good as you any day in the week."

"Give me my leg," she said.

He pushed it farther away with his foot. "Come on now, let's begin to have us a good time," he said coaxingly. "We ain't got to know one another good yet."

"Give me my leg!" she screamed and tried to lunge for it but he pushed her   140
down easily.

"What's the matter with you all of a sudden?" he asked, frowning as he screwed the top on the flask and put it quickly back inside the Bible. "You just a while ago said you didn't believe in nothing. I thought you was some girl!"

Her face was almost purple. "You're a Christian!" she hissed. "You're a fine Christian! You're just like them all—say one thing and do another. You're a perfect Christian, you're…"

The boy's mouth was set angrily. "I hope you don't think," he said in a lofty indignant tone, "that I believe in that crap! I may sell Bibles but I know which end is up and I wasn't born yesterday and I know where I'm going!"

"Give me my leg!" she screeched. He jumped up so quickly that she barely saw him sweep the cards and the blue box back into the Bible and throw the Bible into the valise. She saw him grab the leg and then she saw it for an instant slanted forlornly across the inside of the suitcase with a Bible at either side of its opposite ends. He slammed the lid shut and snatched up the valise and swung it down the hole and then stepped through himself.

When all of him had passed but his head, he turned and regarded her with a   145
look that no longer had any admiration in it. "I've gotten a lot of interesting things," he said. "One time I got a woman's glass eye this way. And you needn't to think you'll catch me because Pointer ain't really my name. I use a different name at every house I call at and don't stay nowhere long. And I'll tell you another thing, Hulga," he said, using the name as if he didn't think much of it, "you ain't so smart. I been believing in nothing ever since I was born!" and then the toast-colored hat disappeared down the hole and the girl was left, sitting on the straw in the dusty sunlight. When she turned her churning face toward the opening, she saw his blue figure struggling successfully over the green speckled lake.

Mrs. Hopewell and Mrs. Freeman, who were in the back pasture, digging up onions, saw him emerge a little later from the woods and head across the meadow toward the highway. "Why, that looks like that nice dull young man that tried to sell me a Bible yesterday," Mrs. Hopewell said, squinting. "He must have been selling them to the Negroes back in there. He was so simple," she said, "but I guess the world would be better off if we were all that simple."

Mrs. Freeman's gaze drove forward and just touched him before he disappeared under the hill. Then she returned her attention to the evil-smelling onion shoot she was lifting from the ground. "Some can't be that simple," she said. "I know I never could."

(1955)

PREWRITING

Understanding the theme of a piece of literature involves figuring out what the whole work means. Your prewriting task here is, as usual, to ask yourself questions that will lead to the meaning of the story you just read.

Figuring Out the Theme

Reread "Good Country People" and formulate specific leading questions about the following elements of the story. For example, you might ask yourself, "How does the title apply to the characters in the story?" or "Do the characters' names seem appropriate? Do they describe the characters in any way? Are they straightforward or satiric?" Consider the following:

1. The title.
2. The setting, especially the descriptions of the Hopewells' house and their living situation.
3. The characters in the story, especially their names, their physical descriptions, and their relationships with one another.
4. Any significant objects, such as Hulga's artificial leg and Manley's Bible, as well as repeated uses of language like the platitudes that Mrs. Hopewell strings together and Hulga's academic comments and references.

5. Any changes that you notice in the characters and their feelings toward themselves or one another.
6. Any reversals or surprises that occur.
7. Any comments or observations the narrator makes about the characters and their actions.
8. The ending.

Stating the Theme

After writing out the answers to the questions you have set for yourself, try to sum up the theme in a complete sentence. You may need to rewrite the sentence several times until you can express the theme satisfactorily. Then state the theme in another way, using other words. Are both statements valid? Are there any secondary themes that enrich the story and add to the primary theme? Write those down, too.

Take one of the statements of theme that you have formulated, and write it at the top of a blank sheet of paper. Fill the page with freewriting about this idea, expressing as quickly as you can your thoughts and feelings about O'Connor's view of human nature.

WRITING

We have emphasized that your essays should be filled with supporting details from your source. Without specific references to the literary work that you are writing about, your judgments and conclusions will be vague and unconvincing.

Choosing Supporting Details

During a close second reading of a story, pay special attention to details that have potential for symbolic meaning. Thoughtful consideration of the names, places, objects, incidents, and minor characters can guide you to a deeper understanding of the work's theme. In "Good Country People," for example, you may notice how often Hulga's artificial limb is mentioned. Go through the story one more time, and put a check mark next to each mention of the wooden leg. During this third examination, you may also note other references to the human body, such as Hulga's weak heart and short-sighted eyes, the Bible salesman's heart condition, and Mrs. Freeman's intense interest in Carramae's vomit and Glynese's sty. Then try to come up with an insight that expresses the meaning of these details—perhaps something like "All the characters seem preoccupied in one way or another with the physical side of being human." You now have a useful thesis for your paper or a topic sentence for a section of it.

A list of specific examples from the story could support your thesis statement, but a simple list would probably sound mechanical and unrevealing. So, if possible, classify the details. In this case, some of the characters seem fascinated with physical details and others try to ignore them. Quote one or two examples of each kind, and then—most important—explain their significance. In this story, the fascination with the physical seems perverse and superficial, while the avoidance is pretentious and hypocritical. Both attitudes suggest a lack of spiritual awareness.

Approach the following writing ideas by rereading the story with your topic in mind. Jot down any details that seem relevant. Review all your notes on the story and see what general observations you can make; then select appropriate supporting details from your list and show how they support your critical generalizations.

IDEAS FOR WRITING

Ideas for Responsive Writing

1. Do you agree with Mrs. Hopewell that "good country people are the salt of the earth" and that "there aren't enough good country people in the world"? Evaluate the validity of these assertions, especially as they relate to the country people you know and the ones you read about in the story.

2. Have you ever met anyone like Manley Pointer? Do such people really exist? Write a character sketch (an extended description) of Pointer, comparing him to people you have known or met.

3. Rewrite the story from Hulga's point of view. You might put your rewrite in the form of a letter from Hulga to her mother.

Ideas for Critical Writing

1. In the essay "Writing Short Stories," O'Connor wrote that "there is a wooden part of [Hulga's] soul that corresponds to her wooden leg." Write an essay using O'Connor's statement as your major claim.

2. The last two paragraphs of the story, concerning Mrs. Hopewell and Mrs. Freeman, were added at the suggestion of O'Connor's editor. What is the purpose of these paragraphs? Analyze this ending, and explain what it contributes to the story's themes.

3. What does "Good Country People" say about uniqueness ("everybody is different") and imperfection? Write an essay examining the story's messages about one or both of these subjects.

4. CRITICAL APPROACHES: All the characters in "Good Country People" except Manley Pointer are female. Review literary interpretations based on gender (pages 750–51). How is the daily life of the main characters affected by an all-female setting? What would be different if men were in the picture? Why are they mainly absent? Write an essay that argues for or against the importance of gender in this story.

Ideas for Researched Writing

1. When Hulga tells the Bible salesman, "Some of us have taken off our blindfolds and see that there's nothing to see," and he later responds, "I have been believing in nothing since I was born," they are expressing the philosophy of *nihilism*. Look up *nihilism* in a reference work like the *Encyclopedia of Philosophy* or the *Oxford Companion to Philosophy*. With this information, write an essay that demonstrates how Hulga's nihilism, her "spiritual affliction," serves to reveal the story's theme.

2. The theme of "Good Country People" has been defined in a number of ways. Find critical commentaries that offer at least three distinct interpretations of the story and its theme. Write your own essay that evaluates, reconciles, or argues against these differing interpretations.

REWRITING

When you revise, you should make sure that your paper *flows*—that your readers can follow your ideas easily.

Achieving Coherence

The best way to make your writing *coherent*—to make it easy to follow—is to have a clear thesis and to make sure that all your subpoints pertain to that thesis. If you organize the development of your ideas carefully, your paragraphs should unfold in a logical, connected way. Continuity also evolves from thinking through your ideas completely and developing them adequately. Leaps in thought and shifts in meaning often result from too much generalization and too little development.

Checking for Coherence

Type up or print out a clean copy of the latest draft of your essay. In the margins, write a word or phrase that labels the point or describes the function of every group of related sentences. These words and phrases are called *glosses*. (You can even use short sentences.) To help write glosses for your sentences and paragraphs, ask yourself these questions: What have I said here? How many ideas are in this passage? What does this sentence/paragraph do?

When you have finished putting glosses in the margins of your essay, go back and review the glosses. Can you see a clear sequence of points? Are there any sentences or passages that you could not write a gloss for? Is there any place where you digress or introduce an unrelated idea? Using the glosses as a guide, make revisions that will improve the coherence of your essay: fill in gaps, combine repetitive sentences, cut out irrelevant material, add transitions. (See Chart 4–2, "Transitional Terms for All Occasions," page 57.)

EDITING

Here are some other ways to help you strengthen the flow and coherence of your sentences.

Repeat Words and Synonyms

Repeat key words for coherence as well as for emphasis:

> I do not want to *read another gothic romance. I especially do not want to read another long gothic romance.*

If repetition is tiresome or you want more variety, use a synonym:

> It was a rare *caper*, planned to the last second. Such elaborate *heists* seem to come right from a detective novel.

Take care when using repetition. Repeated words should be important or emphatic. Do not repeat a common, limp term because you are too tired to find a synonym. Be aware, however, that synonyms are not always interchangeable; check the meaning of any word you are not sure of. The following introduction to a student paper suffers because the writer needlessly repeats the same uninteresting verb (which we have italicized):

> Shirley Jackson's "The Lottery" is a complex story that deals with a fundamental part of human psychology, the *using* of scapegoats. Scapegoats have been *used* throughout history to justify actions. Many times scapegoats are *used* to conceal human errors or prejudices. Scapegoats are, in fact, still *used* today.

Notice that the repetition of the key word *scapegoats* emphasizes the main idea of the paper. But the ineffective repetition should be revised (our substituted verbs are italicized in the following revision):

> Shirley Jackson's "The Lottery" is a complex story that deals with a fundamental element of human psychology—using scapegoats. Scapegoats have been *created* throughout history to justify actions. Many times they are *employed* to conceal human errors or prejudices. In fact, scapegoats still *exist* today.

Try Parallel Structure

Repeat a grammatical pattern to tie points and details together:

> In the morning Emma Bovary ate breakfast with her husband; in the afternoon she picnicked with her paramour.

The play was about to end: the villain stalked off, the lovers kissed, the curtain fell, and the audience applauded wildly.

Be sure that your grammatical patterns actually are parallel. If your phrases or clauses do not follow the same structure, you will lose the good effect.

Not parallel	In "The Lottery" these characteristics include *unwillingness to change, sticking to tradition, fear of peer pressure,* and *just plain being afraid.*
Parallel	In "The Lottery" these characteristics include *unwillingness to change, enslavement to tradition, fear of peer pressure,* and *fear of the unknown.*
Not parallel	Many times scapegoats are invoked to conceal *human errors* or *the way people unfairly judge one another.*
Parallel	Many times scapegoats are used to conceal *human errors* and *prejudices.*

ANTHOLOGY
of Short Fiction

Nathaniel Hawthorne   1804–1864

Nathaniel Hawthorne ranks with the great writers of fiction in English. He wrote richly symbolic novels and tales, often involving the supernatural, yet he once declared, "I am not quite sure that I entirely comprehend my own meaning in some of these blasted allegories." The appearance of his masterpiece of hidden guilt and redemption, *The Scarlet Letter* (1850), secured his position as America's foremost romancer. His last years were troubled by the outbreak of the Civil War, and he vehemently declared himself "a man of peace."

The Birthmark

In the latter part of the last century, there lived a man of science—an eminent proficient in every branch of natural philosophy—who, not long before our story opens, had made experience of a spiritual affinity, more attractive than any chemical one. He had left his laboratory to the care of an assistant, cleared his fine countenance from the furnace-smoke, washed the stain of acids from his fingers, and persuaded a beautiful woman to become his wife. In those days, when the comparatively recent discovery of electricity, and other kindred mysteries of nature, seemed to open paths into the region of miracle, it was not unusual for the love of science to rival the love of woman, in its depth and absorbing energy. The higher intellect, the imagination, the spirit, and even the heart, might all find their congenial aliment in pursuits which, as some of their ardent votaries believed, would ascend from one step of powerful intelligence to another, until the philosopher should lay his hand on the secret of creative force, and perhaps make new worlds for himself. We know not whether Aylmer possessed this degree of faith in man's ultimate control over nature. He had devoted himself, however, too unreservedly to scientific studies, ever to be weaned from them by any second passion. His love for his young wife might prove the stronger of the two; but it could only be by intertwining itself with his love of science, and uniting the strength of the latter to its own.

Such a union accordingly took place, and was attended with truly remarkable consequences, and a deeply impressive moral. One day, very soon after their marriage, Aylmer sat gazing at his wife, with a trouble in his countenance that grew stronger, until he spoke.

"Georgiana," said he, "has it never occurred to you that the mark upon your cheek might be removed?"

"No, indeed," said she, smiling; but perceiving the seriousness of his manner, she blushed deeply. "To tell you the truth, it has been so often called a charm, that I was simple enough to imagine it might be so."

"Ah, upon another face, perhaps it might," replied her husband. "But never   5 on yours! No, dearest Georgiana, you came so nearly perfectly from the hand of Nature, that this slightest possible defect—which we hesitate whether to term a defect or a beauty—shocks me, as being the visible mark of earthly imperfection."

"Shocks you, my husband!" cried Georgiana, deeply hurt; at first reddening with momentary anger, but then bursting into tears. "Then why did you take me from my mother's side? You cannot love what shocks you!"

To explain this conversation, it must be mentioned, that, in the centre of Georgiana's left cheek, there was a singular mark, deeply interwoven, as it were, with the texture and substance of her face. In the usual state of her complexion—a healthy, though delicate bloom—the mark wore a tint of deeper crimson, which imperfectly defined its shape amid the surrounding rosiness. When she blushed, it gradually became more indistinct, and finally vanished amid the triumphant rush of blood, that bathed the whole cheek with its brilliant glow. But, if any shifting emotion caused her to turn pale, there was the mark again, a crimson stain upon the snow, in what Aylmer sometimes deemed an almost fearful distinctness. Its shape bore not a little similarity to the human hand, though of the smallest pigmy size. Georgiana's lovers were wont to say, that some fairy, at her birth-hour, had laid her tiny hand upon the infant's cheek, and left this impress there, in token of the magic endowments that were to give her such sway over all hearts. Many a desperate swain would have risked life for the privilege of pressing his lips to the mysterious hand. It must not be concealed, however, that the impression wrought by this fairy sign-manual varied exceedingly, according to the difference of temperament in the beholders. Some fastidious persons—but they were exclusively of her own sex—affirmed that the Bloody Hand, as they chose to call it, quite destroyed the effect of Georgiana's beauty, and rendered her countenance even hideous. But it would be as reasonable to say, that one of those small blue stains, which sometimes occur in the purest statuary marble, would convert the Eve of Powers to a monster. Masculine observers, if the birthmark did not heighten their admiration, contented themselves with wishing it away, that the world might possess one living specimen of ideal loveliness, without the semblance of a flaw. After his marriage—for he thought little or nothing of the matter before—Aylmer discovered that this was the case with himself.

Had she been less beautiful—if Envy's self could have found aught else to sneer at—he might have felt his affection heightened by the prettiness of this mimic hand, now vaguely portrayed, now lost, now stealing forth again, and glimmering to-and-fro with every pulse of emotion that throbbed within her heart. But, seeing her otherwise so perfect, he found this one defect grow more and more intolerable, with every moment of their united lives. It was the fatal flaw of humanity, which Nature, in one shape or another, stamps ineffaceably on all her productions, either to imply that they are temporary and finite, or that their perfection must be wrought by toil and pain. The Crimson Hand expressed the ineludible gripe, in which mortality clutches the highest and purest of earthly mould, degrading them into kindred with the lowest, and even with the very brutes, like whom their visible frames return to dust. In this manner, selecting it as the symbol of his wife's liability to sin, sorrow, decay, and death, Alymer's sombre imagination was not long in rendering the birthmark a frightful object, causing him more trouble and horror than ever Georgiana's beauty, whether of soul or sense, had given him delight.

At all the seasons which should have been their happiest, he invariably, and without intending it—nay, in spite of a purpose to the contrary—reverted to this one disastrous topic. Trifling as it at first appeared, it so connected itself with innumerable trains of thought, and modes of feeling, that it became the central point of all. With the morning twilight, Aylmer opened his eyes upon his wife's face, and recognized the symbol of imperfection; and when they sat together at the evening hearth, his eyes wandered stealthily to her cheek, and beheld, flickering with the blaze of the wood fire, the spectral Hand that wrote mortality, where he would fain have worshipped. Georgiana soon learned to shudder at his gaze. It needed but a glance, with the peculiar expression that his face often wore, to change the roses of her cheek into a deathlike paleness, amid which the Crimson Hand was brought strongly out, like a bas-relief of ruby on the whitest marble.

Late, one night, when the lights were growing dim, so as hardly to betray the   10
stain on the poor wife's cheek, she herself, for the first time, voluntarily took up the subject.

"Do you remember, my dear Aylmer," said she, with a feeble attempt at a smile—"have you any recollection of a dream, last night, about this odious Hand?"

"None!—none whatever!" replied Aylmer, starting; but then he added in a dry, cold tone, affected for the sake of concealing the real depth of his emotion:—"I might well dream of it; for before I fell asleep, it had taken a pretty firm hold of my fancy."

"And you did dream of it," continued Georgiana, hastily; for she dreaded lest a gush of tears should interrupt what she had to say—"A terrible dream! I wonder that you can forget it. Is it possible to forget this one expression?—'It is in her heart now—we must have it out!'—Reflect, my husband; for by all means I would have you recall that dream."

The mind is in a sad note, when Sleep, the all-involving, cannot confine her spectres within the dim region of her sway, but suffers them to break forth, affrighting this actual life with secrets that perchance belong to a deeper one. Aylmer now remembered his dream. He had fancied himself with his servant Aminadab, attempting an operation for the removal of the birthmark. But the deeper went the knife, the deeper sank the Hand, until at length its tiny grasp appeared to have caught hold of Georgiana's heart; whence, however, her husband was inexorably resolved to cut or wrench it away.

When the dream had shaped itself perfectly in his memory, Aylmer sat in his   15
wife's presence with a guilty feeling. Truth often finds its way to the mind close-muffled in robes of sleep, and then speaks with uncompromising directness of matters in regard to which we practise an unconscious self-deception, during our waking moments. Until now, he had not been aware of the tyrannizing influence acquired by one idea over his mind, and of the lengths which he might find in his heart to go, for the sake of giving himself peace.

"Aylmer," resumed Georgiana, solemnly, "I know not what may be the cost to both of us, to rid me of this fatal birthmark. Perhaps its removal may cause cureless deformity. Or, it may be, the stain goes as deep as life itself. Again, do we know that there is a possibility, on any terms, of unclasping the firm gripe of this little Hand, which was laid upon me before I came into the world?"

"Dearest Georgiana, I have spent much thought upon the subject," hastily interrupted Aylmer—"I am convinced of the perfect practicability of its removal."

"If there be the remotest possibility of it," continued Georgiana, "let the attempt be made, at whatever risk. Danger is nothing to me; for life—while this hateful mark makes me the object of your horror and disgust—life is a burthen which I would fling down with joy. Either remove this dreadful Hand, or take my wretched life! You have deep science! All the world bears witness of it. You have achieved great wonders! Cannot you remove this little, little mark, which I cover with the tips of two small fingers? Is this beyond your power, for the sake of your own peace, and to save your poor wife from madness?"

"Noblest—dearest—tenderest wife!" cried Aylmer, rapturously. "Doubt not my power. I have already given this matter the deepest thought—thought which might almost have enlightened me to create a being less perfect than yourself. Georgiana, you have led me deeper than ever into the heart of science. I feel myself fully competent to render this dear cheek as faultless as its fellow; and then, most beloved, what will be my triumph, when I shall have corrected what Nature left imperfect, in her fairest work! Even Pygmalion, when his sculptured woman assumed life, felt not greater ecstasy than mine will be."

"It is resolved, then," said Georgiana, faintly smiling,—"And, Aylmer, spare me not, though you should find the birthmark take refuge in my heart at last." 20

Her husband tenderly kissed her cheek—her right cheek—not that which bore the impress of the Crimson Hand.

The next day, Aylmer apprized his wife of a plan that he had formed, whereby he might have opportunity for the intense thought and constant watchfulness, which the proposed operation would require; while Georgiana, likewise, would enjoy the perfect repose essential to its success. They were to seclude themselves in the extensive apartments occupied by Aylmer as a laboratory, and where, during his toilsome youth, he had made discoveries in the elemental powers of nature that had roused the admiration of all the learned societies in Europe. Seated calmly in this laboratory, the pale philosopher had investigated the secrets of the highest cloud-region, and of the profoundest mines; he had satisfied himself of the causes that kindled and kept alive the fires of the volcano; and had explained the mystery of fountains, and how it is that they gush forth, some so bright and pure, and others with such rich medicinal virtues, from the dark bosom of the earth. Here, too, at an earlier period, he had studied the wonders of the human frame, and attempted to fathom the very process by which Nature assimilates all her precious influences from earth and air, and from the spiritual world, to create and foster Man, her masterpiece. The latter pursuit, however, Aylmer had long laid aside, in unwilling recognition of the truth, against which all seekers sooner or later stumble, that our great creative Mother, while she amuses us with apparently working in the broadest sunshine, is yet severely careful to keep her own secrets, and, in spite of her pretended openness, shows us nothing but results. She permits us indeed, to mar, but seldom to mend, and, like a jealous patentee, on no account to make. Now, however, Aylmer resumed these half-forgotten investigations; not, of course, with such hopes or wishes as first suggested them; but because they involved much physiological truth, and lay in the path of his proposed scheme for the treatment of Georgiana.

As he led her over the threshold of the laboratory, Georgiana was cold and tremulous. Aylmer looked cheerfully into her face, with intent to reassure her, but was so startled with the intense glow of the birthmark upon the whiteness of her cheek, that he could not restrain a strong convulsive shudder. His wife fainted.

"Aminadab! Aminadab!" shouted Aylmer, stamping violently on the floor.

Forthwith, there issued from an inner apartment a man of low stature, but 25 bulky frame, with shaggy hair hanging about his visage, which was grimed with the vapors of the furnace. This personage had been Aylmer's under-worker during his whole scientific career, and was admirably fitted for that office by his great mechanical readiness, and the skill with which, while incapable of comprehending a single principle, he executed all the practical details of his master's experiments. With his vast strength, his shaggy hair, his smoky aspect, and the indescribable earthiness that incrusted him, he seemed to represent man's physical nature; while Aylmer's slender figure, and pale, intellectual face, were no less apt a type of the spiritual element.

"Throw open the door of the boudoir, Aminadab," said Aylmer, "and burn a pastille."

"Yes, master," answered Aminadab, looking intently at the lifeless form of Georgiana; and then he muttered to himself:—"If she were my wife, I'd never part with that birthmark."

When Georgiana recovered consciousness, she found herself breathing an atmosphere of penetrating fragrance, the gentle potency of which had recalled her from her deathlike faintness. The scene around her looked like enchantment. Aylmer had converted those smoky, dingy, sombre rooms, where he had spent his brightest years in recondite pursuits, into a series of beautiful apartments, not unfit to be the secluded abode of a lovely woman. The walls were hung with gorgeous curtains, which imparted the combination of grandeur and grace, that no other species of adornment can achieve; and as they fell from the ceiling to the floor, their rich and ponderous folds, concealing all angles and straight lines, appeared to shut in the scene from infinite space. For aught Georgiana knew, it might be a pavilion among the clouds. And Aylmer, excluding the sunshine, which would have interfered with his chemical processes, had supplied its place with perfumed lamps, emitting flames of various hue, but all uniting in a soft, empurpled radiance. He now knelt by his wife's side, watching her earnestly, but without alarm; for he was confident in his science, and felt that he could draw a magic circle round her, within which no evil might intrude.

"Where am I?—Ah, I remember!" said Georgiana, faintly; and she placed her hand over her cheek, to hide the terrible mark from her husband's eyes.

"Fear not, dearest!" exclaimed he. "Do not shrink from me! Believe me, 30 Georgiana, I even rejoice in this single imperfection, since it will be such rapture to remove it."

"Oh, spare me!" sadly replied his wife—"Pray do not look at it again. I never can forget that convulsive shudder."

In order to soothe Georgiana, and, as it were, to release her mind from the burthen of actual things, Aylmer now put in practice some of the light and playful secrets, which science had taught him among its profounder lore. Airy figures, absolutely bodiless ideas, and forms of unsubstantial beauty came and danced before her, imprinting their momentary footsteps on beams of light. Though she had some indistinct idea of the method of these optical phenomena, still the illusion was almost perfect enough to warrant the belief, that her husband possessed sway over the spiritual world. Then again, when she felt a wish to look forth from her seclusion, immediately, as if her thoughts were answered, the procession of external existence flitted across a screen. The scenery and the figures of actual life were perfectly represented, but with that bewitching, yet indescribable difference, which always makes a picture, an image, or a shadow, so much more attractive than the original. When wearied of this, Aylmer bade her cast her eyes upon a vessel, containing a quantity of earth. She did so, with little interest at first, but was soon startled to perceive the germ of a plant, shooting upward from the soil. Then came the slender stalk—the leaves gradually unfolded themselves—and amid them was a perfect and lovely flower.

"It is magical!" cried Georgiana, "I dare not touch it."

"Nay, pluck it," answered Aylmer, "pluck it, and inhale its brief perfume while you may. The flower will wither in a few moments, and leave nothing save its brown seed-vessels—but thence may be perpetuated a race as ephemeral as itself."

But Georgiana had no sooner touched the flower than the whole plant suf- 35
fered a blight, its leaves turning coal-black, as if by the agency of fire.

"There was too powerful a stimulus," said Aylmer thoughtfully.

To make up for this abortive experiment, he proposed to take her portrait by a scientific process of his own invention. It was to be effected by rays of light striking upon a polished plate of metal. Georgiana assented—but, on looking at the result, was affrighted to find the features of the portrait blurred and indefinable; while the minute figure of a hand appeared where the cheek should have been. Aylmer snatched the metallic plate, and threw it into a jar of corrosive acid.

Soon, however, he forgot these mortifying failures. In the intervals of study and chemical experiment, he came to her, flushed and exhausted, but seemed invigorated by her presence, and spoke in glowing language of the resources of his art. He gave a history of the long dynasty of the Alchemists, who spent so many ages in quest of the universal solvent, by which the Golden Principle might be elicted from all things vile and base. Aylmer appeared to believe that, by the plainest scientific logic, it was altogether within the limits of possibility to discover this long-sought medium; but, he added, a philosopher who should go deep enough to acquire the power, would attain too lofty a wisdom to stoop to the exercise of it. Not less singular were his opinions in regard to the Elixir Vitæ. He more than intimated, that it was his option to concoct a liquid that should prolong life for years—perhaps interminably—but that it would produce a discord in nature, which all the world, and chiefly the quaffer of the immortal nostrum, would find cause to curse.

"Aylmer, are you in earnest?" asked Georgiana, looking at him with amazement and fear; "it is terrible to possess such power, or even to dream of possessing it!"

"Oh, do not tremble, my love!" said her husband, "I would not wrong either 40
you or myself by working such inharmonious effects upon our lives. But I would have you consider how trifling, in comparison, is the skill requisite to remove this little Hand."

At the mention of the birthmark, Georgiana, as usual, shrank, as if a red-hot iron had touched her cheek.

Again Aylmer applied himself to his labors. She could hear his voice in the distant furnace-room, giving directions to Aminadab, whose harsh, uncouth, misshapen tones were audible in response, more like the grunt or growl of a brute than human speech. After hours of absence, Aylmer reappeared, and proposed that she should now examine his cabinet of chemical products, and natural treasures of the earth. Among the former he showed her a small vial, in which, he remarked, was contained a gentle yet most powerful fragrance, capable of impregnating all the breezes that blow across a kingdom. They were of inestimable value, the contents of that little vial; and, as he said so, he threw some of the perfume into the air, and filled the room with piercing and invigorating delight.

"And what is this?" asked Georgiana, pointing to a small crystal globe, containing a gold-colored liquid. "It is so beautiful to the eye, that I could imagine it the Elixir of Life."

"In one sense it is," replied Aylmer, "or rather the Elixir of Immortality. It is the most precious poison that ever was concocted in this world. By its aid, I could apportion the lifetime of any mortal at whom you might point your finger. The strength of the dose would determine whether he were to linger out years, or drop dead in the midst of a breath. No king, on his guarded throne, could keep his life, if I, in my private station, should deem that the welfare of millions justified me in depriving him of it."

"Why do you keep such a terrific drug?" inquired Georgiana in horror. 45

"Do not mistrust me, dearest!" said her husband, smiling; "its virtuous potency is yet greater than its harmful one. But, see! here is a powerful cosmetic. With a few drops of this, in a vase of water, freckles may be washed away as easily as the hands are cleansed. A stronger infusion would take the blood out of the cheek, and leave the rosiest beauty a pale ghost."

"Is it with this lotion that you intend to bathe my cheek?" asked Georgiana anxiously.

"Oh, no!" hastily replied her husband—"this is merely superficial. Your case demands a remedy that shall go deeper."

In his interviews with Georgiana, Aylmer generally made minute inquiries as to her sensations, and whether the confinement of the rooms, and the temperature of the atmosphere, agreed with her. These questions had such a particular drift, that Georgiana began to conjecture that she was already subjected to certain physical influences, either breathed in with the fragrant air, or taken with her food. She fancied, likewise—but it might be altogether fancy—that there was a stirring up of her system—a strange indefinite sensation creeping through her veins, and tingling, half painfully, half pleasurably, at her heart. Still, whenever she dared to look into the mirror, there she beheld herself, pale as a white rose, and with the crimson birthmark stamped upon her cheek. Not even Aylmer now hated it so much as she.

To dispel the tedium of the hours which her husband found it necessary to 50 devote to the processes of combination and analysis, Georgiana turned over the volumes of his scientific library. In many dark old tomes, she met with chapters full of romance and poetry. They were the works of the philosophers of the middle ages, such as Albertus Magnus, Cornelius Agrippa, Paracelsus, and the famous friar who created the prophetic Brazen Head. All these antique naturalists stood in advance of their centuries, yet were imbued with some of their credulity, and therefore were believed, and perhaps imagined themselves, to have acquired from the investigation of nature a power above nature, and from physics a sway over the spiritual world. Hardly less curious and imaginative were the early volumes of the Transactions of the Royal Society, in which the members, knowing little of the limits of natural possibility, were continually recording wonders, or proposing methods whereby wonders might be wrought.

But, to Georgiana, the most engrossing volume was a large folio from her husband's own hand, in which he had recorded every experiment of his scientific career, with its original aim, the methods adopted for its development, and its final success or failure, with the circumstances to which either event was attributable. The book, in truth, was both the history and emblem of his ardent, ambitious, imaginative, yet practical and laborious, life. He handled physical details, as if there were nothing beyond them; yet spiritualized them all, and redeemed himself from materialism, by his strong and eager aspiration towards the infinite. In his grasp, the veriest clod of earth assumed a soul. Georgiana, as she read, reverenced Aylmer, and loved him more profoundly than ever, but with a less entire dependence on his judgment than heretofore. Much as he had accomplished, she could not but observe that his most splendid successes were almost invariably failures, if compared with the ideal at which he aimed. His brightest diamonds were the merest pebbles, and felt to be so by himself, in comparison with the inestimable gems which lay hidden beyond his reach. The volume, rich with achievements that had won renown for its author, was yet as melancholy a record as ever mortal hand had penned. It was the sad confession, and continual exemplification, of the short-comings of the composite man—the spirit burthened with clay and working in matter—and of the despair that assails the higher nature, at finding itself so miserably thwarted by the earthly part. Perhaps every man of genius, in whatever sphere, might recognize the image of his own experience in Aylmer's journal.

So deeply did these reflections affect Georgiana, that she laid her face upon the open volume, and burst into tears. In this situation she was found by her husband.

"It is dangerous to read in a sorcerer's books," said he, with a smile, though his countenance was uneasy and displeased. "Georgiana, there are pages in that volume, which I can scarcely glance over and keep my senses. Take heed lest it prove as detrimental to you!"

"It has made me worship you more than ever," said she.

"Ah! wait for this one success," rejoined he, "then worship me if you will. I shall deem myself hardly unworthy of it. But, come! I have sought you for the luxury of your voice. Sing to me, dearest!"   55

So she poured out the liquid music of her voice to quench the thirst of his spirit. He then took his leave, with a boyish exuberance of gaiety, assuring her that her seclusion would endure but a little longer, and that the result was already certain. Scarcely had he departed, when Georgiana felt irresistibly impelled to follow him. She had forgotten to inform Aylmer of a symptom, which, for two or three hours past, had begun to excite her attention. It was a sensation in the fatal birthmark, not painful, but which induced a restlessness throughout her system. Hastening after her husband, she intruded, for the first time, into the laboratory.

The first thing that struck her eye was the furnace, that hot and feverish worker, with the intense glow of its fire, which, by the quantities of soot clustered above it, seemed to have been burning for ages. There was a distilling apparatus in full operation. Around the room were retorts, tubes, cylinders, crucibles, and other apparatus of chemical research. An electrical machine stood ready for immediate use. The atmosphere felt oppressively close, and was tainted with gaseous odors, which had been tormented forth by the processes of science. The severe and homely simplicity of the apartment, with its naked walls and brick

pavement, looked strange, accustomed as Georgiana had become to the fantastic
elegance of her boudoir. But what chiefly, indeed almost solely, drew her attention, was the aspect of Aylmer himself.

He was pale as death, anxious, and absorbed, and hung over the furnace as if it
depended upon his utmost watchfulness whether the liquid, which it was distilling,
should be the draught of immortal happiness or misery. How different from the
sanguine and joyous mien that he had assumed for Georgiana's encouragement!

"Carefully now, Aminadab! Carefully, thou human machine! Carefully, thou
man of clay!" muttered Aylmer, more to himself than his assistant. "Now, if
there be a thought too much or too little, it is all over!"

"Hoh! hoh!" mumbled Aminadab—"look, master, look!"   60

Aylmer raised his eyes hastily, and at first reddened, then grew paler than
ever, on beholding Georgiana. He rushed towards her, and seized her arm with
a gripe that left the print of his fingers upon it.

"Why do you come hither? Have you no trust in your husband?" cried he impetuously. "Would you throw the blight of that fatal birthmark over my labors?
It is not well done. Go, prying woman, go!"

"Nay, Aylmer," said Georgiana, with the firmness of which she possessed no
stinted endowment, "it is not you that have a right to complain. You mistrust
your wife! You have concealed the anxiety with which you watch the development of this experiment. Think not so unworthily of me, my husband! Tell me
all the risk we run; and fear not that I shall shrink, for my share in it is far less
than your own!"

"No, no, Georgiana!" said Aylmer impatiently, "it must not be."

"I submit," replied she calmly. "And, Aylmer, I shall quaff whatever draught   65
you bring me; but it will be on the same principle that would induce me to take
a dose of poison, if offered by your hand."

"My noble wife," said Aylmer, deeply moved, "I knew not the height and depth
of your nature, until now. Nothing shall be concealed. Know, then, that this
Crimson Hand, superficial as it seems, has clutched its grasp into your being, with
a strength of which I had no previous conception. I have already administered
agents powerful enough to do aught except to change your entire physical system.
Only one thing remains to be tried. If that fail us, we are ruined!"

"Why did you hesitate to tell me this?" asked she.

"Because, Georgiana," said Aylmer, in a low voice, "there is danger!"

"Danger? There is but one danger—that this horrible stigma shall be left
upon my cheek!" cried Georgiana. "Remove it! remove it!—whatever be the
cost—or we shall both go mad!"

"Heaven knows, your words are too true," said Aylmer, sadly. "And now,   70
dearest, return to your boudoir. In a little while, all will be tested."

He conducted her back, and took leave of her with a solemn tenderness,
which spoke far more than his words how much was now at stake. After his
departure, Georgiana became wrapt in musings. She considered the character of
Aylmer, and did it completer justice than at any previous moment. Her heart
exulted, while it trembled, at his honorable love, so pure and lofty that it would
accept nothing less than perfection, nor miserably make itself contented with an
earthlier nature than he had dreamed of. She felt how much more precious was
such a sentiment, than that meaner kind which would have borne with the
imperfection for her sake, and have been guilty of treason to holy love, by
degrading its perfect idea to the level of the actual. And, with her whole spirit,

she prayed, that, for a single moment, she might satisfy his highest and deepest conception. Longer than one moment, she well knew, it could not be; for his spirit was ever on the march—ever ascending—and each instant required something that was beyond the scope of the instant before.

The sound of her husband's footsteps aroused her. He bore a crystal goblet, containing a liquor colorless as water, but bright enough to be the draught of immortality. Aylmer was pale; but it seemed rather the consequence of a highly wrought state of mind, and tension of spirit, than of fear or doubt.

"The concoction of the draught has been perfect," said he, in answer to Georgiana's look. "Unless all my science have deceived me, it cannot fail."

"Save on your account, my dearest Aylmer," observed his wife, "I might wish to put off this birthmark of mortality by relinquishing mortality itself, in preference to any other mode. Life is but a sad possession to those who have attained precisely the degree of moral advancement at which I stand. Were I weaker and blinder, it might be happiness. Were I stronger, it might be endured hopefully. But, being what I find myself, methinks I am of all mortals the most fit to die."

"You are fit for heaven without tasting death!" replied her husband. "But why do we speak of dying? The draught cannot fail. Behold its effect upon this plant!"   75

On the window-seat there stood a geranium, diseased with yellow blotches, which had overspread all its leaves. Aylmer poured a small quantity of the liquid upon the soil in which it grew. In a little time, when the roots of the plant had taken up the moisture, the unsightly blotches began to be extinguished in a living verdure.

"There needed no proof," said Georgiana, quietly. "Give me the goblet. I joyfully stake all upon your word."

"Drink, then, thou lofty creature!" exclaimed Aylmer, with fervid admiration. "There is no taint of imperfection on thy spirit. Thy sensible frame, too, shall soon be all perfect!"

She quaffed the liquid, and returned the goblet to his hand.

"It is grateful," said she, with a placid smile. "Methinks it is like water from a heavenly fountain; for it contains I know not what of unobtrusive fragrance and deliciousness. It allays feverish thirst, that had parched me for many days. Now, dearest, let me sleep. My earthly senses are closing over my spirit, like the leaves round the heart of a rose, at sunset."   80

She spoke the last words with a gentle reluctance, as if it required almost more energy than she could command to pronounce the faint and lingering syllables. Scarcely had they loitered through her lips, ere she was lost in slumber. Aylmer sat by her side, watching her aspect with the emotions proper to a man, the whole value of whose existence was involved in the process now to be tested. Mingled with this mood, however, was the philosophic investigation, characteristic of the man of science. Not the minutest symptom escaped him. A heightened flush of the cheek—a slight irregularity of breath—a quiver of the eyelid—a hardly perceptible tremor through the frame—such were the details which, as the moments passed, he wrote down in his folio volume. Intense thought had set its stamp upon every previous page of that volume; but the thoughts of years were all concentrated upon the last.

While thus employed, he failed not to gaze often at the fatal Hand, and not without a shudder. Yet once, by a strange and unaccountable impulse, he pressed it with his lips. His spirit recoiled, however, in the very act, and Georgiana, out of the midst of her deep sleep, moved uneasily and murmured, as if in remonstrance. Again, Aylmer resumed his watch. Nor was it without avail. The Crimson Hand, which at first had been strongly visible upon the marble paleness of Georgiana's cheek now grew more faintly outlined. She remained not less pale than ever; but the birthmark, with every breath that came and went, lost somewhat of its former distinctness. Its presence had been awful; its departure was more awful still. Watch the stain of the rainbow fading out of the sky; and you will know how that mysterious symbol passed away.

"By Heaven, it is well nigh gone!" said Aylmer to himself, in almost irrepressible ecstasy. "I can scarcely trace it now. Success! Success! And now it is like the faintest rose-color. The slightest flush of blood across her cheek would overcome it. But she is so pale!"

He drew aside the window-curtain, and suffered the light of natural day to fall into the room, and rest upon her cheek. At the same time, he heard a gross, hoarse chuckle, which he had long known as his servant Aminadab's expression of delight.

"Ah, clod! Ah, earthly mass!" cried Aylmer, laughing in a sort of frenzy.   85
"You have served me well! Matter and Spirit—Earth and Heaven—have both done their part in this! Laugh, thing of senses! You have earned the right to laugh."

These exclamations broke Georgiana's sleep. She slowly unclosed her eyes, and gazed into the mirror, which her husband had arranged for that purpose. A faint smile flitted over her lips, when she recognized how barely perceptible was now that Crimson Hand, which had once blazed forth with such disastrous brilliancy as to scare away all their happiness. But then her eyes sought Aylmer's face, with a trouble and anxiety that he could by no means account for.

"My poor Aylmer!" murmured she.

"Poor? Nay, richest! Happiest! Most favored!" exclaimed he. "My peerless bride, it is successful! You are perfect!"

"My poor Aylmer!" she repeated, with a more than human tenderness. "You have aimed loftily!—you have done nobly! Do not repent, that, with so high and pure a feeling, you have rejected the best that earth could offer. Aylmer—dearest Aylmer—I am dying!"

Alas, it was too true! The fatal Hand had grappled with the mystery of life,   90
and was the bond by which an angelic spirit kept itself in union with a mortal frame. As the last crimson tint of the birthmark—that sole token of human imperfection—faded from her cheek, the parting breath of the now perfect woman passed into the atmosphere, and her soul, lingering a moment near her husband, took its heavenward flight. Then a hoarse, chuckling laugh was heard again! Thus ever does the gross Fatality of Earth exult in its invariable triumph over the immortal essence, which, in this dim sphere of half-development, demands the completeness of a higher state. Yet, had Aylmer reached a profounder wisdom, he need not thus have flung away the happiness, which would have woven his mortal life of the self-same texture with the celestial. The momentary circumstance was too strong for him; he failed to look beyond the shadowy scope of Time, and living once for all in Eternity to find the perfect Future in the present.

(1843)

Questions for Discussion and Writing

1. This story is often seen as a partial allegory. What concepts does each of the three characters stand for? In what way is each one flawed?
2. Is it significant that the birthmark is in the shape of a hand?
3. How would you state the conflict in the story?
4. What is the meaning of the allegory? In other words, what is Hawthorne's theme? Is it still relevant today?
5. Write an essay arguing that Georgiana is complicit in her own fate by encouraging Aylmer's folly.

Kate Chopin 1851–1904

Kate Chopin was born Kate O'Flaherty in St. Louis. After her father died in a train accident when she was four, she was raised by her mother, grandmother, and great-grandmother—all widows. In 1870 she married Oscar Chopin, the son of a wealthy cotton-growing family. After their marriage, they lived in New Orleans, where she had five boys and two girls, all before she was twenty-eight. When Oscar died of swamp fever in 1882, Kate returned to St. Louis, and to support her young family, began to write stories about people she had known in Louisiana. Her explorations of female sexuality and her championing of women's self-worth in her fiction were so shocking that she was denied membership in the St. Louis Literary Society.

The Story of an Hour

Knowing that Mrs. Mallard was afflicted with a heart trouble, great care was taken to break to her as gently as possible the news of her husband's death.

It was her sister Josephine who told her, in broken sentences; veiled hints that revealed in half concealing. Her husband's friend Richards was there, too, near her. It was he who had been in the newspaper office when intelligence of the railroad disaster was received, with Brently Mallard's name leading the list of "killed." He had only taken the time to assure himself of its truth by a second telegram, and had hastened to forestall any less careful, less tender friend in bearing the sad message.

She did not hear the story as many women have heard the same, with a paralyzed inability to accept its significance. She wept at once, with sudden, wild abandonment, in her sister's arms. When the storm of grief had spent itself she went away to her room alone. She would have no one follow her.

There stood, facing the open window, a comfortable, roomy armchair. Into this she sank, pressed down by a physical exhaustion that haunted her body and seemed to reach into her soul.

She could see in the open square before her house the tops of trees that were 5
all aquiver with the new spring life. The delicious breath of rain was in the air.
In the street below a peddler was crying his wares. The notes of a distant song
which some one was singing reached her faintly, and countless sparrows were
twittering in the eaves.

There were patches of blue sky showing here and there through the clouds
that had met and piled one above the other in the west facing her window.

She sat with her head thrown back upon the cushion of the chair, quite
motionless, except when a sob came up into her throat and shook her, as a child
who has cried itself to sleep continues to sob in its dreams.

She was young, with a fair, calm face, whose lines bespoke repression and
even a certain strength. But now there was a dull stare in her eyes, whose gaze
was fixed away off yonder on one of those patches of blue sky. It was not a glance
of reflection, but rather indicated a suspension of intelligent thought.

There was something coming to her and she was waiting for it, fearfully.
What was it? She did not know; it was too subtle and elusive to name. But she
felt it, creeping out of the sky, reaching toward her through the sounds, the
scents, the color that filled the air.

Now her bosom rose and fell tumultuously. She was beginning to recognize 10
this thing that was approaching to possess her, and she was striving to beat it
back with her will—as powerless as her two white slender hands would have
been.

When she abandoned herself a little whispered word escaped her slightly
parted lips. She said it over and over under her breath: "free, free, free!" The vacant stare and the look of terror that had followed it went from her eyes. They
stayed keen and bright. Her pulses beat fast, and the coursing blood warmed
and relaxed every inch of her body.

She did not stop to ask if it were or were not a monstrous joy that held her.
A clear and exalted perception enabled her to dismiss the suggestion as trivial.

She knew that she would weep again when she saw the kind, tender hands
folded in death; the face that had never looked save with love upon her, fixed
and gray and dead. But she saw beyond that bitter moment a long procession of
years to come that would belong to her absolutely. And she opened and spread
her arms out to them in welcome.

There would be no one to live for her during those coming years; she
would live for herself. There would be no powerful will bending hers in that
blind persistence with which men and women believe they have a right to
impose a private will upon a fellow-creature. A kind intention or a cruel intention made the act seem no less a crime as she looked upon it in that brief
moment of illumination.

And yet she had loved him—sometimes. Often she had not. What did it mat- 15
ter! What could love, the unsolved mystery, count for in face of this possession
of self-assertion which she suddenly recognized as the strongest impulse of her
being!

"Free! Body and soul free!" she kept whispering.

Josephine was kneeling before the closed door with her lips to the keyhole,
imploring for admission. "Louise, open the door! I beg; open the door—you
will make yourself ill. What are you doing, Louise? For heaven's sake open
the door."

"Go away. I am not making myself ill." No; she was drinking in a very elixir of life through that open window.

Her fancy was running riot along those days ahead of her. Spring days, and summer days, and all sorts of days that would be her own. She breathed a quick prayer that life might be long. It was only yesterday she had thought with a shudder that life might be long.

She arose at length and opened the door to her sister's importunities. There 20 was a feverish triumph in her eyes, and she carried herself unwittingly like a goddess of Victory. She clasped her sister's waist, and together they descended the stairs. Richards stood waiting for them at the bottom.

Some one was opening the front door with a latchkey. It was Brently Mallard who entered, a little travel-stained, composedly carrying his grip-sack and umbrella. He had been far from the scene of accident, and did not even know there had been one. He stood amazed at Josephine's piercing cry; at Richards' quick motion to screen him from the view of his wife.

But Richards was too late.

When the doctors came they said she had died of heart disease—of joy that kills.

(1894)

Questions for Discussion and Writing

1. What is the double meaning of Mrs. Mallard's "heart trouble," mentioned in the first line of the story?
2. Discuss the function of the imagery in paragraphs 4, 5, and 6.
3. Discuss the dual irony of the final line.
4. Does this exceedingly short story have a theme? If so, can you state one?
5. Write an essay arguing that Mrs. Mallard is (or is not) a sympathetic character.

Sherwood Anderson 1876–1941

Sherwood Anderson, who grew up poor in Clyde, Ohio, delved into the dark side of small-town American life, exposing the psychological deformity and frustration beneath the placid surface. At age thirty-six, he just walked out on his thriving paint business, abandoning his wife and three children, and went to Chicago to become a writer. After the 1919 publication of *Winesburg, Ohio*, a collection of twenty-three linked stories, Anderson became financially comfortable, but he did not achieve a happy marriage until his third try in 1933. While traveling to South America in 1941, he died from peritonitis after swallowing a toothpick in an hors d'oeuvre. His writing influenced Faulkner, Hemingway, and Steinbeck.

Hands

Upon the half decayed veranda of a small frame house that stood near the edge of a ravine near the town of Winesburg, Ohio, a fat little old man walked nervously up and down. Across a long field that had been seeded for clover but that had produced only a dense crop of yellow mustard weeds, he could see the public highway along which went a wagon filled with berry pickers returning from the fields. The berry pickers, youths and maidens, laughed and shouted boisterously. A boy, clad in a blue shirt, leaped from the wagon and attempted to drag after him one of the maidens who screamed and protested shrilly. The feet of the boy in the road kicked up a cloud of dust that floated across the face of the departing sun. Over the long field came a thin girlish voice. "Oh, you Wing Biddlebaum, comb your hair, it's falling into your eyes," commanded the voice to the man, who was bald and whose nervous little hands fiddled about the bare white forehead as though arranging a mass of tangled locks.

Wing Biddlebaum, forever frightened and beset by a ghostly band of doubts, did not think of himself as in any way a part of the life of the town where he had lived for twenty years. Among all the people of Winesburg but one had come close to him. With George Willard, son of Tom Willard, the proprietor of the New Willard House, he had formed something like a friendship. George Willard was the reporter on the *Winesburg Eagle* and sometimes in the evening he walked out along the highway to Wing Biddlebaum's house. Now, as the old man walked up and down on the veranda, his hands moving nervously about, he was hoping that George Willard would come and spend the evening with him. After the wagon containing the berry pickers had passed, he went across the field through the tall mustard weeds and climbing a rail fence peered anxiously along the road to the town. For a moment he stood thus, rubbing his hands together and looking up and down the road, and then, fear overcoming him, ran back to walk again upon the porch of his own house.

In the presence of George Willard, Wing Biddlebaum, who for twenty years had been the town mystery, lost something of his timidity, and his shadowy personality, submerged in a sea of doubts, came forth to look at the world. With the young reporter at his side, he ventured in the light of day into Main Street or strode up and down on the rickety front porch of his own house talking excitedly. The voice that had been low and trembling became shrill and loud. The bent figure straightened. With a kind of wriggle, like a fish returned to the brook by the fisherman, Biddlebaum the silent began to talk, striving to put into words the ideas that had been accumulated by his mind during long years of silence.

Wing Biddlebaum talked much with his hands. The slender expressive fingers, forever active, forever striving to conceal themselves in his pockets or behind his back, came forth and became the piston rods of his machinery of expression.

The story of Wing Biddlebaum is a story of hands. Their restless activity, like unto the beating of the wings of an imprisoned bird, had given him his name. Some obscure "poet" of the town had thought of it. The hands alarmed their owner. He wanted to keep them hidden away and looked with amazement at the quiet inexpressive hands of other men who worked beside him in the fields, or passed driving sleepy teams on country roads.

5

When he talked to George Willard, Wing Biddlebaum closed his fists and beat with them upon a table or on the walls of his house. The action made him more comfortable. If the desire to talk came to him when the two were walking in the fields, he sought out a stump or the top board of a fence and with his hands pounding busily talked with renewed ease.

The story of Wing Biddlebaum's hands is worth a book in itself. Sympathetically set forth it would tap many strange, beautiful qualities in obscure men. It is a job for a poet. In Winesburg the hands had attracted attention merely because of their activity. With them Wing Biddlebaum had picked as high as a hundred and forty quarts of strawberries in a day. They became his distinguishing feature, the source of his fame. Also they made more grotesque an already grotesque and elusive individuality. Winesburg was proud of the hands of Wing Biddlebaum in the same spirit in which it was proud of Banker White's new stone house and Wesley Moyer's bay stallion, Tony Tip, that had won the two-fifteen trot at the fall races in Cleveland.

As for George Willard, he had many times wanted to ask about the hands. At times an almost overwhelming curiosity had taken hold of him. He felt that there must be a reason for their strange activity and their inclination to keep hidden away and only a growing respect for Wing Biddlebaum kept him from blurting out the questions that were often in his mind.

Once he had been on the point of asking. The two were walking in the fields on a summer afternoon and had stopped to sit upon a grassy bank. All afternoon Wing Biddlebaum had talked as one inspired. By a fence he had stopped and beating like a giant woodpecker upon the top board had shouted at George Willard, condemning his tendency to be too much influenced by the people about him. "You are destroying yourself," he cried. "You have the inclination to be alone and to dream and you are afraid of dreams. You want to be like others in town here. You hear them talk and you try to imitate them."

On the grassy bank Wing Biddlebaum had tried again to drive his point home. 10 His voice became soft and reminiscent, and with a sigh of contentment he launched into a long rambling talk, speaking as one lost in a dream.

Out of the dream Wing Biddlebaum made a picture for George Willard. In the picture men lived again in a kind of pastoral golden age. Across a green open country came clean-limbed young men, some afoot, some mounted upon horses. In crowds the young men came to gather about the feet of an old man who sat beneath a tree in a tiny garden and who talked to them.

Wing Biddlebaum became wholly inspired. For once he forgot the hands. Slowly they stole forth and lay upon George Willard's shoulders. Something new and bold came into the voice that talked. "You must try to forget all you have learned," said the old man. "You must begin to dream. From this time on you must shut your ears to the roaring of the voices."

Pausing in his speech, Wing Biddlebaum looked long and earnestly at George Willard. His eyes glowed. Again he raised the hands to caress the boy and then a look of horror swept over his face.

With a convulsive movement of his body Wing Biddlebaum sprang to his feet and thrust his hands deep into his trousers pockets. Tears came to his eyes. "I must be getting along home. I can talk no more with you," he said nervously.

Without looking back, the old man had hurried down the hillside and across 15 a meadow, leaving George Willard perplexed and frightened upon the grassy slope. With a shiver of dread the boy arose and went along the road toward town. "I'll not ask him about his hands," he thought, touched by the memory of the terror he had seen in the man's eyes. "There's something wrong, but I don't want to know what it is. His hands have something to do with his fear of me and of everyone."

And George Willard was right. Let us look briefly into the story of the hands. Perhaps our talking of them will arouse the poet who will tell the hidden wonder story of the influence for which the hands were but fluttering pennants of promise.

In his youth Wing Biddlebaum had been a school teacher in a town in Pennsylvania. He was not then known as Wing Biddlebaum but went by the less euphonic name of Adolph Myers. As Adolph Myers he was much loved by the boys of his school.

Adolph Myers was meant by nature to be a teacher of youth. He was one of those rare little-understood men who rule by a power so gentle that it passes as a lovable weakness. In their feeling for the boys under their charge such men are not unlike the finer sort of women in their love of men.

And yet that is but crudely stated. It needs the poet there. With the boys of his school, Adolph Myers had walked in the evening or had sat talking until dusk upon the school house steps, lost in a kind of dream. Here and there went his hands, caressing the shoulders of the boys, playing about the tousled heads. As he talked his voice became soft and musical. There was a caress in that also. In a way the voice and the hands, the stroking of the shoulders and the touching of the hair were a part of the school master's effort to carry a dream into the young minds. By the caress that was in his fingers he expressed himself. He was one of those men in whom the force that creates life is diffused, not centralized. Under the caress of his hands doubt and disbelief went out of the minds of the boys and they began also to dream.

And then the tragedy. A halfwitted boy of the school became enamored of the young master. In his bed at night he imagined unspeakable things and in the morning went forth to tell his dreams as facts. Strange hideous accusations fell from his loose-hung lips. Through the Pennsylvania town went a shiver. Hidden shadowy doubts that had been in men's minds concerning Adolph Myers were galvanized into beliefs. 20

The tragedy did not linger. Trembling lads were jerked out of bed and questioned. "He put his arms about me," said one. "His fingers were always playing in my hair," said another.

One afternoon a man of the town, Henry Bradford, who kept a saloon, came to the school house door. Calling Adolph Myers into the school yard he began to beat him with his fists. As his hard knuckles beat down into the frightened face of the schoolmaster, his wrath became more and more terrible. Screaming with dismay, the children ran here and there like disturbed insects. "I'll teach you to put your hands on my boy, you beast," roared the saloon keeper, who, tired of beating the master, had begun to kick him about the yard.

Adolph Myers was driven from the Pennsylvania town in the night. With lanterns in their hands a dozen men came to the door of the house where he lived alone and commanded that he dress and come forth. It was raining and one of the men had a rope in his hands. They had intended to hang the school master, but something in his figure, so small, white, and pitiful, touched their hearts and they let him escape. As he ran away into the darkness they repented of their weakness and ran after him, swearing and throwing sticks and great balls of soft mud at the figure that screamed and ran faster and faster into the darkness.

For twenty years Adolph Myers had lived alone in Winesburg. He was but forty but looked sixty-five. The name of Biddlebaum he got from a box of goods seen at a freight station as he hurried through an eastern Ohio town. He had an aunt in Winesburg, a black-toothed old woman who raised chickens, and with her he lived until she died. He had been ill for a year after the experience in Pennsylvania, and after his recovery worked as a day laborer in the fields, going timidly about and striving to conceal his hands. Although he did not understand what had happened he felt that the hands must be to blame. Again and again the fathers of the boys talked of the hands. "Keep your hands to yourself," the saloon keeper had roared, dancing with fury in the school house yard.

Upon the veranda of his house by the ravine, Wing Biddlebaum continued to   25 walk up and down until the sun had disappeared and the road beyond the field was lost in the grey shadows. Going into his house he cut slices of bread and spread honey upon them. When the rumble of the evening train that took away the express cars loaded with the day's harvest of berries had passed and restored the silence of the summer night, he went again to walk upon the veranda. In the darkness he could not see the hands and they became quiet. Although he still hungered for the presence of the boy, who was the medium through which he expressed his love of man, the hunger became again a part of his loneliness and his waiting. Lighting a lamp Wing Biddlebaum washed the few dishes soiled by his simple meal and, setting up a folding cot by the screen door that led to the porch, prepared to undress for the night. A few stray white bread crumbs lay on the cleanly washed floor by the table; putting the lamp upon a low stool he began to pick up the crumbs, carrying them to his mouth one by one with unbelievable rapidity. In the dense blotch of light beneath the table, the kneeling figure looked like a priest engaged in some service of his church. The nervous expressive fingers, flashing in and out of the light, might well have been mistaken for the fingers of the devotee going swiftly through decade after decade of his rosary.

(1919)

Questions for Discussion and Writing

1. Reread the first paragraph of the story closely. How does the imagery of the scene forecast themes developed later?

2. Why does the author say more than once that the story of Wing's hands is material for a poet? In what ways do you think a poem is different from a story?

3. What did the men of the Pennsylvania town decide about Adolph Myers? Why did they have such a rabid reaction? What is the significance of the source of the rumors? Why do you think the first confrontation came from the saloon keeper? Have you ever witnessed a situation like this?

4. What is Wing trying to tell George in their talks? What does he mean by "You must begin to dream"? Why do you think the content of Wing's teachings is left vague?

5. How do you reconcile the final image of Wing with the rest of the story? What emotional tone does it convey to you?

D. H. Lawrence   1885–1930

D[avid] H[erbert] Lawrence, son of a coal miner, was raised in poverty and said of his parents, "Their marriage life has been one carnal, bloody fight. I was born hating my father: as early as ever I can remember, I shivered with horror when he touched me." In 1912, he fell in love with a married woman who abandoned her husband and three children to live with Lawrence in exile. He never ceased to rebel against Puritanism and social conventions, a rebellion that led to some of the most famous censorship trials of the twentieth century. His controversial novel *Lady Chatterley's Lover* (1928), for example, was banned as pornographic in both Britain and the United States until 1960.

The Rocking-Horse Winner

There was a woman who was beautiful, who started with all the advantages, yet she had no luck. She married for love, and the love turned to dust. She had bonny children, yet she felt they had been thrust upon her, and she could not love them. They looked at her coldly, as if they were finding fault with her. And hurriedly she felt she must cover up some fault in herself. Yet what it was that she must cover up she never knew. Nevertheless, when her children were present, she always felt the centre of her heart go hard. This troubled her, and in her manner she was all the more gentle and anxious for her children, as if she loved them very much. Only she herself knew that at the centre of her heart was a hard little place that could not feel love, no, not for anybody. Everybody else said of her: "She is such a good mother. She adores her children." Only she herself, and her children themselves, knew it was not so. They read it in each other's eyes.

There were a boy and two little girls. They lived in a pleasant house, with a garden, and they had discreet servants, and felt themselves superior to anyone in the neighbourhood.

Although they lived in style, they felt always an anxiety in the house. There was never enough money. The mother had a small income, and the father had a small income, but not nearly enough for the social position which they had to keep up. The father went into town to some office. But though he had good prospects, these prospects never materialised. There was always the grinding sense of the shortage of money, though the style was always kept up.

At last the mother said: "I will see if *I* can't make something." But she did not know where to begin. She racked her brains, and tried this thing and the other, but could not find anything successful. The failure made deep lines come into her face. Her children were growing up, they would have to go to school. There must be more money, there must be more money. The father, who was always very handsome and expensive in his tastes, seemed as if he never *would* be able to do anything worth doing. And the mother, who had a great belief in herself, did not succeed any better, and her tastes were just as expensive.

And so the house came to be haunted by the unspoken phrase: *There must be   5 more money! There must be more money!* The children could hear it all the time, though nobody said it aloud. They heard it at Christmas, when the expensive and splendid toys filled the nursery. Behind the shining modern rocking-horse, behind the smart doll's house, a voice would start whispering: "There *must* be more money! There *must* be more money!" And the children would stop playing, to listen for a moment. They would look into each other's eyes, to see if they had all heard. And each one saw in the eyes of the other two that they too had heard. "There *must* be more money! There *must* be more money!"

It came whispering from the springs of the still-swaying rocking-horse, and even the horse, bending his wooden, champing head, heard it. The big doll, sitting so pink and smirking in her new pram,[1] could hear it quite plainly, and seemed to be smirking all the more self-consciously because of it. The foolish puppy, too, that took the place of the teddybear, he was looking so extraordinarily foolish for no other reason but that he heard the secret whisper all over the house: "There *must* be more money!"

Yet nobody ever said it aloud. The whisper was everywhere, and therefore no one spoke it. Just as no one ever says: "We are breathing!" in spite of the fact that breath is coming and going all the time.

"Mother," said the boy Paul one day, "why don't we keep a car of our own? Why do we always use uncle's, or else a taxi?"

"Because we're the poor members of the family," said the mother.

"But why *are* we, mother?"   10

"Well—I suppose," she said slowly and bitterly, "it's because your father has no luck."

The boy was silent for some time.

"Is luck money, mother?" he asked, rather timidly.

"No, Paul. Not quite. It's what causes you to have money."

"Oh!" said Paul vaguely. "I thought when Uncle Oscar said *filthy lucker*, it   15
meant money."

"*Filthy lucre* does mean money," said the mother. "But it's lucre, not luck."

"Oh!" said the boy. "Then what *is* luck, mother?"

"It's what causes you to have money. If you're lucky you have money. That's why it's better to be born lucky than rich. If you're rich, you may lose your money. But if you're lucky, you will always get more money."

"Oh! Will you? And is father not lucky?"

"Very unlucky, I should say," she said bitterly.   20

The boy watched her with unsure eyes.

"Why?" he asked.

"I don't know. Nobody ever knows why one person is lucky and another unlucky."

"Don't they? Nobody at all? Does *nobody* know?"

"Perhaps God. But He never tells."   25

"He ought to, then. And aren't you lucky either, mother?"

"I can't be, if I married an unlucky husband."

"But by yourself, aren't you?"

"I used to think I was, before I married. Now I think I am very unlucky indeed."

"Why?"   30

"Well—never mind! Perhaps I'm not really," she said.

---

[1]Baby carriage.

The child looked at her to see if she meant it. But he saw, by the lines of her mouth, that she was only trying to hide something from him.

"Well, anyhow," he said stoutly, "I'm a lucky person."

"Why?" said his mother, with a sudden laugh.

He stared at her. He didn't even know why he had said it.   35

"God told me," he asserted, brazening it out.

"I hope He did, dear!" she said, again with a laugh, but rather bitter.

"He did, mother!"

"Excellent!" said the mother, using one of her husband's exclamations.

The boy saw she did not believe him; or rather, that she paid no attention to   40
his assertion. This angered him somewhat, and made him want to compel her attention.

He went off by himself, vaguely, in a childish way, seeking for the clue to "luck." Absorbed, taking no heed of other people, he went about with a sort of stealth, seeking inwardly for luck. He wanted luck, he wanted it, he wanted it. When the two girls were playing dolls in the nursery, he would sit on his big rocking-horse, charging madly into space, with a frenzy that made the little girls peer at him uneasily. Wildly the horse careered, the waving dark hair of the boy tossed, his eyes had a strange glare in them. The little girls dared not speak to him.

When he had ridden to the end of his mad little journey, he climbed down and stood in front of his rocking-horse, staring fixedly into its lowered face. Its red mouth was slightly open, its big eye was wide and glassy-bright.

"Now!" he would silently command the snorting steed. "Now, take me to where there is luck! Now take me!"

And he would slash the horse on the neck with the little whip he had asked Uncle Oscar for. He *knew* the horse could take him to where there was luck, if only he forced it. So he would mount again and start on his furious ride, hoping at last to get there. He knew he could get there.

"You'll break your horse, Paul!" said the nurse.   45

"He's always riding like that! I wish he'd leave off!" said his elder sister Joan.

But he only glared down on them in silence. Nurse gave him up. She could make nothing of him. Anyhow, he was growing beyond her.

One day his mother and his Uncle Oscar came in when he was on one of his furious rides. He did not speak to them.

"Hallo, you young jockey! Riding a winner?" said his uncle.

"Aren't you growing too big for a rocking-horse? You're not a very little boy   50
any longer, you know," said his mother.

But Paul only gave a blue glare from his big, rather close-set eyes. He would speak to nobody when he was in full tilt. His mother watched him with an anxious expression on her face.

At last he suddenly stopped forcing his horse into the mechanical gallop and slid down.

"Well, I got there!" he announced fiercely, his blue eyes still flaring, and his sturdy long legs straddling apart.

"Where did you get to?" asked his mother.

"Where I wanted to go," he flared back at her.   55

"That's right, son!" said Uncle Oscar. "Don't you stop till you get there. What's the horse's name?"

"He doesn't have a name," said the boy.

"Gets on without all right?" asked the uncle.

"Well, he has different names. He was called Sansovino last week."

"Sansovino, eh? Won the Ascot.[2] How did you know this name?"　60

"He always talks about horse-races with Bassett," said Joan.

The uncle was delighted to find that his small nephew was posted with all the racing news. Bassett, the young gardener, who had been wounded in the left foot in the war and had got his present job through Oscar Cresswell, whose batman[3] he had been, was a perfect blade of the "turf." He lived in the racing events, and the small boy lived with him.

Oscar Cresswell got it all from Bassett.

"Master Paul comes and asks me, so I can't do more than tell him, sir," said Bassett, his face terribly serious, as if he were speaking of religious matters.

"And does he ever put anything on a horse he fancies?"　65

"Well—I don't want to give him away—he's a young sport, a fine sport, sir. Would you mind asking him himself? He sort of takes a pleasure in it, and perhaps he'd feel I was giving him away, sir, if you don't mind."

Bassett was serious as a church.

The uncle went back to his nephew and took him off for a ride in the car.

"Say, Paul, old man, do you ever put anything on a horse?" the uncle asked.

The boy watched the handsome man closely.　70

"Why, do you think I oughtn't to?" he parried.

"Not a bit of it! I thought perhaps you might give me a tip for the Lincoln."[4]

The car sped on into the country, going down to Uncle Oscar's place in Hampshire.

"Honour bright?" said the nephew.

"Honour bright, son!" said the uncle.　75

"Well, then, Daffodil."

"Daffodil! I doubt it, sonny. What about Mirza?"

"I only know the winner," said the boy. "That's Daffodil."

"Daffodil, eh?"

There was a pause. Daffodil was an obscure horse comparatively.　80

"Uncle!"

"Yes, son?"

"You won't let it go any further, will you? I promised Bassett."

"Bassett be damned, old man! What's he got to do with it?"

"We're partners. We've been partners from the first. Uncle, he lent me my first　85 five shillings, which I lost. I promised him, honour bright, it was only between me and him; only you gave me that ten shilling note I started winning with, so I thought you were lucky. You won't let it go any further, will you?"

The boy gazed at his uncle from those big, hot, blue eyes, set rather close together. The uncle stirred and laughed uneasily.

"Right you are, son! I'll keep your tip private. Daffodil, eh? How much are you putting on him?"

"All except twenty pounds," said the boy. "I keep that in reserve."

The uncle thought it a good joke.

---

[2] A famous horse race run near Ascot in England.

[3] A military officer's orderly or assistant.

[4] A horse race run at Lincoln Downs.

"You keep twenty pounds in reserve, do you, you young romancer! What are   90
you betting, then?"

"I'm betting three hundred," said the boy gravely. "But it's between you and
me, Uncle Oscar! Honour bright?"

The uncle burst into a roar of laughter.

"It's between you and me all right, you young Nat Gould,"[5] he said, laughing.
"But where's your three hundred?"

"Bassett keeps it for me. We're partners."

"You are, are you! And what is Bassett putting on Daffodil?"   95

"He won't go quite as high as I do, I expect. Perhaps he'll go a hundred and
fifty."

"What, pennies?" laughed the uncle.

"Pounds," said the child, with a surprised look at his uncle. "Bassett keeps a
bigger reserve than I do."

Between wonder and amusement Uncle Oscar was silent. He pursued the
matter no further, but he determined to take his nephew with him to the
Lincoln races.

"Now, son," he said, "I'm putting twenty on Mirza, and I'll put five on for   100
you on any horse you fancy. What's your pick?"

"Daffodil, uncle."

"No, not the fiver on Daffodil!"

"I should if it was my own fiver," said the child.

"Good! Good! Right you are! A fiver for me and a fiver for you on Daffodil."

The child had never been to a race-meeting before, and his eyes were blue   105
fire. He pursed his mouth tight and watched. A Frenchman just in front had put
his money on Lancelot. Wild with excitement, he flayed his arms up and down,
yelling, *"Lancelot! Lancelot!"* in his French accent.

Daffodil came in first, Lancelot second, Mirza third. The child, flushed and
with eyes blazing, was curiously serene. His uncle brought him four five-pound
notes, four to one.

"What am I to do with these?" he cried, waving them before the boy's eyes.

"I suppose we'll talk to Bassett," said the boy. "I expect I have fifteen hundred
now; and twenty in reserve; and this twenty."

His uncle studied him for some moments.

"Look here, son!" he said. "You're not serious about Bassett and that fifteen   110
hundred, are you?"

"Yes, I am. But it's between you and me, uncle. Honour bright?"

"Honour bright all right, son! But I must talk to Bassett."

"If you'd like to be a partner, uncle, with Bassett and me, we could all be partners.
Only, you'd have to promise, honour bright, uncle, not to let it go beyond us three.
Bassett and I are lucky, and you must be lucky, because it was your ten shillings
I started winning with…"

Uncle Oscar took both Bassett and Paul into Richmond Park for an afternoon, and there they talked.

"It's like this, you see, sir," Bassett said. "Master Paul would get me talking   115
about racing events, spinning yarns, you know, sir. And he was always keen on
knowing if I'd made or if I'd lost. It's about a year since, now, that I put five

---

[5]Nathaniel Gould, a popular writer who specialized in fiction and articles about horse racing.

shillings on Blush of Dawn for him: and we lost. Then the luck turned, with that ten shillings he had from you: that we put on Singhalese. And since that time, it's been pretty steady, all things considering. What do you say, Master Paul?"

"We're all right when we're sure," said Paul. "It's when we're not quite sure that we go down."

"Oh, but we're careful then," said Bassett.

"But when are you *sure?*" smiled Uncle Oscar.

"It's Master Paul, sir," said Bassett in a secret, religious voice. "It's as if he had it from heaven. Like Daffodil, now, for the Lincoln. That was as sure as eggs."

"Did you put anything on Daffodil?" asked Oscar Cresswell.   120

"Yes, sir. I made my bit."

"And my nephew?"

Bassett was obstinately silent, looking at Paul.

"I made twelve hundred, didn't I, Bassett? I told uncle I was putting three hundred on Daffodil."

"That's right," said Bassett, nodding.   125

"But where's the money?" asked the uncle.

"I keep it safe locked up, sir. Master Paul he can have it any minute he likes to ask for it."

"What, fifteen hundred pounds?"

"And twenty! And *forty*, that is, with the twenty he made on the course."

"It's amazing!" said the uncle.   130

"If Master Paul offers you to be partners, sir, I would, if I were you: if you'll excuse me," said Bassett.

Oscar Cresswell thought about it.

"I'll see the money," he said.

They drove home again, and, sure enough, Bassett came round to the garden-house with fifteen hundred pounds in notes. The twenty pounds reserve was left with Joe Glee, in the Turf Commission deposit.

"You see, it's all right, uncle, when I'm *sure!* Then we go strong, for all we're   135
worth. Don't we, Bassett?"

"We do that, Master Paul."

"And when are you sure?" said the uncle, laughing.

"Oh, well, sometimes I'm *absolutely* sure, like about Daffodil," said the boy; "and sometimes I have an idea; and sometimes I haven't even an idea, have I, Bassett? Then we're careful, because we mostly go down."

"You do, do you! And when you're sure, like about Daffodil, what makes you sure, sonny?"

"Oh, well, I don't know," said the boy uneasily. "I'm sure, you know, uncle;   140
that's all."

"It's as if he had it from heaven, sir," Bassett reiterated.

"I should say so!" said the uncle.

But he became a partner. And when the Leger[6] was coming on Paul was "sure" about Lively Spark, which was a quite inconsiderable horse. The boy in- sisted on putting a thousand on the horse, Bassett went for five hundred, and Oscar Cresswell two hundred. Lively Spark came in first, and the betting had been ten to one against him. Paul had made ten thousand.

---

[6]The St. Leger Stakes race.

"You see," he said, "I was absolutely sure of him."
Even Oscar Cresswell had cleared two thousand.   145
"Look here, son," he said, "this sort of thing makes me nervous."
"It needn't, uncle! Perhaps I shan't be sure again for a long time."
"But what are you going to do with your money?" asked the uncle.
"Of course," said the boy, "I started it for mother. She said she had no
luck, because father is unlucky, so I thought if *I* was lucky, it might stop
whispering."
"What might stop whispering?"   150
"Our house. I *hate* our house for whispering."
"What does it whisper?"
"Why—why"—the boy fidgeted—"why, I don't know. But it's always short of
money, you know, uncle."
"I know it, son, I know it."
"You know people send mother writs,[7] don't you, uncle?"   155
"I'm afraid I do," said the uncle.
"And then the house whispers, like people laughing at you behind your back.
It's awful, that is! I thought if I was lucky—"
"You might stop it," added the uncle.
The boy watched him with big blue eyes, that had an uncanny cold fire in
them, and he said never a word.
"Well, then!" said the uncle. "What are we doing?"   160
"I shouldn't like mother to know I was lucky," said the boy.
"Why not, son?"
"She'd stop me."
"I don't think she would."
"Oh"—and the boy writhed in an odd way—"I *don't* want her to know, uncle."   165
"All right, son! We'll manage it without her knowing."
They managed it very easily. Paul, at the other's suggestion, handed over five
thousand pounds to his uncle, who deposited it with the family lawyer, who was
then to inform Paul's mother that a relative had put five thousand pounds into
his hands, which sum was to be paid out a thousand pounds at a time, on the
mother's birthday, for the next five years.
"So she'll have a birthday present of a thousand pounds for five successive
years," said Uncle Oscar. "I hope it won't make it all the harder for her later."
Paul's mother had her birthday in November. The house had been "whispering"
worse than ever lately, and, even in spite of his luck, Paul could not bear up against
it. He was very anxious to see the effect of the birthday letter, telling his mother
about the thousand pounds.
When there were no visitors, Paul now took his meals with his parents, as he   170
was beyond the nursery control. His mother went into town nearly every day.
She had discovered that she had an odd knack of sketching furs and dress materials, so she worked secretly in the studio of a friend who was the chief "artist"
for the leading drapers. She drew the figures of ladies in furs and ladies in silk
and sequins for the newspaper advertisements. This young woman artist earned
several thousand pounds a year, but Paul's mother only made several hundreds,

---

[7]Requests for payment from creditors.

and she was again dissatisfied. She so wanted to be first in something, and she did not succeed, even in making sketches for drapery advertisements.

She was down to breakfast on the morning of her birthday. Paul watched her face as she read her letters. He knew the lawyer's letter. As his mother read it, her face hardened and became more expressionless. Then a cold, determined look came on her mouth. She hid the letter under the pile of others, and said not a word about it.

"Didn't you have anything nice in the post for your birthday, mother?" said Paul.

"Quite moderately nice," she said, her voice cold and absent.

She went away to town without saying more.

But in the afternoon Uncle Oscar appeared. He said Paul's mother had had a 175 long interview with the lawyer, asking if the whole five thousand could not be advanced at once, as she was in debt.

"What do you think, uncle?" asked the boy.

"I leave it to you, son."

"Oh, let her have it, then! We can get some more with the other," said the boy.

"A bird in the hand is worth two in the bush, laddie!" said Uncle Oscar.

"But I'm sure to *know* for the Grand National; or the Lincolnshire; or else 180 the Derby.[8] I'm sure to know for *one* of them," said Paul.

So Uncle Oscar signed the agreement, and Paul's mother touched the whole five thousand. Then something very curious happened. The voices in the house suddenly went mad, like a chorus of frogs on a spring evening. There were certain new furnishings, and Paul had a tutor. He was *really* going to Eton, his father's school, in the following autumn. There were flowers in the winter, and a blossoming of the luxury Paul's mother had been used to. And yet the voices in the house, behind the sprays of mimosa and almond-blossom, and from under the piles of iridescent cushions, simply trilled and screamed in a sort of ecstasy: "There *must* be more money! Oh-h-h; there *must* be more money. Oh, now, now-w! Now-w-w—there *must* be more money!—more than ever! More than ever!"

It frightened Paul terribly. He studied away at his Latin and Greek with his tutor. But his intense hours were spent with Bassett. The Grand National had gone by: he had not "known," and had lost a hundred pounds. Summer was at hand. He was in agony for the Lincoln. But even for the Lincoln he didn't "know," and he lost fifty pounds. He became wild-eyed and strange, as if something were going to explode in him.

"Let it alone, son! Don't you bother about it!" urged Uncle Oscar. But it was as if the boy couldn't really hear what his uncle was saying.

"I've got to know for the Derby! I've got to know for the Derby!" the child reiterated, his big blue eyes blazing with a sort of madness.

His mother noticed how overwrought he was. 185

"You'd better go to the seaside. Wouldn't you like to go now to the seaside, instead of waiting? I think you'd better," she said, looking down at him anxiously, her heart curiously heavy because of him.

But the child lifted his uncanny blue eyes.

"I couldn't possibly go before the Derby, mother!" he said. "I couldn't possibly!"

---

[8]All important horse races.

"Why not?" she said, her voice becoming heavy when she was opposed. "Why not? You can still go from the seaside to see the Derby with your Uncle Oscar, if that's what you wish. No need for you to wait here. Besides, I think you care too much about these races. It's a bad sign. My family has been a gambling family, and you won't know till you grow up how much damage it has done. But it has done damage. I shall have to send Bassett away, and ask Uncle Oscar not to talk racing to you, unless you promise to be reasonable about it: go away to the seaside and forget it. You're all nerves!"

"I'll do what you like, mother, so long as you don't send me away till after the Derby," the boy said.

"Send you away from where? Just from this house?"

"Yes," he said, gazing at her.

"Why, you curious child, what makes you care about this house so much, suddenly? I never knew you loved it."

He gazed at her without speaking. He had a secret within a secret, something he had not divulged, even to Bassett or to his Uncle Oscar.

But his mother, after standing undecided and a little bit sullen for some moments, said:

"Very well, then! Don't go to the seaside till after the Derby, if you don't wish it. But promise me you won't let your nerves go to pieces. Promise you won't think so much about horse-racing and *events*, as you call them!"

"Oh no," said the boy casually. "I won't think much about them, mother. You needn't worry. I wouldn't worry, mother, if I were you."

"If you were me and I were you," said his mother, "I wonder what we *should* do!"

"But you know you needn't worry, mother, don't you?" the boy repeated.

"I should be awfully glad to know it," she said wearily.

"Oh, well, you *can*, you know. I mean, you *ought* to know you needn't worry," he insisted.

"Ought I? Then I'll see about it," she said.

Paul's secret of secrets was his wooden horse, that which had no name. Since he was emancipated from a nurse and a nursery-governess, he had had his rocking-horse removed to his own bedroom at the top of the house.

"Surely you're too big for a rocking-horse!" his mother had remonstrated.

"Well, you see, mother, till I can have a *real* horse, I like to have *some* sort of animal about," had been his quaint answer.

"Do you feel he keeps you company?" she laughed.

"Oh yes! He's very good, he always keeps me company, when I'm there," said Paul.

So the horse, rather shabby, stood in an arrested prance in the boy's bedroom.

The Derby was drawing near, and the boy grew more and more tense. He hardly heard what was spoken to him, he was very frail, and his eyes were really uncanny. His mother had sudden strange seizures of uneasiness about him. Sometimes, for half an hour, she would feel a sudden anxiety about him that was almost anguish. She wanted to rush to him at once, and know he was safe.

Two nights before the Derby, she was at a big party in town, when one of her rushes of anxiety about her boy, her first born, gripped her heart till she could hardly speak. She fought with the feeling, might and main, for she believed in common sense. But it was too strong. She had to leave the dance and go downstairs to telephone to the country. The children's nursery-governess was terribly surprised and startled at being rung up in the night.

"Are the children all right, Miss Wilmot?"

"Oh yes, they are quite all right."

"Master Paul? Is he all right?"

"He went to bed as right as a trivet. Shall I run up and look at him?"

"No," said Paul's mother reluctantly. "No! Don't trouble. It's all right. Don't   215
sit up. We shall be home fairly soon." She did not want her son's privacy intruded upon.

"Very good," said the governess.

It was about one o'clock when Paul's mother and father drove up to their
house. All was still. Paul's mother went to her room and slipped off her white fur
cloak. She had told her maid not to wait up for her. She heard her husband
downstairs, mixing a whisky and soda.

And then, because of the strange anxiety at her heart, she stole upstairs to her
son's room. Noiselessly she went along the upper corridor. Was there a faint
noise? What was it?

She stood, with arrested muscles, outside his door, listening. There was a
strange, heavy, and yet not loud noise. Her heart stood still. It was a soundless
noise, yet rushing and powerful. Something huge, in violent, hushed motion.
What was it? What in God's name was it? She ought to know. She felt that she
knew the noise. She knew what it was.

Yet she could not place it. She couldn't say what it was. And on and on it   220
went, like a madness.

Softly, frozen with anxiety and fear, she turned the door-handle.

The room was dark. Yet in the space near the window, she heard and saw
something plunging to and fro. She gazed in fear and amazement.

Then suddenly she switched on the light, and saw her son, in his green pyja-
mas, madly surging on the rocking-horse. The blaze of light suddenly lit him
up, as he urged the wooden horse, and lit her up, as she stood, blonde, in her
dress of pale green and crystal, in the doorway.

"Paul!" she cried. "Whatever are you doing?"

"It's Malabar!" he screamed in a powerful, strange voice. "It's Malabar!"   225

His eyes blazed at her for one strange and senseless second, as he ceased urging
his wooden horse. Then he fell with a crash to the ground, and she, all her tormented motherhood flooding upon her, rushed to gather him up.

But he was unconscious, and unconscious he remained, with some brain-fever.
He talked and tossed, and his mother sat stonily by his side.

"Malabar! Malabar! Bassett, Bassett, I *know*! It's Malabar!"

So the child cried, trying to get up and urge the rocking-horse that gave him
his inspiration.

"What does he mean by Malabar?" asked the heart-frozen mother.   230

"I don't know," said the father stonily.

"What does he mean by Malabar?" she asked her brother Oscar.

"It's one of the horses running for the Derby," was the answer.

And, in spite of himself, Oscar Cresswell spoke to Bassett, and himself put a
thousand on Malabar: at fourteen to one.

The third day of the illness was critical: they were waiting for a change.   235
The boy, with his rather long, curly hair, was tossing ceaselessly on the pillow. He neither slept nor regained consciousness, and his eyes were like blue
stones. His mother sat, feeling her heart had gone, turned actually into a
stone.

In the evening, Oscar Cresswell did not come, but Bassett sent a message, saying could he come up for one moment, just one moment? Paul's mother was very angry at the intrusion, but on second thoughts she agreed. The boy was the same. Perhaps Bassett might bring him to consciousness.

The gardener, a shortish fellow with a little brown mustache and sharp little brown eyes, tiptoed into the room, touched his imaginary cap to Paul's mother, and stole to the bedside, staring with glittering, smallish eyes at the tossing, dying child.

"Master Paul!" he whispered. "Master Paul! Malabar came in first all right, a clean win. I did as you told me. You've made over seventy thousand pounds, you have; you've got over eighty thousand. Malabar came in all right, Master Paul."

"Malabar! Malabar! Did I say Malabar, mother? Did I say Malabar? Do you think I'm lucky, mother? I knew Malabar, didn't I? Over eighty thousand pounds! I call that lucky, don't you, mother? Over eighty thousand pounds! I knew, didn't I know I knew? Malabar came in all right. If I ride my horse till I'm sure, then I tell you, Bassett, you can go as high as you like. Did you go for all you were worth, Bassett?"

"I went a thousand on it, Master Paul."   240

"I never told you, mother, that if I can ride my horse, and *get there*, then I'm absolutely sure—oh, absolutely! Mother, did I ever tell you? I *am* lucky!"

"No, you never did," said his mother.

But the boy died in the night.

And even as he lay dead, his mother heard her brother's voice saying to her: "My God, Hester, you're eighty thousand to the good, and a poor devil of a son to the bad. But, poor devil, poor devil, he's best gone out of a life where he rides his rocking-horse to find a winner."

(1932)

Questions for Discussion and Writing

1. How did you respond to the supernatural elements of "The Rocking-Horse Winner"? If you were able to suspend your disbelief as you read the story, what do you think allowed you to do so? If the unbelievable elements impaired your acceptance of the story, why? Why do you think the supernatural elements are used in the story?

2. What happens when Paul manages to present some money to his mother? Why do the voices become louder, rather than softer, over the course of the story? What does money represent to Paul and to his mother?

3. The story seems to criticize both people who think that success and failure are purely a matter of luck and those who pursue control zealously, as Paul does. How can these two criticisms be reconciled?

4. Why must Paul die in the end?

5. Most readers see the cold-hearted mother as the villain of the story. However, Oscar and Bassett take meaningful roles, too. Present a reading of the story in which you argue that the unfit mother is not the source of all evil.

William Faulkner   1897–1962

William Faulker lived most of his life in Oxford, Mississippi. He never graduated from high school or college and was rejected by the U.S. army during World War I for being too short. He worked briefly at the local post office but quit, saying he refused to be "at the beck and call of every son of a bitch with two cents in his pocket." In an interview he once observed, "The writer's only responsibility is to his art. He will be completely ruthless if he is a good one. ... If a writer has to rob his mother, he wil not hesitate; the 'Ode on a Grecian Urn' is worth any number of old ladies." He won two Pulitzer Prizes, and in 1949 he was awarded the Nobel Prize for Literature.

A Rose for Emily

I

When Miss Emily Grierson died, our whole town went to her funeral: the men through a sort of respectful affection for a fallen monument, the women mostly out of curiosity to see the inside of her house, which no one save an old manservant—a combined gardener and cook—had seen in at least ten years.

It was a big, squarish frame house that had once been white, decorated with cupolas[1] and spires and scrolled balconies in the heavily lightsome style of the seventies, set on what had once been our most select street. But garages and cotton gins had encroached and obliterated even the august names of that neighborhood; only Miss Emily's house was left, lifting its stubborn and coquettish decay above the cotton wagons and the gasoline pumps—an eyesore among eyesores. And now Miss Emily had gone to join the representatives of those august names where they lay in the cedar-bemused cemetery among the ranked and anonymous graves of Union and Confederate soldiers who fell at the battle of Jefferson.

Alive, Miss Emily had been a tradition, a duty, and a care; a sort of hereditary obligation upon the town, dating from that day in 1894 when Colonel Sartoris, the mayor—he who fathered the edict that no Negro woman should appear on the streets without an apron—remitted her taxes, the dispensation dating from the death of her father on into perpetuity. Not that Miss Emily would have accepted charity. Colonel Sartoris invented an involved tale to the effect that Miss Emily's father had loaned money to the town, which the town, as a matter of business, preferred this way of repaying. Only a man of Colonel Sartoris' generation and thought could have invented it, and only a woman could have believed it.

When the next generation, with its more modern ideas, became mayors and aldermen, this arrangement created some little dissatisfaction. On the first of the year they mailed her a tax notice. February came, and there was no reply. They wrote her a formal letter, asking her to call at the sheriff's office at her

---

[1]Ornamental turrets on a roof.

convenience. A week later the mayor wrote her himself, offering to call or to send his car for her, and received in reply a note on paper of an archaic shape, in a thin, flowing calligraphy in faded ink, to the effect that she no longer went out at all. The tax notice was also enclosed, without comment.

They called a special meeting of the Board of Aldermen. A deputation waited   5
upon her, knocked at the door through which no visitor had passed since she ceased giving china-painting lessons eight or ten years earlier. They were admitted by the old Negro into a dim hall from which a stairway mounted into still more shadow. It smelled of dust and disuse—a close, dank smell. The Negro led them into the parlor. It was furnished in heavy, leather-covered furniture. When the Negro opened the blinds of one window, they could see that the leather was cracked; and when they sat down, a faint dust rose sluggishly about their thighs, spinning with slow motes in the single sun-ray. On a tarnished gilt easel before the fireplace stood a crayon portrait of Miss Emily's father.

They rose when she entered—a small, fat woman in black, with a thin gold chain descending to her waist and vanishing into her belt, leaning on an ebony cane with a tarnished gold head. Her skeleton was small and spare; perhaps that was why what would have been merely plumpness in another was obesity in her. She looked bloated, like a body long submerged in motionless water, and of that pallid hue. Her eyes, lost in the fatty ridges of her face, looked like two small pieces of coal pressed into a lump of dough as they moved from one face to another while the visitors stated their errand.

She did not ask them to sit. She just stood in the door and listened quietly until the spokesman came to a stumbling halt. Then they could hear the invisible watch ticking at the end of the gold chain.

Her voice was dry and cold. "I have no taxes in Jefferson. Colonel Sartoris explained it to me. Perhaps one of you can gain access to the city records and satisfy yourselves."

"But we have. We are the city authorities, Miss Emily. Didn't you get a notice from the sheriff, signed by him?"

"I received a paper, yes," Miss Emily said. "Perhaps he considers himself the   10
sheriff....I have no taxes in Jefferson."

"But there is nothing on the books to show that, you see. We must go by the—"

"See Colonel Sartoris. I have no taxes in Jefferson."

"But, Miss Emily—"

"See Colonel Sartoris." (Colonel Sartoris had been dead almost ten years.) "I have no taxes in Jefferson. Tobe!" The Negro appeared. "Show these gentlemen out."

II

So she vanquished them, horse and foot, just as she had vanquished their   15
fathers thirty years before about the smell. That was two years after her father's death and a short time after her sweetheart—the one we believed would marry her—had deserted her. After her father's death she went out very little; after her sweetheart went away, people hardly saw her at all. A few of the ladies had the temerity to call, but were not received, and the only sign of life about the place was the Negro man—a young man then—going in and out with a market basket.

"Just as if a man—any man—could keep a kitchen properly," the ladies said; so they were not surprised when the smell developed. It was another link between the gross, teeming world and the high and mighty Griersons.

A neighbor, a woman, complained to the mayor, Judge Stevens, eighty years old. "But what will you have me do about it, madam?" he said.

"Why, send her word to stop it," the woman said. "Isn't there a law?"

"I'm sure that won't be necessary," Judge Stevens said. "It's probably just a snake or a rat that nigger of hers killed in the yard. I'll speak to him about it."   20

The next day he received two more complaints, one from a man who came in diffident deprecation. "We really must do something about it, Judge. I'd be the last one in the world to bother Miss Emily, but we've got to do something." That night the Board of Aldermen met—three graybeards and one younger man, a member of the rising generation.

"It's simple enough," he said. "Send her word to have her place cleaned up. Give her a certain time to do it in, and if she don't...."

"Dammit, sir," Judge Stevens said, "will you accuse a lady to her face of smelling bad?"

So the next night, after midnight, four men crossed Miss Emily's lawn and slunk about the house like burglars, sniffing along the base of the brickwork and at the cellar openings while one of them performed a regular sowing motion with his hand out of a sack slung from his shoulder. They broke open the cellar door and sprinkled lime there, and in all the outbuildings. As they recrossed the lawn, a window that had been dark was lighted and Miss Emily sat in it, the light behind her, and her upright torso motionless as that of an idol. They crept quietly across the lawn and into the shadow of the locusts that lined the street. After a week or two the smell went away.

That was when people had begun to feel really sorry for her. People in our town, remembering how old lady Wyatt, her great-aunt, had gone completely crazy at last, believed that the Griersons held themselves a little too high for what they really were. None of the young men were quite good enough for Miss Emily and such. We had long thought of them as a tableau,[2] Miss Emily a slender figure in white in the background, her father a spraddled silhouette in the foreground, his back to her and clutching a horsewhip, the two of them framed by the back-flung front door. So when she got to be thirty and was still single, we were not pleased exactly, but vindicated; even with insanity in the family she wouldn't have turned down all of her chances if they had really materialized.   25

When her father died, it got about that the house was all that was left to her; and in a way, people were glad. At last they could pity Miss Emily. Being left alone, and a pauper, she had become humanized. Now she too would know the old thrill and the old despair of a penny more or less.

The day after his death all the ladies prepared to call at the house and offer condolence and aid, as is our custom. Miss Emily met them at the door, dressed as usual and with no trace of grief on her face. She told them that her father was not dead. She did that for three days, with the ministers calling on her, and the doctors, trying to persuade her to let them dispose of the body. Just as they were about to resort to law and force, she broke down, and they buried her father quickly.

---

[2]A living picture created by silent, motionless actors.

We did not say she was crazy then. We believed she had to do that. We remembered all the young men her father had driven away, and we knew that with nothing left, she would have to cling to that which had robbed her, as people will.

III

She was sick for a long time. When we saw her again, her hair was cut short, making her look like a girl, with a vague resemblance to those angels in colored church windows—sort of tragic and serene.

The town had just let the contracts for paving the sidewalks, and in the 30 summer after her father's death they began the work. The construction company came with niggers and mules and machinery, and a foreman named Homer Barron, a Yankee—a big, dark, ready man, with a big voice and eyes lighter than his face. The little boys would follow in groups to hear him cuss the niggers, and the niggers singing in time to the rise and fall of picks. Pretty soon he knew everybody in town. Whenever you heard a lot of laughing anywhere about the square, Homer Barron would be in the center of the group. Presently, we began to see him and Miss Emily on Sunday afternoons driving in the yellow-wheeled buggy and the matched team of bays from the livery stable.

At first we were glad that Miss Emily would have an interest, because the ladies all said, "Of course a Grierson would not think seriously of a Northerner, a day laborer." But there were still others, older people, who said that even grief could not cause a real lady to forget *noblesse oblige*[3]—without calling it *noblesse oblige*. They just said, "Poor Emily. Her kinsfolk should come to her." She had some kin in Alabama; but years ago her father had fallen out with them over the estate of old lady Wyatt, the crazy woman, and there was no communication between the two families. They had not even been represented at the funeral.

And as soon as the old people said, "Poor Emily," the whispering began. "Do you suppose it's really so?" they said to one another. "Of course it is. What else could…" This behind their hands; rustling of craned silk and satin behind jalousies[4] closed upon the sun of Sunday afternoon as the thin, swift clop-clop-clop of the matched team passed: "Poor Emily."

She carried her head high enough—even when we believed that she was fallen. It was as if she demanded more than ever the recognition of her dignity as the last Grierson; as if it had wanted that touch of earthiness to reaffirm her imperviousness. Like when she bought the rat poison, the arsenic. That was over a year after they had begun to say "Poor Emily," and while the two female cousins were visiting her.

"I want some poison," she said to the druggist. She was over thirty then, still a slight woman, though thinner than usual, with cold, haughty black eyes in a face the flesh of which was strained across the temples and about the eye-sockets as you imagine a lighthouse-keeper's face ought to look. "I want some poison," she said.

"Yes, Miss Emily. What kind? For rats and such? I'd recom—" 35
"I want the best you have. I don't care what kind."

---

[3]The obligation of those of noble birth to behave honorably.
[4]Window blinds with slats that open and close.

The druggist named several. "They'll kill anything up to an elephant. But what you want is—"

"Arsenic," Miss Emily said. "Is that a good one?"

"Is...arsenic? Yes, ma'am. But what you want—"

"I want arsenic."   40

The druggist looked down at her. She looked back at him, erect, her face like a strained flag. "Why, of course," the druggist said. "If that's what you want. But the law requires you to tell what you are going to use it for."

Miss Emily just stared at him, her head tilted back in order to look him eye for eye, until he looked away and went and got the arsenic and wrapped it up. The Negro delivery boy brought her the package; the druggist didn't come back. When she opened the package at home there was written on the box, under the skull and bones: "For rats."

IV

So the next day we all said, "She will kill herself"; and we said it would be the best thing. When she had first begun to be seen with Homer Barron, we had said, "She will marry him." Then we said, "She will persuade him yet," because Homer himself had remarked—he liked men, and it was known that he drank with the younger men in the Elks' Club—that he was not a marrying man. Later we said, "Poor Emily" behind the jalousies as they passed on Sunday afternoon in the glittering buggy, Miss Emily with her head high and Homer Barron with his hat cocked and a cigar in his teeth, reins and whip in a yellow glove.

Then some of the ladies began to say that it was a disgrace to the town and a bad example to the young people. The men did not want to interfere, but at last the ladies forced the Baptist minister—Miss Emily's people were Episcopal—to call upon her. He would never divulge what happened during that interview, but he refused to go back again. The next Sunday they again drove about the streets, and the following day the minister's wife wrote to Miss Emily's relations in Alabama.

So she had blood-kin under her roof again and we sat back to watch devel-   45
opments. At first nothing happened. Then we were sure that they were to be married. We learned that Miss Emily had been to the jeweler's and ordered a man's toilet set in silver, with the letters H.B. on each piece. Two days later we learned that she had bought a complete outfit of men's clothing, including a nightshirt, and we said, "They are married." We were really glad. We were glad because the two female cousins were even more Grierson than Miss Emily had ever been.

So we were not surprised when Homer Barron—the streets had been finished some time since—was gone. We were a little disappointed that there was not a pub-lic blowing-off, but we believed that he had gone on to prepare for Miss Emily's coming, or to give her a chance to get rid of the cousins. (By that time it was a cabal, and we were all Miss Emily's allies to help circumvent the cousins.) Sure enough, after another week they departed. And, as we had expected all along, within three days Homer Barron was back in town. A neighbor saw the Negro man admit him at the kitchen door at dusk one evening.

And that was the last we saw of Homer Barron. And of Miss Emily for some time. The Negro man went in and out with the market basket, but the front door remained closed. Now and then we would see her at the window for a moment, as the men did that night when they sprinkled the lime, but for almost six months she did not appear on the streets. Then we knew that this was to be expected too; as if that quality of her father which had thwarted her woman's life so many times had been too virulent and too furious to die.

When we next saw Miss Emily, she had grown fat and her hair was turning gray. During the next few years it grew grayer and grayer until it attained an even pepper-and-salt iron-gray, when it ceased turning. Up to the day of her death at seventy-four it was still that vigorous iron-gray, like the hair of an active man.

From that time on her front door remained closed, save during a period of six or seven years, when she was about forty, during which she gave lessons in china-painting. She fitted up a studio in one of the downstairs rooms, where the daughters and granddaughters of Colonel Sartoris' contemporaries were sent to her with the same regularity and in the same spirit that they were sent to church on Sundays with a twenty-five-cent piece for the collection plate. Meanwhile her taxes had been remitted.

Then the newer generation became the backbone and the spirit of the town, 50 and the painting pupils grew up and fell away and did not send their children to her with boxes of color and tedious brushes and pictures cut from the ladies' magazines. The front door closed upon the last one and remained closed for good. When the town got free postal delivery, Miss Emily alone refused to let them fasten the metal numbers above her door and attach a mailbox to it. She would not listen to them.

Daily, monthly, yearly we watched the Negro grow grayer and more stooped, going in and out with the market basket. Each December we sent her a tax notice, which would be returned by the post office a week later, unclaimed. Now and then we would see her in one of the downstairs windows—she had evidently shut up the top floor of the house—like the carven torso of an idol in a niche, looking or not looking at us, we could never tell which. Thus she passed from generation to generation—dear, inescapable, impervious, tranquil, and perverse.

And so she died. Fell ill in the house filled with dust and shadows, with only a doddering Negro man to wait on her. We did not even know she was sick; we had long since given up trying to get any information from the Negro. He talked to no one, probably not even to her, for his voice had grown harsh and rusty, as if from disuse.

She died in one of the downstairs rooms, in a heavy walnut bed with a curtain, her gray head propped on a pillow yellow and moldy with age and lack of sunlight.

V

The Negro met the first of the ladies at the front door and let them in, with their hushed, sibilant voices and their quick, curious glances, and then he disappeared. He walked right through the house and out the back and was not seen again.

The two female cousins came at once. They held the funeral on the second 55 day, with the town coming to look at Miss Emily beneath a mass of bought flowers, with the crayon face of her father musing profoundly above the bier and the ladies sibilant and macabre; and the very old men—some in their brushed Confederate uniforms—on the porch and the lawn, talking of Miss Emily as if she had been a contemporary of theirs, believing that they had danced with her and courted her perhaps, confusing time with its mathematical progression, as the old do, to whom all the past is not a diminishing road but, instead, a huge meadow which no winter ever quite touches, divided from them now by the narrow bottle-neck of the most recent decade of years.

Already we knew that there was one room in that region above stairs which no one had seen in forty years, and which would have to be forced. They waited until Miss Emily was decently in the ground before they opened it.

The violence of breaking down the door seemed to fill this room with pervading dust. A thin, acrid pall as of the tomb seemed to lie everywhere upon this room decked and furnished as for a bridal: upon the valance curtains of faded rose color, upon the rose-shaded lights, upon the dressing table, upon the delicate array of crystal and the man's toilet things backed with tarnished silver, silver so tarnished that the monogram was obscured. Among them lay a collar and tie, as if they had just been removed, which, lifted, left upon the surface a pale crescent in the dust. Upon a chair hung the suit, carefully folded; beneath it the two mute shoes and the discarded socks.

The man himself lay in the bed.

For a long while we just stood there, looking down at the profound and fleshless grin. The body had apparently once lain in the attitude of an embrace, but now the long sleep that outlasts love, that conquers even the grimace of love, had cuckolded him. What was left of him, rotted beneath what was left of the nightshirt, had become inextricable from the bed in which he lay; and upon him and upon the pillow beside him lay that even coating of the patient and biding dust.

Then we noticed that in the second pillow was the indentation of a head. 60 One of us lifted something from it, and leaning forward, that faint and invisible dust dry and acrid in the nostrils, we saw a long strand of iron-gray hair.

(1931)

Questions for Discussion and Writing

1. What does Faulkner achieve by disrupting the chronology of Miss Emily's story?
2. How would you describe the point of view here? Do you find it effective? Why or why not?
3. What kind of person is Emily Grierson? Why does she live in the past? How do the townspeople feel about her? How do you feel about her?
4. What kind of person is Homer Barron? Why do the townspeople consider him not good enough for Miss Emily?
5. Write an essay arguing that Emily Grierson's relationship with her father contributed to her tragedy.

Ernest Hemingway 1899–1961

Ernest Hemingway was born in Oak Park, a Chicago suburb he described as a "town of wide lawns and narrow minds." Rather than attend college, he became a newspaper reporter, a job that helped develop his spare, forceful writing style. As a volunteer ambulance driver in World War I, Hemingway was seriously wounded. He married the first of his four wives in

1921 and took her to Paris, where he worked as a foreign correspondent, wrote fiction, and became a voice of the "Lost Generation" of American expatriates. In 1954 he won the Nobel Prize for Literature. When he was sixty-two and terminally ill with cancer, he committed suicide by shooting himself with a shotgun.

Hills Like White Elephants*

The hills across the valley of the Ebro[1] were long and white. On this side there was no shade and no trees and the station was between two lines of rails in the sun. Close against the side of the station there was the warm shadow of the building and a curtain, made of strings of bamboo beads, hung across the open door into the bar, to keep out flies. The American and the girl with him sat at a table in the shade, outside the building. It was very hot and the express from Barcelona would come in forty minutes. It stopped at this junction for two minutes and went on to Madrid.

"What should we drink?" the girl asked. She had taken off her hat and put it on the table.

"It's pretty hot," the man said.

"Let's drink beer."

"Dos cervezas," the man said into the curtain.   5

"Big ones?" a woman asked from the doorway.

"Yes. Two big ones."

The woman brought two glasses of beer and two felt pads. She put the felt pads and the beer glasses on the table and looked at the man and the girl. The girl was looking off at the line of hills. They were white in the sun and the country was brown and dry.

"They look like white elephants," she said.

"I've never seen one," the man drank his beer.   10

"No, you wouldn't have."

"I might have," the man said. "Just because you say I wouldn't have doesn't prove anything."

The girl looked at the bead curtain. "They've painted something on it," she said. "What does it say?"

"Anis del Toro. It's a drink."

"Could we try it?"   15

The man called "Listen" through the curtain. The woman came out from the bar.

"Four reales."[2]

"We want two Anis del Toro."

"With water?"

"Do you want it with water?"   20

"I don't know," the girl said. "Is it good with water?"

---

[1]A river in Spain.
[2]Spanish coins.

"It's all right."

"You want them with water?" asked the woman.

"Yes, with water."

"It tastes like licorice," the girl said and put the glass down.   25

"That's the way with everything."

"Yes," said the girl. "Everything tastes of licorice. Especially all the things you've waited so long for, like absinthe."

"Oh, cut it out."

"You started it," the girl said. "I was being amused. I was having a fine time."

"Well, let's try and have a fine time."   30

"All right. I was trying. I said the mountains looked like white elephants. Wasn't that bright?"

"That was bright."

"I wanted to try this new drink. That's all we do, isn't it—look at things and try new drinks?"

"I guess so."

The girl looked across at the hills.   35

"They're lovely hills," she said. "They don't really look like white elephants. I just meant the coloring of their skin through the trees."

"Should we have another drink?"

"All right."

The warm wind blew the bead curtain against the table.

"The beer's nice and cool," the man said.   40

"It's lovely," the girl said.

"It's really an awfully simple operation, Jig," the man said. "It's not really an operation at all."

The girl looked at the ground the table legs rested on.

"I know you wouldn't mind it, Jig. It's really not anything. It's just to let the air in."

The girl did not say anything.

"I'll go with you and I'll stay with you all the time. They just let the air in and   45
then it's all perfectly natural."

"Then what will we do afterward?"

"We'll be fine afterward. Just like we were before."

"What makes you think so?"

"That's the only thing that bothers us. It's the only thing that's made us unhappy."   50

The girl looked at the bead curtain, put her hand out and took hold of two of the strings of beads.

"And you think then we'll be all right and be happy."

"I know we will. You don't have to be afraid. I've known lots of people that have done it."

"So have I," said the girl. "And afterward they were all so happy."

"Well," the man said, "if you don't want to you don't have to. I wouldn't have you do it if you didn't want to. But I know it's perfectly simple."   55

"And you really want to?"

"I think it's the best thing to do. But I don't want you to do it if you don't really want to."

"And if I do it you'll be happy and things will be like they were and you'll love me?"

"I love you now. You know I love you."

"I know. But if I do it, then it will be nice again if I say things are like white   60
elephants, and you'll like it?"

"I'll love it. I love it now but I just can't think about it. You know how I get
when I worry."

"If I do it you won't ever worry?"

"I won't worry about that because it's perfectly simple."

"Then I'll do it. Because I don't care about me."

"What do you mean?"   65

"I don't care about me."

"Well, I care about you."

"Oh, yes. But I don't care about me. And I'll do it and then everything will be
fine."

"I don't want you to do it if you feel that way."

The girl stood up and walked to the end of the station. Across, on the other   70
side, were fields of grain and trees along the banks of the Ebro. Far away, beyond the river, were mountains. The shadow of a cloud moved across the field
of grain and she saw the river through the trees.

"And we could have all this," she said. "And we could have everything and
every day we make it more impossible."

"What did you say?"

"I said we could have everything."

"We can have everything."

"No, we can't."   75

"We can have the whole world."

"No, we can't."

"We can go everywhere."

"No, we can't. It isn't ours any more."

"It's ours."   80

"No, it isn't. And once they take it away, you never get it back."

"But they haven't taken it away."

"We'll wait and see."

"Come on back in the shade," he said. "You mustn't feel that way."

"I don't feel any way," the girl said. "I just know things."   85

"I don't want you to do anything that you don't want to do—"

"Nor that isn't good for me," she said. "I know. Could we have another
beer?"

"All right. But you've got to realize—"

"I realize," the girl said. "Can't we maybe stop talking?"

They sat down at the table and the girl looked across at the hills on the dry   90
side of the valley and the man looked at her and at the table.

"You've got to realize," he said, "that I don't want you to do it if you don't
want to. I'm perfectly willing to go through with it if it means anything to you."

"Doesn't it mean anything to you? We could get along."

"Of course it does. But I don't want anybody but you. I don't want anyone
else. And I know it's perfectly simple."

"Yes, you know it's perfectly simple."

"It's all right for you to say that, but I do know it."   95

"Would you do something for me now?"

"I'd do anything for you."

"Would you please please please please please please please stop talking?"

He did not say anything but looked at the bags against the wall of the station. There were labels on them from all the hotels where they had spent nights.

"But I don't want you to," he said. "I don't care anything about it." 100

"I'll scream," the girl said.

The woman came out through the curtains with two glasses of beer and put them down on the damp felt pads. "The train comes in five minutes," she said.

"What did she say?" asked the girl.

"That the train is coming in five minutes."

The girl smiled brightly at the woman, to thank her. 105

"I'd better take the bags over to the other side of the station," the man said. She smiled at him.

"All right. Then come back and we'll finish the beer."

He picked up the two heavy bags and carried them around the station to the other tracks. He looked up the tracks but could not see the train. Coming back, he walked through the barroom, where people waiting for the train were drinking. He drank an Anis at the bar and looked at the people. They were all waiting reasonably for the train. He went out through the bead curtain. She was sitting at the table and smiled at him.

"Do you feel better?" he asked.

"I feel fine," she said. "There's nothing wrong with me. I feel fine." 110

(1927)

Questions for Discussion and Writing

1. How would you describe the point of view in this story?
2. The number *two* is used ten times in the story. What is the significance of this repetition? (Note especially the two parallel train tracks and the two strings of beads that do not intersect: Do they suggest anything about the characters' lives?)
3. What is the main point or theme of the story? What is the central issue between the lovers?
4. What is a "white elephant"? Explain the story's title.
5. Write an essay in which you argue that Jig will (or will not) do what her lover wants.

John Steinbeck   *1902–1968*

John Steinbeck was born in Salinas, California, where he worked as a fruit-picker, hod carrier, and ranch hand. After high school graduation, he continued working at menial jobs while taking classes in marine biology at Stanford University. In 1925, he went to New York City to become a writer. He got a job as a laborer on the building of Madison Square Garden but could not get published, so he moved back to California. His early works met with little success, but *Tortilla Flat* (1935) became a best seller and received the California Commonwealth Club's Gold Medal for best novel by a California author. Steinbeck went on to write a number of highly successful novels and stories. In 1962 he was awarded the Nobel Prize for Literature.

The Chrysanthemums

The high gray-flannel fog of winter closed off the Salinas Valley from the sky and from all the rest of the world. On every side it sat like a lid on the mountains and made of the great valley a closed pot. On the broad, level land floor the gang plows bit deep and left the black earth shining like metal where the shares had cut. On the foothill ranches across the Salinas River, the yellow stubble fields seemed to be bathed in pale cold sunshine, but there was no sunshine in the valley now in December. The thick willow scrub along the river flamed with sharp and positive yellow leaves.

It was a time of quiet and of waiting. The air was cold and tender. A light wind blew up from the southwest so that the farmers were mildly hopeful of a good rain before long; but fog and rain do not go together.

Across the river, on Henry Allen's foothill ranch there was little work to be done, for the hay was cut and stored and the orchards were plowed up to receive the rain deeply when it should come. The cattle on the higher slopes were becoming shaggy and rough-coated.

Elisa Allen, working in her flower garden, looked down across the yard and saw Henry, her husband, talking to two men in business suits. The three of them stood by the tractor shed, each man with one foot on the side of the little Fordson. They smoked cigarettes and studied the machine as they talked.

Elisa watched them for a moment and then went back to her work. She 5 was thirty-five. Her face was lean and strong and her eyes were as clear as water. Her figure looked blocked and heavy in her gardening costume, a man's black hat pulled down over her eyes, clodhopper shoes, a figured print dress almost completely covered by a big corduroy apron with four big pockets to hold the snips, the trowel and scratcher, the seeds and the knife she worked with. She wore heavy leather gloves to protect her hands while she worked.

She was cutting down the old year's chrysanthemum stalks with a pair of short and powerful scissors. She looked down toward the men by the tractor shed now and then. Her face was eager and mature and handsome; even her work with the scissors was over-eager, over-powerful. The chrysanthemum stems seemed too small and easy for her energy.

She brushed a cloud of hair out of her eyes with the back of her glove, and left a smudge of earth on her cheek in doing it. Behind her stood the neat white farm house with red geraniums close-banked around it as high as the windows. It was a hard-swept looking little house, with hard-polished windows, and a clean mud-mat on the front steps.

Elisa cast another glance toward the tractor shed. The strangers were getting into their Ford coupe. She took off a glove and put her strong fingers down into the forest of new green chrysanthemum sprouts that were growing around the old roots. She spread the leaves and looked down among the close-growing stems. No aphids were there, no sowbugs or snails or cutworms. Her terrier fingers destroyed such pests before they could get started.

Elisa started at the sound of her husband's voice. He had come near quietly, and he leaned over the wire fence that protected her flower garden from cattle and dogs and chickens.

"At it again," he said. "You've got a strong new crop coming." 10

Elisa straightened her back and pulled on the gardening glove again. "Yes. They'll be strong this coming year." In her tone and on her face there was a little smugness.

"You've got a gift with things," Henry observed. "Some of those yellow chrysanthemums you had this year were ten inches across. I wish you'd work out in the orchard and raise some apples that big."

Her eyes sharpened. "Maybe I could do it, too. I've a gift with things, all right. My mother had it. She could stick anything in the ground and make it grow. She said it was having planters' hands that knew how to do it."

"Well, it sure works with flowers," he said.

"Henry, who were those men you were talking to?" 15

"Why, sure, that's what I came to tell you. They were from the Western Meat Company. I sold them those thirty head of three-year-old steers. Got nearly my own price, too."

"Good," she said. "Good for you."

"And I thought," he continued, "I thought how it's Saturday afternoon, and we might go into Salinas for dinner at a restaurant, and then to a picture show— to celebrate, you see."

"Good," she repeated. "Oh, yes. That will be good."

Henry put on his joking tone. "There's fights tonight. How'd you like to go 20 to the fights?"

"Oh, no," she said breathlessly. "No, I wouldn't like fights."

"Just fooling, Elisa. We'll go to a movie. Let's see. It's two now. I'm going to take Scotty and bring down those steers from the hill. It'll take us maybe two hours. We'll go in town about five and have dinner at the Cominos Hotel. Like that?"

"Of course I'll like it. It's good to eat away from home."

"All right, then. I'll go get up a couple of horses."

She said, "I'll have plenty of time to transplant some of these sets, I guess." 25

She heard her husband calling Scotty down by the barn. And a little later she saw the two men ride up the pale yellow hillside in search of the steers.

There was a little square sandy bed kept for rooting the chrysanthemums. With her trowel she turned the soil over and over, and smoothed it and patted it firm. Then she dug ten parallel trenches to receive the sets. Back at the chrysanthemum bed she pulled out the little crisp shoots, trimmed off the leaves of each one with her scissors and laid it on a small orderly pile.

A squeak of wheels and plod of hoofs came from the road. Elisa looked up. The country road ran along the dense bank of willows and cottonwoods that bordered the river, and up this road came a curious vehicle, curiously drawn. It was an old spring-wagon, with a round canvas top on it like the cover of a prairie schooner. It was drawn by an old bay horse and a little gray-and-white burro. A big stubble-bearded man sat between the cover flaps and drove the crawling team. Underneath the wagon, between the hind wheels, a lean and rangy mongrel dog walked sedately. Words were painted on the canvas, in clumsy, crooked letters. "Pots, pans, knives, sisors, lawn mores, Fixed." Two rows of articles, and the triumphantly definitive "Fixed" below. The black paint had run down in little sharp points beneath each letter.

Elisa, squatting on the ground, watched to see the crazy, loose-jointed wagon pass by. But it didn't pass. It turned into the farm road in front of her house, crooked old wheels skirling and squeaking. The rangy dog darted from between the wheels and ran ahead. Instantly the two ranch shepherds flew out at him. Then all three stopped, and with stiff and quivering tails, with taut straight legs, with ambassadorial dignity, they slowly circled, sniffing daintily. The caravan pulled up to Elisa's wire fence and stopped. Now the newcomer dog, feeling out-numbered, lowered his tail and retired under the wagon with raised hackles and bared teeth.

The man on the wagon seat called out, "That's a bad dog in a fight when he gets started."   30

Elisa laughed. "I see he is. How soon does he generally get started?"

The man caught up her laughter and echoed it heartily. "Sometimes not for weeks and weeks," he said. He climbed stiffly down, over the wheel. The horse and the donkey drooped like unwatered flowers.

Elisa saw that he was a very big man. Although his hair and beard were gray-ing, he did not look old. His worn black suit was wrinkled and spotted with grease. The laughter had disappeared from his face and eyes the moment his laughing voice ceased. His eyes were dark, and they were full of the brooding that gets in the eyes of teamsters and of sailors. The calloused hands he rested on the wire fence were cracked, and every crack was a black line. He took off his battered hat.

"I'm off my general road, ma'am," he said. "Does this dirt road cut over across the river to the Los Angeles highway?"

Elisa stood up and shoved the thick scissors in her apron pocket. "Well, yes, it does, but it winds around and then fords the river. I don't think your team could pull through the sand."   35

He replied with some asperity, "It might surprise you what them beasts can pull through."

"When they get started?" she asked.

He smiled for a second. "Yes. When they get started."

"Well," said Elisa, "I think you'll save time if you go back to the Salinas road and pick up the highway there."

He drew a big finger down the chicken wire and made it sing. "I ain't in any hurry, ma'am. I go from Seattle to San Diego and back every year. Takes all my time. About six months each way. I aim to follow nice weather."   40

Elisa took off her gloves and stuffed them in the apron pocket with the scissors. She touched the under edge of her man's hat, searching for fugitive hairs. "That sounds like a nice kind of way to live," she said.

He leaned confidentially over the fence. "Maybe you noticed the writing on my wagon. I mend pots and sharpen knives and scissors. You got any of them things to do?"

"Oh, no," she said quickly. "Nothing like that." Her eyes hardened with resistance.

"Scissors is the worst thing," he explained. "Most people just ruin scissors trying to sharpen 'em, but I know how. I got a special tool. It's a little bobbit kind of thing, and patented. But it sure does the trick."

"No. My scissors are all sharp."   45

"All right, then. Take a pot," he continued earnestly, "a bent pot, or a pot with a hole. I can make it like new so you don't have to buy no new ones. That's a saving for you."

"No," she said shortly. "I tell you I have nothing like that for you to do."

His face fell to an exaggerated sadness. His voice took on a whining undertone. "I ain't had a thing to do today. Maybe I won't have no supper tonight. You see I'm off my regular road. I know folks on the highway clear from Seattle to San Diego. They save their things for me to sharpen up because they know I do it so good and save them money."

"I'm sorry," Elisa said irritably. "I haven't anything for you to do."

His eyes left her face and fell to searching the ground. They roamed about 50 until they came to the chrysanthemum bed where she had been working. "What's them plants, ma'am?"

The irritation and resistance melted from Elisa's face. "Oh, those are chrysanthemums, giant whites and yellows. I raise them every year, bigger than anybody around here."

"Kind of a long-stemmed flower? Looks like a quick puff of colored smoke?" he asked.

"That's it. What a nice way to describe them."

"They smell kind of nasty till you get used to them," he said.

"It's a good bitter smell," she retorted, "not nasty at all." 55

He changed his tone quickly. "I like the smell myself."

"I had ten-inch blooms this year," she said.

The man leaned farther over the fence. "Look. I know a lady down the road a piece, has got the nicest garden you ever seen. Got nearly every kind of flower but no chrysanthemums. Last time I was mending a copper-bottom washtub for her (that's a hard job but I do it good), she said to me, 'If you ever run acrost some nice chrysanthemums I wish you'd try to get me a few seeds.' That's what she told me."

Elisa's eyes grew alert and eager. "She couldn't have known much about chrysanthemums. You *can* raise them from seed, but it's much easier to root the little sprouts you see there."

"Oh," he said. "I s'pose I can't take none to her, then." 60

"Why yes you can," Elisa cried. "I can put some in damp sand, and you can carry them right along with you. They'll take root in the pot if you keep them damp. And then she can transplant them."

"She'd sure like to have some, ma'am. You say they're nice ones?"

"Beautiful," she said. "Oh, beautiful." Her eyes shone. She tore off the battered hat and shook out her dark pretty hair. "I'll put them in a flower pot, and you can take them right with you. Come into the yard."

While the man came through the picket gate Elisa ran excitedly along the geranium-bordered path to the back of the house. And she returned carrying a big red flower pot. The gloves were forgotten now. She kneeled on the ground by the starting bed and dug up the sandy soil with her fingers and scooped it into the bright new flower pot. Then she picked up the little pile of shoots she had prepared. With her strong fingers she pressed them into the sand and tamped around them with her knuckles. The man stood over her. "I'll tell you what to do," she said. "You remember so you can tell the lady."

"Yes, I'll try to remember." 65

"Well, look. These will take root in about a month. Then she must set them out, about a foot apart in good rich earth like this, see?" She lifted a handful of dark soil for him to look at. "They'll grow fast and tall. Now remember this: In July tell her to cut them down, about eight inches from the ground."

"Before they bloom?" he asked.

"Yes, before they bloom." Her face was tight with eagerness. "They'll grow right up again. About the last of September the buds will start."

She stopped and seemed perplexed. "It's the budding that takes the most care," she said hesitantly. "I don't know how to tell you." She looked deep into his eyes, searchingly. Her mouth opened a little, and she seemed to be listening. "I'll try to tell you," she said. "Did you ever hear of planting hands?"

"Can't say I have, ma'am."

"Well, I can only tell you what it feels like. It's when you're picking off the buds you don't want. Everything goes right down into your fingertips. You watch your fingers work. They do it themselves. You can feel how it is. They pick and pick the buds. They never make a mistake. They're with the plant. Do you see? Your fingers and the plant. You can feel that, right up your arm. They know. They never make a mistake. You can feel it. When you're like that you can't do anything wrong. Do you see that? Can you understand that?"

She was kneeling on the ground looking up at him. Her breast swelled passionately.

The man's eyes narrowed. He looked away self-consciously. "Maybe I know," he said. "Sometimes in the night in the wagon there—"

Elisa's voice grew husky. She broke in on him, "I've never lived as you do, but I know what you mean. When the night is dark—why, the stars are sharp-pointed, and there's quiet. Why, you rise up and up! Every pointed star gets driven into your body. It's like that. Hot and sharp and—lovely."

Kneeling there, her hand went out toward his legs in the greasy black trousers. Her hesitant fingers almost touched the cloth. Then her hand dropped to the ground. She crouched low like a fawning dog.

He said, "It's nice, just like you say. Only when you don't have no dinner, it ain't."

She stood up then, very straight, and her face was ashamed. She held the flower pot out to him and placed it gently in his arms. "Here. Put it in your wagon, on the seat, where you can watch it. Maybe I can find something for you to do."

At the back of the house she dug in the can pile and found two old and battered aluminum saucepans. She carried them back and gave them to him. "Here, maybe you can fix these."

His manner changed. He became professional. "Good as new I can fix them." At the back of his wagon he set a little anvil, and out of an oily tool box dug a small machine hammer. Elisa came through the gate to watch him while he pounded out the dents in the kettles. His mouth grew sure and knowing. At a difficult part of the work he sucked his underlip.

"You sleep right in the wagon?" Elisa asked.

"Right in the wagon, ma'am. Rain or shine I'm dry as a cow in there."

"It must be nice," she said. "It must be very nice. I wish women could do such things."

"It ain't the right kind of life for a woman."

Her upper lip raised a little, showing her teeth. "How do you know? How can you tell?" she said.

"I don't know, ma'am," he protested. "Of course I don't know. Now here's your kettles, done. You don't have to buy no new ones."

"How much?"

"Oh, fifty cents'll do. I keep my prices down and my work good. That's why I have all them satisfied customers up and down the highway."

Elisa brought him a fifty-cent piece from the house and dropped it in his hand. "You might be surprised to have a rival some time. I can sharpen scissors, too. And I can beat the dents out of little pots. I could show you what a woman might do."

He put his hammer back in the oily box and shoved the little anvil out of sight. "It would be a lonely life for a woman, ma'am, and a scary life, too, with animals creeping under the wagon all night." He climbed over the singletree, steadying himself with a hand on the burro's white rump. He settled himself in the seat, picked up the lines. "Thank you kindly, ma'am," he said. "I'll do like you told me; I'll go back and catch the Salinas road."

"Mind," she called, "if you're long in getting there, keep the sand damp."   90

"Sand, ma'am? ... Sand? Oh, sure. You mean around the chrysanthemums. Sure I will." He clucked his tongue. The beasts leaned luxuriously into their collars. The mongrel dog took his place between the back wheels. The wagon turned and crawled out the entrance road and back the way it had come, along the river.

Elisa stood in front of her wire fence watching the slow progress of the caravan. Her shoulders were straight, her head thrown back, her eyes half-closed, so that the scene came vaguely into them. Her lips moved silently, forming the words "Good-bye—good-bye." Then she whispered, "That's a bright direction. There's a glowing there." The sound of her whisper startled her. She shook herself free and looked about to see whether anyone had been listening. Only the dogs had heard. They lifted their heads toward her from their sleeping in the dust, and then stretched out their chins and settled asleep again. Elisa turned and ran hurriedly into the house.

In the kitchen she reached behind the stove and felt the water tank. It was full of hot water from the noonday cooking. In the bathroom she tore off her soiled clothes and flung them into the corner. And then she scrubbed herself with a little block of pumice, legs and thighs, loins and chest and arms, until her skin was scratched and red. When she had dried herself she stood in front of a mirror in her bedroom and looked at her body. She tightened her stomach and threw out her chest. She turned and looked over her shoulder at her back.

After a while she began to dress slowly. She put on her newest underclothing and her nicest stockings and the dress which was the symbol of her prettiness. She worked carefully on her hair, penciled her eyebrows and rouged her lips.

Before she was finished she heard the little thunder of hoofs and the shouts of   95
Henry and his helper as they drove the red steers into the corral. She heard the gate bang shut and set herself for Henry's arrival.

His steps sounded on the porch. He entered the house calling, "Elisa, where are you?"

"In my room, dressing. I'm not ready. There's hot water for your bath. Hurry up. It's getting late."

When she heard him splashing in the tub, Elisa laid his dark suit on the bed, and shirt and socks and tie beside it. She stood his polished shoes on the floor beside the bed. Then she went to the porch and sat primly and stiffly down. She looked toward the river road where the willow-line was still yellow with frosted leaves so that under the high gray fog they seemed a thin band of sunshine. This was the only color in the gray afternoon. She sat unmoving for a long time. Her eyes blinked rarely.

Henry came banging out of the door, shoving his tie inside his vest as he came. Elisa stiffened and her face grew tight. Henry stopped short and looked at her. "Why—why, Elisa. You look so nice!"

"Nice? You think I look nice? What do you mean by 'nice'?"   100

Henry blundered on. "I don't know. I mean you look different, strong and happy."

"I am strong? Yes, strong. What do you mean 'strong'?"

He looked bewildered. "You're playing some kind of a game," he said helplessly. "It's a kind of a play. You look strong enough to break a calf over your knee, happy enough to eat it like a watermelon."

For a second she lost her rigidity. "Henry! Don't talk like that. You didn't know what you said." She grew complete again. "I'm strong," she boasted. "I never knew before how strong."

Henry looked down toward the tractor shed, and when he brought his eyes   105
back to her, they were his own again. "I'll get out the car. You can put on your coat while I'm starting."

Elisa went into the house. She heard him drive to the gate and idle down his motor, and then she took a long time to put on her hat. She pulled it here and pressed it there. When Henry turned the motor off she slipped into her coat and went out.

The little roadster bounced along on the dirt road by the river, raising the birds and driving the rabbits into the brush. Two cranes flapped heavily over the willow-line and dropped into the riverbed.

Far ahead on the road Elisa saw a dark speck. She knew.

She tried not to look as they passed it, but her eyes would not obey. She whispered to herself sadly, "He might have thrown them off the road. That wouldn't have been much trouble, not very much. But he kept the pot," she explained. "He had to keep the pot. That's why he couldn't get them off the road."

The roadster turned a bend and she saw the caravan ahead. She swung full   110
around toward her husband so she could not see the little covered wagon and the mismatched team as the car passed them.

In a moment it was over. The thing was done. She did not look back.

She said loudly, to be heard above the motor, "It will be good, tonight, a good dinner."

"Now you're changed again," Henry complained. He took one hand from the wheel and patted her knee. "I ought to take you in to dinner oftener. It would be good for both of us. We get so heavy out on the ranch."

"Henry," she asked, "could we have wine at dinner?"

"Sure we could. Say! That will be fine."   115

She was silent for a while; then she said, "Henry, at those prize fights, do the men hurt each other very much?"

"Sometimes a little, not often. Why?"

"Well, I've read how they break noses, and blood runs down their chests. I've read how the fighting gloves get heavy and soggy with blood."

He looked around at her. "What's the matter, Elisa? I didn't know you read things like that." He brought the car to a stop, then turned to the right over the Salinas River bridge.

"Do any women ever go to the fights?" she asked.   120

"Oh, sure, some. What's the matter, Elisa? Do you want to go? I don't think you'd like it, but I'll take you if you really want to go."

MARITAL RATING SCALE
WIFE'S CHART
George W. Crane, Ph.D., M.D.
(copyright 1939)

In computing the score, check the various items under DEMERITS which fit the wife, and add the total. Each item counts as one point unless specifically weighted as in parentheses. Then check the items under MERITS which apply; now subtract the DEMERIT score from the MERIT score. The result is the wife's raw score. Interpret it according to this table:

RAW SCORES	INTERPRETATION
0–24	Very Poor (Failures)
25–41	Poor
42–58	Average
59–75	Superior
76 and up	Very Superior

DEMERITS		MERITS	
1. Slow in coming to bed—delays til husband is almost asleep.		1. A good hostess—even to unexpected guests.	
2. Doesn't like children. (5)		2. Has supper on time.	
3. Fails to sew on buttons or clean socks regularly.		3. Can carry on interesting conversation.	
4. Wears soiled or ragged dresses and aprons around the house.		4. Can play a musical instrument, as piano, violin, etc.	
5. Wears red nail polish.		5. Dresses for breakfast.	
6. Often late for appointments. (5)		6. Neat housekeeper—tidy and clean.	
7. Seams in hose often crooked.		7. Personally puts children to bed.	
8. Goes to bed with curlers on her hair or much face cream.		8. Never goes to bed angry, always makes up first . (5)	
9. Puts her cold feet on husband at night to warm them.		9. Asks husband's opinion regarding important decisions and purchases.	
10. Is a back seat driver.		10. Good sense of humor—jolly and gay.	
11. Flirts with other men at parties or in restaurants. (5)		11. Religious—sends children to church or Sunday school and goes herself. (10)	
12. Is suspicious and jealous. (5)		12. Lets husband sleep late on Sunday and holidays.	

During the period of this story, women were often asked in popular magazines to review their performance as wives using scales like this one.

She relaxed limply in the seat. "Oh, no. No. I don't want to go. I'm sure I don't." Her face was turned away from him. "It will be enough if we can have wine. It will be plenty." She turned up her coat collar so he could not see that she was crying weakly—like an old woman.

(1938)

Questions for Discussion and Writing

1. The chrysanthemums are clearly a symbol. What do they represent? Write an essay that makes a claim about the symbolism of the chrysanthemums.
2. How does the description of the setting at the beginning relate to the condition of Elisa's life?
3. Discuss the interactions between Elisa and the two males in the story. How do the men manipulate her? How does she try to manipulate them?
4. Why is Elisa interested in the prize fights? Why does she ask, "Do the men hurt each other very much?"
5. How do you think Elisa would respond to the "Wife's Chart" on page 251? In what ways does Steinbeck's characterization of Elisa act as a rebuttal to the values articulated in the chart?

Richard Wright   1908–1960

Richard Wright was born poor near Natchez, Mississippi, and conditions worsened after his father deserted the family. As a child he collected coal along the railroad tracks to heat their house. Although the family moved often, he did well in school while working at menial jobs to help pay the bills. After making it to Chicago, he landed a job with the postal service and joined the Federal Writers' Project. Like many writers of the time, he joined the Communist Party but quit after several years and rejected the party line. In 1946, alienated by the racism in the United States, he moved to Paris where he spent the last fourteen years of his life. His first novel, *Native Son* (1940), dramatizes the brutality of racial conflict and has become an American classic.

The Man Who Was Almost a Man

Dave struck out across the fields, looking homeward through paling light. Whut's the use of talkin wid em niggers in the field? Anyhow, his mother was putting supper on the table. Them niggers can't understan nothing. One of these days he was going to get a gun and practice shooting, then they couldn't talk to him as though he were a little boy. He slowed, looking at the ground. Shucks, Ah ain scareda them even ef they are biggern me! Aw, Ah know whut Ahma do. Ahm going by ol Joe's sto n git that Sears Roebuck catlog n look at them guns. Mebbe Ma will lemme buy one when she gits mah pay from ol man Hawkins. Ahma beg her t gimme some money. Ahm ol ernough to hava gun. Ahm seventeen. Almost a man. He strode, feeling his long loose-jointed limbs. Shucks, a man oughta hava little gun aftah he done worked hard all day.

He came in sight of Joe's store. A yellow lantern glowed on the front porch. He mounted the steps and went through the screen door, hearing it bang behind him. There was a strong smell of coal oil and mackerel fish. He felt very confident until he saw fat Joe walk in through the rear door, then his courage began to ooze.

"Howdy, Dave! Whutcha want?"

"How yuh, Mistah Joe? Aw, Ah don wanna buy nothing. Ah jus wanted t see ef yuhd lemme look at tha catlog erwhile."

"Sure! You wanna see it here?"   5

"Nawsuh. Ah wans t take it home wid me. Ah'll bring it back termorrow when Ah come in from the fiels."

"You plannin on buying something?"

"Yessuh."

"Your ma lettin you have your own money now?"

"Shucks. Mistah Joe, Ahm gittin t be a man like anybody else!"   10

Joe laughed and wiped his greasy white face with a red bandanna.

"Whut you plannin on buyin?"

Dave looked at the floor, scratched his head, scratched his thigh, and smiled. Then he looked up shyly.

"Ah'll tell yuh, Mistah Joe, ef yuh promise yuh won't tell."

"I promise."   15

"Waal, Ahma buy a gun."

"A gun? Whut you want with a gun?"

"Ah wanna keep it."

"You ain't nothing but a boy. You don't need a gun."

"Aw, lemme have the catlog, Mistah Joe. Ah'll bring it back."   20

Joe walked through the rear door. Dave was elated. He looked around at barrels of sugar and flour. He heard Joe coming back. He craned his neck to see if he were bringing the book. Yeah, he's got it. Gawddog, he's got it!

"Here, but be sure you bring it back. It's the only one I got."

"Sho, Mistah Joe."

"Say, if you wanna buy a gun, why don't you buy one from me? I gotta gun to sell."

"Will it shoot?"   25

"Sure it'll shoot."

"Whut kind is it?"

"Oh, it's kinda old … a left-hand Wheeler. A pistol. A big one."

"Is it got bullets in it?"

"It's loaded."   30

"Kin Ah see it?"

"Where's your money?"

"Whut yuh wan fer it?"

"I'll let you have it for two dollars."

"Just two dollahs? Shucks, Ah could buy tha when Ah git mah pay."   35

"I'll have it here when you want it."

"Awright, suh. Ah be in fer it."

He went through the door, hearing it slam again behind him. Ahma git some money from Ma n buy me a gun! Only two dollahs! He tucked the thick catalogue under his arm and hurried.

"Where yuh been, boy?" His mother held a steaming dish of black-eyed peas.

"Aw, Ma, Ah jus stopped down the road t talk wid the boys."   40

"Yuh know bettah t keep suppah waitin."

He sat down, resting the catalogue on the edge of the table.

"Yuh git up from there and git to the well n wash yoself! Ah ain feedin no hogs in mah house!"

She grabbed his shoulder and pushed him. He stumbled out of the room, then came back to get the catalogue.

"Whut this?"   45

"Aw, Ma, it's jusa catlog."

"Who yuh git it from?"

"From Joe, down at the sto."

"Waal, thas good. We kin use it in the outhouse."

"Naw, Ma." He grabbed for it. "Gimme ma catlog, Ma."   50

She held onto it and glared at him.

"Quit hollerin at me! Whut's wrong wid yuh? Yuh crazy?"

"But Ma, please. It ain mine! It's Joe's! He tol me t bring it back t im termorrow."

She gave up the book. He stumbled down the back steps, hugging the thick book under his arm. When he had splashed water on his face and hands, he groped back to the kitchen and fumbled in a corner for the towel. He bumped into a chair; it clattered to the floor. The catalogue sprawled at his feet. When he had dried his eyes he snatched up the book and held it again under his arm. His mother stood watching him.

"Now, ef yuh gonna act a fool over that ol book, Ah'll take it n burn it up."   55

"Naw, Ma, please."

"Waal, set down n be still!"

He sat down and drew the oil lamp close. He thumbed page after page, unaware of the food his mother set on the table. His father came in. Then his small brother.

"Whutcha got there, Dave?" his father asked.

"Jusa catlog," he answered, not looking up.   60

"Yeah, here they is!" His eyes glowed at blue-and-black revolvers. He glanced up, feeling sudden guilt. His father was watching him. He eased the book under the table and rested it on his knees. After the blessing was asked, he ate. He scooped up peas and swallowed fat meat without chewing. Buttermilk helped to wash it down. He did not want to mention money before his father. He would do much better by cornering his mother when she was alone. He looked at his father uneasily out of the edge of his eye.

"Boy, how come yuh don quit foolin wid tha book n eat yo suppah?"

"Yessuh."

"How you n ol man Hawkins gitten erlong?"

"Suh?"   65

"Can't yuh hear? Why don yuh lissen? Ah ast yu how wuz yuh n ol man Hawkins gittin erlong?"

"Oh, swell, Pa. Ah plows mo lan than anybody over there."

"Waal, yuh oughta keep yo mind on whut yuh doin."

"Yessuh."

He poured his plate full of molasses and sopped it up slowly with a chunk of   70
cornbread. When his father and brother had left the kitchen, he still sat and
looked again at the guns in the catalogue, longing to muster courage enough to
present his case to his mother. Lawd, ef Ah only had tha pretty one! He could
almost feel the slickness of the weapon with his fingers. If he had a gun like that
he would polish it and keep it shining so it would never rust. N Ah'd keep it
loaded, by Gawd!

"Ma?" His voice was hesitant.

"Hunh?"

"Ol man Hawkins give yuh mah money yit?"

"Yeah, but ain no usa yuh thinking bout throwin nona it erway. Ahm keepin
tha money sos yuh kin have cloes t go to school this winter."

He rose and went to her side with the open catalogue in his palms. She was   75
washing dishes, her head bent low over a pan. Shyly he raised the book. When
he spoke, his voice was husky, faint.

"Ma, Gawd knows Ah wans one of these."

"One of whut?" she asked, not raising her eyes.

"One of these," he said again, not daring even to point. She glanced up at the
page, then at him with wide eyes.

"Nigger, is yuh gone plumb crazy?"

"Aw, Ma—"   80

"Git outta here! Don yuh talk t me bout no gun! Yuh a fool!"

"Ma, Ah kin buy one fer two dollahs."

"Not ef Ah knows it, yuh ain!"

"But yuh promised me one—"

"Ah don care whut Ah promised! Yuh ain nothing but a boy yit!"   85

"Ma, ef yuh lemme buy one Ah'll *never* ast yuh fer nothing no mo."

"Ah tol yuh t git outta here! Yuh ain gonna toucha penny of tha money fer no
gun! Thas how come Ah has Mistah Hawkins t pay yo wages t me, cause Ah
knows yuh ain got no sense."

"But, Ma, we needa gun. Pa ain got no gun. We needa gun in the house. Yuh
kin never tell whut might happen."

"Now don yuh try to maka fool outta me, boy! Ef we did hava gun, yuh
wouldn't have it!"

He laid the catalogue down and slipped his arm around her waist.   90

"Aw, Ma, Ah done worked hard alla summer n ain ast yuh fer nothin, is
Ah, now?"

"Thas whut yuh spose t do!"

"But Ma, Ah wans a gun. Yuh kin lemme have two dollahs outta mah money.
Please, Ma. I kin give it to Pa.... Please, Ma! Ah loves yuh, Ma."

When she spoke her voice came soft and low.

"Whut yu wan wida gun, Dave? Yuh don need no gun. Yuh'll git in trouble.   95
N ef yo pa jus thought Ah let yuh have money t buy a gun he'd hava fit."

"Ah'll hide it, Ma. It ain but two dollahs."

"Lawd, chil, whut's wrong wid yuh?"

"Ain nothin wrong, Ma. Ahm almos a man now. Ah wans a gun."

"Who gonna sell yuh a gun?"

"Ol Joe at the sto."   100

"N it don cos but two dollahs?"

"Thas all, Ma. Jus two dollahs. Please, Ma."

She was stacking the plates away; her hands moved slowly, reflectively. Dave kept an anxious silence. Finally, she turned to him.

"Ah'll let yuh git tha gun ef yuh promise me one thing."

"Whut's tha, Ma?"

"Yuh bring it straight back t me, yuh hear? It be fer Pa."

"Yessum! Lemme go now, Ma."

She stopped, turned slightly to one side, raised the hem of her dress, rolled down the top of her stocking, and came up with a slender wad of bills.

"Here," she said. "Lawd knows yuh don need no gun. But yer pa does. Yuh bring it right back t me, yuh hear? Ahma put it up. Now ef yuh don, Ahma have yuh pa lick yuh so hard yuh won fergit it."

"Yessum."

He took the money, ran down the steps, and across the yard.

"Dave! Yuuuuuh Daaaaave!"

He heard, but he was not going to stop now. "Naw, Lawd!"

The first movement he made the following morning was to reach under his pillow for the gun. In the gray light of dawn he held it loosely, feeling a sense of power. Could kill a man with a gun like this. Kill anybody, black or white. And if he were holding his gun in his hand, nobody could run over him; they would have to respect him. It was a big gun, with a long barrel and a heavy handle. He raised and lowered it in his hand, marveling at its weight.

He had not come straight home with it as his mother had asked; instead he had stayed out in the fields, holding the weapon in his hand, aiming it now and then at some imaginary foe. But he had not fired it; he had been afraid that his father might hear. Also he was not sure he knew how to fire it.

To avoid surrendering the pistol he had not come into the house until he knew that they were all asleep. When his mother had tiptoed to his bedside late that night and demanded the gun, he had first played possum; then he had told her that the gun was hidden outdoors, that he would bring it to her in the morning. Now he lay turning it slowly in his hands. He broke it, took out the cartridges, felt them, and then put them back.

He slid out of bed, got a long strip of old flannel from a trunk, wrapped the gun in it, and tied it to his naked thigh while it was still loaded. He did not go in to breakfast. Even though it was not yet daylight, he started for Jim Hawkins' plantation. Just as the sun was rising he reached the barns where the mules and plows were kept.

"Hey! That you, Dave?"

He turned. Jim Hawkins stood eying him suspiciously.

"What're yuh doing here so early?"

"Ah didn't know Ah wuz gittin up so early, Mistah Hawkins. Ah wuz fixin t hitch up ol Jenny n take her t the fiels."

"Good. Since you're so early, how about plowing that stretch down by the woods?"

"Suits me, Mistah Hawkins."

"O.K. Go to it!"

He hitched Jenny to a plow and started across the fields. Hot dog! This was just what he wanted. If he could get down by the woods, he could shoot his gun and nobody would hear. He walked behind the plow, hearing the traces creaking, feeling the gun tied tight to his thigh.

When he reached the woods, he plowed two whole rows before he decided to take out the gun. Finally, he stopped, looked in all directions, then untied the gun and held it in his hand. He turned to the mule and smiled.

"Know whut this is, Jenny? Naw, yuh wouldn know! Yuhs jusa ol mule! Anyhow, this is a gun, n it kin shoot, by Gawd!"

He held the gun at arm's length. Whut t hell, Ahma shoot this thing! He looked at Jenny again.

"Lissen here, Jenny! When Ah pull this ol trigger, Ah don wan yuh t run n acka fool now!"

Jenny stood with head down, her short ears pricked straight. Dave walked off   130
about twenty feet, held the gun far out from him at arm's length, and turned his head. Hell, he told himself, Ah ain afraid. The gun felt loose in his fingers; he waved it wildly for a moment. Then he shut his eyes and tightened his forefinger. Bloom! A report half deafened him and he thought his right hand was torn from his arm. He heard Jenny whinnying and galloping over the field, and he found himself on his knees, squeezing his fingers hard between his legs. His hand was numb; he jammed it into his mouth, trying to warm it, trying to stop the pain. The gun lay at his feet. He did not quite know what had happened. He stood up and stared at the gun as though it were a living thing. He gritted his teeth and kicked the gun. Yuh almos broke mah arm! He turned to look for Jenny; she was far over the fields, tossing her head and kicking wildly.

"Hol on there, ol mule!"

When he caught up with her she stood trembling, walling her big white eyes at him. The plow was far away; the traces had broken. Then Dave stopped short, looking, not believing. Jenny was bleeding. Her left side was red and wet with blood. He went closer. Lawd, have mercy! Wondah did Ah shoot this mule? He grabbed for Jenny's mane. She flinched, snorted, whirled, tossing her head.

"Hol on now! Hol on."

Then he saw the hole in Jenny's side, right between the ribs. It was round, wet, red. A crimson stream streaked down the front leg, flowing fast. Good Gawd! Ah wuzn't shootin at tha mule. He felt panic. He knew he had to stop that blood, or Jenny would bleed to death. He had never seen so much blood in all his life. He chased the mule for half a mile, trying to catch her. Finally she stopped, breathing hard, stumpy tail half arched. He caught her mane and led her back to where the plow and gun lay. Then he stooped and grabbed handfuls of damp black earth and tried to plug the bullet hole. Jenny shuddered, whinnied, and broke from him.

"Hol on! Hol on now!"   135
He tried to plug it again, but blood came anyhow. His fingers were hot and sticky. He rubbed dirt into his palms, trying to dry them. Then again he attempted to plug the bullet hole, but Jenny shied away, kicking her heels high. He stood helpless. He had to do something. He ran at Jenny; she dodged him. He watched a red stream of blood flow down Jenny's leg and form a bright pool at her feet.

"Jenny...Jenny," he called weakly.

His lips trembled. She's bleeding t death! He looked in the direction of home, wanting to go back, wanting to get help. But he saw the pistol lying in the damp black clay. He had a queer feeling that if he only did something, this would not be; Jenny would not be there bleeding to death.

When he went to her this time, she did not move. She stood with sleepy, dreamy eyes; and when he touched her she gave a low-pitched whinny and knelt to the ground, her front knees slopping in blood.

"Jenny...Jenny..." he whispered. 140

For a long time she held her neck erect; then her head sank, slowly. Her ribs swelled with a mighty heave and she went over.

Dave's stomach felt empty, very empty. He picked up the gun and held it gingerly between his thumb and forefinger. He buried it at the foot of a tree. He took a stick and tried to cover the pool of blood with dirt—but what was the use? There was Jenny lying with her mouth open and her eyes walled and glassy. He could not tell Jim Hawkins he had shot his mule. But he had to tell something. Yeah, Ah'll tell em Jenny started gittin wil n fell on the joint of the plow....But that would hardly happen to a mule. He walked across the field slowly, head down.

It was sunset. Two of Jim Hawkins' men were over near the edge of the woods digging a hole in which to bury Jenny. Dave was surrounded by a knot of people, all of whom were looking down at the dead mule.

"I don't see how in the world it happened," said Jim Hawkins for the tenth time.

The crowd parted and Dave's mother, father, and small brother pushed into the center. 145

"Where Dave?" his mother called.

"There he is," said Jim Hawkins.

His mother grabbed him.

"Whut happened, Dave? Whut yuh done?"

"Nothin." 150

"C'mon, boy, talk," his father said.

Dave took a deep breath and told the story he knew nobody believed.

"Waal," he drawled. "Ah brung ol Jenny down here sos Ah could do mah plowin. Ah plowed bout two rows, just like yuh see." He stopped and pointed at the long rows of upturned earth. "Then somethin musta been wrong wid ol Jenny. She wouldn ack right a-tall. She started snortin n kickin her heels. Ah tried t hol her, but she pulled erway, rearin n goin in. Then when the point of the plow was stickin up in the air, she swung erroun n twisted herself back on it....She stuck herself n started t bleed. N fo Ah could do anything, she wuz dead."

"Did you ever hear of anything like that in all your life?" asked Jim Hawkins.

There were white and black standing in the crowd. They murmured. Dave's mother came close to him and looked hard into his face. "Tell the truth, Dave," she said. 155

"Looks like a bullet hole to me," said one man.

"Dave, whut yuh do wid tha gun?" his mother asked.

The crowd surged in, looking at him. He jammed his hands into his pockets, shook his head slowly from left to right, and backed away. His eyes were wide and painful.

"Did he hava gun?" asked Jim Hawkins.

"By Gawd, Ah tol yuh tha wuz a gun wound," said a man, slapping his thigh. 160

His father caught his shoulders and shook him till his teeth rattled.

"Tell whut happened, yuh rascal! Tell whut…"

Dave looked at Jenny's stiff legs and began to cry.

"Whut yuh do wid tha gun?" his mother asked.

"Whut wuz he doin wida gun?" his father asked.

"Come on and tell the truth," said Hawkins. "Ain't nobody going to hurt   165
you…."

His mother crowded close to him.

"Did yuh shoot tha mule, Dave?"

Dave cried, seeing blurred white and black faces.

"Ahh ddinn gggo tt sshooot hher….Ah ssswear ffo Gawd Ahh ddin….Ah
wuz a-tryin t sssee ef the old gggun would sshoot—"

"Where yuh git the gun from?" his father asked.   170

"Ah got it from Joe, at the sto."

"Where yuh git the money?"

"Ma give it t me."

"He kept worryin me, Bob. Ah had t. Ah tol im t bring the gun right back t
me….It was fer yuh, the gun."

"But how yuh happen to shoot that mule?" asked Jim Hawkins.   175

"Ah wuzn shootin at the mule, Mistah Hawkins. The gun jumped when Ah
pulled the trigger….N fo Ah knowed anythin Jenny was there a-bleedin."

Somebody in the crowd laughed. Jim Hawkins walked close to Dave and
looked into his face.

"Well, looks like you have bought you a mule, Dave."

"Ah swear fo Gawd, Ah didn go t kill the mule, Mistah Hawkins!"

"But you killed her!"   180

All the crowd was laughing now. They stood on tiptoe and poked heads over
one another's shoulders.

"Well, boy, looks like yuh done bought a dead mule! Hahaha!"

"Ain tha ershame."

"Hohohohoho."

Dave stood, head down, twisting his feet in the dirt.   185

"Well, you needn't worry about it, Bob," said Jim Hawkins to Dave's father.
"Just let the boy keep on working and pay me two dollars a month."

"Whut yuh wan fer yo mule, Mistah Hawkins?"

Jim Hawkins screwed up his eyes.

"Fifty dollars."

"Whut yuh do wid tha gun?" Dave's father demanded.   190

Dave said nothing.

"Yuh wan me t take a tree n beat yuh till yuh talk!"

"Nawsuh!"

"Whut yuh do wid it?"

"Ah throwed it erway."   195

"Where?"

"Ah…Ah throwed it in the creek."

"Waal, c'mon home. N firs thing in the mawnin git to tha creek n fin tha gun."

"Yessuh."

"Whut yuh pay fer it?"   200

"Two dollahs."

"Take tha gun n git yo money back n carry it t Mistah Hawkins, yuh hear? N don
fergit Ahma lam you black bottom good fer this! Now march yosef on home, suh!"

Dave turned and walked slowly. He heard people laughing. Dave glared, his eyes welling with tears. Hot anger bubbled in him. Then he swallowed and stumbled on.

That night Dave did not sleep. He was glad that he had gotten out of killing the mule so easily, but he was hurt. Something hot seemed to turn over inside him each time he remembered how they had laughed. He tossed on his bed, feeling his hard pillow. N Pa says he's gonna beat me....He remembered other beatings, and his back quivered. Naw, naw, Ah sho don wan im t beat me tha way no mo. Dam em all! Nobody ever gave him anything. All he did was work. They treat me like a mule, n then they beat me. He gritted his teeth. N Ma had t tell on me.

Well, if he had to, he would take old man Hawkins that two dollars. But   205
that meant selling the gun. And he wanted to keep that gun. Fifty dollars for a dead mule.

He turned over, thinking how he had fired the gun. He had an itch to fire it again. Ef other men kin shoota gun, by Gawd, Ah kin! He was still, listening. Mebbe they all sleepin now. The house was still. He heard the soft breathing of his brother. Yes, now! He would go down and get that gun and see if he could fire it! He eased out of bed and slipped into overalls.

The moon was bright. He ran almost all the way to the edge of the woods. He stumbled over the ground, looking for the spot where he had buried the gun. Yeah, here it is. Like a hungry dog scratching for a bone, he pawed it up. He puffed his black cheeks and blew dirt from the trigger and barrel. He broke it and found four cartridges unshot. He looked around; the fields were filled with silence and moonlight. He clutched the gun stiff and hard in his fingers. But, as soon as he wanted to pull the trigger, he shut his eyes and turned his head. Naw, Ah can't shoot wid mah eyes closed n mah head turned. With effort he held his eyes open; then he squeezed. *Blooooom!* He was stiff, not breathing. The gun was still in his hands. Dammit, he'd done it! He fired again. *Blooooom!* He smiled. *Blooooom! Blooooom! Click, click.* There! It was empty. If anybody could shoot a gun, he could. He put the gun into his hip pocket and started across the fields.

When he reached the top of a ridge he stood straight and proud in the moonlight, looking at Jim Hawkins' big white house, feeling the gun sagging in his pocket. Lawd, ef Ah had just one mo bullet Ah'd taka shot at tha house. Ah'd like t scare ol man Hawkins jusa little....Jusa enough t let im know Dave Saunders is a man.

To his left the road curved, running to the tracks of the Illinois Central. He jerked his head, listening. From far off came a faint *hoooof-hoooof; hoooof-hoooof; hoooof-hoooof*....He stood rigid. Two dollahs a mont. Les see now....Tha means it'll take bout two years. Shucks! Ah'll be dam!

He started down the road, toward the tracks. Yeah, here she comes! He stood   210
beside the track and held himself stiffly. Here she comes, erroun the ben....C mon, yuh slow poke! C mon! He had his hand on his gun; something quivered in his stomach. Then the train thundered past, the gray and brown box cars rumbling and clinking. He gripped the gun tightly; then he jerked his hand out of his pocket. Ah betcha Bill wouldn't do it! Ah betcha.... The cars slid past, steel grinding upon steel. Ahm ridin yuh ternight, so hep me Gawd! He was hot all over. He hesitated just a moment; then he grabbed, pulled atop of a car, and lay flat. He felt his pocket; the gun was still there. Ahead the long rails were glinting in the moonlight, stretching away, away to somewhere, somewhere where he could be a man....

(1940)

Questions for Discussion and Writing

1. What needs does Dave hope to satisfy by owning a gun? What are the sources of Dave's needs?
2. What does the accidental shooting of Jenny reveal about Dave? In what ways could this "accident" be seen as a subconscious act of rebellion against exploitation and shame? Is there any other evidence of Dave's rebelliousness or hostility?
3. What do the descriptions of the field, the store, and the house suggest about Dave's environment? How much do these living and working conditions affect Dave's attitudes and behavior?
4. What do you think of the story's ending?
5. Compare Dave's decision to leave town to Sammy's decision to quit his job (in the story "A & P"—pages 285–89).

Eudora Welty 1909–2001

Eudora Welty was born in Jackson, Mississippi, to devoted and prosperous parents who encouraged her literary bent. She recalled, "Any room in our house, at any time of day, was there to read in, or to be read to." She left Jackson to attend the University of Wisconsin and Columbia University, but returned to Jackson in 1932 to work for a radio station, several newspapers, and the WPA before launching her literary career. Welty's humor and astute observations give her portraits of small-town life a universal reality. One critic has observed, "Welty's career would seem to prove that an artist can thrive without benefit of poverty, obscurity, and neglect." She never married and when asked why, replied, "It never came up." The e-mail software Eudora was named after Welty because of her story "Why I Live at the P.O."

Why I Live at the P.O.

I was getting along fine with Mama, Papa-Daddy and Uncle Rondo until my sister Stella-Rondo just separated from her husband and came back home again. Mr. Whitaker! Of course I went with Mr. Whitaker first, when he first appeared here in China Grove, taking "Pose Yourself" photos, and Stella-Rondo broke us up. Told him I was one-sided. Bigger on one side than the other, which is a deliberate, calculated falsehood: I'm the same. Stella-Rondo is exactly twelve months to the day younger than I am and for that reason she's spoiled.

She's always had anything in the world she wanted and then she'd throw it away. Papa-Daddy gave her this gorgeous Add-a-Pearl necklace when she was eight years old and she threw it away playing baseball when she was nine, with only two pearls.

So as soon as she got married and moved away from home the first thing she did was separate! From Mr. Whitaker! This photographer with the popeyes she said she trusted. Came home from one of those towns up in Illinois and to our complete surprise brought this child of two.

Mama said she like to made her drop dead for a second. "Here you had this marvelous blonde child and never so much as wrote your mother a word about it," says Mama. "I'm thoroughly ashamed of you." But of course she wasn't.

Stella-Rondo just calmly takes off this *hat*, I wish you could see it. She says, "Why, Mama, Shirley-T.'s adopted, I can prove it."   5

"How?" says Mama, but all I says was, "H'm!" There I was over the hot stove, trying to stretch two chickens over five people and a completely unexpected child into the bargain, without one moment's notice.

"What do you mean—'H'm!'?" says Stella-Rondo, and Mama says, "I heard that, Sister."

I said that oh, I didn't mean a thing, only that whoever Shirley-T. was, she was the spit-image of Papa-Daddy if he'd cut off his beard, which of course he'd never do in the world. Papa-Daddy's Mama's papa and sulks.

Stella-Rondo got furious! She said, "Sister, I don't need to tell you you got a lot of nerve and always did have and I'll thank you to make no future reference to my adopted child whatsoever."

"Very well," I said. "Very well, very well. Of course I noticed at once she   10
looks like Mr. Whitaker's side too. That frown. She looks like a cross between Mr. Whitaker and Papa-Daddy."

"Well, all I can say is she isn't."

"She looks exactly like Shirley Temple to me," says Mama, but Shirley-T. just ran away from her.

So the first thing Stella-Rondo did at the table was turn Papa-Daddy against me.

"Papa-Daddy," she says. He was trying to cut up his meat. "Papa-Daddy!" I was taken completely by surprise. Papa-Daddy is about a million years old and's got this long-long beard. "Papa-Daddy, Sister says she fails to understand why you don't cut off your beard."

So Papa-Daddy l-a-y-s down his knife and fork! He's real rich. Mama says he   15
is, he says he isn't. So he says, "Have I heard correctly? You don't understand why I don't cut off my beard?"

"Why," I says, "Papa-Daddy, of course I understand, I did not say any such of a thing, the idea!"

He says, "Hussy!"

I says, "Papa-Daddy, you know I wouldn't any more want you to cut off your beard than the man in the moon. It was the farthest thing from my mind! Stella Rondo sat there and made that up while she was eating breast of chicken."

But he says, "So the postmistress fails to understand why I don't cut off my beard. Which job I got you through my influence with the government. 'Bird's nest'—is that what you call it?"

Not that it isn't the next to smallest P.O. in the entire state of Mississippi.   20

I says, "Oh, Papa-Daddy," I says, "I didn't say any such of a thing, I never dreamed it was a bird's nest, I have always been grateful though this is the next to smallest P.O. in the state of Mississippi, and I do not enjoy being referred to as a hussy by my own grandfather."

But Stella-Rondo says, "Yes, you did say it too. Anybody in the world could of heard you, that had ears."

"Stop right there," says Mama, looking at me.

So I pulled my napkin straight back through the napkin ring and left the table.

As soon as I was out of the room Mama says, "Call her back, or she'll starve to death," but Papa-Daddy says, "This is the beard I started growing on the Coast when I was fifteen years old." He would of gone on till nightfall if Shirley-T. hadn't lost the Milky Way she ate in Cairo.

So Papa-Daddy says, "I am going out and lie in the hammock, and you can all sit here and remember my words: I'll never cut off my beard as long as I live, even one inch, and I don't appreciate it in you at all." Passed right by me in the hall and went straight out and got in the hammock.

It would be a holiday. It wasn't five minutes before Uncle Rondo suddenly appeared in the hall in one of Stella-Rondo's flesh-colored kimonos, all cut on the bias, like something Mr. Whitaker probably thought was gorgeous.

"Uncle Rondo!" I says. "I didn't know who that was! Where are you going?"

"Sister," he says, "get out of my way, I'm poisoned."

"If you're poisoned stay away from Papa-Daddy," I says. "Keep out of the hammock. Papa-Daddy will certainly beat you on the head if you come within forty miles of him. He thinks I deliberately said he ought to cut off his beard after he got me the P.O., and I've told him and told him and told him, and he acts like he just don't hear me. Papa-Daddy must of gone stone deaf."

"He picked a fine day to do it then," says Uncle Rondo, and before you could say "Jack Robinson" flew out in the yard.

What he'd really done, he'd drunk another bottle of that prescription. He does it every single Fourth of July as sure as shooting, and it's horribly expensive. Then he falls over in the hammock and snores. So he insisted on zigzagging right on out to the hammock, looking like a half-wit.

Papa-Daddy woke up with this horrible yell and right there without moving an inch he tried to turn Uncle Rondo against me. I heard every word he said. Oh, he told Uncle Rondo I didn't learn to read till I was eight years old and he didn't see how in the world I ever got the mail put up at the P.O., much less read it all, and he said if Uncle Rondo could only fathom the lengths he had gone to get me that job! And he said on the other hand he thought Stella-Rondo had a brilliant mind and deserved credit for getting out of town. All the time he was just lying there swinging as pretty as you please and looping out his beard, and poor Uncle Rondo was pleading with him to slow down the hammock, it was making him as dizzy as a witch to watch it. But that's what Papa-Daddy likes about a hammock. So Uncle Rondo was too dizzy to get turned against me for the time being. He's Mama's only brother and is a good case of a one-track mind. Ask anybody. A certified pharmacist.

Just then I heard Stella-Rondo raising the upstairs window. While she was married she got this peculiar idea that it's cooler with the windows shut and locked. So she has to raise the window before she can make a soul hear her outdoors.

So she raises the window and says, "Oh!" You would have thought she was mortally wounded.

Uncle Rondo and Papa-Daddy didn't even look up, but kept right on with what they were doing. I had to laugh.

I flew up the stairs and threw the door open! I says, "What in the wide world's the matter, Stella-Rondo? You mortally wounded?"

"No," she says, "I am not mortally wounded but I wish you would do me the favor of looking out that window there and telling me what you see."

So I shade my eyes and look out the window.   40

"I see the front yard," I says.

"Don't you see any human beings?" she says.

"I see Uncle Rondo trying to run Papa-Daddy out of the hammock," I says. "Nothing more. Naturally, it's so suffocating-hot in the house, with all the windows shut and locked, everybody who cares to stay in their right mind will have to go out and get in the hammock before the Fourth of July is over."

"Don't you notice anything different about Uncle Rondo?" asks Stella-Rondo.

"Why, no, except he's got on some terrible-looking flesh-colored contraption I wouldn't be found dead in, is all I can see," I says.

"Never mind, you won't be found dead in it, because it happens to be part of   45
my trousseau, and Mr. Whitaker took several dozen photographs of me in it," say Stella-Rondo. "What on earth could Uncle Rondo *mean* by wearing part of my trousseau out in the broad open daylight without saying so much as 'Kiss my foot,' *knowing* I only got home this morning after my separation and hung my negligee up on the bathroom door, just as nervous as I could be?"

"I'm sure I don't know, and what do you expect me to do about it?" I says. "Jump out the window?"

"No, I expect nothing of the kind. I simply declare that Uncle Rondo looks like a fool in it, that's all," she says. "It makes me sick to my stomach."

"Well, he looks as good as he can," I says. "As good as anybody in reason could." I stood up for Uncle Rondo, please remember. And I said to Stella Rondo, "I think I would do well not to criticize so freely if I were you and came home with a two-year-old child I had never said a word about, and no explanation whatever about my separation."

"I asked you the instant I entered this house not to refer one more time to my adopted child, and you gave me your word of honor you would not," was all Stella-Rondo would say, and started pulling out every one of her eyebrows with some cheap Kress tweezers.

So I merely slammed the door behind me and went down and made some   50
green-tomato pickle. Somebody had to do it. Of course Mama had turned both the niggers loose; she always said no earthly power could hold one anyway on the Fourth of July, so she wouldn't even try. It turned out that Jaypan fell in the lake and came within a very narrow limit of drowning.

So Mama trots in. Lifts up the lid and says, "H'm! Not very good for your Uncle Rondo in his precarious condition, I must say. Or poor little adopted Shirley-T. Shame on you!"

That made me tired. I says, "Well, Stella-Rondo had better thank her lucky stars it was her instead of me came trotting in with that very peculiar-looking child. Now if it had been me that trotted in from Illinois and brought a peculiar-looking child of two, I shudder to think of the reception I'd of got, much less controlled the diet of an entire family."

"But you must remember, Sister, that you were never married to Mr. Whitaker in the first place and didn't go up to Illinois to live," says Mama, shaking a spoon in my face. "If you had I would of been just as overjoyed to see you and your little adopted girl as I was to see Stella-Rondo, when you wound up with your separation and came on back home."

"You would not," I says.

"Don't contradict me, I would," says Mama.

But I said she couldn't convince me though she talked till she was blue in the face. Then I said, "Besides, you know as well as I do that that child is not adopted."

"She most certainly is adopted," says Mama, stiff as a poker.

I says, "Why, Mama, Stella-Rondo had her just as sure as anything in this world, and just too stuck up to admit it."

"Why, Sister," said Mama. "Here I thought we were going to have a pleasant Fourth of July, and you start right out not believing a word your own baby sister tells you!"

"Just like Cousin Annie Flo. Went to her grave denying the facts of life," I remind Mama.

"I told you if you ever mentioned Annie Flo's name I'd slap your face," says Mama, and slaps my face.

"All right, you wait and see," I says.

"I," says Mama, "I prefer to take my children's word for anything when it's humanly possible." You ought to see Mama, she weighs two hundred pounds and has real tiny feet.

Just then something perfectly horrible occurred to me.

"Mama," I says, "can that child talk?" I simply had to whisper! "Mama, I wonder if that child can be—you know—in any way? Do you realize," I says, "that she hasn't spoken one single, solitary word to a human being up to this minute? This is the way she looks," I says, and I looked like this.

Well, Mama and I just stood there and stared at each other. It was horrible!

"I remember well that Joe Whitaker frequently drank like a fish," says Mama. "I believed to my soul he drank *chemicals.*" And without another word she marches to the foot of the stairs and calls Stella-Rondo.

"Stella-Rondo? O-o-o-o-o! Stella-Rondo!"

"What?" says Stella-Rondo from upstairs. Not even the grace to get up off the bed.

"Can that child of yours talk?" asks Mama.

Stella-Rondo says, "Can she what?"

"Talk! Talk!" says Mama. "Burdyburdyburdyburdy!"

So Stella-Rondo yells back, "Who says she can't talk?"

"Sister says so," says Mama.

"You didn't have to tell me, I know whose word of honor don't mean a thing in this house," says Stella-Rondo.

And in a minute the loudest Yankee voice I ever heard in my life yells out, "OE'm Pop-OE the Sailor-r-r-r Ma-a-an!" and then somebody jumps up and down in the upstairs hall. In another second the house would of fallen down.

"Not only talks, she can tap-dance!" calls Stella-Rondo, "Which is more than some people I won't name can do."

"Why, the little precious darling thing!" Mama says, so surprised. "Just as smart as she can be!" Starts talking baby talk right there. Then she turns on me. "Sister, you ought to be thoroughly ashamed! Run upstairs this instant and apologize to Stella-Rondo and Shirley-T."

"Apologize for what?" I says. "I merely wondered if the child was normal, that's all. Now that she's proved she is, why, I have nothing further to say."

But Mama just turned on her heel and flew out, furious. She ran right upstairs and hugged the baby. She believed it was adopted. Stella-Rondo hadn't done a thing but turn her against me from upstairs while I stood there helpless over the hot stove. So that made Mama, Papa-Daddy, and the baby all on Stella-Rondo's side.

Next, Uncle Rondo.

I must say that Uncle Rondo has been marvelous to me at various times in the past and I was completely unprepared to be made to jump out of my skin, the way it turned out. Once Stella-Rondo did something perfectly horrible to him—broke a chain letter from Flanders Field—and he took the radio back he had given her and gave it to me. Stella-Rondo was furious! For six months we all had to call her Stella instead of Stella-Rondo, or she wouldn't answer. I always thought Uncle Rondo had all the brains of the entire family. Another time he sent me to Mammoth Cave, with all expenses paid.

But this would be the day he was drinking that prescription, the Fourth of July.

So at supper Stella-Rondo speaks up and says she thinks Uncle Rondo ought to try to eat a little something. So finally Uncle Rondo said he would try a little cold biscuits and ketchup, but that was all. So she brought it to him.

"Do you think it wise to disport with ketchup in Stella-Rondo's flesh-colored kimono?" I says. Trying to be considerate! If Stella-Rondo couldn't watch out for her trousseau, somebody had to.

"Any objections?" asks Uncle Rondo, just about to pour out all the ketchup.

"Don't mind what she says, Uncle Rondo," says Stella-Rondo. "Sister has been devoting this solid afternoon to sneering out my bedroom window at the way you look."

"What's that?" says Uncle Rondo. Uncle Rondo has got the most terrible temper in the world. Anything is liable to make him tear the house down if it comes at the wrong time.

So Stella-Rondo says, "Sister says, 'Uncle Rondo certainly does look like a fool in that pink kimono!'"

Do you remember who it was really said that?

Uncle Rondo spills out all the ketchup and jumps out of his chair and tears off the kimono and throws it down on the dirty floor and puts his foot on it. It had to be sent all the way to Jackson to the cleaners and re-pleated.

"So that's your opinion of your Uncle Rondo, is it?" he says. "I look like a fool, do I? Well, that's the last straw. A whole day in this house with nothing to do, and then to hear you come out with a remark like that behind my back!"

"I didn't say any such of a thing, Uncle Rondo," I says, "and I'm not saying who did, either. Why, I think you look all right. Just try to take care of yourself and not talk and eat at the same time," I says. "I think you better go lie down."

"Lie down my foot," says Uncle Rondo. I ought to of known by that he was fixing to do something perfectly horrible.

So he didn't do anything that night in the precarious state he was in—just played Casino with Mama and Stella-Rondo and Shirley-T and gave Shirley-T. a nickel with a head on both sides. It tickled her nearly to death, and she called him "Papa." But at 6:30 A.M. the next morning, he threw a whole five-cent package of some unsold one-inch firecrackers from the store as hard as he could into my bedroom and they every one went off. Not one bad one in the string. Anybody else, there'd be one that wouldn't go off.

Well, I'm just terribly susceptible to noise of any kind, the doctor has always told me I was the most sensitive person he had ever seen in his whole life, and I was simply prostrated. I couldn't eat! People tell me they heard it as far as the cemetery, and old Aunt Jep Patterson, that had been holding her own so good, thought it was Judgment Day and she was going to meet her whole family. It's usually so quiet here.

And I'll tell you it didn't take me any longer than a minute to make up my mind what to do. There I was with the whole entire house on Stella-Rondo's side and turned against me. If I have anything at all I have pride.

So I just decided I'd go straight down to the P.O. There's plenty of room there in the back, I says to myself.

Well! I made no bones about letting the family catch on to what I was up to. I didn't try to conceal it.

The first thing they knew, I marched in where they were all playing Old 100 Maid and pulled the electric oscillating fan out by the plug, and everything got real hot. Next I snatched the pillow I'd done the needlepoint on right off the davenport from behind Papa-Daddy. He went "Ugh!" I beat Stella-Rondo up the stairs and finally found my charm bracelet in her bureau drawer under a picture of Nelson Eddy.

"So that's the way the land lies," says Uncle Rondo. There he was, piecing on the ham. "Well, Sister, I'll be glad to donate my army cot if you got any place to set it up, providing you'll leave right this minute and let me get some peace." Uncle Rondo was in France.

"Thank you kindly for the cot and 'peace' is hardly the word I would select if I had to resort to firecrackers at 6:30 A.M. in a young girl's bedroom," I says back to him. "And as to where I intend to go, you seem to forget my position as postmistress of China Grove, Mississippi," I says. "I've always got the P.O."

Well, that made them all sit up and take notice.

I went out front and started digging up some four-o'clocks to plant around the P.O.

"Ah-ah-ah!" says Mama, raising the window. "Those happen to be my 105 four-o'clocks. Everything planted in that star is mine. I've never known you to make anything grow in your life."

"Very well," I says. "But I take the fern. Even you, Mama, can't stand there and deny that I'm the one watered that fern. And I happen to know where I can send in a box top and get a packet of one thousand mixed seeds, no two the same kind, free."

"Oh, where?" Mama wants to know.

But I says, "Too late. You 'tend to your house, and I'll 'tend to mine. You hear things like that all the time if you know how to listen to the radio. Perfectly marvelous offers. Get anything you want free."

So I hope to tell you I marched in and got that radio, and they could of all bit a nail in two, especially Stella-Rondo, that it used to belong to, and she well knew she couldn't get it back, I'd sue for it like a shot. And I very politely took the sewing-machine motor I helped pay the most on to give Mama for Christmas back in 1929, and a good big calendar, with the first-aid remedies on it. The thermometer and the Hawaiian ukulele certainly were rightfully mine, and I stood on the step-ladder and got all my watermelon-rind preserves and every fruit and vegetable I'd put up, every jar. Then I began to pull the tacks out of the bluebird wall vases on the archway to the dining room.

"Who told you you could have those, Miss Priss?" says Mama, fanning as 110 hard as she could.

"I bought 'em and I'll keep track of 'em," I says. "I'll tack 'em up one on each side the post-office window, and you can see 'em when you come to ask me for your mail, if you're so dead to see 'em."

"Not I! I'll never darken the door to that post office again if I live to be a hundred," Mama says. "Ungrateful child! After all the money we spent on you at the Normal."

"Me either," says Stella-Rondo. "You can just let my mail lie there and *rot*, for all I care. I'll never come and relieve you of a single, solitary piece."

"I should worry," I says. "And who you think's going to sit down and write you all those big fat letters and postcards, by the way? Mr. Whitaker? Just because he was the only man ever dropped down in China Grove and you got him— unfairly—is he going to sit down and write you a lengthy correspondence after you come home giving no rhyme nor reason whatsoever for your separation and no explanation for the presence of that child? I may not have your brilliant mind, but I fail to see it."

So Mama says, "Sister, I've told you a thousand times that Stella-Rondo simply 115 got homesick, and this child is far too big to be hers," and she says, "Now, why don't you all just sit down and play Casino?"

Then Shirley-T. sticks out her tongue at me in this perfectly horrible way. She has no more manners than the man in the moon. I told her she was going to cross her eyes like that some day and they'd stick.

"It's too late to stop me now," I says. "You should have tried that yesterday. I'm going to the P.O. and the only way you can possibly see me is to visit me there."

So Papa-Daddy says, "You'll never catch me setting foot in that post office, even if I should take a notion into my head to write a letter some place." He says, "I won't have you reachin' out of that little old window with a pair of shears and cuttin' off any beard of mine. I'm too smart for you!"

"We all are," says Stella-Rondo.

But I said, "If you're so smart, where's Mr. Whitaker?" 120

So then Uncle Rondo says, "I'll thank you from now on to stop reading all the orders I get on postcards and telling everybody in China Grove what you think is the matter with them," but I says, "I draw my own conclusions and will continue in the future to draw them." I says, "If people want to write their inmost secrets on penny postcards, there's nothing in the wide world you can do about it, Uncle Rondo."

"And if you think we'll ever *write* another postcard you're sadly mistaken," says Mama.

"Cutting off your nose to spite your face then," I says. "But if you're all determined to have no more to do with the U.S. mail, think of this: What will Stella-Rondo do now, if she wants to tell Mr. Whitaker to come after her?"

"Wah!" says Stella-Rondo. I knew she'd cry. She had a conniption fit right there in the kitchen.

"It will be interesting to see how long she holds out," I says. "And now— I am 125 leaving."

"Good-by," says Uncle Rondo.

"Oh, I declare," says Mama, "to think that a family of mine should quarrel on the Fourth of July, or the day after, over Stella-Rondo leaving old Mr. Whitaker and having the sweetest little adopted child! It looks like we'd all be glad!"

"Wah!" says Stella-Rondo, and has a fresh conniption fit.

"He left *her*—you mark my words," I says. "That's Mr. Whitaker. I know Mr. Whitaker. After all, I knew him first. I said from the beginning he'd up and leave her. I foretold every single thing that's happened."

"Where did he go?" asks Mama. 130

"Probably to the North Pole, if he knows what's good for him," I says.

But Stella-Rondo just bawled and wouldn't say another word. She flew to her room and slammed the door.

"Now look what you've gone and done, Sister," says Mama. "You go apologize."

"I haven't got time, I'm leaving," I says.

"Well, what are you waiting around for?" asks Uncle Rondo. 135

So I just picked up the kitchen clock and marched off, without saying "Kiss my foot" or anything, and never did tell Stella-Rondo good-by.

There was a nigger girl going along on a little wagon right in front.

"Nigger girl," I says, "come help me haul these things down the hill, I'm going to live in the post office."

Took her nine trips in her express wagon. Uncle Rondo came out on the porch and threw her a nickel.

And that's the last I've laid eyes on any of my family or my family laid eyes on 140 me for five solid days and nights. Stella-Rondo may be telling the most horrible tales in the world about Mr. Whitaker, but I haven't heard them. As I tell everybody, I draw my own conclusions.

But oh, I like it here. It's ideal, as I've been saying. You see, I've got everything cater-cornered, the way I like it. Hear the radio? All the war news. Radio, sewing machine, book ends, ironing board, and that great big piano lamp—peace, that's what I like. Butter-bean vines planted all along the front where the strings are.

Of course, there's not much mail. My family are naturally the main people in China Grove, and if they prefer to vanish from the face of the earth, for all the mail they get or the mail they write, why, I'm not going to open my mouth. Some of the folks here in town are taking up for me and some turned against me. I know which is which. There are always people who will quit buying stamps just to get on the right side of Papa-Daddy.

But here I am, and here I'll stay. I want the world to know I'm happy.

And if Stella-Rondo should come to me this minute, on bended knees, and *attempt* to explain the incidents of her life with Mr. Whitaker, I'd simply put my fingers in both my ears and refuse to listen.

(1941)

Questions for Discussion and Writing

1. What are some of the verbal tactics that Sister uses to get us on her side as she tells this story? Find several examples of hyperbole and colloquial expressions that contribute to the humor of the story.

2. What does Sister's use of the racial epithet "nigger" tell you about her character? What does the last sentence in the story tell you about her?

3. How does Stella-Rondo's behavior intensify the sibling rivalry? Why do you think Mama takes her side against Sister?

4. When the family swears they will boycott the post office, Sister says, "Cutting off your nose to spite your face then." In what way is her response ironic?

5. Write a paper using evidence from the story making the claim that Sister was unfairly treated by her family or showing that Sister brought most of the trouble on herself.

Tillie Olsen   1913–2007

Tillie Olsen was born in Omaha, Nebraska, the daughter of political refugees from the repression of Czarist Russia. In her book *Silences* (1978), Olsen explains how gender, race, and class can render people inarticulate. Her own life illustrates the problem. She began working on a novel before she was twenty, but then she married, had four children, worked, participated in union activities, and did not resume writing until the 1950s, when her youngest daughter started school. The completed novel, *Yonnondio*, was finally published in 1974. Her long story "Tell Me a Riddle" won the O. Henry Prize in 1961. Olsen has said that she felt no personal guilt as a working parent because "guilt is a word used far too sloppily, to cover up harmful situations in society that must be changed."

I Stand Here Ironing

I stand here ironing, and what you asked me moves tormented back and forth with the iron.

"I wish you would manage the time to come in and talk with me about your daughter. I'm sure you can help me understand her. She's a youngster who needs help and whom I'm deeply interested in helping."

"Who needs help?" Even if I came what good would it do? You think because I am her mother I have a key, or that in some way you could use me as a key? She has lived for nineteen years. There is all that life that has happened outside of me, beyond me.

And when is there time to remember, to sift, to weigh, to estimate, to total? I will start and there will be an interruption and I will have to gather it all together again. Or I will become engulfed with all I did or did not do, with what should have been and what cannot be helped.

She was a beautiful baby. The first and only one of our five that was beautiful at birth. You do not guess how new and uneasy her tenancy in her now-loveliness. You did not know her all those years she was thought homely, or see her poring over her baby pictures, making me tell her over and over how beautiful she had

5

been—and would be, I would tell her—and was now, to the seeing eye. But the seeing eyes were few or nonexistent. Including mine.

I nursed her. They feel that's important nowadays. I nursed all the children, but with her, with all the fierce rigidity of first motherhood, I did like the books then said. Though her cries battered me to trembling and my breasts ached with swollenness, I waited till the clock decreed.

Why do I put that first? I do not even know if it matters, or if it explains anything.

She was a beautiful baby. She blew shining bubbles of sound. She loved motion, loved light, loved color and music and textures. She would lie on the floor in her blue overalls patting the surface so hard in ecstasy her hands and feet would blur. She was a miracle to me, but when she was eight months old I had to leave her daytimes with the woman downstairs to whom she was no miracle at all, for I worked or looked for work and for Emily's father, who "could no longer endure" (he wrote in his good-by note) "sharing want with us."

I was nineteen. It was the pre-relief, pre-WPA world of the depression. I would start running as soon as I got off the streetcar, running up the stairs, the place smelling sour, and awake or asleep to startle awake, when she saw me she would break into a clogged weeping that could not be comforted, a weeping I can yet hear.

After a while I found a job hashing at night so I could be with her days, and it 10 was better. But it came to where I had to bring her to his family and leave her.

It took a long time to raise the money for her fare back. Then she got chicken pox and I had to wait longer. When she finally came, I hardly knew her, walking quick and nervous like her father, looking like her father, thin, and dressed in a shoddy red that yellowed her skin and glared at the pockmarks. All the baby loveliness gone.

She was two. Old enough for nursery school they said, and I did not know then what I know now—the fatigue of the long day, and the lacerations of group life in the kinds of nurseries that are only parking places for children.

Except that it would have made no difference if I had known. It was the only place there was. It was the only way we could be together, the only way I could hold a job.

And even without knowing, I knew. I knew the teacher that was evil because all these years it has curdled into my memory, the little boy hunched in the corner, her rasp, "why aren't you outside, because Alvin hits you? that's no reason, go out, scaredy." I knew Emily hated it even if she did not clutch and implore "don't go Mommy" like the other children, mornings.

She always had a reason why we should stay home. Momma, you look sick. 15 Momma, I feel sick. Momma, the teachers aren't there today, they're sick. Momma, we can't go, there was a fire there last night. Momma, it's a holiday today, no school, they told me.

But never a direct protest, never rebellion. I think of our others in their three-, four-year-oldness—the explosions, the tempers, the denunciations, the demands—and I feel suddenly ill. I put the iron down. What in me demanded that goodness in her? And what was the cost, the cost to her of such goodness?

The old man living in the back once said in his gentle way: "You should smile at Emily more when you look at her." What *was* in my face when I looked at her? I loved her. There were all the acts of love.

It was only with the others I remembered what he said, so that it was the face of joy, and not of care or tightness or worry I turned to them—too late for Emily. She does not smile easily, let alone almost always as her brothers and sisters do. Her face is closed and somber, but when she wants, how fluid. You must have seen it in her pantomimes, you spoke of her rare gift for comedy on the stage that rouses a laughter out of the audience so dear they applaud and applaud and do not want to let her go.

Where does it come from, that comedy? There was none of it in her when she came back to me that second time, after I had had to send her away again. She had a new daddy now to learn to love, and I think perhaps it was a better time.

Except when we left her alone nights, telling ourselves she was old enough.   20

"Can't you go some other time, Mommy, like tomorrow?" she would ask. "Will it be just a little while you'll be gone? Do you promise?"

The time we came back, the front door open, the clock on the floor in the hall. She rigid awake. "It wasn't just a little while. I didn't cry. Three times I called you, just three times, and then I ran downstairs to open the door so you could come faster. The clock talked loud, I threw it away, it scared me when it talked."

She said the clock talked loud that night I went to the hospital to have Susan. She was delirious with the fever that comes before red measles, but she was fully conscious all the week I was gone and the week after we were home when she could not come near the new baby or me.

She did not get well. She stayed skeleton thin, not wanting to eat, and night after night she had nightmares. She would call for me, and I would sleepily call back, "you're all right, darling, go to sleep, it's just a dream," and if she still called, in a sterner voice, "now go to sleep, Emily, there's nothing to hurt you." Twice, only twice, when I had to get up for Susan anyway, I went in to sit with her.

Now when it is too late (as if she would let me hold and comfort her like I do   25 the others) I get up and go to her at her moan or restless stirring. "Are you awake? Can I get you something?" And the answer is always the same: "No, I'm all right, go back to sleep, Mother."

They persuaded me at the clinic to send her away to a convalescent home in the country where "she can have the kind of food and care you can't manage for her, and you'll be free to concentrate on the new baby." They still send children to that place. I see pictures on the society page of sleek young women planning affairs to raise money for it, or dancing at the affairs, or decorating Easter eggs or filling Christmas stockings for children.

They never have a picture of the children so I do not know if they still wear those gigantic red bows and the ravaged looks on the every other Sunday when parents can come to visit "unless otherwise notified"—as we were notified the first six weeks.

Oh it is a handsome place, green lawns and tall trees and fluted flower beds. High up on the balconies of each cottage the children stand, the girls in their red bows and white dresses, the boys in white suits and giant red ties. The parents stand below shrieking up to be heard and the children shriek down to be heard, and between them the invisible wall "Not To Be Contaminated by Parental Germs or Physical Affection."

There was a tiny girl who always stood hand in hand with Emily. Her parents never came. One visit she was gone. "They moved her to Rose Cottage," Emily shouted in explanation. "They don't like you to love anybody here."

She wrote once a week, the labored writing of a seven-year-old. "I am fine. How   30
is the baby. If I write my leter nicly I will have a star. Love." There was never a star.
We wrote every other day, letters she could never hold or keep but only hear
read—once. "We simply do not have room for children to keep any personal pos-
sessions," they patiently explained when we pieced one Sunday's shrieking together
to plead how much it would mean to Emily to keep her letters and cards.

Each visit she looked frailer. "She isn't eating," they told us.

(They had runny eggs for breakfast or mush with lumps, Emily said later, I'd
hold it in my mouth and not swallow. Nothing ever tasted good, just when they
had chicken.)

It took us eight months to get her released home, and only the fact that she
gained back so little of her seven lost pounds convinced the social worker.

I used to try to hold and love her after she came back, but her body would
stay stiff, and after a while she'd push away. She ate little. Food sickened her,
and I think much of life too. Oh she had physical lightness and brightness, twin-
kling by on skates, bouncing like a ball up and down up and down over the jump
rope, skimming over the hill; but these were momentary.

She fretted about her appearance, thin and dark and foreign-looking at a   35
time when every little girl was supposed to look or thought she should look a
chubby blond replica of Shirley Temple. The doorbell sometimes rang for her,
but no one seemed to come and play in the house or be a best friend. Maybe
because we moved so much.

There was a boy she loved painfully through two school semesters. Months later
she told me how she had taken pennies from my purse to buy him candy. "Licorice
was his favorite and I bought him some every day, but he still liked Jennifer better'n
me. Why, Mommy?" The kind of question for which there is no answer.

School was a worry to her. She was not glib or quick in a world where glibness
and quickness were easily confused with ability to learn. To her over-worked and
exasperated teachers she was an over-conscientious "slow learner" who kept
trying to catch up and was absent entirely too often.

I let her be absent, though sometimes the illness was imaginary. How different
from my now-strictness about attendance with the others. I wasn't working. We
had a new baby, I was home anyhow. Sometimes, after Susan grew old enough,
I would keep her home from school, too, to have them all together.

Mostly Emily had asthma, and her breathing, harsh and labored, would fill
the house with a curiously tranquil sound. I would bring the two old dresser mirrors
and her boxes of collections to her bed. She would select beads and single earrings,
bottle tops and shells, dried flowers and pebbles, old postcards and scraps, all sorts
of oddments; then she and Susan would play Kingdom, setting up landscapes and
furniture, peopling them with action.

Those were the only times of peaceful companionship between her and   40
Susan. I have edged away from it, that poisonous feeling between them, that terrible balancing of hurts and needs I had to do between the two, and did so badly,
those earlier years.

Oh there are conflicts between the others too, each one human, needing,
demanding, hurting, taking—but only between Emily and Susan, no, Emily
toward Susan that corroding resentment. It seems so obvious on the surface, yet it
is not obvious. Susan, the second child, Susan, golden and curly haired and chubby,
quick and articulate and assured, everything in appearance and manner Emily was
not; Susan, not able to resist Emily's precious things, losing or sometimes clumsily

breaking them; Susan telling jokes and riddles to company for applause while Emily sat silent (to say to me later: that was *my* riddle, Mother, I told it to Susan); Susan, who for all the five years' difference in age was just a year behind Emily in developing physically.

I am glad for that slow physical development that widened the difference between her and her contemporaries, though she suffered over it. She was too vulnerable for that terrible world of youthful competition, of preening and parading, of constant measuring of yourself against every other, of envy: "If I had that copper hair," or "If I had that skin...." She tormented herself enough about not looking like the others, there was enough of the unsureness, the having to be conscious of words before you speak, the constant caring—what are they thinking of me? what kind of an impression am I making?—without having it all magnified unendurably by the merciless physical drives.

Ronnie is calling. He is wet and I change him. It is rare there is such a cry now. That time of motherhood is almost behind me when the ear is not one's own but must always be racked and listening for the child cry, the child call. We sit for a while and I hold him, looking out over the city spread in charcoal with its soft aisles of light. "*Shoogily*," he breathes and curls closer. I carry him back to bed, asleep. *Shoogily*. A funny word, a family word, inherited from Emily, invented by her to say: *comfort*.

In this and other ways she leaves her seal, I say aloud. And startle at my saying it. What do I mean? What did I start to gather together, to try and make coherent? I was at the terrible, growing years. War years. I do not remember them well. I was working again, there were four smaller ones now, there was no time for her. She had to help be a mother, and housekeeper, and shopper. She had to set her seal. Mornings of crisis and near hysteria trying to get lunches packed, hair combed, coats and shoes found, everyone to school or Child Care on time, the baby ready for transportation. And always the paper scribbled on by a smaller one, the book looked at by Susan then mislaid, the homework not done. Running out to that huge school where she was one, she was lost, she was a drop; suffering over her unpreparedness, stammering and unsure in her classes.

There was so little left at night after the kids were bedded down. She would   45 struggle over her books, always eating (it was in those years she developed her enormous appetite that is legendary in our family) and I would be ironing, or preparing food for the next day, or writing V-mail[1] to Bill, or tending the baby. Sometimes, to make me laugh, or out of her despair, she would imitate happenings or types at school.

I think I said once: "Why don't you do something like this in the school amateur show?" One morning she phoned me at work, hardly understandable through the weeping: "Mother, I did it. I won, I won; they gave me first prize; they clapped and clapped and wouldn't let me go."

Now suddenly she was Somebody, and as imprisoned in her difference as she had been in her anonymity.

She began to be asked to perform at other high schools, even in colleges, then at city and state-wide affairs. The first one we went to, I only recognized her that first moment when thin, shy, she almost drowned herself into the curtains. Then: Was this Emily? The control, the command, the convulsing and deadly clowning, the spell, then the roaring, stamping audience, unwilling to let this rare and precious laughter out of their lives.

---

[1]Victory mail; letter written to personnel in the armed forces overseas during World War II.

Afterwards: You ought to do something about her with a gift like that—but without money or knowing how, what does one do? We have left it all to her, and the gift has as often eddied inside, clogged and clotted, as been used and growing.

She is coming. She runs up the stairs two at a time with her light graceful step, and I know she is happy tonight. Whatever it was that occasioned your call did not happen today.

"Aren't you ever going to finish the ironing, Mother? Whistler painted his mother in a rocker. I'd have to paint mine standing over an ironing board." This is one of the communicative nights and she tells me everything and nothing as she fixes herself a plate of food out of the icebox.

She is so lovely. Why did you want me to come in at all? Why were you concerned? She will find her way.

She starts up the stairs to bed. "Don't get *me* up with the rest in the morning." "But I thought you were having midterms." "Oh, those," she comes back in, kisses me, and says quite lightly, "in a couple of years when we'll all be atom-dead they won't matter a bit."

She has said it before. She *believes* it. But because I have been dredging the past, and all that compounds a human being is so heavy and meaningful in me, I cannot endure it tonight.

I will never total it all. I will never come in to say: She was a child seldom smiled at. Her father left me before she was a year old. I had to work away from her her first six years when there was work, or I sent her home and to his relatives. There were years she had care she hated. She was dark and thin and foreign-looking in a world where the prestige went to blondness and curly hair and dimples, she was slow where glibness was prized. She was a child of anxious, not proud, love. We were poor and could not afford for her the soil of easy growth. I was a young mother, I was a distracted mother. There were the other children pushing up, demanding. Her younger sister seemed all that she was not. There were years she did not want me to touch her. She kept too much in herself, her life was such she had to keep too much in herself. My wisdom came too late. She has much to her and probably little will come of it. She is a child of her age, of depression, of war, of fear.

Let her be. So all that is in her will not bloom—but in how many does it? There is still enough left to live by. Only help her to know—help make it so there is cause for her to know—that she is more than this dress on the ironing board, helpless before the iron.

(1961)

Questions for Discussion and Writing

1. The story is a monologue. What is the speaker's situation? Where is she and to whom is she talking?

2. Identify some of the conflicts in the story. Are any of them resolved?

3. How is personal responsibility portrayed in this story? To what extent is the speaker responsible for Emily's character and success in life? To what extent are circumstances responsible? To what extent is Emily herself responsible?

4. Write an essay in which you argue that this story reflects the common experiences of millions of people.

5. Rewrite the story from Emily's point of view.

Hisaye Yamamoto 1921–

Hisaye Yamamoto was born in Redondo Beach, California, the daughter of Japanese immigrants. She loved to read as a child and majored in foreign languages when she attended community college. During World War II, she and her family were forcibly interned in a relocation center in Arizona. While the family was confined, her brother Johnny, a soldier in the U.S. army, was killed in action in Italy. After returning to California, she became a housewife and mother, too busy to write much. "Most of the time I am cleaning house, or cooking or doing yard work," she once explained. "Very little time is spent writing. But if somebody told me I couldn't write, it would probably grieve me very much."

Seventeen Syllables

The first Rosie knew that her mother had taken to writing poems was one evening when she finished one and read it aloud for her daughter's approval. It was about cats, and Rosie pretended to understand it thoroughly and appreciate it no end, partly because she hesitated to disillusion her mother about the quantity and quality of Japanese she had learned in all the years now that she had been going to Japanese school every Saturday (and Wednesday, too, in the summer). Even so, her mother must have been skeptical about the depth of Rosie's understanding, because she explained afterwards about the kind of poem she was trying to write.

See, Rosie, she said, it was a *haiku*, a poem in which she must pack all her meaning into seventeen syllables only, which were divided into three lines of five, seven, and five syllables. In the one she had just read, she had tried to capture the charm of a kitten, as well as comment on the superstition that owning a cat of three colors meant good luck.

"Yes, yes, I understand. How utterly lovely," Rosie said, and her mother, either satisfied or seeing through the deception and resigned, went back to composing.

The truth was that Rosie was lazy; English lay ready on the tongue but Japanese had to be searched for and examined, and even then put forth tentatively (probably to meet with laughter). It was so much easier to say yes, yes, even when one meant no, no. Besides, this was what was in her mind to say: I was looking through one of your magazines from Japan last night, Mother, and towards the back I found some *haiku* in English that delighted me. There was one that made me giggle off and on until I fell asleep—

> It is morning, and lo!
> I lie awake, comme il faut,[1]
> sighing for some dough.

Now, how to reach her mother, how to communicate the melancholy song? 5
Rosie knew formal Japanese by fits and starts, her mother had even less English, no French. It was much more possible to say yes, yes.

---

[1]In good form; proper. Pronounced *come il fō*.

It developed that her mother was writing the *haiku* for a daily newspaper, the *Mainichi Shimbun*, that was published in San Francisco. Los Angeles, to be sure, was closer to the farming community in which the Hayashi family lived and several Japanese vernaculars were printed there, but Rosie's parents said they preferred the tone of the northern paper. Once a week, the *Mainichi* would have a section devoted to *haiku*, and her mother became an extravagant contributor, taking for herself the blossoming pen name, Ume Hanazono.

So Rosie and her father lived for awhile with two women, her mother and Ume Hanazono. Her mother (Tome Hayashi by name) kept house, cooked, washed, and, along with her husband and the Carrascos, the Mexican family hired for the harvest, did her ample share of picking tomatoes out in the sweltering fields and boxing them in tidy strata in the cool packing shed. Ume Hanazono, who came to life after the dinner dishes were done, was an earnest, muttering stranger who often neglected speaking when spoken to and stayed busy at the parlor table as late as midnight scribbling with pencil on scratch paper or carefully copying characters on good paper with her fat, pale green Parker.

The new interest had some repercussions on the household routine. Before, Rosie had been accustomed to her parents and herself taking their hot baths early and going to bed almost immediately afterwards, unless her parents challenged each other to a game of flower cards or unless company dropped in. Now if her father wanted to play cards, he had to resort to solitaire (at which he always cheated fearlessly), and if a group of friends came over, it was bound to contain someone who was also writing *haiku*, and the small assemblage would be split in two, her father entertaining the non-literary members and her mother comparing ecstatic notes with the visiting poet.

If they went out, it was more of the same thing. But Ume Hanazono's life span, even for a poet's, was very brief—perhaps three months at most.

One night they went over to see the Hayano family in the neighboring town to the west, an adventure both painful and attractive to Rosie. It was attractive because there were four Hayano girls, all lovely and each one named after a season of the year (Haru, Natsu, Aki, Fuyu), painful because something had been wrong with Mrs. Hayano ever since the birth of her first child. Rosie would sometimes watch Mrs. Hayano, reputed to have been the belle of her native village, making her way about a room, stooped, slowly shuffling, violently trembling (*always* trembling), and she would be reminded that this woman, in this same condition, had carried and given issue to three babies. She would look wonderingly at Mr. Hayano, handsome, tall, and strong, and she would look at her four pretty friends. But it was not a matter she could come to any decision about.

On this visit, however, Mrs. Hayano sat all evening in the rocker, as motionless and unobtrusive as it was possible for her to be, and Rosie found the greater part of the evening practically anaesthetic. Too, Rosie spent most of it in the girls' room, because Haru, the garrulous one, said almost as soon as the bows and other greetings were over, "Oh, you must see my new coat!"

It was a pale plaid of grey, sand, and blue, with an enormous collar, and Rosie, seeing nothing special in it, said, "Gee, how nice."

Migrant workers harvesting a field in central California.

"Nice?" said Haru, indignantly. "Is that all you can say about it? It's gorgeous! And so cheap, too. Only seventeen-ninety-eight, because it was a sale. The saleslady said it was twenty-five dollars regular."

"Gee," said Rosie. Natsu, who never said much and when she said anything said it shyly, fingered the coat covetously and Haru pulled it away.

"Mine," she said, putting it on. She minced in the aisle between the two large beds and smiled happily. "Let's see how your mother likes it."   15

She broke into the front room and the adult conversation and went to stand in front of Rosie's mother, while the rest watched from the door. Rosie's mother was properly envious. "May I inherit it when you're through with it?"

Haru, pleased, giggled and said yes, she could, but Natsu reminded gravely from the door, "You promised me, Haru."

Everyone laughed but Natsu, who shamefacedly retreated into the bedroom. Haru came in laughing, taking off the coat. "We were only kidding, Natsu," she said. "Here, you try it on now."

After Natsu buttoned herself into the coat, inspected herself solemnly in the bureau mirror, and reluctantly shed it, Rosie, Aki, and Fuyu got their turns, and Fuyu, who was eight, drowned in it while her sisters and Rosie doubled up in amusement. They all went into the front room later, because Haru's mother quaveringly called to her to fix the tea and rice cakes and open a can of sliced peaches for everybody. Rosie noticed that her mother and Mr. Hayano were talking together at the little table—they were discussing a *haiku* that Mr. Hayano was planning to send to the *Mainichi*, while her father was sitting at one end of the sofa looking through a copy of *Life*, the new picture magazine. Occasionally, her father would comment on a photograph, holding it toward Mrs. Hayano and speaking to her as he always did—loudly, as though he thought someone such as she must surely be at least a trifle deaf also.

The five girls had their refreshments at the kitchen table, and it was while Rosie 20 was showing the sisters her trick of swallowing peach slices without chewing (she chased each slippery crescent down with a swig of tea) that her father brought his empty teacup and untouched saucer to the sink and said, "Come on, Rosie, we're going home now."

"Already?" asked Rosie.

"Work tomorrow," he said.

He sounded irritated, and Rosie, puzzled, gulped one last yellow slice and stood up to go, while the sisters began protesting, as was their wont.

"We have to get up at five-thirty," he told them, going into the front room quickly, so that they did not have their usual chance to hang onto his hands and plead for an extension of time.

Rosie, following, saw that her mother and Mr. Hayano were sipping tea and 25 still talking together, while Mrs. Hayano concentrated, quivering, on raising the handless Japanese cup to her lips with both her hands and lowering it back to her lap. Her father, saying nothing, went out the door, onto the bright porch, and down the steps. Her mother looked up and asked, "Where is he going?"

"Where is he going?" Rosie said. "He said we were going home now."

"Going home?" Her mother looked with embarrassment at Mr. Hayano and his absorbed wife and then forced a smile. "He must be tired," she said.

Haru was not giving up yet. "May Rosie stay overnight?" she asked, and Natsu, Aki, and Fuyu came to reinforce their sister's plea by helping her make a circle around Rosie's mother. Rosie, for once having no desire to stay, was relieved when her mother, apologizing to the perturbed Mr. and Mrs. Hayano for her father's abruptness at the same time, managed to shake her head no at the quartet, kindly but adamant, so that they broke their circle and let her go.

Rosie's father looked ahead into the windshield as the two joined him. "I'm sorry," her mother said. "You must be tired." Her father, stepping on the starter, said nothing. "You know how I get when it's *haiku*," she continued, "I forget what time it is." He only grunted.

As they rode homeward silently, Rosie, sitting between, felt a rush of hate for 30 both—for her mother for begging, for her father for denying her mother. I wish this old Ford would crash, right now, she thought, then immediately, no, no, I wish my father would laugh, but it was too late: already the vision had passed through her mind of the green pick-up crumpled in the dark against one of the mighty eucalyptus trees they were just riding past, of the three contorted, bleeding bodies, one of them hers.

Rosie ran between two patches of tomatoes, her heart working more rambunctiously than she had ever known it to. How lucky it was that Aunt Taka and Uncle Gimpachi had come tonight, though, how very lucky. Otherwise she might not have really kept her half-promise to meet Jesus Carrasco. Jesus was going to be a senior in September at the same school she went to, and his parents were the ones helping with the tomatoes this year. She and Jesus, who hardly remembered seeing each other at Cleveland High where there were so many other people and two whole grades between them, had become great friends this summer—he always had a joke for her when he periodically drove the loaded pick-up up from the fields to the shed where she was usually sorting while her mother and father did the packing, and they laughed a great deal together over infinitesimal repartee during the afternoon break for chilled watermelon or ice cream in the shade of the shed.

What she enjoyed most was racing him to see which could finish picking a double row first. He, who could work faster, would tease her by slowing down until she thought she would surely pass him this time, then speeding up furiously to leave her several sprawling vines behind. Once he had made her screech hideously by crossing over, while her back was turned, to place atop the tomatoes in her green-stained bucket a truly monstrous, pale green worm (it had looked more like an infant snake). And it was when they had finished a contest this morning, after she had pantingly pointed a green finger at the immature tomatoes evident in the lugs at the end of his row and he had returned the accusation (with justice), that he had startlingly brought up the matter of their possibly meeting outside the range of both their parents' dubious eyes.

"What for?" she had asked.

"I've got a secret I want to tell you," he said.

"Tell me now," she demanded.   35

"It won't be ready till tonight," he said.

She laughed. "Tell me tomorrow then."

"It'll be gone tomorrow," he threatened.

"Well, for seven hakes, what is it?" she had asked, more than twice, and when he had suggested that the packing shed would be an appropriate place to find out, she had cautiously answered maybe. She had not been certain she was going to keep the appointment until the arrival of mother's sister and her husband. Their coming seemed a sort of signal of permission, of grace, and she had definitely made up her mind to lie and leave as she was bowing them welcome.

So as soon as everyone appeared settled back for the evening, she announced   40
loudly that she was going to the privy outside. "I'm going to the *benjo!*" and slipped out the door. And now that she was actually on her way, her heart pumped in such an undisciplined way that she could hear it with her ears. It's because I'm running, she told herself, slowing to a walk. The shed was up ahead, one more patch away, in the middle of the fields. Its bulk, looming in the dimness, took on a sinisterness that was funny when Rosie reminded herself that it was only a wooden frame with a canvas roof and three canvas walls that made a slapping noise on breezy days.

Jesus was sitting on the narrow plank that was the sorting platform and she went around to the other side and jumped backwards to seat herself on the rim of a packing stand. "Well, tell me," she said without greeting, thinking her voice sounded reassuringly familiar.

"I saw you coming out the door," Jesus said. "I heard you running part of the way, too."

"Uh-huh," Rosie said. "Now tell me the secret."

"I was afraid you wouldn't come," he said.

Rosie delved around on the chicken-wire bottom of the stall for number two   45
tomatoes, ripe, which she was sitting beside, and came up with a left-over that felt edible. She bit into it and began sucking out the pulp and seeds. "I'm here," she pointed out.

"Rosie, are you sorry you came?"

"Sorry? What for?" she said. "You said you were going to tell me something."

"I will, I will," Jesus said, but his voice contained disappointment, and Rosie fleetingly felt the older of the two, realizing a brand-new power which vanished without category under her recognition.

"I have to go back in a minute," she said. "My aunt and uncle are here from Wintersburg. I told them I was going to the privy."

Jesus laughed. "You funny thing," he said. "You slay me!"   50

"Just because you have a bathroom *inside*," Rosie said. "Come on, tell me."

Chuckling, Jesus came around to lean on the stand facing her. They still could not see each other very clearly, but Rosie noticed that Jesus became very sober again as he took the hollow tomato from her hand and dropped it back into the stall. When he took hold of her empty hand, she could find no words to protest; her vocabulary had become distressingly constricted and she thought desperately that all that remained intact now was yes and no and oh, and even these few sounds would not easily out. Thus, kissed by Jesus, Rosie fell for the first time entirely victim to a helplessness delectable beyond speech. But the terrible, beautiful sensation lasted no more than a second, and the reality of Jesus' lips and tongue and teeth and hands made her pull away with such strength that she nearly tumbled.

Rosie stopped running as she approached the lights from the windows of home. How long since she had left? She could not guess, but gasping yet, she went to the privy in back and locked herself in. Her own breathing deafened her in the dark, close space, and she sat and waited until she could hear at last the nightly calling of the frogs and crickets. Even then, all she could think to say was oh, my, and the pressure of Jesus' face against her face would not leave.

No one had missed her in the parlor, however, and Rosie walked in and through quickly, announcing that she was next going to take a bath. "Your father's in the bathhouse," her mother said, and Rosie, in her room, recalled that she had not seen him when she entered. There had been only Aunt Taka and Uncle Gimpachi with her mother at the table, drinking tea. She got her robe and straw sandals and crossed the parlor again to go outside. Her mother was telling them about the *haiku* competition in the *Mainichi* and the poem she had entered.

Rosie met her father coming out of the bathhouse. "Are you through,   55
Father?" she asked. "I was going to ask you to scrub my back."

"Scrub your own back," he said shortly, going toward the main house.

"What have I done now?" she yelled after him. She suddenly felt like doing a lot of yelling. But he did not answer, and she went into the bathhouse. Turning on the dangling light, she removed her denims and T-shirt and threw them in the big carton for dirty clothes standing next to the washing machine. Her other things she took with her into the bath compartment to wash after her bath. After she had scooped a basin of hot water from the square wooden tub, she sat on the grey cement of the floor and soaped herself at exaggerated leisure, singing "Red Sails in the Sunset" at the top of her voice and using da-da-da where she suspected her words. Then, standing up, still singing, for she was possessed by the notion that any attempt now to analyze would result in spoilage and she believed that the larger her volume the less she would be able to hear herself think, she obtained more hot water and poured it on until she was free of lather. Only then did she allow herself to step into the steaming vat, one leg first, then the remainder of her body inch by inch until the water no longer stung and she could move around at will.

She took a long time soaking, afterwards remembering to go around outside to stoke the embers of the tin-lined fireplace beneath the tub and to throw on a few more sticks so that the water might keep its heat for her mother, and when she finally returned to the parlor, she found her mother still talking *haiku* with her aunt and uncle, the three of them on another round of tea. Her father was nowhere in sight.

At Japanese school the next day (Wednesday, it was), Rosie was grave and giddy by turns. Preoccupied at her desk in the row for students on Book Eight, she made up for it at recess by performing wild mimicry for the benefit of her friend Chizuko. She held her nose and whined a witticism or two in what she considered was the manner of Fred Allen; she assumed intoxication and a British accent to go over the climax of the Rudy Vallee recording of the pub conversation about William Ewart Gladstone; she was the child Shirley Temple piping, "On the Good Ship Lollipop"; she was the gentleman soprano of the Four Inkspots trilling, "If I Didn't Care." And she felt reasonably satisfied when Chizuko wept and gasped, "Oh, Rosie, you ought to be in the movies!"

Her father came after her at noon, bringing her sandwiches of minced ham   60
and two nectarines to eat while she rode, so that she could pitch right into the sorting when they got home. The lugs were piling up, he said, and the ripe tomatoes in them would probably have to be taken to the cannery tomorrow if they were not ready for the produce haulers tonight. "This heat's not doing them any good. And we've got no time for a break today."

It *was* hot, probably the hottest day of the year, and Rosie's blouse stuck damply to her back even under the protection of the canvas. But she worked as efficiently as a flawless machine and kept the stalls heaped, with one part of her mind listening in to the parental murmuring about the heat and the tomatoes and with another part planning the exact words she would say to Jesus when he drove up with the first load of the afternoon. But when at last she saw that the pick-up was coming, her hands went berserk and the tomatoes started falling in the wrong stalls, and her father said, "Hey, hey! Rosie, watch what you're doing!"

"Well, I have to go to the *benjo*," she said, hiding panic.

"Go in the weeds over there," he said, only half-joking.

"Oh, Father!" she protested.

"Oh, go on home," her mother said. "We'll make out for awhile."   65

In the privy Rosie peered through a knothole toward the fields, watching as much as she could of Jesus. Happily she thought she saw him look in the direction of the house from time to time before he finished unloading and went back toward the patch where his mother and father worked. As she was heading for the shed, a very presentable black car purred up the dirt driveway to the house and its driver motioned to her. Was this the Hayashi home, he wanted to know. She nodded. Was she a Hayashi? Yes, she said, thinking that he was a good-looking man. He got out of the car with a huge, flat package and she saw that he warmly wore a business suit. "I have something here for your mother then," he said, in a more elegant Japanese than she was used to.

She told him where her mother was and he came along with her, patting his face with an immaculate white handkerchief and saying something about the coolness of San Francisco. To her surprised mother and father, he bowed and introduced himself as, among other things, the *haiku* editor of the

Mainichi Shimbun, saying that since he had been coming as far as Los Angeles anyway, he had decided to bring her the first prize she had won in the recent contest.

"First prize?" her mother echoed, believing and not believing, pleased and overwhelmed. Handed the package with a bow, she bobbed her head up and down numerous times to express her utter gratitude.

"It is nothing much," he added, "but I hope it will serve as a token of our great appreciation for your contributions and our great admiration of your considerable talent."

"I am not worthy," she said, falling easily into his style. "It is I who should 70 make some sign of my humble thanks for being permitted to contribute."

"No, no, to the contrary," he said, bowing again.

But Rosie's mother insisted, and then saying that she knew she was being unorthodox, she asked if she might open the package because her curiosity was so great. Certainly she might. In fact, he would like her reaction to it, for personally, it was one of his favorite *Hiroshiges*.

Rosie thought it was a pleasant picture, which looked to have been sketched with delicate quickness. There were pink clouds, containing some graceful calligraphy, and a sea that was a pale blue except at the edges, containing four sampans with indications of people in them. Pines edged the water and on the far-off beach there was a cluster of thatched huts towered over by pine-dotted mountains of grey and blue. The frame was scalloped and gilt.

After Rosie's mother pronounced it without peer and somewhat prodded her father into nodding agreement, she said Mr. Kuroda must at least have a cup of tea after coming all this way, and although Mr. Kuroda did not want to impose, he soon agreed that a cup of tea would be refreshing and went along with her to the house, carrying the picture for her.

"Ha, your mother's crazy!" Rosie's father said, and Rosie laughed uneasily as 75 she resumed judgment on the tomatoes. She had emptied six lugs when he broke into an imaginary conversation with Jesus to tell her to go and remind her mother of the tomatoes, and she went slowly.

Mr. Kuroda was in his shirtsleeves expounding some *haiku* theory as he munched a rice cake, and her mother was rapt. Abashed in the great man's presence, Rosie stood next to her mother's chair until her mother looked up inquiringly, and then she started to whisper the message, but her mother pushed her gently away and reproached, "You are not being very polite to our guest."

"Father says the tomatoes..." Rosie said aloud, smiling foolishly.

"Tell him I shall only be a minute," her mother said, speaking the language of Mr. Kuroda.

When Rosie carried the reply to her father, he did not seem to hear and she said again, "Mother says she'll be back in a minute."

"All right, all right," he nodded, and they worked again in silence. But sud- 80 denly, her father uttered an incredible noise, exactly like the cork of a bottle popping, and the next Rosie knew, he was stalking angrily toward the house, almost running in fact, and she chased after him crying, "Father! Father! What are you going to do?"

He stopped long enough to order her back to the shed. "Never mind!" he shouted. "Get on with the sorting!"

And from the place in the fields where she stood, frightened and vacillating, Rosie saw her father enter the house. Soon Mr. Kuroda came out alone, putting on his coat. Mr. Kuroda got into his car and backed out down the driveway onto the highway. Next her father emerged, also alone, something in his arms (it was the picture, she realized), and, going over to the bathhouse woodpile, he threw the picture on the ground and picked up the axe. Smashing the picture, glass and all (she heard the explosion faintly), he reached over for the kerosene that was used to encourage the bath fire and poured it over the wreckage. I am dreaming, Rosie said to herself, I am dreaming, but her father, having made sure that his act of cremation was irrevocable, was even then returning to the fields.

Rosie ran past him and toward the house. What had become of her mother? She burst into the parlor and found her mother at the back window watching the dying fire. They watched together until there remained only a feeble smoke under the blazing sun. Her mother was very calm.

"Do you know why I married your father?" she said without turning.

"No," said Rosie. It was the most frightening question she had ever been 85 called upon to answer. Don't tell me now, she wanted to say, tell me tomorrow, tell me next week, don't tell me today. But she knew she would be told now, that the telling would combine with the other violence of the hot afternoon to level her life, her world to the very ground.

It was like a story out of the magazines illustrated in sepia, which she had consumed so greedily for a period until the information had somehow reached her that those wretchedly unhappy autobiographies, offered to her as the testimonials of living men and women, were largely inventions: Her mother, at nineteen, had come to America and married her father as an alternative to suicide.

At eighteen she had been in love with the first son of one of the well-to-do families in her village. The two had met whenever and wherever they could, secretly, because it would not have done for his family to see him favor her—her father had no money; he was a drunkard and a gambler besides. She had learned she was with child; an excellent match had already been arranged for her lover. Despised by her family, she had given premature birth to a stillborn son, who would be seventeen now. Her family did not turn her out, but she could no longer project herself in any direction without refreshing in them the memory of her indiscretion. She wrote to Aunt Taka, her favorite sister in America, threatening to kill herself if Aunt Taka would not send for her. Aunt Taka hastily arranged a marriage with a young man of whom she knew, but lately arrived from Japan, a young man of simple mind, it was said, but of kindly heart. The young man was never told why his unseen betrothed was so eager to hasten the day of meeting.

The story was told perfectly, with neither groping for words nor untoward passion. It was as though her mother had memorized it by heart, reciting it to herself so many times over that its nagging vileness had long since gone.

"I had a brother then?" Rosie asked, for this was what seemed to matter now; she would think about the other later, she assured herself, pushing back the illumination which threatened all that darkness that had hitherto been merely mysterious or even glamorous. "A half-brother?"

"Yes."   90

"I would have liked a brother," she said.

Suddenly, her mother knelt on the floor and took her by the wrists. "Rosie," she said urgently, "Promise me you will never marry!" Shocked more by the request than the revelation, Rosie stared at her mother's face. Jesus, Jesus, she called silently, not certain whether she was invoking the help of the son of the Carrascos or of God, until there returned sweetly the memory of Jesus' hand, how it had touched her and where. Still her mother waited for an answer, holding her wrists so tightly that her hands were going numb. She tried to pull free. Promise, her mother whispered fiercely, promise. Yes, yes, I promise, Rosie said. But for an instant she turned away, and her mother, hearing the familiar glib agreement, released her. Oh, you, you, you, her eyes and twisted mouth said, you fool. Rosie, covering her face, began at last to cry, and the embrace and consoling hand came much later than she expected.

(1949)

Questions for Discussion and Writing

1. What conflicts between the mother and teenaged daughter are set up in the opening section of the story? Why are these conflicts and Rosie's way of dealing with them important to the story as a whole?

2. How does Ume's talent affect her husband? How does he express his feelings about it? How does he finally end her career as a poet?

3. What does Rosie feel for Jesus? List the various feelings she has and how she deals with them. Why are these feelings important when Tome finally tells Rosie the story of her marriage?

4. What are the connections between the episodes in the story about Rosie and those about her mother?

5. What does the visit to the Hayanos contribute to your understanding of Rosie, her mother, and her father?

6. Why does Rosie find that "the embrace and consoling hand came much later than she expected" at the end of the story?

John Updike   1932–2009

John Updike grew up in Pennsylvania, an only child who loved reading but suffered from stammering and psoriasis. He went to Harvard on a scholarship, got married during his junior year, and graduated summa cum laude in 1954. He briefly studied art at Oxford, then worked on the staff of the *New Yorker*, but after two years moved to Massachusetts. His prodigious output caused one critic to complain, "Updike can write faster than I can read." He has twice won the Pulitzer Prize, twice appeared on the cover of *Time*, and twice received the National Medal of Honor. Updike died of lung cancer in 2009 at the age of seventy-six.

A & P

In walks these three girls in nothing but bathing suits. I'm in the third checkout slot, with my back to the door, so I don't see them until they're over by the bread. The one that caught my eye first was the one in the plaid green two-piece. She was a chunky kid, with a good tan and a sweet broad soft-looking can with those two crescents of white just under it, where the sun never seems to hit, at the top of the backs of her legs. I stood there with my hand on a box of HiHo crackers trying to remember if I rang it up or not. I ring it up again and the customer starts giving me hell. She's one of these cash-register-watchers, a witch about fifty with rouge on her cheekbones and no eyebrows, and I know it made her day to trip me up. She'd been watching cash registers for fifty years and probably never seen a mistake before.

By the time I got her feathers smoothed and her goodies into a bag—she gives me a little snort in passing, if she'd been born at the right time they would have burned her over in Salem—by the time I get her on her way the girls had circled around the bread and were coming back, without a pushcart, back my way along the counters, in the aisle between the checkouts and the Special bins. They didn't even have shoes on. There was this chunky one, with the two-piece—it was bright green and the seams on the bra were still sharp and her belly was still pretty pale so I guessed she just got it (the suit)—there was this one, with one of those chubby berry-faces, the lips all bunched together under her nose, this one, and a tall one, with black hair that hadn't quite frizzed right, and one of these sunburns right across under the eyes and a chin that was too long—you know, the kind of girl other girls think is very "striking" and "attractive" but never quite makes it, as they very well know, which is why they like her so much—and then the third one, that wasn't quite so tall. She was the queen. She kind of led them, the other two peeking around and making their shoulders round. She didn't look around, not this queen, she just walked straight on slowly, on these long white prima-donna legs. She came down a little hard on her heels, as if she didn't walk in bare feet that much, putting down her heels and then letting the weight move along to her toes as if she was testing the floor with every step, putting a little deliberate extra action into it. You never know for sure how girls' minds work (do you really think it's a mind in there or just a little buzz like a bee in a glass jar?) but you got the idea she had talked the other two into coming in here with her, and now she was showing them how to do it, walk slow and hold yourself straight.

She had on a kind of dirty-pink—beige maybe, I don't know—bathing suit with a little nubble all over it and, what got me, the straps were down. They were off her shoulders looped loose around the cool tops of her arms, and I guess as a result the suit had slipped a little on her, so all around the top of the cloth there was this shining rim. If it hadn't been there you wouldn't have known there could have been anything whiter than those shoulders. With the straps pushed off, there was nothing between the top of the suit and the top of her head except just *her*, this clean bare plane of the top of her chest down from the shoulder bones like a dented sheet of metal tilted in the light. I mean, it was more than pretty.

She had a sort of oaky hair that the sun and salt had bleached, done up in a bun that was unraveling, and a kind of prim face. Walking into the A & P with your straps down, I suppose it's the only kind of face you *can* have. She held her head so high her neck, coming up out of those white shoulders, looked kind of stretched, but I didn't mind. The longer her neck was, the more of her there was.

She must have felt in the corner of her eye me and over my shoulder Stokesie 5 in the second slot watching, but she didn't tip. Not this queen. She kept her eyes moving across the racks, and stopped, and turned so slow it made my stomach rub the inside of my apron, and buzzed to the other two, who kind of huddled against her for relief, and then they all three of them went up the cat-and-dog-food-breakfast-cereal-macaroni-rice-raisins-seasonings-spreads-spaghetti-soft-drinks-crackers-and-cookies aisle. From the third slot I look straight up this aisle to the meat counter, and I watched them all the way. The fat one with the tan sort of fumbled with the cookies, but on second thought she put the package back. The sheep pushing their carts down the aisle—the girls were walking against the usual traffic (not that we have one-way signs or anything)—were pretty hilarious. You could see them, when Queenie's white shoulders dawned on them, kind of jerk, or hop, or hiccup, but their eyes snapped back to their own baskets and on they pushed. I bet you could set off dynamite in an A & P and the people would by and large keep reaching and checking oatmeal off their lists and muttering "Let me see, there was a third thing, began with A, aspara-gus, no, ah, yes, applesauce!" or whatever it is they do mutter. But there was no doubt, this jiggled them. A few houseslaves in pin curlers even looked around after pushing their carts past to make sure what they had seen was correct.

You know, it's one thing to have a girl in a bathing suit down on the beach, where what with the glare nobody can look at each other much anyway, and an-other thing in the cool of the A & P, under the fluorescent lights, against all those stacked packages, with her feet paddling along naked over our checker-board green-and-cream rubber-tile floor.

"Oh Daddy," Stokesie said beside me. "I feel so faint."

"Darling," I said. "Hold me tight." Stokesie's married, with two babies chalked up on his fuselage already, but as far as I can tell that's the only difference. He's twenty-two, and I was nineteen this April.

"Is it done?" he asks, the responsible married man finding his voice. I forgot to say he thinks he's going to be manager some sunny day, maybe in 1990 when it's called the Great Alexandrov and Petrooshki Tea Company or something.

What he meant was, our town is five miles from a beach, with a big summer colony out on the Point, but we're right in the middle of town, and the women generally put on a shirt or shorts or something before they get out of the car into the street. And anyway these are usually women with six children and vari-cose veins mapping their legs and nobody, including them, could care less. As I say, we're right in the middle of town, and if you stand at our front doors you can see two banks and the Congregational church and the newspaper store and three real-estate offices and about twenty-seven old freeloaders tearing up Central Street because the sewer broke again. It's not as if we're on the Cape; we're north of Boston and there's people in this town haven't seen the ocean for twenty years.

The girls had reached the meat counter and were asking McMahon some-thing. He pointed, they pointed, and they shuffled out of sight behind a pyramid of Diet Delight peaches. All that was left for us to see was old McMahon patting his mouth and looking after them sizing up their joints. Poor kids, I began to feel sorry for them, they couldn't help it.

Now here comes the sad part of the story, at least my family says it's sad, but I don't think it's so sad myself. The store's pretty empty, it being Thursday after-noon, so there was nothing much to do except lean on the register and wait for the girls to show up again. The whole store was like a pinball machine and I didn't know which tunnel they'd come out of. After a while they come around out of the

10

far aisle, around the light bulbs, records at discount of the Caribbean Six or Tony Martin Sings or some such gunk you wonder they waste the wax on, six-packs of candy bars, and plastic toys done up in cellophane that fall apart when a kid looks at them anyway. Around they come, Queenie still leading the way, and holding a little gray jar in her hand. Slots Three through Seven are unmanned and I could see her wondering between Stokes and me, but Stokesie with his usual luck draws an old party in baggy gray pants who stumbles up with four giant cans of pineapple juice (what do these bums *do* with all that pineapple juice? I've often asked myself) so the girls come to me. Queenie puts down the jar and I take it into my fingers icy cold. Kingfish Fancy Herring Snacks in Pure Sour Cream: 49¢. Now her hands are empty, not a ring or a bracelet, bare as God made them, and I wonder where the money's coming from. Still with that prim look she lifts a folded dollar bill out of the hollow at the center of her nubbled pink top. The jar went heavy in my hand. Really, I thought that was so cute.

Then everybody's luck begins to run out. Lengel comes in from haggling with a truck full of cabbages on the lot and is about to scuttle into that door marked MANAGER behind which he hides all day when the girls touch his eye. Lengel's pretty dreary, teaches Sunday school and the rest, but he doesn't miss that much. He comes over and says, "Girls, this isn't the beach."

Queenie blushes, though maybe it's just a brush of sunburn I was noticing for the first time, now that she was so close. "My mother asked me to pick up a jar of herring snacks." Her voice kind of startled me, the way voices do when you see the people first, coming out so flat and dumb yet kind of tony, too, the way it ticked over "pick up" and "snacks." All of a sudden I slid right down her voice into her living room. Her father and the other men were standing around in ice-cream coats and bow ties and the women were in sandals picking up herring snacks on toothpicks off a big glass plate and they were all holding drinks the color of water with olives and sprigs of mint in them. When my parents have somebody over they get lemonade and if it's a real racy affair Schlitz in tall glasses with "They'll Do It Every Time" cartoons stencilled on.

"That's all right," Lengel said. "But this isn't the beach." His repeating this 15 struck me as funny, as if it had just occurred to him, and he had been thinking all these years the A & P was a great big dune and he was the head lifeguard. He didn't like my smiling—as I say he doesn't miss much—but he concentrates on giving the girls that sad Sunday-school-superintendent stare.

Queenie's blush is no sunburn now, and the plump one in plaid, that I liked better from the back—a really sweet can—pipes up, "We weren't doing any shopping. We just came in for the one thing."

"That makes no difference," Lengel tells her, and I could see from the way his eyes went that he hadn't noticed she was wearing a two-piece before. "We want you decently dressed when you come in here."

"We *are* decent," Queenie says suddenly, her lower lip pushing, getting sore now that she remembers her place, a place from which the crowd that runs the A & P must look pretty crummy. Fancy Herring Snacks flashed in her very blue eyes.

"Girls, I don't want to argue with you. After this come in here with your shoulders covered. It's our policy." He turns his back. That's policy for you. Policy is what the kingpins want. What the others want is juvenile delinquency.

All this while, the customers had been showing up with their carts but, you 20 know, sheep, seeing a scene, they had all bunched up on Stokesie, who shook open a paper bag as gently as peeling a peach, not wanting to miss a word. I could feel in the silence everybody getting nervous, most of all Lengel, who asks me, "Sammy, have you rung up their purchase?"

I thought and said "No" but it wasn't about that I was thinking. I go through the punches, 4, 9, GROC, TOT—it's more complicated than you think, and after you do it often enough, it begins to make a little song, that you hear words to, in my case "Hello (*bing*) there, you (*gung*) hap-py *pee-pul* (*splat*)!"—the *splat* being the drawer flying out. I uncrease the bill, tenderly as you may imagine, it just having come from between the two smoothest scoops of vanilla I had ever known there were, and pass a half and a penny into her narrow pink palm, and nestle the herrings in a bag and twist its neck and hand it over, all the time thinking.

The girls, and who'd blame them, are in a hurry to get out, so I say "I quit" to Lengel quick enough for them to hear, hoping they'll stop and watch me, their unsuspected hero. They keep right on going, into the electric eye; the door flies open and they flicker across the lot to their car, Queenie and Plaid and Big Tall Goony-Goony (not that as raw material she was so bad), leaving me with Lengel and a kink in his eyebrow.

"Did you say something, Sammy?"

"I said I quit."

"I thought you did." 25

"You didn't have to embarrass them."

"It was they who were embarrassing us."

I started to say something that came out "Fiddle-de-do." It's a saying of my grandmother's, and I know she would have been pleased.

"I don't think you know what you're saying," Lengel said.

"I know you don't," I said. "But I do." 30

I pull the bow at the back of my apron and start shrugging it off my shoulders. A couple of customers that had been heading for my slot begin to knock against each other, like scared pigs in a chute.

Lengel sighs and begins to look very patient and old and gray. He's been a friend of my parents for years. "Sammy, you don't want to do this to your Mom and Dad," he tells me. It's true, I don't. But it seems to me that once you begin a gesture it's fatal not to go through with it. I fold the apron, "Sammy" stitched in red on the pocket, and put it on the counter, and drop the bow tie on top of it. The bow tie is theirs, if you've ever wondered. "You'll feel this for the rest of your life," Lengel says, and I know that's true, too, but remembering how he made that pretty girl blush makes me so scrunchy inside I punch the No Sale tab and the machine whirs "pee-pul" and the drawer splats out. One advantage to this scene taking place in summer, I can follow this up with a clean exit, there's no fumbling around getting your coat and galoshes, I just saunter into the electric eye in my white shirt that my mother ironed the night before, and the door heaves itself open, and outside the sunshine is skating around on the asphalt.

I look around for my girls, but they're gone, of course. There wasn't anybody but some young married screaming with her children about some candy they didn't get by the door of a powder-blue Falcon station wagon. Looking back in the big windows, over the bags of peat moss and aluminum lawn furniture stacked on the pavement, I could see Lengel in my place in the slot, checking the sheep through. His face was dark gray and his back stiff, as if he's just had an injection of iron, and my stomach kind of fell as I felt how hard the world was going to be to me hereafter.

(1962)

Questions for Discussion and Writing

1. What is Sammy's attitude toward his job, the people he works with, and his customers? List some of his descriptions, especially the metaphors (like "I got her feathers smoothed"), that reveal these attitudes.
2. Why does Sammy quit his job? Does he have more than one reason? Why does he see it as an act of heroism? Is it?
3. As the story closes, Sammy thinks "how hard the world was going to be to me hereafter." Will it? Why or why not?
4. Why do some readers find the story offensively sexist? Write an essay arguing your position on this question.
5. Rewrite a section of the story from a different point of view: Queenie's, Lengel's, the other shoppers', or an objective position. Show how point of view makes a difference in the story's interpretation.

Joyce Carol Oates   1938–

Joyce Carol Oates grew up during the depression on a farm in upstate New York. She won a scholarship to Syracuse University, where she became valedictorian of her graduating class. Oates has achieved a prodigious literary output, publishing more than eighty books of fiction, poetry, drama, essays, and literary criticism. Wryly, she once suggested that her epitaph could read, "She certainly tried." Oates has said she writes about "real people in a real society," but her fiction frequently centers on the connection between violence and sexual obsession.

Where Are You Going, Where Have You Been?

For Bob Dylan[1]

Her name was Connie. She was fifteen and she had a quick, nervous giggling habit of craning her neck to glance into mirrors or checking other people's faces to make sure her own was all right. Her mother, who noticed everything and knew everything and who hadn't much reason any longer to look at her own face, always scolded Connie about it. "Stop gawking at yourself. Who are you? You think you're so pretty?" she would say. Connie would raise her eyebrows at these familiar complaints and look right through her mother, into a shadowy vision of herself as she was right at that moment: she knew she was pretty and that was everything. Her mother had been pretty once too, if you could believe those old

---

[1]Bob Dylan (b. 1941), the composer, author, and singer who devised and popularized folk rock during the 1960s.

snapshots in the album, but now her looks were gone and that was why she was always after Connie.

"Why don't you keep your room clean like your sister? How've you got your hair fixed—what the hell stinks? Hair spray? You don't see your sister using that junk."

Her sister June was twenty-four and still lived at home. She was a secretary in the high school Connie attended, and if that wasn't bad enough—with her in the same building—she was so plain and chunky and steady that Connie had to hear her praised all the time by her mother and her mother's sisters. June did this, June did that, she saved money and helped clean the house and cooked and Connie couldn't do a thing, her mind was all filled with trashy daydreams. Their father was away at work most of the time and when he came home he wanted supper and he read the newspaper at supper and after supper he went to bed. He didn't bother talking much to them, but around his bent head Connie's mother kept picking at her until Connie wished her mother was dead and she herself was dead and it was all over. "She makes me want to throw up sometimes," she complained to her friends. She had a high, breathless, amused voice that made everything she said sound a little forced, whether it was sincere or not.

There was one good thing: June went places with girl friends of hers, girls who were just as plain and steady as she, and so when Connie wanted to do that her mother had no objections. The father of Connie's best girl friend drove the girls the three miles to town and left them off at a shopping plaza so they could walk through the stores or go to a movie, and when he came to pick them up again at eleven he never bothered to ask what they had done.

They must have been familiar sights, walking around the shopping plaza in   5
their shorts and flat ballerina slippers that always scuffed the sidewalk, with charm bracelets jingling on their thin wrists; they would lean together to whisper and laugh secretly if someone passed who amused or interested them. Connie had long dark blond hair that drew anyone's eye to it, and she wore part of it pulled up on her head and puffed out and the rest of it she let fall down her back. She wore a pull-over jersey blouse that looked one way when she was at home and another way when she was away from home. Everything about her had two sides to it, one for home and one for anywhere that was not home: her walk, which could be childlike and bobbing, or languid enough to make anyone think she was hearing music in her head; her mouth, which was pale and smirking most of the time, but bright and pink on these evenings out; her laugh, which was cynical and drawling at home—"Ha, ha, very funny"—but high-pitched and nervous anywhere else, like the jingling of the charms on her bracelet.

Sometimes they did go shopping or to a movie, but sometimes they went across the highway, ducking fast across the busy road, to a drive-in restaurant where older kids hung out. The restaurant was shaped like a big bottle, though squatter than a real bottle, and on its cap was a revolving figure of a grinning boy who held a hamburger aloft. One night in mid-summer they ran across, breathless with daring, and right away someone leaned out a car window and invited them over, but it was just a boy from high school they didn't like. It made them feel good to be able to ignore him. They went up through the maze of parked and cruising cars to the bright-lit, fly-infested restaurant, their faces pleased and expectant as if they were entering a sacred building that loomed up out of the night to give them what haven and blessing they yearned for. They sat at the counter and crossed their legs at the ankles, their thin shoulders rigid with excitement, and listened to the music that made everything so good: the music was always in the background, like music at a church service; it was something to depend upon.

A boy named Eddie came in to talk with them. He sat backwards on his stool, turning himself jerkily around in semi-circles and then stopping and turning again, and after a while he asked Connie if she would like something to eat. She said she would and so she tapped her friend's arm on her way out—her friend pulled her face up into a brave, droll look—and Connie said she would meet her at eleven, across the way. "I just hate to leave her like that," Connie said earnestly, but the boy said that she wouldn't be alone for long. So they went out to his car, and on the way Connie couldn't help but let her eyes wander over the windshields and faces all around her, her face gleaming with a joy that had nothing to do with Eddie or even this place; it might have been the music. She drew her shoulders up and sucked in her breath with the pure pleasure of being alive, and just at that moment she happened to glance at a face just a few feet from hers. It was a boy with shaggy black hair, in a convertible jalopy painted gold. He stared at her and then his lips widened into a grin. Connie slit her eyes at him and turned away, but she couldn't help glancing back and there he was still watching her. He wagged a finger and laughed and said, "Gonna get you, baby," and Connie turned away again without Eddie noticing anything.

She spent three hours with him, at the restaurant where they ate hamburgers and drank Cokes in wax cups that were always sweating, and then down an alley a mile or so away, and when he left her off at five to eleven only the movie house was still open at the plaza. Her girl friend was there, talking with a boy. When Connie came up, the two girls smiled at each other and Connie said, "How was the movie?" and the girl said, "*You* should know." They rode off with the girl's father, sleepy and pleased, and Connie couldn't help but look back at the darkened shopping plaza with its big empty parking lot and its signs that were faded and ghostly now, and over at the drive-in restaurant where cars were still circling tirelessly. She couldn't hear the music at this distance.

Next morning June asked her how the movie was and Connie said, "So-so."

She and that girl and occasionally another girl went out several times a   10 week, and the rest of the time Connie spent around the house—it was summer vacation—getting in her mother's way and thinking, dreaming about the boys she met. But all the boys fell back and dissolved into a single face that was not even a face, but an idea, a feeling, mixed up with the urgent insistent pounding of the music and the humid night air of July. Connie's mother kept dragging her back to the daylight by finding things for her to do or saying, suddenly, "What's this about the Pettinger girl?"

And Connie would say nervously, "Oh, her. That dope." She always drew thick clear lines between herself and such girls, and her mother was simple and kind enough to believe her. Her mother was so simple, Connie thought, that it was maybe cruel to fool her so much. Her mother went scuffling around the house in old bedroom slippers and complained over the telephone to one sister about the other, then the other called up and the two of them complained about the third one. If June's name was mentioned her mother's tone was approving, and if Connie's name was mentioned it was disapproving. This did not really mean she disliked Connie, and actually Connie thought that her mother preferred her to June just because she was prettier, but the two of them kept up a pretense of exasperation, a sense that they were tugging and struggling over something of little value to either of them. Sometimes, over coffee, they were almost friends, but something would come up—some vexation that was like a fly buzzing suddenly around their heads—and their faces went hard with contempt.

One Sunday Connie got up at eleven—none of them bothered with church— and washed her hair so that it could dry all day long in the sun. Her parents and sister were going to a barbecue at an aunt's house and Connie said no, she wasn't interested, rolling her eyes to let her mother know just what she thought of it. "Stay home alone then," her mother said sharply. Connie sat out back in a lawn chair and watched them drive away, her father quiet and bald, hunched around so that he could back the car out, her mother with a look that was still angry and not at all softened through the windshield, and in the back seat poor old June, all dressed up as if she didn't know what a barbecue was, with all the running yelling kids and the flies. Connie sat with her eyes closed in the sun, dreaming and dazed with the warmth about her as if this were a kind of love, the caresses of love, and her mind slipped over onto thoughts of the boy she had been with the night before and how nice he had been, how sweet it always was, not the way someone like June would suppose but sweet, gentle, the way it was in movies and promised in songs; and when she opened her eyes she hardly knew where she was, the back yard ran off into weeds and a fence-like line of trees and behind it the sky was perfectly blue and still. The asbestos "ranch house" that was now three years old startled her—it looked small. She shook her head as if to get awake.

It was too hot. She went inside the house and turned on the radio to drown out the quiet. She sat on the edge of her bed, barefoot, and listened for an hour and a half to a program called XYZ Sunday Jamboree, record after record of hard, fast, shrieking songs she sang along with, interspersed by exclamations from "Bobby King": "An' look here, you girls at Napoleon's—Son and Charley want you to pay real close attention to this song coming up!"

And Connie paid close attention herself, bathed in a glow of slow-pulsed joy that seemed to rise mysteriously out of the music itself and lay languidly about the airless little room, breathed in and breathed out with each gentle rise and fall of her chest.

After a while she heard a car coming up the drive. She sat up at once, startled, because it couldn't be her father so soon. The gravel kept crunching all the way in from the road—the driveway was long—and Connie ran to the window. It was a car she didn't know. It was an open jalopy, painted a bright gold that caught the sunlight opaquely. Her heart began to pound and her fingers snatched at her hair, checking it, and she whispered, "Christ. Christ," wondering how bad she looked. The car came to a stop at the side door and the horn sounded four short taps, as if this were a signal Connie knew. 15

She went into the kitchen and approached the door slowly, then hung out the screen door, her bare toes curling down off the step. There were two boys in the car and now she recognized the driver: he had shaggy, shabby black hair that looked crazy as a wig and he was grinning at her.

"I ain't late, am I?" he said.

"Who the hell do you think you are?" Connie said.

"Toldja I'd be out, didn't I?"

"I don't even know who you are." 20

She spoke sullenly, careful to show no interest or pleasure, and he spoke in a fast, bright monotone. Connie looked past him to the other boy, taking her time. He had fair brown hair, with a lock that fell onto his forehead. His sideburns gave him a fierce, embarrassed look, but so far he hadn't even bothered to glance at her. Both boys wore sunglasses. The driver's glasses were metallic and mirrored everything in miniature.

"You wanta come for a ride?" he said.

Connie smirked and let her hair fall loose over one shoulder.

"Don'tcha like my car? New paint job," he said. "Hey."

"What?"   25

"You're cute."

She pretended to fidget, chasing flies away from the door.

"Don'tcha believe me, or what?" he said.

"Look, I don't even know who you are," Connie said in disgust.

"Hey, Ellie's got a radio, see. Mine's broke down." He lifted his friend's arm and   30
showed her the little transistor radio the boy was holding, and now Connie began to hear the music. It was the same program that was playing inside the house.

"Bobby King?" she said.

"I listen to him all the time. I think he's great."

"He's kind of great," Connie said reluctantly.

"Listen, that guy's *great*. He knows where the action is."

Connie blushed a little, because the glasses made it impossible for her to see   35
just what this boy was looking at. She couldn't decide if she liked him or if he was just a jerk, and so she dawdled in the doorway and wouldn't come down or go back inside. She said, "What's all that stuff painted on your car?"

"Can'tcha read it?" He opened the door very carefully, as if he were afraid it might fall off. He slid out just as carefully, planting his feet firmly on the ground, the tiny metallic world in his glasses slowing down like gelatine hardening and in the midst of it Connie's bright green blouse. "This here is my name to begin with," he said. ARNOLD FRIEND was written in tarlike black letters on the side, with a drawing of a round, grinning face that reminded Connie of a pumpkin, except it wore sunglasses. "I wanta introduce myself. I'm Arnold Friend and that's my real name and I'm gonna be your friend, honey, and inside the car's Ellie Oscar, he's kinda shy." Ellie brought his transistor radio up to his shoulder and balanced it there. "Now these numbers are a secret code, honey," Arnold Friend explained. He read off the numbers 33, 19, 17 and raised his eyebrows at her to see what she thought of that, but she didn't think much of it. The left rear fender had been smashed and around it was written, on the gleaming gold background: DONE BY CRAZY WOMAN DRIVER. Connie had to laugh at that. Arnold Friend was pleased at her laughter and looked up at her. "Around the other side's a lot more— you wanta come and see them?"

"No."

"Why not?"

"Why should I?"

"Don'tcha wanta see what's on the car? Don'tcha wanta go for a ride?"   40

"I don't know."

"Why not?"

"I got things to do."

"Like what?"

"Things."   45

He laughed as if she had said something funny. He slapped his thigh. He was standing in a strange way, leaning back against the car as if he were balancing himself. He wasn't tall, only an inch or so taller than she would be if she came down to him. Connie liked the way he was dressed, which was the way all of them dressed: tight faded jeans stuffed into black, scuffed boots, a belt that pulled his waist in and showed how lean he was, and a white pull-over shirt that was a little soiled and showed the hard small muscles of his arms and shoulders. He looked as if he probably did hard work, lifting and carrying things. Even his neck looked muscular. And his face was a familiar face, somehow: the jaw and chin and cheeks slightly darkened because he hadn't shaved for a day or two, and the nose long and hawklike, sniffing as if she were a treat he was going to gobble up and it was all a joke.

"Connie, you ain't telling the truth. This is your day set aside for a ride with me and you know it," he said, still laughing. The way he straightened and recovered from his fit of laughing showed that it had been all fake.

"How do you know what my name is?" she said suspiciously.

"It's Connie."

"Maybe and maybe not."   50

"I know my Connie," he said, wagging his finger. Now she remembered him even better, back at the restaurant, and her cheeks warmed at the thought of how she had sucked in her breath just at the moment she passed him—how she must have looked to him. And he had remembered her. "Ellie and I come out here especially for you," he said. "Ellie can sit in back. How about it?"

"Where?"

"Where what?"

"Where're we going?"

He looked at her. He took off the sunglasses and she saw how pale the skin   55
around his eyes was, like holes that were not in shadow but instead in light. His eyes were chips of broken glass that catch the light in an amiable way. He smiled. It was as if the idea of going for a ride somewhere, to some place, was a new idea to him.

"Just for a ride, Connie sweetheart."

"I never said my name was Connie," she said.

"But I know what it is. I know your name and all about you, lots of things," Arnold Friend said. He had not moved yet but stood still leaning back against the side of his jalopy. "I took a special interest in you, such a pretty girl, and found out all about you—like I know your parents and sister are gone some-wheres and I know where and how long they're going to be gone, and I know who you were with last night, and your best girl friend's name is Betty. Right?"

He spoke in a simple lilting voice, exactly as if he were reciting the words to a song. His smile assured her that everything was fine. In the car Ellie turned up the volume on his radio and did not bother to look around at them.

"Ellie can sit in the back seat," Arnold Friend said. He indicated his friend with a   60
casual jerk of his chin, as if Ellie did not count and she should not bother with him.

"How'd you find out all that stuff?" Connie said.

"Listen: Betty Schultz and Tony Fitch and Jimmy Pettinger and Nancy Pettinger," he said in a chant. "Raymond Stanley and Bob Hutter—"

"Do you know all those kids?"

"I know everybody."

"Look, you're kidding. You're not from around here."   65

"Sure."

"But—how come we never saw you before?"

"Sure you saw me before," he said. He looked down at his boots, as if he were a little offended. "You just don't remember."

"I guess I'd remember you," Connie said.

"Yeah?" He looked up at this, beaming. He was pleased. He began to mark time   70
with the music from Ellie's radio, tapping his fists lightly together. Connie looked
away from his smile to the car, which was painted so bright it almost hurt her eyes
to look at it. She looked at that name, ARNOLD FRIEND. And up at the front fender
was an expression that was familiar—MAN THE FLYING SAUCERS. It was an expression kids had used the year before but didn't use this year. She looked at it for a
while as if the words meant something to her that she did not yet know.

"What're you thinking about? Huh?" Arnold Friend demanded. "Not worried
about your hair blowing around in the car, are you?"

"No."

"Think I maybe can't drive good?"

"How do I know?"

"You're a hard girl to handle. How come?" he said. "Don't you know I'm your   75
friend? Didn't you see me put my sign in the air when you walked by?"

"What sign?"

"My sign." And he drew an X in the air, leaning out toward her. They were
maybe ten feet apart. After his hand fell back to his side the X was still in the air,
almost visible. Connie let the screen door close and stood perfectly still inside it,
listening to the music from her radio and the boy's blend together. She stared at
Arnold Friend. He stood there so stiffly relaxed, pretending to be relaxed, with
one hand idly on the door handle as if he were keeping himself up that way and
had no intention of ever moving again. She recognized most things about him,
the tight jeans that showed his thighs and buttocks and the greasy leather boots
and the tight shirt, and even that slippery friendly smile of his, that sleepy
dreamy smile that all the boys used to get across ideas they didn't want to put
into words. She recognized all this and also the singsong way he talked, slightly
mocking, kidding, but serious and a little melancholy, and she recognized the
way he tapped one fist against the other in homage to the perpetual music behind
him. But all these things did not come together.

She said suddenly, "Hey, how old are you?"

His smile faded. She could see then that he wasn't a kid, he was much older—
thirty, maybe more. At this knowledge her heart began to pound faster.

"That's a crazy thing to ask. Can'tcha see I'm your own age?"   80

"Like hell you are."

"Or maybe a coupla years older. I'm eighteen."

"Eighteen?" she said doubtfully.

He grinned to reassure her and lines appeared at the corners of his mouth.
His teeth were big and white. He grinned so broadly his eyes became slits and
she saw how thick the lashes were, thick and black as if painted with a black
tar-like material. Then, abruptly, he seemed to become embarrassed and looked
over his shoulder at Ellie. "*Him*, he's crazy," he said. "Ain't he a riot? He's a nut,
a real character." Ellie was still listening to the music. His sunglasses told nothing about what he was thinking. He wore a bright orange shirt unbuttoned
halfway to show his chest, which was a pale, bluish chest and not muscular
like Arnold Friend's. His shirt collar was turned up all around and the very tips
of the collar pointed out past his chin as if they were protecting him. He was
pressing the transistor radio up against his ear and sat there in a kind of daze,
right in the sun.

"He's kinda strange," Connie said.   85

"Hey, she says you're kinda strange! Kinda strange!" Arnold Friend cried. He pounded on the car to get Ellie's attention. Ellie turned for the first time and Connie saw with shock that he wasn't a kid either—he had a fair, hairless face, cheeks reddened slightly as if the veins grew too close to the surface of his skin, the face of a forty-year-old baby. Connie felt a wave of dizziness rise in her at this sight and she stared at him as if waiting for something to change the shock of the moment, make it all right again. Ellie's lips kept shaping words, mumbling along with the words blasting in his ear.

"Maybe you two better go away," Connie said faintly.

"What? How come?" Arnold Friend cried. "We come out here to take you for a ride. It's Sunday." He had the voice of the man on the radio now. It was the same voice, Connie thought. "Don'tcha know it's Sunday all day? And honey, no matter who you were with last night, today you're with Arnold Friend and don't you forget it! Maybe you better step out here," he said, and this last was in a different voice. It was a little flatter, as if the heat was finally getting to him.

"No. I got things to do."

"Hey."   90

"You two better leave."

"We ain't leaving until you come with us."

"Like hell I am—"

"Connie, don't fool around with me. I mean—I mean, don't fool *around*," he said, shaking his head. He laughed incredulously. He placed his sunglasses on top of his head, carefully, as if he were indeed wearing a wig, and brought the stems down behind his ears. Connie stared at him, another wave of dizziness and fear rising in her so that for a moment he wasn't even in focus but was just a blur standing there against his gold car, and she had the idea that he had driven up the driveway all right but had come from nowhere before that and belonged nowhere and that everything about him and even about the music that was so familiar to her was only half real.

"If my father comes and sees you—"   95

"He ain't coming. He's at a barbecue."

"How do you know that?"

"Aunt Tillie's. Right now they're—uh—they're drinking. Sitting around," he said vaguely, squinting as if he were staring all the way to town and over to Aunt Tillie's back yard. Then the vision seemed to get clear and he nodded energetically. "Yeah. Sitting around. There's your sister in a blue dress, huh? And high heels, the poor sad bitch—nothing like you, sweetheart! And your mother's helping some fat woman with the corn, they're cleaning the corn—husking the corn—"

"What fat woman?" Connie cried.

"How do I know what fat woman. I don't know every goddamn fat woman in   100
the world!" Arnold Friend laughed.

"Oh, that's Mrs. Hornsby....Who invited her?" Connie said. She felt a little light-headed. Her breath was coming quickly.

"She's too fat. I don't like them fat. I like them the way you are, honey," he said, smiling sleepily at her. They stared at each other for a while through the screen door. He said softly, "Now, what you're going to do is this: you're going to come out that door. You're going to sit up front with me and Ellie's going to sit in the back, the hell with Ellie, right? This isn't Ellie's date. You're my date. I'm your lover, honey."

"What? You're crazy—"

"Yes, I'm your lover. You don't know what that is but you will," he said. "I know that too. I know all about you. But look: it's real nice and you couldn't ask for nobody better than me, or more polite. I always keep my word. I'll tell you how it is, I'm always nice at first, the first time. I'll hold you so tight you won't think you have to try to get away or pretend anything because you'll know you can't. And I'll come inside you where it's all secret and you'll give in to me and you'll love me—"

"Shut up! You're crazy!" Connie said. She backed away from the door. She put 105
her hands up against her ears as if she'd heard something terrible, something not meant for her. "People don't talk like that, you're crazy," she muttered. Her heart was almost too big now for her chest and its pumping made sweat break out all over her. She looked out to see Arnold Friend pause and then take a step toward the porch, lurching. He almost fell. But, like a clever drunken man, he managed to catch his balance. He wobbled in his high boots and grabbed hold of one of the porch posts.

"Honey?" he said. "You still listening?"

"Get the hell out of here!"

"Be nice, honey. Listen."

"I'm going to call the police—"

He wobbled again and out of the side of his mouth came a fast spat curse, an 110
aside not meant for her to hear. But even this "Christ!" sounded forced. Then he began to smile again. She watched this smile come, awkward as if he were smiling from inside a mask. His whole face was a mask, she thought wildly, tanned down to his throat but then running out as if he had plastered makeup on his face but had forgotten about his throat.

"Honey—? Listen, here's how it is. I always tell the truth and I promise you this: I ain't coming in that house after you."

"You better not! I'm going to call the police if you—if you don't—"

"Honey," he said, talking right through her voice, "honey, I'm not coming in there but you are coming out here. You know why?"

She was panting. The kitchen looked like a place she had never seen before, some room she had run inside but that wasn't good enough, wasn't going to help her. The kitchen window had never had a curtain, after three years, and there were dishes in the sink for her to do—probably—and if you ran your hand across the table you'd probably feel something sticky there.

"You listening honey? Hey?" 115

"—going to call the police—"

"Soon as you touch the phone I don't need to keep my promise and can come inside. You won't want that."

She rushed forward and tried to lock the door. Her fingers were shaking. "But why lock it," Arnold Friend said gently, talking right into her face. "It's just a screen door. It's just nothing." One of his boots was at a strange angle, as if his foot wasn't in it. It pointed out to the left, bent at the ankle. "I mean, anybody can break through a screen door and glass and wood and iron or anything else if he needs to, anybody at all, and specially Arnold Friend. If the place got lit up with a fire, honey, you'd come runnin' out into my arms, right into my arms an' safe at home—like you knew I was your lover and'd stopped fooling around. I don't mind a nice shy girl but I don't like no fooling around." Part of those words were spoken with a slight rhythmic lilt, and Connie somehow recognized them—the echo of a song from last year, about a girl rushing into her boy friend's arms and coming home again—

Connie stood barefoot on the linoleum floor, staring at him. "What do you want?" she whispered.

"I want you," he said.   120

"What?"

"Seen you that night and thought, that's the one, yes sir. I never needed to look anymore."

"But my father's coming back. He's coming to get me. I had to wash my hair first—" She spoke in a dry, rapid voice, hardly raising it for him to hear.

"No, your daddy is not coming and yes, you had to wash your hair and you washed it for me. It's nice and shining and all for me. I thank you sweetheart," he said with a mock bow, but again he almost lost his balance. He had to bend and adjust his boots. Evidently his feet did not go all the way down; the boots must have been stuffed with something so that he would seem taller. Connie stared out at him and behind him at Ellie in the car, who seemed to be looking off toward Connie's right, into nothing. This Ellie said, pulling the words out of the air one after another as if he were just discovering them, "You want me to pull out the phone?"

"Shut your mouth and keep it shut," Arnold Friend said, his face red from   125
bending over or maybe from embarrassment because Connie had seen his boots. "This ain't none of your business."

"What—what are you doing? What do you want?" Connie said. "If I call the police they'll get you, they'll arrest you—"

"Promise was not to come in unless you touch that phone, and I'll keep that promise," he said. He resumed his erect position and tried to force his shoulders back. He sounded like a hero in a movie, declaring something important. But he spoke too loudly and it was as if he were speaking to someone behind Connie. "I ain't made plans for coming in that house where I don't belong but just for you to come out to me, the way you should. Don't you know who I am?"

"You're crazy," she whispered. She backed away from the door but did not want to go into another part of the house, as if this would give him permission to come through the door. "What do you...you're crazy, you...."

"Huh? What're you saying, honey?"

Her eyes darted everywhere in the kitchen. She could not remember what it   130
was, this room.

"This is how it is, honey: you come out and we'll drive away, have a nice ride. But if you don't come out we're gonna wait till your people come home and then they're all going to get it."

"You want that telephone pulled out?" Ellie said. He held the radio away from his ear and grimaced, as if without the radio the air was too much for him.

"I toldja shut up, Ellie," Arnold Friend said, "you're deaf, get a hearing aid, right? Fix yourself up. This little girl's no trouble and's gonna be nice to me, so Ellie keep to yourself, this ain't your date—right? Don't hem in on me, don't hog, don't crush, don't bird dog, don't trail me," he said in a rapid, meaningless voice, as if he were running through all the expressions he'd learned but was no longer sure which of them was in style, then rushing on to new ones, making them up with his eyes closed. "Don't crawl under my fence, don't squeeze in my chipmunk hole, don't sniff my glue, suck my popsicle, keep your own greasy fingers on yourself!" He shaded his eyes and peered in at Connie, who was backed against the kitchen table. "Don't mind him, honey, he's just a creep. He's a dope. Right? I'm the boy for you and like I said, you come out here nice like a lady and give me your hand, and nobody else gets hurt, I mean, your nice old bald-headed daddy and your mummy and your sister in her high heels. Because listen: why bring them in this?"

"Leave me alone," Connie whispered.

"Hey, you know that old woman down the road, the one with the chickens and stuff—you know her?"   135

"She's dead!"

"Dead? What? You know her?" Arnold Friend said.

"She's dead—"

"Don't you like her?"

"She's dead—she's—she isn't here any more—"?   140

"But don't you like her, I mean, you got something against her? Some grudge or something?" Then his voice dipped as if he were conscious of a rudeness. He touched the sunglasses perched up on top of his head as if to make sure they were still there. "Now, you be a good girl."

"What are you going to do?"

"Just two things, or maybe three," Arnold Friend said. "But I promise it won't last long and you'll like me that way you get to like people you're close to. You will. It's all over for you here, so come on out. You don't want your people in any trouble, do you?"

She turned and bumped against a chair or something, hurting her leg, but she ran into the back room and picked up the telephone. Something roared in her ear, a tiny roaring, and she was so sick with fear that she could do nothing but listen to it—the telephone was clammy and very heavy and her fingers groped down to the dial but were too weak to touch it. She began to scream into the phone, into the roaring. She cried out, she cried for her mother, she felt her breath start jerking back and forth in her lungs as if it were something Arnold Friend was stabbing her with again and again with no tenderness. A noisy sorrowful wailing rose all about her and she was locked inside it the way she was locked inside this house.

After a while she could hear again. She was sitting on the floor with her wet   145
back against the wall.

Arnold Friend was saying from the door, "That's a good girl. Put the phone back."

She kicked the phone away from her.

"No, honey. Pick it up. Put it back right."

She picked it up and put it back. The dial tone stopped.

"That's a good girl. Now, you come outside."   150

She was hollow with what had been fear but what was now just an emptiness. All that screaming had blasted it out of her. She sat, one leg cramped under her, and deep inside her brain was something like a pinpoint of light that kept going and would not let her relax. She thought, I'm not going to see my mother again. She thought, I'm not going to sleep in my bed again. Her bright green blouse was all wet.

Arnold Friend said, in a gentle-loud voice that was like a stage voice, "The place where you came from ain't there any more, and where you had in mind to go is cancelled out. This place you are now—inside your daddy's house—is nothing but a cardboard box I can knock down any time. You know that and always did know it. You hear me?"

She thought, I have got to think. I have to know what to do.

"We'll go out to a nice field, out in the country here where it smells so nice and it's sunny," Arnold Friend said. "I'll have my arms tight around you so you won't need to try to get away and I'll show you what love is like, what it does. The hell with this house! It looks solid all right," he said. He ran a fingernail down the screen and the noise did not make Connie shiver, as it would have the day before. "Now, put your hand on your heart, honey. Feel that? That feels solid too but we know better. Be nice to me, be sweet like you can because what else is there for a girl like you but to be sweet and pretty and give in?—and get away before her people come back?"

She felt her pounding heart. Her hand seemed to enclose it. She thought for the first time in her life that it was nothing that was hers, that belonged to her, but just a pounding, living thing inside this body that wasn't really hers either. 155

"You don't want them to get hurt," Arnold Friend went on. "Now, get up, honey. Get up all by yourself."

She stood.

"Now, turn this way. That's right. Come over here to me—Ellie, put that away, didn't I tell you? You dope. You miserable creepy dope," Arnold Friend said. His words were not angry but only part of an incantation. The incantation was kindly. "Now, come out through the kitchen to me, honey, and let's see a smile, try it, you're a brave, sweet little girl and now they're eating corn and hot dogs cooked to bursting over an outdoor fire, and they don't know one thing about you and never did and honey, you're better than them because not a one of them would have done this for you."

Connie felt the linoleum under her feet; it was cool. She brushed her hair back out of her eyes. Arnold Friend let go of the post tentatively and opened his arms for her, his elbows pointing in toward each other and his wrists limp, to

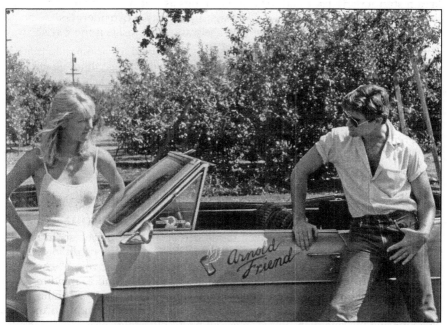

Laura Dern as Connie and Treat Williams as Arnold Friend in *Smooth Talk*, the 1985 film version of "Where Are You Going, Where Have You Been?"

show that this was an embarrassed embrace and a little mocking, he didn't want to make her self-conscious.

She put out her hand against the screen. She watched herself push the door   160 slowly open as if she were back safe somewhere in the other doorway, watching this body and this head of long hair moving out into the sunlight where Arnold Friend waited.

"My sweet little blue-eyed girl," he said in a half-sung sigh that had nothing to do with her brown eyes but was taken up just the same by the vast sunlit reaches of the land behind him and on all sides of him—so much land that Connie had never seen before and did not recognize except to know that she was going to it.

(1966)

Questions for Discussion and Writing

1. Explain the title. Why is it in the form of a question, and why are there two parts to the question? Who does "you" refer to?
2. Who is the story's main character, Connie or Arnold Friend?
3. What do you think of the various members of Connie's family? Why has Oates limited their roles in the story?
4. Where does Arnold take Connie, and what happens to her? Write your own continuation of the story.
5. Write a comparison between Connie and Eveline (see pages 4–7). Argue that these seemingly different protagonists are similar in several significant ways.

Raymond Carver   1938–1988

Raymond Carver grew up poor in Yakima, Washington. Married at nineteen and a father of two by twenty, he moved to California, worked nights, attended college, divorced, and, as he put it, "took up drinking as a serious pursuit." At age thirty-nine, though, he gave up alcohol and observed, "In this second life, this post-drinking life, I still retain a certain sense of pessimism." But he did not give up smoking, declaring himself "a cigarette with a body attached to it." Two years before dying of lung cancer at age fifty, he and his partner, the poet Tess Gallagher, were married in a Reno chapel in a ceremony he described as a "high tacky affair."

What We Talk About When We Talk About Love

My friend Mel McGinnis was talking. Mel McGinnis is a cardiologist, and sometimes that gives him the right.

The four of us were sitting around his kitchen table drinking gin. Sunlight filled the kitchen from the big window behind the sink. There were Mel and me and his second wife, Teresa—Terri, we called her—and my wife, Laura. We lived in Albuquerque then. But we were all from somewhere else.

There was an ice bucket on the table. The gin and the tonic water kept going around, and we somehow got on the subject of love. Mel thought real love was nothing less than spiritual love. He said he'd spent five years in a seminary before quitting to go to medical school. He said he still looked back on those years in the seminary as the most important years in his life.

Terri said the man she lived with before she lived with Mel loved her so much he tried to kill her. Then Terri said, "He beat me up one night. He dragged me around the living room by my ankles. He kept saying, 'I love you, I love you, you bitch.' He went on dragging me around the living room. My head kept knocking on things." Terri looked around the table. "What do you do with love like that?"

She was a bone-thin woman with a pretty face, dark eyes, and brown hair that 5 hung down her back. She liked necklaces made of turquoise, and long pendant earrings.

"My God, don't be silly. That's not love, and you know it," Mel said. "I don't know what you'd call it, but I sure know you wouldn't call it love."

"Say what you want to, but I know it was," Terri said. "It may sound crazy to you, but it's true just the same. People are different, Mel. Sure, sometimes he may have acted crazy. Okay. But he loved me. In his own way maybe, but he loved me. There was love there, Mel. Don't say there wasn't."

Mel let out his breath. He held his glass and turned to Laura and me. "The man threatened to kill me," Mel said. He finished his drink and reached for the gin bottle. "Terri's a romantic. Terri's of the kick-me-so-I'll-know-you-love-me school. Terri, hon, don't look that way." Mel reached across the table and touched Terri's cheek with his fingers. He grinned at her.

"Now he wants to make up," Terri said.

"Make up what?" Mel said. "What is there to make up? I know what I know. 10 That's all."

"How'd we get started on this subject, anyway?" Terri said. She raised her glass and drank from it. "Mel always has love on his mind," she said. "Don't you, honey?" She smiled, and I thought that was the last of it.

"I just wouldn't call Ed's behavior love. That's all I'm saying, honey," Mel said. "What about you guys?" Mel said to Laura and me. "Does that sound like love to you?"

"I'm the wrong person to ask," I said. "I didn't even know the man. I've only heard his name mentioned in passing. I wouldn't know. You'd have to know the particulars. But I think what you're saying is that love is an absolute."

Mel said, "The kind of love I'm talking about is. The kind of love I'm talking about, you don't try to kill people."

Laura said, "I don't know anything about Ed, or anything about the situation. 15 But who can judge anyone else's situation?"

I touched the back of Laura's hand. She gave me a quick smile. I picked up Laura's hand. It was warm, the nails polished, perfectly manicured. I encircled the broad wrist with my fingers, and I held her.

"When I left, he drank rat poison," Terri said. She clasped her arms with her hands. "They took him to the hospital in Santa Fe. That's where we lived then, about ten miles out. They saved his life. But his gums went crazy from it. I mean they pulled away from his teeth. After that, his teeth stood out like fangs. My God," Terri said. She waited a minute, then let go of her arms and picked up her glass.

"What people won't do!" Laura said.

"He's out of the action now," Mel said. "He's dead."

Mel handed me the saucer of limes. I took a section, squeezed it over my 20 drink, and stirred the ice cubes with my finger.

"It gets worse," Terri said. "He shot himself in the mouth. But he bungled that too. Poor Ed," she said. Terri shook her head.

"Poor Ed nothing," Mel said. "He was dangerous."

Mel was forty-five years old. He was tall and rangy with curly soft hair. His face and arms were brown from the tennis he played. When he was sober, his gestures, all his movements, were precise, very careful.

"He did love me though, Mel. Grant me that," Terri said. "That's all I'm asking. He didn't love me the way you love me. I'm not saying that. But he loved me. You can grant me that, can't you?"

"What do you mean, he bungled it?" I said.   25

Laura leaned forward with her glass. She put her elbows on the table and held her glass in both hands. She glanced from Mel to Terri and waited with a look of bewilderment on her open face, as if amazed that such things happened to people you were friendly with.

"How'd he bungle it when he killed himself?" I said.

"I'll tell you what happened," Mel said. "He took this twenty-two pistol he'd bought to threaten Terri and me with. Oh, I'm serious, the man was always threatening. You should have seen the way we lived in those days. Like fugitives. I even bought a gun myself. Can you belive it? A guy like me? But I did. I bought one for self-defense and carried it in the glove compartment. Sometimes I'd have to leave the apartment in the middle of the night. To go to the hospital, you know? Terri and I weren't married then, and my first wife had the house and kids, the dog, everything, and Terri and I were living in this apartment here. Sometimes, as I say, I'd get a call in the middle of the night and have to go in to the hospital at two or three in the morning. It'd be dark out there in the parking lot, and I'd break into a sweat before I could even get to my car. I never knew if he was going to come up out of the shrubbery or from behind a car and start shooting. I mean, the man was crazy. He was capable of wiring a bomb, anything. He used to call my service at all hours and say he needed to talk to the doctor, and when I'd return the call, he'd say, 'Son of a bitch, your days are numbered.' Little things like that. It was scary, I'm telling you."

"I still feel sorry for him," Terri said.

"It sounds like a nightmare," Laura said. "But what exactly happened after he   30
shot himself?"

Laura is a legal secretary. We'd met in a professional capacity. Before we knew it, it was a courtship. She's thirty-five, three years younger than I am. In addition to being in love, we like each other and enjoy one another's company. She's easy to be with.

"What happened?" Laura said.

Mel said, "He shot himself in the mouth in his room. Someone heard the shot and told the manager. They came in with a passkey, saw what had happened, and called an ambulance. I happened to be there when they brought him in, alive but past recall. The man lived for three days. His head swelled up to twice the size of a normal head. I'd never seen anything like it, and I hope I never do again. Terri wanted to go in and sit with him when she found out about it. We had a fight over it. I didn't think she should see him like that. I didn't think she should see him, and I still don't."

"Who won the fight?" Laura said.

"I was in the room with him when he died," Terri said. "He never came up 35
out of it. But I sat with him. He didn't have anyone else."

"He was dangerous," Mel said. "If you call that love, you can have it."

"It was love," Terri said. "Sure, it's abnormal in most people's eyes. But he
was willing to die for it. He did die for it."

"I sure as hell wouldn't call it love," Mel said. "I mean, no one knows what he
did it for. I've seen a lot of suicides, and I couldn't say anyone ever knew what
they did it for."

Mel put his hands behind his neck and tilted his chair back. "I'm not interested
in that kind of love," he said. "If that's love, you can have it."

Terri said, "We were afraid. Mel even made a will out and wrote to his 40
brother in California who used to be a Green Beret. Mel told him who to look
for if something happened to him."

Terri drank from her glass. She said, "But Mel's right—we lived like fugitives.
We were afraid. Mel was, weren't you, honey? I even called the police at one point,
but they were no help. They said they couldn't do anything until Ed actually did
something. Isn't that a laugh?" Terri said.

She poured the last of the gin into her glass and waggled the bottle. Mel got
up from the table and went to the cupboard. He took down another bottle.

"Well, Nick and I know what love is," Laura said. "For us, I mean," Laura
said. She bumped my knee with her knee. "You're supposed to say something
now," Laura said, and turned her smile on me.

For an answer, I took Laura's hand and raised it to my lips. I made a big production out of kissing her hand. Everyone was amused.

"We're lucky," I said. 45

"You guys," Terri said. "Stop that now. You're making me sick. You're still on
the honeymoon, for God's sake. You're still gaga, for crying out loud. Just wait.
How long have you been together now? How long has it been? A year? Longer
than a year?"

"Going on a year and a half," Laura said, flushed and smiling.

"Oh, now," Terri said. "Wait awhile."

She held her drink and gazed at Laura.

"I'm only kidding," Terri said. 50

Mel opened the gin and went around the table with the bottle.

"Here, you guys," he said. "Let's have a toast. I want to propose a toast. A
toast to love. To true love," Mel said.

We touched glasses.

"To love," we said.

Outside in the backyard, one of the dogs began to bark. The leaves of the 55
aspen that leaned past the window ticked against the glass. The afternoon sun
was like a presence in this room, the spacious light of ease and generosity. We
could have been anywhere, somewhere enchanted. We raised our glasses
again and grinned at each other like children who had agreed on something
forbidden.

"I'll tell you what real love is," Mel said. "I mean, I'll give you a good example.
And then you can draw your own conclusions." He poured more gin into his glass.
He added an ice cube and a sliver of lime. We waited and sipped our drinks. Laura
and I touched knees again. I put a hand on her warm thigh and left it there.

"What do any of us really know about love?" Mel said. "It seems to me we're just beginners at love. We say we love each other and we do, I don't doubt it. I love Terri and Terri loves me, and you guys love each other too. You know the kind of love I'm talking about now. Physical love, that impulse that drives you to someone special, as well as love of the other person's being, his or her essence, as it were. Carnal love and, well, call it sentimental love, the day-to-day caring about the other person. But sometimes I have a hard time accounting for the fact that I must have loved my first wife too. But I did, I know I did. So I suppose I am like Terri in that regard. Terri and Ed." He thought about it and then he went on. "There was a time when I thought I loved my first wife more than life itself. But now I hate her guts. I do. How do you explain that? What happened to that love? What happened to it, is what I'd like to know. I wish someone could tell me. Then there's Ed. Okay, we're back to Ed. He loves Terri so much he tries to kill her and he winds up killing himself." Mel stopped talking and swallowed from his glass. "You guys have been together eighteen months and you love each other. It shows all over you. You glow with it. But you both loved other people before you met each other. You've both been married before, just like us. And you probably loved other people before that too, even. Terri and I have been together five years, been married for four. And the terrible thing, the terrible thing is, but the good thing too, the saving grace, you might say, is that if something happened to one of us—excuse me for saying this—but if something happened to one of us tomorrow, I think the other one, the other person, would grieve for a while, you know, but then the surviving party would go out and love again, have someone else soon enough. All this, all of this love we're talking about, it would just be a memory. Maybe not even a memory. Am I wrong? Am I way off base? Because I want you to set me straight if you think I'm wrong. I want to know. I mean, I don't know anything, and I'm the first one to admit it."

"Mel, for God's sake," Terri said. She reached out and took hold of his wrist. "Are you getting drunk? Honey? Are you drunk?"

"Honey, I'm just talking," Mel said. "All right? I don't have to be drunk to say what I think. I mean, we're all just talking, right?" Mel said. He fixed his eyes on her.

"Sweetie, I'm not criticizing," Terri said.   60

She picked up her glass.

"I'm not on call today," Mel said. "Let me remind you of that. I am not on call," he said.

"Mel, we love you," Laura said.

Mel looked at Laura. He looked at her as if he could not place her, as if she was not the woman she was.

"Love you too, Laura," Mel said. "And you, Nick, love you too. You know   65 something?" Mel said. "You guys are our pals," Mel said.

He picked up his glass.

Mel said, "I was going to tell you about something. I mean, I was going to prove a point. You see, this happened a few months ago, but it's still going on right now, and it ought to make us feel ashamed when we talk like we know what we're talking about when we talk about love."

"Come on now," Terri said. "Don't talk like you're drunk if you're not drunk."

"Just shut up for once in your life," Mel said very quietly. "Will you do me a favor and do that for a minute? So as I was saying, there's this old couple who had this car wreck out on the interstate. A kid hit them and they were all torn to shit and nobody was giving them much chance to pull through."

Terri looked at us and then back at Mel. She seemed anxious, or maybe that's too strong a word.   70

Mel was handing the bottle around the table.

"I was on call that night," Mel said. "It was May or maybe it was June. Terri and I had just sat down to dinner when the hospital called. There'd been this thing out on the interstate. Drunk kid, teenager, plowed his dad's pickup into this camper with this old couple in it. They were up in their mid-seventies, that couple. The kid—eighteen, nineteen, something—he was DOA. Taken the steering wheel through his sternum. The old couple, they were alive, you understand. I mean, just barely. But they had everything. Multiple fractures, internal injuries, hemorrhaging, contusions, lacerations, the works, and they each of them had themselves concussions. They were in a bad way, believe me. And, of course, their age was two strikes against them. I'd say she was worse off than he was. Ruptured spleen along with everything else. Both kneecaps broken. But they'd been wearing their seatbelts and, God knows, that's what saved them for the time being."

"Folks, this is an advertisement for the National Safety Council," Terri said. "This is your spokesman, Dr. Melvin R. McGinnis, talking." Terri laughed. "Mel," she said, "sometimes you're just too much. But I love you, hon," she said.

"Honey, I love you," Mel said.

He leaned across the table. Terri met him halfway. They kissed.   75

"Terri's right," Mel said as he settled himself again. "Get those seatbelts on. But seriously, they were in some shape, those oldsters. By the time I got down there, the kid was dead, as I said. He was off in a corner, laid out on a gurney. I took one look at the old couple and told the ER nurse to get me a neurologist and an orthopedic man and a couple of surgeons down there right away."

He drank from his glass. "I'll try to keep this short," he said. "So we took the two of them up to the OR and worked like fuck on them most of the night. They had these incredible reserves, those two. You see that once in a while. So we did everything that could be done, and toward morning we're giving them a fifty-fifty chance, maybe less than that for her. So here they are, still alive the next morning. So, okay, we move them into the ICU, which is where they both kept plugging away at it for two weeks, hitting it better and better on all the scopes. So we transfer them out to their own room."

Mel stopped talking. "Here," he said, "let's drink this cheapo gin the hell up. Then we're going to dinner, right? Terri and I know a new place. That's where we'll go, to this new place we know about. But we're not going until we finish up this cut-rate, lousy gin."

Terri said, "We haven't actually eaten there yet. But it looks good. From the outside, you know."

"I like food," Mel said. "If I had it to do all over again, I'd be a chef, you know? Right, Terri?" Mel said.   80

He laughed. He fingered the ice in his glass.

"Terri knows," he said. "Terri can tell you. But let me say this. If I could come back again in a different life, a different time and all, you know what? I'd like to come back as a knight. You were pretty safe wearing all that armor. It was all right being a knight until gunpowder and muskets and pistols came along."

"Mel would like to ride a horse and carry a lance," Terri said.

"Carry a woman's scarf with you everywhere," Laura said.

"Or just a woman," Mel said.   85

"Shame on you," Laura said.

Terri said, "Suppose you came back as a serf. The serfs didn't have it so good in those days," Terri said.

"The serfs never had it good," Mel said. "But I guess even the knights were vessels to someone. Isn't that the way it worked? But then everyone is always a vessel to someone. Isn't that right? Terri? But what I liked about knights, besides their ladies, was that they had that suit of armor, you know, and they couldn't get hurt very easy. No cars in those days, you know? No drunk teenagers to tear into your ass."

"Vassals," Terri said.

"What?" Mel said.   90

"Vassals," Terri said. "They were called vassals, not vessels."

"Vassals, vessels," Mel said, "what the fuck's the difference? You knew what I meant anyway. All right," Mel said. "So I'm not educated. I learned my stuff. I'm a heart surgeon, sure, but I'm just a mechanic. I go in and fuck around and I fix things. Shit," Mel said.

"Modesty doesn't become you," Terri said.

"He's just a humble sawbones," I said. "But sometimes they suffocated in all that armor, Mel. They'd even have heart attacks if it got too hot and they were too tired and worn out. I read somewhere that they'd fall off their horses and not be able to get up because they were too tired to stand with all that armor on them. They got trampled by their own horses sometimes."

"That's terrible," Mel said. "That's a terrible thing, Nicky. I guess they'd just lay   95 there and wait until somebody came along and made a shish kebab out of them."

"Some other vessel," Terri said.

"That's right," Mel said. "Some vassal would come along and spear the bastard in the name of love. Or whatever the fuck it was they fought over in those days."

"Same things we fight over these days," Terri said.

Laura said, "Nothing's changed."

The color was still high in Laura's cheeks. Her eyes were bright. She brought   100 her glass to her lips.

Mel poured himself another drink. He looked at the label closely as if studying a long row of numbers. Then he slowly put the bottle down on the table and slowly reached for the tonic water.

"What about the old couple?" Laura said. "You didn't finish that story you started."

Laura was having a hard time lighting her cigarette. Her matches kept going out.

The sunshine inside the room was different now, changing, getting thinner. But the leaves outside the window were still shimmering, and I stared at the pattern they made on the panes and on the Formica counter. They weren't the same patterns, of course.

"What about the old couple?" I said.   105

"Older but wiser," Terri said.

Mel stared at her.

Terri said, "Go on with your story, hon. I was only kidding. Then what happened?"

"Terri, sometimes," Mel said.

"Please, Mel," Terri said. "Don't always be so serious, sweetie. Can't you take   110
a joke?"

"Where's the joke?" Mel said.

He held his glass and gazed steadily at his wife.

"What happened?" Laura said.

Mel fastened his eyes on Laura. He said, "Laura, if I didn't have Terri and if
I didn't love her so much, and if Nick wasn't my best friend, I'd fall in love with
you. I'd carry you off, honey," he said.

"Tell your story," Terri said. "Then we'll go to that new place, okay?"   115

"Okay," Mel said. "Where was I?" he said. He started at the table and then he
began again.

"I dropped in to see each of them every day, sometimes twice a day if I was up
doing other calls anyway. Casts and bandages, head to foot, the both of them.
You know, you've seen it in the movies. That's just the way they looked, just like
in the movies. Little eye-holes and nose-holes and mouth-holes. And she had to
have her legs slung up on top of it. Well, the husband was very depressed for the
longest while. Even after he found out that his wife was going to pull through,
he was still very depressed. Not about the accident, though. I mean, the accident
was one thing, but it wasn't everything. I'd get up to his mouth-hole, you know,
and he'd say no, it wasn't the accident exactly but it was because he couldn't see
her through his eye-holes. He said that was what was making him feel so bad.
Can you imagine? I'm telling you, the man's heart was breaking because he
couldn't turn his goddamn head and *see* his goddamn wife."

Mel looked around the table and shook his head at what he was going to say.

"I mean, it was killing the old fart just because he couldn't *look* at the fucking
woman."

We all looked at Mel.   120

"Do you see what I'm saying?" he said.

Maybe we were a little drunk by then. I know it was hard keeping things in
focus. The light was draining out of the room, going back through the window
where it had come from. Yet nobody made a move to get up from the table to
turn on the overhead light.

"Listen," Mel said. "Let's finish this fucking gin. There's about enough here
for one shooter all around. Then let's go eat. Let's go to the new place."

"He's depressed," Terri said. "Mel, why don't you take a pill?"

Mel shook his head. "I've taken everything there is."   125

"We all need a pill now and then," I said.

"Some people are born needing them," Terri said.

She was using her finger to rub at something on the table. Then she stopped
rubbing.

"I think I want to call my kids," Mel said. "Is that all right with everybody?
I'll call my kids," he said.

Terri said, "What if Marjorie answers the phone? You guys, you've heard us   130
on the subject of Marjorie? Honey, you know you don't want to talk to
Marjorie. It'll make you feel even worse."

"I don't want to talk to Marjorie," Mel said. "But I want to talk to my kids."

"There isn't a day goes by that Mel doesn't say he wishes she'd get married again.
Or else die," Terri said. "For one thing," Terri said, "she's bankrupting us. Mel says

it's just to spite him that she won't get married again. She has a boyfriend who lives with her and the kids, so Mel is supporting the boyfriend too."

"She's allergic to bees," Mel said. "If I'm not praying she'll get married again, I'm praying she'll get herself stung to death by a swarm of fucking bees."

"Shame on you," Laura said.

"Bzzzzzzz," Mel said, turning his fingers into bees and buzzing them at   135
Terri's throat. Then he let his hands drop all the way to his sides.

"She's vicious," Mel said. "Sometimes I think I'll go up there dressed like a beekeeper. You know, that hat that's like a helmet with the plate that comes down over your face, the big gloves, and the padded coat? I'll knock on the door and let loose a hive of bees in the house. But first I'd make sure the kids were out, of course."

He crossed one leg over the other. It seemed to take him a lot of time to do it. Then he put both feet on the floor and leaned forward, elbows on the table, his chin cupped in his hands.

"Maybe I won't call the kids, after all. Maybe it isn't such a hot idea. Maybe we'll just go eat. How does that sound?"

"Sounds fine to me," I said. "Eat or not eat. Or keep drinking. I could head right on out into the sunset."

"What does that mean, honey?" Laura said.   140

"It just means what I said," I said. "It means I could just keep going. That's all it means."

"I could eat something myself," Laura said. "I don't think I've ever been so hungry in my life. Is there something to nibble on?"

"I'll put out some cheese and crackers," Terri said.

But Terri just sat there. She did not get up to get anything.

Mel turned his glass over. He spilled it out on the table.   145

"Gin's gone," Mel said.

Terri said, "Now what?"

I could hear my heart beating. I could hear everyone's heart. I could hear the human noise we sat there making, not one of us moving, not even when the room went dark.

(1981)

Questions for Discussion and Writing

1. What different definitions and descriptions of love come up during the conversation? Do the characters ever get anywhere with the subject? Why or why not?

2. What distinguishes this story from other stories you have read in this course? Do you think you could recognize another Raymond Carver story? How?

3. When the narrator says of himself and Laura, "In addition to being in love, we like each other and enjoy one another's company," what is he saying about his definition of love?

4. Reread the first two paragraphs of the story. What expository information do you get in these few sentences?

5. Is this story optimistic or pessimistic about love? Write an essay arguing your answer to this question.

Toni Cade Bambara   1939–1995

Toni Cade Bambara wrote under the name Toni Cade until 1970, when she adopted the African name Bambara. Early on, she championed the civil rights struggle and the women's liberation movement and, in the 1970s, visited both Cuba and Vietnam to meet with women's groups there. In her fiction, her colorful characters speak in black dialect, which she spoke of as "riffs" or "be-bop." For a while, she said, writing seemed to her "rather frivolous, like something you did because you didn't feel like doing any work. But...I've come to appreciate that it is a perfectly legitimate way to participate in a struggle." She fought colon cancer but died in 1995 at age fifty-six.

The Lesson

Back in the days when everyone was old and stupid or young and foolish and me and Sugar were the only ones just right, this lady moved on our block with nappy hair and proper speech and no makeup. And quite naturally we laughed at her, laughed the way we did at the junk man who went about his business like he was some big-time president and his sorry-ass horse his secretary. And we kinda hated her too, hated the way we did the winos who cluttered up our parks and pissed on our handball walls and stank up our hallways and stairs so you couldn't halfway play hide-and-seek without a goddamn gas mask. Miss Moore was her name. The only woman on the block with no first name. And she was black as hell, cept for her feet, which were fish white and spooky. And she was always planning these boring-ass things for us to do, us being my cousin, mostly, who lived on the block cause we all moved North the same time and to the same apartment then spread out gradual to breathe. And our parents would yank our heads into some kinda shape and crisp up our clothes so we'd be presentable for travel with Miss Moore, who always looked like she was going to church, though she never did. Which is just one of the things the grownups talked about when they talked behind her back like a dog. But when she came calling with some sachet she'd sewed up or some gingerbread she'd made or some book, why then they'd all be too embarrassed to turn her down and we'd get handed over all spruced up. She'd been to college and said it was only right that she should take responsibility for the young ones' education, and she not even related by marriage or blood. So they'd go for it. Specially Aunt Gretchen. She was the main gofer in the family. You got some ole dumb shit foolishness you want somebody to go for, you send for Aunt Gretchen. She been screwed into the go-along for so long, it's a blood-deep natural thing with her. Which is how she got saddled with me and Sugar and Junior in the first place while our mothers were in a la-de-da apartment up the block having a good ole time.

So this one day Miss Moore rounds us all up at the mailbox and it's puredee hot and she's knockin herself out about arithmetic. And school suppose to let up in summer I heard, but she don't never let up. And the starch in my pinafore scratching the shit outta me and I'm really hating this nappy-head bitch and her goddamn college degree. I'd much rather go to the pool or to the show where it's cool. So me and Sugar leaning on the mailbox being surly, which is a Miss Moore word. And Flyboy checking out what everybody brought for lunch. And Fat Butt already wasting his peanut-butter-and-jelly sandwich like the pig he is. And Junebug punchin on Q.T.'s arm for potato chips. And Rosie Giraffe shifting from one hip to the other waiting for somebody to step on her foot or ask her if she from Georgia so she can kick ass, preferably Mercedes'. And Miss Moore asking us do we know what money is, like we a bunch of retards. I mean real money, she say, like it's only poker chips or monopoly papers we lay on the grocer. So right away I'm tired of this and say so. And would much rather snatch Sugar and go to the Sunset and terrorize the West Indian kids and take their hair ribbons and their money too. And Miss Moore files that remark away for next week's lesson on brotherhood, I can tell. And finally I say we oughta get to the subway cause it's cooler and besides we might meet some cute boys. Sugar done swiped her mama's lipstick, so we ready.

So we heading down the street and she's boring us silly about what things cost and what our parents make and how much goes for rent and how money ain't divided up right in this country. And then she gets to the part about we all poor and live in the slums, which I don't feature. And I'm ready to speak on that, but she steps out in the street and hails two cabs just like that. Then she hustles half the crew in with her and hands me a five-dollar bill and tells me to calculate 10 percent tip for the driver. And we're off. Me and Sugar and Junebug and Flyboy hanging out the window and hollering to everybody, putting lipstick on each other cause Flyboy a faggot anyway, and making farts with our sweaty armpits. But I'm mostly trying to figure how to spend this money. But they all fascinated with the meter ticking and Junebug starts laying bets as to how much it'll read when Flyboy can't hold his breath no more. Then Sugar lays bets as to how much it'll be when we get there. So I'm stuck. Don't nobody want to go for my plan, which is to jump out at the next light and run off to the first bar-b-que we can find. Then the driver tells us to get the hell out cause we there already. And the meter reads eighty-five cents. And I'm stalling to figure out the tip and Sugar say give him a dime. And I decide he don't need it as bad as I do, so later for him. But then he tries to take off with Junebug still in the door so we talk about his mama something ferocious. Then we check out that we on Fifth Avenue and everybody dressed up in stockings. One lady in a fur coat, hot as it is. White folks crazy.

"This is the place," Miss Moore say, presenting it to us in the voice she uses at the museum. "Let's look in the windows before we go in."

"Can we steal?" Sugar asks very serious like she's getting the ground rules squared away before she plays. "I beg your pardon," say Miss Moore, and we fall out. So she leads us around the windows of the toy store and me and Sugar screamin, "This is mine, that's mine. I gotta have that, that was made for me, I was born for that," till Big Butt drowns us out.

"Hey, I'm going to buy that there."

"That there? You don't even know what it is, stupid."

"I do so," he say punchin on Rosie Giraffe. "It's a microscope."

"Whatcha gonna do with a microscope, fool?"

"Look at things."

"Like what, Ronald?" asks Miss Moore. And Big Butt ain't got the first notion. So here go Miss Moore gabbing about the thousands of bacteria in a drop of water and the somethinorother in a speck of blood and the million and one living things in the air around us is invisible to the naked eye. And what she say that for? Junebug go to town on that "naked" and we rolling. Then Miss Moore ask what it cost. So we all jam into the window smudgin it up and the price tag say $300. So then she ask how long'd take for Big Butt and Junebug to save up their allowances. "Too long," I say. "Yeh," adds Sugar, "outgrown it by that time." And Miss Moore say no, you never outgrow learning instruments. "Why, even medical students and interns and," blah, blah, blah. And we ready to choke Big Butt for bringing it up in the first damn place.

"This here costs four hundred eighty dollars," say Rosie Giraffe. So we pile up all over her to see what she pointin out. My eyes tell me it's a chunk of glass cracked with something heavy, and different-color inks dripped into the splits, then the whole thing put into a oven or something. But for $480 it don't make sense.

"That's a paperweight made of semi-precious stones fused together under tremendous pressure," she explains slowly, with her hands doing the mining and all the factory work.

"So what's a paperweight?" asks Rosie Giraffe.

"To weigh paper with, dumbbell," say Flyboy, the wise man from the East.   15

"Not exactly," say Miss Moore, which is what she say when you warm or way off too. "It's to weigh paper down so it won't scatter and make your desk untidy." So right away me and Sugar curtsey to each other and then to Mercedes who is more the tidy type.

"We don't keep paper on top of the desk in my class," say Junebug, figuring Miss Moore crazy or lyin one.

"At home, then," she say. "Don't you have a calendar and a pencil case and a blotter and a letter-opener on your desk at home where you do your homework?" And she know damn well what our homes look like cause she nosys around in them every chance she gets.

"I don't even have a desk," say Junebug. "Do we?"

"No. And I don't get no homework neither," say Big Butt.   20

"And I don't even have a home," say Flyboy like he do at school to keep the white folks off his back and sorry for him. Send this poor kid to camp posters, is his specialty.

"I do," says Mercedes. "I have a box of stationery on my desk and a picture of my cat. My godmother bought the stationery and the desk. There's a big rose on each sheet and the envelopes smell like roses."

"Who wants to know about your smelly-ass stationery," say Rosie Giraffe fore I can get my two cents in.

"It's important to have a work area all your own so that...."

"Will you look at this sailboat, please," say Flyboy, cuttin her off and pointin   25 to the thing like it was his. So once again we tumble all over each other to gaze at this magnificent thing in the toy store which is just big enough to maybe sail two kittens across the pond if you strap them to the posts tight. We all start reciting the price tag like we in assembly. "Handcrafted sailboat of fiberglass at one thousand one hundred ninety-five dollars."

"Unbelievable," I hear myself say and am really stunned. I read it again for myself just in case the group recitation put me in a trance. Same thing. For some reason this pisses me off. We look at Miss Moore and she looking at us, waiting for I dunno what.

The interior of F.A.O. Schwartz, a glittering festival of toys that
overwhelms Sylvia and the other underprivileged children in
"The Lesson."

Who'd pay all that when you can buy a sailboat set for a quarter at Pop's,
a tube of glue for a dime, and a ball of string for eight cents? "It must have a
motor and a whole lot else besides," I say. "My sailboat cost me about fifty
cents."

"But will it take water?" says Mercedes with her smart ass.

"Took mine to Alley Pond Park once," say Flyboy. "String broke. Lost it. Pity."

"Sailed mine in Central Park and it keeled over and sank. Had to ask my   30
father for another dollar."

"And you got the strap," laughs Big Butt. "The jerk didn't even have a string
on it. My old man wailed on his behind."

Little Q.T. was staring hard at the sailboat and you could see he wanted it
bad. But he too little and somebody'd just take it from him. So what the hell.
"This boat for kids, Miss Moore?"

"Parents silly to buy something like that just to get all broke up," say Rosie
Giraffe.

"That much money it should last forever," I figure.

"My father'd buy it for me if I wanted it."   35

"Your father, my ass," say Rosie Giraffe getting a chance to finally push Mercedes.

"Must be rich people shop here," say Q.T.

"You are a very bright boy," say Flyboy. "What was your first clue?" And he rap him on the head with the back of his knuckles, since Q.T. the only one he could get away with. Though Q.T. liable to come up behind you years later and get his licks in when you half expect it.

"What I want to know is," I says to Miss Moore though I never talk to her, I wouldn't give the bitch that satisfaction, "is how much a real boat costs? I figure a thousand'd get you a yacht any day."

"Why don't you check that out," she says, "and report back to the group?"   40
Which really pains my ass. If you gonna mess up a perfectly good swim day least you could do is have some answers. "Let's go in," she say like she got something up her sleeve. Only she don't lead the way. So me and Sugar turn the corner to where the entrance is, but when we get there I kinda hang back. Not that I'm scared, what's there to be afraid of, just a toy store. But I feel funny, shame. But what I got to be shamed about? Got as much right to go in as anybody. But somehow I can't seem to get hold of the door, so I step away for Sugar to lead. But she hangs back too. And I look at her and she looks at me and this is ridiculous. I mean, damn, I have never ever been shy about doing nothing or going nowhere. But then Mercedes steps up and then Rosie Giraffe and Big Butt crowd in behind and shove, and next thing we all stuffed into the doorway with only Mercedes squeezing past us, smoothing out her jumper and walking right down the aisle. Then the rest of us tumble in like a glued-together jigsaw done all wrong. And people lookin at us. And it's like the time me and Sugar crashed into the Catholic church on a dare. But once we got in there and everything so hushed and holy and the candles and the bowin and the handkerchiefs on all the drooping heads, I just couldn't go through with the plan. Which was for me to run up to the altar and do a tap dance while Sugar played the nose flute and messed around in the holy water. And Sugar kept giving me the elbow. Then later teased me so bad I tied her up in the shower and turned it on and locked her in. And she'd be there till this day if Aunt Gretchen hadn't finally figured I was lyin about the boarder takin a shower.

Same thing in the store. We all walkin on tiptoe and hardly touchin the games and puzzles and things. And I watched Miss Moore who is steady watchin us like she waitin for a sign. Like Mama Drewery watches the sky and sniffs the air and takes note of just how much slant is in the bird formation. Then me and Sugar bump smack into each other, so busy gazing at the toys, 'specially the sailboat. But we don't laugh and go into our fat-lady bump-stomach routine. We just stare at that price tag. Then Sugar run a finger over the whole boat. And I'm jealous and want to hit her. Maybe not her, but I sure want to punch somebody in the mouth.

"Watcha bring us here for, Miss Moore?"

"You sound angry, Sylvia. Are you mad about something?" Givin me one of them grins like she tellin a grown-up joke that never turns out to be funny. And she's lookin very closely at me like maybe she plannin to do my portrait from memory. I'm mad, but I won't give her that satisfaction. So I slouch around the store bein very bored and say, "Let's go."

Me and Sugar at the back of the train watchin the tracks whizzin by large then small then gettin gobbled up in the dark. I'm thinkin about this tricky toy I saw in the store. A clown that somersaults on a bar then does chin-ups just cause you yank lightly at his leg. Cost $35. I could see me askin my mother for a $35 birthday clown. "You wanna who that costs what?" she'd say, cocking her head to the side to get a better view of the hole in my head. Thirty-five dollars could buy new bunk beds for Junior and Gretchen's boy. Thirty-five dollars and the whole household could go visit Granddaddy Nelson in the country. Thirty-five dollars would pay for the rent and the piano bill too. Who are these people that spend that much for performing clowns and $1,000 for toy sailboats? What kinda work they do and how they live and how come we ain't in on it? Where we are is who we are, Miss Moore always pointin out. But it don't necessarily have to be that way, she always adds then waits for somebody to say that poor people have to wake up and demand their share of the pie and don't one of us know what kind of pie she talkin about in the first damn place. But she ain't so smart cause I still got her four dollars from the taxi and she sure ain't gettin it. Messin up my day with this shit. Sugar nudges me in my pocket and winks.

Miss Moore lines us up in front of the mailbox where we started from, seem like   45
years ago, and I got a headache for thinkin so hard. And we lean all over each other so we can hold up under the draggy-ass lecture she always finishes us off with at the end before we thank her for borin us to tears. But she just looks at us like she readin tea leaves. Finally she say, "Well, what did you think of F.A.O. Schwartz?"

Rosie Giraffe mumbles, "White folks crazy."

"I'd like to go there again when I get my birthday money," says Mercedes, and we shove her out the pack so she has to lean on the mailbox by herself.

"I'd like a shower. Tiring day," say Flyboy.

Then Sugar surprises me by sayin, "You know, Miss Moore, I don't think all of us here put together eat in a year what that sailboat costs." And Miss Moore lights up like somebody goosed her. "And?" she say, urging Sugar on. Only I'm standin on her foot so she don't continue.

"Imagine for a minute what kind of society it is in which some people can spend   50
on a toy what it would cost to feed a family of six or seven. What do you think?"

"I think," say Sugar pushing me off her feet like she never done before, cause I whip her ass in a minute, "that this is not much of a democracy if you ask me. Equal chance to pursue happiness means an equal crack at the dough, don't it?" Miss Moore is besides herself and I am disgusted with Sugar's treachery. So I stand on her foot one more time to see if she'll shove me. She shuts up, and Miss Moore looks at me, sorrowfully I'm thinkin. And somethin weird is goin on, I can feel it in my chest.

"Anybody else learn anything today?" lookin dead at me. I walk away and Sugar has to run to catch up and don't even seem to notice when I shrug her arm off my shoulder.

"Well, we got four dollars anyway," she says.

"Uh hunh."

"We could go to Hascombs and get half a chocolate layer and then go to the   55
Sunset and still have plenty money for potato chips and ice-cream sodas."

"Uh hunh."

"Race you to Hascombs," she say.

We start down the block and she gets ahead which is O.K. by me cause I'm goin to the West End and then over to the Drive to think this day through. She can run if she want to and even run faster. But ain't nobody gonna beat me at nuthin.

(1972)

Questions for Discussion and Writing

1. How would you characterize Sylvia? What makes her first-person point of view effective? Is she a reliable narrator?
2. How would you characterize Miss Moore? Why doesn't Sylvia admire her, as the adults do? Why does Sugar not feel hostile toward Miss Moore, as Sylvia does?
3. Why doesn't Sylvia get the point of the lesson being taught by the visit to the expensive toy store? Why is she so angry that she wants "to punch somebody in the mouth"?
4. What is the significance of the last line of the story? How does it relate to the lesson Sylvia was supposed to learn?
5. Write an essay explaining how Bambara manages to convey her revolutionary "lesson" without seeming didactic or preachy.

Bharati Mukherjee   1940–

Bharati Mukherjee, born in India in 1940 to wealthy parents, taught herself to read and write when only three years old. She was educated in Calcutta, but desiring to become a writer, she attended the Writer's Workshop at the University of Iowa in 1961, where she met her future husband. They were married after a whirlwind courtship of only two weeks. Now a naturalized U.S. citizen, she is a Distinguished Professor of English at the University of California–Berkeley, and her husband teaches at the University of Iowa. Her fiction frequently explores the tensions in multicultural relationships.

A Father

One Wednesday morning in mid-May Mr. Bhowmick woke up as he usually did at 5:43 A.M., checked his Rolex against the alarm clock's digital readout, punched down the alarm (set for 5:45), then nudged his wife awake. She worked as a claims investigator for an insurance company that had an office in a nearby shopping mall. She didn't really have to leave the house until 8:30, but she liked to get up early and cook him a big breakfast. Mr. Bhowmick had to drive a long way to work. He was a naturally dutiful, cautious man, and he set the alarm clock early enough to accommodate a margin for accidents.

While his wife, in a pink nylon negligee she had paid for with her own MasterCard card, made him a new version of French toast from a clipping ("Eggs-cellent Recipes!") Scotchtaped to the inside of a kitchen cupboard, Mr. Bhowmick brushed his teeth. He brushed, he gurgled with the loud, hawking noises that he and his brother had been taught as children to make in order to flush clean not merely teeth but also tongue and palate.

After that he showered, then, back in the bedroom again, he recited prayers in Sanskrit to Kali, the patron goddess of his family, the goddess of wrath and vengeance. In the pokey flat of his childhood in Ranchi, Bihar, his mother had given over a whole bedroom to her collection of gods and goddesses. Mr. Bhowmick couldn't be that extravagant in Detroit. His daughter, twenty-six and an electrical engineer, slept in the other of the two bedrooms in his apartment. But he had done his best. He had taken Woodworking I and II at a nearby recreation center and built a grotto for the goddess. Kali-Mata was eight inches tall, made of metal and painted a glistening black so that the metal glowed like the oiled, black skin of a peasant woman. And though Kali-Mata was totally nude except for a tiny gilt crown and a garland strung together from sinners' chopped off heads, she looked warm, cozy, *pleased*, in her makeshift wooden shrine in Detroit. Mr. Bhowmick had gathered quite a crowd of admiring, fellow wood-workers in those final weeks of decoration.

"Hurry it up with the prayers," his wife shouted from the kitchen. She was an agnostic, a believer in ambition, not grace. She frequently complained that his prayers had gotten so long that soon he wouldn't have time to go to work, play duplicate bridge with the Ghosals, or play the tabla in the Bengali Association's one Sunday per month musical soirees. Lately she'd begun to drain him in a wholly new way. He wasn't praying, she nagged; he was shutting her out of his life. There'd be no peace in the house until she hid Kali-Mata in a suitcase.

She nagged, and he threatened to beat her with his shoe as his father had threatened his mother: it was the thrust and volley of marriage. There was no question of actually taking off a shoe and applying it to his wife's body. She was bigger than he was. And, secretly, he admired her for having the nerve, the agnosticism, which as a college boy in backward Bihar he too had claimed.

"I have time," he shot at her. He was still wrapped in a damp terry towel.

"You have time for everything but domestic life."

It was the fault of the shopping mall that his wife had started to buy pop psychology paperbacks. These paperbacks preached that for couples who could sit down and talk about their "relationship," life would be sweet again. His engineer daughter was on his wife's side. She accused him of holding things in.

"Face it, Dad," she said. "You have an affect deficit."

But surely everyone had feelings they didn't want to talk about or talk over. He definitely did not want to blurt out anything about the sick-in-the-guts sensations that came over him most mornings and that he couldn't bubble down with Alka-Seltzer or smother with Gas-X. The women in his family were smarter than him. They were cheerful, outgoing, more American somehow.

How could he tell these bright, mocking women that in the 5:43 A.M. darkness, he sensed invisible presences: gods and snakes frolicked in the master bedroom, little white sparks of cosmic static crackled up the legs of his pajamas. Something was out there in the dark, something that could invent accidents and coincidences to remind mortals that even in Detroit they were no more than mortal. His wife would label this paranoia and dismiss it. Paranoia, premonition: whatever it was, it had begun to undermine his composure.

Take this morning. Mr. Bhowmick had woken up from a pleasant dream about a man taking a Club Med vacation, and the postdream satisfaction had lasted through the shower, but when he'd come back to the shrine in the bedroom, he'd noticed all at once how scarlet and saucy was the tongue that

Kali-Mata stuck out at the world. Surely he had not lavished such alarming detail, such admonitory colors on that flap of flesh.

Watch out, ambulatory sinners. Be careful out there, the goddess warned him, and not with the affection of Sergeant Esterhaus,[1] either.

"French toast must be eaten hot-hot," his wife nagged. "Otherwise they'll taste like rubber."

Mr. Bhowmick laid the trousers of a two-trouser suit he had bought on sale   15 that winter against his favorite tweed jacket. The navy stripes in the trousers and the small, navy tweed flecks in the jacket looked quite good together. So what if the Chief Engineer had already started wearing summer cottons?

"I am coming, I am coming," he shouted back. "You want me to eat hot-hot, you start the frying only when I am sitting down. You didn't learn anything from Mother in Ranchi?"

"Mother cooked French toast from fancy recipes? I mean French Sandwich Toast with complicated filling?"

He came into the room to give her his testiest look. "You don't know the meaning of complicated cookery. And mother had to get the coal fire of the *chula* going first."

His daughter was already at the table. "Why don't you break down and buy her a microwave oven? That's what I mean about sitting down and talking things out." She had finished her orange juice. She took a plastic measure of Slim-Fast out of its can and poured the powder into a glass of skim milk. "It's ridiculous."

Babli was not the child he would have chosen as his only heir. She was brighter cer-   20 tainly than the sons and daughters of the other Bengalis he knew in Detroit, and she had been the only female student in most of her classes at Georgia Tech, but as she sat there in her beige linen business suit, her thick chin dropping into a polkadotted cravat, he regretted again that she was not the child of his dreams. Babli would be able to help him out moneywise if something happened to him, something so bad that even his pension plans and his insurance policies and his money market schemes wouldn't be enough. But Babli could never comfort him. She wasn't womanly or tender the way that unmarried girls had been in the wistful days of his adolescence. She could sing Hindi film songs, mimicking exactly the high, artificial voice of Lata Mungeshkar, and she had taken two years of dance lessons at Sona Devi's Dance Academy in Southfield, but these accomplishments didn't add up to real femininity. Not the kind that had given him palpitations in Ranchi.

Mr. Bhowmick did his best with his wife's French toast. In spite of its filling of marshmallows, apricot jam and maple syrup, it tasted rubbery. He drank two cups of Darjeeling tea, said, "Well, I'm off," and took off.

All might have gone well if Mr. Bhowmick hadn't fussed longer than usual about putting his briefcase and his trenchcoat in the backseat. He got in behind the wheel of his Oldsmobile, fixed his seatbelt and was just about to turn the key in the ignition when his neighbor, Al Stazniak, who was starting up his Buick Skylark, sneezed. A sneeze at the start of a journey brings bad luck. Al Stazniak's sneeze was fierce, made up of five short bursts, too loud to be ignored.

---

[1]A character from *Hill Street Blues*, a popular television program in the 1980s, who began each episode telling his officers, "Be careful out there."

Be careful out there! Mr. Bhowmick could see the goddess's scarlet little tongue tip wagging at him.

He was a modern man, an intelligent man. Otherwise he couldn't have had the options in life that he did have. He couldn't have given up a good job with perks in Bombay and found a better job with General Motors in Detroit. But Mr. Bhowmick was also a prudent enough man to know that some abiding truth lies bunkered within each wanton Hindu superstition. A sneeze was more than a sneeze. The heedless are carried off in ambulances. He had choices to make. He could ignore the sneeze, and so challenge the world unseen by men. Perhaps Al Stazniak had hay fever. For a sneeze to be a potent omen, surely it had to be unprovoked and terrifying, a thunderclap cleaving the summer skies. Or he could admit the smallness of mortals, undo the fate of the universe by starting over, and go back inside the apartment, sit for a second on the sofa, then re-start his trip.

Al Stazniak rolled down his window. "Everything okay?"   25

Mr. Bhowmick nodded shyly. They weren't really friends in the way neighbors can sometimes be. They talked as they parked or pulled out of their adjacent parking stalls. For all Mr. Bhowmick knew, Al Stazniak had no legs. He had never seen the man out of his Skylark.

He let the Buick back out first. Everything was okay, yes, please. All the same he undid his seatbelt. Compromise, adaptability, call it what you will. A dozen times a day he made these small trade-offs between new-world reasonableness and old-world beliefs.

While he was sitting in his parked car, his wife's ride came by. For fifty dollars a month, she was picked up and dropped off by a hard up, newly divorced woman who worked at a florist's shop in the same mall. His wife came out the front door in brown K-Mart pants and a burgundy windbreaker. She waved to him, then slipped into the passenger seat of the florist's rusty Japanese car.

He was a metallurgist. He knew about rust and ways of preventing it, secret ways, thus far unknown to the Japanese.

Babli's fiery red Mitsubishi was still in the lot. She wouldn't leave for work for   30 another eight minutes. He didn't want her to know he'd been undone by a sneeze. Babli wasn't tolerant of superstitions. She played New Wave music in her tapedeck. If asked about Hinduism, all she'd ever said to her American friends was that "it's neat." Mr. Bhowmick had heard her on the phone years before. The cosmos balanced on the head of a snake was like a beachball balanced on the snout of a circus seal. "This Hindu myth stuff," he'd heard her say, "is like a series of super graphics."

He'd forgiven her. He could probably forgive her anything. It was her way of surviving high school in a city that was both native to her, and alien.

There was no question of going back where he'd come from. He hated Ranchi. Ranchi was no place for dreamers. All through his teenage years, Mr. Bhowmick had dreamed of success abroad. What form that success would take he had left vague. Success had meant to him escape from the constant plotting and bitterness that wore out India's middle class.

Babli should have come out of the apartment and driven off to work by now. Mr. Bhowmick decided to take a risk, to dash inside and pretend he'd left his briefcase on the coffee table.

When he entered the living room, he noticed Babli's spring coat and large vinyl pocketbook on the sofa. She was probably sorting through the junk jewelry on her dresser to give her business suit a lift. She read hints about dressing in women's magazines and applied them to her person with seriousness. If his luck held, he could sit on the sofa, say a quick prayer and get back to the car without her catching on.

It surprised him that she didn't shout out from her bedroom, "Who's there?" What if he had been a rapist? 35

Then he heard Babli in the bathroom. He heard unladylike squawking noises. She was throwing up. A squawk, a spitting, then the horrible gurgle of a waterfall.

A revelation came to Mr. Bhowmick. A woman vomiting in the privacy of the bathroom could mean many things. She was coming down with the flu. She was nervous about a meeting. But Mr. Bhowmick knew at once that his daughter, his untender, unloving daughter whom he couldn't love and hadn't tried to love, was not, in the larger world of Detroit, unloved. Sinners are everywhere, even in the bosom of an upright, unambitious family like the Bhowmicks. It was the goddess sticking out her tongue at him.

The father sat heavily on the sofa, shrinking from contact with her coat and pocketbook. His brisk, bright engineer daughter was pregnant. Someone had taken time to make love to her. Someone had thought her tender, feminine. Someone even now was perhaps mooning over her. The idea excited him. It was so grotesque and wondrous. At twenty-six Babli had found the man of her dreams; whereas at twenty-six Mr. Bhowmick had given up on truth, beauty and poetry and exchanged them for two years at Carnegie Tech.

Mr. Bhowmick's tweed-jacketed body sagged against the sofa cushions. Babli would abort, of course. He knew his Babli. It was the only possible option if she didn't want to bring shame to the Bhowmick family. All the same, he could see a chubby baby boy on the rug, crawling to his granddaddy. Shame like that was easier to hide in Ranchi. There was always a barren womb sanctified by marriage that could claim sudden fructifying by the goddess Parvati. Babli would do what she wanted. She was headstrong and independent and he was afraid of her.

Babli staggered out of the bathroom. Damp stains ruined her linen suit. It was the first time he had seen his daughter look ridiculous, quite unprofessional. She didn't come into the living room to investigate the noises he'd made. He glimpsed her shoeless stockinged feet flip-flop on collapsed arches down the hall to her bedroom. 40

"Are you all right?" Mr. Bhowmick asked, standing in the hall. "Do you need Sinutab?"

She wheeled around. "What're you doing here?"

He was the one who should be angry. "I'm feeling poorly too," he said. "I'm taking the day off."

"I feel fine," Babli said.

Within fifteen minutes Babli had changed her clothes and left. Mr. Bhowmick had the apartment to himself all day. All day for praising or cursing the life that had brought him along with its other surprises an illegitimate grandchild. 45

It was his wife that he blamed. Coming to America to live had been his wife's idea. After the wedding, the young Bhowmicks had spent two years in Pittsburgh on his student visa, then gone back home to Ranchi for nine years. Nine crushing years. Then the job in Bombay had come through. All during those nine years his wife had screamed and wept. She was a woman of wild, progressive ideas—she'd called them her "American" ideas—and she'd been martyred by her neighbors for them. American *memsahib. Markin mem, Markin mem.* In bazaars the beggar boys had trailed her and hooted. She'd done provocative things. She'd hired a *chamar* woman who by caste rules was forbidden to cook for higher caste families, especially for widowed mothers of decent men. This had caused a blowup in the neighborhood. She'd made other, lesser errors. While other wives shopped and cooked every day, his wife had cooked the whole week's menu on weekends.

"What's the point of having a refrigerator, then?" She'd been scornful of the Ranchi women.

His mother, an old-fashioned widow, had accused her of trying to kill her by poisoning. "You are in such a hurry? You want to get rid of me quick-quick so you can go back to the States?"

Family life had been turbulent.

He had kept aloof, inwardly siding with his mother. He did not love his wife 50 now, and he had not loved her then. In any case, he had not defended her. He felt some affection, and he felt guilty for having shunned her during those unhappy years. But he had thought of it then as revenge. He had wanted to marry a beautiful woman. Not being a young man of means, only a young man with prospects, he had had no right to yearn for pure beauty. He cursed his fate and after a while, settled for a barrister's daughter, a plain girl with a wide, flat plank of a body and myopic eyes. The barrister had sweetened the deal by throwing in an all-expenses-paid two years' study at Carnegie Tech to which Mr. Bhowmick had been admitted. Those two years had changed his wife from pliant girl to ambitious woman. She wanted America, nothing less.

It was his wife who had forced him to apply for permanent resident status in the U.S. even though he had a good job in Ranchi as a government engineer. The putting together of documents for the immigrant visa had been a long and humbling process. He had had to explain to a chilly clerk in the Embassy that, like most Indians of his generation, he had no birth certificate. He had to swear out affidavits, suffer through police checks, bribe orderlies whose job it was to move his dossier from desk to desk. The decision, the clerk had advised him, would take months, maybe years. He hadn't dared hope that merit might be rewarded. Merit could collapse under bad luck. It was for grace that he prayed.

While the immigration papers were being processed, he had found the job in Bombay. So he'd moved his mother in with his younger brother's family, and left his hometown for good. Life in Bombay had been lighthearted, almost fulfilling. His wife had thrown herself into charity work with the same energy that had offended the Ranchi women. He was happy to be in a big city at last. Bombay was the Rio de Janeiro of the East; he'd read that in a travel brochure. He drove out to Nariman Point at least once a week to admire the necklace of municipal lights, toss coconut shells into the dark ocean, drink beer at the Oberoi-Sheraton where overseas Indian girls in designer jeans beckoned him in sly ways. His nights were full. He played duplicate bridge, went to the movies, took his wife to Bingo nights at his club. In Detroit he was a lonelier man.

Then the green card had come through. For him, for his wife, and for the daughter who had been born to them in Bombay. He sold what he could sell, and put in his brother's informal trust what he couldn't to save on taxes. Then he had left for America, and one more start.

All through the week, Mr. Bhowmick watched his daughter. He kept furtive notes on how many times she rushed to the bathroom and made hawking, wrenching noises, how many times she stayed late at the office, calling her mother to say she'd be taking in a movie and pizza afterwards with friends.

He had to tell her that he knew. And he probably didn't have much time. She   55
shouldn't be on Slim-Fast in her condition. He had to talk things over with her. But what would he say to her? What position could he take? He had to choose between public shame for the family, and murder.

For three more weeks he watched her and kept his silence. Babli wore shifts to the office instead of business suits, and he liked her better in those garments. Perhaps she was dressing for her young man, not from necessity. Her skin was pale and blotchy by turn. At breakfast her fingers looked stiff, and she had trouble with silverware.

Two Saturdays running, he lost badly at duplicate bridge. His wife scolded him. He had made silly mistakes. When was Babli meeting this man? Where? He must be American; Mr. Bhowmick prayed only that he was white. He pictured his grandson crawling to him, and the grandson was always fat and brown and buttery-skinned, like the infant Krishna. An American son-in-law was a terrifying notion. Why was she not mentioning men, at least, preparing the way for the major announcement? He listened sharply for men's names, rehearsed little lines like, "Hello, Bob, I'm Babli's old man," with a cracked little laugh. Bob, Jack, Jimmy, Tom. But no names surfaced. When she went out for pizza and a movie it was with the familiar set of Indian girls and their strange, unpopular, American friends, all without men. Mr. Bhowmick tried to be reasonable. Maybe she had already gotten married and was keeping it secret. "Well, Bob, you and Babli sure had Mrs. Bhowmick and me going there, heh-heh," he mumbled one night with the Sahas and Ghosals, over cards. "Pardon?" asked Pronob Saha. Mr. Bhowmick dropped two tricks, and his wife glared. "Such stupid blunders," she fumed on the drive back. A new truth was dawning; there would be no marriage for Babli. Her young man probably was not so young and not so available. He must be already married. She must have yielded to passion or been raped in the office. His wife seemed to have noticed nothing. Was he a murderer, or a conspirator? He kept his secret from his wife; his daughter kept her decision to herself.

Nights, Mr. Bhowmick pretended to sleep, but as soon as his wife began her snoring—not real snores so much as loud, gaspy gulpings for breath—he turned on his side and prayed to Kali-Mata.

In July, when Babli's belly had begun to push up against the waistless dresses she'd bought herself, Mr. Bhowmick came out of the shower one weekday morning and found the two women screaming at each other. His wife had a rolling pin in one hand. His daughter held up a *National Geographic* as a shield for her head. The crazy look that had been in his wife's eyes when she'd shooed away beggar kids was in her eyes again.

"Stop it!" His own boldness overwhelmed him. "Shut up! Babli's pregnant, so   60
what? It's your fault, you made us come to the States."

Girls like Babli were caught between rules, that's the point he wished to make. They were too smart, too impulsive for a backward place like Ranchi, but not tough nor smart enough for sex-crazy places like Detroit.

"My fault?" his wife cried. "I told her to do hanky-panky with boys? I told her to shame us like this?"

She got in one blow with the rolling pin. The second glanced off Babli's shoulder and fell on his arm which he had stuck out for his grandson's sake.

"I'm calling the police," Babli shouted. She was out of the rolling pin's range. "This is brutality. You can't do this to me."

"Shut up! Shut your mouth, foolish woman." He wrenched the weapon 65 from his wife's fist. He made a show of taking off his shoe to beat his wife on the face.

"What do you know? You don't know anything." She let herself down slowly on a dining chair. Her hair, curled overnight, stood in wild whorls around her head. "Nothing."

"And you do!" He laughed. He remembered her tormentors, and laughed again. He had begun to enjoy himself. Now *he* was the one with the crazy, progressive ideas.

"Your daughter is pregnant, yes," she said, "any fool knows that. But ask her the name of the father. Go, ask."

He stared at his daughter who gazed straight ahead, eyes burning with hate, jaw clenched with fury.

"Babli?" 70

"Who needs a man?" she hissed. "The father of my baby is a bottle and a syringe. Men louse up your lives. I just want a baby. Oh, don't worry—he's a certified fit donor. No diseases, college graduate, above average, and he made the easiest twenty-five dollars of his life—"

"Like animals," his wife said. For the first time he heard horror in her voice. His daughter grinned at him. He saw her tongue, thick and red, squirming behind her row of perfect teeth.

"Yes, yes, yes," she screamed, "like livestock. Just like animals. You should be happy—that's what marriage is all about, isn't it? Matching bloodlines, matching horoscopes, matching castes, matching, matching, matching…" and it was difficult to know if she was laughing or singing, or mocking and like a madwoman.

Mr. Bhowmick lifted the rolling pin high above his head and brought it down hard on the dome of Babli's stomach. In the end, it was his wife who called the police.

(1985)

Questions for Discussion and Writing

1. What kind of person is the father in this story? What details in the story reveal his character? How does his religion cause trouble in the family?
2. What kind of person is the mother? How is her character revealed?
3. What do we know about the grown daughter, Babli? How do you respond to her character?
4. How does the father regard his wife? How does he feel about his daughter? Do you think he has good reason to react this way?
5. Why does it seem unlikely that the events in this story would have happened if the family had remained in India?

Louise Erdrich   1954–

Louise Erdrich was raised as a member of the Turtle Mountain Chippewas in North Dakota with her grandfather as the tribal chief. Growing up, she worked as a farmhand, a waitress, a lifeguard, and a construction worker. After graduating from Dartmouth, she eventually married one of her professors, the writer Michael Dorris. She was having no luck getting her first novel accepted until he sent submission letters on stationery he made himself with "Michael Dorris Agency" as the letterhead. The book became a best-seller, but the couple later separated, and he committed suicide. Erdrich presently lives, writes, and owns a bookstore in Minneapolis.

The Red Convertible

Lyman Lamartine

I was the first one to drive a convertible on my reservation. And of course it was red, a red Olds. I owned that car along with my brother Henry Junior. We owned it together until his boots filled with water on a windy night and he bought out my share. Now Henry owns the whole car, and his youngest brother Lyman (that's myself), Lyman walks everywhere he goes.

How did I earn enough money to buy my share in the first place? My own talent was I could always make money. I had a touch for it, unusual in a Chippewa. From the first I was different that way, and everyone recognized it. I was the only kid they let in the American Legion Hall to shine shoes, for example, and one Christmas I sold spiritual bouquets for the mission door to door. The nuns let me keep a percentage. Once I started, it seemed the more money I made the easier the money came. Everyone encouraged it. When I was fifteen I got a job washing dishes at the Joliet Cafe, and that was where my first big break happened.

It wasn't long before I was promoted to busing tables, and then the short-order cook quit and I was hired to take her place. No sooner than you know it I was managing the Joliet. The rest is history. I went on managing. I soon became part owner, and of course there was no stopping me then. It wasn't long before the whole thing was mine.

After I'd owned the Joliet for one year, it blew over in the worst tornado ever seen around here. The whole operation was smashed to bits. A total loss. The fryalator was up in a tree, the grill torn in half like it was paper. I was only sixteen. I had it all in my mother's name, and I lost it quick, but before I lost it I had every one of my relatives, and their relatives, to dinner, and I also bought that red Olds I mentioned, along with Henry.

The first time we saw it! I'll tell you when we first saw it. We had gotten a   5 ride to Winnipeg, and both of us had money. Don't ask me why, because we never mentioned a car or anything, we just had all our money. Mine was cash, a big bankroll from the Joliet's insurance. Henry had two checks—a week's extra pay for being laid off, and his regular check from the Jewel Bearing Plant.

We were walking down Portage anyway, seeing the sights, when we saw it. There it was, parked, large as life. Really as *if* it was alive. I thought of the word *repose*, because the car wasn't simply stopped, parked, or whatever. That car reposed, calm and gleaming, a FOR SALE sign in its left front window. Then, before we had thought it over at all, the car belonged to us and our pockets were empty. We had just enough money for gas back home.

We went places in that car, me and Henry. We took off driving all one whole summer. We started off toward the Little Knife River and Mandaree in Fort Berthold and then we found ourselves down in Wakpala somehow, and then suddenly we were over in Montana on the Rocky Boy, and yet the summer was not even half over. Some people hang on to details when they travel, but we didn't let them bother us and just lived our everyday lives here to there.

I do remember this place with willows. I remember I laid under those trees and it was comfortable. So comfortable. The branches bent down all around me like a tent or a stable. And quiet, it was quiet, even though there was a pow-wow close enough so I could see it going on. The air was not too still, not too windy either. When the dust rises up and hangs in the air around dancers like that, I feel good. Henry was asleep with his arms thrown wide. Later on, he woke up and we started driving again. We were somewhere in Montana, or maybe on the Blood Reserve—it could have been anywhere. Anyway it was where we met the girl.

All her hair was in buns around her ears, that's the first thing I noticed about her. She was posed alongside the road with her arm out, so we stopped. That girl was short, so short her lumber shirt looked comical on her, like a nightgown. She had jeans on and fancy moccasins and she carried a little suitcase.

"Hop on in," says Henry. So she climbs in between us.   10

"We'll take you home," I says. "Where do you live?"

"Chicken," she says.

"Where the hell's that?" I ask her.

"Alaska."

"Okay," says Henry, and we drive.   15

We got up there and never wanted to leave. The sun doesn't truly set there in summer, and the night is more a soft dusk. You might doze off, sometimes, but before you know it you're up again, like an animal in nature. You never feel like you have to sleep hard or put away the world. And things would grow up there. One day just dirt or moss, the next day flowers and long grass. The girl's name was Susy. Her family really took to us. They fed us and put us up. We had our own tent to live in by their house, and the kids would be in and out of there all day and night. They couldn't get over me and Henry being brothers, we looked so different. We told them we knew we had the same mother, anyway.

One night Susy came in to visit us. We sat around in the tent talking of this and that. The season was changing. It was getting darker by that time, and the cold was even getting just a little mean. I told her it was time for us to go. She stood up on a chair.

"You never seen my hair," Susy said.

That was true. She was standing on a chair, but still, when she unclipped her buns the hair reached all the way to the ground. Our eyes opened. You couldn't tell how much hair she had when it was rolled up so neatly. Then my brother Henry did something funny. He went up to the chair and said, "Jump on my shoulders." So she did that, and her hair reached down past his waist, and he started twirling, this way and that, so her hair was flung out from side to side.

"I always wondered what it was like to have long pretty hair," Henry says.   20
Well, we laughed. It was a funny sight, the way he did it. The next morning we got up and took leave of those people.

On to greener pastures, as they say. It was down through Spokane and across Idaho then Montana and very soon we were racing the weather right along under the Canadian border through Columbus, Des Lacs, and then were in Bottineau County and soon home. We'd made most of the trip, that summer, without putting up the car hood at all. We got home just in time.

I don't wonder that the army was so glad to get my brother that they turned him into a Marine. He was built like a brick outhouse anyway. We liked to tease him that they really wanted him for his Indian nose. He had a nose big and sharp as a hatchet, like the nose on Red Tomahawk, the Indian who killed Sitting Bull, whose profile is on signs all along the North Dakota highways. Henry went off to training camp, came home once during Christmas, then the next thing you know we got an overseas letter from him. It was 1970, and he said he was stationed up in the northern hill country. Whereabouts I did not know. He wasn't such a hot letter writer, and only got off two before the enemy caught him. I could never keep it straight, which direction those good Vietnam soldiers were from.

I wrote him back several times, even though I didn't know if those letters would get through. I kept him informed all about the car. Most of the time I had it up on blocks in the yard or half taken apart, because that long trip did a hard job on it under the hood.

I always had good luck with numbers, and never worried about the draft myself. I never even had to think about what my number was. But Henry was never lucky in the same way as me. It was at least three years before Henry came home. By then I guess the whole war was solved in the government's mind, but for him it would keep on going. In those years I'd put his car into almost perfect shape. I always thought of it as his car while he was gone, even though when he left he said, "Now it's yours," and threw me his key.

"Thanks for the extra key," I'd said. "I'll put it in your drawer just in case I need   25
it." He laughed.

When he came home, though, Henry was very different, and I'll say this: the change was no good. You could hardly expect him to change for the better, I know. But he was quiet, so quiet, and never comfortable sitting still anywhere but always up and moving around. I thought back to times we'd sat still for whole afternoons, never moving a muscle, just shifting our weight along the ground, talking to whoever sat with us, watching things. He'd always had a joke, then, too, and now you couldn't get him to laugh, or when he did it was more the sound of a man choking, a sound that stopped up the throats of other people around him. They got to leaving him alone most of the time, and I didn't blame them. It was a fact: Henry was jumpy and mean.

I'd bought a color TV set for my mom and the rest of us while Henry was away. Money still came very easy. I was sorry I'd ever bought it though, because of Henry. I was also sorry I'd bought color, because with black-and-white the pictures seem older and farther away. But what are you going to do? He sat in front of it, watching it, and that was the only time he was completely still. But it was the kind of stillness that you see in a rabbit when it freezes and before it will bolt. He was not easy. He sat in his chair gripping the armrests with all his might, as if the chair itself was moving at a high speed and if he let go at all he would rocket forward and maybe crash right through the set.

Once I was in the room watching TV with Henry and I heard his teeth click at something. I looked over, and he'd bitten through his lip. Blood was going down his chin. I tell you right then I wanted to smash that tube to pieces. I went over to it but Henry must have known what I was up to. He rushed from his chair and shoved me out of the way, against the wall. I told myself he didn't know what he was doing.

My mom came in, turned the set off real quiet, and told us she had made something for supper. So we went and sat down. There was still blood going down Henry's chin, but he didn't notice it and no one said anything, even though every time he took a bite of his bread his blood fell onto it until he was eating his own blood mixed in with the food.

While Henry was not around we talked about what was going to happen to   30
him. There were no Indian doctors on the reservation, and my mom couldn't come around to trusting the old man, Moses Pillager, because he courted her long ago and was jealous of her husbands. He might take revenge through her son. We were afraid that if we brought Henry to a regular hospital they would keep him.

"They don't fix them in those places," Mom said; "they just give them drugs."

"We wouldn't get him there in the first place," I agreed, "so let's just forget about it."

Then I thought about the car.

Henry had not even looked at the car since he'd gotten home, though like I said, it was in tip-top condition and ready to drive. I thought the car might bring the old Henry back somehow. So I bided my time and waited for my chance to interest him in the vehicle.

One night Henry was off somewhere. I took myself a hammer. I went out to   35
that car and I did a number on its underside. Whacked it up. Bent the tail pipe double. Ripped the muffler loose. By the time I was done with the car it looked worse than any typical Indian car that has been driven all its life on reservation roads, which they always say are like government promises—full of holes. It just about hurt me, I'll tell you that! I threw dirt in the carburetor and I ripped all the electric tape off the seats. I made it look just as beat up as I could. Then I sat back and waited for Henry to find it.

Still, it took him over a month. That was all right, because it was just getting warm enough, not melting, but warm enough to work outside.

"Lyman," he says, walking in one day, "that red car looks like shit."

"Well, it's old," I says. "You got to expect that."

"No way!" says Henry. "That car's a classic! But you went and ran the piss right out of it, Lyman, and you know it don't deserve that. I kept that car in A-one shape. You don't remember. You're too young. But when I left, that car was running like a watch. Now I don't even know if I can get it to start again, let alone get it anywhere near its old condition."

"Well, you try," I said, like I was getting mad, "but I say it's a piece of junk."   40

Then I walked out before he could realize I knew he'd strung together more than six words at once.

After that I thought he'd freeze himself to death working on that car. He was out there all day, and at night he rigged up a little lamp, ran a cord out the window, and had himself some light to see by while he worked. He was better than he had been before, but that's still not saying much. It was easier for him to do the things the rest of us did. He ate more slowly and didn't jump up and down during the meal to get this or that or look out the window. I put my hand in the back of the TV set, I admit, and fiddled around with it good, so that it was almost impossible now to get a clear picture. He didn't look at it very often anyway. He was always out with that car or going off to get parts for it. By the time it was really melting outside, he had it fixed.

I had been feeling down in the dumps about Henry around this time. We had always been together before. Henry and Lyman. But he was such a loner now that I didn't know how to take it. So I jumped at the chance one day when Henry seemed friendly. It's not that he smiled or anything. He just said, "Let's take that old shit-box for a spin." Just the way he said it made me think he could be coming around.

We went out to the car. It was spring. The sun was shining very bright. My only sister, Bonita, who was just eleven years old, came out and made us stand together for a picture. Henry leaned his elbow on the red car's windshield, and he took his other arm and put it over my shoulder, very carefully, as though it was heavy for him to lift and he didn't want to bring the weight down all at once.

"Smile," Bonita said, and he did.

45

That picture. I never look at it anymore. A few months ago, I don't know why, I got his picture out and tacked it on the wall. I felt good about Henry at the time, close to him. I felt good having his picture on the wall, until one night when I was looking at television. I was a little drunk and stoned. I looked up at the wall and Henry was staring at me. I don't know what it was, but his smile had changed, or maybe it was gone. All I know is I couldn't stay in the same room with that picture. I was shaking. I got up, closed the door, and went into the kitchen. A little later my friend Ray came over and we both went back into that room. We put the picture in a brown bag, folded the bag over and over tightly, then put it way back in a closet.

I still see that picture now, as if it tugs at me, whenever I pass that closet door. The picture is very clear in my mind. It was so sunny that day Henry had to squint against the glare. Or maybe the camera Bonita held flashed like a mirror, blinding him, before she snapped the picture. My face is right out in the sun, big and round. But he might have drawn back, because the shadows on his face are deep as holes. There are two shadows curved like little hooks around the ends of his smile, as if to frame it and try to keep it there—that one, first smile that looked like it might have hurt his face. He has his field jacket on and the wornin clothes he'd come back in and kept wearing ever since. After Bonita took the picture, she went into the house and we got into the car. There was a full cooler in the trunk. We started off, east, toward Pembina and the Red River because Henry said he wanted to see the high water.

The trip over there was beautiful. When everything starts changing, drying up, clearing off, you feel like your whole life is starting. Henry felt it, too. The top was down and the car hummed like a top. He'd really put it back in shape, even the tape on the seats was very carefully put down and glued back in layers. It's not that he smiled again or even joked, but his face looked to me as if it was clear, more peaceful. It looked as though he wasn't thinking of anything in particular except the bare fields and windbreaks and houses we were passing.

The river was high and full of winter trash when we got there. The sun was still out, but it was colder by the river. There were still little clumps of dirty snow here and there on the banks. The water hadn't gone over the banks yet, but it would, you could tell. It was just at its limit, hard swollen, glossy like an old gray scar. We made ourselves a fire, and we sat down and watched the current go. As I watched it I felt something squeezing inside me and tightening and trying to let go all at the same time. I knew I was not just feeling it myself; I knew I was feeling what Henry was going through at that moment. Except that I couldn't stand it, the closing and opening. I jumped to my feet. I took Henry by the shoulders and I started shaking him. "Wake up," I says, "wake up, wake up, wake up!" I didn't know what had come over me. I sat down beside him again.

His face was totally white and hard. Then it broke, like stones break all of a 50 sudden when water boils up inside them.

"I know it," he says. "I know it. I can't help it. It's no use."

We start talking. He said he knew what I'd done with the car. It was obvious it had been whacked out of shape and not just neglected. He said he wanted to give the car to me for good now, it was no use. He said he'd fixed it just to give it back and I should take it.

"No way," I says. "I don't want it."

"That's okay," he says, "you take it."

"I don't want it, though," I says back to him, and then to emphasize, just to 55 emphasize, you understand, I touch his shoulder. He slaps my hand off.

"Take that car," he says.

"No," I say. "Make me," I say, and then he grabs my jacket and rips the arm loose. That jacket is a class act, suede with tags and zippers. I push Henry backwards, off the log. He jumps up and bowls me over. We go down in a clinch and come up swinging hard, for all we're worth, with our fists. He socks my jaw so hard I feel like it swings loose. Then I'm at his rib cage and land a good one under his chin so his head snaps back. He's dazzled. He looks at me and I look at him and then his eyes are full of tears and blood and at first I think he's crying. But no, he's laughing. "Ha, ha!" he says. "Ha! Ha! Take good care of it."

"Okay," I says. "Okay, no problem. Ha! Ha!"

I can't help it, and I start laughing, too. My face feels fat and strange, and after a while I get a beer from the cooler in the trunk, and when I hand it to Henry he takes his shirt and wipes my germs off. "Hoof-and-mouth disease," he says. For some reason this cracks me up, and so we're really laughing for a while, and then we drink all the rest of the beers one by one and throw them in the river and see how far, how fast, the current takes them before they fill up and sink.

"You want to go on back?" I ask after a while. "Maybe we could snag a couple 60 nice Kashpaw girls."

He says nothing. But I can tell his mood is turning again.

"They're all crazy, the girls up here, every damn one of them."

"You're crazy too," I say, to jolly him up. "Crazy Lamartine boys!"

He looks as though he will take this wrong at first. His face twists, then clears, and he jumps up on his feet. "That's right!" he says. "Crazier 'n hell. Crazy Indians!"

I think it's the old Henry again. He throws off his jacket and starts springing 65
his legs up from the knees like a fancy dancer. He's down doing something between a grass dance and a bunny hop, no kind of dance I ever saw before, but
neither has anyone else on all this green growing earth. He's wild. He wants to
pitch whoopee! He's up and at me and all over. All this time I'm laughing so
hard, so hard my belly is getting tied up in a knot.

"Got to cool me off!" he shouts all of a sudden. Then he runs over to the
river and jumps in.

There's boards and other things in the current. It's so high. No sound comes
from the river after the splash he makes, so I run right over. I look around. It's
getting dark. I see he's halfway across the water already, and I know he didn't
swim there but the current took him. It's far. I hear his voice, though, very
clearly across it.

"My boots are filling," he says.

He says this in a normal voice, like he just noticed and he doesn't know what
to think of it. Then he's gone. A branch comes by. Another branch. And I go in.

By the time I get out of the river, off the snag I pulled myself onto, the sun is 70
down. I walk back to the car, turn on the high beams, and drive it up the bank. I put
it in first gear and then I take my foot off the clutch. I get out, close the door, and
watch it plow softly into the water. The headlights reach in as they go down,
searching, still lighted even after the water swirls over the back end. I wait. The
wires short out. It is all finally dark. And then there is only the water, the sound of
it going and running and going and running and running.

(1984)

Questions for Discussion and Writing

1. How does the red Oldsmobile function as the story's central symbol? What
   changes does the car go through? How do these changes stand for what
   Lyman and Henry are going through?

2. Why is Lyman upset by the picture of himself and his brother? When does
   the picture begin to bother Lyman—before or after Henry's death? Do we
   know for sure? Does it make any difference?

3. Why does Lyman send the car into the river? Why are the car's lights left on?

4. Write an essay that makes a major claim about the brothers' relationship.

5. Analyze a single episode in the story (such as the visit to Alaska or Henry's
   watching TV), and discuss its relation to the story as a whole.

PART III

Writing About Poetry

The language of poetry is even more compressed than the language of the short story. You need to give yourself willingly to the understanding of poetry. The pleasure of reading it derives from the beauty of the language—the delight of the sounds and the images—as well as the power of the emotion and the depth of the insights conveyed. Poetry may seem difficult, but it can also be intensely rewarding.

12

How Do I Read Poetry?

In order to enjoy discovering the meaning of poetry, you must approach it with a positive attitude—a willingness to understand. Poetry invites your creative participation. More than any other form of literature, poetry allows you as reader to inform its meaning as you bring your own knowledge and experience to bear in interpreting images, motifs, and symbols.

Begin by reading the poem aloud—or at least by sounding the words aloud in your mind. Rhyme and rhythm work in subtle ways to emphasize key words and clarify meaning. As you reread, go slowly, paying careful attention to every word, looking up in a good dictionary any words that are unclear, and examining again and again any difficult lines.

Get the Literal Meaning First: Paraphrase

Before you begin interpreting a poem, you must be sure that you understand the literal meaning. Because one of the delights of poetry stems from the unusual ways in which poets put words together, you may sometimes need to straighten out the syntax. For instance, Thomas Hardy writes

> And why unblooms the best hope ever sown?

The usual way of expressing that question would be something like this:

> And why does the best hope ever sown not bloom?

Occasionally you may need to fill in words that the poet has deliberately omitted through ellipsis. When Walt Whitman writes

> But I with mournful tread,
> Walk the deck my Captain lies,
> Fallen cold and dead,

we can tell that he means "the deck on which my Captain lies, / Fallen cold and dead."

Pay close attention to punctuation; it can provide clues to meaning. But do not be distressed if you discover that poets (like Emily Dickinson and Stevie Smith) sometimes use punctuation in strange ways or (like E. E. Cummings) not at all. Along with the deliberate fracturing of syntax, this unusual use of punctuation comes under the heading of poetic license.

Always you must look up any words that you do not know—as well as any familiar words that fail to make complete sense in the context. When you read this line from Whitman:

> Passing the apple-tree blows of white and pink in the orchards,

the word "blows" seems a strange choice. If you consult your dictionary, you will discover an unusual definition of blows: "masses of blossoms," a meaning which fits exactly.

Make Associations for Meaning

Once you understand the literal meaning of a poem, you can begin to expand that meaning into an interpretation. As you do so, keep asking yourself questions: Who is the speaker? Who is being addressed? What is the message? What do the images contribute? What do the symbols suggest? How does it all fit together?

When, for instance, Emily Dickinson in the following lines envisions "Rowing in Eden," how do you respond to this image?

> Rowing in Eden—
> Ah, the Sea!
> Might I but moor—Tonight—
> In Thee!

Can she mean *literally* rowing in Eden? Not unless you picture a lake in the Garden, which is, of course, a possibility. What do you associate with Eden? Complete bliss? Surely. Innocence, perhaps—the innocence of Adam and Eve before the Fall? Or their lustful sensuality after the Fall? Given the opening lines of the poem,

> Wild Nights—Wild Nights!
> Were I with thee
> Wild Nights should be
> Our luxury!

one fitting response might be that "Rowing in Eden" suggests paddling through sexual innocence in a far from chaste anticipation of reaching the port of ecstasy: to "moor—Tonight— / In Thee!"

Sometimes poems, like stories and plays, contain *allusions* (indirect references to famous persons, events, places, or to other works of literature) that add to the meaning. Some allusions are fairly easy to perceive. When Eliot's Prufrock, in his famous love song, observes

> No! I am not Prince Hamlet, nor was meant to be,

we know that he declines to compare himself with Shakespeare's Hamlet, a character who also had difficulty taking decisive action. Some allusions, though, are more subtle. You need to know these lines from Ernest Dowson:

> Last night, ah, yesternight, betwixt her lips and mine,
> There fell thy shadow, Cynara!

in order to catch the allusion to them in Eliot's "The Hollow Men":

> Between the motion
> And the act
> Falls the shadow.

Many allusions you can simply look up. If you are puzzled by Swinburne's line

> Thou has conquered, O pale Galilean,

your dictionary will identify the Galilean as Jesus Christ. For less well-known figures or events, you may need to consult a dictionary of biblical characters, a dictionary of classical mythology, or a good encyclopedia.

Other valuable reference tools are Sir James Frazer's *The Golden Bough*, which discusses preclassical myth, magic, and religion, and Cirlot's *A Dictionary of Symbols*, which traces through mythology and world literature the significance of various **archetypal** (i.e., universal) symbols—the sea, the seasons, colors, numbers, islands, serpents, and a host of others.

Thus, learning to understand poetry—like learning to understand any imaginative literature—involves asking yourself questions and then speculating and researching until you come up with satisfying answers. Chart 12-1 on the next page will give you a starting list of questions.

Chart 12-1   Critical Questions for Reading Poetry

Before planning an analysis of any selection in the anthology of poetry, write out your answers to the following questions to confirm your understanding of the poem and to generate material for the paper.

1. Can you paraphrase the poem if necessary?
2. Who is the speaker in the poem? How would you describe this persona?
3. What is the speaker's tone? Which words reveal this tone? Is the poem perhaps ironic?
4. What heavily connotative words are used? What words have unusual or special meanings? Are any words or phrases repeated? If so, why? Which words do you need to look up?
5. What images does the poet use? How do the images relate to one another? Do these images form a unified pattern (a motif) throughout the poem? Is there a central, controlling image?
6. What figures of speech are used? How do they contribute to the tone and meaning of the poem?
7. Are there any symbols? What do they mean? Are they universal symbols, or do they arise from the particular context of this poem?
8. Is the occasion for or the setting of the poem important in understanding its meaning? If so, why?
9. What is the theme (the central idea) of this poem? Can you state it in a single sentence?
10. How important is the role of metrics (sound effects), such as rhyme and rhythm? How do they affect tone and meaning?
11. How important is the contribution of form, such as rhyme scheme and line arrangement? How does the form influence the overall effect of the poem?

13

Writing About Persona and Tone

Tone, which can be important in analyzing a short story, is crucial to the interpretation of poetry. Persona is closely related to tone. In order to identify persona and determine tone, you need (as usual) to ask yourself questions about the poem.

Who Is Speaking?

A good question to begin with is this: Who is the speaker in the poem? Often the most obvious answer seems to be "The poet," especially if the poem is written in the first person. When Emily Dickinson begins

> This is my letter to the world
> That never wrote to me—

we can be fairly sure that she is writing in her own voice—that the poem itself is her "letter to the world." But poets often adopt a *persona*; that is, they speak through the voice of a character they have created. Stevie Smith, herself a middle-aged woman, adopts a persona of a different age and of the opposite sex in these lines:

> An old man of seventy-three
> I lay with my young bride in my arms....

Thomas Hardy in "The Ruined Maid" (on page 342) composes a dramatic monologue with a dual persona (or two personae), two young women who converse throughout the poem. The speaker in Auden's "The Unknown Citizen" (on page 343) is apparently a spokesperson for the bureaucracy—but most certainly is not Auden himself. Thus, in order to be strictly accurate, you should avoid "The poet says..." and use instead "The speaker in the poem says..." or "The persona in the poem says...."

What Is Tone?

After deciding who the speaker is, your next question might be "What is the tone of this poetic voice?" *Tone* in poetry is essentially the same as in fiction, drama, or expository prose: the attitude of the writer toward the subject matter of the work—the poem, story, play, or essay. And tone in a piece of writing is always similar to tone of voice in speaking. If a friend finds you on the verge of tears and comments, "You certainly look cheerful today," her tone of voice—as well as the absurdity of the statement—lets you know that your friend is using *verbal irony*; that is, she means the opposite of what she says.

Recognizing Verbal Irony

Because verbal irony involves a reversal of meaning, it is the most important tone to recognize. To miss the irony is to miss the meaning in many cases. When Stephen Crane begins a poem

> Do not weep, maiden, for war is kind,

an alert reader will catch the ironic tone at once from the word *kind*, which war definitely is not. But irony can at times be much more subtle. Sometimes you need to put together a number of verbal clues in order to perceive the irony. W. H. Auden's poem "The Unknown Citizen," which appears in this chapter, is such a poem. Gradually as you read, you realize that the tribute being paid to this model worker (identified by number rather than name) is not the eulogy you are led to expect but an ironic commentary on the regimented society that molded the man. By the time you reach the last two lines, the irony has become apparent.

Describing Tone

One of the chief problems in identifying tone involves finding exactly the right word or words to describe it. Even after you have detected that a work's tone is ironic, you may need to decide whether the irony is gentle or bitter, or whether it is light or scathing in tone. Remember that you are trying to identify the tone of the poetic voice, just as you would identify the tone of anyone speaking to you.

You need a number of adjectives at your command to pinpoint tone. As you analyze poetic tone, keep the following terms in mind to see whether any may prove useful: *humorous, joyous, playful, light, hopeful, brisk, lyrical, admiring, celebratory, laudatory, expectant, wistful, sad, mournful, dreary, tragic, elegiac, solemn, somber, poignant, earnest, blasé, disillusioned, straightforward, curt, hostile, sarcastic, cynical, ambivalent, ambiguous.*

Looking at Persona and Tone

Read the following five poems for pleasure. Then, as you read through them again slowly and carefully, pay attention to the persona and try to identify the tone of this speaker's voice. Is the speaker angry, frightened, astonished, admiring? Or perhaps sincere, sarcastic, humorous, deceptive?

Theodore Roethke *1908–1963*

Born in Saginaw, Michigan, Theodore Roethke was strongly influenced by his father, Otto, and his father's brother, stern German immigrants who co-owned a twenty-five-acre greenhouse complex. Much of the poet's childhood and adolescence was spent working there, as reflected by the images of nature and growth that pervade his poetry. In 1923, when Theodore was only fifteen, his uncle committed suicide and his father died from cancer. While an undergraduate at the University of Michigan, Roethke decided to pursue both poetry and teaching. He was awarded the Pulitzer Prize for poetry in 1953.

My Papa's Waltz

The whiskey on your breath
Could make a small boy dizzy;
But I hung on like death:
Such waltzing was not easy.

We romped until the pans   5
Slid from the kitchen shelf;
My mother's countenance
Could not unfrown itself.

The hand that held my wrist
Was battered on one knuckle;   10
At every step you missed
My right ear scraped a buckle.

You beat time on my head
With a palm caked hard by dirt,
Then waltzed me off to bed   15
Still clinging to your shirt.

(1948)

Thomas Hardy *1840–1928*

An architect in London, Thomas Hardy first became interested in literature at age thirty, when he began to write novels. Among the sixteen he produced, the best-known are *The Return of the Native* (1878) and *Tess of the D'Urbervilles* (1891). When his novel *Jude the Obscure* (1895) was called immoral for criticizing marriage, Hardy became so angry that he wrote nothing but poetry for the rest of his life. Many modern poets, including W. H. Auden, Philip Larkin, and Dylan Thomas, were influenced by Hardy's use of irony and spoken language.

The Ruined Maid

"O 'Melia, my dear, this does everything crown!
Who could have supposed I should meet you in Town?
And whence such fair garments, such prosperi-ty?"—
"O didn't you know I'd been ruined?" said she.

—"You left us in tatters, without shoes or socks,   5
Tired of digging potatoes, and spudding up docks;
And now you've gay bracelets and bright feathers three!"—
"Yes: that's how we dress when we're ruined," said she.

—"At home in the barton° you said 'thee' and 'thou,'
And 'thik oon,' and 'theas oon,' and 't'other'; but now   10
Your talking quite fits 'ee for high compa-ny!"—
"Some polish is gained with one's ruin," said she.

—"Your hands were like paws then, your face blue and bleak,
But now I'm bewitched by your delicate cheek,
And your little gloves fit as on any la-dy!"—   15
"We never do work when we're ruined," said she.

—"You used to call home-life a hag-ridden dream,
And you'd sigh, and you'd sock,° but at present you seem
To know not of megrims° or melancho-ly!"—
"True. One's pretty lively when ruined," said she.   20

—"I wish I had feathers, a fine sweeping gown,
And a delicate face, and could strut about Town!"—
"My dear—a raw country girl, such as you be,
Cannot quite expect that. You ain't ruined," said she.

(1866)

---

9 barton Farmyard.   **18 sock** Moan.   **19 megrims** Sadness.

W. H. Auden   1907–1973

Although born and raised in England, W(ystan) H(ugh) Auden became a U.S. citizen in 1946. An extremely talented poet, he was the major literary voice of the 1930s, an "age of anxiety" that faced world war and global depression. Influenced by Freud, Auden often wrote about human guilt and fear, but he also celebrated the power of love to overcome anxiety. His volume of poetry *The Age of Anxiety* (1947) won the Pulitzer Prize. Auden also collaborated on verse plays and wrote librettos for operas.

The Unknown Citizen

(To JS/07/M/378
This Marble Monument
Is Erected by the State)

He was found by the Bureau of Statistics to be
One against whom there was no official complaint,
And all the reports on his conduct agree
That, in the modern sense of an old-fashioned word, he was a saint,
For in everything he did he served the Greater Community.   5
Except for the War till the day he retired
He worked in a factory and never got fired,
But satisfied his employers, Fudge Motors Inc.
Yet he wasn't a scab or odd in his views,
For his Union reports that he paid his dues,   10
(Our report on his Union shows it was sound)
And our Social Psychology workers found
That he was popular with his mates and liked a drink.
The Press are convinced that he bought a paper every day
And that his reactions to advertisements were normal in every way.   15
Policies taken out in his name prove that he was fully insured,
And his Health-card shows he was once in hospital but left it cured.
Both Producers Research and High-Grade Living declare
He was fully sensible to the advantages of the Installment Plan
And had everything necessary to the Modern Man,   20
A phonograph, a radio, a car and a frigidaire.
Our researchers into Public Opinion are content
That he held the proper opinions for the time of year;
When there was peace, he was for peace; when there was war, he went.
He was married and added five children to the population,   25
Which our Eugenist says was the right number for a parent of
    his generation,
And our teachers report that he never interfered with their education.
Was he free? Was he happy? The question is absurd:
Had anything been wrong, we should certainly have heard.

(1940)

Edmund Waller   1606–1687

Edmund Waller was an English poet and a wealthy member of parliament. In 1643 he was
arrested for his part in a plot to turn London over to the exiled king, Charles I. By betraying
his co-conspirations and by making lavish bribes, Waller avoided death. His smooth, graceful verses were extremely popular and included both love poems and tributes to important
public figures of the day.

Go, Lovely Rose

Go, lovely Rose,
Tell her that wastes her time and me,
   that now she knows,
When I resemble her to thee,
How sweet and fair she seems to be.   5

Tell her that's young,
And shuns to have her graces spied,
   that had'st thou sprung
In deserts where no men abide,
Thou must have uncommended died.   10

Small is the worth
Of beauty from the light retir'd:
   Bid her come forth,
Suffer herself to be desir'd,
And not blush so to be admir'd.   15

Then die, that she
The common fate of all things rare
   May read in thee,
How small a part of time they share,
That are so wondrous sweet and fair.   20
          (1645)

Dorothy Parker   *1893–1967*

Known best for her acerbic wit, Dorothy Parker was actually a serious editor and writer. Fired from *Vanity Fair* for writing harsh theater reviews, she reviewed books for the *New Yorker*, which also published her stories, poems, and articles for over thirty years. Her lasting literary contributions include short stories such as "Big Blonde" and "The Waltz" and several collections of sardonic verse.

One Perfect Rose

A single flow'r he sent me, since we met.
   All tenderly his messenger he chose;
Deep-hearted, pure, with scented dew still wet—
   One perfect rose.

I knew the language of the floweret;   5
   "My fragile leaves," it said, "his heart enclose."

Love long has taken for his amulet
   One perfect rose.

Why is it no one ever sent me yet
   One perfect limousine, do you suppose?   10
Ah no, it's always just my luck to get
   One perfect rose.

                (1926)

PREWRITING

As you search for a fuller understanding of a poem and for a possible writing thesis, remember to keep rereading the poem (or at least pertinent parts of it). The questions you pose for yourself will become easier to answer and your responses more enlightened.

Asking Questions About the Speaker in "My Papa's Waltz"

If a poem lends itself to an approach through persona or tone, you will, of course, find something unusual or perhaps puzzling about the speaker or the poetic voice. Consider Theodore Roethke's "My Papa's Waltz," which you just read. Ask yourself first "Who is the speaker?" You know from line 2: "a small boy." But the past tense verbs suggest that the boy may be grown now, remembering a childhood experience. Sometimes this adult perspective requires additional consideration.

Next, ask yourself "What is the speaker's attitude toward his father?" The boy's feelings about his father become the crucial issue in determining the tone of the poem. You need to look carefully at details and word choice to discover your answer. Consider, for instance, these questions:

1. Try to recapture your own childhood perspective on some interaction with adults: being kissed and hugged by relatives, encountering an adult who acted oddly, relating to your first schoolteacher, meeting a babysitter. Was it fun? Were you uncomfortable? Write a description of the experience that includes only your point of view as a child.

2. Is it pleasant or unpleasant to be made dizzy from the smell of whiskey on someone's breath?

3. Does it sound like fun to hang on "like death"?

4. How does it change the usually pleasant experience of waltzing to call it "not easy"?

5. What sort of "romping" would be necessary to cause pans to slide from a shelf?

6. Is it unusual to hold your dancing partner by the wrist? How is this different from being held by the hand?

7. Would it be enjoyable or painful to have your ear scraped repeatedly by a buckle?
8. Would you like or resent having someone "beat time" on your head with a hard, dirty hand?
9. If the father is gripping the boy's wrist with one hand and thumping his head with the other, does this explain why the boy must hang on for dear life?
10. What other line in the poem does the last line echo?

If your answers to these questions lead you to conclude that this waltzing was not fun for the boy, then you could describe the tone as ironic (because of the discrepancy between the pleasant idea of the waltz and the boy's unpleasant experience). You could, possibly, describe the tone as detached, because the boy gives no clear indication of his feelings. We have to deduce them from details in the poem. You could even describe the tone as reminiscent, but this term is too general to indicate the meaning carried by the tone.

We all bring our own experience to bear in interpreting a poem. What you should be careful about is allowing your personal experience to carry too much weight in your response. If, for instance, you had an abusive father, you might so strongly identify with the boy's discomfort that you would call the tone resentful. On the other hand, if you enjoyed a loving relationship with your father, you might well find, as does X. J. Kennedy, "the speaker's attitude toward his father warmly affectionate" and take this recollection of childhood to be a happy one. Kennedy cites as evidence "the rollicking rhythms of the poem; the playfulness of a rhyme like *dizzy* and *easy*; the joyful suggestions of the words *waltz, waltzing,* and *romped*." He suggests that a reader who sees the tone as resentful fails "to visualize this scene in all its comedy, with kitchen pans falling and the father happily using his son's head for a drum." Kennedy also feels in the last line the suggestion of "the boy *still clinging* with persistent love."[1]

Devising a Thesis

Since your prewriting questioning has been directed toward discovering the attitude of the speaker in the poem, you could formulate a thesis that allows you to argue for the need to understand the persona in order to perceive the tone of the poem. Of course, the way you interpret the poem will determine the way you state your thesis. You could write a convincing paper on any one of the following claims:

The tone of Roethke's "My Papa's Waltz" reveals the speaker's ambivalent feelings toward his father.

The tone of Roethke's "My Papa's Waltz" subtly conveys the speaker's resentment toward his father.

The speaker's affection for his father is effectively captured in the tone of Roethke's "My Papa's Waltz."

---

[1]*An Introduction to Poetry*, 4th ed. (Boston: Little, Brown, 1971), 10.

If you wrote on the first claim, you would focus on the conflicting evidence suggesting that the boy is delighted by his father's attention but frightened by the coercion of the dance. If you wrote on the second claim, you would cite evidence of the boy's discomfort and argue that the "waltz" in the title and the rollicking meter are thus clearly ironic. If you wrote on the last claim, you would emphasize the sprightly meter and playful rhymes, which present the dance as a frisky romp and show that the boy is having a splendid time.

Describing the Tone in "The Ruined Maid"

You can see by now that speaker and tone are all but impossible to separate. In order to get at the tone of Hardy's poem, write out responses to the following questions and be prepared to discuss the tone in class.

1. Who are the two speakers in this poem?
2. What does the term *maid* mean in the title? Look it up in your dictionary if you are not sure.
3. What different meanings does your dictionary give for *ruined?* Which one applies in the poem?
4. How does the ruined maid probably make her living? What details suggest this?
5. Describe how the tone of the country maid's speeches changes during the course of the poem.
6. What tone does the ruined maid use in addressing her former friend?
7. How does the final line undercut the ruined maiden's boast that she gained "polish" with her ruin?
8. What is Hardy's tone—that is, the tone of the poem itself?

Discovering a Thesis

If you are going to write on tone in "The Ruined Maid," you might devise a major claim focusing on the way we, as readers, discover the irony in the poem. Your claim could read something like this:

> In Hardy's poem the discrepancy between the supposedly "ruined" woman's present condition and her previous wretched state reveals the ironic tone.

If you wanted, instead, to write about the dual personae in the poem, you might think about how they function—to figure out why Hardy chose to present the poem through two speakers instead of the usual one. Perhaps he chose this technique because the two voices enable him to convey his theme convincingly. You might invent a claim along these lines:

> Hardy employs dual personae in "The Ruined Maid" to convince us that prostitution, long considered "a fate worse than death," is actually much preferable to grinding poverty.

In each paper, although your focus would be different, the evidence you use in presenting the contrast would be essentially the same.

Describing the Tone in "The Unknown Citizen"

1. "The Unknown Citizen" begins with the citizen's epitaph. In a five- to ten-line poem, write your own epitaph as it might appear if you died in the next year. Think about what you would like to emphasize and what you prefer to downplay. Would you try to get a message across to people who read your gravestone?
2. How is the "he" being referred to in the poem identified in the italicized epigraph?
3. Who is the speaker in the poem? Why does the speaker use *our* and *we* instead of *my* and *I?*
4. Is *Fudge Motors Inc.* a serious name for a corporation? What is the effect of rhyming *Inc.* (line 8) with *drink* (line 13)?
5. Why does Auden capitalize so many words and phrases that normally would not be capitalized (like *Greater Community, Installment Plan, Modern Man,* and *Public Opinion*)?
6. What is the attitude of the poetic voice toward the Unknown Citizen? What is Auden's attitude toward the Unknown Citizen? What is Auden's attitude toward the speaker in the poem?
7. What, then, is the tone of the poem?

Discovering a Thesis

If you were going to write on tone in Auden's "The Unknown Citizen," you would focus on the features of the poem that reveal that tone— beginning or ending perhaps with the epigraph in which he is referred to as a number, not a name. You might frame a claim something like this:

> Auden's sharply ironic tone reveals to us that the Unknown Citizen is being honored not for his accomplishments but for being a model of conformity to the policies of the state.

As you develop this claim, you can focus on the discrepancies you recognize between the solemn praise offered by the speaker and your recognition of these qualities as far from admirable.

Discovering Tone in "Go, Lovely Rose"

1. What has happened between the speaker and the woman before the poem was written?
2. Why does he choose a rose to carry his message?
3. What does *uncommended* mean in line 10?
4. Can you detect a tone slightly different in lines 2 and 7 from the speaker's admiring tone in the poem as a whole?
5. How do you respond to his telling the rose to die so that the woman may be reminded of how quickly her beauty will also die?

6. Does the title "Song," as the poem is sometimes called, convey any hint about the tone?

7. How would you describe the tone of this poem?

Discovering Tone in "One Perfect Rose"

1. Think of a time when you received a gift that was not what you'd hoped for, or a gift that showed severe misjudgment of your preferences. Write a paragraph about your public and your private reactions to the gift.

2. What are the similarities between Parker's poem and Waller's?

3. What are the major differences?

4. Why does Parker put an apostrophe in *flow'r?*

5. What is an amulet?

6. How does the tone of the poem change in the last stanza? Can you explain why this happens?

7. What is the tone of the entire poem?

WRITING

Because you may find poetry more difficult to write about than short stories, first be sure that you understand the poem. If the poem is difficult, write a complete ***paraphrase*** in which you straighten out the word order and replace any unfamiliar words or phrases with everyday language. Yes, you damage the poem when you paraphrase it, but the poem will survive.

After you are sure you have a firm grasp on the literal level, you can then begin to examine the images, make associations, and flesh out the meanings that will eventually lead you to an interpretation of the poem. By this time, you should have generated sufficient material to write about the work. The writing process is essentially the same as it is for analyzing a short story.

Explicating and Analyzing

In explicating a poem, you proceed carefully through the text, interpreting it, usually, line by line. Because of the attention to detail, ***explication*** is best suited to writing about a short poem or a key section of a longer work. As an explicator you may look at any or all elements of the poem—tone, persona, images, symbolism, metrics—as you discuss the way these elements function together to form the poem. Although you may paraphrase an occasional line, your explication will be concerned mainly with revealing hidden meanings in the poem. Probably most of your class discussions involve a kind of informal explication of poems, stories, or plays.

A written explication is easy to organize: you start with the first line and work straight through the poem. But explicating well requires a discerning eye. You have to make numerous decisions about what to comment on and how far to pursue a point, and you also have to pull various strands together in the end to arrive at a conclusion involving a statement of the theme or purpose of the poem. This approach, if poorly handled, can be a mechanical task, but if well done, explication can prove a rewarding way to examine a rich and complex work.

A written *analysis* involves explication but differs by focusing on some element of the poem and examining how that element (tone, persona, imagery, symbolism, metrics) contributes to an understanding of the meaning or purpose of the whole. You can see that an analysis is more challenging to write because you must exercise more options in selecting and organizing your material. Your instructor will let you know if it matters which type of paper you compose.

IDEAS FOR WRITING

Ideas for Responsive Writing

1. Were you ever frightened or hurt as a child, like the boy in Roethke's poem, by being handled too roughly by an adult? Describe the experience, explaining not only how you felt but also what you now think the adult's motives might have been.

2. Using Dorothy Parker's "One Perfect Rose" as a guide, write an ironic or humorous response to Christopher Marlowe's "The Passionate Shepherd to His Love" (pages 544–45) or compose the woman's reply to Andrew Marvell's "To His Coy Mistress" (pages 399–400).

3. Do you know anyone well who is a conformist, a person very much like Auden's Unknown Citizen? If so, write an updated ironic tribute to the type of person who always goes along with the crowd. Write your satirical praise as a speech, an essay, or a poem.

Ideas for Critical Writing

1. Choose one of the sample claims included in the "Prewriting" section of this chapter and write an essay defending that claim.

2. Both "My Papa's Waltz" (page 341) by Theodore Roethke and "Piano" by D. H. Lawrence (page 413) concern the childhood experience of a young boy. Study both poems until you are sure you understand them; then compare or contrast their tones.

3. Compare Waller's "Go, Lovely Rose" with Parker's parody "One Perfect Rose" by focusing on the differences in tone.

4. Stevie Smith's "Not Waving but Drowning" (page 419) seems difficult until you realize that two voices are speaking—the "I" of the first and third stanzas and the "they" of the second. Once you understand the implications of this dual perspective, write an explication of the poem.

5. Explain the satirical effectiveness of Auden's deadpan narrator in "The Unknown Citizen."

6. CRITICAL APPROACHES: Review the formalist approach to literary interpretation (page 748). Using evidence only from within "Go, Lovely Rose," explain the reasoning the narrator is presenting. What is his goal? What comparisons does he encourage the reader ("her") to make between herself and the rose? What point of argument is developed in each stanza?

Ideas for Researched Writing

1. To discover more about tone, consult reference works such as *A Handbook to Literature*, the *New Princeton Encyclopedia of Poetry and Poetics*, or the online *Glossary of Poetic Terms* at www.poeticbyway.com/glossary.html. Apply what you learn in an essay analyzing the tone of E. E. Cummings's "next to of course god america i" (pages 467–68).

2. Investigate the difference of opinion about the tone of "My Papa's Waltz." Locate at least three different interpretations, and write an essay in which you respond to and evaluate these views.

EDITING

In this section we will explain a few conventions that you should observe in writing about poetry. If you have often written papers analyzing poetry, you probably incorporate these small but useful bits of mechanical usage automatically. If not, take time during the revising or editing stage to get them right.

Quoting Poetry in Essays

The following are the main conventions to observe when quoting poetry in writing:

Inserting Slash Marks When quoting only a couple of lines, use a slash mark to indicate the end of each line (except the last).

Whitman similarly describes the soul's position in the universe in these lines: "And you O my soul where you stand, / Surrounded, detached, in measureless oceans of space" (6–7).

Citing Line Numbers Cite line numbers in parentheses after the quotation marks and before the period when quoting complete lines, as in the previous example. When quoting only a phrase, cite the line number immediately after closing the quotation marks, even if your sentence continues.

In the italicized portion of the poem, the bird sings a carol in praise of "lovely and soothing death" (135) to help the persona overcome his grief.

Adjusting End Punctuation   Because you are using the lines you quote in a different context from that in the poem, you may adjust the punctuation of the last line you quote to make it fit your sentence. Here is a line from Whitman's "When Lilacs Last in the Dooryard Bloom'd":

> To adorn the burial-house of him I love?

Notice how the end punctuation is dropped in order to suit the writer's sentence:

> The persona brings visions of the varying beauty of the entire country, as he says, "To adorn the burial-house of him I love" (80).

Using Ellipsis Dots   To show omissions when quoting poetry, use three dots, just as you would if quoting prose.

> The poet's sympathies are not for the living but for the dead: "They themselves were fully at rest.... / The living remain'd and suffer'd..." (181–82).

Using Square Brackets   If you need to change a word, a capital letter, or some punctuation *within* the line or lines you quote, enclose the changed letter or mark of punctuation in square brackets (not parentheses).

> The persona brings visions of the varying beauty of the entire country "[t]o adorn the burial-house of him [he] love[s]" (80).

Remember that you do not have to quote complete lines. Rather than clutter your sentence with three sets of brackets, you could quote only the telling phrase in that line.

> The persona brings visions of the varying beauty of the entire country to "adorn the burial-house" (80) of the one he loves.

Quoting Multiple Lines   If you are quoting more than two or three lines, indent ten spaces and omit the quotation marks (since the indention tells your readers that the material is quoted).

> After describing the carnage of war dead, the persona realizes that his sympathies have been misplaced:
>
>> They themselves were fully at rest, they suffer'd not,
>> The living remain'd and suffer'd, the mother suffer'd,
>> And the wife and the child and the musing comrade suffer'd
>> And the armies that remain'd suffer'd. (181–84)

The indented material should still be double-spaced (unless your instructor asks you to single-space the lines).

Sample Student Response: Persona and Tone

The following student paper was written in response to A. E. Housman's poem "To an Athlete Dying Young" and is included here not as a model but to generate class discussion. Read the poem, which appears on pages 407–08, and then decide whether you agree with the student's claims about the tone and persona of Housman's poem.

Sample Student Response: Persona and Tone

Kenric L. Bond

Professor Funk

English 1002

2 October 2005

Death at an Early Age

Wouldn't it be great to die in your prime, not to be remembered as old and feeble but as still strong and vibrant? A. E. Housman's poem "To an Athlete Dying Young" tells of an athlete who died a hero not too long after winning a record-setting race.

The first stanza tells of an athlete coming home after winning a race: "The time you won your town the race / We chaired you through the market-place" (1–2). But the next stanza begins, "To-day, the road all runners come, / Shoulder-high we bring you home" (5–6). The similarity between these two scenes is startling. We would not ordinarily link the picture of pallbearers carrying the deceased home in a casket with a hero being carried on the shoulders of his cheering fans. These first two stanzas set up the contrast between triumph and death that continues through the rest of the poem.

The third stanza deals with this issue of dying in one's prime by mentioning "the laurel," which grows "early" but "withers quicker than the rose" (11–12). The laurel represents fame for winning the race, but it is forgotten sooner than the brief life of a rose. This point about the brevity of fame is repeated in the last stanza:

> And round that early-laurelled head
> Will flock to gaze the strengthless dead,
> And find unwithered on its curls
> The garland briefer than a girl's. (25–28)

Bond 2

The victory garland, awarded after the race, is still green with life on the dead athlete's head; the fame of winning the race is shorter than a girl's innocence and purity. So, Housman implies, the time to die is while the recent victory is still being discussed among the living in the area coffee shops and beauty salons.

During the poem, A. E. Housman tries to convince us that it is best to die young: "Smart lad, to slip betimes away / From fields where glory does not stay" (9–10). Housman calls the athlete smart for dying while the memory of victory is still fresh in the minds of a society where positive accomplishments are easily forgotten. The poet also applauds the athlete's death because then the runner won't have to face the disheartening sight of a new runner breaking his records and stealing the glory he once enjoyed: "Eyes the shady night has shut / Cannot see the record cut" (13–14).

As a runner myself, I know that I will someday see all the records that I set in high school broken. I have already witnessed a few of my marks reset by other runners. If I had died right after my high school years, I could have missed these superficial disappointments. But an athlete shouldn't be so shallow that he or she can't bear to live and see such trivial things as records broken. They are just names on a wall or trophies in a case. I hope that somebody does break my records because that's why I made them—to be broken.

Housman seems to think that setting records and living in the limelight are all that athletes are looking for in their lives. The poet suggests that it would be too difficult for an athlete to live and see the record books rewritten and that a victorious athlete would be

Bond 3

vain enough to worry about what other people think of his physical state after he's dead. Well, I think the poet is wrong. I'm one athlete who has more than records and glory to live for.

Analyzing the Student Response

After rereading Housman's poem, write an analysis of the preceding student response. (Or, if you prefer, write your own interpretation of "To an Athlete Dying Young.") The following questions may help you:

1. Does the student have a clear understanding of the poem's main theme? Where does he state the theme? Do you agree with his statement of the theme?
2. Does the student identify the speaker in the poem? Are the speaker and the poet the same person? How do you know?
3. Does the student identify the poem's tone? Could the speaker's attitude toward death be ironic? Does the student see any irony in the poem? Does the student ever use any irony himself?
4. Do you agree with the student's claim about Housman's purpose (first sentence of paragraph 5)? How does this claim relate to the student's interpretation of the poem's tone?
5. How do the student's own experiences influence his responses to the poem? How does the student feel about the poet's attitude toward athletes? Do you agree with the reactions expressed in the last two paragraphs?

14

Writing About Poetic Language

In no other form of literature are words so important as in poetry. As you study the language of poetry—its freshness, precision, and beauty— you can learn ways in which to use words effectively in your own prose writing.

What Do the Words Suggest?

Your sensitivity to poetic language will be enhanced if you learn the meaning of a few terms in literary criticism. (The important term *allusion* is defined in Chapter 12, page 337.)

Connotation and Denotation

Many single words carry a rich load of meaning, both denotative and connotative. The **denotation** of a word is the definition you will find in the dictionary. The **connotation** of a word is the emotional overtone you may feel when encountering the term. Consider the word *mother*. Most people would respond positively with feelings of warmth, security, and love associated with bedtime stories, a warm lap, and fresh apple pies. So, when Stephen Crane includes the word in these moving lines:

> Mother whose heart hung humble as a button
> On the bright splendid shroud of your son,
> Do not weep.
> War is kind,

the connotations of the word *mother* probably account for part of our emotional response.

Figures of Speech

The most common figures of speech—metaphor, simile, and personification—appear in our everyday language. You might say, if you keep forgetting things, "My mind is a sieve," creating a metaphor. Or you might note, "That dog looks like a dust mop without a handle," making a simile. Or you might complain, "My computer can't spell worth a darn," using personification. Of course, poets use figures of speech that are much fresher and more imaginative than the kind most of us employ—one of the cardinal reasons for considering them poets.

Metaphor and Simile

A *metaphor* is an imaginative comparison that makes use of the connotative values of words. When Shakespeare writes to a young lover, "Thy eternal summer shall not fade," he is comparing youth to the joys of summertime. In "Dulce et Decorum Est" (pages 466–67), a compelling antiwar poem, Wilfred Owen uses the metaphors "drunk with fatigue," "blood-shod," "like old beggars under sacks," "coughing like hags," "flound'ring like a man in fire or lime," and "his hanging face, like a devil's sick of sin." The last four of these singularly grim comparisons would usually be called *similes* because they include the connective *like*, but you can also find similes that use *as* and other explicitly comparative words. In fact, many people use the broader term *metaphor* to refer to any figure of speech that involves a comparison.

A metaphor goes beyond descriptive detail by making an association that can *only* be imaginary, one that is impossible in reality. A person's life does not have seasons except in a metaphorical way; nor do people really become intoxicated with fatigue. However, the mental stretch these comparisons demand is part of their power. "Drunk with fatigue" makes many imaginative associations: the tired soldiers have lost their ability to think straight; they are staggering along about to fall over; they are not physiologically alert. In the poem, it is this state that makes one of them unable to don his mask quickly when a chlorine gas bomb strikes. His reaction time is fatally impaired, just like a drunk's. You can see how the metaphor packs in meaning and guides our response to the poem's narrative.

These metaphorical ideas—life having seasons or people feeling drunk with fatigue—are not difficult to grasp, because they resonate with our own experiences. Some critics would say that the best metaphors demand a more intellectual leap, having a shocking or puzzling aspect. An example from "Dulce et Decorum Est" might be the description of the soldiers' hurry to grab their gas masks as "an ecstasy of fumbling." We usually associate "ecstasy" with happiness, yet this cannot be the meaning here. We are forced to think beyond the obvious, to the features of ecstasy that do apply—intensity, overpowering emotion, lack of thought, lack of conscious control. The student paper beginning on page 368 explicates several such unusual metaphors in John Donne's "A Valediction: Forbidding Mourning."

In this chapter, the poem "In the Long Hall" provides an example of an *extended metaphor*. An extended metaphor is exactly what it sounds like: an imaginative comparison worked out through several lines or perhaps even an entire poem, accruing meaning as it goes along. In this case, your understanding of the poem hinges on your understanding of the metaphor it develops.

Personification

"Daylight is nobody's friend," writes Anne Sexton in a metaphor that compares daylight to a friend. More exactly it is a *personification*, because it makes a nonhuman thing sound like a human being. T. S. Eliot uses personification when he writes "the afternoon, the evening, sleeps so peacefully," as does Andrew Marvell in "Fate with jealous eyes does see."

Imagery

Perhaps personification is so widely used in poetry because it gives us a clear image of something otherwise vague or abstract, like daylight or fate. *Imagery* is the term we use to speak of these sensory impressions literature gives us. Robert Frost, in a famous poem, describes a sleigh driver "stopping here / To watch his woods fill up with snow," providing a visual image that most readers find easy to picture. In the same poem, Frost gives us an apt auditory image: "The only other sound's the sweep / Of easy wind and downy flake." And anyone who has spent time in a big airport surely agrees with Yvor Winters's image of one: "the light gives perfect vision, false and hard; / The metal glitters, deep and bright."

Symbol

A *symbol* is an image that becomes so suggestive that it takes on much more meaning than its descriptive value. The connotations of the words, the repetition, the placement, and the meaning it may gather from the rest of the poem help identify an image as a symbol. Blue skies and fresh spring breezes can certainly be just that, but they can also symbolize freedom. Look at the first stanza of a W. H. Auden poem:

> As I walked out one evening
> Walking down Bristol Street
> The people on the pavement
> Were fields of harvest wheat.

The image in lines 3 and 4 is descriptive: you can envision a crowd of moving people seeming to ripple like wheat. The observation is also symbolic, because harvest wheat is just about to be cut down; the rest of the poem endorses a rather dim view of human hopes and dreams.

Paradox

The same poem says, "You shall love your crooked neighbor / With your crooked heart." An inexperienced reader might say, "Now, that doesn't make any sense! *Crooked heart* and *love* seem contradictory." Others, though, would be sensitive to the paradox in those lines. A *paradox* is a phrase or statement that on the surface seems contradictory but makes some kind of emotional sense. Looking back at Yvor Winters's description of the San Francisco airport at night, you will find the phrase "perfect vision, false and hard." How can perfect vision be false instead of true? Only as a paradox. Paradoxical also are the "sounds of silence," which is the title of a Paul Simon song. And popular singer Carly Simon tells her lover paradoxically that "Nobody does it better / Makes me feel bad so good." The standard Christian paradox is stated in the motto of Mary, Queen of Scots: "In my end is my beginning." In order to make sense of that statement, all we need to know is the customary Christian belief that after death begins a better life in heaven.

Oxymoron

Another figure of speech that appears occasionally in both poetry and prose is an *oxymoron*, an extreme paradox in which two words having opposite meanings are juxtaposed, as in "deafening silence" or "elaborately simple."

Looking at Poetic Language

The five poems you are about to study exemplify elements of poetic language. As you read them over several times, identify figures of speech, imagery, symbol, and paradox.

Walt Whitman 1819–1892

Born on an impoverished farm in Long Island, Whitman moved with his family to Brooklyn, where he worked for many years as a printer, teacher, journalist, and carpenter. In 1855, he published his own book of poetry, *Leaves of Grass*, a collection of twelve long poems, which he expanded and revised throughout his life. His work as a volunteer nurse in the Civil War inspired his next collection of poems, *Drum Taps* (1865). Whitman's bold experiments with free verse and his celebration of human sexuality shocked his contemporaries—but liberated American poetry and influenced generations of modern poets.

A Noiseless Patient Spider

A noiseless patient spider,
I mark'd where on a little promontory it stood isolated,

Mark'd how to explore the vacant vast surrounding,
It launched forth filament, filament, filament, out of itself,
Ever unreeling them, ever tirelessly speeding them.   5

And you O my soul where you stand,
Surrounded, detached, in measureless oceans of space,
Ceaselessly musing, venturing, throwing, seeking the
    spheres to connect them,
Till the bridge you will need be form'd, till the ductile anchor hold,
Till the gossamer thread you fling catch somewhere,   10
    O my soul.

                                      (1881)

William Shakespeare 1564–1616

See page 584 for a biographical note about this author.

Shall I Compare Thee to a Summer's Day?

Shall I compare thee to a summer's day?
Thou art more lovely and more temperate:
Rough winds do shake the darling buds of May,
And summer's lease hath all too short a date:
Sometimes too hot the eye of heaven shines,   5
And often is his gold complexion dimmed;
And every fair from fair sometimes declines,
By chance or nature's changing course untrimmed;
But thy eternal summer shall not fade,
Nor lose possession of that fair thou ow'st;   10
Nor shall death brag thou wander'st in his shade,
When in eternal lines to time thou grow'st:
So long as men can breathe, or eyes can see,
So long lives this, and this gives life to thee.
                         (1609)

Kay Ryan 1945–

While a student at UCLA, Kay Ryan was denied membership in the university poetry club. In 2004 she was awarded the $100,000 Ruth Lilly Poetry Prize and in 2008 was named Poet Laureate of the United States. "All of us want instant success," she says. "I'm glad I was on a sort of slow drip." A lifetime Californian, she lives in Marin

County with her partner, Carol Adair, and has taught remedial English at the College of Marin for thirty years.

———◆———

Turtle

Who would be a turtle who could help it?
A barely mobile hard roll, a four-oared helmet,
She can ill afford the chances she must take
In rowing toward the grasses that she eats.
Her track is graceless, like dragging   5
A packing-case places, and almost any slope
Defeats her modest hopes. Even being practical,
She's often stuck up to the axle on her way
To something edible. With everything optimal,
She skirts the ditch which would convert   10
Her shell into a serving dish. She lives
Below luck-level, never imagining some lottery
Will change her load of pottery to wings.
Her only levity is patience,
The sport of truly chastened things.   15

(1994)

Hayden Carruth   1921–2008

Hayden Carruth, who held a master's degree from the University of Chicago, spent eighteen months in his thirties in what he called "the loony bin," recovering from agoraphobia so severe that for five years he huddled in the attic of his parents' house, barely able to write—"like squeezing old glue out of the tube." Eventually he moved to Vermont, where he scraped out a hard living—chopping wood, smoking pigs, and typing manuscripts for a dollar a page. Married four times, he declared, "The women in my life got me through." He won the National Book Award in 1996 for his collection *Scrambled Eggs & Whiskey.*

———◆———

In the Long Hall

On his knees he was weaving a tapestry
which was unraveling behind him. At first
he didn't mind it; the work was flawed,
loose ends, broken threads, a pattern
he could not control; but as his skill   5
improved he began to resent the way
his tapestry was undoing itself.
He resolved not to look back

but to keep going ahead, as he did
successfully for a long time. Still   10
later, however, he began to notice
that the part of the tapestry in front
of him was unraveling too; threads
he had just knotted became loose.
He tied them again. But before long   15
he could not keep up, his hands
were too slow, his fingers too weak.
The unraveling in front pushed
him toward the unraveling in back
until he found himself isolated   20
on a small part of the tapestry whose
pattern he could not see because
it was beneath his own body. He spun
this way and that. He worked as fast as
he could with trembling fingers   25
in futility, in frenzy, in despair.

(1978)

Donald Hall   1928–

Donald Hall was born in Connecticut and educated at Exeter Academy and at Harvard and Oxford universities. He met and married the poet Jane Kenyon in 1972, and the couple moved to Eagle Pond Farm in rural New Hampshire, where Hall remains affiliated with Bennington College. In 1989, he was diagnosed with colon cancer and given a slim chance of surviving five years. In 1994 Kenyon developed leukemia and died within fifteen months. Hall's collection *Without: Poems* (1998) focuses on her illness and death. In 2006, he was named Poet Laureate of the United States.

My Son My Executioner

My son, my executioner,
   I take you in my arms,
Quiet and small and just astir,
   And whom my body warms.

Sweet death, small son, our instrument   5
   Of immortality,
Your cries and hungers document
   Our bodily decay.

We twenty-five and twenty-two,
   Who seemed to live forever,   10
Observe enduring life in you
   And start to die together.

(1955)

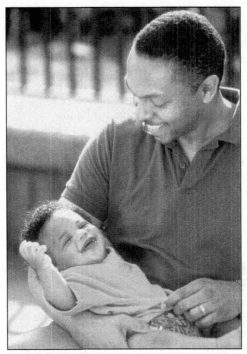

Father holding his son, who looks nothing like an executioner.

PREWRITING

The following exercises will help you analyze the use of language in the poems that you just read in preparation for writing a paper focusing on that approach.

Examining Poetic Language

1. Why could one say that "Shall I Compare Thee to a Summer's Day?" presents contrast rather than comparison?

2. In a group of classmates, attempt to write a companion poem to "Shall I Compare Thee to a Summer's Day?" using instead the extended metaphor "Shall I compare thee to a winter's day?" Try to use connotative language.

3. What is the main comparison made in "A Noiseless Patient Spider"? What is personified? Using a thesaurus, paraphrase the poem, substituting near synonyms for some of the original words. Comment on the differences in meaning and tone you create. (Imagine, for example, if the spider "launched forth string, string, string, out of itself.")

4. "Turtle" contains a number of figures of speech. Identify as many as you can. Which ones do you find fresh and effective? Which ones are less successful in your opinion?

5. What metaphor is developed through "In the Long Hall"? It may help you to fill in the blank: "_____ is like weaving a tapestry." Within this metaphor, what do changes in the process of weaving mean?
6. Explain the paradox that is central to "My Son My Executioner."

WRITING

Poetic language is one of the richest veins of material for writing. You could, for example, analyze the role of nature imagery in "Turtle," in "Shall I Compare Thee to a Summer's Day?" or in "A Noiseless Patient Spider." Or you could examine the cumulative effect of the extended metaphor in "In the Long Hall."

Comparing and Contrasting

Noticing similarities and differences between poems will sharpen your sensitivity to each of them. If you listed all the words in the short poem "My Son My Executioner" and scrambled them and then listed all the words in "Turtle" and scrambled them, putting the two lists side by side, you might see for the first time that "Turtle" has few words longer than two syllables, that it has few abstract terms, and that in contrast with "My Son My Executioner" it has few words that convey emotion. Taking the comparison further, you might say that "Turtle" focuses on creating a strong, sensual image while "My Son My Executioner" focuses on expression of ideas and feelings.

The following writing assignments suggest some meaningful comparisons to explore.

IDEAS FOR WRITING

Ideas for Responsive Writing

1. Whitman's poem comparing the explorations of the spider to the searchings of his soul makes the totally abstract idea of the soul's search for meaning clear and concrete. Think of some abstraction that you might want to explain to a five-year-old child—something like gentleness, aggression, wisdom, slyness, or perseverance. Then think of an appropriate animal or insect to illustrate the quality, and write a poem or a fable to show the child why the quality is good or bad. Remember to keep your vocabulary simple and your lines or sentences short.
2. Who is the "he," the weaver, in "In the Long Hall"? Write an essay explaining whether "he" is everyone, a certain type of person, or a specific character created by Carruth. Be specific about how you came to your conclusion.
3. Write a detailed description of an animal, using personification and metaphors the way Kay Ryan does in her poem "Turtle."

Ideas for Critical Writing

1. In your study of literature and in your everyday life, you have come across many metaphors and similes for the life span (for example, the idea that life is a journey). Explain the extended metaphor in "In the Long Hall" in terms of similarities to and differences from other figures of speech that describe the life span.

2. Compare the two kinds of love described in "A Valediction: Forbidding Mourning" (pages 398–99), using the images associated with each kind, to discover what John Donne considers the nature of true love.

3. Interpret the symbol of the spider in "Design" (page 412) and in "A Noiseless Patient Spider" (pages 360–61).

4. Compare and contrast the nature imagery in Shakespeare's Sonnet 18 ("Shall I Compare Thee to a Summer's Day?" on page 361) and Sonnet 73 ("That Time of Year Thou Mayst in Me Behold" on page 396).

5. CRITICAL APPROACHES: Review the psychological approach to interpreting literature (pages 749–50). Read D. H. Lawrence's "Piano" (page 413), looking for clues to the narrator's conscious and unconscious motivations, defenses, inner conflicts, and symbolic representations. Write an explication of the poem from a psychological point of view.

Ideas for Researched Writing

1. In the early twentieth century, a prominent group of poets developed an identity as *imagists*, dedicated to concrete, concentrated poetic language. The movement was called *imagism*. Several of these poets are represented in the poetry anthology in this text. Consult reference works and article databases for information about this movement and its followers. Write a paper explaining the principles of the movement, using examples from imagist poets.

2. Critic I. A. Richards coined two terms—*vehicle* and *tenor*—to describe the relationship between a writer's ideas and the metaphors used to objectify the ideas. Find out more about Richards's explanation of these terms. Then write a report explaining to your classmates how the terms can be used to analyze and understand metaphors. Use several poems from this book to illustrate your points.

REWRITING: STYLE

After looking so closely at poetic language, you should have a grasp of how important every word is to the total effect of a piece of writing.

Choosing Vivid, Descriptive Terms

Dudley Randall's "To the Mercy Killers" (page 428) draws its strength almost exclusively from the vividness of its language. He describes himself as "a clot, an aching clench, / a stub, a stump, a butt, a scab, a knob, / a screaming pain, a putrefying stench." While your expository prose should not be quite so packed with arresting terminology, it can probably be improved by some attention to descriptive wording. Look at several of your back papers from this class. See whether you can identify your favorite vacant words. Do you always express positive evaluations with *nice* or *beautiful*? Do you usually intensify an adjective with the word *very*? Do you refer to everything from ideas to irises as *things*? And do you describe anything that causes a faint stir in your being as *interesting*, causing you to come up with vapid sentences like "This beautiful poem is full of very interesting things"? If so, you need to find livelier, more exact terms.

Sample Student Paper: Poetic Language

Here are the second and final drafts of an Eastern Illinois University student's essay analyzing the love imagery in Donne's "A Valediction: Forbidding Mourning" (pages 398–99).

Comparison Exercise

After you have read both drafts, go over them again, making point-by-point comparisons. Notice that the writer went beyond the instructor's specific suggestions in her final revision. Write your response to the following topics, and be prepared to discuss your findings in class.

1. Identify five cases in which the writer made changes in word choice (diction). Using a dictionary, explain the rationale for the changes.
2. Identify two sentences that have been significantly changed. Explain the reasons for the changes.
3. Closely analyze all the alterations in the third paragraph of the essay.

Sample Student Paper: Second Draft

Weaver 1

Sonya Weaver

Professor Funk

English 1002

April 3 2005

Images of a Love

The speaker in John Donne's poem "A Valediction: Forbidding Mourning" is an unromantic man who is sternly forbidding his wife to be sorrowful at his parting. This description is not true of course, but it is the way the speaker might be perceived if all comparisons, contrasts, and images were taken out of the poem. In order to appreciate the beauty of this poem and interpret it correctly, it is necessary to take a close look at each image or comparison.

punct.

wordy sentence.

The first comparison we come to likens the speaker's parting to the quiet and easy death of virtuous men. The speaker paints a picture of a virtuous or upright man who, because he does not fear it, is passing peacefully into death. His deathbed is surrounded by his friends who are having trouble deciding if he has actually passed away or if he is still quietly breathing. The speaker says that his departure from his wife should be just as calm. He says, "let us melt" (5) which implies slowly and easily parting without any noise or tears. He explains that showing great emotion would expose their love to the common people and he does not want (this) because he believes their love is special, and that exposure would <u>lower</u> their love.

vague reference

best word choice?

Weaver 2

The speaker next contrasts their love to the love of common people. He states that common people notice earthquakes, but not trepidations or tremblings that take place among the stars. He is illustrating that common people's love is earthly, but that (their) love is heavenly. He goes on to say that "sublunary" (13) or earthly lovers cannot be apart from each other because when they are, they lose their love because it is only physical. He claims that he and his wife are not like (this.) He feels that their love (his and his wife's) is spiritual and refined and that it is so great that it is above their under-standing ("ourselves know not what it is" [18]). They do not have to worry about their spouse being unfaithful, as earthly lovers do, because their love is not just physical.

misleading reference?

needs rephrasing

weak reference

rephrase

Next the speaker compares the malleability of gold to the distance that their souls can stretch (21–24). The speaker says that temporary separation should not be viewed as a break. He believes that even though they may be many miles apart, they are still one. He claims their souls can expand over distances equal to the malleability of gold or 250 square feet. This is a truly beautiful image.

maybe expand with other associa-tions of gold

clarify

The last image is another very beautiful one. It compares their two souls to twin compasses (25–36). The speaker believes that if their souls are two (in-stead of one), they are still linked to each other, as are the parts of a compass. He likens his wife to the foot in the center. She makes no attempt on her own to move. She does so only if he does. She is also like the center foot in that if he leaves, she leans after him

Weaver 3

and then becomes upright when he returns home as does the center foot of a compass when the outer foot is at a distance drawing a circle. He says that there will be times when he must leave but that he will always return to her even as a compass returns to its starting point upon completion of a circle.

Without its images, this poem would be nothing more than a husband prohibiting his wife from being sad at his departure. However, Donne's images transform this rough message into a beautiful and romantic love poem. Images are important! *Weak closing line*

Be sure to add Work Cited (on a separate page).

This is a good second draft showing sensitivity to the images. I have marked a few places where your style needs more clarity and grace as well as one paragraph that could be expanded.

Sample Student Paper: Final Draft

Sonya Weaver

Professor Funk

English 1002

10 April 2005

Images of a Love

The speaker in John Donne's poem "A Valediction: Forbidding Mourning" is an unromantic man who is sternly forbidding his love to be sorrowful at his parting. This description is not true, of course, but it is the way the speaker might be perceived if all comparisons, contrasts, and images were taken out of the poem. In order to appreciate the beauty of this poem and interpret it accurately, each image or comparison must be closely analyzed.

The first comparison we come to likens the speaker's parting to the quiet and easy death of virtuous men. The speaker paints a picture of a virtuous or upright man who, because he does not fear it, is passing peacefully into death. His deathbed is surrounded by his friends, who are having trouble deciding if he has actually passed away or if he is still quietly breathing. The speaker suggests that his departure from his wife should be just as calm. He says, "let us melt" (5), which implies slow and easy movement, without any clamor or sobbing. He explains that showing great emotion would display their love to the common people, and he does not want this display because he believes it would make their special love seem common.

Weaver 2

The speaker next contrasts their special love to common love. He states that common people notice earthquakes, but not trepidations or tremblings that take place among the stars. He is illustrating that common people's love is earthly, but that the love between him and his wife is heavenly. He goes on to say that "sublunary" (13) or earthly lovers mourn physical separation because their love is limited to the physical realm. He claims that he and his wife are not thus limited. Their love is so spiritual and refined that it is even beyond their own understanding ("ourselves know not what it is" [18]). They do not have to worry about unfaithfulness, as earthly lovers do, because their love is not merely defined by the physical.

Next the speaker compares their love to the rare, precious, and beautiful metal gold (21–24). The comparison suggests not only that their love shares these three qualities, but also that it shares gold's malleability. An ounce of gold can be spread thin enough to cover 250 square feet. The speaker compares this span to the distance that their souls can stretch. The speaker says that temporary separation should not be viewed as a break. He believes that even though they may be many miles apart, they are still one, like a continuous sheet of spread gold—an unusual and expressive image.

The last image is another quite eloquent one. It compares their two souls to twin compasses (25–36). The speaker believes that if their souls are two (instead of one), they are still linked to each other, as are the parts of a drafting compass. He likens his wife to the foot in the center. She makes no attempt on her own to move but does so only if he does. She is also

Weaver 3

like the center foot in that if he leaves, she leans after him and then becomes upright when he returns home, behaving like the center foot of a compass when the outer foot draws a circle and then folds into the center. He says that there will be times when he must leave but that he will always return to her even as a compass returns to its starting point upon completion of a circle.

Without its images, this poem would be nothing more than a husband's prohibiting his wife from being sad at his departure. However, Donne's often extraordinary images transform this austere message into a beautiful and romantic love poem.

Weaver 4

Work Cited

Donne, John. "A Valediction: Forbidding Mourning."
    Literature and the Writing Process. Ed. Elizabeth
    McMahan, Susan X Day, and Robert Funk. 7th ed.
    Upper Saddle River: Prentice, 2005. 427. Print.

15

Writing About Poetic Form

When we say that poetry has *form*, we mean it has design or structure. All poems have some kind of form. Many elements go into making the forms of poetry, but they all involve arranging the words in patterns. Sometimes sound controls the pattern; sometimes the number of words or the length of the lines determines the form.

What Are the Forms of Poetry?

Poetic forms can be divided into those that use sound effects (rhythm, rhyme), those that involve the length and organization of lines (stanza), and those that artistically manipulate word order (syntax).

Rhythm and Rhyme

Sound effects are produced by organized repetition. Stressing or accenting words and syllables produces *rhythm*; repeating similar sounds in an effective scheme produces *rhyme*. Both effects intensify the meaning of a poem, arouse interest, and give pleasure. Once we notice a pattern of sound we expect it to continue, and this expectation makes us more attentive to subtleties in the entire poem.

Rhythm can affect us powerfully. We respond almost automatically to the beat of a drum, the thumping of our heart, the pulsing of an engine. Poetic rhythm, usually more subtle, is created by repeating stresses and pauses. Rhythm conveys no verbal meaning itself, but when used skillfully it reinforces the meaning and tone of a poem. Consider how Theodore Roethke captures the raucous spirit of "My Papa's Waltz" in the recurring three-stress rhythm of these lines.

> We rómped untíl the páns
> Slíd from the kítchen shélf;
>
> Then wáltzed me óff to béd
> Still clínging tó your shírt.

Chart 15-1   Rhythm and Meter in Poetry

When the rhythm has a regular pattern—that is, when the stress recurs at regular intervals—the result is *meter*. Not all poems are metered, but many are written in one dominant pattern.

Number of Feet   Poetic meter is measured in feet, units of stressed and unstressed syllables. A line of poetry may be written in monometer (having one foot), dimeter (two feet), trimeter (three feet), tetrameter (four feet), pentameter (five feet), hexameter (six feet), and so on.

Kinds of Feet   The syllables in a line can occur in regular patterns. The most common pattern for poetry written in English is *iambic*, an unstressed syllable (˘) followed by a stressed one (´). This line is written in iambic pentameter; it has five iambic feet:

My mis | tress' eyes | are no | thing like | the sun

Three other meters are of some importance in English poetry.

Trochaic (a stressed syllable followed by an unstressed one):

Tell me | not in | mourn ful | num bers

Anapestic (two unstressed syllables followed by a stressed one):

'Twas the night | be fore Christ | mas and all | through the house

Dactylic (a stressed syllable followed by two unstressed ones):

Hig gle dy | pig gle dy | Pres i dent | Jeff er son

For more details about the rhythms of poetry, see the above chart on meter.

Rhyme, a recurring pattern of similar sounds, also enhances tone and meaning. Because rhymed language is special language, it helps to set poetry apart from ordinary expression and calls attention to the sense, feeling, and tone of the words. Rhyme also gives a certain pleasure to the reader by fulfilling the expectation of the sound patterns. Rhyme, which usually depends on sound, not spelling, occurs when accented syllables contain the same or a similar vowel sound with identical consonant sounds following the vowel: *right* and *bite, knuckle* and *buckle*. Rhymes are commonly used at regular intervals within a poem, often at the ends of lines:

> Yet he wasn't a scab or odd in his views,
> For his Union reports that he paid his dues.

Alliteration, Assonance, and Consonance

Closely allied to rhyme are other verbal devices that depend on the correspondence of sounds. *Alliteration* is the repetition of consonant sounds either at the beginning of words or in stressed syllables: "The Soul selects her own Society—" or "Nature's first green is gold, /Her hardest hue to hold." *Assonance* is the repetition of similar vowel sounds that are not followed by identical consonant sounds: *grave* and *gain*, *shine* and *bright*. *Consonance* is a kind of half-rhyme in which the consonants are parallel but the vowels change: *blade* and *blood*, *flash* and *flesh*. Alliteration, assonance, and consonance are likely to be used occasionally and not in regular, recurring patterns; but these devices of sound do focus our attention and affect the tone, melody, and tempo of poetic expression.

Exercise on Poetic Form

Listen to a favorite popular song and copy down the lyrics (you may have to listen several times). Now arrange the lines on the page as you think they would be printed. What patterns of rhythm and sound do you see? Did you notice them before you wrote the words down and arranged the lines? Does the lineation (the arrangement into lines of poetry) help make the meaning any clearer? If possible, compare your written version with a printed one (on the CD cover or album liner or online lyrics site).

Stanzas: Closed and Open Forms

In the past, almost all poems were written in *closed form*: poetry with lines of equal length arranged in fixed patterns of stress and rhyme. Although these elements of form are still much in evidence today, modern poets prefer the greater freedom of *open-form poetry*, which uses lines of varying length and avoids prescribed patterns of rhyme or rhythm.

Closed forms give definition and shape to poetic expression. *Rhyme schemes* and *stanza patterns* demand the careful arrangement of words and lines into units of meaning that guide both writer and reader in understanding poetry.

Couplets and Quatrains Stanzas can be created on the basis of the number of lines, the length of the lines, the pattern of stressed syllables (the meter), and the rhyme scheme (the order in which rhymed words recur). The simplest stanza form is the *couplet*: two rhymed lines, usually of equal length and similar meter. W. H. Auden's "The Unknown Citizen" (page 343) is written in rhyming couplets, although the lines vary in length and sometimes in rhythm. The most common stanza in English poetry is the **quatrain**, a group of four lines with any number of rhyme schemes. "The Ruined Maid" (page 342) is composed of six quatrains in which the lines rhyme as couplets (critics indicate this pattern of rhyme with letters: *a a b b*). The same rhyme scheme and stanza form are used in "Aunt Jennifer's Tigers" (page 432), while the quatrains of "My Papa's Waltz" (page 341) employ an alternating rhyme pattern (*a b a b*). Longer stanza patterns are used, of course, but the quatrain and the couplet remain the basic components of closed-form poetry.

Sonnets The fixed form that has been used most frequently by the greatest variety of notable poets in England and America is the **sonnet**. Originated in Italy in the fourteenth century, the sonnet became a staple of English poetry in the sixteenth century and has continued to attract practitioners ever since.

The form of the sonnet is firmly fixed: fourteen lines, with ten syllables per line, arranged in a set rhyme scheme. The *Shakespearean sonnet* uses the rhyme scheme most common for sonnets in English: *a b a b, c d c d, e f e f, g g*. You will notice the rhyme scheme falls into three quatrains and an ending couplet, with a total of seven rhymes. "Shall I Compare Thee to a Summer's Day?" (page 361) and "That Time of Year Thou Mayst in Me Behold" (page 396) are splendid examples of Shakespeare's mastery of the sonnet (he wrote 154 of them) and illustrate why this traditional verse form continues to entice and stir both poets and readers. Dudley Randall's "To the Mercy Killers" (page 428) is an intriguing example of a modern Shakespearean sonnet.

The Italian sonnet, not very common in English poetry, uses fewer rhymes (five) and has only two groupings of lines, the first eight called the *octave* and the last six the *sestet*. Robert Frost created a chilling Italian sonnet in "Design" (page 412).

Free Verse A poem written in **free verse** or *open form* generally has no rhyme scheme and no basic meter for the entire selection. Rhyme and rhythm do occur, of course, but not in the fixed patterns that are required of stanzas and sonnets. Many readers think that open-form poetry is easy to write, but that is not the case. Only careless poetry is easy to write, and even closed forms can be sloppily written. Open forms demand their own special arrangements; without the fixed patterns of traditional forms to guide them, modern poets must discover these structures on their own. Walt Whitman's "A Noiseless Patient Spider" (pages 360–61) demonstrates how open form still uses sound and rhythm to create tone, enhance meaning, and guide the responses of the reader.

Poetic Syntax

Rhyme, rhythm, and stanza are not the only resources of form available to poets. Writers can also manipulate the way the words are arranged into sentences. For instance, the short, staccato sentences of "We Real Cool" (page 380) impress us in a way entirely different from the effect of the intricate expression of "The Silken Tent" (page 384), which is a single sentence stretching over fourteen lines. Words in English sentences must be arranged in fairly standard patterns. If we reverse the order of "John struck the ball" to "The ball struck John," the words take on a new meaning altogether. As with stanza form and rhyme scheme, poets can either stick with the rigidity of English sentence structure (syntax) or try to achieve unusual effects through inversion. E. E. Cummings, for example, forces his readers to pay close attention to the line "anyone lived in a pretty how town" by rearranging the words in an unexpected way. (In the standard pattern of an exclamation, the line would read "How pretty a town anyone lived in!")

Visual Poetry

Someone once defined poetry as "lines of words that don't go all the way to the margin." *Concrete poetry*, however, makes extensive use of line breaks and spatial arrangements. A mix of conventional poetry and graphic art, a concrete poem takes on the shape of its subject. Some famous examples include George Herbert's "Easter Wings," which looks like a pair of wings on the page, and John Hollander's "Swan and Shadow," which arranges the words and lines to create the outline of a swan and its reflection in the water. More recent concrete poetry pays greater attention to the visual effect than to the content, such as the construction that uses only the phrase "au pair girl" displayed in the shape of a pear.

Looking at the Forms of Poetry

The following poems illustrate many of the variations of sound and organization that we have just discussed. As you read these poems, be alert for the special effects that the poets create with rhythm, rhyme, stanza form, and syntax. You may have to read some selections several times to appreciate how thoroughly form and meaning work together.

Gwendolyn Brooks   1917–2000

Gwendolyn Brooks once confessed that as a child she "was very ill-adjusted. I couldn't skate, I was never a good rope-jumper, and I can remember thinking I must be a very inferior kind of child since I couldn't play jacks." Although she grew up as a middle-class African American, in her poetry Brooks identified with the poor blacks of Chicago (where she spent most of her life) and the simplicity of her poetic voice successfully conveys the meager circumstance of her subjects. In 1950 she became the first black woman to win the Pulitzer Prize.

Looking cool shooting pool at the local hangout.

We Real Cool

The Pool Players
Seven at the Golden Shovel

We real cool. We
Left school. We

Lurk late. We
Strike straight. We

Sing sin. We   5
Thin gin. We

Jazz June. We
Die soon.
(1960)

A. E. Housman   1859–1936

After failing his finals at Oxford, A(lfred) E(dward) Housman became a clerk in the London Patent Office. An extremely capable scholar, he published several studies of classical authors and was eventually appointed a professor of Latin at London University and then at Cambridge University. Housman's own poetry, admired for its exquisite simplicity and penetrating feeling, often deals with the tragedy of doomed youth. His poetic works include *A Shropshire Lad* (1896) and *Last Poems* (1922).

Eight O'Clock

He stood, and heard the steeple
  Sprinkle the quarters on the morning town.
One, two, three, four, to market-place and people
  It tossed them down.

Strapped, noosed, nighing his hour,   5
  He stood and counted them and cursed his luck;
And then the clock collected in the tower
  Its strength, and struck.

                                        (1922)

E. E. Cummings   *1894–1962*

Born in Cambridge, Massachusetts, E(dward) E(stlin) Cummings is perhaps best known for his eccentric antipathy toward capital letters—a style copied by many poetry students. His volumes of poetry include *Tulips and Chimneys* (1923) and *95 Poems* (1958). During World War I, Cummings served as an ambulance driver in France and was mistakenly committed to a French prison camp for three months, an experience he recounted in the prose journal *The Enormous Room* (1922).

anyone lived in a pretty how town

anyone lived in a pretty how town
(with up so floating many bells down)
spring summer autumn winter
he sang his didn't he danced his did.

Women and men (both little and small)   5
cared for anyone not at all
they sowed their isn't they reaped their same
sun moon stars rain

children guessed (but only a few
and down they forgot as up they grew   10
autumn winter spring summer)
that noone loved him more by more

when by now and tree by leaf
she laughed his joy she cried his grief
bird by snow and stir by still   15
anyone's any was all to her

someones married their everyones
laughed their cryings and did their dance
(sleep wake hope and then) they
said their nevers they slept their dream   20

stars rain sun moon
(and only the snow can begin to explain
how children are apt to forget to remember
with up so floating many bells down)

one day anyone died i guess   25
(and noone stooped to kiss his face)
busy folk buried them side by side
little by little and was by was

all by all and deep by deep
and more by more they dream their sleep   30
noone and anyone earth by april
wish by spirit and if by yes.

Women and men (both dong and ding)
summer autumn winter spring
reaped their sowing and went their came   35
sun moon stars rain
                                        (1940)

Wole Soyinka 1934–

Wole Soyinka was born in Isara, Nigeria. An outspoken social critic, Soyinka had to flee Nigeria several times for criticizing the government and has been jailed twice. Educated at Leeds University in England, he has written twenty plays, two novels, five books of poetry, and numerous works of literary and social criticism. His works often concern the struggle between tradition and modernization in Africa. In 1986 he became the first black African to be awarded the Nobel Prize for Literature.

Telephone Conversation

The price seemed reasonable, location
Indifferent. The landlady swore she lived
Off premises. Nothing remained
But self-confession. 'Madam,' I warned,

'I hate a wasted journey—I am African.'   5
Silence. Silenced transmission of
Pressurized good-breeding. Voice, when it came,
Lipstick coated, long gold-rolled
Cigarette-holder pipped.° Caught I was, foully.
'HOW DARK?'...I had not misheard...'ARE YOU LIGHT   10
OR VERY DARK?' Button B. Button A. Stench
Of rancid breath of public hide-and-speak.
Red booth. Red pillar-box. Red double-tiered
Omnibus squelching tar. It *was* real! Shamed
By ill-mannered silence, surrender   15
Pushed dumbfoundment to beg simplification.
Considerate she was, varying the emphasis—
'ARE YOU DARK? OR VERY LIGHT?' Revelation came.
'You mean—like plain or milk chocolate?'
Her assent was clinical, crushing in its light   20
Impersonality. Rapidly, wave-length adjusted,
I chose. 'West African sepia'—and as afterthought,
'Down in my passport.' Silence for spectroscopic
Flight of fancy, till truthfulness clanged her accent
Hard on the mouthpiece. 'WHAT'S THAT?' conceding   25
'DON'T KNOW WHAT THAT IS.' 'Like brunette.'
'THAT'S DARK, ISN'T IT?' 'Not altogether.
Facially, I am brunette, but madam, you should see
The rest of me. Palm of my hand, soles of my feet
Are a peroxide blond. Friction, caused—   30
Foolishly madam—by sitting down, has turned
My bottom raven black—One moment madam!'—sensing
Her receiver rearing on the thunderclap
About my ears—'Madam,' I pleaded, 'wouldn't you rather
See for yourself?'   35

                                                              (1960)

---

⁹**pipped** Made a short, high-pitched sound (British usage).

Robert Frost   1874–1963

One of the most popular and honored of American poets, Robert Frost was born in San Francisco, but as a young boy his family moved east, and much of his work reflects a love of the New England landscape. Before gaining success as a poet, Frost worked as a teacher, a chicken farmer, and a handyman. His poems are characterized by colloquial, restrained language that implies messages rather than openly stating them. Frost was awarded four Pulitzer Prizes for his poetry.

The Silken Tent

She is as in a field a silken tent
At midday when the sunny summer breeze
Has dried the dew and all its ropes relent,
So that in guys it gently sways at ease,
And its supporting central cedar pole,   5
That is its pinnacle to heavenward
And signifies the sureness of the soul,
Seems to owe naught to any single cord,
But strictly held by none, is loosely bound
By countless silken ties of love and thought   10
To everything on earth the compass round,
And only by one's going slightly taut
In the capriciousness of summer air
Is of the slightest bondage made aware.

(1943)

Billy Collins   1941–

Born in New York City, William James (Billy) Collins has lived there ever since. His father is an electrician, his mother a nurse. Selected as Poet Laureate of the United States in 2000, he served two terms. He has managed to combine critical approval with unprecedented popular success: his last three collections of poems have broken sales records for poetry. "Usually," he says, "I try to create a hospitable tone at the beginning of the poem. Stepping from the title to the first lines is like stepping into a canoe. A lot of things can go wrong."

Sonnet

All we need is fourteen lines, well thirteen now,
and after this one just a dozen
to launch a little ship on love's storm-tossed seas,
then only ten more left like rows of beans.
How easily it goes unless you get Elizabethan   5
and insist the iambic bongos must be played
and rhymes positioned at the ends of lines,
one for every station of the cross.
But hang on here while we make the turn
into the final six where all will be resolved,   10
where longing and heartache will find an end,
where Laura will tell Petrarch to put down his pen,
take off those crazy medieval tights,
blow out the lights, and come at last to bed.

(1999)

Roger McGough   1937–

Award-winning poet, playwright, broadcaster, and children's author, Roger McGough has been one of the most successful poets in England for more than thirty years. His 1960s poems captured the verve and irreverence of that era. McGough has always used his wit to undermine the sad disappointments of life.

————◆————

40 ----------------- Love	
middle	aged
couple	playing
ten	nis
when	the
game	ends
and	they
go	home
the	net
will	still
be	be-
tween	them
	(1971)

PREWRITING

Writing about poetic form is challenging. Because it is impossible to separate form from meaning, you must be sure that you understand what a poem says before you try to analyze how its formal characteristics contribute to your understanding and appreciation. In completing the following exercises, you should read the poems aloud, if possible, and reread the difficult passages a number of times before you decide on your answers.

Experimenting with Poetic Forms

1. Examine "We Real Cool" by Gwendolyn Brooks (page 380). How would you describe the rhythm of this poem? How does the rhythm affect your perception of the speakers (the "We" of the poem)? Why are all the sentences in the last four stanzas only three words long? What is the effect of placing the subject of those sentences ("We") at the ends of the lines?

2. Look at the alliteration in "Eight O'Clock" by A. E. Housman (page 381). What events or feelings are emphasized by alliteration? How do other elements of form—rhyme, stress, stanza pattern—influence the tone and

point of the brief drama described in the poem? Write an objective account of the events in "Eight O'Clock." What did you have to leave out of your account?

3. Study the rhyme schemes and line variations of the following poems, all of which are written in quatrains:

—"Eight O'Clock" (page 381)
—"My Son My Executioner" (page 363)
—"anyone lived in a pretty how town" (pages 381–82)
—"One Perfect Rose" (pages 344–45)
—"Piano" (page 413)
—"A Valediction: Forbidding Mourning" (pages 398–99)

In which of the poems do the stanza divisions indicate a change of time or a shift in thought? Do any of the poets disregard the stanza patterns? Try to decide why all of these poets used quatrains.

4. Rewrite the following lines—from "The Unknown Citizen" and "anyone lived in a pretty how town"—putting them in the word order you would expect them to follow in ordinary speech:

For in everything he did he served the Greater Community.

Except for the War till the day he retired
He worked in a factory....

anyone lived in a pretty how town
(with up so floating many bells down)

Women and men (both little and small)
cared for anyone not at all

WRITING

Because rhythm, rhyme, syntax, and stanza convey no meaning in themselves, you probably will not write an entire essay on form alone. Instead you can use what you have learned about poetic form to help you analyze and interpret a poem (or poems) with greater understanding and confidence.

Relating Form to Meaning

You can use observations about form to confirm and develop your ideas about the meaning or theme of a poem. Looking at a poem's formal characteristics will help you to answer such important questions as these: What is the tone? Is the speaker being ironic? What are the key words and images? And how does the main idea advance through the poem?

Specifically, elements of form offer clues like these:

1. Close, obvious rhyme often indicates a comic or ironic tone. Subtle rhymes support more serious tones.
2. Heavy stress can be humorous, but it can also suggest anger, defiance, strength, or fear.
3. Alliteration can be humorous, but it can also be chillingly serious; it serves to provide emphasis by slowing the reading of the line.
4. Assonance can provide a rich, solemn effect, a certain grandeur perhaps, or even a sensuous effect.
5. Rhythm and repetition emphasize key words.
6. Stanzas and rhyme schemes mark out patterns of thought and can serve as guides to development of theme.
7. Important images are often underscored with rhyme and stress.
8. Inverted or unusual syntax calls attention to complex ideas.
9. Various elements of form can be used to indicate a change in speaker or a shift in thought or tone.
10. Typographical effects can call attention to significant feelings or ideas.

This list does not exhaust the possibilities, but it should alert you to the various ways that form relates to thought and meaning in poetry.

IDEAS FOR WRITING

Ideas for Expressive Writing

1. Write an original haiku. A *haiku* is a rhymeless Japanese poem. Its form is based on syllables: seventeen syllables usually arranged in three lines, often following a pattern of five, seven, and five. Haiku written in English, however, do not always follow the original Japanese syllable pattern and may even be rhymed. Because of their brevity, haiku compress their expression by focusing on images and letting the closely observed details suggest the feelings and meanings. The following haiku, translated from Japanese originals and some written in English, provide a variety of models for you to follow.

> The piercing chill I feel:
>   my dead wife's comb, in our bedroom,
>   under my heel...
>   —Taniguchi Buson (trans. Harold G. Henderson)

> Sprayed with strong poison
>   my roses are crisp this year
> in the crystal vase.
>   —Paul Goodman

>   the old woman holds
>   lilac buds
>   to her good ear—
>
> —Raymond Roseliep

>   Heat-lightning streak—
>   through darkness pierces
>   the heron's shriek.
>
> —Matsuo Basho

Notice that the images in these haiku convey strong sensory experiences implying a great deal more than a mere description would suggest.

2. Write a concrete poem. Decide on a topic (an object, an activity, or an emotion), and then imagine how to make the appearance of the words on the page reflect what they mean. For example, if you were to write about running or driving, you might runthewordstogetherlikethis to suggest speed, or you could arrange the letters in the word *staircase* so they actually climb up the page. You can vary the typeface to represent different ways to emphasize the words, such as boldface to suggest anger or all capitals to indicated loudness. You might write the poem out first and then use your computer to format the type and the spaces to represent the meaning.

Ideas for Critical Writing

1. Explain how rhythm, repetition, and rhyme affect the tone and meaning in "We Real Cool" and "Eight O'Clock." Are the effects the same in both poems?

2. Write an interpretation of "anyone lived in a pretty how town" or "Telephone Conversation." Give particular attention to the way that meter, rhyme, alliteration, syntax, and stanza form contribute to your understanding of the poem.

3. CRITICAL APPROACHES: Review the discussion of the deconstructionists' approach to interpreting literature (pages 751–52). Then analyze the poem "Sonnet" explaining how Billy Collins deconstructs the form and purposes of a traditional sonnet at the same time he uses them. Is the poem a parody or a clever treatment of the conventional form—or both?

4. Compare one of Shakespeare's sonnets (page 361 or page 395) with a modern sonnet, such as Frost's "Design" (page 412) or Randall's "To the Mercy Killers" (page 428). Why do the modern poems *not* seem like sonnets? Pay close attention to the syntax and the way the rhyme scheme subdivides each poem.

5. Explain how the spacing and the arrangement of words contribute to the tone and meaning of "40 - - - Love" (page 385). You probably need to find out what "40-love" means in tennis.

Ideas for Researched Writing

1. What is a *villanelle* or a *sestina* or a *cinquain*? Examine the rules for writing one of these closed forms of poetry and read a number of examples.

Consult a reference work such as *The New Princeton Encyclopedia of Poetry* or *The Teachers & Writers Handbook of Poetic Forms*. Using illustrative examples, write a paper in which you describe the form to an audience of classmates and general readers.

2. Research the phenomenon of *slam poetry*. What happens at these events? What kinds of poetry do they produce? You might include the *spoken word movement*, which is a spinoff of slam poetry, in your investigation.

REWRITING: STYLE

As a writer, you must choose your words carefully. Many English words are to some extent synonymous, even interchangeable, but often the distinctions between synonyms are as important as their similarities. "The difference between the right word and the almost right word," said Mark Twain, "is the difference between lightning and the lightning bug." When you revise your essay, focus on the accuracy and precision of the words you use.

Finding the Exact Word

You must take care that both the denotations and the connotations of the words you use are the ones you intend. You do not want to write *heroics* when you really mean *heroism*. You do not want to "*expose* three main topics" when you really intend to *explore* them. The following are some problem areas to consider as you look at the words you have used in your essay.

1. **Distinguish among synonyms.**
   Exact writing demands that you choose among different shades of meaning. Although *feeling* and *sensation* are synonyms, they are certainly not interchangeable. Neither are *funny* and *laughable* or *famous* and *notorious*. Consult your dictionary for help in choosing the word that says exactly what you mean.

   Explain the differences in meaning among the following groups of words and phrases:

   a. a *renowned* politician, a *famous* politician, a *notorious* politician
   b. an *indifferent* parent, a *detached* parent, an *unconcerned* parent
   c. to *condone* an action, to *excuse* an action, to *forgive* an action
   d. *pilfer, steal, rob, burglarize, loot, ransack*
   e. an *apparent* error, a *visible* error, an *egregious* error

2. **Watch out for words with similar sound or spelling.**
   Homophones (words that have the same pronunciation but different meanings and different spellings) are sometimes a source of confusion.

The student who wrote that a song conveyed the composer's "piece of mind" let the sound of the word override her knowledge of spelling and meaning. Words that are similar in sound and spelling can also be confusing. If you are not careful, you can easily confuse *eminent* with *imminent* or write *quiet* when you mean *quite*.

Explain the difference in meaning in the following pairs of words:

a. *apprise, appraise*   h. *idol, idle*
b. *anecdote, antidote*   i. *accept, except*
c. *elicit, illicit*   j. *simple, simplistic*
d. *martial, marital*   k. *beside, besides*
e. *statue, statute*   l. *weather, whether*
f. *human, humane*   m. *incidence, incident*
g. *lose, loose*   n. *angle, angel*

3. **Choose the precise adjective form.**

   Many words have two or more adjective forms: a *questioning* remark is not the same as a *questionable* remark. As with homophones and other words that sound alike, do not let the similarity in spelling and pronunciation mislead you.

   Point out the connotative differences in meaning in the following pairs of adjectives.

   a. an *intelligible* essay, an *intelligent* essay
   b. a *hateful* sibling, a *hated* sibling
   c. a *likely* roommate, a *likable* roommate
   d. an *informed* speaker, an *informative* speaker
   e. a *workable* thesis, a *working* thesis

4. **Watch out for malapropisms.**

   Misused words are often unintentionally funny. These humorous confusions and near misses are called *malapropisms*. You may get a laugh from your readers if you write "My car insurance collapsed last week," but you will not be impressing them with your command of the language.

   In the following sentences, what do you think the writer probably meant to say?

   a. He has only a *supercilious* knowledge of the subject.
   b. She was the *pineapple* of perfection.
   c. They burned the *refuge*.
   d. He passed his civil service *eliminations*.
   e. They are in for a *shrewd* awakening.

5. **Be sure the words fit the context.**

   Sentences can be disconcerting if all the words do not have the same emotional associations. For instance, "The thief brandished his gun and angrily requested the money" is confusing because *brandished* and *angrily* suggest a different emotion from *requested*. A better word choice would be "*demanded* the money."

Explain why the italicized words are inappropriate in the following sentences. What words would you use as replacements?

a. Her *stubbornness* in the face of danger saved our lives.

b. The use of violence to obtain a goal is too *poignantly* barbaric for most people to *sympathize* with.

c. The mob shouted in *displeasure*.

Sample Student Paper on Poetic Form

The following paper, written by a student at Eastern Illinois University, advances several claims about Robert Frost's use of the sonnet form in "The Silken Tent" (page 384).

Elizabeth Curvey

Professor Coleman

English 1003

12 December 2008

Consistency of Character and Form in
"The Silken Tent"

The speaker in Robert Frost's poem "The Silken Tent" compares a woman he admires to a flexible shelter. In an extended metaphor, he conveys two distinct impressions: the soft femininity of a delicate fabric (silk) and the protective toughness of a tent. The speaker admires his subject, the woman, for being feminine and strong at the same time; but it is her seamless, genuine character that inspires his praise most. This inspiration is expressed in both the content and the form of the poem.

Frost's speaker uses detailed descriptions of the tent to illustrate the personality traits that he most admires. The woman's poise and self-confidence are first conveyed in the description of the tent's movements: "it gently sways at ease" (4), without rigidity. And the depiction of the tent's "supporting central cedar pole" (5) seems to stress the woman's pride and integrity. By comparing the woman's soul to a "pinnacle"—a sharp, straight, upright object—that points "heavenward" (6-7), the speaker reinforces his admiration of her firmness of character.

The admiration is intensified by the speaker's realization that everything the woman has and stands for is her own creation from materials in the world around her. This notion is expressed in the line "Seems to owe naught to any single cord" (8), a remark that implies that the woman is self-sustaining,

Curvey 2

not relying on someone else for her esteem. Yet the woman's self-confidence has not made her insensitive to others. She is connected "By countless silken ties of love and thought / To everything on earth the compass round" (10-11). The speaker suggests that the woman is capable of loving generously because she is self-assured.

Perhaps the most significant compliment comes in the last three lines of the poem, where the speaker comments on the woman's temperament:

And only by one's going slightly taut

In the capriciousness of summer air

Is of the slightest bondage made aware. (12-14)

Using the image of a summer breeze to suggest the tugs of change, the speaker indicates that the woman handles her obligations with ease and composure.

The form of "The Silken Tent" is a traditional Shakespearean sonnet: three quatrains with *abab*, *cdcd*, *efef* rhyme schemes, followed by a *gg* couplet. In the conventional sonnet, each quatrain expresses its own statement, topic, or question. The couplet sums up all the quatrains with a concluding comment. However, in "The Silken Tent" the thoughts and observations are not divided up into the conventional units set out by the patterns of rhyme.

The quatrains do not end with terminal punctuation: periods, semicolons, question marks, or colons. Instead, the whole poem comprises one long sentence. So the logic flows smoothly from one section into the next—for example, the last three lines (quoted above) are a logical unit, not the last two lines. The continuity and inner logic of the sonnet reflect the

Curvey 3

speaker's appraisal of the woman, as being both conventional and unique, a person with a wholeness and unity all her own. Though influenced by the demands of custom, she remains splendidly herself.

ANTHOLOGY
of Poetry

William Shakespeare 1564–1616

See page 584 for a biographical note about this author.

When in Disgrace with Fortune and Men's Eyes

When, in disgrace with fortune and men's eyes,
I all alone beweep my outcast state,
And trouble deaf heaven with my bootless° cries,
And look upon myself, and curse my fate,
Wishing me like to one more rich in hope,   5
Featured like him, like him with friends possessed,
Desiring this man's art and that man's scope,
With what I most enjoy contented least;
Yet in these thoughts myself almost despising,
Haply I think on thee—and then my state,°   10
Like to the lark at break of day arising
From sullen earth, sings hymns at heaven's gate;
For thy sweet love remembered such wealth brings
That then I scorn to change my state with kings.

(1609)

---

3 bootless Helpless.   **10 state** Condition.

Questions for Discussion and Writing

1. Is it believable that the mere thought of his beloved could change the speaker's whole outlook on life?
2. Summarize the speaker's state of mind before the shift that occurs in line 10.
3. How does the meaning of the poem change if the reader interprets "thee" (line 10) and "thy" (line 13) to refer to God instead of a romantic lover?

That Time of Year Thou Mayst in Me Behold

That time of year thou mayst in me behold
When yellow leaves, or none, or few, do hang
Upon those boughs which shake against the cold,
Bare ruined choirs, where late the sweet birds sang.
In me thou see'st the twilight of such day   5
As after sunset fadeth in the west,
Which by and by black night doth take away,
Death's second self that seals up all in rest.
In me thou see'st the glowing of such fire,
That on the ashes of his youth doth lie,   10
As the death-bed, whereon it must expire
Consumed with that which it was nourished by.
This thou perceiv'st, which makes thy love more strong
To love that well, which thou must leave ere long.
                                                (1609)

Questions for Discussion and Writing

1. How does the speaker portray himself in this sonnet?
2. What are the controlling metaphors in each of the quatrains? How are they
   related?
3. How do you explain the idea expressed in the last two lines? Why would the
   loved one's love grow stronger when he/she sees that the speaker is getting older?

My Mistress' Eyes Are Nothing Like the Sun

My mistress' eyes are nothing like the sun;
Coral is far more red than her lips' red;
If snow be white, why then her breasts are dun;
If hairs be wires, black wires grow on her head.
I have seen roses damask'd, red and white,   5
But no such roses see I in her cheeks,
And in some perfumes there is more delight
Than in the breath that from my mistress reeks.
I love to hear her speak, yet well I know
That music hath a far more pleasing sound.   10
I grant I never saw a goddess go;
My mistress, when she walks, treads on the ground:
And yet, by heaven, I think my love as rare
As any she belied with false compare.
                                                (1609)

Questions for Discussion and Writing

1. The comparisons that Shakespeare uses negatively in this sonnet were familiar enough in his time to be considered clichés even then. What is the poet's point in cataloging these overused images?
2. What is the speaker's attitude toward his mistress? Is he making fun of her? Do the "if…then" constructions help you to figure out the distinction the speaker is making between the artificial comparisons and his real-life girlfriend?
3. Paraphrase the last two lines of the poem.
4. Write your own parody of some form of writing that you think is sometimes overdone (such as advice columns, sports articles, celebrity profiles, articles in sensational tabloids like the *National Enquirer*, horoscopes).

 John Donne 1572–1631

The first and perhaps greatest of the metaphysical poets, John Donne wrote erotic lyrics and cynical love poems in his youth. A politically disastrous marriage ruined his civil career, but in 1615 he converted to Anglicanism and later became dean of St. Paul's Cathedral, the most influential preacher in England. In later years, he wrote religious sonnets, elegies, epigrams, and verse letters. Donne's use of complex conceits and compressed phrasing influenced many twentieth-century poets, especially T. S. Eliot.

Death, Be Not Proud

Death, be not proud, though some have callèd thee
Mighty and dreadful, for thou art not so,
For those whom thou think'st thou dost overthrow
Die not, poor Death, nor yet canst thou kill me.
From rest and sleep, which but thy pictures be,   5
Much pleasure, then from thee much more must flow;
And soonest our best men with thee do go—
Rest of their bones and souls' delivery!
Thou'rt slave to fate, chance, kings, and desperate men,
And dost with poison, war, and sickness dwell,   10
And poppy or charms can make us sleep as well,
And better than thy stroke; why swell'st thou then?
One short sleep past, we wake eternally,
And death shall be no more: Death, thou shalt die!
(1633)

Questions for Discussion and Writing

1. What is the speaker's attitude toward Death in this poem?
2. How are paradox and personification used in this sonnet to signify a victory over Death?
3. Summarize each step in the argument that "proves" Death not to be very powerful.
4. Upon what beliefs does the success of the argument depend? In what senses are the speaker's final claims about Death not justified?

A Valediction: Forbidding Mourning

As virtuous men pass mildly away,
    And whisper to their souls, to go,
Whilst some of their sad friends do say,
    "The breath goes now," and some say, "No,"

So let us melt, and make no noise,   5
    No tear-floods, nor sigh-tempests move,

'Twere profanation of our joys
    To tell the laity our love.

Moving of th' earth brings harms and fears,
    Men reckon what it did and meant;   10
But trepidation of the spheres,
    Though greater far, is innocent.°

Dull sublunary lovers' love
    (Whose soul is sense) cannot admit
Absence, because it doth remove   15
    Those things which elemented° it.

But we, by a love so much refined
    That our selves know not what it is,
Inter-assurèd of the mind,
    Care less, eyes, lips, and hands to miss.   20

Our two souls therefore, which are one,
    Though I must go, endure not yet
A breach, but an expansion,
    Like gold to airy thinness beat.

If they be two, they are two so   25
    As stiff twin compasses are two:
Thy soul, the fixed foot, makes no show
    To move, but doth, if th' other do.

---

12 innocent Innocuous, harmless.   **16 elemented** Composed.

And though it in the center sit,
    Yet when the other far doth roam, 30
It leans, and hearkens after it,
    And grows erect, as that comes home.

Such wilt thou be to me, who must
    Like th' other foot, obliquely run;
Thy firmness makes my circle just, 35
    And makes me end, where I begun.
                (1633)

Questions for Discussion and Writing

1. What is a "valediction"? And why does the speaker forbid mourning?
2. Explain how the simile about the passing away of virtuous men (lines 1–4) relates to the couple (in lines 5–8).
3. What distinction does the speaker make between "dull sublunary lovers" and the love that he and his beloved share?
4. According to the speaker, why will he end where he began? Can you explain his reasons?

Andrew Marvell   1621–1678

Though not a Puritan himself, Andrew Marvell supported the Puritan cause in the English Civil War. He held a number of posts during the Commonwealth and was instrumental in saving John Milton from punishment after the Restoration. One of the metaphysical poets, Marvell is best known for his witty lyrics that often present a tacit debate about opposing values. He has been called "the most major minor poet" in English.

To His Coy Mistress

Had we but world enough, and time,
This coyness,° lady, were no crime.
We would sit down, and think which way
To walk, and pass our long love's day.
Thou by the Indian Ganges' side 5
Shouldst rubies find; I by the tide
Of Humber° would complain. I would

---

2 coyness Modesty, reluctance.   **7 Humber** A river in northern England.

Love you ten years before the Flood:
And you should if you please refuse
Till the conversion of the Jews.   10
My vegetable love should grow
Vaster than empires, and more slow.
An hundred years should go to praise
Thine eyes, and on thy forehead gaze.
Two hundred to adore each breast: 15
But thirty thousand to the rest.
An age at least to every part,
And the last age should show your heart.
For, lady, you deserve this state;
Nor would I love at lower rate.   20
     But at my back I always hear
Time's wingèd chariot hurrying near:
And yonder all before us lie
Deserts of vast eternity.
Thy beauty shall no more be found,   25
Nor, in thy marble vault, shall sound
My echoing song; then worms shall try
That long preserved virginity:
And your quaint honour turn to dust;
And into ashes all my lust.   30
The grave's a fine and private place,
But none, I think, do there embrace.
     Now therefore, while the youthful hue
Sits on thy skin like morning dew,
And while thy willing soul transpires   35
At every pore with instant fires,
Now let us sport us while we may;
And now, like amorous birds of prey,
Rather at once our time devour,
Than languish in his slow-chapped° pow'r.   40
Let us roll all our strength, and all
Our sweetness, up into one ball:
And tear our pleasures with rough strife,
Through the iron gates of life.
Thus, though we cannot make our sun
Stand still, yet we can make him run.

                                                      (1681)

---

40 slow-chapped Slow chewing

Questions for Discussion and Writing

1. What is the tone of the assertion in the first 20 lines? How does the speaker's tone change after line 20?
2. In the second stanza (lines 21–23), why is time behind the speaker and eternity in front of him?

3. What words contribute to a second change in tone (after line 32)?
4. In the 17th century, a cannonball was simply called a "ball." What is the point, then, of the description of a cannonball ripping through the gates of a fortified city?
5. What universal human concern does this poem reflect? What basic human needs might be said to motivate the speaker?

John Keats   *1795–1821*

A major figure in the romantic period of English poetry, John Keats began writing at age eighteen and died of tuberculosis in Italy at age twenty-five, after having seen both his mother and brother die of the disease. His poems, which are rich in imagery and dignified in expression, include "Ode on a Grecian Urn," "To Autumn," and "The Eve of St. Agnes."

Ode on a Grecian Urn

Thou still unravished bride of quietness,
    Thou foster-child of silence and slow time,
Sylvan historian, who canst thus express
    A flowery tale more sweetly than our rhyme:
What leaf-fringed legend haunts about thy shape   5
Of deities or mortals, or of both,
    In Tempe° or the dales of Arcady?°
What men or gods are these? What maidens loth?
    What mad pursuit? What struggle to escape?
      What pipes and timbrels? What wild ecstasy?   10

Heard melodies are sweet, but those unheard
    Are sweeter; therefore, ye soft pipes, play on;
Not to the sensual ear, but, more endeared,
    Pipe to the spirit ditties of no tone:
Fair youth, beneath the trees, thou canst not leave   15
    Thy song, nor ever can those trees be bare;
      Bold Lover, never, never canst thou kiss,
Though winning near the goal—yet, do not grieve;
    She cannot fade, though thou hast not thy bliss,
      For ever wilt thou love, and she be fair!   20

---

7 Tempe Valley in Thessaly, noted for its natural beauty.   **Arcady** Region in Greece, a traditional setting for pastoral poetry.

Ah, happy, happy boughs! that cannot shed
 Your leaves, nor ever bid the spring adieu;
And, happy melodist, unwearièd,
 For ever piping songs for ever new;
More happy love! more happy, happy love!   25
For ever warm and still to be enjoyed,
 For ever panting, and for ever young;
  All breathing human passion far above,
That leaves a heart high-sorrowful and cloyed,
 A burning forehead, and a parching tongue.   30

Who are these coming to the sacrifice?
 To what green altar, O mysterious priest,
Lead'st thou that heifer lowing at the skies,
 And all her silken flanks with garlands dressed?
What little town by river or sea shore,   35
 Or mountain-built with peaceful citadel,
  Is emptied of this folk, this pious morn?
And, little town, thy streets for evermore
 Will silent be; and not a soul to tell
  Why thou art desolate, can e'er return.   40
O Attic° shape! Fair attitude! with brede°
 Of marble men and maidens overwrought,
With forest branches and the trodden weed;
 Thou, silent form, dost tease us out of thought
As doth eternity: Cold Pastoral!   45
 When old age shall this generation waste,
 Thou shalt remain, in midst of other woe
Than ours, a friend to man, to whom thou say'st,
 "Beauty is truth, truth beauty,"—that is all
  Ye know on earth, and all ye need to know.   50
        (1819)

---

41 Attic Of Attica, thus, classic in grace and simplicity.   **brede** Design, decoration.

Questions for Discussion and Writing

1. How can unheard melodies be sweeter than heard ones?
2. Why are the figures so lucky to exist on the urn (lines 15–27)? What disadvantages do living lovers experience (lines 28–30)?
3. How is the urn a "Cold Pastoral"? How is it a "friend to man"?
4. Explain the closing line and give your reactions to this assertion about beauty and truth.

Walt Whitman   1819–1892

See page 360 for a biographical note about this author.

Song of Myself

SECTION 11
Twenty-eight young men bathe by the shore,
Twenty-eight young men and all so friendly;
Twenty-eight years of womanly life and all so lonesome.

She owns the fine house by the rise of the bank,
She hides handsome and richly drest aft the blinds of the window.   5

Which of the young men does she like the best?
Ah the homeliest of them is beautiful to her.

Where are you off to, lady? for I see you,
You splash in the water there, yet stay stock still in your room.

Dancing and laughing along the beach came the twenty-ninth bather,   10
The rest did not see her, but she saw them and loved them.

The beards of the young men glisten'd with wet, it ran from their long hair,
Little streams pass'd all over their bodies.

An unseen hand also pass'd over their bodies,
It descended tremblingly from their temples and ribs.   15

The young men float on their backs, their white bellies bulge to the
     sun, they do not ask who seizes fast to them,
They do not know who puffs and declines with pendant and bending arch,
They do not think whom they souse with spray.

                                                    (1881)

Questions for Discussion and Writing

1. Why does the woman hide "handsome and richly drest" behind the window blinds? What sort of life do you think she leads?
2. How can the woman splash in the water and also "stay stock still" in her room?
3. What is the sexual implication of the phrase "souse with spray"? What other sexually charged language is there in these lines?
4. What does this episode imply about the sexual differences between men and women? Do you think these implications are valid?
5. What is the effect of the repetition and the unusually long lines of verse?

Matthew Arnold   *1822–1888*

Matthew Arnold was born in Middlesex, England, studied classics at Oxford, and later taught there. He was appointed inspector of schools for England and remained at that post for thirty-five years. As a poet, Arnold took his inspiration from Greek tragedies, Keats, and Wordsworth. An eminent social and literary critic in later years, he lectured in America in 1883 and 1886.

Dover Beach

The sea is calm to-night,
The tide is full, the moon lies fair
Upon the Straits;—on the French coast, the light
Gleams, and is gone; the cliffs of England stand,
Glimmering and vast, out in the tranquil bay.   5
Come to the window, sweet is the night air!
Only, from the long line of spray
Where the sea meets the moon-blanched sand,
Listen! you hear the grating roar
Of pebbles which the waves draw back, and fling,   10
At their return, up the high strand,
Begin, and cease, and then again begin,

With tremulous cadence slow, and bring
The eternal note of sadness in.
Sophocles° long ago   15
Heard it on the Aegean, and it brought
Into his mind the turbid ebb and flow
Of human misery; we
Find also in the sound a thought,
Hearing it by this distant northern sea.   20

The Sea of Faith
Was once, too, at the full, and round earth's shore
Lay like the folds of a bright girdle furled;
But now I only hear
Its melancholy, long, withdrawing roar,   25
Retreating to the breath
Of the night-wind down the vast edges drear
And naked shingles° of the world.

Ah, love, let us be true
To one another! for the world, which seems   30
To lie before us like a land of dreams,
So various, so beautiful, so new,
Hath really neither joy, nor love, nor light,
Nor certitude, nor peace, nor help for pain;

---

15 Sophocles In *Antigone* the Greek dramatist likens the curse of heaven to the ebb and flow of the sea.   **28 shingles** Gravel beaches.

And we are here as on a darkling° plain   35
Swept with confused alarms of struggle and flight,
Where ignorant armies clash by night.

(1867)

---

35 darkling Darkened.

Questions for Discussion and Writing

1. Describe the setting of the poem. To whom is the persona speaking?
2. What could have caused the "Sea of Faith" to be retreating like the tide? Note the date of the poem.
3. What does the persona pose as a solution to the loss of religious faith?
4. Write an essay in which you argue that the images of sound and sight—or lack of sight—contribute to the effectiveness of the poem.

 Emily Dickinson 1830–1886

Emily Dickinson is among the greatest of American poets. During most of her adult life, she was a recluse, confining herself to her father's home in Amherst, Massachusetts, wearing only white and shunning company. She produced more than 1,700 lyrics, which are characterized by startling imagery, ellipses, and unexpected juxtapositions. Only seven of her poems were published in her lifetime—and those without her permission. Her influence is still felt in modern poetry.

Much Madness Is Divinest Sense

Much Madness is divinest Sense—
To a discerning Eye—
Much Sense—the starkest Madness—
'Tis the Majority
In this, as All, prevail—   5
Assent—and you are sane—
Demur—you're straightway dangerous—
And handled with a Chain—

(ca. 1862)

Questions for Discussion and Writing

1. Can you think of an example, perhaps historical, of something that was considered madness that turned out to be the truth?
2. Can you think of something that is accepted by most people in society that you consider "madness"?
3. What does Dickinson mean by "handled with a Chain"?

Because I Could Not Stop for Death

Because I could not stop for Death—
He kindly stopped for me—
The Carriage held but just Ourselves—
And Immortality—

We slowly drove—He knew no haste   5
And I had put away
My labor and my leisure too,
For His Civility—

We passed the School, where Children strove
At Recess—in the Ring—   10
We passed the Fields of Gazing Grain—
We passed the Setting Sun—

Or rather—He passed Us—
The Dews drew quivering and chill—
For only Gossamer,° my Gown   15
My Tippet°—only Tulle°—

We paused before a House that seemed
A Swelling of the Ground—
The Roof was scarcely visible—
The Cornice—in the Ground—   20

Since then—'tis Centuries—and yet
Feels shorter than the Day
I first surmised the Horses' Heads
Were toward Eternity—

(ca. 1863)

---

15 Gossamer Thin, sheer.   **16 Tippet** Short cape covering just the shoulders.   **Tulle** Soft net fabric.

Questions for Discussion and Writing

1. What is the action described in the poem? What do the images in stanza 3 suggest? What is the "House" in lines 17–20?
2. Death is personified in the poem. What sort of person is he?
3. What is the persona's attitude toward death?
4. Can you state a theme for the poem?

Wild Nights—Wild Nights!

Wild Nights—Wild Nights!
Were I with thee
Wild Nights should be
Our luxury!

Futile—the Winds—   5
To a Heart in port—
Done with the Compass—
Done with the Chart!
Rowing in Eden—   10
Ah, the Sea!
Might I but moor—Tonight—
In Thee!

(1861)

Questions for Discussion and Writing

1. What is the speaker looking forward to in this poem?
2. What does the word *luxury* mean in line 4?
3. Paraphrase the second stanza, adding any words that may have been omitted.
4. Explain the image of "a Heart in port" in stanza 2.
5. What does the speaker long for in the last two lines?

A. E. Housman   *1859–1936*

See pages 380–81 for a biographical note about this author.

To an Athlete Dying Young

The time you won your town the race
We chaired you through the market-place;
Man and boy stood cheering by,
And home we brought you shoulder-high.

To-day, the road all runners come,   5
Shoulder-high we bring you home,
And set you at your threshold down,
Townsman of a stiller town.

Smart lad, to slip betimes away
From fields where glory does not stay,   10
And early though the laurel grows
It withers quicker than the rose.

Eyes the shady night has shut
Cannot see the record cut,

And silence sounds no worse than cheers   15
After earth has stopped the ears.

Now you will not swell the rout
Of lads that wore their honors out,
Runners whom renown outran
And the name died before the man.   20

So set, before its echoes fade,
The fleet foot on the sill of shade,
And hold to the low lintel° up
The still-defended challenge-cup.

And round that early-laurelled° head   25
Will flock to gaze the strengthless dead,
And find unwithered on its curls
The garland briefer than a girl's.

                                                        (1896)

---

23 lintel Horizontal support above a door.   **25 laurelled** In ancient times victors were crowned with laurel wreaths.

Questions for Discussion and Writing

1. What is "the road all runners come" in line 5? What is that "stiller town" the road leads to? What is the significance of the laurel in line 11?
2. How valuable is the approbation the lad receives in the final stanza? Would it have been worth dying for?
3. What point do you think Housman is making here?

William Butler Yeats   *1865–1939*

One of the most important poets of the twentieth century, William Butler Yeats was born near Dublin, attended art school for a time, but quit to devote himself to poetry, plays, and politics. He served as a senator in the Irish Free State (1922–1928), helped found the Irish National Theatre Society at the now famous Abbey Theatre, and was awarded the Nobel Prize for Literature in 1923.

The Second Coming

Turning and turning in the widening gyre°
The falcon cannot hear the falconer;
Things fall apart; the centre cannot hold;

---

1 gyre A spiral motion, used by Yeats to suggest the cycles of history.

Mere anarchy is loosed upon the world,
The blood-dimmed tide is loosed, and everywhere 5
The ceremony of innocence is drowned;
The best lack all conviction, while the worst
Are full of passionate intensity.

Surely some revelation is at hand;
Surely the Second Coming is at hand. 10
The Second Coming! Hardly are those words out
When a vast image out of *Spiritus Mundi°*
Troubles my sight: somewhere in sands of the desert
A shape with lion body and the head of a man,
A gaze blank and pitiless as the sun, 15
Is moving its slow thighs, while all about it
Reel shadows of the indignant desert birds.
The darkness drops again; but now I know
That twenty centuries of stony sleep
Were vexed to nightmare by a rocking cradle, 20
And what rough beast, its hour come round at last,
Slouches towards Bethlehem to be born?

(1921)

---

12 Spiritus Mundi The Soul of the World, a collective unconscious from which humans draw memories, symbols, dreams.

Questions for Discussion and Writing

1. What is the state of the world being described by the speaker in the first stanza?
2. What does the "ceremony of innocence" suggest?
3. Why does Yeats envision the "rough beast" as coming from the desert? What associations can you make with a desert?
4. Can you explain lines 19 and 20? Whose rocking cradle is it?
5. Write a brief essay explaining what the beast represents.

Edwin Arlington Robinson   *1869–1935*

Edwin Arlington Robinson was born in Tide Head, Maine. Though now considered an important poet, Robinson spent many years depending on friends for a livelihood. The publication of his narrative poem *Tristram* (1927) brought him wide recognition and some measure of financial independence. Although his verse is traditional in form, he anticipated many twentieth-century poets with his emphasis on themes of alienation and failure. His poetry won three Pulitzer Prizes—in 1921, 1924, and 1927.

Richard Cory

Whenever Richard Cory went downtown,
We people on the pavement looked at him;
He was a gentleman from sole to crown,
Clean favored, and imperially slim.

And he was always quietly arrayed,   5
And he was always human when he talked;
But still he fluttered pulses when he said,
"Good-morning," and he glittered when he walked.

And he was rich—yes, richer than a king—
And admirably schooled in every grace: 10
In fine,° we thought that he was everything
To make us wish that we were in his place.

So on we worked, and waited for the light,
And went without the meat, and cursed the bread;
And Richard Cory, one calm summer night,   15
Went home and put a bullet through his head.

                                                       (1896)

---

11 **In fine** In short.

Questions for Discussion and Writing

1. Who is the speaker in this poem?
2. What sort of person is Richard Cory? What does it mean to be "a gentleman from sole to crown"?
3. Trace the motif of images of royalty in the poem. What do they suggest about Richard Cory and those who admired him?

Robert Frost   *1874–1963*

See page 383 for a biographical note about this poet.

Mending Wall

Something there is that doesn't love a wall,
That sends the frozen-ground-swell under it
And spills the upper boulders in the sun,
And makes gaps even two can pass abreast.

The work of hunters is another thing: 5
I have come after them and made repair
Where they have left not one stone on a stone,
But they would have the rabbit out of hiding,
To please the yelping dogs. The gaps I mean,
No one has seen them made or heard them made, 10
But at spring mending-time we find them there.
I let my neighbor know beyond the hill;
And on a day we meet to walk the line
And set the wall between us once again.
We keep the wall between us as we go. 15
To each the boulders that have fallen to each.
And some are loaves and some so nearly balls
We have to use a spell to make them balance:
"Stay where you are until our backs are turned!"
We wear our fingers rough with handling them. 20
Oh, just another kind of outdoor game,
One on a side. It comes to little more:
There where it is we do not need the wall:
He is all pine and I am apple orchard.
My apple trees will never get across 25
And eat the cones under his pines, I tell him.
He only says, "Good fences make good neighbors."
Spring is the mischief in me, and I wonder
If I could put a notion in his head:
"*Why* do they make good neighbors? Isn't it 30
Where there are cows? But here there are no cows.
Before I built a wall I'd ask to know
What I was walling in or walling out,
And to whom I was like to give offense.
Something there is that doesn't love a wall, 35
That wants it down." I could say "Elves" to him,
But it's not elves exactly, and I'd rather
He said it for himself. I see him there,
Bringing a stone grasped firmly by the top
In each hand, like an old-stone savage armed. 40
He moves in darkness as it seems to me,
Not of woods only and the shade of trees.
He will not go behind his father's saying,
And he likes having thought of it so well
He says again, "Good fences make good neighbors." 45

(1914)

Questions for Discussion and Writing

1. Who is the speaker in the poem? What sort of person is he or she? What sort of person is the neighbor?
2. The line "Something there is that doesn't love a wall" appears twice. Why? What does the line mean? Does it state the poem's theme?

3. How does the speaker feel about walls? About hunters?
4. Do "Good fences make good neighbors," or are they "like to give offense"? Write an essay arguing your views on this issue.

Design

I found a dimpled spider, fat and white,
On a white heal-all,° holding up a moth
Like a white piece of rigid satin cloth—
Assorted characters of death and blight
Mixed ready to begin the morning right,   5
Like the ingredients of a witches' broth—
A snow-drop spider, a flower like a froth,
And dead wings carried like a paper kite.

What had that flower to do with being white,
The wayside blue and innocent heal-all?   10
What brought the kindred spider to that height,
Then steered the white moth thither in the night?
What but design of darkness to appall?—
If design govern in a thing so small.

(1936)

---

2 heal-all A low-growing plant, usually having violet-blue flowers.

Questions for Discussion and Writing

1. How does the title relate to the poem?
2. What associations do you get from the words used to describe the spider? How do you usually think of spiders?
3. What do the speaker's questions lead you to consider? What answers does the poem suggest?
4. Write an essay interpreting Frost's ironic use of white in the poem.

 D. H. Lawrence   1885–1930

See page 222 for a biographical note about this author.

Piano

Softly, in the dusk, a woman is singing to me;
Taking me back down the vista of years, till I see
A child sitting under the piano, in the boom of the tingling strings
And pressing the small, poised feet of a mother who smiles as she sings.

In spite of myself, the insidious mastery of song   5
Betrays me back, till the heart of me weeps to belong
To the old Sunday evenings at home, with winter outside
And hymns in the cozy parlour, the tinkling piano our guide.

So now it is vain for the singer to burst into clamour
With the great black piano appassionato. The glamour   10
Of childish days is upon me, my manhood is cast
Down in the flood of remembrance, I weep like a child for the past.

(1918)

Questions for Discussion and Writing

1. Where is the speaker in the first line of the poem? In line 3?
2. Who is the woman in the first line? In line 4?
3. The speaker resists crying because in 1918 it was considered unmanly to weep. Does he try for any other reason to stem "the flood of remembrance"?

T. S. Eliot   1888–1965

Born in St. Louis, T(homas) S(tearns) Eliot studied at Harvard and emigrated to London, where he worked as a bank clerk and as an editor. In 1927 he became a British citizen and joined the Church of England. His landmark poem *The Waste Land* (1922) influenced a generation of young poets. As a critic, he revived interest in John Donne and other metaphysical poets. In later years, he wrote verse plays, such as *Murder in the Cathedral* (1935) and *The Cocktail Party* (1950), and won the Nobel Prize for Literature in 1948.

The Love Song of J. Alfred Prufrock

S'io credesse che mia risposta fosse
A persona che mai tornasse al mondo,
Questa fiamma staria senza piu scosse.
Ma perciocche giammai di questo fondo

Non torno vivo alcun, s'i'odo il vero,
Senze tema d'infamia ti rispondo.°

Let us go then, you and I,
When the evening is spread out against the sky
Like a patient etherised upon a table;
Let us go, through certain half-deserted streets,
The muttering retreats   5
Of restless nights in one-night cheap hotels
And sawdust restaurants with oyster-shells:
Streets that follow like a tedious argument
Of insidious intent
To lead you to an overwhelming question…   10
Oh, do not ask, "What is it?"
Let us go and make our visit.

In the room the women come and go
Talking of Michelangelo.

The yellow fog that rubs its back upon the window-panes,   15
The yellow smoke that rubs its muzzle on the window-panes
Licked its tongue into the corners of the evening,
Lingered upon the pools that stand in drains,
Let fall upon its back the soot that falls from chimneys,
Slipped by the terrace, made a sudden leap,   20
And seeing that it was a soft October night,
Curled once about the house, and fell asleep.

And indeed there will be time
For the yellow smoke that slides along the street
Rubbing its back upon the window-panes;   25
There will be time, there will be time
To prepare a face to meet the faces that you meet;
There will be time to murder and create,
And time for all the works and days of hands
That lift and drop a question on your plate;   30
Time for you and time for me,
And time yet for a hundred indecisions,
And for a hundred visions and revisions,
Before the taking of a toast and tea.

In the room the women come and go   35
Talking of Michelangelo.

And indeed there will be time
To wonder, "Do I dare? " and, "Do I dare?"
Time to turn back and descend the stair,
With a bald spot in the middle of my hair—   40
(They will say: "How his hair is growing thin!")
My morning coat, my collar mounting firmly to the chin,

Epigraph: From Dante's *Inferno*—the speech of one dead and damned, Count Guido da Montefe,
who thinks his hearer is also going to remain in hell; he offers to tell Dante his story: "If I thought my
reply were to someone who could ever return to the world, this flame would waver no more. But
since, I'm told, nobody ever escapes from this pit, I'll tell you without fear of ill fame."

My necktie rich and modest, but asserted by a simple pin—
(They will say: "But how his arms and legs are thin!")
Do I dare   45
Disturb the universe?
In a minute there is time
For decisions and revisions which a minute will reverse.

For I have known them all already, known them all—
Have known the evenings, mornings, afternoons,   50
I have measured out my life with coffee spoons;
I know the voices dying with a dying fall
Beneath the music from a farther room.
      So how should I presume?

And I have known the eyes already, known them all—   55
The eyes that fix you in a formulated phrase,
And when I am formulated, sprawling on a pin,
When I am pinned and wriggling on the wall,
Then how should I begin
To spit out all the butt-ends of my days and ways?   60
      And how should I presume?

And I have known the arms already, known them all—
Arms that are braceleted and white and bare
(But in the lamplight, downed with light brown hair!)
Is it perfume from a dress   65
That makes me so digress?
Arms that lie along a table, or wrap about a shawl.
      And should I then presume?
      And how should I begin?

. . . .

Shall I say, I have gone at dusk through narrow streets   70
And watched the smoke that rises from the pipes
Of lonely men in shirt-sleeves, leaning out of windows? ...
I should have been a pair of ragged claws
Scuttling across the floors of silent seas.

. . . .

And the afternoon, the evening, sleeps so peacefully!   75
Smoothed by long fingers,
Asleep ... tired ... or it malingers,
Stretched on the floor, here beside you and me.
Should I, after tea and cakes and ices,
Have the strength to force the moment to its crisis?   80
But though I have wept and fasted, wept and prayed,
Though I have seen my head (grown slightly bald) brought in upon a
      platter,°
I am no prophet—and here's no great matter;
I have seen the moment of my greatness flicker,

---

82 upon a platter The head of John the Baptist was presented to Salome on a platter. See
Matthew 14:1–11.

And I have seen the eternal Footman hold my coat, and snicker,   85
And in short, I was afraid.

And would it have been worth it, after all,
After the cups, the marmalade, the tea,
Among the porcelain, among some talk of you and me,
Would it have been worth while,   90
To have bitten off the matter with a smile,
To have squeezed the universe into a ball
To roll it toward some overwhelming question,
To say: "I am Lazarus,°come from the dead,
Come back to tell you all, I shall tell you all"—   95
If one, settling a pillow by her head,
     Should say: "That is not what I meant at all;
     That is not it, at all."
And would it have been worth it, after all,
Would it have been worth while,   100
After the sunsets and the dooryards and the sprinkled streets,
After the novels, after the teacups, after the skirts that trail along the
     floor—
And this, and so much more?—
It is impossible to say just what I mean!
But as if a magic lantern threw the nerves in patterns on a screen: 105
Would it have been worth while
If one, settling a pillow or throwing off a shawl,
And turning toward the window, should say:
"That is not it at all,
That is not what I meant, at all."   110
                    . . . .

No! I am not Prince Hamlet, nor was meant to be;
Am an attendant lord, one that will do
To swell a progress, start a scene or two,
Advise the prince; no doubt, an easy tool,
Deferential, glad to be of use,   115
Politic, cautious, and meticulous;
Full of high sentence, but a bit obtuse;
At times, indeed, almost ridiculous—
Almost, at times, the Fool.

I grow old...I grow old...   120
I shall wear the bottoms of my trousers rolled.

Shall I part my hair behind? Do I dare to eat a peach?
I shall wear white flannel trousers, and walk upon the beach.
I have heard the mermaids singing, each to each.

I do not think that they will sing to me.   125

I have seen them riding seaward on the waves
Combing the white hair of the waves blown back
When the wind blows the water white and black.

---

94 Lazarus Jesus raised Lazarus from the dead. See John 11:1–41.

We have lingered in the chambers of the sea
By sea-girls wreathed with seaweed red and brown   130
Till human voices wake us, and we drown.
                                                    (1917)

Questions for Discussion and Writing

1. Who is speaking in the poem and to whom?
2. What is the situation depicted?
3. What sort of person is J. Alfred Prufrock? Why is he so wary about going to this party? Why does he consider parting his hair behind? What does it mean to measure out one's life with coffee spoons? Why do women make him so nervous? Why does he think he should have been a crab, "Scuttling across the floors of silent seas"? Why does he exaggerate so? Is he right in deciding that he's more like Polonius than Hamlet? Why does he wonder if he dares to eat a peach? Why does he decide the mermaids will not sing to him?

Claude McKay 1890–1948

Claude McKay was born in Sunny Ville, Jamaica. At the age of twenty-three, he moved to the United States, where he encountered the strong racial prejudice prevalent during this period. A prominent figure in the Harlem Renaissance, McKay was a catalyst among African American writers, preaching black vitality and social reform. He wrote four volumes of poetry, including *If We Must Die* (1919); a novel, *Home to Harlem* (1928); and an autobiography, *A Long Way from Home* (1937).

America

Although she feeds me bread of bitterness,
And sinks into my throat her tiger's tooth,
Stealing my breath of life, I will confess
I love this cultured hell that tests my youth!
Her vigor flows like tides into my blood,   5
Giving me strength erect against her hate.
Her bigness sweeps my being like a flood,
Yet as a rebel fronts a king in state,
I stand within her walls with not a shred
Of terror, malice, not a word of jeer.   10
Darkly I gaze into the days ahead,
And see her might and granite wonders there,
Beneath the touch of Time's unerring hand,
Like priceless treasures sinking in the sand.
                                                    (1920)

Questions for Discussion and Writing

1. Who is speaking in this poem?
2. Explain the metaphors in the first three lines.
3. What does the speaker love about America? What does he regard as a threat to her strength?

 Jean Toomer   1894–1967

Jean Toomer grew up in Washington, D.C., attended several colleges, and worked briefly as the headmaster of a black school in Georgia. His best-known work, *Cane* (1923), combines poetry, fiction, and drama into an artistic vision of the black American experience. Widely acclaimed for its innovative style and penetrating insights, *Cane* is one of the most important works of the Harlem Renaissance, although Toomer later disavowed any connection with that movement.

Reapers

Black reapers with the sound of steel on stones
Are sharpening scythes. I see them place the hones°
In their hip-pockets as a thing that's done,
And start their silent swinging, one by one.

Black horses drive a mower through the weeds,   5
And there, a field rat, startled, squealing bleeds,
His belly close to ground. I see the blade,
Blood-stained, continue cutting weeds and shade.

(1923)

---

2 hones Whetstones for sharpening blades.

Questions for Discussion and Writing

1. Read the poem aloud. Notice several patterns of sound. How do they relate to the picture described in the poem?
2. Does the speaker of the poem, the viewer of the scene, see life as a joyful romp, a dashing adventure, or a predetermined grind? How do you know?
3. Death is sometimes called "The Grim Reaper." Do you think Toomer had this in mind when he wrote "Reapers"? Why?

Stevie Smith   *1902–1971*

Born Florence Margaret Smith in Hull, England, Stevie Smith worked as a secretary and occasionally as a writer and broadcaster for the BBC. She began publishing verse, which she often illustrated herself, in the 1930s but did not gain much recognition until 1962, when her *Selected Poems* appeared. Noted for her eccentricity and humor, Smith often aimed her satirical barbs at religion and made unexpected use of traditional hymns, songs, and nursery rhymes in her poems.

Not Waving but Drowning

Nobody heard him, the dead man,
But still he lay moaning:
I was much further out than you thought
And not waving but drowning.

Poor chap, he always loved larking   5
And now he's dead
It must have been too cold for him his heart gave way,
They said.

Oh, no no no, it was too cold always
(Still the dead one lay moaning)   10
I was much too far out all my life
And not waving but drowning.

(1957)

Questions for Discussion and Writing

1. Who are the two speakers in the poem? How does one misunderstand the other?
2. The lines "I was much too far out all my life /And not waving but drowning" are obviously meant to carry more than a literal meaning. What does the dead man mean?
3. In what ways might your outward demeanor be contrary to the "inner you"? Write an essay about how you or someone you know might give a false impression to others.

Langston Hughes   *1902-1967*

Born in Joplin, Missouri, Hughes spent his youth in the Midwest. After a brief time in Mexico in 1920 in an attempt to reunite with his estranged father, Hughes moved to New York, where he spent one unhappy year at Columbia University. He then embarked on a series of world travels as a seaman and menial worker in Africa and Europe before returning to the United States to graduate in 1929 from the nation's first black college, Lincoln University in Pennsylvania. Hughes was a leading figure in the Harlem Renaissance, celebrating the vitality of African American culture in poetry, stories, novels, autobiographies, children's books, radio plays, musicals, operettas, and newspaper columns. He also nurtured the talents of many other black writers and gained international admiration for his efforts.

Harlem (A Dream Deferred)

What happens to a dream deferred?

Does it dry up
like a raisin in the sun?
Or fester like a sore—
And then run?   5
Does it stink like rotten meat?
Or crust and sugar over—
like a syrupy sweet?

Maybe it just sags
like a heavy load.   10

Or does it explode?

(1951)

Langston Hughes, a leading figure of the Harlem Renaissance in the 1920s and 1930s, who celebrated the vitality of African American culture in many genres. (The New York Public Library/Art Resource. Schomburg Collection of the New York Public Library.)

Questions for Discussion and Writing

1. What is the "dream deferred" mentioned in the opening line?
2. What effect do all the visual images describe?
3. How do these consequences culminate in the meaning of the final line?
4. Examine the similes Hughes employs to evoke the effects of the deferred dream, and write an essay discussing the social implications these images convey.

Theme for English B

The instructor said,

   Go home and write
   a page tonight.
   And let that page come out of you—
   Then, it will be true.   5

I wonder if it's that simple?
I am twenty-two, colored, born in Winston-Salem.
I went to school there, then Durham, then here
to this college on the hill above Harlem.
I am the only colored student in my class.   10
The steps from the hill lead down into Harlem,
through a park, then I cross St. Nicholas,
Eighth Avenue, Seventh, and I come to the Y,
the Harlem Branch Y, where I take the elevator
up to my room, sit down, and write this page: 15
It's not easy to know what is true for you or me
at twenty-two, my age. But I guess I'm what
I feel and see and hear, Harlem, I hear you:
hear you, hear me—we two—you, me, talk on this page.
(I hear New York, too.) Me—who?   20
Well, I like to eat, sleep, drink, and be in love.
I like to work, read, learn, and understand life.
I like a pipe for a Christmas present,
or records—Bessie,° bop,° or Bach.
I guess being colored doesn't make me *not* like   25
the same things other folks like who are other races.
So will my page be colored that I write?
Being me, it will not be white.
But it will be
a part of you, instructor.   30
You are white—
yet a part of me, as I am a part of you.
That's American.
Sometimes perhaps you don't want to be a part of me.
Nor do I often want to be a part of you.   35

---

24 Bessie (Smith, 1894–1937), African American blues singer.   **bop** A kind of jazz; also called be-bop.

But we are, that's true!
I guess you learn from me—
although you're older—and white—
and somewhat more free.

This is my page for English B. 40

(1951)

Questions for Discussion and Writing

1. What would you write if you had the assignment that the speaker's teacher gives the class? How would you decide what to include?
2. What is the student's attitude toward the assignment? How can you tell?
3. The teacher says, "And let that page come out of you—then, it will be true." What do you think she means by this? What ideas about writing does she probably hold?
4. Do you think the racial difference is an important part of this poem? Or do you think the main point is about how the teacher and the student look at things differently?

Countee Cullen   1903–1946

Countee Cullen was adopted by a Methodist minister and raised in Harlem. His first volume of poems, *Color* (1925), was published when he was a student at New York University. His early work established him as a leader of the Harlem Renaissance, but his collection *Copper Sun* (1927), which featured love poems, disappointed black nationalists. Cullen stopped writing poetry after he published *The Black Christ* in 1929. He taught school in New York City for the rest of his life.

Incident

(For Eric Walrond)

Once riding in old Baltimore,
    Heart-filled, head-filled with glee,
I saw a Baltimorean
    Keep looking straight at me.

Now I was eight and very small, 5
    And he was no whit bigger,
And so I smiled, but he poked out
    His tongue, and called me, "Nigger."

I saw the whole of Baltimore
    From May until December; 10

Of all the things that happened there
That's all that I remember.

(1925)

Questions for Discussion and Writing

1. Though the main point of "Incident" is unstated, its theme is clear. How would you state it in a sentence?
2. "Incident" is very simple in form and language. Why do you think the author chose this simplicity?
3. Write an essay about your own introduction into a part of the adult world that you weren't aware of as a child or youth.

 Theodore Roethke   1908–1963

See page 341 for a biographical note about this author.

I Knew a Woman

I knew a woman, lovely in her bones,
When small birds sighed, she would sigh back at them;
Ah, when she moved, she moved more ways than one:
The shapes a bright container can contain!
Of her choice virtues only gods should speak,   5
Or English poets who grew up on Greek
(I'd have them sing in chorus, cheek to cheek).

How well her wishes went! She stroked my chin,
She taught me Turn, and Counter-turn, and Stand;
She taught me Touch, that undulant white skin;   10
I nibbled meekly from her proffered hand;
She was the sickle; I, poor I, the rake,
Coming behind her for her pretty sake
(But what prodigious mowing we did make).

Love likes a gander, and adores a goose: 15
Her full lips pursed, the errant note to seize;
She played it quick, she played it light and loose;
My eyes, they dazzled at her flowing knees;
Her several parts could keep a pure repose,
Or one hip quiver with a mobile nose   20
(She moved in circles, and those circles moved).

Let seed be grass, and grass turn into hay:
I'm martyr to a motion not my own;
What's freedom for? To know eternity.
I swear she cast a shadow white as stone.   25
But who would count eternity in days?
These old bones live to learn her wanton ways:
(I measure time by how a body sways).

(1958)

Questions for Discussion and Writing

1. List some of the things that the woman is compared to. What do they have in common? What comparisons strike you as unusual in a love poem?
2. Explain the image of the sickle and rake in stanza two.
3. Write an essay explaining how the speaker of the poem gently makes fun of himself for his obsession with the woman.

Elizabeth Bishop   1911–1979

Elizabeth Bishop was born in Massachusetts. Her father died when she was a baby and her mother was committed as insane when Elizabeth was five; she was raised by relatives in New England and Nova Scotia. Educated at Vassar, she lived mainly in Key West and in Brazil. Bishop's poetry, known for its understanding of the natural world, often provides meticulously detailed descriptions that focus on external reality. Her first book, *North & South*, was published in 1946; collected with her second book, *Cold Spring*, it won the 1955 Pulitzer Prize.

One Art

The art of losing isn't hard to master;
so many things seem filled with the intent
to be lost that their loss is no disaster.
Lose something every day. Accept the fluster
of lost door keys, the hour badly spent.   5
The art of losing isn't hard to master.

Then practice losing farther, losing faster:
places, and names, and where it was you meant
to travel. None of these will bring disaster.

I lost my mother's watch. And look! my last, or   10
next-to-last, of three loved houses went.
The art of losing isn't hard to master.

I lost two cities, lovely ones. And, vaster,
some realms I owned, two rivers, a continent.
I miss them, but it wasn't a disaster. 15

—Even losing you (the joking voice, a gesture
I love) I shan't have lied. It's evident
the art of losing's not too hard to master
though it may look like (*Write it!*) like disaster.
(1976)

Questions for Discussion and Writing

1. What is the form of this poem? What effect does the repetition have on the tone and point of the poem?
2. What experiences does the poem relate?
3. What kinds of loss does the speaker mention?
4. Is losing an art? Is it really "easy"? How does one "master" it? Has the speaker mastered it?

May Sarton 1912–1995

A prolific writer of poetry, novels, autobiography, screenplays, and journals, May Sarton was born in Belgium but emigrated to the United States in 1916. Sarton supported herself mainly through visiting professorships, poetry readings, and lectures. Her work deals with private human concerns such as love, loneliness, and creativity. Sarton's clear, simple style only appears effortless: she said some of her poems went through sixty drafts. Her poetry is compiled in *Collected Poems, 1930–1973* (1974) and *Selected Poems* (1978).

AIDS

We are stretched to meet a new dimension
Of love, a more demanding range
Where despair and hope must intertwine.
How grow to meet it? Intention
Here can neither move nor change 5
The raw truth. Death is on the line.
It comes to separate and estrange
Lover from lover in some reckless design.
Where do we go from here?

Fear. Fear. Fear. Fear. 10

Our world has never been more stark
Or more in peril.

It is very lonely now in the dark.
Lonely and sterile.
And yet in the simple turn of a head   15
Mercy lives. I heard it when someone said
"I must go now to a dying friend.
Every night at nine I tuck him into bed,
And give him a shot of morphine,"
And added, "I go where I have never been."   20
I saw he meant into a new discipline
He had not imagined before, and a new grace.

Every day now we meet face to face.
Every day now devotion is the test.
Through the long hours, the hard, caring nights   25
We are forging a new union. We are blest.

As closed hands open to each other
Closed lives open to strange tenderness.
We are learning the hard way how to mother.
Who says it is easy? But we have the power.   30
I watch the faces deepen all around me.
It is the time of change, the saving hour.
The word is not fear, the word we live,
But an old word suddenly made new,
As we learn it again, as we bring it alive: 35

Love. Love. Love. Love.

                                                        (1988)

Questions for Discussion and Writing

1. Who is the "we" in the poem?
2. When the friend in stanza four says, "I go where I have never been," what does he mean? How does his experience relate to the rest of the poem?
3. What does the line "We are blest" mean? How does the speaker manage to pull a positive meaning out of the AIDS experience? Do you know of other, similar experiences that bring about "a new grace"?

Octavio Paz   *1914–1998*

The first Mexican to be awarded the Nobel Prize for Literature (1990), Octavio Paz was born in Mexico City, the son and grandson of prominent political activists. For twenty years, Paz served as a diplomat for the Mexican government with posts in New York, Paris, India, and Japan. In 1968, however, he resigned from the diplomatic service in protest against the government's violent suppression of the student demonstrations during the Olympic Games in Mexico. After that, Paz worked as an editor and publisher, founding two important magazines dedicated to the arts and politics. In 1980, he was named honorary doctor at Harvard University.

The Street

Translated by Muriel Rukeyser

A long silent street.
I walk in blackness and I stumble and fall
and rise, and I walk blind, my feet
stepping on silent stones and dry leaves.
Someone behind me also stepping on stones, leaves: 5
if I slow down, he slows;
if I run, he runs. I turn: nobody.
Everything dark and doorless.
Turning and turning among these corners
which lead forever to the street   10
where nobody waits for, nobody follows me,
where I pursue a man who stumbles
and rises and says when he sees me: nobody.

(1963)

Questions for Discussion and Writing

1. Reread the first four lines of the poem. What is familiar about this scene? How does it make you feel?
2. What are the main sensory appeals of the poem? List the words that carry this appeal.
3. Why do you think the leaves are dry rather than wet? What about the choice of the word "doorless" in line 8?

Dudley Randall   1914–2000

Dudley Randall was born in Washington, D.C., and graduated from Wayne State and the University of Michigan, where he earned degrees in English and library science. In 1969 he became librarian and poet-in-residence at the University of Detroit. A pioneer in the movement to publish the work of African-American writers, Randall founded Broadside Press, one of the most influential small publishing houses in America. Collections of his work include *Cities Burning* (1968), *More to Remember* (1971), *After the Killing* (1973), and *A Litany of Friends* (1981).

To the Mercy Killers

If ever mercy move you murder me,
I pray you, kindly killers, let me live.
Never conspire with death to set me free,
but let me know such life as pain can give.
Even though I be a clot, an aching clench,   5
a stub, a stump, a butt, a scab, a knob,
a screaming pain, a putrefying stench,
still let me live, so long as life shall throb.
Even though I turn such traitor to myself
as beg to die, do not accomplice me.   10
Even though I seem not human, a mute shelf
of glucose, bottled blood, machinery
to swell the lung and pump the heart—even so,
do not put out my life. Let me still glow.

(1973)

Questions for Discussion and Writing

1. Point out the ironic word choice in the first two lines of the poem.
2. Why does the speaker want to be allowed to live even when enduring the horrors he describes? Do you agree with his position?
3. What is the implied comparison in the last line?
4. Write a short response in which you agree or disagree with the poem's main argument.

Dylan Thomas 1914–1953

Dylan Thomas was born in Wales. Shunning school to pursue a writing career, he published his first book of poetry at age twenty. Limited by his lack of a degree, he had trouble making a living as a writer, and his early life was marked by poverty and heavy drinking. Calling his poetry a "record of my struggle from darkness towards some measure of light," Thomas delighted in sound, sometimes at the expense of sense.

Do Not Go Gentle into That Good Night

Do not go gentle into that good night,
Old age should burn and rave at close of day;
Rage, rage against the dying of the light.

Though wise men at their end know dark is right,
Because their words had forked no lightning they   5
Do not go gentle into that good night.

Good men, the last wave by, crying how bright
Their frail deeds might have danced in a green bay,
Rage, rage against the dying of the light.

Wild men who caught and sang the sun in flight, 10
And learn, too late, they grieved it on its way,
Do not go gentle into that good night.

Grave men, near death, who see with blinding sight
Blind eyes could blaze like meteors and be gay,
Rage, rage against the dying of the light. 15

And you, my father, there on the sad height,
Curse, bless, me now with your fierce tears, I pray.
Do not go gentle into that good night.
Rage, rage against the dying of the light.

(1952)

Questions for Discussion and Writing

1. What do the repeated images "that good night" and "dying of the light" stand for?
2. What repeated pattern can you see in stanzas two through five? What kinds of people are described in these stanzas?
3. Explain the seeming contradiction in line 17.

 Gwendolyn Brooks   1917–2000

See page 379 for a biographical note about this author.

Sadie and Maud

Maud went to college.
Sadie stayed at home.
Sadie scraped life
With a fine-tooth comb.

She didn't leave a tangle in. 5
Her comb found every strand.
Sadie was one of the livingest chits°
In all the land.

---

7 chits A pert, lively young woman.

Sadie bore two babies
Under her maiden name.   10
Maud and Ma and Papa
Nearly died of shame.

When Sadie said her last so-long
Her girls struck out from home.
(Sadie had left as heritage   15
Her fine-tooth comb.)

Maud, who went to college,
Is a thin brown mouse.
She is living all alone
In this old house.   20

(1945)

Questions for Discussion and Writing

1. What is the attitude of the speaker toward each young woman, Sadie and Maud?
2. What was Sadie's legacy, symbolized by her "fine-tooth comb"?
3. What is the meaning of the poem? Write an explication.
4. Do you agree with Brooks's theme? Why or why not?

The Bean Eaters

They eat beans mostly, this old yellow pair.
Dinner is a casual affair.
Plain chipware on a plain and creaking wood,
Tin flatware.

Two who are Mostly Good.   5
Two who have lived their day,
But keep on putting on their clothes
And putting things away.

And remembering...
Remembering, with twinklings and twinges,   10
As they lean over the beans in their rented back room that
        is full of beads and receipts and dolls and cloths,
        tobacco crumbs, vases and fringes.

(1945)

Questions for Discussion and Writing

1. Why is the couple eating beans? How do you know?
2. What overall impression does the list at the end of the poem give you?

3. Why does the writer include the phrase "Mostly Good"? Why aren't the people described as "Good"?
4. What is the significance of "putting on their clothes /And putting things away"?

Anne Sexton 1928–1974

Instead of attending college, Anne Sexton eloped at nineteen, became a housewife and mother, and worked briefly as a fashion model. She suffered her first nervous breakdown when she was twenty-eight, and for the rest of her life, she was "in and out of mental institutions, on and off psychiatric drugs." Her psychiatrist suggested writing poetry as therapy. She did, and her highly introspective poetry won her a wide and loyal audience. Sexton once wrote that poetry "should be a shock to the senses. It should hurt." Her collection of poems *Live or Die* (1966) won a Pulitzer Prize. She committed suicide at age forty-six.

You All Know the Story of the Other Woman

It's a little Walden.
She is private in her breathbed
as his body takes off and flies,
flies straight as an arrow.
But it's a bad translation.   5
Daylight is nobody's friend.
God comes in like a landlord
and flashes on his brassy lamp.
Now she is just so-so.
He puts his bones back on,   10
turning the clock back an hour.
She knows flesh, that skin balloon,
the unbound limbs, the boards,
the roof, the removable roof.
She is his selection, part time.   15
You know the story too! Look,
when it is over he places her,
like a phone, back on the hook.
                    (1967)

Questions for Discussion and Writing

1. Concentrate on the title. Do you all know the story of the other woman? What is "the conventional wisdom" about what happens to the other woman?

2. This poem depends on metaphors and similes for its meaning. Identify and explain five of them. Why does the last simile make the point unmistakable?

3. How does the man behave after he has had sex with the woman? Write a paraphrase of lines 6 through 14.

Adrienne Rich   *1929–*

Born in Baltimore, Adrienne Rich graduated from Radcliffe College in 1951, the same year that her first book of poetry, *A Change in the World*, appeared in the Yale Series of Younger Poets. The Vietnam War and her teaching experience with minority youth in New York City heightened Rich's political awareness, and she became increasingly involved in the women's movement. Her poetry collection *Diving into the Wreck* (1973) won the National Book Award.

Aunt Jennifer's Tigers

Aunt Jennifer's tigers prance across a screen,
Bright topaz denizens of a world of green.
They do not fear the men beneath the tree;
They pace in sleek chivalric certainty.

Aunt Jennifer's fingers fluttering through her wool   5
Find even the ivory needle hard to pull.
The massive weight of Uncle's wedding band
Sits heavily upon Aunt Jennifer's hand.

When Aunt is dead, her terrified hands will lie
Still ringed with ordeals she was mastered by.   10
The tigers in the panel that she made
Will go on prancing, proud and unafraid.

                          (1951)

Questions for Discussion and Writing

1. What human traits do the tigers possess? What kind of life do they lead? What does "prancing" suggest?

2. What kind of life does Aunt Jennifer lead? How do the tigers help you to understand her plight? Why might she have chosen them for her tapestry?

3. What does Aunt Jennifer's wedding band symbolize? What is a wedding ring supposed to symbolize?

4. One critic says that the speaker in the poem is "almost callous in her disregard for Aunt's death," that the speaker cares more for the gorgeous tigers than for Aunt Jennifer. Argue your response to this interpretation.

Sylvia Plath   *1932–1963*

Sylvia Plath was born in Boston, where her father taught at Boston University. Her early years were filled with honors and awards. She won a Fulbright Scholarship to Cambridge, where she met and married English poet Ted Hughes. But beneath the conventional success was a woman whose acute perceptions and intolerable pain led her to commit suicide at age thirty. Plath produced three volumes of powerful poetry and an autobiographical novel, *The Bell Jar* (1963).

Mirror

I am silver and exact. I have no preconceptions.
Whatever I see I swallow immediately
Just as it is, unmisted by love or dislike.
I am not cruel, only truthful—
The eye of a little god, four-cornered.   5
Most of the time I meditate on the opposite wall.
It is pink, with speckles. I have looked at it so long
I think it is a part of my heart. But it flickers.
Faces and darkness separate us over and over.

Now I am a lake. A woman bends over me,   10
Searching my reaches for what she really is.
Then she turns to those liars, the candles or the moon.
I see her back, and reflect it faithfully.
She rewards me with tears and an agitation of hands.
I am important to her. She comes and goes.   15
Each morning it is her face that replaces the darkness.
In me she has drowned a young girl, and in me an old woman
Rises toward her day after day, like a terrible fish.

                                                                                     (1963)

Questions for Discussion and Writing

1. Consider the use of personification in this poem. What difference would it make if the mirror had no voice—for example, if the poem began "The mirror is silver and exact. It has no preconceptions"?

2. What reason can you see for the stanza division? What two characters does the mirror choose to describe itself?

3. Why does the mirror call candles and the moon "those liars"?

John Updike   *1932–2009*

See page 285 for a biographical note about this author.

Ex-Basketball Player

Pearl Avenue runs past the high-school lot,
Bends with the trolley tracks, and stops, cut off
Before it has a chance to go two blocks,
At Colonel McComsky Plaza. Berth's Garage
Is on the corner facing west, and there,   5
Most days, you'll find Flick Webb, who helps Berth out.

Flick stands tall among the idiot pumps—
Five on a side, the old bubble-head style,°
Their rubber elbows hanging loose and low.
One's nostrils are two S's, and his eyes   10
An E and O.°And one is squat, without
A head at all—more of a football type.

Once Flick played for the high-school team, the Wizards.
He was good: in fact, the best. In '46
He bucketed three hundred ninety points,   15
A county record still. The ball loved Flick.
I saw him rack up thirty-eight or forty
In one home game. His hands were like wild birds.

He never learned a trade, he just sells gas,
Checks oil, and changes flats. Once in a while,   20
As a gag, he dribbles an inner tube,
But most of us remember anyway.
His hands are fine and nervous on the lug wrench.
It makes no difference to the lug wrench, though.

---

8 bubble-head style Gasoline pumps with round glass globes on top.
11 E and O ESSO—a major oil company in the 1940s, the time frame of the poem.

An "old bubble-head" ESSO gasoline pump.

Off work, he hangs around Mae's luncheonette.   25
Grease-gray and kind of coiled, he plays pinball,
Smokes those thin cigars, nurses lemon phosphates.
Flick seldom says a word to Mae, just nods
Beyond her face toward bright applauding tiers
Of Necco Wafers, Nibs, and Juju Beads.   30

(1958)

Questions for Discussion and Writing

1. What is the story of Flick Webb's life? How do both his first and last names
   fit his life story?
2. Who is the narrator (the "I") of the poem? How old is he? Where does
   he live?
3. Though the poem has no regular rhyme, it follows patterns. Explain the logic
   of the stanza breaks and line breaks.
4. Do you think Flick would agree with this assessment of his life?

Marge Piercy   1936–

Marge Piercy was born in Detroit, Michigan. Concerned with depicting and dignifying women's experiences, Piercy has been accused of politicizing her work. In the introduction to her book of poetry *Circles on the Water* (1982), she explains how her writing can be "of use" to women: "To find ourselves spoken for in art gives dignity to our pain, our anger, our lust, our losses." Among her popular novels are *Small Changes* (1973), *Woman on the Edge of Time* (1976), and *Gone to Soldiers* (1987).

Barbie Doll

This girlchild was born as usual
and presented dolls that did pee-pee
and miniature GE stoves and irons
and wee lipsticks the color of cherry candy.
Then in the magic of puberty, a classmate said: 5
You have a great big nose and fat legs.

She was healthy, tested intelligent,
possessed strong arms and back,
abundant sexual drive and manual dexterity.
She went to and fro apologizing.   10
Everyone saw a fat nose on thick legs.

She was advised to play coy,
exhorted to come on hearty,
exercise, diet, smile and wheedle.
Her good nature wore out   15
like a fan belt.
So she cut off her nose and her legs
and offered them up.

In the casket displayed on satin she lay
with the undertaker's cosmetics painted on,   20
a turned-up putty nose,
dressed in a pink and white nightie.
Doesn's she look pretty? everyone said.
Consummation at last.
To every woman a happy ending.   25

(1973)

Questions for Discussion and Writing

1. What led to the suicide in the poem? In what way is it a happy ending?
2. Why is the poem titled "Barbie Doll"? What qualities do you associate with Barbie?

3. This poem was written in 1973. Do you think its view of female socialization is still relevant today? Write a paper arguing your answer to this question.

Lucille Clifton   1936–2010

Lucille Clifton grew up in Buffalo, New York, the child of parents without much formal schooling who instilled in their children the value of education and the love of reading. She began writing as a child but later remarked that "the only writers I ever saw in the New York public schools were portraits on the wall of old dead white men with beards from New England." But she developed the "respect and wonder and love for language" that enabled her to become a poet. "The only reason to write poetry," she declares, "is to assert the importance of being human."

homage to my hips

these hips are big hips.
they need space to
move around in.
they don't fit into little
petty places. these hips   5
are free hips.
they don't like to be held back.
these hips have never been enslaved.
they go where they want to go.
they do what they want to do.   10
these hips are mighty hips.
these hips are magic hips.
i have known them
to put a spell on a man and
spin him like a top!   15

(1987)

Questions for Discussion and Writing

1. What is the unexpected element in "homage to my hips"? Point out examples.
2. Any big-hipped woman could appreciate the speaker's sentiments on some level. Do you think that knowing that Lucille Clifton is African American adds anything to your appreciation of the poem? What details stand out when you think of the author's race? Do you think this attention is fair or unfair? Argue for your answer.

3. Why are the last three lines especially impressive concerning the power of the speaker's hips?
4. Identify one of your physical or emotional qualities that others might see as a negative but that you believe makes you a stronger or better person. Write an essay arguing your point.

Seamus Heaney 1939–

Cited as Ireland's best poet since Yeats, Seamus Heaney was born on a farm in Northern Ireland, and his early poetry communicates a strong sense of the physical environment of his youth. His later work, often dense and poignant, concerns the cultural implications of words and their historical contexts. Heaney now divides his time between Dublin and the United States, where he teaches at Harvard. His most recent books of poetry are *The Haw Lantern* (1987) and *Electric Light* (2001). He received the Nobel Prize for Literature in 1995.

Digging

Between my finger and my thumb
The squat pen rests; snug as a gun.

Under my window, a clean rasping sound
When the spade sinks into gravelly ground:
My father, digging. I look down   5

Till his straining rump among the flowerbeds
Bends low, comes up twenty years away
Stooping in rhythm through potato drills
Where he was digging.

The coarse boot nestled on the lug, the shaft   10
Against the inside knee was levered firmly.
He rooted out tall tops, buried the bright edge deep
To scatter new potatoes that we picked
Loving their cool hardness in our hands.

By God, the old man could handle a spade.   15
Just like his old man.

My grandfather cut more turf° in a day
Than any other man on Toner's bog.
Once I carried him milk in a bottle
Corked sloppily with paper. He straightened up   20
To drink it, then fell to right away
Nicking and slicing neatly, heaving sods

---

17 turf Peat, used for fuel in Ireland.

Over his shoulder, going down and down
For the good turf. Digging.

The cold smell of potato mould, the squelch and slap   25
Of soggy peat, the curt cuts of an edge
Through living roots awaken in my head.
But I've no spade to follow men like them.

Between my finger and my thumb
The squat pen rests.   30
I'll dig with it.

(1966)

Questions for Discussion and Writing

1. What does the speaker of the poem admire about his forefathers? Make a list
   of the qualities he seems to revere.
2. Do you have any feelings about carrying on the work of your parents or
   grandparents? Do you think most people do?
3. The speaker has chosen a profession very different from potato farming.
   He implies, though, in the last line, that it is similar. How is it the same?

Billy Collins   1941–

Born in New York City, William James (Billy) Collins has lived there ever since. His father
is an electrician, his mother a nurse. Selected as Poet Laureate of the United States in 2000,
he served two terms. He has managed to combine critical approval with unprecedented
popular success. His last three collections of poems have broken sales records for poetry.
"Usually," he says, "I try to create a hospitable tone at the beginning of a poem. Stepping
from the title to the first lines is like stepping into a canoe. A lot of things can go wrong."

Introduction to Poetry

I ask them to take a poem
and hold it up to the light
like a color slide

or press an ear against its hive.

I say drop a mouse into a poem   5
and watch him probe his way out,

or walk inside the poem's room
and feel the walls for a light switch.

I want them to water-ski
across the surface of a poem   10
waving at the author's name on the shore.

But all they want to do
is tie the poem to a chair with a rope
and torture a confession out of it.

They begin beating it with a hose   15
to find out what it really means.
                                                 (1988)

Questions for Discussion and Writing

1. Who is "I" in the poem? Who are "they"? Does the title help you identify
   who these people represent? In what two different ways could you take
   the title?
2. The "I" presents five metaphors as possible approaches to understanding a
   poem. Can you explain what type of approach each metaphor suggests? Even
   if not, can you identify which approach *you* usually take when studying a poem?
   How would you describe your usual process if you don't understand a poem
   right away?
3. While the "I" uses five metaphors, the "they" present only one metaphor.
   What is it? Why is the last metaphor humorous? Can you explain more than
   one reason why this metaphor for understanding a poem represents a bad
   approach?

Sharon Olds   1942–

Sharon Olds, born in San Francisco and educated at Stanford University, is the author of
several books of poetry. Because of her intense focus on family and sexual relationships,
she is often compared to confessional poets Sylvia Plath and Anne Sexton. Olds teaches
creative writing at New York University and at the Goldwater Hospital, a facility for the
physically disabled. A review of her book *The Unswept Room* (2002) calls her poetry "fiery,
penetrating, and unnerving."

Sex Without Love

How do they do it, the ones who make love
without love? Beautiful as dancers,
gliding over each other like ice-skaters
over the ice, fingers hooked
inside each other's bodies, faces   5
red as steak, wine, wet as the
children at birth whose mothers are going to
give them away. How do they come to the

come to the   come to the   God   come to the
still waters, and not love   10
the one who came there with them, light
rising slowly as steam off their joined
skin? These are the true religious,
the purists, the pros, the ones who will not
accept a false Messiah, love the   15
priest instead of the God. They do not
mistake the lover for their own pleasure,
they are like great runners: they know they are alone
with the road surface, the cold, the wind,
the fit of their shoes, their over-all cardio-   20
vascular health—just factors, like the partner
in the bed, and not the truth, which is the
single body alone in the universe
against its own best time.

                                                        (1984)

Questions for Discussion and Writing

1. What other kinds of people are those who have sex without love compared
   with? Would you call these comparisons positive, negative, or mixed?
2. What do you think is the speaker's attitude toward people who have sex without love? What in the poem contributes to your opinion?
3. What ideas about love and sex are challenged in this poem?

Susan Ludvigson   1942–

Writing poetry in both open and closed forms, Susan Ludvigson is renowned for giving
voice to an astonishing range of characters in her works: rural women in Wisconsin with
dark secrets, little girls playing house, the mistress of sculptor Auguste Robin, a young man
attempting suicide in the Paris Metro, a Japanese film crew building a sand castle. When
Ludvigson was a child, her father owned two restaurants in a small town in Wisconsin, and
images from that period may influence the poem here.

Inventing My Parents

After Edward Hopper's *Nighthawks* (1942)

They sit in the bright cafe
discussing Hemingway, and how
this war will change them.
Sinclair Lewis' name comes up,
and Kay Boyle's, and then Fitzgerald's.   5

They disagree about the American Dream.
My mother, her bare arms
silver under fluorescent lights,
says she imagines it a hawk
flying over, its shadow sweeping   10
every town. Their coffee's getting cold
but they hardly notice. My mother's face
is lit by ideas. My father's gestures
are a Frenchman's. When he concedes
a point, he shrugs, an elaborate lift   15
of the shoulders, his hands and smile
declaring an open mind.

I am five months old, at home with a sitter
this August night, when the air outside
is warm as a bath. They decide,   20
though the car is parked nearby,
to walk the few blocks home, savoring
the fragrant night, their being alone together.
As they go out the door, he's reciting
Donne's "Canonization": "For God's sake   25
hold your tongue, and let me love,"
and she's laughing, light
as summer rain when it begins.

                                                                (1992)

Questions for Discussion and Writing

1. Look up an image if the painting *Nighthawks* by Edward Hopper. What
   tone does Ludvigson's envisioning of the painting create? Does this tone
   agree with the impression you get from the scene?
2. What do the details of the couple's conversation reveal about the kind of people the parents are?
3. What adjectives would you choose to describe the mother? Which might you
   choose to describe the father? Explain the reasoning behind your choices.
4. Does Ludvigson's poem change the way you view Edward Hopper's
   Nighthawks? Or does the painting still seem to present the bleak café and
   alienated patrons seen by many viewers? Consider the title Hopper chose.

Gina Valdés   1943–

Gina Valdés was born in Los Angeles, spent her childhood in Mexico, and returned to
Los Angeles during adolescence. She attended the University of California, San Diego,
and still lives in San Diego today. Her stories and poetry often focus on the plight of
undocumented workers, Chicano alienation in the United States and the status of
Chicanas. Her collection *Puentes y fronteras* [*Bridges and Frontiers*] (1982) takes the form

of *coplas*, four-line stanzas from traditional Mexican folk poetry, with Valdés substituting a female for the conventional male narrator. In *Comiendo lumbre: Eating Fire* (1986), she experiments with alternating between Spanish and English in each poem.

My Mother Sews Blouses

My mother sews blouses
for a dollar a piece.
They must be working on
black cloth again, I see
her fingers sliding on   5
her eyelids.

Six months ago she went
to the old oculist, the
one who "knows all about
eyes," who turned her   10
eyelids inside out and
scraped them with a tiny
knife to get the black
lint out.

Her eyes were bright and   15
clear for a few months.
She's blinking now,
talking about night
school.

(1986)

Women working in an apparel-industry sweatshop.

Questions for Discussion and Writing

1. Why do you think the mother is so poorly paid for her sewing?
2. Consider possible symbolism in the poem. What do we usually associate with the inability to see? What could the black lint symbolize?
3. Why is the woman "thinking about night school"? What effect will her current job have on this goal? Does the poem suggest that she will succeed or fail? Explain.

Edward Hirsch   1950–

Edward Hirsch was born in Chicago. When he was eight years old, he "wandered down to the basement of our house to pick through some of my grandfather's forgotten books" and read a verse (by Emily Bronte) that captivated him. It was the beginning of a lifelong love affair with poetry, which he explored at Grinnell College and the University of Pennsylvania, where he received a Ph.D. in folklore. His book *How to Read a Poem and Fall in Love with Poetry* was a surprise bestseller in 1999 and remains in print today.

Execution

The last time I saw my high school football coach
He had cancer stenciled into his face
Like pencil marks from the sun, like intricate
Drawings on the chalkboard, small x's and o's
That he copied down in a neat numerical hand   5
Before practice in the morning. By day's end
The board was a spiderweb of options and counters,
Blasts and sweeps, a constellation of players
Shining under his favorite word, Execution,
Underlined in the upper right-hand corner of things.   10
He believed in football like a new religion
And had perfect unquestioning faith in the fundamentals
Of blocking and tackling, the idea of warfare
Without suffering or death, the concept of teammates
Moving in harmony like the planets—and yet   15
Our awkward adolescent bodies were always canceling
The flawless beauty of Saturday afternoons in September,
Falling away from the particular grace of autumn,
The clear weather, the ideal game he imagined.
And so he drove us through punishing drills   20
On weekday afternoons, and doubled our practice time,
And challenged us to hammer him with forearms,
And devised elaborate, last-second plays—a flea-

Flicker, a triple reverse—to save us from defeat.
Almost always they worked. He despised losing   25
And loved winning more than his own body, maybe even
More than himself. But the last time I saw him
He looked wobbly and stunned by illness,
And I remembered the game in my senior year
When we met a downstate team who loved hitting   30
More than we did, who battered us all afternoon
With a vengeance, who destroyed us with timing
And power, with deadly, impersonal authority,
Machine-like fury, perfect execution.

(1989)

Questions for Discussion and Writing

1. How does the coach feel about football? What comparisons does the speaker use to describe the coach's feelings?
2. What is the significance of the game with the downstate team (lines 29–34)? Why did the speaker remember that game the last time he saw the coach?
3. What do you think of the lines "He despised losing / And loved winning more than his own body"? What is the speaker implying?
4. What is the speaker's attitude toward his coach? Do you think he likes or admires him? Write a paper arguing your position on this issue.
5. Explain the ironies that you find in this poem. Start with the title.

Rita Dove   1952–

Rita Dove was born in Akron, Ohio, and educated at Miami University, the University of Tübingen, and the University of Iowa. She has earned praise for plainspoken poems that reflect her life and the experiences of African-Americans in general. In 1987 she won the Pulitzer Prize for *Thomas and Beulah*, a series of poems about the lives of the title characters, from their southern origins through their lives in Akron in the 1960s. In 1992 Dove was named Poet Laureate of the United States, the youngest person ever to be appointed to this post.

Daystar

She wanted a little room for thinking:
but she saw diapers steaming on the line,
a doll slumped behind the door.
So she lugged a chair behind the garage
to sit out the children's naps.   5

Sometimes there were things to watch—
the pinched armor of a vanished cricket,

a floating maple leaf. Other days
she stared until she was assured
when she closed her eyes   10
she'd see only her own vivid blood.

She had an hour, at best, before Liza appeared
pouting from the top of the stairs.
And just *what* was mother doing
out back with the field mice? Why,   15

building a palace. Later
that night when Thomas rolled over and
lurched into her, she would open her eyes
and think of the place that was hers
for an hour—where   20
she was nothing,
pure nothing, in the middle of the day.

                                                                    (1986)

Questions for Discussion and Writing

1. What is a "daystar" and how does it apply to this poem?
2. Did you identify with the woman in the poem? When, if ever, do you want solitude? Why? Why does the persona want it?
3. Who are Liza and Thomas? Are they important characters? Why does the writer refrain from identifying them? Why is the woman not identified by name, as they are?
4. What is happening in the last stanza? Why would the woman want to be "pure nothing" while having sex?

Alberto Ríos   1952–

The son of a Guatemalan father and an English mother, Alberto Ríos grew up on the American side of the city of Nogales, Arizona, on the Mexican border. Having earned an M.F.A. in creative writing at the University of Arizona, he is the author of nine books of poems, three short-story collections, and a memoir. He won the Walt Whitman Award for his poetry, which has been adapted to dance and both classical and popular music. Ríos was also featured in the documentary *Birthwrite: Growing Up Hispanic* (1989). Since 1994, he has been Regents' Professor of English at Arizona State University.

In Second Grade Miss Lee I Promised Never to Forget You and I Never Did

In a letting-go moment
Miss Lee the Teacher
Who was not married
And who the next year was not at school,
Said to us, her second grade,   5
French lovers in the morning
Keep an apple next to the bed,
Each taking a bite
On first waking, to take away
The blackish breath of the night,   10
You know the kind.
A bite and then kissing,
And kissing like that was better.

I saw her once more
When she came to sell encyclopedias.   15
I was always her favorite—
The erasers, and the way she looked at me.
I promised, but not to her face,
Never to forget
The story of the apples.   20
Miss Lee all blond hair and thin,
Like *a real movie star*
If she would have just combed herself more.
Miss Lee, I promised,
I would keep apples   25
For you.

                              (2002)

Questions for Discussion and Writing

1. Put together a profile of Miss Lee from the details you know about her. Why do you think she was not at school the year after the time in the poem?

2. How old are second grade students? Why did the narrator remember forever the apple story Miss Lee told? Do you remember any single classroom incident from your grade school years? Why? Generally, what kinds of incidents stand out in a child's mind?

3. How does Ríos sustain the child's point of view in the poem? What would be different from an adult's point of view? For example, what would the point of view of the child's parents include?

Jimmy Santiago Baca   1952–

Jimmy Santiago Baca endured a family life shattered by matricide, a childhood in a state orphanage, and years in a state prison for supposed drug crimes. Baca managed to teach himself to read and write between state-ordered electroshock sessions to curb his combative nature. His poetry, especially that about prison life, has won him critical acclaim.

There Are Black

There are black guards slamming cell gates
on black men,
          And brown guards saying hello to brown men
with numbers on their backs,
          And white guards laughing with white cons,
          and red guards, few, say nothing
to red inmates as they walk by to chow and cells.   5

          There you have it, the little antpile...
convicts marching in straight lines, guards flying
on badged wings, permits to sting, to glut themselves
at the cost of secluding themselves from their people...
          Turning off their minds like watertaps   10
wrapped in gunnysacks that insulate the pipes
carrying the pale weak water to their hearts.

          It gets bad when you see these same guards
carrying buckets of blood out of cells,
see them puking at the smell, the people,   15
their own people slashing their wrists,
hanging themselves with belts from light outlets;
it gets bad to see them clean up the mess,
carry the blue cold body out under sheets,
and then retake their places in guard cages,
watching their people maul and mangle themselves,   20

          And over this blood-rutted land,
the sun shines, the guards talk of horses and guns,
go to the store and buy new boots,
and the longer they work here the more powerful they become,
taking on the presence of some ancient mummy,   25
down in the dungeons of prison, a mummy
that will not listen, but has a strange power
in this dark world, to be so utterly disgusting in ignorance,
and yet so proudly command so many men....

          And the convicts themselves, at the mummy's   30
feet, blood-splattered leather, at this one's feet,
they become cobras sucking life out of their brothers,

they fight for rings and money and drugs,
in this pit of pain their teeth bare fangs,
to fight for what morsels they can....   35

      And the other convicts, guilty
of nothing but their born color, guilty of being innocent,
they slowly turn to dust in the nightly winds here,
flying in the wind back to their farms and cities.
From the gash in their hearts, sand flies up spraying   40
over houses and through trees,

      look at the sand blow over this deserted place,
you are looking at them.

           (1979)

Questions for Discussion and Writing

1. What is it about the prison guards that horrifies the speaker in "There Are Black"?
2. The speaker understands what motivates the guards to keep their jobs. What are their motivations?
3. What are the two types of convicts described in stanzas five and six?
4. Do you think that this subject matter is appropriate for poetry? Why or why not?

Judith Ortiz Cofer   *1952–*

Judith Ortiz Cofer was born in Puerto Rico; her family emigrated to the United States when she was six. This mixed heritage animates her writing, which often describes the experience of balancing two cultures in one life. Cofer wrote poetry as a graduate student and began focusing on prose in the late 1980s, publishing the novel *The Line of the Sun*, which was nominated for a 1989 Pulitzer Prize. She has also written widely published essays and a volume of stories for young adults.

Latin Women Pray

Latin women pray
In incense sweet churches
They pray in Spanish to an Anglo God
With a Jewish heritage.
And this Great White Father   5
Imperturbable in his marble pedestal
Looks down upon his brown daughters
Votive candles shining like lust
In his all seeing eyes
Unmoved by their persistent prayers.   10

Yet year after year
Before his image they kneel
Margarita Josefina Maria and Isabel
All fervently hoping
That if not omnipotent
At least he be bilingual   15

(1987)

Questions for Discussion and Writing

1. To what religion do the women belong? How can you tell?
2. List words that describe the God worshipped in the poem and words that describe the women. How are the two lists opposites? Do they contain any similarities? What other views of God may be compared with this one?
3. What are the women probably praying for "year after year"? Why do they never get it? Why do they persist?
4. Of all the ways possible to describe the reflection of votive candles in a statue's eyes, the writer chose the image "shining like lust." What does this image contribute to our understanding of the God in the poem?

Dorianne Laux   1952–

Dorianne Laux worked at lowly service jobs from the age of eighteen until thirty, raising a daughter as a single mother and taking writing classes and workshops at the local college when she could. Obtaining scholarships and grants, she was able to return to school full-time and graduated with honors from Mills College in 1988. In a 2006 interview with *Southern Hum*, Laux asserted, "It seems to me that all poems are odes in one way or another. Even poems of desperation or loss are odes to human emotion and endurance, to the spirit that rages quietly on."

What I Wouldn't Do

The only job I didn't like, quit
after the first shift, was selling
subscriptions to *TV Guide* over the phone.
Before that it was fast food, all
the onion rings I could eat, handing   5
sacks of deep fried burritos through
the sliding window, the hungry hands
grabbing back. And at the laundromat,
plucking bright coins from a palm
or pressing them into one, kids   10

screaming from the bathroom and twenty
dryers on high. Cleaning houses was fine,
polishing the knick-knacks of the rich.
I liked holding the hand-blown glass bell
from Czechoslovakia up to the light,   15
the jewelled clapper swinging lazily
from side to side, its foreign,
A-minor ping. I drifted, an itinerant,
from job to job, the sanatorium
where I pureed peas and carrots   20
and stringy beets, scooped them,
like pudding, onto flesh-colored
plastic plates, or the gas station
where I dipped the ten-foot measuring stick
into the hole in the blacktop,   25
pulled it up hand over hand
into the twilight, dripping
its liquid gold, pink-tinged.
I liked the donut shop best, 3 AM,
alone in the kitchen, surrounded   30
by sugar and squat mounds of dough,
the flashing neon sign strung from wire
behind the window, gilding my white uniform
yellow, then blue, then drop-dead red.
It wasn't that I hated calling them, hour   35
after hour, stuck in a booth with a list
of strangers' names, dialing their numbers
with the eraser end of a pencil and them
saying hello. It was that moment
of expectation, before I answered back,   40
the sound of their held breath,
their disappointment when they realized
I wasn't who they thought I was,
the familiar voice, or the voice they loved
and had been waiting all day to hear.   45

(1994)

Questions for Discussion and Writing

1. List the jobs the narrator describes before her telemarketing job. What do
they have in common? What is similar in the way she describes each one?

2. What can you infer about the narrator by the way she describes the jobs?
Why do you think she liked them all right?

3. How does the *TV Guide* job contrast with the others in the poem? Can you
explain why she quit after the first shift? Does the nature of *TV Guide* play a
role in the poem's meaning?

4. Write a descriptive paragraph or poem about a job you enjoyed or hated.

Martín Espada   1957–

Martin Espada came from a family of Puerto Rican immigrants, and his many volumes of poetry reflect these origins. His writing is openly political, expressing anger at injustice and racism. The poems often tell stories from the points of view of gutsy, vivid Latino characters, such as janitors, junkies, prisoners, or mental patients. Humor and empathy infuse his depictions of these characters' struggles. Espada's third book of poetry, *Rebellion Is the Circle of a Lover's Hands*, won the 1990 PEN/Revson Award and the Paterson Poetry Prize.

Bully

Boston, Massachusetts, 1987

In the school auditorium
the Theodore Roosevelt statue
is nostalgic
for the Spanish American War,
each fist lonely for a saber   5
or the reins of anguished horses,
or a podium to clatter with speeches
glorying in the malaria of conquest.

But now the Roosevelt school
is pronounced *Hernandez.*   10
Puerto Rico has invaded Roosevelt
with its army of Spanish-singing children
in the hallways,
brown children devouring
the stockpiles of the cafeteria,   15
children painting *Taíno* ancestors
that leap naked across murals.

Roosevelt is surrounded
by all the faces
he ever shoved in eugenic spite   20
and cursed as mongrels, skin of one race,
hair and cheekbones of another.

Once Marines tramped
from the newsreel of his imagination;
now children plot to spray graffiti   25
in parrot-brilliant colors
across the Victorian mustache
and monocle.
                          (1990)

Questions for Discussion and Writing

1. The poet depends on our knowing at least a few things about Teddy Roosevelt, the Spanish-American War, eugenics, and Taíno Puerto Rican ancestors. If you aren't familiar with any of this history, use an encyclopedia to fill in the gaps, and then explain how this information helps you to read the poem. Can you understand his main theme without these insights?

2. There are several surprising images in the poem, created by unexpected word combinations—for example, the linking of "lonely" and "fist," as well as "statue" and "nostalgic." Find other examples and discuss the tone created by these images.

3. There are four stanzas in the poem. Summarize the main point of each, and explain the reasons for the order in which Espada places his ideas.

4. Who is the "bully" in the poem? Why did Espada select this title? Why did he include "Boston, Massachusetts, 1987"? Write an essay in which you argue your position on these questions.

PAIRED POEMS FOR COMPARISON

Poets are often inspired by the work of other poets. This section contains three pairs of poems that respond to each other in some way. In the first pair, the speaker in the second poem replies directly to the enticements offered by the speaker in the first poem. In the second pair, the response is a *parody*—an imitation that copies some features of the first poem, but changes the subject matter and diction for humorous effect. And in the last pair the two poets present differing perspectives on the same topic. As you read these poems, think about what each poet has to say and how the second poem modifies or complements the intent and meaning of the first one.

Christopher Marlowe   *1564–1593*

The son of a Canterbury shoemaker, Christopher Marlowe was one of the leading poets and dramatists of his day. His major plays, which include *Tamburlaine the Great* (1587), *Dr. Faustus* (1588), and *Edward II* (1592), concern heroic figures who are brought down by their own extravagant passions. He was one of the first to use blank verse in his plays, a practice that Shakespeare perfected. Marlowe's lyric poetry is graceful and warmly sensuous. He was killed in a quarrel over a tavern bill.

The Passionate Shepherd to His Love

Come live with me and be my love,
And we will all the pleasures prove,
That valleys, groves, hills and fields,
Woods, or steepy mountain yields.

And we will sit upon the rocks,   5
And see the shepherds feed their flocks,
By shallow rivers to whose falls
Melodious birds sing madrigals.

And I will make thee beds of roses
With a thousand fragrant posies,   10
A cap of flowers, and a kirtle
Embroidered all with leaves of myrtle;

A gown made of the finest wool
Which from our pretty lambs we pull;

Fair lined slippers for the cold,   15
With buckles of the purest gold;

A belt of straw and ivy buds,
With coral clasps and amber studs:
And if these pleasures may thee move,
Come live with me and be my love.   20

The shepherds' swains shall dance and sing
For thy delight each May morning:
If these delights thy mind may move,
Then live with me and be my love.

(1600)

Questions for Discussion and Writing

1. How does the young lover vary his appeals? Is there an implication that the object of his invitation is rejecting him?
2. Does the speaker go too far ("buckles of the purest gold") and lose credibility? Or is credibility even an issue in this kind of poem?
3. By the end of the poem, how convincing do you find the Shepherd's appeal? Just how "passionate" is he?

Sir Walter Raleigh   ca. 1552–1618

Sir Walter Raleigh was an English soldier, explorer, courtier, and man of letters. A favorite of Queen Elizabeth I, he organized the colonizing expeditions to North America that ended tragically with the lost colony of Roanoke Island. Imprisoned for thirteen years in the Tower of London by James I, Raleigh was released to search for gold in South America. When he returned empty-handed, he was executed. A true court poet, he circulated his poems in manuscript; as a result, only a few have survived.

The Nymph's Reply to the Shepherd

If all the world and love were young,
And truth in every shepherd's tongue,
These pretty pleasures might me move,
To live with thee, and be thy love.

Time drives the flocks from field to fold,   5
When rivers rage, and rocks grow cold,
And Philomel becometh dumb,
The rest complains of cares to come.

The flowers do fade, and wanton fields,
To wayward winter reckoning yields: 10
A honey tongue, a heart of gall,
Is fancy's spring, but sorrow's fall.

Thy gowns, thy shoes, thy beds of roses,
Thy cap, thy kirtle, and thy posies,
Soon break, soon wither, soon forgotten: 15
In folly ripe, in reason rotten.

Thy belt of straw and ivy buds,
Thy coral clasps and amber studs,
All these in me no means can move,
To come to thee, and be thy love.   20

But could youth last, and love still breed,
Had joys no date, nor age no need,
Then these delights my mind might move
To live with thee and be thy love.
                                    (1600)

Questions for Discussion and Writing

1. How does the nymph counter the shepherd's pleasant pastoral images?
2. Note how the nymph mentions all of the images drawn from nature that were used in the Marlowe poem. But what does she do with them?
3. Which of the two lovers, the shepherd or the nymph, do you like better? Which approach to love do you find more attractive? Write a comparison essay in which you defend your choice.

Robert Browning *1812–1889*

Robert Browning was an English poet who experimented with diction and rhythm as well as with psychological portraits in verse. He secretly married Elizabeth Barrett, and they moved to Italy in 1846, partly to avoid her domineering father. Browning was a master of dramatic monologues, exemplified in "My Last Duchess" and "Porphyria's Lover." After the death of his wife, Browning returned to England where he wrote what some consider his masterwork, *The Ring and the Book* (1868–1869).

My Last Duchess

Ferrara

That's my last Duchess painted on the wall,
Looking as if she were alive; I call
That piece a wonder, now: Frà Pandolf's° hands
Worked busily a day, and there she stands.
Will't please you sit and look at her? I said 5
"Frà Pandolf" by design, for never read
Strangers like you that pictured countenance,
The depth and passion of its earnest glance,
But to myself they turned (since none puts by
The curtain I have drawn for you, but I) 10
And seemed as they would ask me, if they durst,
How such a glance came there; so, not the first
Are you to turn and ask thus. Sir, 'twas not
Her husband's presence only, called that spot
Of joy into the Duchess' cheek: perhaps 15
Frà Pandolf chanced to say "Her mantle laps
Over my Lady's wrist too much," or "Paint
Must never hope to reproduce the faint
Half-flush that dies along her throat": such stuff
Was courtesy, she thought, and cause enough 20
For calling up that spot of joy. She had
A heart—how shall I say?—too soon made glad,
Too easily impressed; she liked whate'er
She looked on, and her looks went everywhere.
Sir, 'twas all one! My favor at her breast, 25
The dropping of the daylight in the West,
The bough of cherries some officious fool
Broke in the orchard for her, the white mule
She rode with round the terrace—all and each
Would draw from her alike the approving speech, 30
Or blush, at least. She thanked men,—good; but thanked
Somehow—I know not how—as if she ranked
My gift of a nine-hundred-years-old name
With anybody's gift. Who'd stoop to blame
This sort of trifling? Even had you skill 35
In speech—(which I have not)—to make your will
Quite clear to such an one, and say, "Just this

---

3 Frà Pandolf's A fictitious artist.

Or that in you disgusts me; here you miss,
Or there exceed the mark"—and if she let
Herself be lessoned so, nor plainly set   40
Her wits to yours, forsooth, and made excuse,
—E'en then would be some stooping, and I choose
Never to stoop. Oh, Sir, she smiled, no doubt,
Whene'er I passed her; but who passed without
Much the same smile? This grew; I gave commands;   45
Then all smiles stopped together. There she stands
As if alive. Will't please you rise? We'll meet
The company below, then. I repeat,
The Count your Master's known munificence
Is ample warrant that no just pretence   50
Of mine for dowry will be disallowed;
Though his fair daughter's self, as I avowed
At starting, is my object. Nay, we'll go
Together down, Sir! Notice Neptune, though,
Taming a sea-horse, thought a rarity,   55
Which Claus of Innsbruck° cast in bronze for me.

                                                        (1842)

---

56 Claus of Innsbruck Another fictitious artist.

Questions for Discussion and Writing

1. Who is speaking to whom? What is the situation?
2. According to the Duke, what were the Duchess's faults? Do you trust the speaker's account of the Duchess and her "failings"?
3. Does the Duke's carefully controlled composure slip as he relates his story about the last duchess? Or is he intentionally letting the emissary know his (the Duke's) feelings about women and wives?
4. If you were the emissary for the Count whose daughter the Duke hopes to marry, what would you report to your master?

Gabriel Spera   1966–

Gabriel Spera is a technical writer and the director of the Aerospace Press in El Segundo, California. He was born in New York, grew up in New Jersey, and holds a B.A. from Cornell University and an M.F.A. from the University of North Carolina. His first collection of poems, *The Standing Wave*, received the 2004 PEN Center USA Literary Award. According to one critic, Spera's poetry "distinguishes itself with intelligence, wit, impeccable technique, and openness, and it has real substance to impart."

My Ex-Husband

That's my ex-husband pictured on the shelf,
Smiling as if in love. I took it myself
With his Leica, and stuck it in that frame
We got for our wedding. Kind of a shame
To waste it on him, but what could I do?   5
(Since I haven't got a photograph of you.)
I know what's on your mind—you want to know
Whatever could have made me let him go—
He seems like any woman's perfect catch,
What with his ruddy cheeks, the thin mustache,   10
Those close-set, baggy eyes, that tilted grin.
But snapshots don't show what's beneath the skin!
He had a certain charm, charisma, style,
That passionate, earnest glance he struck, meanwhile
Whispering the sweetest things, like "Your lips   15
Are like plump rubies, eyes like diamond chips,"
Could flush the throat of any woman, not
Just mine. He knew the most romantic spots
In town, where waiters, who all knew his face,
Reserved an intimately dim-lit place   20
Half-hidden in a corner nook. Such stuff
Was all too well rehearsed, I soon enough
Found out. He had an attitude—how should
I put it—smooth, self-satisfied, too good
For the rest of the world, too easily   25
Impressed with his officious self. And he
flirted—fine! but flirted somehow a bit
Too ardently, too blatantly, as if,
If someone ever noticed, no one cared
How slobbishly he carried on affairs.   30
Who'd lower herself to put up with shit
Like that? Even if you'd the patience—which
I have not—to go and see some counsellor
And say, "My life's a living hell," or
"Everything he does disgusts, the lout!"—   35
And even if you'd somehow worked things out,
Took a long trip together, made amends,
Let things get back to normal, even then
You'd still be on the short end of the stick;
And I choose never ever to get stuck.   40
Oh, no doubt, it always made my limbs go
Woozy when he kissed me, but what bimbo
In the steno pool went without the same
Such kisses? So, I made some calls, filed some claims,
All kisses stopped together. There he grins,   45
Almost lovable. Shall we go? I'm in
The mood for Chez Pierre's, perhaps, tonight,
Though anything you'd like would be all right

As well, of course, though I'd prefer not to go
To any place with checkered tables. No,   50
We'll take my car. By the way, have I shown
You yet these lovely champagne flutes, hand blown,
Imported from Murano, Italy,
Which Claus got in the settlement for me!

(1992)

Questions for Discussion and Writing

1. Look at this poem alongside the original, Browning's "My Last
   Duchess," and note the similarities. Make a list of parallels in
   the form and tone of the two poems. Then discuss parallels in
   content: what changes are made in the details of the situation?
2. What do the speakers of the poems have in common? What
   does the persona of "My Ex-Husband" do rather than have the
   spouse murdered?
3. Is there a difference in the ways you respond to the speakers? If
   so, how do you account for the difference?

Robert Hayden   1913–1980

Born Asa Bundy Sheffey in Detroit, Robert Hayden was renamed by his
foster parents. In the poetry of his first collection, *Heart-Shape in the Dust*
(1940), he used facts about African American history that he unearthed as
a researcher for the Federal Writers' Project (1936–40). Educated at
Wayne State and the University of Michigan, Hayden taught at Fisk
University and returned to teach at Michigan. He considered his writing
"a form of prayer—a prayer for illumination, perfection."

Those Winter Sundays

Sundays too my father got up early
and put his clothes on in the blueblack cold,
then with cracked hands that ached
from labor in the weekday weather made
banked fires blaze. No one ever thanked him.   5

I'd wake and hear the cold splintering, breaking.
When the rooms were warm, he'd call,
and slowly I would rise and dress,
fearing the chronic angers of that house,

Speaking indifferently to him,   10
who had driven out the cold
and polished my good shoes as well.
What did I know, what did I know
of love's austere and lonely offices°?

(1966)

---

14 offices Duties.

Questions for Discussion and Writing

1. The speaker is clearly looking back at a pattern of life experienced as a child. What does the speaker know now that he or she didn't know then?
2. What kind of home was the speaker's? How do you know?
3. What are the various expressions of love? Which ones are "austere and lonely"?
4. What is the religious meaning of the word "office"? How does that connotation fit the use of the word in this poem?

George Bilgere   1951–

George Bligere survived an unhappy childhood in Riverside, California. His father was a drunk, his parents divorced, then his mother died. Yet he came out of it as a basically contented individual. Dealing with the pain of his own divorce, he has said, enabled him to use more "open" language in his poetry. Billy Collins observes that the poems are "balanced between humor and seriousness, between the sadness of loss and the joy of being alive to experience it. Whenever a parade of Bilgere poems goes by, I'll be there waving my little flag."

Like Riding a Bicycle

I would like to write a poem
About how my father taught me
To ride a bicycle one soft twilight,
A poem in which he was tired
And I was scared, unable to disbelieve   5

In gravity and believe in him,
As the fireflies were coming out
And only enough light remained
For one more run, his big hand at the small
Of my back, pulling away like the gantry   10
At a missile launch, and this time, this time
I wobbled into flight, caught a balance
I would never lose, and pulled away
From him as he eased, laughing, to a stop,
A poem in which I said that even today   15
As I make some perilous adult launch,
Like pulling away from my wife
Into the fragile new balance of our life
Apart, I can still feel that steadying hand,
Still hear that strong voice telling me   20
To embrace the sweet fall forward
Into the future's blue
Equilibrium. But,

Of course, he was drunk that night,
Still wearing his white shirt   25
And tie from the office, the air around us
Sick with scotch, and the challenge
Was keeping his own balance
As he coaxed his bulk into a trot
Beside me in the hot night, sweat   30
Soaking his armpits, the eternal flame
Of his cigarette flaring as he gasped
And I fell, again and again, entangled
In my gleaming Schwinn, until
He swore and stomped off   35
Into the house to continue
Working with my mother
On their own divorce, their balance
Long gone and the hard ground already
Rising up to smite them   40
While I stayed outside in the dark,
Still falling, until at last I wobbled
Into the frail, upright delight
Of feeling sorry for myself, riding
Alone down the neighborhood's   45
Black street like the lonely western hero
I still catch myself in the act
Of performing.

And yet, having said all this,
I must also say that this summer evening   50
Is very beautiful, and I am older
Than my father ever was
As I coast the Pacific shoreline
On my old bike, the gears clicking

Like years, the wind   55
Touching me for the first time, it seems,
In a very long time,
With soft urgency all over.

(2002)

Questions for Discussion and Writing

1. What is a "gantry" (line 10)? Explain why "gantry" is a perfect word choice in the poem.
2. How would you describe the boy's relationship with his father? On what specific words and phrases in the poem do you base your interpretation?
3. Why does the poet place the stanza breaks where they are? Summarize the meaning of each of the three stanzas.
4. Write an essay comparing this poem with Hayden's "Those Winter Sundays." Focus on the speaker's attitude toward his father in each poem.

A PORTFOLIO OF WAR POETRY

War stirs powerful feelings and has inspired an abundance of powerful poetry. Admirable emotions—courage, honor, bravery—are aroused by the excitement and passion of war. But at the same time, negative emotions—grief, anger, misery—are stoked by the senseless slaughter of war. Perhaps this emotional duality helps somewhat to explain why the eloquence and power of antiwar poems have done so little to halt humans' willingness to engage in war, despite its destruction and its staggering toll.

Richard Lovelace   1618–1657

A wealthy, handsome Cavalier poet and a loyal supporter of King Charles I, Richard Lovelace was twice imprisoned by the Puritan Parliament during the English Civil War. He died in poverty in a London slum. Much of Lovelace's poetry is labored and lifeless, but he did write several charming, graceful lyrics, such as "To Althea from Prison," "To Amarantha, That She Would Dishevel Her Hair," and "To Lucasta, on Going to the Wars."

To Lucasta, on Going to the Wars

Tell me not, sweet, I am unkind,
　That from the nunnery
Of thy chaste breast and quiet mind
　To war and arms I fly.

True, a new mistress now I chase,　　　　　　　　　　　5
　The first foe in the field;
And with stronger faith embrace
　A sword, a horse, a shield.

Yet this inconstancy is such
　As thou shalt adore;　　　　　　　　　　　　　　　　10
I could not love thee, dear, so much,
　Loved I not honor more.

(1649)

Questions for Discussion and Writing

1. What seems to be the speaker's attitude toward war? How old do you imagine the speaker to be?
2. Who is the speaker's "new mistress"?
3. What values or virtues are contrasted in the poem?

Stephen Crane   1871–1900

Stephen Crane was born in Newark, New Jersey, the fourteenth child of a Methodist minister who died when Crane was nine. Leaving college early, he moved to New York City, where he observed firsthand the boozers and prostitutes who inhabited the slums. Crane's first novel, *Maggie: A Girl of the Streets* (1893), drew on these observations. At age twenty-four, and with no military experience, he wrote *The Red Badge of Courage* (1895), a Civil War novel that became an American classic and made Crane famous.

War Is Kind

Do not weep, maiden, for war is kind.
Because your lover threw wild hands toward the sky
And the affrighted steed ran on alone,
Do not weep.
War is kind.   5

    Hoarse, booming drums of the regiment,
    Little souls who thirst for fight,
    These men were born to drill and die.
    The unexplained glory flies above them,
    Great is the Battle-God, great, and his Kingdom—   10
    A field where a thousand corpses lie.

Do not weep, babe, for war is kind.
Because your father tumbled in the yellow trenches,
Raged at his breast, gulped and died,
Do not weep.   15
War is kind.

    Swift blazing flag of the regiment,
    Eagle with crest of red and gold,
    These men were born to drill and die.
    Point for them the virtue of slaughter,   20
    Make plain to them the excellence of killing
    And a field where a thousand corpses lie.

Mother whose heart hung humble as a button
On the bright splendid shroud of your son,
Do not weep.   25
War is kind.

(1899)

Questions for Discussion and Writing

1. Why do you think stanzas 2 and 4 are indented?

2. Why is the flag referred to as "the unexplained glory" (line 9)?
3. What is the tone of the poem? And the theme?

Wilfred Owen   1893–1918

Wilfred Owen began writing poetry at the University of London. After teaching English in France for a few years, he returned to England and joined the army. Owen was wounded in 1917 and killed in action a few days before the armistice was declared in 1918. Owen's poems, published only after his death, are some of the most powerful and vivid accounts of the horrors of war to emerge from World War I.

Dulce et Decorum Est

Bent double, like old beggars under sacks,
Knock-kneed, coughing like hags, we cursed through sludge,
Till on the haunting flares we turned our backs
And towards our distant rest began to trudge.
Men marched asleep. Many had lost their boots   5
But limped on, blood-shod. All went lame; all blind;
Drunk with fatigue; deaf even to the hoots
Of tired, outstripped Five-Nines° that dropped behind.

Gas! Gas! Quick, boys!—An ecstasy of fumbling,
Fitting the clumsy helmets just in time;   10

John Singer Sargent's painting *Gassed* (1918) depicts World War I soldiers blinded by mustard gas being led back to hospital tents and dressing stations. *Source:* Imperial War Museum Negative Number Q1460.

---

8 Five-Nines Poison gas shells.

But someone still was yelling out and stumbling
And flound'ring like a man in fire or lime...
Dim, through the misty panes and thick green light,
As under a green sea, I saw him drowning.
In all my dreams before my helpless sight,   15
He plunges at me, guttering, choking, drowning.

If in some smothering dreams you too could pace
Behind the wagon that we flung him in,
And watch the white eyes writhing in his face,
His hanging face, like a devil's sick of sin;   20
If you could hear, at every jolt, the blood
Come gargling from the froth-corrupted lungs,
Obscene as cancer, bitter as the cud
Of vile, incurable sores on innocent tongues,—
My friend, you would not tell with such high zest   25
To children ardent for some desperate glory,
The old Lie: Dulce et decorum est
Pro patria mori.°

                                                        (1920)

27–28 The old Lie The quotation is from the Latin poet Horace, meaning "It is sweet and fitting to die for one's country."

Questions for Discussion and Writing

1. What are "Five-Nines"? Why does the speaker describe them as "tired"?
2. To whom is this poem addressed (the "you" in the third stanza)? What is the tone of the phrase "My friend" (line 25)?
3. What is the "desperate glory" mentioned in line 26? Can you think of any examples of it from books or movies?
4. What is "the old Lie," and do people still tell it?

E. E. Cummings   *1894–1962*

See page 381 for a biographical note about this author.

---

next to of course god america i

"next to of course god america i
love you land of the pilgrims' and so forth oh
say can you see by the dawn's early my
country 'tis of centuries come and go

and are no more what of it we should worry   5
in every language even deafanddumb
thy sons acclaim your glorious name by gorry
by jingo by gee by gosh by gum
why talk of beauty what could be more beautiful
than these heroic happy dead   10
who rushed like lions to the roaring slaughter
they did not stop to think they died instead
then shall the voice of liberty be mute?"

He spoke. And drank rapidly a glass of water
                                        (1926)

Questions for Discussion and Writing

1. Why does the poem begin with quotation marks?
2. At what point in the poem did you figure out that it is a parody? What is
   being parodied?
3. Point out several patriotic clichés in the quoted lines. Why are they jumbled
   together? Which ones contradict each other?
4. What does the last line of the poem reveal to you?

Peg Lauber   1938–

Born and reared in Detroit, Michigan, Peg Lauber now spends summers in Wisconsin
and winters in New Orleans raising sandhill cranes. One critic says that in her collection,
New Orleans Suite, she "captures the river, the birds, the fish, the snakes, the barge traffic,
the strippers and prostitutes—all the sweetness and squalor, the festivity and fever, the
miracle and mayhem of the human spectacle."

Six National Guardsmen Blown Up Together

Today the six come home for good,
those who grew up together on the bayous,
like those boys in the Civil War
who enlisted together, died together,
sometimes leaving small towns   5
with no young men—
a whole generation gone. These six hunted,
fished, trapped together, but someone
tracked them, hunted them
a world away from their usual prey—   10
alligators, nutrias, crawfish, bass.

Right across the canal out front
is the Naval base's runway approach
where we'll hear or even see
the big cargo plane carrying   15
what is left of the men coming in,
rumbling and lumbering along, scaring
the brown pelican and his mate
flying low up the channel
and scattering seventeen members   20
of the Cajun Air Force,
those bigger white pelicans,
cruising, then banking away.

Only the gulls will remain
gliding around with mournful   25
screeches, appropriate requiem.
Then silence, all planes grounded
in respect for the relatives, the wives
who huddle on folding chairs, bent
weeping into their small children's hair,   30
the children frightened, weeping with them,
now understanding that their father
in that flag-draped box will not,
like a Jack, pop out
if they touch a button—   35
that nothing, nothing
will ever be the same.

                                              (2006)

Questions for Discussion and Writing

1. Why did the poet select the title "Six National Guardsmen Blown Up Together"? How does it shape your expectations for the poem?
2. What is the setting for this poem? How many different kinds of local animals are mentioned? How does their presence affect your feelings about the people and events in the poem?
3. What do you think of the Jack-in-the-Box simile in the final lines? How effectively does it capture the events and feelings of the moment being described?

Yusef Komunyakaa 1947–

Born James Willie Brown Jr., Yusef Komunyakaa was born and grew up in Bogalusa, Louisiana, just as the civil rights movement was gathering momentum. He later reclaimed the name *Komunyakaa* from his great-grandparents, who had been stowaways in a ship from Trinidad. He served in the U.S. Army in Vietnam from 1965 to 1967, and his war poems rank with the best on the subject. Komunyakaa has said, "Poetry is a kind of distilled insinuation. It's a way of expanding and talking around an idea or question.

Sometimes more actually gets said through such a technique than a full-frontal assault."
His collection *Neon Vernacular* won the Pulitzer Prize for poetry in 1994.

Facing It

My black face fades,
hiding inside the black granite.
I said I wouldn't,
Dammit: No tears.
I'm stone. I'm flesh.   5
My clouded reflection eyes me
like a bird of prey, the profile of night
slanted against morning. I turn
this way—the stone lets me go.

The Vietnam Veterans Memorial in Washington, D. C., contains 58,325
names of the killed and missing from the Vietnam war. The wall's mirror-
like surface (polished black granite) reflects the images of surrounding
trees, lawns, monuments, and visitors. (Alan Schein/Corbis/Stock
Market.)

I turn that way—I'm inside   10
the Vietnam Veterans Memorial
again, depending on the light
to make a difference.
I go down the 58,002 names,
half-expecting to find   15
my own in letters like smoke.
I touch the name Andrew Johnson;
I see the booby trap's white flash.
Names shimmer on a woman's blouse
but when she walks away   20
the names stay on the wall.
Brushstrokes flash, a red bird's
wings cutting across my stare.
The sky. A plane in the sky.
A white vet's image floats   25
closer to me, then his pale eyes
look through mine. I'm a window.
He's lost his right arm
inside the stone. In the black mirror
a woman's trying to erase names: 30
No, she's brushing a boy's hair.

                       (1988)

Questions for Discussion and Writing

1. Explain the title of the poem. What is "It"?
2. Why is the speaker "half-expecting to find my own [name] in letters like smoke" (lines 15–16)?
3. From line 19 on, the speaker describes images he sees reflected in the Wall. Can you explain the choice of these particular images?
4. What is the significance of the error in perception that the speaker makes at the end of the poem? Why are the woman and boy present? How is their activity symbolic?

Dwight Okita 1958–

Dwight Okita, born in Chicago and still a resident there, describes himself as a gay Japanese American Buddhist. His parents were sent as teenagers to a relocation camp at the onset of World War II, and his mother served as the model for the young girl in the following poem. Okita explains that at the time of the experience she thought "the term 'camp' always sounded like fun, like summer camp. So I wrote the poem in the form of a kind of thank-you letter, which I imagined she might've written to the American government."

In Response to Executive Order 9066
All Americans of Japanese Descent Must
Report to Relocation Centers

Dear Sirs:
Of course I'll come. I've packed my galoshes
and three packets of tomato seeds. Denise calls them
love apples. My father says where we're going
they won't grow.   5

I am a fourteen-year-old girl with bad spelling
and a messy room. If it helps any, I will tell you
I have always felt funny using chopsticks
and my favorite food is hot dogs.
My best friend is a white girl named Denise—   10
we look at boys together. She sat in front of me
all through grade school because of our names:
O'Connor, Ozawa. I know the back of Denise's head very well.
I tell her she's going bald. She tells me I copy on tests.
We're best friends.   15

I saw Denise today in Geography class.
She was sitting on the other side of the room.
"You're trying to start a war," she said, "giving secrets away

May 1942, Hayward, California—A Japanese American family, tagged and waiting for the bus that will take them to an internment camp.

to the Enemy. Why can't you keep your big mouth shut?"
I didn't know what to say.   20
I gave her a packet of tomato seeds
and asked her to plant them for me, told her
when the first tomato ripened
she'd miss me.

(1983)

Questions for Discussion and Writing

1. Log on to "YouTube Executive Order 9066," and watch a movie about the Japanese internment in 1942. Why is it ironic that the speaker in the poem is packing her galoshes?
2. Why does the first-person persona of a fourteen-year-old girl provide an effective voice for the poem?
3. Why does she mention that she has "always felt funny using chopsticks" (line 8) and that her favorite food is hot dogs?
4. What has happened to cause her "best friend" Denise to shun her? Why does the speaker not "know what to say" (line 20)? Do you think the tomato seeds she gives Denise are in any way symbolic?

Making Connections

1. Compare the speaker's attitude toward war in "To Lucasta, on Going to the Wars" with the attitudes of the speakers in at least three other poems in this portfolio.
2. Write a paper discussing the ways in which the memorial in Washington to the Vietnam War dead differs from the usual monuments honoring dead soldiers. Consider why some patriotic groups at first were offended by the monument.
3. Discuss the meaning of the phrases "desperate glory" (from "Dulce et Decorum Est"), "unexplained glory" (from "War Is Kind"), and "your glorious name" (from "next to of course god america i") to show how these phrases reinforce the themes of their poems.
4. Several poems directly or indirectly attack the causes of war. Make a list of as many of these causes as you can. Which ones seem valid to you? Which do you question?

PART IV

Writing About Drama

This section, focusing on drama and including brief discussions of its beginnings and more recent developments in contemporary theater, completes our literary and rhetorical instruction.

16

How Do I Read a Play?

A play is written to be performed. Although most drama begins with a written script, the author of a play counts on the collaboration of others—actors, directors, set designers, costumers, makeup artists, lighting and sound engineers—to translate the written words into a performance on stage or film or videotape. Unlike novelists and poets, playwrights do not necessarily expect their words to be read by the audience.

The performance goal of drama does not mean, however, that you cannot read and study a play as you would a story or a poem. Plays share many literary qualities with other types of creative writing: character, plot, structure, atmosphere, theme, symbolism, and point of view. But it is important to recognize the differences between reading a play and seeing one performed.

Listen to the Lines

The major difference between reading and watching a play is that, as a reader, you do not have the actors' voices and gestures to interpret the lines and establish the characters for you. Because playwrights rely almost entirely on speeches or conversations (called *dialogue*) to define character, develop plot, and convey theme, it will be your task as a reader to listen to the lines in your mind. Read the dialogue as you would expect to hear it spoken. For example, when you read Antigone's response to Creon,

> So for me, at least, to meet this doom of yours
> is precious little pain. But if I had allowed
> my own mother's son to rot, an unburied corpse—
> that would have been an agony!

do you hear the assurance and passion in her voice? Or when you read the speech that Troy Maxson directs to "Mr. Death," do you detect the mixture of defiance and anger and fear in his words?

I'm gonna tell you what I'm gonna do. I'm gonna take and build me a fence around this yard. See? I'm gonna build me a fence around what belongs to me. And then I want you to stay on the other side. See? You stay over there until you're ready for me. Then you come on. Bring your army. Bring your sickle. Bring your wrestling clothes. I ain't gonna fall down on my vigilance this time. You ain't gonna sneak up on me no more.

Of course, the tone of these lines is not as clear when they are taken out of context, but even these brief quotations illustrate the charged nature of language you should expect when you read a play.

You can actually read the lines out loud to yourself or enlist some fellow students to act out some scenes with you. These oral readings will force you to decide how to interpret the words. Most of the time, however, you will have to use your imagination to re-create the sound of the spoken medium. If you do get to see a performance of a play you are reading or to hear a recording of it, you will appreciate the extraordinary liveliness of dramatic literature when it is lifted from the page and provided with sound and action.

Reading a play does have some advantage over viewing a live performance. Unlike a theatergoer, a reader can stop and return to lines or speeches that seem especially complicated or meaningful. Close reading gives you the opportunity to examine and consider the playwright's exact words, which often fly by quickly, sometimes in altered form, in an actual performance.

Visualize the Scene

In addition to imagining the sound of the dialogue, you will want to picture in your mind what the stage looks like. In a traditional theater the audience sits out front while the actors perform on a raised stage separated from the viewers by a curtain and perhaps an orchestra. The arch from which the curtain hangs is called the *proscenium*; the space extending from the bottom of the curtain to the footlights is the *apron*. The stage directions (printed in italics) indicate where the playwright wants the actors to move. *Upstage* means toward the back; *downstage* means toward the apron. A traditional set, made of canvas-covered frames called *flats*, will look like a room—with one wall removed for the audience to see through. Sometimes the set will be constructed to resemble the battlements of a castle, an opening in a forest, or a lifeboat on the ocean. Occasionally the setting is only suggested: a character climbs a ladder to deliver lines supposedly from a balcony or from an upstairs room. In one modern play, the two protagonists are presented on a bare stage speaking throughout the production (with only their heads visible) from inside garbage cans.

Another kind of stage, called *theater in the round* or an *arena stage*, puts the audience in raised seats on all sides with the players performing in the round space in the middle. After the audience is seated, the lights are extinguished, and the actors enter through the same aisles used earlier by the audience. When the actors are in position, the lights come up, illuminating only the stage, and the play begins. At the end of a scene or an act, the lights go down again, signifying the fall of the curtain and allowing the actors to leave. Stagehands come on between acts or scenes, if needed, to rearrange the setting. Not all plays are suited to this intimate staging, of course, but the audience at an arena production gains an immediacy, a feeling almost of being involved in the action, that cannot be achieved in a traditional theater.

Envision the Action

Poet and playwright Ezra Pound pointed out that the "medium of drama is not words, but persons moving about on a stage using words." This observation underlines the importance of movement, gesture, and setting in the performance of a play. These nonverbal elements of the language of drama are sometimes described in the author's stage directions. Often, though, you will find the cues for gestures, movements, and facial expressions in the words themselves, just as the director and the actors do when they are preparing a script for production. For example, these lines of Othello, spoken when he has been roused from his bed by a fight among his men, suggest the physical performance that would accompany the words:

> Why, how now, ho! from whence ariseth this?
> Are we turn'd Turks, and to ourselves do that
> Which heaven hath forbid the Ottomites?
> For Christian shame, put by this barbarous brawl
> He that stirs next to carve for his own rage
> Holds his soul light; he dies upon his motion.
> Silence that dreadful bell.

Reading this speech with an actor's or director's imagination, you can see in your mind the character stride angrily into the fight scene, gesture threateningly at the men who are poised to continue the fight, and then point suddenly offstage in the direction of the clamoring alarm bell. Such a detailed reading will take time, but you will be rewarded by the fun and satisfaction of catching the full dramatic quality of the play.

In more recent years, playwrights like August Wilson have tried to keep artistic control over the interpretations of their works by including detailed stage directions in their scripts. The extensive production notes for Wilson's *Fences* sometimes read like descriptions from a novel or an essay.

Troy is fifty-three years old, a large man with thick, heavy hands; it is his largeness that he strives to fill out and make an accommodation with. Together with his blackness, his largeness informs his sensibilities and the choices he has made in his life.

With or without notes like this, your imagination will be working full time when you read a play. You will not be at the mercy of some designer's taste or the personal interpretation of a director or actor. You will be free to produce the play in the theater of your mind.

Drama on Film

Many plays are available on videotape or digital videodiscs. These include filmed versions of stage performances, such as the Laurence Olivier production of Shakespeare's *Othello*, and movies adapted from plays, such as the several screen versions of *A Doll's House*.

You can often gain insight and special pleasure from seeing a dramatic work on film. A video production provides you with an opportunity to compare your responses to the play as you read it with your responses as you watch the video. You will also be able to think about the decisions that the film director has made. Here are some points to consider when comparing a film to the written text of a play:

- What scenes or characters, if any, have been cut? What, if anything, has been added? Why do you think these changes were made? What is their effect?
- Are the characters portrayed as you imagined they would be? Has the film changed your perception of the characters or your understanding of the plot?
- Would you have cast the same actors in these roles? If not, whom would you have chosen? What difference do you think your choices would make?
- Does the film focus your attention on certain characters or actions through such techniques as close-ups or reaction shots? What are the results of these uses of the camera?
- How is the setting different from what you imagined as you read the play? Did the filmmaker take liberties with the setting suggested by the playwright? (For example, were indoor play scenes transferred outdoors in the film?)
- Does the play transfer effectively from the page to the screen? Do you think the play is better suited to the stage?
- Does the film version clarify the play for you? Does it enhance your appreciation of the play? Can you explain why or why not?
- Do you think the playwright would be pleased with the film version? Why or why not?

• Imagine that you are directing a film version of a play that you have read. What important decisions about character, setting, and pacing of the action would you have to make? Would you cut any scenes? Would you add any new scenes? What advice would you give to the performers about their roles?

Before writing about a play or a film, be sure to respond to the critical questions in Chart 16-1.

Chart 16-1   Critical Questions for Reading Plays

Before planning an analysis of any of the plays in this text, write out your answers to the following questions to be sure you understand the play and to help you generate material for your paper.

1. What is the central conflict in the play? How is it resolved?
2. Does the play contain any secondary conflicts (subplots)? How do they relate to the main conflict?
3. Does the play follow a traditional dramatic structure (see Chapter 17)? What is the climax? Is there a denouement?
4. Who is the main character or protagonist (see Chapter 17)? What sort of person is he or she? Does this protagonist have a fatal flaw? Is the protagonist a hero (see Chapter 18)?
5. Is the antagonist (the one who opposes the protagonist) a person, an environment, or a social force (see Chapter 17)? If a person, does the antagonist cause conflict intentionally?
6. Do the other characters provide exposition (background information)? Are they used as *foils* to oppose, contrast, criticize, and thus help develop the main characters?
7. What are the time and setting of the play? How important are these elements? Could the play be set just as effectively in another time or place?
8. Does the title provide any clues to an understanding of the play? If you had to give the play another title, what would it be?
9. What is the theme of the play? Can you state it in a single sentence?
10. Is the play a tragedy, a comedy, or a mixture (see Chapter 18)? Is this classification important?
11. Is the presentation realistic? Does the playwright use any special theatrical devices (such as lighting, music, costumes, distinctive or surreal settings)? If so, what effect do they have on your impression of the play?

17

Writing About Dramatic Structure

D rama is not as flexible as other forms of literature. A writer of fiction can take as much time as needed to inform the reader about character, setting, motivation, or theme. The dramatist must do everything quickly and clearly. Audiences will not sit through a tedious first act; neither can they stop the play, pick it up tomorrow, or go back to Act I to refresh their memories. Even with the technology of video recording, most plays, including film and television drama, are seen in a single, relatively brief sitting.

What Is Dramatic Structure?

More than two thousand years ago the Greek philosopher Aristotle pointed out that the most important element of drama is the *fable,* what we call the *story,* or *plot.* The fable, said Aristotle, has to have a beginning, a middle, and an end. As obvious as this observation seems, it emphasizes the dramatist's special need to engage an audience early and keep it engaged until the conclusion of the play.

Recognizing the drama's strict time limits, Aristotle set down a number of conditions for developing the fable, or plot, in a clear and interesting way. According to Aristotle, the heart of the dramatic story is the *agon,* or *argument,* and the conflict surrounding this argument creates tension and incites interest. The two sides of the conflict, the pros and cons of the argument, are represented on stage by the *protagonist* and the *antagonist.* The protagonist may be one person or many, and the antagonist may be a person, a group, a thing, or a force (supernatural or natural). We often call the protagonist of a play its *hero* or *heroine,* and sometimes the antagonist is also the *villain.*

The fundamental struggle between the protagonist and the antagonist is developed according to a set pattern that theater audiences have come to recognize and expect. This conventional structure can be varied, of course, but most dramatic literature contains the following components:

1. *Point of attack:* the starting point from which the dramatist leads the audience into the plot. A playwright can begin at the story's beginning and allow the audience to discover what is going on at the same time the characters do; or the writer can begin in the middle of things (*in medias res*), or even near the end, and gradually reveal the events that have already taken place.
2. *Exposition:* the revelation of facts, circumstances, and past events. The essential facts about the characters and the conflict can be established in a number of ways, from having minor characters reveal information through conversation to plunging the audience right into the action.
3. *Rising action:* the building of interest through complication of the conflict. In this stage, the protagonist and antagonist move steadily toward a confrontation.
4. *Climax:* the play's high point, the decisive showdown between protagonist and antagonist. The climax—the play's turning point—can be a single moment or a series of events, but once reached, it becomes a point of no return.
5. *Falling action:* the unraveling of the plot, where events fall into place and the conflict moves toward final resolution.
6. *Denouement:* the play's conclusion, the explanation or outcome of the action. The term *denouement* (literally an "untying") may be applied to both comedy and tragedy, but the Greeks used the word *catastrophe* for a tragic denouement, probably because it involved the death of the hero or heroine. Comedies, of course, end happily, often with a wedding.

Whatever it is called, the denouement marks the end of the play: the lovers kiss, the bodies are carried off the stage, and the audience goes home. Most dramatists employ this traditional pattern. Even when they mix in other devices, rearrange elements, and invent new ways to exhibit their materials, dramatists still establish a conflict, develop both sides of the argument, and reach a credible conclusion. After centuries of theater history, the basic structure of drama has changed very little.

Looking at Dramatic Structure

As you read *Antigone*, written in 442 B.C., notice that the play's central conflict is introduced, developed, and resolved according to the pattern we have just described.

Although written first, *Antigone* is the third and last play in the chronology of events composing Sophocles's Oedipus cycle; the first two plays are *Oedipus the King* and *Oedipus at Colonus.*

According to Greek legend, King Laius of Thebes and his descendants were doomed by the god Apollo. Warned by the Oracle of Delphi that his own son would kill him, Laius leaves the son, Oedipus, to die in the mountains. But Oedipus survives and unknowingly kills his father, whom he encounters on the road to Thebes. Oedipus solves the riddle of the Sphinx for the Thebans and becomes their king, unwittingly marrying his mother, Jocasta, the widow of Laius. Several years later, when he learns what he has done, Oedipus blinds himself and leaves Thebes. Creon, brother of Jocasta, becomes the ruler of Thebes and is entrusted with caring for Oedipus's two daughters, Antigone and Ismene. Oedipus's two sons, Polynices and Eteocles, reject their father and struggle for power in Thebes. Polynices is driven from the city but returns with an army; in the ensuing battle he and Eteocles kill each other, while Creon succeeds to the throne. As the play opens, Antigone and Ismene are discussing Creon's first official decree.

Sophocles   *ca. 496–ca. 405* B.C.

Sophocles wrote more than 120 plays, but only 7 have survived. Born in Colonus, near Athens, he studied under Aeschylus, the master of Greek tragedy. Sophocles did not question the justice of the gods; his plays assume a divine order that humans must follow. His strong-willed protagonists end tragically because of pride and lack of self-knowledge. His works include *Oedipus the King, Antigone, Electra,* and *Ajax.*

Antigone

Translated by Robert Fagles

CHARACTERS

ANTIGONE, *daughter of Oedipus*
  and Jocasta
ISMENE, *sister of Antigone*
A CHORUS *of old Theban*
  citizens and their LEADER
CREON, *king of Thebes, uncle of*
  Antigone and Ismene
A SENTRY

HAEMON, *son of Creon and*
  Eurydice
TIRESIAS, *a blind prophet*
A MESSENGER
EURYDICE, *wife of Creon*
GUARDS, ATTENDANTS, *and*
  A BOY

TIME AND SCENE

The royal house of Thebes. It is still night, and invading armies have just been driven from the city. Fighting on opposite sides, the sons of Oedipus, Eteocles and Polynices, have killed each other in combat. Their uncle, CREON, is now king of Thebes.

Enter ANTIGONE, slipping through the central doors of the palace. She motions to her sister, ISMENE, who follows her cautiously toward an altar at the center of the stage.

The opening scene from a modern-dress production (1946) of *Anitgone*, with Katharine Cornell in the title role. Antigone is seated alone to the left, with the Narrator, a substitute for the Greek chorus, gesturing in the center and Haemon and Ismene standing at the right. (AP/Wide World Photos)

ANTIGONE. My own flesh and blood—dear sister, dear Ismene,
    how many griefs our father Oedipus handed down!
    Do you know one, I ask you, one grief
    that Zeus[1] will not perfect for the two of us
    while we still live and breathe? There's nothing,
    no pain—our lives are pain—no private shame,
    no public disgrace, nothing I haven't seen
    in your griefs and mine. And now this:
    an emergency decree, they say, the Commander
    has just declared for all of Thebes.   10
    What, haven't you heard? Don't you see?
    The doom reserved for enemies
    marches on the ones we love the most.
ISMENE. Not I, I haven't heard a word, Antigone.
    Nothing of loved ones,
    no joy or pain has come my way, not since
    the two of us were robbed of our two brothers,
    both gone in a day, a double blow—
    not since the armies of Argos vanished,
    just this very night. I know nothing more,   20
    whether our luck's improved or ruin's still to come.
ANTIGONE. I thought so. That's why I brought you out here,
    past the gates, so you could hear in private.
ISMENE. What's the matter? Trouble, clearly...
    you sound so dark, so grim.

---

[1]**Zeus** The highest Olympian deity.

ANTIGONE. Why not? Our own brothers' burial!
  Hasn't Creon graced one with all the rites,
  disgraced the other? Eteocles, they say,
  has been given full military honors,
  rightly so—Creon's laid him in the earth   30
  and he goes with glory down among the dead.
  But the body of Polynices, who died miserably—
  why, a city-wide proclamation, rumor has it,
  forbids anyone to bury him, even mourn him.
  He's to be left unwept, unburied, a lovely treasure
  for birds that scan the field and feast to their heart's content.

  Such, I hear, is the martial law our good Creon
  lays down for you and me—yes, me, I tell you—
  and he's coming here to alert the uninformed
  in no uncertain terms,   40
  and he won't treat the matter lightly. Whoever
  disobeys in the least will die, his doom is sealed:
  stoning to death inside the city walls!

  There you have it. You'll soon show what you are,
  worth your breeding, Ismene, or a coward—
  for all your royal blood.
ISMENE. My poor sister, if things have come to this,
  who am I to make or mend them, tell me,
  what good am I to you?
ANTIGONE.   Decide.
  Will you share the labor, share the work?   50
ISMENE. What work, what's the risk? What do you mean?
ANTIGONE.
     Raising her hands.
  Will you lift up his body with these bare hands
  and lower it with me?
ISMENE.   What? You'd bury him—
  when a law forbids the city?
ANTIGONE.   Yes!
  He is my brother and—deny it as you will—
  your brother too.
  No one will ever convict me for a traitor.
ISMENE. So desperate, and Creon has expressly—
ANTIGONE.   No,
  he has no right to keep me from my own.
ISMENE. Oh my sister, think—   60
  think how our own father died, hated,
  his reputation in ruins, driven on
  by the crimes he brought to light himself
  to gouge out his eyes with his own hands—
  then mother...his mother and wife, both in one,
  mutilating her life in the twisted noose—
  and last, our two brothers dead in a single day,

both shedding their own blood, poor suffering boys,
battling out their common destiny hand-to-hand.

Now look at the two of us, left so alone... 70
think what a death we'll die, the worst of all
if we violate the laws and override
the fixed decree of the throne, its power—
we must be sensible. Remember we are women,
we're not born to contend with men. Then too,
we're underlings, ruled by much stronger hands,
so we must submit in this, and things still worse.

I, for one, I'll beg the dead to forgive me—
I'm forced, I have no choice—I must obey
the ones who stand in power. Why rush to extremes? 80
It's madness, madness.
ANTIGONE.   I won't insist,
no, even if you should have a change of heart,
I'd never welcome you in the labor, not with me.
So, do as you like, whatever suits you best—
I'll bury him myself.
And even if I die in the act, that death will be a glory.
I'll lie with the one I love and loved by him—
an outrage sacred to the gods! I have longer
to please the dead than please the living here:
in the kingdom down below I'll lie forever. 90
Do as you like, dishonor the laws
the gods hold in honor.
ISMENE.   I'd do them no dishonor...
but defy the city? I have no strength for that.
ANTIGONE. You have your excuses. I am on my way,
I'll raise a mound for him, for my dear brother.
ISMENE. Oh Antigone, you're so rash—I'm so afraid for you!
ANTIGONE. Don't fear for me. Set your own life in order.
ISMENE. Then don't, at least, blurt this out to anyone.
Keep it a secret. I'll join you in that, I promise.
ANTIGONE . Dear god, shout it from the rooftops. I'll hate you 100
all the more for silence—tell the world!
ISMENE. So fiery—and it ought to chill your heart.
ANTIGONE. I know I please where I must please the most.
ISMENE. Yes, if you can, but you're in love with impossibility.
ANTIGONE. Very well then, once my strength gives out
I will be done at last.
ISMENE.   You're wrong from the start.
You're off on a hopeless quest.
ANTIGONE. If you say so, you will make me hate you,
and the hatred of the dead, by all rights,
will haunt you night and day. 110
But leave me to my own absurdity, leave me
to suffer this—dreadful thing. I'll suffer

nothing as great as death without glory.
Exit to the side.
ISMENE. Then go if you must, but rest assured,
wild, irrational as you are, my sister,
you are truly dear to the ones who love you.
Withdrawing to the palace. Enter a CHORUS, *the old citizens of Thebes,*
chanting as the sun begins to rise.
CHORUS. Glory!—great beam of sun, brightest of all
that ever rose on the seven gates of Thebes,
    you burn through night at last!
        Great eye of the golden day,   120
mounting the Dirce's[2] banks you throw him back—
the enemy out of Argos, the white shield, the man of bronze—
he's flying headlong now
        the bridle of fate stampeding him with pain!

    And he had driven against our borders,
    launched by the warring claims of Polynices—
    like an eagle screaming, winging havoc
    over the land, wings of armor
    shielded white as snow,
    a huge army massing,   130
    crested helmets bristling for assault.

He hovered above our roofs, his vast maw gaping
closing down around our seven gates,
    his spears thirsting for the kill
            but now he's gone, look,
before he could glut his jaws with Theban blood
or the god of fire put our crown of towers to the torch.
He grappled the Dragon none can master—Thebes—
        the clang of our arms like thunder at his back!

    Zeus hates with a vengeance all bravado,   140
    the mighty boasts of men. He watched them
    coming on in a rising flood, the pride
    of their golden armor ringing shrill—
    and brandishing his lightning
    blasted the fighter just at the goal,
    rushing to shout his triumph from our walls.

Down from the heights he crashed, pounding down on the earth!
And a moment ago, blazing torch in hand—
        mad for attack, ecstatic
he breathed his rage, the storm   150
    of his fury hurling at our heads!

---

[2]**Dirce** A river near Thebes.

But now his high hopes have laid him low
and down the enemy ranks the iron god of war
    deals his rewards, his stunning blows—Ares[3]
    rapture of battle, our right arm in the crisis.

    Seven captains marshaled at seven gates
    seven against their equals, gave
    their brazen trophies up to Zeus,
    god of the breaking rout of battle,
    all but two: those blood brothers,   160
    one father, one mother—matched in rage,
    spears matched for the twin conquest—
    clashed and won the common prize of death.

But now for Victory! Glorious in the morning,
joy in her eyes to meet our joy
    she is winging down to Thebes,
our fleets of chariots wheeling in her wake—
    Now let us win oblivion from the wars,
thronging the temples of the gods
in singing, dancing choirs through the night!   170
    Lord Dionysus,[4] god of the dance
    that shakes the land of Thebes, now lead the way!
Enter CREON *from the palace, attended by his guard.*
    But look, the king of the realm is coming,
    Creon, the new man for the new day,
    whatever the gods are sending now…
    what new plan will he launch?
    Why this, this special session?
    Why this sudden call to the old men
    summoned at one command?
CREON.   My countrymen,
    the ship of state is safe. The gods who rocked her,   180
after a long, merciless pounding in the storm,
have righted her once more.
                  Out of the whole city
I have called you here alone. Well I know,
first, your undeviating respect
for the throne and royal power of King Laius.
Next, while Oedipus steered the land of Thebes,
and even after he died, your loyalty was unshakable,
you still stood by their children. Now then,
since the two sons are dead—two blows of fate
in the same day, cut down by each other's hands,   190
both killers, both brothers stained with blood—
as I am next in kin to the dead,
I now possess the throne and all its powers.
Of course you cannot know a man completely,

---

[3]**Ares** God of war.
[4]**Dionysus** God of fertility and wine.

his character, his principles, sense of judgment,
not till he's shown his colors, ruling the people,
making laws. Experience, there's the test.
As I see it, whoever assumes the task,
the awesome task of setting the city's course,
and refuses to adopt the soundest policies   200
but fearing someone, keeps his lips locked tight,
he's utterly worthless. So I rate him now,
I always have. And whoever places a friend
above the good of his own country, he is nothing:
I have no use for him. Zeus my witness,
Zeus who sees all things, always—
I could never stand by silent, watching destruction
march against our city, putting safety to rout,
nor could I ever make that man a friend of mine
who menaces our country. Remember this: 210
our country *is* our safety.
Only while she voyages true on course
can we establish friendships, truer than blood itself.
Such are my standards. They make our city great.

Closely akin to them I have proclaimed,
just now, the following decree to our people
concerning the two sons of Oedipus.
Eteocles, who died fighting for Thebes,
excelling all in arms: he shall be buried,
crowned with a hero's honors, the cups we pour   220
to soak the earth and reach the famous dead.

But as for his blood brother, Polynices,
who returned from exile, home to his father-city
and the gods of his race, consumed with one desire—
to burn them roof to roots—who thirsted to drink
his kinsmen's blood and sell the rest to slavery:
that man—a proclamation has forbidden the city
to dignify him with burial, mourn him at all.
No, he must be left unburied, his corpse
carrion for the birds and dogs to tear,   230
an obscenity for the citizens to behold!

These are my principles. Never at my hands
will the traitor be honored above the patriot.
But whoever proves his loyalty to the state:
I'll prize that man in death as well as life.
LEADER. If this is your pleasure, Creon, treating
our city's enemy and our friend this way...
The power is yours, I suppose, to enforce it
with the laws, both for the dead and all of us,
the living.

CREON. Follow my orders closely then,   240
   be on your guard.
LEADER.   We're too old.
   Lay that burden on younger shoulders.
CREON.   No, no,
   I don't mean the body—I've posted guards already.
LEADER. What commands for us then? What other service?
CREON. See that you never side with those who break my orders.
LEADER. Never. Only a fool could be in love with death.
CREON. Death is the price—you're right. But all too often
   the mere hope of money has ruined many men.
     A SENTRY *enters from the side.*
SENTRY.   My lord,
   I can't say I'm winded from running, or set out
   with any spring in my legs either—no sir,   250
   I was lost in thought, and it made me stop, often,
   dead in my tracks, wheeling, turning back,
   and all the time a voice inside me muttering,
   "Idiot, why? You're going straight to your death."
   Then muttering, "Stopped again, poor fool?
   If somebody gets the news to Creon first,
   what's to save your neck?"

                  And so,
   mulling it over, on I trudged, dragging my feet,
   you can make a short road take forever...
   but at last, common sense won out,   260
   I'm here, and I'm all yours,
   and even though I come empty-handed
   I'll tell my story just the same, because
   I've come with a good grip on one hope,
   what will come will come, whatever fate—
CREON. Come to the point!
   What's wrong—why so afraid?
SENTRY. First, myself, I've got to tell you,
   I didn't do it, didn't see who did—
   Be fair, don't take it out on me.   270
CREON. You're playing it safe, soldier,
   barricading yourself from any trouble.
   It's obvious, you've something strange to tell.
SENTRY. Dangerous too, and danger makes you delay
   for all you're worth.
CREON. Out with it—then dismiss!
SENTRY. All right, here it comes. The body—
   someone's just buried it, then run off...
   sprinkled some dry dust on the flesh,
   given it proper rites.
CREON.   What?   280
   What man alive would dare—

SENTRY.   I've no idea, I swear it.
There was no mark of a spade, no pickaxe there,
no earth turned up, the ground packed hard and dry,
unbroken, no tracks, no wheelruts, nothing,
the workman left no trace. Just at sunup
the first watch of the day points it out—
it was a wonder! We were stunned...
a terrific burden too, for all of us, listen:
you can't see the corpse, not that it's buried,
really, just a light cover of road-dust on it,   290
as if someone meant to lay the dead to rest
and keep from getting cursed.
Not a sign in sight that dogs or wild beasts
had worried the body, even torn the skin.

But what came next! Rough talk flew thick and fast,
guard grilling guard—we'd have come to blows
at last, nothing to stop it; each man for himself
and each the culprit, no one caught red-handed,
all of us pleading ignorance, dodging the charges,
ready to take up red-hot iron in our fists,   300
go through fire, swear oaths to the gods—
"I didn't do it, I had no hand in it either,
not in the plotting, not in the work itself!"

Finally, after all this wrangling came to nothing,
one man spoke out and made us stare at the ground,
hanging our heads in fear. No way to counter him,
no way to take his advice and come through
safe and sound. Here's what he said:
"Look, we've got to report the facts to Creon,
we can't keep this hidden." Well, that won out,   310
and the lot fell on me, condemned me,
unlucky as ever, I got the prize. So here I am,
against my will and yours too, well I know—
no one wants the man who brings bad news.
LEADER.   My king,
ever since he began I've been debating in my mind,
could this possibly be the work of the gods?
CREON.   Stop—
before you make me choke with anger—the gods!
You, you're senile, must you be insane?
You say—why it's intolerable—say the gods
could have the slightest concern for that corpse?   320
Tell me, was it for meritorious service
they proceeded to bury him, prized him so? The hero
who came to burn their temples ringed with pillars,
their golden treasures—scorch their hallowed earth
and fling their laws to the winds.
Exactly when did you last see the gods
celebrating traitors? Inconceivable!

No, from the first there were certain citizens
who could hardly stand the spirit of my regime,
grumbling against me in the dark, heads together, 330
tossing wildly, never keeping their necks beneath
the yoke, loyally submitting to their king.
These are the instigators, I'm convinced—
they've perverted my own guard, bribed them
to do their work.
               Money! Nothing worse
in our lives, so current, rampant, so corrupting.
Money—you demolish cities, root men from their homes,
you train and twist good minds and set them on
to the most atrocious schemes. No limit,
you make them adept at every kind of outrage, 340
every godless crime—money!
                    Everyone—
the whole crew bribed to commit this crime,
they've made one thing sure at least:
sooner or later they will pay the price.
   Wheeling on the SENTRY.
                        You—
I swear to Zeus as I still believe in Zeus,
if you don't find the man who buried that corpse,
the very man, and produce him before my eyes,
simple death won't be enough for you,
not till we string you up alive
and wring the immorality out of you. 350
Then you can steal the rest of your days,
better informed about where to make a killing.
You'll have learned, at last, it doesn't pay
to itch for rewards from every hand that beckons.
Filthy profits wreck most men, you'll see—
they'll never save your life.
SENTRY.   Please,
   may I say a word or two, or just turn and go?
CREON. Can't you tell? Everything you say offends me.
SENTRY. Where does it hurt you, in the ears or in the heart?
CREON. And who are you to pinpoint my displeasure? 360
SENTRY. The culprit grates on your feelings,
   I just annoy your ears.
CREON.   Still talking?
   You talk too much! A born nuisance—
SENTRY.   Maybe so,
   but I never did this thing, so help me!
CREON.   Yes, you did—
   what's more, you squandered your life for silver!
SENTRY. Oh it's terrible when the one who does the judging
   judges things all wrong.
CREON.   Well now,
   you just be clever about your judgments—

if you fail to produce the criminals for me,
you'll swear your dirty money brought you pain.
Turning sharply, reentering the palace.   370
SENTRY. I hope he's found. Best thing by far.
But caught or not, that's in the lap of fortune;
I'll never come back, you've seen the last of me.
I'm saved, even now, and I never thought,
I never hoped—
dear gods, I owe you all my thanks!
Rushing out.
CHORUS.   Numberless wonders
terrible wonders walk the world but none the match for man—
that great wonder crossing the heaving gray sea,
           driven on by the blasts of winter
on through breakers crashing left and right,   380
     holds his steady course
and the oldest of the gods he wears away—
the Earth, the immortal, the inexhaustible—
as his plows go back and forth, year in, year out
     with the breed of stallions turning up the furrows.

And the blithe, lightheaded race of birds he snares,
the tribes of savage beasts, the life that swarms the depths—
           with one fling of his nets
woven and coiled tight, he takes them all,
     man the skilled, the brilliant!   390
He conquers all, taming with his techniques
the prey that roams the cliffs and wild lairs,
training the stallion, clamping the yoke across
     his shaggy neck, and the tireless mountain bull.

And speech and thought, quick as the wind
and the mood and mind for law that rules the city—
     all these he has taught himself
and shelter from the arrows of the frost
when there's rough lodging under the cold clear sky
and the shafts of lashing rain—   400
           ready, resourceful man!
                    Never without resources
never an impasse as he marches on the future—
only Death, from Death alone he will find no rescue
but from desperate plagues he has plotted his escapes.

Man the master, ingenious past all measure
past all dreams, the skills within his grasp—
     he forges on, now to destruction
now again to greatness. When he weaves in
the laws of the land, and the justice of the gods   410
that binds his oaths together
           he and his city rise high—
                    but the city casts out

that man who weds himself to inhumanity
thanks to reckless daring. Never share my hearth
never think my thoughts, whoever does such things.
    Enter ANTIGONE *from the side, accompanied by the* SENTRY.
Here is a dark sign from the gods—
what to make of this? I know her,
how can I deny it? That young girl's Antigone!
Wretched child of a wretched father,   420
Oedipus. Look, is it possible?
They bring you in like a prisoner—
why? did you break the king's laws?
Did they take you in some act of mad defiance?
SENTRY. She's the one, she did it single-handed—
    we caught her burying the body. Where's Creon?
    Enter CREON *from the palace.*
LEADER. Back again, just in time when you need him.
CREON. In time for what? What is it?
SENTRY.   My king,
    there's nothing you can swear you'll never do—
    second thoughts make liars of us all.   430
    I could have sworn I wouldn't hurry back
    (what with your threats, the buffeting I just took),
    but a stroke of luck beyond our wildest hopes,
    what a joy, there's nothing like it. So,
    back I've come, breaking my oath, who cares?
    I'm bringing in our prisoner—this young girl—
    we took her giving the dead the last rites.
    But no casting lots this time; this is *my* luck,
    my prize, no one else's.
                     Now, my lord,
    here she is. Take her, question her,   440
    cross-examine her to your heart's content.
    But set me free, it's only right—
    I'm rid of this dreadful business once for all.
CREON. Prisoner! Her? You took her—where, doing what?
SENTRY. Burying the man. That's the whole story.
CREON.   What?
    You mean what you say, you're telling me the truth?
SENTRY. She's the one. With my own eyes I saw her
    bury the body, just what you've forbidden.
    There. Is that plain and clear?
CREON. What did you see? Did you catch her in the act?   450
SENTRY. Here's what happened. We went back to our post,
    those threats of yours breathing down our necks—
    we brushed the corpse clean of the dust that covered it,
    stripped it bare...it was slimy, going soft,
    and we took to high ground, backs to the wind
    so the stink of him couldn't hit us;
    jostling, baiting each other to keep awake,
    shouting back and forth—no napping on the job,

not this time. And so the hours dragged by
until the sun stood dead above our heads,   460
a huge white ball in the noon sky, beating,
blazing down, and then it happened—
suddenly, a whirlwind!
Twisting a great dust-storm up from the earth,
a black plague of the heavens, filling the plain,
ripping the leaves off every tree in sight,
choking the air and sky. We squinted hard
and took our whipping from the gods.

And after the storm passed—it seemed endless—
there, we saw the girl!   470
And she cried out a sharp, piercing cry,
like a bird come back to an empty nest,
peering into its bed, and all the babies gone...
Just so, when she sees the corpse bare
she bursts into a long, shattering wail
and calls down withering curses on the heads
of all who did the work. And she scoops up dry dust,
handfuls, quickly, and lifting a fine bronze urn,
lifting it high and pouring, she crowns the dead
with three full libations.
                     Soon as we saw   480
we rushed her, closed on the kill like hunters,
and she, she didn't flinch. We interrogated her,
charging her with offenses past and present—
she stood up to it all, denied nothing. I tell you,
it made me ache and laugh in the same breath.
It's pure joy to escape the worst yourself,
it hurts a man to bring down his friends.
But all that, I'm afraid, means less to me
than my own skin. That's the way I'm made.

CREON.
    Wheeling on ANTIGONE
                             You,   490
with your eyes fixed on the ground—speak up.
Do you deny you did this, yes or no?
ANTIGONE. I did it. I don't deny a thing.
CREON.
    To the SENTRY.
You, get out, wherever you please—
you're clear of a very heavy charge.
    He leaves; CREON *turns back to* ANTIGONE.
You, tell me briefly, no long speeches—
were you aware a decree had forbidden this?
ANTIGONE. Well aware. How could I avoid it? It was public.
CREON. And still you had the gall to break this law?
ANTIGONE. Of course I did. It wasn't Zeus, not in the least,   500
who made this proclamation—not to me.
Nor did that Justice, dwelling with the gods

beneath the earth, ordain such laws for men.
Nor did I think your edict had such force
that you, a mere mortal, could override the gods,
the great unwritten, unshakable traditions.
They are alive, not just today or yesterday:
they live forever, from the first of time,
and no one knows when they first saw the light.

These laws—I was not about to break them,
not out of fear of some man's wounded pride, 510
and face the retribution of the gods.
Die I must, I've known it all my life—
how could I keep from knowing?—even without
your death-sentence ringing in my ears.
And if I am to die before my time
I consider that a gain. Who on earth,
alive in the midst of so much grief as I,
could fail to find his death a rich reward?
So for me, at least, to meet this doom of yours
is precious little pain. But if I had allowed 520
my own mother's son to rot, an unburied corpse—
that would have been an agony! This is nothing.
And if my present actions strike you as foolish,
let's just say I've been accused of folly
by a fool.
LEADER.   Like father like daughter,
passionate, wild...
she hasn't learned to bend before adversity.
CREON. No? Believe me, the stiffest stubborn wills
fall the hardest; the toughest iron,
tempered strong in the white-hot fire, 530
you'll see it crack and shatter first of all.
And I've known spirited horses you can break
with a light bit—proud, rebellious horses.
There's no room for pride, not in a slave,
not with the lord and master standing by.

This girl was an old hand at insolence
when she overrode the edicts we made public.
But once she'd done it—the insolence,
twice over—to glory in it, laughing,
mocking us to our face with what she'd done. 540
I'm not the man, not now: she is the man
if this victory goes to her and she goes free.

Never! Sister's child or closer in blood
than all my family clustered at my altar
worshiping Guardian Zeus—she'll never escape,
she and her blood sister, the most barbaric death.
Yes, I accuse her sister of an equal part
in scheming this, this burial.

To his ATTENDANTS.

                                              Bring her here!
I just saw her inside, hysterical, gone to pieces.
It never fails: the mind convicts itself   550
in advance, when scoundrels are up to no good,
plotting in the dark. Oh but I hate it more
when a traitor, caught red-handed,
tries to glorify his crimes.
ANTIGONE. Creon, what more do you want
    than my arrest and execution?
CREON. Nothing. Then I have it all.
ANTIGONE. Then why delay? Your moralizing repels me,
    every word you say—pray god it always will.
    So naturally all I say repels you too.
                                              Enough.   560
Give me glory! What greater glory could I win
than to give my own brother decent burial?
These citizens here would all agree,
    To the CHORUS.
they'd praise me too
if their lips weren't locked in fear.
    Pointing to CREON.
Lucky tyrants—the perquisites of power!
Ruthless power to do and say whatever pleases *them*.
CREON. You alone, of all the people in Thebes,
    see things that way.
ANTIGONE.   They see it just that way
    but defer to you and keep their tongues in leash.   570
CREON. And you, aren't you ashamed to differ so from them?
    So disloyal!
ANTIGONE.   Not ashamed for a moment,
    not to honor my brother, my own flesh and blood.
CREON. Wasn't Eteocles a brother too—cut down, facing him?
ANTIGONE. Brother, yes, by the same mother, the same father.
CREON. Then how can you render his enemy such honors,
    such impieties in his eyes?
ANTIGONE. He'll never testify to that,
    Eteocles dead and buried.
CREON.   He will—
    if you honor the traitor just as much as him.   580
ANTIGONE. But it was his brother, not some slave that died—
CREON. Ravaging our country!—
    but Eteocles died fighting in our behalf.
ANTIGONE. No matter—Death longs for the same rites for all.
CREON. Never the same for the patriot and the traitor.
ANTIGONE. Who, Creon, who on earth can say the ones below
    don't find this pure and uncorrupt?
CREON. Never. Once an enemy, never a friend,
    not even after death.

ANTIGONE. I was born to join in love, not hate— 590
    that is my nature.
CREON.   Go down below and love,
    if love you must—love the dead! While I'm alive,
    no woman is going to lord it over me.
      Enter ISMENE *from the palace, under guard.*
CHORUS.   Look,
    Ismene's coming, weeping a sister's tears,
    loving sister, under a cloud…
    her face is flushed, her cheeks streaming.
    Sorrow puts her lovely radiance in the dark.
CREON.   You—
    in my house, you viper, slinking undetected,
    sucking my life-blood! I never knew
    I was breeding twin disasters, the two of you 600
    rising up against my throne. Come, tell me,
    will you confess your part in the crime or not?
    Answer me. Swear to me.
ISMENE.   I did it, yes—
    if only she consents—I share the guilt,
    the consequences too.
ANTIGONE.   No,
    Justice will never suffer that—not you,
    you were unwilling. I never brought you in.
ISMENE. But now you face such dangers…I'm not ashamed
    to sail through trouble with you,
    make your troubles mine.
ANTIGONE.   Who did the work? 610
    Let the dead and the god of death bear witness!
    I've no love for a friend who loves in words alone.
ISMENE. Oh no, my sister, don't reject me, please,
    let me die beside you, consecrating
    the dead together.
ANTIGONE.   Never share my dying,
    don't lay claim to what you never touched.
    My death will be enough.
ISMENE. What do I care for life, cut off from you?
ANTIGONE. Ask Creon. Your concern is all for him.
ISMENE. Why abuse me so? It doesn't help you now.
ANTIGONE.   You're right— 620
    if I mock you, I get no pleasure from it,
    only pain.
ISMENE.   Tell me, dear one,
    what can I do to help you, even now?
ANTIGONE. Save yourself. I don't grudge you your survival.
ISMENE. Oh no, no, denied my portion in your death?
ANTIGONE. You chose to live, I chose to die.
ISMENE.   Not, at least,
    without every kind of caution I could voice.

ANTIGONE. Your wisdom appealed to one world—mine, another.

ISMENE. But look, we're both guilty, both condemned to death.

ANTIGONE. Courage! Live your life. I gave myself to death,   630
    long ago, so I might serve the dead.

CREON. They're both mad, I tell you, the two of them.
    One's just shown it, the other's been that way
    since she was born.

ISMENE.   True, my king,
    the sense we were born with cannot last forever . . .
    commit cruelty on a person long enough
    and the mind begins to go.

CREON.   Yours did,
    when you chose to commit your crimes with her.

ISMENE. How can I live alone, without her?

CREON.   Her?
    Don't even mention her—she no longer exists.   640

ISMENE. What? You'd kill your own son's bride?

CREON.   Absolutely:
    there are other fields for him to plow.

ISMENE.   Perhaps,
    but never as true, as close a bond as theirs.

CREON. A worthless woman for my son? It repels me.

ISMENE. Dearest Haemon, your father wrongs you so!

CREON. Enough, enough—you and your talk of marriage!

ISMENE. Creon—you're really going to rob your son of Antigone?

CREON. Death will do it for me—break their marriage off.

LEADER. So, it's settled then? Antigone must die?

CREON. Settled, yes—we both know that.
    To the GUARDS.
    Stop wasting time. Take them in.   650
    From now on they'll act like women.
    Tie them up, no more running loose;
    even the bravest will cut and run,
    once they see Death coming for their lives.
    The GUARDS *escort* ANTIGONE *and* ISMENE *into the palace.* CREON
    remains while the old citizens form their chorus.

CHORUS. Blest, they are the truly blest who all their lives
    have never tasted devastation. For others, once
    the gods have rocked a house to its foundations
          the ruin will never cease, cresting on and on
    from one generation on throughout the race—   660
    like a great mounting tide
    driven on by savage northern gales,
          surging over the dead black depths
    roiling up from the bottom dark heaves of sand
    and the headlands, taking the storm's onslaught full-force,
    roar, and the low moaning
                  echoes on and on
                         and now
    as in ancient times I see the sorrows of the house,

the living heirs of the old ancestral kings,
piling on the sorrows of the dead
      and one generation cannot free the next— 670
some god will bring them crashing down,
the race finds no release.
And now the light, the hope
      springing up from the late last root
in the house of Oedipus, that hope's cut down in turn
by the long, bloody knife swung by the gods of death
by a senseless word
             by fury at the heart.
                    Zeus,
yours is the power, Zeus, what man on earth
can override it, who can hold it back?
Power that neither Sleep, the all-ensnaring 680
      no, nor the tireless months of heaven
can ever overmaster—young through all time,
mighty lord of power, you hold fast
      the dazzling crystal mansions of Olympus.
And throughout the future, late and soon
as through the past, your law prevails:
no towering form of greatness
      enters into the lives of mortals
            free and clear of ruin.
                    True,
our dreams, our high hopes voyaging far and wide 690
bring sheer delight to many, to many others
      delusion, blithe, mindless lusts
and the fraud steals on one slowly...unaware
till he trips and puts his foot into the fire.
      He was a wise old man who coined
the famous saying: "Sooner or later
foul is fair, fair is foul
to the man the gods will ruin"—
      He goes his way for a moment only
             free of blinding ruin.
    Enter HAEMON *from the palace.*
Here's Haemon now, the last of all your sons. 700
Does he come in tears for his bride,
his doomed bride, Antigone—
bitter at being cheated of their marriage?
CREON. We'll soon know, better than seers could tell us.
    Turning to HAEMON.
Son, you've heard the final verdict on your bride?
Are you coming now, raving against your father?
Or do you love me, no matter what I do?
HAEMON. Father, I'm your *son*...you in your wisdom
set my bearings for me—I obey you. 710
No marriage could ever mean more to me than you,
whatever good direction you may offer.

CREON.   Fine, Haemon.
That's how you ought to feel within your heart,
subordinate to your father's will in every way.
That's what a man prays for: to produce good sons—
households full of them, dutiful and attentive,
so they can pay his enemy back with interest
and match the respect their father shows his friend.
But the man who rears a brood of useless children,
what has he brought into the world, I ask you?   720
Nothing but trouble for himself, and mockery
from his enemies laughing in his face.
                                        Oh Haemon,
never lose your sense of judgment over a woman.
The warmth, the rush of pleasure, it all goes cold
in your arms, I warn you...a worthless woman
in your house, a misery in your bed.
What wound cuts deeper than a loved one
turned against you? Spit her out,
like a mortal enemy—let the girl go.
Let her find a husband down among the dead.   730

Imagine it: I caught her in naked rebellion,
the traitor, the only one in the whole city.
I'm not about to prove myself a liar,
not to my people, no, I'm going to kill her!
That's right—so let her cry for mercy, sing her hymns
to Zeus who defends all bonds of kindred blood.
Why, if I bring up my own kin to be rebels,
think what I'd suffer from the world at large.
Show me the man who rules his household well:
I'll show you someone fit to rule the state.   740
That good man, my son,
I have every confidence he and he alone
can give commands and take them too. Staunch
in the storm of spears he'll stand his ground,
a loyal, unflinching comrade at your side.

But whoever steps out of line, violates the laws
or presumes to hand out orders to his superiors,
he'll win no praise from me. But that man
the city places in authority, his orders
must be obeyed, large and small   750
right and wrong.
                    Anarchy—
show me a greater crime in all the earth!
She, she destroys cities, rips up houses,
breaks the ranks of spearmen into headlong rout.
But the ones who last it out, the great mass of them
owe their lives to discipline. Therefore
we must defend the men who live by law,

never let some woman triumph over us.
Better to fall from power, if fall we must,
at the hands of a man—never be rated 760
inferior to a woman, never.
LEADER.   To us,
unless old age has robbed us of our wits,
you seem to say what you have to say with sense.
HAEMON. Father, only the gods endow a man with reason,
the finest of all their gifts, a treasure.
Far be it from me—I haven't the skill,
and certainly no desire, to tell you when,
if ever, you make a slip in speech...though
someone else might have a good suggestion.

Of course it's not for you, 770
in the normal run of things, to watch
whatever men say or do, or find to criticize.
The man in the street, you know, dreads your glance,
he'd never say anything displeasing to your face.
But it's for me to catch the murmurs in the dark,
the way the city mourns for this young girl.
"No woman," they say, "ever deserved death less,
and such a brutal death for such a glorious action.
She, with her own dear brother lying in his blood—
she couldn't bear to leave him dead, unburied, 780
food for the wild dogs or wheeling vultures.
Death? She deserves a glowing crown of gold!"
So they say, and the rumor spreads in secret,
darkly...
                        I rejoice in your success, father—
nothing more precious to me in the world.
What medal of honor brighter to his children
than a father's growing glory? Or a child's
to his proud father? Now don't, please,
be quite so single-minded, self-involved
or assume the world is wrong and you are right. 790
Whoever thinks that he alone possesses intelligence,
the gift of eloquence, he and no one else,
and character too...such men, I tell you,
spread them open—and you will find them empty.
                                             No,
it's no disgrace for a man, even a wise man,
to learn many things and not to be too rigid.
You've seen trees by a raging winter torrent,
how many sway with the flood and salvage every twig,
but not the stubborn—they're ripped out, roots and all.
Bend or break. The same when a man is sailing: 800
haul your sheets too taut, never give an inch,
you'll capsize, go the rest of the voyage
keel up and the rowing-benches under.

Oh give way. Relax your anger—change!
I'm young, I know, but let me offer this:
it would be best by far, I admit,
if a man were born infallible, right by nature.
If not—and things don't often go that way,
it's best to learn from those with good advice.

LEADER. You'd do well, my lord, if he's speaking to the point,   810
to learn from him,
> *Turning to* HAEMON.

                      and you, my boy, from him.
You both are talking sense.

CREON.   So,
men our age, we're to be lectured, are we?—
schooled by a boy his age?

HAEMON. Only in what is right. But if I seem young,
look less to my years and more to what I do.

CREON. Do? Is admiring rebels an achievement?

HAEMON. I'd never suggest that you admire treason.

CREON.   Oh?—
isn't that just the sickness that's attacked her?

HAEMON. The whole city of Thebes denies it, to a man.   820

CREON. And is Thebes about to tell me how to rule?

HAEMON. Now, you see? Who's talking like a child?

CREON. Am I to rule this land for others—or myself?

HAEMON. It's no city at all, owned by one man alone.

CREON. What? The city *is* the king's—that's the law!

HAEMON. What a splendid king you'd make of a desert island—
you and you alone.

CREON.
> *To the* CHORUS.

                      This boy, I do believe,
is fighting on her side, the woman's side.

HAEMON. If you are a woman, yes;
my concern is all for you.   830

CREON. Why, you degenerate—bandying accusations,
threatening me with justice, your own father!

HAEMON. I see my father offending justice—wrong.

CREON.   Wrong?
To protect my royal rights?

HAEMON.   Protect your rights?
When you trample down the honors of the gods?

CREON. You, you soul of corruption, rotten through—
woman's accomplice!

HAEMON.   That may be,
but you'll never find me accomplice to a criminal.

CREON. That's what *she* is,
and every word you say is a blatant appeal for her—   840

HAEMON. And you, and me, and the gods beneath the earth.

CREON. You'll never marry her, not while she's alive.

HAEMON. Then she'll die... but her death will kill another.

CREON. What, brazen threats? You go too far!

HAEMON.   What threat?
   Combating your empty, mindless judgments with a word?
CREON. You'll suffer for your sermons, you and your empty wisdom!
HAEMON. If you weren't my father, I'd say you were insane.
CREON. Don't flatter me with Father—you woman's slave!
HAEMON. You really expect to fling abuse at me
   and not receive the same?
CREON.   Is that so!   850
   Now, by heaven, I promise you, you'll pay—
   taunting, insulting me! Bring her out,
   that hateful—she'll die now, here,
   in front of his eyes, beside her groom!
HAEMON. No, no, she will never die beside me—
   don't delude yourself. And you will never
   see me, never set eyes on my face again.
   Rage your heart out, rage with friends
   who can stand the sight of you.
     Rushing out.
LEADER. Gone, my king, in a burst of anger.   860
   A temper young as his…hurt him once,
   he may do something violent.
CREON.   Let him do—
   dream up something desperate, past all human limit!
   Good riddance. Rest assured,
   he'll never save those two young girls from death.
LEADER. Both of them, you really intend to kill them both?
CREON. No, not her, the one whose hands are clean;
   you're quite right.
LEADER.   But Antigone—
   what sort of death do you have in mind for her?
CREON. I'll take her down some wild, desolate path   870
   never trod by men, and wall her up alive
   in a rocky vault, and set out short rations,
   just a gesture of piety
   to keep the entire city free of defilement.
   There let her pray to the one god she worships:
   Death—who knows?—may just reprieve her from death.
   Or she may learn at last, better late than never,
   what a waste of breath it is to worship Death.
     Exit to the palace.
CHORUS. Love, never conquered in battle
   Love the plunderer laying waste the rich!   880
   Love standing the night-watch
          guarding a girl's soft cheek,
 you range the seas, the shepherds' steadings off in the wilds—
 not even the deathless gods can flee your onset,
 nothing human born for a day—
 whoever feels your grip is driven mad.
                Love
 you wrench the minds of the righteous into outrage,
 swerve them to their ruin—you have ignited this,

this kindred strife, father and son at war
              and Love alone the victor—   890
warm glance of the bride triumphant, burning with desire!
Throned in power, side-by-side with the mighty laws!
Irresistible Aphrodite,[5] never conquered—
Love, you mock us for your sport.
        ANTIGONE *is brought from the palace under guard.*
               But now, even I'd rebel against the king,
               I'd break all bounds when I see this—
               I fill with tears, can't hold them back,
               not any more... I see Antigone make her way
               to the bridal vault where all are laid to rest.
ANTIGONE. Look at me, men of my fatherland,   900
        setting out on the last road
looking into the last light of day
the last I'll ever see...
the god of death who puts us all to bed
takes me down to the banks of Acheron[6] alive—
        denied my part in the wedding-songs,
no wedding-song in the dusk has crowned my marriage—
I go to wed the lord of the dark waters.
CHORUS. Not crowned with glory, crowned with a dirge,
        you leave for the deep pit of the dead.   910
        No withering illness laid you low,
        no strokes of the sword—no law to yourself,
        alone, no mortal like you, ever, you go down
        to the halls of Death alive and breathing.
ANTIGONE. But think of Niobe[7]—well I know her story—
        think what a living death she died,
Tantalus' daughter, stranger queen from the east:
there on the mountain heights, growing stone
binding as ivy, slowly walled her round
and the rains will never cease, the legends say   920
the snows will never leave her...
        wasting away, under her brows the tears
showering down her breasting ridge and slopes—
a rocky death like hers puts me to sleep.
CHORUS. But she was a god, born of gods,
        and we are only mortals born to die.
        And yet, of course, it's a great thing
        for a dying girl to hear, just hear
        she shares a destiny equal to the gods,
        during life and later, once she's dead.
ANTIGONE.   O you mock me!   930
Why, in the name of all my fathers' gods
why can't you wait till I am gone—
        must you abuse me to my face?

---

[5]**Aphrodite** Goddess of love.
[6]**Acheron** A river in the underworld, to which the dead go.
[7]**Niobe** A queen of Thebes who was punished by the gods for her pride and was turned into stone.

O my city, all your fine rich sons!
And you, you springs of the Dirce,
holy grove of Thebes where the chariots gather,
      you at least, you'll bear me witness, look,
unmourned by friends and forced by such crude laws
I go to my rockbound prison, strange new tomb—
    always a stranger, O dear god,   940
    I have no home on earth and none below,
      not with the living, not with the breathless dead.
CHORUS. You went too far, the last limits of daring—
    smashing against the high throne of Justice!
        Your life's in ruins, child—I wonder…
    do you pay for your father's terrible ordeal?
ANTIGONE. There—at last you've touched it, the worst pain
  the worst anguish! Raking up the grief for father
    three times over, for all the doom
  that's struck us down, the brilliant house of Laius.   950
O mother, your marriage-bed
the coiling horrors, the coupling there—
    you with your own son, my father—doomstruck mother!
Such, such were my parents, and I their wretched child.
I go to them now, cursed, unwed, to share their home—
    I am a stranger! O dear brother, doomed
    in your marriage—your marriage murders mine,
      your dying drags me down to death alive!
    Enter CREON.
CHORUS. Reverence asks some reverence in return—
    but attacks on power never go unchecked,   960
      not by the man who holds the reins of power.
    Your own blind will, your passion has destroyed you.
ANTIGONE. No one to weep for me, my friends,
      no wedding-song—they take me away
      in all my pain…the road lies open, waiting.
      Never again, the law forbids me to see
      the sacred eye of day. I am agony!
    No tears for the destiny that's mine,
      no loved one mourns my death.
CREON.   Can't you see?
  If a man could wail his own dirge *before* he dies,   970
  he'd never finish.
    To the GUARDS.
                Take her away, quickly!
Wall her up in the tomb, you have your orders.
Abandon her there, alone, and let her choose—
death or a buried life with a good roof for shelter.
As for myself, my hands are clean. This young girl—
dead or alive, she will be stripped of her rights,
her stranger's rights, here in the world above.
ANTIGONE. O tomb, my bridal-bed—my house, my prison
  cut in the solid rock, my everlasting watch!
  I'll soon be there, soon embrace my own,   980

the great growing family of our dead
Persephone[8] has received among her ghosts.
                                              I,
the last of them all, the most reviled by far,
go down before my destined time's run out.
But still I go, cherishing one good hope:
my arrival may be dear to father,
dear to you, my mother,
dear to you, my loving brother, Eteocles—
When you died I washed you with my hands,
I dressed you all, I poured the cups   990
across your tombs. But now, Polynices,
because I laid your body out as well,
this, this is my reward. Nevertheless
I honored you—the decent will admit it—
well and wisely too.
                          Never, I tell you,
if I had been the mother of children
or if my husband died, exposed and rotting—
I'd never have taken this ordeal upon myself,
never defied our people's will. What law,
you ask, do I satisfy with what I say?   1000
A husband dead, there might have been another.
A child by another too, if I had lost the first.
But mother and father both lost in the halls of Death,
no brother could ever spring to light again.

For this law alone I held you first in honor.
For this, Creon, the king, judges me a criminal
guilty of dreadful outrage, my dear brother!
And now he leads me off, a captive in his hands,
with no part in the bridal-song, the bridal-bed,
denied all joy of marriage, raising children—   1010
deserted so by loved ones, struck by fate,
I descend alive to the caverns of the dead.

What law of the mighty gods have I transgressed?
Why look to the heavens any more, tormented as I am?
Whom to call, what comrades now? Just think,
my reverence only brands me for irreverence!
Very well: if this is the pleasure of the gods,
once I suffer I will know that I was wrong.
But if these men are wrong, let them suffer
nothing worse than they mete out to me—   1020
these masters of injustice!
LEADER. Still the same rough winds, the wild passion
raging through the girl.

---

[8]**Persephone** Queen of the underworld.

CREON.
> *To the* GUARDS.
>   Take her away.
> You're wasting time—you'll pay for it too.
ANTIGONE. Oh god, the voice of death. It's come, it's here.
CREON. True. Not a word of hope—your doom is sealed.
ANTIGONE. Land of Thebes, city of all my fathers—
>   O you gods, the first gods of the race!
>   They drag me away, now, no more delay.
>   Look on me, you noble sons of Thebes—   1030
>   the last of a great line of kings,
>   I alone, see what I suffer now
>   at the hands of what breed of men—
>   all for reverence, my reverence for the gods!
> *She leaves under guard; the* CHORUS *gathers.*
CHORUS. Danaë, Danaë[9]—
> even she endured a fate like yours,
>   in all her lovely strength she traded
> the light of day for the bolted brazen vault—
> buried within her tomb, her bridal-chamber,
> wed to the yoke and broken.   1040
>   But she was of glorious birth
>   my child, my child
> and treasured the seed of Zeus within her womb,
> the cloudburst streaming gold!
>   The power of fate is a wonder,
>   dark, terrible wonder—
>   neither wealth nor armies
>   towered walls nor ships
>   black hulls lashed by the salt
>   can save us from that force.   1050

> The yoke tamed him too
>   young Lycurgus[10] flaming in anger
> king of Edonia, all for his mad taunts
> Dionysus clamped him down, encased
> in the chain-mail of rock
>   and there his rage
>   his terrible flowering rage burst—
> sobbing, dying away...at last that madman
> came to know his god—
>   the power he mocked, the power   1060
>   he taunted in all his frenzy
>   trying to stamp out
>   the women strong with the god—
>   the torch, the raving sacred cries—

---

[9]**Danaë** Locked in a cell by her father because it was prophesied that her son would kill him, but visited by Zeus in the form of a shower of gold. Their son was Perseus.
[10]**Lycurgus** Punished by Dionysus because he would not worship him.

enraging the Muses[11] who adore the flute.
And far north where the Black Rocks
    cut the sea in half
and murderous straits
split the coast of Thrace
      a forbidding city stands   1070
where once, hard by the walls
the savage Ares thrilled to watch
a king's new queen, a Fury rearing in rage
      against his two royal sons—
        her bloody hands, her dagger-shuttle
stabbing out their eyes—cursed, blinding wounds—
their eyes blind sockets screaming for revenge!

They wailed in agony, cries echoing cries
      the princes doomed at birth...
and their mother doomed to chains,   1080
walled off in a tomb of stone—
      but she traced her own birth back
to a proud Athenian line and the high gods
and off in caverns half the world away,
born of the wild North Wind
      she sprang on her father's gales,
        racing stallions up the leaping cliffs—
child of the heavens. But even on her the Fates
the gray everlasting Fates rode hard
my child, my child.
    Enter TIRESIAS, *the blind prophet, led by a* BOY.
TIRESIAS.   Lords of Thebes,   1090
  I and the boy have come together,
  hand in hand. Two see with the eyes of one...
  so the blind must go, with a guide to lead the way.
CREON. What is it, old Tiresias? What news now?
TIRESIAS. I will teach you. And you obey the seer.
CREON.   I will,
  I've never wavered from your advice before.
TIRESIAS. And so you kept the city straight on course.
CREON. I owe you a great deal, I swear to that.
TIRESIAS. Then reflect, my son: you are poised,
  once more, on the razor-edge of fate.   1100
CREON. What is it? I shudder to hear you.
TIRESIAS.   You will learn
  when you listen to the warnings of my craft.
  As I sat on the ancient seat of augury,[12]
  in the sanctuary where every bird I know
  will hover at my hands—suddenly I heard it,
  a strange voice in the wingbeats, unintelligible,

---

[11]**Muses** Goddesses of the arts.
[12]**Seat of augury** Where Tiresias looked for omens among birds.

barbaric, a mad scream! Talons flashing, ripping,
they were killing each other—that much I knew—
the murderous fury whirring in those wings
made that much clear!
                              I was afraid,   1110
I turned quickly, tested the burnt-sacrifice,
ignited the altar at all points—but no fire,
the god in the fire never blazed.
Not from those offerings...over the embers
slid a heavy ooze from the long thighbones,
smoking, sputtering out, and the bladder
puffed and burst—spraying gall into the air—
and the fat wrapping the bones slithered off
and left them glistening white. No fire!
The rites failed that might have blazed the future   1120
with a sign. So I learned from the boy here;
he is my guide, as I am guide to others.
                              And it's you—
your high resolve that sets this plague on Thebes.
The public altars and sacred hearths are fouled,
one and all, by the birds and dogs with carrion
torn from the corpse, the doomstruck son of Oedipus!
And so the gods are deaf to our prayers, they spurn
the offerings in our hands, the flame of holy flesh.
No birds cry out an omen clear and true—
they're gorged with the murdered victim's blood and fat.   1130
Take these things to heart, my son, I warn you.
All men make mistakes, it is only human.
But once the wrong is done, a man
can turn his back on folly, misfortune too,
if he tries to make amends, however low he's fallen,
and stops his bullnecked ways. Stubbornness
brands you for stupidity—pride is a crime.
No, yield to the dead!
Never stab the fighter when he's down.
Where's the glory, killing the dead twice over?   1140

I mean you well. I give you sound advice.
It's best to learn from a good adviser
when he speaks for your own good:
it's pure gain.
CREON.   Old man—all of you! So,
you shoot your arrows at my head like archers at the target—
I even have *him* loosed on me, this fortune-teller.
Oh his ilk has tried to sell me short
and ship me off for years. Well,
drive your bargains, traffic—much as you like—
in the gold of India, silver-gold of Sardis.   1150
You'll never bury that body in the grave,
not even if Zeus's eagles rip the corpse

and wing their rotten pickings off to the throne of god!
Never, not even in fear of such defilement
will I tolerate his burial, that traitor.
Well I know, we can't defile the gods—
no mortal has the power.
                    No,
reverend old Tiresias, all men fall,
it's only human, but the wisest fall obscenely
when they glorify obscene advice with rhetoric—   1160
all for their own gain.
TIRESIAS. Oh god, is there a man alive
   who knows, who actually believes...
CREON.   What now?
   What earth-shattering truth are you about to utter?
TIRESIAS. ...just how much a sense of judgment, wisdom
   is the greatest gift we have?
CREON.   Just as much, I'd say,
   as a twisted mind is the worst affliction going.
TIRESIAS. You are the one who's sick, Creon, sick to death.
CREON. I am in no mood to trade insults with a seer.
TIRESIAS. You have already, calling my prophecies a lie.
CREON.   Why not?   1170
   You and the whole breed of seers are mad for money!
TIRESIAS. And the whole race of tyrants lusts to rake it in.
CREON. This slander of yours—
   are you aware you're speaking to the king?
TIRESIAS. Well aware. Who helped you save the city?
CREON.   You—
   you have your skills, old seer, but you lust for injustice!
TIRESIAS. You will drive me to utter the dreadful secret in my heart.
CREON. Spit it out! Just don't speak it for profit.
TIRESIAS. Profit? No, not a bit of profit, not for you.
CREON. Know full well, you'll never buy off my resolve.   1180
TIRESIAS. Then know this too, learn this by heart!
   The chariot of the sun will not race through
so many circuits more, before you have surrendered
one born of your own loins, your own flesh and blood,
a corpse for corpses given in return, since you have thrust
to the world below a child sprung for the world above,
ruthlessly lodged a living soul within the grave—
then you've robbed the gods below the earth,
keeping a dead body here in the bright air,
unburied, unsung, unhallowed by the rites.   1190

You, you have no business with the dead,
nor do the gods above—this is violence
you have forced upon the heavens.
And so the avengers, the dark destroyers late
but true to the mark, now lie in wait for you,
the Furies sent by the gods and the god of death

to strike you down with the pains that you perfected!
There. Reflect on that, tell me I've been bribed.
The day comes soon, no long test of time, not now,
that wakes the wails for men and women in your halls. 1200
Great hatred rises against you—
cities in tumult, all whose mutilated sons
the dogs have graced with burial, or the wild beasts,
some wheeling crow that wings the ungodly stench of carrion
back to each city, each warrior's hearth and home.

These arrows for your heart! Since you've raked me
I loose them like an archer in my anger,
arrows deadly true. You'll never escape
their burning, searing force.
        Motioning to his escort.
Come, boy, take me home. 1210
So he can vent his rage on younger men,
and learn to keep a gentler tongue in his head
and better sense than what he carries now.
        Exit to the side.
LEADER. The old man's gone, my king—
        terrible prophecies. Well I know,
        since the hair on this old head went gray,
        he's never lied to Thebes.
CREON. I know it myself—I'm shaken, torn.
        It's a dreadful thing to yield...but resist now?
        Lay my pride bare to the blows of ruin? 1220
        That's dreadful too.
LEADER.   But good advice,
        Creon, take it now, you must.
CREON. What should I do? Tell me...I'll obey.
LEADER. Go! Free the girl from the rocky vault
        and raise a mound for the body you exposed.
CREON. That's your advice? You think I should give in?
LEADER. Yes, my king, quickly. Disasters sent by the gods
        cut short our follies in a flash.
CREON.   Oh it's hard,
        giving up the heart's desire...but I will do it—
        no more fighting a losing battle with necessity. 1230
LEADER. Do it now, go, don't leave it to others.
CREON. Now—I'm on my way! Come, each of you,
        take up axes, make for the high ground,
        over there, quickly! I and my better judgment
        have come round to this—I shackled her,
        I'll set her free myself. I am afraid...
        it's best to keep the established laws
        to the very day we die.
        Rushing out, followed by his entourage. The CHORUS *clusters around the
        altar.*
CHORUS. God of a hundred names!

                    Great Dionysus—
Son and glory of Semele! Pride of Thebes—   1240
Child of Zeus whose thunder rocks the clouds—
Lord of the famous lands of evening—
King of the Mysteries!
                    King of Eleusis, Demeter's plain[13]
her breasting hills that welcome in the world—
Great Dionysus!
                    Bacchus,[14] living in Thebes
the mother-city of all your frenzied women—
                                        Bacchus
        living along the Ismenus'[15] rippling waters
standing over the field sown with the Dragon's teeth!

You—we have seen you through the flaring smoky fires,
        your torches blazing over the twin peaks   1250
where nymphs of the hallowed cave climb onward
                    fired with you, your sacred rage—
we have seen you at Castalia's running spring[16]
and down from the heights of Nysa[17] crowned with ivy
the greening shore rioting vines and grapes
            down you come in your storm of wild women
                    ecstatic, mystic cries—
                                Dionysus—
down to watch and ward the roads of Thebes!

First of all cities, Thebes you honor first
you and your mother, bride of the lightning—   1260
come, Dionysus! now your people lie
in the iron grip of plague,
come in your racing, healing stride
                    down Parnassus' slopes[18]
or across the moaning straits.
                    Lord of the dancing—
dance, dance the constellations breathing fire!
Great master of the voices of the night!
Child of Zeus, God's offspring, come, come forth!
Lord, king, dance with your nymphs, swirling, raving
arm-in-arm in frenzy through the night   1270
they dance you, Iacchus[19]—

---

[13]**Demeter's plain** The goddess of grain was worshiped at Eleusis, near Athens.
[14]**Bacchus** Another name for Dionysus.
[15]**Ismenus** A river near Thebes where the founders of the city were said to have sprung from a dragon's teeth.
[16]**Castalia's running spring** The sacred spring of Apollo's oracle at Delphi.
[17]**Nysa** A mountain where Dionysus was worshiped.
[18]**Parnassus** A mountain in Greece that was sacred to Dionysus as well as other gods and goddesses.
[19]**Iacchus** Dionysus.

Dance, Dionysus
giver of all good things!
    Enter a MESSENGER *from the side.*

MESSENGER.   Neighbors,
friends of the house of Cadmus[20] and the kings,
there's not a thing in this life of ours
I'd praise or blame as settled once for all.
Fortune lifts and Fortune fells the lucky
and unlucky every day. No prophet on earth
can tell a man his fate. Take Creon:
there was a man to rouse your envy once,
as I see it. He saved the realm from enemies;   1280
taking power, he alone, the lord of the fatherland,
he set us true on course—flourished like a tree
with the noble line of sons he bred and reared...
and now it's lost, all gone.

                    Believe me,
when a man has squandered his true joys,
he's good as dead, I tell you, a living corpse.
Pile up riches in your house, as much as you like—
live like a king with a huge show of pomp,
but if real delight is missing from the lot,
I wouldn't give you a wisp of smoke for it,   1290
not compared with joy.

LEADER.   What now?
What new grief do you bring the house of kings?
MESSENGER. Dead, dead—and the living are guilty of their death!
LEADER. Who's the murderer? Who is dead? Tell us.
MESSENGER. Haemon's gone, his blood spilled by the very hand—
LEADER. His father's or his own?
MESSENGER.   His own...
raging mad with his father for the death—
LEADER.   Oh great seer,
you saw it all, you brought your word to birth!
MESSENGER. Those are the facts. Deal with them as you will.
    As he turns to go, EURYDICE *enters from the palace.*
LEADER. Look, Eurydice. Poor woman, Creon's wife,   1300
so close at hand. By chance perhaps,
unless she's heard the news about her son.
EURYDICE.   My countrymen,
all of you—I caught the sound of your words
as I was leaving to do my part,
to appeal to queen Athena[21] with my prayers.
I was just loosing the bolts, opening the doors,
when a voice filled with sorrow, family sorrow,
struck my ears, and I fell back, terrified,

---

[20]**Cadmus** The legendary founder of Thebes.
[21]**Athena** Goddess of wisdom and protector of Greek cities.

into the women's arms—everything went black.
Tell me the news, again, whatever it is... 1310
sorrow and I are hardly strangers;
I can bear the worst.
MESSENGER.   I—dear lady,
I'll speak as an eye-witness. I was there.
And I won't pass over one word of the truth.
Why should I try to soothe you with a story,
only to prove a liar in a moment?
Truth is always best.
               So,
I escorted your lord, I guided him
to the edge of the plain where the body lay,
Polynices, torn by the dogs and still unmourned. 1320
And saying a prayer to Hecate of the Crossroads,
Pluto[22] too, to hold their anger and be kind,
we washed the dead in a bath of holy water
and plucking some fresh branches, gathering...
what was left of him, we burned them all together
and raised a high mound of native earth, and then
we turned and made for that rocky vault of hers,
the hollow, empty bed of the bride of Death.
And far off, one of us heard a voice,
a long wail rising, echoing 1330
out of that unhallowed wedding-chamber;
he ran to alert the master and Creon pressed on,
closer—the strange, inscrutable cry came sharper,
throbbing around him now, and he let loose
a cry of his own, enough to wrench the heart,
"Oh god, am I the prophet now? going down
the darkest road I've ever gone? My son—
it's *his* dear voice, he greets me! Go, men,
closer, quickly! Go through the gap,
the rocks are dragged back— 1340
right to the tomb's very mouth—and look,
see if it's Haemon's voice I think I hear,
or the gods have robbed me of my senses."

The king was shattered. We took his orders,
went and searched, and there in the deepest,
dark recesses of the tomb we found her...
hanged by the neck in a fine linen noose,
strangled in her veils—and the boy,
his arms flung around her waist,
clinging to her, wailing for his bride, 1350
dead and down below, for his father's crimes

---

[22]**Hecate, Pluto** Gods of the underworld.

and the bed of his marriage blighted by misfortune.
When Creon saw him, he gave a deep sob,
he ran in, shouting, crying out to him,
"Oh my child—what have you done? what seized you,
what insanity? what disaster drove you mad?
Come out, my son! I beg you on my knees!"
But the boy gave him a wild burning glance,
spat in his face, not a word in reply,
he drew his sword—his father rushed out,   1360
running as Haemon lunged and missed!—
and then, doomed, desperate with himself,
suddenly leaning his full weight on the blade,
he buried it in his body, halfway to the hilt.
And still in his senses, pouring his arms around her,
he embraced the girl and breathing hard,
released a quick rush of blood,
bright red on her cheek glistening white.
And there he lies, body enfolding body...
he has won his bride at last, poor boy,   1370
not here but in the houses of the dead.

Creon shows the world that of all the ills
afflicting men the worst is lack of judgment.
    EURYDICE *turns and reenters the palace.*
LEADER. What do you make of that? The lady's gone,
    without a word, good or bad.
MESSENGER.   I'm alarmed too
    but here's my hope—faced with her son's death,
    she finds it unbecoming to mourn in public.
    Inside, under her roof, she'll set her women
    to the task and wail the sorrow of the house.
    She's too discreet. She won't do something rash.   1380
LEADER. I'm not so sure. To me, at least,
    a long heavy silence promises danger,
    just as much as a lot of empty outcries.
MESSENGER. We'll see if she's holding something back,
    hiding some passion in her heart.
    I'm going in. You may be right—who knows?
    Even too much silence has its dangers.
    Exit to the palace. Enter CREON *from the side, escorted by* ATTENDANTS
    carrying HAEMON's *body on a bier.*
LEADER. The king himself! Coming toward us,
       look, holding the boy's head in his hands.
       Clear, damning proof, if it's right to say so—   1390
       proof of his own madness, no one else's,
         no, his own blind wrongs.
CREON.   Ohhh,
    so senseless, so insane...my crimes,
    my stubborn, deadly—

Look at us, the killer, the killed,
father and son, the same blood—the misery!
My plans, my mad fanatic heart,
my son, cut off so young!
Ai, dead, lost to the world,
not through your stupidity, no, my own.

LEADER.   Too late,   1400
   too late, you see what justice means.

CREON.   Oh I've learned
   through blood and tears! Then, it was then,
   when the god came down and struck me—a great weight
   shattering, driving me down that wild savage path,
   ruining, trampling down my joy. Oh the agony!
      the heartbreaking agonies of our lives.
    Enter the MESSENGER *from the palace.*

MESSENGER.   Master,
   what a hoard of grief you have, and you'll have more.
   The grief that lies to hand you've brought yourself—
    Pointing to HAEMON's *body.*
   the rest, in the house, you'll see it all too soon.

CREON. What now? What's worse than this?

MESSENGER.   The queen is dead.   1410
   The mother of this dead boy...mother to the end—
   poor thing, her wounds are fresh.

CREON.   No, no,
   harbor of Death, so choked, so hard to cleanse!—
   why me? why are you killing me?
   Herald of pain, more words, more grief?
   I died once, you kill me again and again!
   What's the report, boy...some news for me?
   My wife dead? O dear god!
   Slaughter heaped on slaughter?
   The doors open; the body of EURYDICE *is brought out on her bier.*

MESSENGER.   See for yourself:
   now they bring her body from the palace.

CREON.   Oh no,   1420
   another, a second loss to break the heart.
   What next, what fate still waits for me?
   I just held my son in my arms and now,
   look, a new corpse rising before my eyes—
      wretched, helpless mother—O my son!

MESSENGER. She stabbed herself at the altar,
   then her eyes went dark, after she'd raised
   a cry for the noble fate of Megareus,[23] the hero
   killed in the first assault, then for Haemon,
   then with her dying breath she called down   1430
   torments on your head—you killed her sons.

---

[23]**Megareus** A son of Creon and Eurydice; he died when Thebes was attacked.

CREON.   Oh the dread,
    I shudder with dread! Why not kill me too?—
    run me through with a good sharp sword?
    Oh god, the misery, anguish—
    I, I'm churning with it, going under.
MESSENGER. Yes, and the dead, the woman lying there,
    piles the guilt of all their deaths on you.
CREON. How did she end her life, what bloody stroke?
MESSENGER. She drove home to the heart with her own hand,
    once she learned her son was dead...that agony.   1440
CREON. And the guilt is all mine—
    can never be fixed on another man,
    no escape for me. I killed you,
    I, god help me, I admit it all!
  To his ATTENDANTS.
    Take me away, quickly, out of sight.
    I don't even exist—I'm no one. Nothing.
LEADER. Good advice, if there's any good in suffering.
    Quickest is best when troubles block the way.
CREON.
  Kneeling in prayer.
    Come, let it come!—that best of fates for me
    that brings the final day, best fate of all.   1450
    Oh quickly, now—
    so I never have to see another sunrise.
LEADER. That will come when it comes;
    we must deal with all that lies before us.
    The future rests with the ones who tend the future.
CREON. That prayer—I poured my heart into that prayer!
LEADER. No more prayers now. For mortal men
    there is no escape from the doom we must endure.
CREON. Take me away, I beg you, out of sight.
    A rash, indiscriminate fool!   1460
    I murdered you, my son, against my will—
    you too, my wife...
            Wailing wreck of a man,
    whom to look to? where to lean for support?
  Desperately turning from HAEMON *to* EURYDICE *on their biers.*
    Whatever I touch goes wrong—once more
    a crushing fate's come down upon my head.
  The MESSENGER *and* ATTENDANTS *lead* CREON *into the palace.*
CHORUS. Wisdom is by far the greatest part of joy,
    and reverence toward the gods must be safeguarded.
    The mighty words of the proud are paid in full
    with mighty blows of fate, and at long last
        those blows will teach us wisdom.   1470
  The old citizens exit to the side.

(ca. 442 B.C.)

PREWRITING

Now that you have read *Antigone* and have some sense of its basic structure, read the play again carefully and write out the answers to the questions below. Your responses will not only help you to sharpen your understanding of dramatic structure; they will also lead you to clarify your reactions to *Antigone's* characters and themes.

Analyzing Dramatic Structure

1. Think about a clash with authority that you have experienced in your own life. What caused the clash? How firmly did you stand your ground in the conflict? What were the consequences of your behavior?

2. What background are we given in the opening scene (lines 1–116)? List the main points of information that this exchange between Antigone and Ismene reveals.

3. What exposition does the Chorus give in lines 117–72?

4. How does Sophocles use the Sentry (lines 249 and following)? Does this character provide more than factual exposition?

5. What do you think the main conflict is? State it as specifically as you can in a single sentence.

6. Identify the protagonist and the antagonist. Is it fair to apply the labels *heroine* and *villain* to them?

7. Where does the climax occur? Identify the scene and describe what happens. Why do you think this is the play's turning point?

8. Does the climax seem to come early in the play? How does Sophocles maintain interest after the turning point? Did you expect such dramatic developments after the climax? Do you think Creon expected them?

9. When does the catastrophe occur? Was this outcome inevitable? Were your feelings about the outcome different the second time you read the play?

10. State what you consider the play's theme to be.

11. A *foil* is a contrasting character who sets off or helps to define another character. How is Ismene a foil to Antigone? Are there any foils to Creon?

12. Why is Eurydice included in the plot? How do you feel about her fate?

Having answered these questions about the structure of *Antigone*, devise a graph or chart that illustrates the pattern of events in the play. Make sure your graph shows the six structural components discussed on page 483.

WRITING

Your understanding of the structure of *Antigone* will enable you to write more easily about the play's arguments. As you watched the conflict develop between Antigone and Creon, you undoubtedly became aware of the opposing values that these two characters represent. As one critic has observed about *Antigone*, "The characters *are* the issues, and the issues the characters."[1] It is now your turn to examine these issues and decide where you stand.

Discovering a Workable Argumentative Thesis

Argument means dispute; it implies that there are opposing sides. Any matter worth arguing will involve at least one "issue"—that is, an essential point in question or disagreement. You need not always take sides, but once you have decided what issues are involved in an argument, you can write an effective paper by taking a stand and explaining why you have chosen one side over the other.

Your approach to *Antigone* will have to take into account the controversial nature of the play's conflict. Review your responses to the prewriting questions about the disagreement and about the antagonist and protagonist. Can you identify an issue that you think is central to the play's meaning? Are there other issues involved in the conflict? Try to get the main issues stated as clearly and specifically as you can before you begin to write. The ideas for writing that follow should help you to work out the important issues of the play.

You can argue an issue in two ways. You can devise a major claim about one side of the question and present reasons and evidence to support your stand. Or you can anticipate the claims of the opposing side and show how the evidence does not support this side, indicating where the fallacies or errors lie in the opposition's reasoning. You will probably want to combine both techniques in writing about *Antigone*.

Whatever your approach, you need to study the evidence and examine the ideas on both sides for flaws in logical thinking. One way to make this examination involves listing the main arguments, pro and con, in two columns on a sheet of paper.

Creon	Antigone
Public interest outweighs private loyalties.	Eternal unwritten laws take precedence.
Polynices made war on his own country.	All the dead deserve honor.

---

[1]Charles Paul Segal, "Sophocles' Praise of Man and the Conflicts of *Antigone*," in *Sophocles: A Collection of Critical Essays*, ed. T. Woodward (Englewood Cliffs, NJ: Prentice-Hall, 1966), 63.

You can make a similar listing of speeches or lines from the play that serve as evidence for the two sides of the argument. For instance, you may want to note such revealing statements by Creon as these:

> [W]hoever places a friend
> above the good of his own country, he is nothing. (203–04)

> [T]hat man
> the city places in authority, his orders
> must be obeyed, large and small,
> right and wrong. (748–51)

Compare these lists and see which side has the stronger arguments and the greater amount of evidence. You can then decide which side you are going to support; you also have a convenient listing of specific ideas and quotations to use in developing your essay.

Quoting from a Play

When writing a paper on a single play, instead of citing page numbers, you need to give act and scene numbers in parentheses at the end of the quoted material; for verse plays give act, scene, and line numbers. Because *Antigone* is not divided into acts and scenes, give the line numbers for the quotations you use. Long quotations (more than three lines) should be indented with *no* quotation marks. Also, indicate the speaker when quoting a passage in which more than one character speaks. Here are some samples:

It is up to Ismene, then, to point out the obvious: "Remember we are women, / we're not born to contend with men" (74–75).

Only two lines are quoted, separated with a slash and enclosed in quotation marks.

During her defense, Antigone declares her defiance:

> This is nothing.
> And if my present actions strike you as foolish,
> let's just say I've been accused of folly
> by a fool. (522–25)

A long quotation is indented with no quotation marks.

For plays *not* written in verse, give act and scene or page numbers in parentheses at the end of the quoted material.

IDEAS FOR WRITING

Ideas for Responsive Writing

1. Do you see yourself as approving of or opposing the rules and norms of the society you live in? How do you support, change, or disobey these rules and norms? Write about one rule or group of related rules (for example, sex roles or parent–child relationships) that you accept or reject.

2. In modern society, what might Creon and Antigone disagree about? Write an essay explaining where the two characters would probably stand on one of today's issues.

Ideas for Critical Writing

1. Is Creon a politician concerned with imposing and maintaining order? Is Antigone an anarchist whose action will destroy that order? Or is she a private citizen determined to follow the dictates of her personal beliefs? Write an essay that interprets *Antigone* as a struggle between public policy and individual conscience, supporting the side that you think is right.

2. CRITICAL APPROACHES: Read about gender-focused approaches to interpreting literature (pages 750–51). Can you explain the conflict between Antigone and Creon as a psychological clash between a woman and a man? Write an essay that develops a claim about the male–female opposition in the play. You may want to work Ismene, Haemon, and Eurydice into your scheme of opposing values.

Ideas for Researched Writing

1. A. R. Gurney wrote *Another Antigone* (1988), an updated version of *Antigone* in which a classics professor and a headstrong college student clash over a term paper on Sophocles. Read this modern *Antigone*, and write an essay comparing and contrasting it to the original. Some topics to consider: What problems did the modern writer encounter in changing the setting? Are the same themes developed in both versions? Are the conflicts resolved in similar ways? Compare and contrast specific scenes. You may want to read reviews of productions of *Another Antigone* to see how critics and audiences respond to it.

2. Other transformations of *Antigone* include two plays with World War II settings: Jean Anouilh's 1942 version, also called *Antigone*, which was first produced in Paris in 1944 during the Nazi occupation of France; and Chiori Miyagawa's *Antigone's Red*, which is set in a Japanese-American internment camp in the 1940s. Find out more about these versions, and write an essay in which you evaluate how effectively the original themes and conflicts are used to comment on modern-day issues. Or write a comparison to the original using the approach previously described.

REWRITING

You will want to be certain that your arguments about *Antigone* are perfectly clear. Take some time to ensure that what you have written cannot be misunderstood. If you can, coax a friend or classmate into reading your first draft; ask your reader to point out sentences that do not make sense or that are unclear.

Avoiding Unclear Language

Multisyllabic words and long, involved sentences may dazzle your readers, but they can also hinder clear communication. Your first goal in writing should be to convey ideas and information. Trying to impress your readers with big words and fancy phrases may lead to one or more forms of unclear expression.

1. *Engfish:* Writing specialist Ken Macrorie uses this term to call attention to artificial language that does not represent a writer's own experience and education. Engfish is phony, pretentious, stuffy, and often impossible to decode. Writers use Engfish, it seems, when they are unsure of which attitude to take toward their subject and their audience. The student who wrote

   Antigone's unacceptable posture toward the designated governmental powers inevitably entailed the termination of her existence,

   no doubt thought that this inflated diction was appropriate for a serious paper on a classical play. But most readers probably would prefer to see that sentence revised to read more clearly, like this one:

   Antigone's defiance led to her death.

   In the long run, clarity will impress your readers more than Engfish ever can.

2. *Jargon:* This term applies to the specialized language used by a particular group of people. Computer operators, sociologists, teenagers, architects, hockey players, mobsters—all sorts of interest groups and professions—employ words and terms that relate only to their particular activities. The problem with jargon is that outsiders do not understand it. Writing about a "love game" or the "ad court" will be all right for an audience of tennis buffs, but you will have to change your language for more general readers. Jargon may not come up in your essay about *Antigone*, but it can creep in from other sources. For instance, the student who wrote

Antigone's behavior is marked by regressive reaction formation toward authoritarian figures

was apparently influenced by the jargon of her psychology class. Unless you are writing for an audience of fellow psychoanalysts, you would do better to say the following:

Antigone sometimes acted like a disobedient daughter.

3. *Abstract words:* Abstract terms and general expressions do not automatically make your writing intellectual and impressive. Although it is true that writing an argumentative essay requires using abstract ideas, your paper will be more persuasive if it is factual, concrete, and clear. Abstractions tend to be hazy and difficult to define. Words like *duty, anarchy, patriotism,* and *truth* have different meanings to different people. When writing about an abstract concept, make certain that you have a definite meaning in your own mind. If, for instance, you write that

Antigone is a woman of honor

it is a good idea to check the dictionary to see if your understanding of the word *honor* coincides with a standard definition. *The American Heritage Dictionary* gives thirteen entries for *honor.* Which one does the above sentence convey? Would "a woman's chastity" be accurate in this context? It might be more meaningful to say

Antigone is a woman of principle and integrity

although those words are also abstract. Try, if possible, to specify the meaning you want when using an abstract term.

Above all, Creon is a master politician—a man of ambition intent on holding his power.

Sample Student Paper

In the following paper, Laurie Dahlberg, a student at Illinois State University, argues that the chief conflict in *Antigone* involves a power struggle between male and female. Notice how she uses and documents quoted material from the play to support her claims.

Sample Student Paper

Laurie Dahlberg

Professor Day

English 102

April 2, 2005

"Never Be Rated Inferior to a Woman":

Gender Conflict in *Antigone*

Antigone is a drama built around two basic conflicts. Beneath the more obvious conflict of the individual versus the state lies a struggle of male against female. The protagonist, Antigone, becomes a criminal by choice but a feminist by chance. The antagonist, Creon, is fighting to retain control over Antigone, not only as king over subject but also as man over woman.

Antigone knows that she has violated the king's order not to bury her brother Polynices, but she seems not to notice that she has also violated the social code by stepping outside the boundaries of acceptable feminine behavior. Her act of defiance is courageous, self-reliant, and completely contrary to the obedience expected of women in her society. She fearlessly assures her sister, Ismene, that Creon "has no right to keep me from my own" (59). It is up to Ismene, then, to point out the obvious: "Remember we are women, / we're not born to contend with men" (74–75). A perfect foil for Antigone, Ismene epitomizes the good Theban woman—she is deferential, passive, and timid. Though she loves Antigone dearly, Ismene is still bound to her male masters and cannot follow her sister: "we're underlings, ruled by much stronger hands," she says. "I must obey / the ones who stand in power" (76, 79–80). Eventually, Ismene is rewarded for her passivity when Creon spares her life.

When Antigone is arrested, King Creon expresses shock that a woman in his court has committed the crime. But his disbelief soon turns to perverse pleasure at the opportunity to punish this woman for her audacity. Creon's threatening speeches to Antigone also bring out his contempt for women:

> Go down below and love,
> if love you must—love the dead!
>   While I'm alive,
> no woman is going to lord it over
>   me. (591–93)

Antigone, however, rises above the pettiness of sexual rivalry by responding only to the conflict between king and subject. Unlike Creon, Antigone acts out of a heartfelt moral obligation, proclaiming that she is "Not ashamed for a moment, / not to honor my brother, my own flesh and blood" (572–73). As Antigone calmly and eloquently argues the righteousness of her action instead of quivering with fear under Creon's threats, the king's feeling of triumph slowly turns to rage. During her defense, Antigone declares her defiance:

>   This is nothing.
> And if my present actions strike you
>   as foolish,
> let's just say I've been accused of
>   folly
> by a fool. (522–25)

To which Creon angrily replies:

> This girl was an old hand at
>   insolence

when she overrode the edicts we made

    public.

But once she'd done it—the

    insolence,

twice over—to glory in it,

    laughing,

mocking us to our face with what

    she'd done.

I'm not the man, not now: she is the

    man

if this victory goes to her and she

    goes free. (536–42)

Though Antigone's illegal act is punishable by death, it is the fact that a mere woman has defied him that enrages Creon. Her death alone will not satisfy him. He needs to master her willfulness and make her regret her arrogance. Instead of killing her, he entombs her, where she will die slowly. This method of execution, Creon says, will teach the woman a lesson:

There let her pray to the one god she

    worships:

Death—who knows?—may just reprieve

    her from death.

Or she may learn at last, better

    late than never,

what a waste of breath it is to

    worship Death. (875–78)

The key to Creon's personality is found in his comment to Haemon when he is explaining why he (the king) has sentenced his son's bride-to-be to death:

we must defend the men who live by

    law,

never let some woman triumph over us.

Better to fall from power, if we

    must,

at the hands of a man—never be

    rated

inferior to a woman, never. (757–61)

Creon refuses to listen to Haemon's reasoning, and the young man, disgusted by his father's cruelty, rejects him. This rejection makes the king even more bitter. Creon's pride has made him blind to his mistake.

    Throughout the course of the play, Creon changes from a strict but competent leader to a wildly insecure man, plagued by imaginary enemies. He has come to suspect that anyone who disagrees with him is involved in a plot against him, as these words to Ismene reveal:

                   You—

in my house, you viper, slinking

    undetected,

sucking my life-blood! I never knew

I was breeding twin disasters, the

    two of you

rising up against my throne. (597–601)

Creon has mistaken Antigone's act of piety for a wild attempt by a power-hungry woman to undermine his rule. Out of his own fear of being beaten by a woman, Creon begins a chain of events which finally destroys him, fulfilling Antigone's prediction:

But if these men are wrong, let them

    suffer

nothing worse than they mete out to

    me—

these masters of injustice! (1019–21)

Work Cited

Sophocles. *Antigone*. Trans. Robert Fagles. *Literature
    and the Writing Process*. Ed. Elizabeth McMahan,
    Susan X Day, and Robert Funk. 7th ed. Upper
    Saddle River: Prentice, 2005. 592–627. Print.

Questions for Discussion

1. Do you think this essay overemphasizes the gender issue in analyzing the conflict between Creon and Antigone? Has the author slighted or ignored more important issues?
2. Can you find any additional evidence that the author of the essay overlooked or chose not to use? Would the case be strengthened by including Eurydice in the analysis?
3. The author says that Antigone rises above sexual rivalry in her defiant behavior. Is this view entirely true? Can you find any evidence to suggest that Antigone is also caught up in the power struggle between male and female?
4. In carrying out her approach, the author of the essay analyzes Creon more than Antigone. Why is that? Is this strategy productive? Do you agree with the conclusion about Creon's character development?

18

Writing About Character

Pondering people's characters comes quite naturally and easily. You will remember that we began our approach to literature with the study of character in the short story. Drama also provides us with carefully drawn examples of human speech and behavior. Whether the presentation is realistic or not, the characters are at the heart of the play.

What Is the Modern Hero?

In everyday life, we use the word *heroic* to describe people who save others' lives while risking their own, acts of great self-sacrifice or self-control, feats that we hold in awe. Before you read on, think of the last time you remember calling something heroic or referring to someone as a hero. Note the situation, and think about what you meant by the word. We often use it lightly—the person who supplies a much needed extension cord or an emergency ten-dollar loan may temporarily be a hero. But drama practically forces us into deeper consideration of what a hero is.

The Classical Tragic Hero

In the fourth century B.C., Aristotle described the classic concept of the tragic hero. He wrote that the hero must be someone "who is highly renowned and prosperous." Classical tragedy involves the inevitable destruction of a noble person by means of a character flaw, usually a disproportionate measure of a specific human attribute such as pride or jealousy or indecision. The Aristotelian definition implies this basic premise: there is a natural, right ordering and proportion of traits within the human being that, if violated, produces calamity. Many critics cite Antigone's "difficult willfulness" as the explanation of her fate. Charles Segal claims that "she can assert what she is only by staking her entire being, her life. It is by this extreme defense of her beliefs that she rises to heroic and deeply tragic stature."[1]

---

[1]Charles Paul Segal, "Sophocles' Praise of Man and the Conflicts of *Antigone*," in *Sophocles: A Collection of Critical Essays*, ed. T. Woodward (Englewood Cliffs, NJ: Prentice-Hall, 1966), 65.

531

The Modern Tragic Hero

In 1949, the famous playwright Arthur Miller described what he considered a new kind of hero. In an article titled "Tragedy and the Common Man" (*New York Times*, 27 Feb. 1949, 3.1.3.), he challenged Aristotle's idea that the hero must be a "highly renowned and prosperous" figure who has a tragic flaw. In contrast to a disorder exclusively within the personal traits of the hero, Miller's idea of the modern hero emphasizes a clash between the character and the environment, especially the social environment. He says that each person has a chosen image of self and position and that tragedy results when the character's environment denies the fulfillment of this self-concept. The hero no longer must be born into the nobility but gains stature in the action of pitting self against cosmos. The tragedy is "the disaster inherent in being torn away from our chosen image of what and who we are in this world." Feelings of displacement and indignity, then, are the driving forces for Miller's modern tragic hero. In his own play *Death of a Salesman*, the character Willy Loman imagines himself as a well-liked, successful, worldly businessman. Tragically, he is really an object of ridicule and contempt, always on the edge of poverty. Such conflicts between ideal self-image and reality occur over and over in the modern play you are about to read.

Looking at the Modern Hero

As you read for pleasure *Fences* by August Wilson, take special note of the characters. Who is the hero? the heroine?—or are there none? To which characters do you respond positively? Are there any to whom you respond negatively?

August Wilson   1945–2005

August Wilson earned fame writing a cycle of ten plays, each set during a decade from 1900 to 1990 in his boyhood home, the economically depressed neighborhood of The Hill in Pittsburgh. He said that his plays offer White Americans a different view of Blacks: "For instance, in *Fences* they see a garbageman, a person they don't really look at, although they see a garbageman every day. By looking at Troy's life, white people find out that the content of this black garbageman's life is affected by the same things—love, honor, beauty, betrayal, duty. Recognizing that these things are as much part of his life as theirs can affect how they think about and deal with black people in their lives." Wilson's plays were so successful and admired on the New York stage that when he died in 2005, Broadway's Virginia Theater was renamed the August Wilson Theater.

Fences

for Lloyd Richards,
who adds to whatever he touches

When the sins of our fathers visit us
We do not have to play host.
We can banish them with forgiveness
As God, in His Largeness and Laws.

—August Wilson

LIST OF CHARACTERS

TROY MAXSON

JIM BONO, *Troy's friend*

ROSE, *Troy's wife*

LYONS, *Troy's oldest son by previous marriage*

GABRIEL, *Troy's brother*

CORY, *Troy and Rose's son*

RAYNELL, *Troy's daughter*

SETTING

The setting is the yard which fronts the only entrance to the Maxson household, an ancient two-story brick house set back off a small alley in a big-city neighborhood. The entrance to the house is gained by two or three steps leading to a wooden porch badly in need of paint.

A relatively recent addition to the house and running its full width, the porch lacks congruence. It is a sturdy porch with a flat roof. One or two chairs of dubious value sit at one end where the kitchen window opens onto the porch. An old-fashioned icebox stands silent guard at the opposite end.

The yard is a small dirt yard, partially fenced, except for the last scene, with a wooden saw horse, a pile of lumber, and other fence-building equipment set off to the side. Opposite is a tree from which hangs a ball made of rags. A baseball bat leans against the tree. Two oil drums serve as garbage receptacles and sit near the house at right to complete the setting.

THE PLAY

Near the turn of the century, the destitute of Europe sprang on the city with tenacious claws and an honest and solid dream. The city devoured them. They swelled its belly until it burst into a thousand furnaces and sewing machines, a thousand butcher shops and bakers' ovens, a thousand churches and hospitals and funeral parlors and money-lenders. The city grew. It nourished itself and offered each man a partnership limited only by his talent, his guile and his willingness and capacity for hard work. For the immigrants of Europe, a dream dared and won true.

The descendants of African slaves were offered no such welcome or participation. They came from places called the Carolinas and the Virginias, Georgia, Alabama, Mississippi, and Tennessee. They came strong, eager, searching. The city rejected them and they fled and settled along the riverbanks and under bridges in shallow, ramshackle houses made of sticks and tarpaper. They collected rags and wood. They sold the use of their muscles and their bodies. They cleaned houses and washed clothes, they shined shoes, and in quiet desperation and vengeful pride, they stole, and lived in pursuit of their own dream. That they could breathe free, finally, and stand to meet life with the force of dignity and whatever eloquence the heart could call upon.

By 1957, the hard-won victories of the European immigrants had solidified the industrial might of America. War had been confronted and won with new energies that used loyalty and patriotism as its fuel. Life was rich, full, and flourishing. The Milwaukee Braves won the World Series, and the hot winds of change that would make the sixties a turbulent, racing, dangerous, and provocative decade had not yet begun to blow full.

ACT 1

SCENE 1

It is 1957. TROY *and* BONO *enter the yard, engaged in conversation.* TROY *is fifty- three years old, a large man with thick, heavy hands; it is this largeness that he strives to fill out and make an accommodation with. Together with his blackness, his largeness informs his sensibilities and the choices he has made in his life.*

Of the two men, BONO *is obviously the follower. His commitment to their friendship of thirty-odd years is rooted in his admiration of* TROY'S *honesty, capacity for hard work, and his strength, which* BONO *seeks to emulate.*

It is Friday night, payday, and the one night of the week the two men engage in a ritual of talk and drink. TROY *is usually the most talkative and at times he can be crude and almost vulgar, though he is capable of rising to profound heights of expression. The men carry lunch buckets and wear or carry burlap aprons and are dressed in clothes suitable to their jobs as garbage collectors.*

BONO. Troy, you ought to stop that lying!

TROY. I ain't lying! The nigger had a watermelon this big. [*He indicates with his hands.*] Talking about…"What watermelon, Mr. Rand?" I liked to fell out! "What watermelon, Mr. Rand?"…And it sitting there big as life.

BONO. What did Mr. Rand say?

TROY. Ain't said nothing. Figure if the nigger too dumb to know he carrying a watermelon, he wasn't gonna get much sense out of him. Trying to hide that great big old watermelon under his coat. Afraid to let the white man see him carry it home.

BONO. I'm like you…I ain't got no time for them kind of people.

TROY. Now what he look like getting mad cause he see the man from the union talking to Mr. Rand?

BONO. He come to me talking about…"Maxson gonna get us fired." I told him to get away from me with that. He walked away from me calling you a troublemaker. What Mr. Rand say?

TROY. Ain't said nothing. He told me to go down the Commissioner's office next Friday. They called me down there to see them.

BONO. Well, as long as you got your complaint filed, they can't fire you. That's what one of them white fellows tell me.

TROY. I ain't worried about them firing me. They gonna fire me cause I asked a question? That's all I did. I went to Mr. Rand and asked him, "Why? Why you got the white mens driving and the colored lifting?" Told him, "What's the matter, don't I count? You think only white fellows got sense enough to drive a truck. That ain't no paper job! Hell, anybody can drive a truck. How come you got all whites driving and the colored lifting?" He told me "take it to the union." Well, hell, that's what I done! Now they wanna come up with this pack of lies.

BONO. I told Brownie if the man come and ask him any questions...just tell the truth! It ain't nothing but something they done trumped up on you cause you filed a complaint on them.

TROY. Brownie don't understand nothing. All I want them to do is change the job description. Give everybody a chance to drive the truck. Brownie can't see that. He ain't got that much sense.

BONO. How you figure he be making out with that gal be up at Taylor's all the time...that Alberta gal?

TROY. Same as you and me. Getting just as much as we is. Which is to say nothing.

BONO. It is, huh? I figure you doing a little better than me...and I ain't saying what I'm doing.

TROY. Aw, nigger, look here...I know you. If you had got anywhere near that gal, twenty minutes later you be looking to tell somebody. And the first one you gonna tell...that you gonna want to brag to...is me.

BONO. I ain't saying that, I see where you be eyeing her.

TROY. I eye all the women. I don't miss nothing. Don't never let nobody tell you Troy Maxson don't eye the women.

BONO. You been doing more than eyeing her. You done bought her a drink or two.

TROY. Hell yeah, I bought her a drink! What that mean? I bought you one, too. What that mean cause I buy her a drink? I'm just being polite.

BONO. It's all right to buy her one drink. That's what you call being polite. But when you wanna be buying two or three...that's what you call eyeing her.

TROY. Look here, as long as you known me...you ever known me to chase after women?

BONO. Hell yeah! Long as I done known you. You forgetting I knew you when.

TROY. Naw, I'm talking about since I been married to Rose?

BONO. Oh, not since you been married to Rose. Now, that's the truth, there, I can say that.

TROY. All right then! Case closed.

BONO. I see you be walking up around Alberta's house. You supposed to be at Taylors' and you be walking up around there.

TROY. What you watching where I'm walking for? I ain't watching after you.

BONO. I seen you walking around there more than once.

TROY. Hell, you liable to see me walking anywhere! That don't mean nothing cause you see me walking around there.

BONO. Where she come from anyway? She just kinda showed up one day.

TROY. Tallahassee. You can look at her and tell she one of them Florida gals. They got some big healthy women down there. Grow them right up out the ground. Got a little bit of Indian in her. Most of them niggers down in Florida got some Indian in them.

BONO. I don't know about that Indian part. But she damn sure big and healthy. Women wear some big stockings. Got them great big old legs and hips as wide as the Mississippi River.

TROY. Legs don't mean nothing. You don't do nothing but push them out of the way. But them hips cushion the ride!

BONO. Troy, you ain't got no sense.

TROY. It's the truth! Like you riding on Goodyears!

ROSE *enters from the house. She is ten years younger than* TROY, *her devotion to him stems from her recognition of the possibilities of her life without him: a succession of abusive men and their babies, a life of partying and running the streets, the Church, or aloneness with its attendant pain and frustration. She recognizes* TROY'S *spirit as a fine and illuminating one and she either ignores or forgives his faults, only some of which she recognizes. Though she doesn't drink, her presence is an integral part of the Friday night rituals. She alternates between the porch and the kitchen, where supper preparations are under way.*

ROSE. What you all out here getting into?

TROY. What you worried about what we getting into for? This is men talk, woman.

ROSE. What I care what you all talking about? Bono, you gonna stay for supper?

BONO. No, I thank you, Rose. But Lucille say she cooking up a pot of pigfeet.

TROY. Pigfeet! Hell, I'm going home with you! Might even stay the night if you got some pigfeet. You got something in there to top them pigfeet, Rose?

ROSE. I'm cooking up some chicken. I got some chicken and collard greens.

TROY. Well, go on back in the house and let me and Bono finish what we was talking about. This is men talk. I got some talk for you later. You know what kind of talk I mean. You go on and powder it up.

ROSE. Troy Maxson, don't you start that now!

TROY [*puts his arm around her*]. Aw, woman...come here. Look here. Bono...when I met this woman...I got out that place, say, "Hitch up my pony, saddle up my mare...there's a woman out there for me somewhere. I looked here. Looked there. Saw Rose and latched on to her." I latched on to her and told her—I'm gonna tell you the truth—I told her, "Baby, I don't wanna marry, I just wanna be your man." Rose told me...tell him what you told me, Rose.

ROSE. I told him if he wasn't the marrying kind, then move out the way so the marrying kind could find me.

TROY. That's what she told me. "Nigger, you in my way. You blocking the view! Move out the way so I can find me a husband." I thought it over two or three days. Come back—

ROSE. Ain't no two or three days nothing. You was back the same night.

TROY. Come back, told her..."Okay, baby...but I'm gonna buy me a banty rooster and put him out there in the backyard...and when he see a stranger come, he'll flap his wings and crow...." Look here, Bono, I could watch the front door by myself...it was that back door I was worried about.

ROSE. Troy, you ought not talk like that. Troy ain't doing nothing but telling a lie.

TROY. Only thing is...when we first got married...forget the rooster...we ain't had no yard!

BONO. I hear you tell it. Me and Lucille was staying down there on Logan Street. Had two rooms with the outhouse in the back. I ain't mind the outhouse none. But when that goddamn wind blow through there in the winter...that's what I'm talking about! To this day I wonder why in the hell I ever stayed down there for six long years. But see, I didn't know I could do no better. I thought only white folks had inside toilets and things.

ROSE. There's a lot of people don't know they can do no better than they doing now. That's just something you got to learn. A lot of folks still shop at Bella's.

TROY. Ain't nothing wrong with shopping at Bella's. She got fresh food.

ROSE. I ain't said nothing about if she got fresh food. I'm talking about what she charge. She charge ten cents more than the A&P.

TROY. The A&P ain't never done nothing for me. I spends my money where I'm treated right. I go down to Bella, say, "I need a loaf of bread, I'll pay you Friday." She give it to me. What sense that make when I got money to go and spend it somewhere else and ignore the person who done right by me? That ain't in the Bible.

ROSE. We ain't talking about what's in the Bible. What sense it make to shop there when she overcharge?

TROY. You shop where you want to. I'll do my shopping where the people been good to me.

ROSE. Well, I don't think it's right for her to overcharge. That's all I was saying.

BONO. Look here...I got to get on. Lucille going be raising all kind of hell.

TROY. Where you going, nigger? We ain't finished this pint. Come here, finish this pint.

BONO. Well, hell, I am...if you ever turn the bottle loose.

TROY [*hands him the bottle*]. The only thing I say about the A&P is I'm glad Cory got that job down there. Help him take care of his school clothes and things. Gabe done moved out and things getting tight around here. He got that job....He can start to look out for himself.

ROSE. Cory done went and got recruited by a college football team.

TROY. I told that boy about that football stuff. The white man ain't gonna let him get nowhere with that football. I told him when he first come to me with it. Now you come telling me he done went and got more tied up in it. He ought to go and get recruited in how to fix cars or something where he can make a living.

ROSE. He ain't talking about making no living playing football. It's just something the boys in school do. They gonna send a recruiter by to talk to you. He'll tell you he ain't talking about making no living playing football. It's a honor to be recruited.

TROY. It ain't gonna get him nowhere. Bono'll tell you that.

BONO. If he be like you in the sports...he's gonna be all right. Ain't but two men ever played baseball as good as you. That's Babe Ruth and Josh Gibson. Them's the only two men ever hit more home runs than you.

TROY. What it ever get me? Ain't got a pot to piss in or a window to throw it out of.

ROSE. Times have changed since you was playing baseball, Troy. That was before the war. Times have changed a lot since then.

TROY. How in hell they done changed?

ROSE. They got lots of colored boys playing ball now. Baseball and football.

BONO. You right about that, Rose. Times have changed, Troy. You just come along too early.

TROY. There ought not never have been no time called too early! Now you take that fellow...What's that fellow they had playing right field for the Yankees back then? You know who I'm talking about, Bono. Used to play right field for the Yankees.

ROSE. Selkirk?

TROY. Selkirk! That's it! Man batting .269, understand? .269. What kind of sense that make? I was hitting .432 with thirty-seven home runs! Man batting .269 and playing right field for the Yankees! I saw Josh Gibson's daughter yesterday. She walking around with raggedy shoes on her feet. Now I bet you Selkirk's daughter ain't walking around with raggedy shoes on the feet! I bet you that!

ROSE. They got a lot of colored baseball players now. Jackie Robinson was the first. Folks had to wait for Jackie Robinson.

TROY. I done seen a hundred niggers play baseball better than Jackie Robinson. Hell, I know some teams Jackie Robinson couldn't even make! What you talking about Jackie Robinson. Jackie Robinson wasn't nobody. I'm talking about if you could play ball then they ought to have let you play. Don't care what color you were. Come telling me I come along too early. If you could play...then they ought to have let you play.

> TROY *takes a long drink from the bottle.*

ROSE. You gonna drink yourself to death. You don't need to be drinking like that.

TROY. Death ain't nothing. I done seen him. Done wrassled with him. You can't tell me nothing about death. Death ain't nothing but a fastball on the outside corner. And you know what I'll do to that! Lookee here, Bono...am I lying? You get one of them fastballs, about waist high, over the outside corner of the plate where you can get the meat of the bat on it...and good god! You can kiss it goodbye. Now, am I lying?

BONO. Naw, you telling the truth there. I seen you do it.

TROY. If I'm lying...that 450 feet worth of lying! [*Pause.*] That's all death is to me. A fastball on the outside corner.

ROSE. I don't know why you want to get on talking about death.

TROY. Ain't nothing wrong with talking about death. That's part of life. Everybody gonna die. You gonna die, I'm gonna die. Bono's gonna die. Hell, we all gonna die.

ROSE. But you ain't got to talk about it. I don't like to talk about it.

TROY. You the one brought it up. Me and Bono was talking about baseball...you tell me I'm gonna drink myself to death. Ain't that right, Bono? You know I don't drink this but one night out of the week. That's Friday night. I'm gonna drink just enough to where I can handle it. Then I cuts it loose. I leave it alone. So don't you worry about me drinking myself to death. 'Cause I ain't worried about Death. I done seen him. I done wrestled with him.

Look here, Bono...I looked up one day and Death was marching straight at me. Like Soldiers on Parade! The Army of Death was marching straight at me. The middle of July, 1941. It got real cold just like it be winter. It seem like Death himself reached out and touched me on the shoulder. He touched me just like I touch you. I got cold as ice and Death standing there grinning at me.

ROSE. Troy, why don't you hush that talk.

TROY. I say...what you want, Mr. Death? You be wanting me? You done brought your army to be getting me? I looked him dead in the eye. I wasn't fearing nothing. I was ready to tangle. Just like I'm ready to tangle now. The Bible say be ever vigilant. That's why I don't get but so drunk. I got to keep watch.

ROSE. Troy was right down there in Mercy Hospital. You remember he had pneumonia? Laying there with a fever talking plumb out of his head.

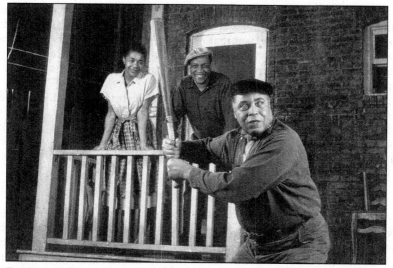

Troy (James Earl Jones) stands ready to take a swing at Death while Rose (Mary Alice) and Bono (Ray Aranha) look on. Photo from the original Broadway production of *Fences*.

TROY. Death standing there staring at me…carrying that sickle in his hand. Finally he say, "You want bound over for another year?" See, just like that…"You want bound over for another year?" I told him, "Bound over hell! Let's settle this now!"

It seem like he kinda fell back when I said that, and all the cold went out of me. I reached down and grabbed that sickle and threw it just as far as I could throw it…and me and him commenced to wrestling.

We wrestled for three days and three nights. I can't say where I found the strength from. Everytime it seemed like he was gonna get the best of me, I'd reach way down deep inside myself and find the strength to do him one better.

ROSE. Everytime Troy tell that story he find different ways to tell it. Different things to make up about it.

TROY. I ain't making up nothing. I'm telling you the facts of what happened. I wrestled with Death for three days and three nights and I'm standing here to tell you about it. [*Pause.*] All right. At the end of the third night we done weakened each other to where we can't hardly move. Death stood up, throwed on his robe…had him a white robe with a hood on it. He throwed on that robe and went off to look for his sickle. Say, "I'll be back." Just like that. "I'll be back." I told him, say, "Yeah, but…you gonna have to find me!" I wasn't no fool. I wasn't going looking for him. Death ain't nothing to play with. And I know he's gonna get me. I know I got to join his army…his camp followers. But as long as I keep my strength and see him coming…as long as I keep up my vigilance…he's gonna have to fight to get me. I ain't going easy.

BONO. Well, look here, since you got to keep up your vigilance…let me have the bottle.

TROY. Aw hell, I shouldn't have told you that part. I should have left out that part.

ROSE. Troy be talking that stuff and half the time don't even know what he be talking about.

TROY. Bono know me better than that.

BONO. That's right. I know you. I know you got some Uncle Remus in your blood. You got more stories than the devil got sinners.

TROY. Aw hell, I done seen him too! Done talked with the devil.

ROSE. Troy, don't nobody wanna be hearing all that stuff.

> LYONS *enters the yard from the street. Thirty-four years old,* TROY'S *son by a previous marriage, he sports a neatly trimmed goatee, sport coat, white shirt, tieless and buttoned at the collar. Though he fancies himself a musician, he is more caught up in the rituals and "idea" of being a musician than in the actual practice of the music. He has come to borrow money from* TROY, *and while he knows he will be successful, he is uncertain as to what extent his lifestyle will be held up to scrutiny and ridicule.*

LYONS. Hey, Pop.

TROY. What you come "Hey, Popping" me for?

LYONS. How you doing, Rose? [*He kisses her.*] Mr. Bono. How you doing?

BONO. Hey, Lyons...how you been?

TROY. He must have been doing all right. I ain't seen him around here last week.

ROSE. Troy, leave your boy alone. He come by to see you and you wanna start all that nonsense.

TROY. I ain't bothering Lyons. [*Offers him the bottle.*] Here...get you a drink. We got an understanding. I know why he come by to see me and he know I know.

LYONS. Come on, Pop...I just stopped by to say hi...see how you was doing.

TROY. You ain't stopped by yesterday.

ROSE. You gonna stay for supper, Lyons? I got some chicken cooking in the oven.

LYONS. No, Rose...thanks. I was just in the neighborhood and thought I'd stop by for a minute.

TROY. You was in the neighborhood all right, nigger. You telling the truth there. You was in the neighborhood 'cause it's my payday.

LYONS. Well, hell, since you mentioned it...let me have ten dollars.

TROY. I'll be damned! I'll die and go to hell and play blackjack with the devil before I give you ten dollars.

BONO. That's what I wanna know about...that devil you done seen.

LYONS. What...Pop done seen the devil? You too much, Pops.

TROY. Yeah, I done seen him. Talked to him too!

ROSE. You ain't seen no devil. I done told you that man ain't had nothing to do with the devil. Anything you can't understand, you want to call it the devil.

TROY. Look here, Bono...I went down to see Hertzberger about some furniture. Got three rooms for two-ninety-eight. That what it say on the radio. "Three rooms...two-ninety-eight." Even made up a little song about it. Go down there...man tell me I can't get no credit. I'm working every day and can't get no credit. What to do? I got an empty house with some raggedy furniture in it. Cory ain't got no bed. He's sleeping on a pile of rags on the floor. Working every day and can't get no credit. Come back here—Rose'll tell you—madder than hell. Sit down...try to figure what I'm gonna do. Come a knock on the door. Ain't been living here but three days. Who know I'm here? Open the door...devil standing there bigger than life. White fellow...got on good clothes and everything. Standing there with a clipboard in his hand. I ain't had to say nothing. First words come out of his mouth was…"I understand you need some furniture and can't get no credit." I liked to fell over. He say, "I'll give you all the credit you want, but you got to pay the interest on it." I told him, "Give me three rooms worth and charge whatever you want." Next day a truck pulled up here and two men unloaded them three rooms. Man what drove the truck give me a book. Say send ten dollars, first of every month to the address in the book and every thing will be all right. Say if I miss a payment the devil was coming back and it'll be hell to pay. That was fifteen years ago. To this day…the first of the month I send my ten dollars, Rose'll tell you.

ROSE. Troy lying.

TROY. I ain't never seen that man since. Now you tell me who else that could have been but the devil? I ain't sold my soul or nothing like that, you understand. Naw, I wouldn't have truck with the devil about nothing like that. I got my furniture and pays my ten dollars the first of the month just like clockwork.

BONO. How long you say you been paying this ten dollars a month?

TROY. Fifteen years!

BONO. Hell, ain't you finished paying for it yet? How much the man done charged you?

TROY. Ah hell, I done paid for it. I done paid for it ten times over! The fact is I'm scared to stop paying it.

ROSE. Troy lying. We got that furniture from Mr. Glickman. He ain't paying no ten dollars a month to nobody.

TROY. Aw hell, woman. Bono know I ain't that big a fool.

LYONS. I was just getting ready to say…I know where there's a bridge for sale.

TROY. Look here, I'll tell you this…it don't matter to me if he was the devil. It don't matter if the devil give credit. Somebody has got to give it.

ROSE. It ought to matter. You going around talking about having truck with the devil…God's the one you gonna have to answer to. He's the one gonna be at the Judgment.

LYONS. Yeah, well, look here, Pop…Let me have that ten dollars. I'll give it back to you. Bonnie got a job working at the hospital.

TROY. What I tell you, Bono? The only time I see this nigger is when he wants something. That's the only time I see him.

LYONS. Come on, Pop, Mr. Bono don't want to hear all that. Let me have the ten dollars. I told you Bonnie working.

TROY. What that mean to me? "Bonnie working." I don't care if she working. Go ask her for the ten dollars if she working. Talking about "Bonnie working." Why ain't you working?

LYONS. Aw, Pop, you know I can't find no decent job. Where am I gonna get a job at? You know I can't get no job.

TROY. I told you I know some people down there. I can get you on the rubbish if you want to work. I told you that the last time you came by here asking me for something.

LYONS. Naw, Pop…thanks. That ain't for me. I don't wanna be carrying nobody's rubbish. I don't wanna be punching nobody's time clock.

TROY. What's the matter, you too good to carry people's rubbish? Where you think that ten dollars you talking about come from? I'm just supposed to haul people's rubbish and give my money to you cause you too lazy to work. You too lazy to work and wanna know why you ain't got what I got.

ROSE. What hospital Bonnie working at? Mercy?

LYONS. She's down at Passavant working in the laundry.

TROY. I ain't got nothing as it is. I give you that ten dollars and I got to eat beans the rest of the week. Naw...you ain't getting no ten dollars here.

LYONS. You ain't got to be eating no beans. I don't know why you wanna say that.

TROY. I ain't got no extra money. Gabe done moved over to Miss Pearl's paying her the rent and things done got tight around here. I can't afford to be giving you every payday.

LYONS. I ain't asked you to give me nothing. I asked you to loan me ten dollars. I know you got ten dollars.

TROY. Yeah, I got it. You know why I got it? 'Cause I don't throw my money away out there in the streets. You living the fast life...wanna be a musician...running around in them clubs and things...then, you learn to take care of yourself. You ain't gonna find me going and asking nobody for nothing. I done spent too many years without.

LYONS. You and me is two different people, Pop.

TROY. I done learned my mistake and learned to do what's right by it. You still trying to get something for nothing. Life don't owe you nothing. You owe it to yourself. Ask Bono. He'll tell you I'm right.

LYONS. You got your way of dealing with the world...I got mine. The only thing that matters to me is the music.

TROY. Yeah, I can see that! It don't matter how you gonna eat...where your next dollar is coming from. You telling the truth there.

LYONS. I know I got to eat. But I got to live too. I need something that gonna help me to get out of the bed in the morning. Make me feel like I belong in the world. I don't bother nobody. I just stay with the music cause that's the only way I can find to live in the world. Otherwise there ain't no telling what I might do. Now I don't come criticizing you and how you live. I just come by to ask you for ten dollars. I don't wanna hear all that about how I live.

TROY. Boy, your mamma did a hell of a job raising you.

LYONS. You can't change me, Pop. I'm thirty-four years old. If you wanted to change me, you should have been there when I was growing up. I come by to see you...ask for ten dollars and you want to talk about how I was raised. You don't know nothing about how I was raised.

ROSE. Let the boy have ten dollars, Troy.

TROY [*to* LYONS]. What the hell you looking at me for? I ain't got no ten dollars. You know what I do with my money. [*To* ROSE.] Give him ten dollars if you want him to have it.

ROSE. I will. Just as soon as you turn it loose.

TROY [*handing* ROSE *the money*]. There it is. Seventy-six dollars and forty-two cents. You see this, Bono? Now, I ain't gonna get but six of that back.

ROSE. You ought to stop telling that lie. Here, Lyons. [*She hands him the money.*]

LYONS. Thanks, Rose. Look...I got to run...I'll see you later.

TROY. Wait a minute. You gonna say, "Thanks, Rose" and ain't gonna look to see where she got that ten dollars from? See how they do me, Bono?

LYONS. I know she got it from you, Pop. Thanks. I'll give it back to you.

TROY. There he go telling another lie. Time I see that ten dollars...he'll be owing me thirty more.

LYONS. See you, Mr. Bono.

BONO. Take care, Lyons!

LYONS. Thanks, Pop. I'll see you again.

LYONS exits the yard.

TROY. I don't know why he don't go and get him a decent job and take care of that woman he got.

BONO. He'll be all right, Troy. The boy is still young.

TROY. The *boy* is thirty-four years old.

ROSE. Let's not get off into all that.

BONO. Look here…I got to be going. I got to be getting on. Lucille gonna be waiting.

TROY [*puts his arm around* ROSE]. See this woman, Bono? I love this woman. I love this woman so much it hurts. I love her so much…I done run out of ways of loving her. So I got to go back to basics. Don't you come by my house Monday morning talking about time to go to work…'cause I'm still gonna be stroking!

ROSE. Troy! Stop it now!

BONO. I ain't paying him no mind, Rose. That ain't nothing but gin-talk. Go on, Troy. I'll see you Monday.

TROY. Don't you come by my house, nigger! I done told you what I'm gonna be doing.

> *The lights go down to black.*

SCENE 2

The lights come up on ROSE *hanging up clothes. She hums and sings softly to herself. It is the following morning.*

ROSE [*sings*].

> Jesus, be a fence all around me every day
> Jesus, I want you to protect me as I travel on my way.
> Jesus, be a fence all around me every day.

> TROY *enters from the house.*

> Jesus, I want you to protect me
> As I travel on my way.

[*To* TROY.] Morning. You ready for breakfast? I can fix it soon as I finish hanging up these clothes.

TROY. I got the coffee on. That'll be all right. I'll just drink some of that this morning.

ROSE. That 651 hit yesterday. That's the second time this month. Miss Pearl hit for a dollar…seem like those that need the least always get lucky. Poor folks can't get nothing.

TROY. Them numbers don't know nobody. I don't know why you fool with them. You and Lyons both.

ROSE. It's something to do.

TROY. You ain't doing nothing but throwing your money away.

ROSE. Troy, you know I don't play foolishly. I just play a nickel here and a nickel there.

TROY. That's two nickels you done thrown away.

ROSE. Now I hit sometimes…that makes up for it. It always comes in handy when I do hit. I don't hear you complaining then.

TROY. I ain't complaining now. I just say it's foolish. Trying to guess out of six hundred ways which way the number gonna come. If I had all the money niggers, these Negroes, throw away on numbers for one week—just one week—I'd be a rich man.

ROSE. Well, you wishing and calling it foolish ain't gonna stop folks from playing numbers. That's one thing for sure. Besides...some good things come from playing numbers. Look where Pope done bought him that restaurant off of numbers.

TROY. I can't stand niggers like that. Man ain't had two dimes to rub together. He walking around with his shoes all run over bumming money for cigarettes. All right. Got lucky there and hit the numbers...

ROSE. Troy, I know all about it.

TROY. Had good sense, I'll say that for him. He ain't throwed his money away. I seen niggers hit the numbers and go through two thousand dollars in four days. Man bought him that restaurant down there...fixed it up real nice...and then didn't want nobody to come in it! A Negro go in there and can't get no kind of service. I seen a white fellow come in there and order a bowl of stew. Pope picked all the meat out of the pot for him. Man ain't had nothing but a bowl of meat! Negro come behind him and ain't got nothing but the potatoes and carrots. Talking about what numbers do for people, you picked a wrong example. Ain't done nothing but make a worser fool out of him than he was before.

ROSE. Troy, you ought to stop worrying about what happened at work yesterday.

TROY. I ain't worried. Just told me to be down there at the Commissioner's office on Friday. Everybody think they gonna fire me. I ain't worried about them firing me. You ain't got to worry about that. [*Pause.*] Where's Cory? Cory in the house? [*Calls.*] Cory?

ROSE. He gone out.

TROY. Out, huh? He gone out 'cause he know I want him to help me with this fence. I know how he is. That boy scared of work.

> GABRIEL *enters. He comes halfway down the alley and, hearing* TROY's *voice, stops.*

TROY [*continues*]. He ain't done a lick of work in his life.

ROSE. He had to go to football practice. Coach wanted them to get in a little extra practice before the season start.

TROY. I got his practice...running out of here before he get his chores done.

ROSE. Troy, what is wrong with you this morning? Don't nothing set right with you. Go on back in there and go to bed...get up on the other side.

TROY. Why something got to be wrong with me? I ain't said nothing wrong with me.

ROSE. You got something to say about everything. First it's the numbers...then it's the way the man runs his restaurant...then you done got on Cory. What's it gonna be next? Take a look up there and see if the weather suits you...or is it gonna be how you gonna put up the fence with the clothes hanging in the yard.

TROY. You hit the nail on the head then.

ROSE. I know you like I know the back of my hand. Go on in there and get you some coffee...see if that straighten you up. 'Cause you ain't right this morning.

> TROY *starts into the house and sees* GABRIEL. GABRIEL *starts singing.* TROY's *brother, he is seven years younger than* TROY. *Injured in World War II, he has a metal plate in his head. He carries an old trumpet tied around his waist and*

believes with every fiber of his being that he is the Archangel Gabriel. He carries a chipped basket with an assortment of discarded fruits and vegetables he has picked up in the strip district and which he attempts to sell.

GABRIEL [*singing*].

> Yes, ma'am I got plums
> You ask me how I sell them
> Oh ten cents apiece
> Three for a quarter
> Come and buy now
> 'Cause I'm here today
> And tomorrow I'll be gone

GABRIEL *enters.*

Hey, Rose!

ROSE. How you doing Gabe?

GABRIEL. There's Troy...Hey, Troy!

TROY. Hey, Gabe.

Exit into kitchen.

ROSE [*to* GABRIEL]. What you got there?

GABRIEL. You know what I got, Rose. I got fruits and vegetables.

ROSE [*looking in basket*]. Where's all these plums you talking about?

GABRIEL. I ain't got no plums today, Rose. I was just singing that. Have some to-morrow. Put me in a big order for plums. Have enough plums tomorrow for St. Peter and everybody.

TROY *reenters from kitchen, crosses to steps.*

[*To* ROSE.] Troy's mad at me.

TROY. I ain't mad at you. What I got to be mad at you about? You ain't done nothing to me.

GABRIEL. I just moved over to Miss Pearl's to keep out from in your way. I ain't mean no harm by it.

TROY. Who said anything about that? I ain't said anything about that.

GABRIEL. You ain't mad at me, is you?

TROY. Naw...I ain't mad at you, Gabe. If I was mad at you I'd tell you about it.

GABRIEL. Got me two rooms. In the basement. Got my own door too. Wanna see my key? [*He holds up a key.*] That's my own key! My two rooms!

TROY. Well, that's good, Gabe. You got your own key...that's good.

ROSE. You hungry, Gabe? I was just fixing to cook Troy his breakfast.

GABRIEL. I'll take some biscuits. You got some biscuits? Did you know when I was in heaven...every morning me and St. Peter would sit down by the gate and eat some big fat biscuits? Oh, yeah! We had us a good time. We'd sit there and eat us them biscuits and then St. Peter would go off to sleep and tell me to wake him up when it's time to open the gates for the judgment.

ROSE. Well, come on...I'll make up a batch of biscuits.

ROSE *exits into the house.*

GABRIEL. Troy...St. Peter got your name in the book. I seen it. It say...Troy Maxson. I say...I know him! He got the same name like what I got. That's my brother!

TROY. How many times you gonna tell me that, Gabe?

GABRIEL. Ain't got my name in the book. Don't have to have my name. I done died and went to heaven. He got your name though. One morning St. Peter was looking at his book...marking it up for the judgment...and he let me see your name. Got it in there under M. Got Rose's name...I ain't seen it like I seen yours...but I know it's in there. He got a great big book. Got everybody's name what was ever been born. That's what he told me. But I seen your name. Seen it with my own eyes.

TROY. Go on in the house there. Rose going to fix you something to eat.

GABRIEL. Oh, I ain't hungry. I done had breakfast with Aunt Jemimah. She come by and cooked me up a whole mess of flapjacks. Remember how we used to eat them flapjacks?

TROY. Go on in the house and get you something to eat now.

GABRIEL. I got to sell my plums. I done sold some tomatoes. Got me two quarters. Wanna see? [*He shows* TROY *his quarters.*] I'm gonna save them and buy me a new horn so St. Peter can hear me when it's time to open the gates. [GABRIEL *stops suddenly. Listens.*] Hear that? That's the hellhounds. I got to chase them out of here. Go on get out of here! Get out!

GABRIEL *exits singing.*

> Better get ready for the judgment
> Better get ready for the judgment
> My Lord is coming down

ROSE *enters from the house.*

TROY. He's gone off somewhere.

GABRIEL [*offstage*].

> Better get ready for the judgment
> Better get ready for the judgment morning
> Better get ready for the judgment
> My God is coming down

ROSE. He ain't eating right. Miss Pearl say she can't get him to eat nothing.

TROY. What you want me to do about it, Rose? I done did everything I can for the man. I can't make him get well. Man got half his head blown away...what you expect?

ROSE. Seem like something ought to be done to help him.

TROY. Man don't bother nobody. He just mixed up from that metal plate he got in his head. Ain't no sense for him to go back into the hospital.

ROSE. Least he be eating right. They can help him take care of himself.

TROY. Don't nobody wanna be locked up, Rose. What you wanna lock him up for? Man go over there and fight the war...messin' around with them Japs, get half his head blow off...and they give him a lousy three thousand dollars. And I had to swoop down on that.

ROSE. Is you fixing to go into that again?

TROY. That's the only way I got a roof over my head...cause of that metal plate.

ROSE. Ain't no sense you blaming yourself for nothing. Gabe wasn't in no condition to manage that money. You done what was right by him. Can't nobody say you ain't done what was right by him. Look how long you took care of him...till he wanted to have his own place and moved over there with Miss Pearl.

TROY. That ain't what I'm saying woman! I'm just stating the facts. If my brother didn't have that metal plate in his head...I wouldn't have a pot to piss in or a window to throw it out of. And I'm fifty-three years old. Now see if you can understand that!

TROY *gets up from the porch and starts to exit the yard.*

ROSE. Where you going off to? You been running out of here every Saturday for weeks. I thought you was gonna work on this fence?

TROY. I'm gonna walk down to Taylors'. Listen to the ball game. I'll be back in a bit. I'll work on it when I get back.

He exits the yard. The lights go to black.

SCENE 3

The lights come up on the yard. It is four hours later. ROSE *is taking down the clothes from the line.* CORY *enters carrying his football equipment.*

ROSE. Your daddy like to had a fit with you running out of here this morning without doing your chores.

CORY. I told you I had to go to practice.

ROSE. He say you were supposed to help him with this fence.

CORY. He been saying that the last four or five Saturdays, and then he don't never do nothing, but go down to Taylors'. Did you tell him about the recruiter?

ROSE. Yeah, I told him.

CORY. What he say?

ROSE. He ain't said nothing too much. You get in there and get started on your chores before he gets back. Go on and scrub down them steps before he gets back here hollering and carrying on.

CORY. I'm hungry. What you got to eat, Mama?

ROSE. Go on and get started on your chores. I got some meat loaf in there. Go on and make you a sandwich...and don't leave no mess in there.

CORY *exits into the house.* ROSE *continues to take down the clothes.* TROY *enters the yard and sneaks up and grabs her from behind.*

Troy! Go on, now. You liked to scared me to death. What was the score of the game? Lucille had me on the phone and I couldn't keep up with it.

TROY. What I care about the game? Come here, woman.

[*He tries to kiss her.*]

ROSE. I thought you went down Taylors' to listen to the game. Go on, Troy! You supposed to be putting up this fence.

TROY [*attempting to kiss her again*]. I'll put it up when I finish with what is at hand.

ROSE. Go on, Troy. I ain't studying you.

TROY [*chasing after her*]. I'm studying you...fixing to do my homework!

ROSE. Troy, you better leave me alone.

TROY. Where's Cory? That boy brought his butt home yet?

ROSE. He's in the house doing his chores.

TROY [*calling*]. Cory! Get your butt out here, boy!

ROSE *exits into the house with the laundry.* TROY *goes over to the pile of wood, picks up a board, and starts sawing.* CORY *enters from the house.*

TROY. You just now coming in here from leaving this morning?

CORY. Yeah, I had to go to football practice.

TROY. Yeah, what?

CORY. Yessir.

TROY. I ain't but two seconds off you noway. The garbage sitting in there overflowing...you ain't done none of your chores...and you come in here talking about "Yeah."

CORY. I was just getting ready to do my chores now, Pop...

TROY. Your first chore is to help me with this fence on Saturday. Everything else come after that. Now get that saw and cut them boards.

> CORY *takes the saw and begins cutting the boards.* TROY *continues working. There is a long pause.*

CORY. Hey, Pop...why don't you buy a TV?

TROY. What I want with a TV? What I want one of them for?

CORY. Everybody got one. Earl, Ba Bra...Jesse!

TROY. I ain't asked you who had one. I say what I want with one?

CORY. So you can watch it. They got lots of things on TV. Baseball games and everything. We could watch the World Series.

TROY. Yeah...and how much this TV cost?

CORY. I don't know. They got them on sale for around two hundred dollars.

TROY. Two hundred dollars, huh?

CORY. That ain't that much, Pop.

TROY. Naw, it's just two hundred dollars. See that roof you got over your head at night? Let me tell you something about that roof. It's been over ten years since that roof was last tarred. See now...the snow come this winter and sit up there on that roof like it is...and it's gonna seep inside. It's just gonna be a little bit...ain't gonna hardly notice it. Then the next thing you know, it's gonna be leaking all over the house. Then the wood rot from all that water and you gonna need a whole new roof. Now, how much you think it cost to get that roof tarred?

CORY. I don't know.

TROY. Two hundred and sixty-four dollars...cash money. While you thinking about a TV, I got to be thinking about the roof...and whatever else go wrong here. Now if you had two hundred dollars, what would you do...fix the roof or buy a TV?

CORY. I'd buy a TV. Then when the roof started to leak...when it needed fixing...I'd fix it.

TROY. Where you gonna get the money from? You done spent it for a TV. You gonna sit up and watch the water run all over your brand new TV.

CORY. Aw, Pop. You got money. I know you do.

TROY. Where I got it at, huh?

CORY. You got it in the bank.

TROY. You wanna see my bankbook? You wanna see that seventy-three dollars and twenty-two cents I got sitting up in there?

CORY. You ain't got to pay for it all at one time. You can put a down payment on it and carry it on home with you.

TROY. Not me. I ain't gonna owe nobody nothing if I can help it. Miss a payment and they come and snatch it right out of your house. Then what you got? Now, soon as I get two hundred dollars clear, then I'll buy a TV. Right now, as soon as I get two hundred and sixty-four dollars, I'm gonna have this roof tarred.

CORY. Aw...Pop!

TROY. You go on and get you two hundred dollars and buy one if ya want it. I got better things to do with my money.

CORY. I can't get no two hundred dollars. I ain't never seen two hundred dollars.

TROY. I'll tell you what...you get you a hundred dollars and I'll put the other hundred with it.

CORY. All right, I'm gonna show you.

TROY. You gonna show me how you can cut them boards right now.

CORY *begins to cut the boards. There is a long pause.*

CORY. The Pirates won today. That makes five in a row.

TROY. I ain't thinking about the Pirates. Got an all-white team. Got that boy...that Puerto Rican boy...Clemente. Don't even half-play him. That boy could be something if they give him a chance. Play him one day and sit him on the bench the next.

CORY. He gets a lot of chances to play.

TROY. I'm talking about playing regular. Playing every day so you can get your timing. That's what I'm talking about.

CORY. They got some white guys on the team that don't play every day. You can't play everybody at the same time.

TROY. If they got a white fellow sitting on the bench...you can bet your last dollar he can't play! That colored guy got to be twice as good before he get on the team. That's why I don't want you to get all tied up in them sports. Man on the team and what it get him? They got colored on the team and don't use them. Same as not having them. All them teams the same.

CORY. The Braves got Hank Aaron and Wes Covington. Hank Aaron hit two home runs today. That makes forty-three.

TROY. Hank Aaron ain't nobody. That what you supposed to do. That's how you supposed to play the game. Ain't nothing to it. It's just a matter of timing...getting the right follow-through. Hell, I can hit forty-three home runs right now!

CORY. Not off no major-league pitching, you couldn't.

TROY. We had better pitching in the Negro leagues. I hit seven home runs off of Satchel Paige. You can't get no better than that!

CORY. Sandy Koufax. He's leading the league in strikeouts.

TROY. I ain't thinking of no Sandy Koufax.

CORY. You got Warren Spahn and Lew Burdette. I bet you couldn't hit no home runs off of Warren Spahn.

TROY. I'm through with it now. You go on and cut them boards. [*Pause.*] Your mama tell me you done got recruited by a college football team? Is that right?

CORY. Yeah. Coach Zellman say the recruiter gonna be coming by to talk to you. Get you to sign the permission papers.

TROY. I thought you supposed to be working down there at the A&P. Ain't you suppose to be working down there after school?

CORY. Mr. Stawicki say he gonna hold my job for me until after the football season. Say starting next week I can work weekends.

TROY. I thought we had an understanding about this football stuff? You suppose to keep up with your chores and hold that job down at the A&P. Ain't been around here all day on a Saturday. Ain't none of your chores done...and now you telling me you done quit your job.

CORY. I'm going to be working weekends.

TROY. You damn right you are! And ain't no need for nobody coming around here to talk to me about signing nothing.

CORY. Hey, Pop…you can't do that. He's coming all the way from North Carolina.

TROY. I don't care where he coming from. The white man ain't gonna let you get nowhere with that football noway. You go on and get your book-learning so you can work yourself up in that A&P or learn how to fix cars or build houses or something, get you a trade. That way you have something can't nobody take away from you. You go on and learn how to put your hands to some good use. Besides hauling people's garbage.

CORY. I get good grades, Pop. That's why the recruiter wants to talk with you. You got to keep up your grades to get recruited. This way I'll be going to college. I'll get a chance…

TROY. First you gonna get your butt down there to the A&P and get your job back.

CORY. Mr. Stawicki done already hired somebody else 'cause I told him I was playing football.

TROY. You a bigger fool than I thought…to let somebody take away your job so you can play some football. Where you gonna get your money to take out your girlfriend and whatnot? What kind of foolishness is that to let somebody take away your job?

CORY. I'm still gonna be working weekends.

TROY. Naw…naw. You getting your butt out of here and finding you another job.

CORY. Come on, Pop! I got to practice. I can't work after school and play football too. The team needs me. That's what Coach Zellman say…

TROY. I don't care what nobody else say. I'm the boss…you understand? I'm the boss around here. I do the only saying what counts.

CORY. Come on, Pop!

TROY. I asked you…did you understand?

CORY. Yeah…

TROY. What?!

CORY. Yessir.

TROY. You go on down there to that A&P and see if you can get your job back. If you can't do both…then you quit the football team. You've got to take the crookeds with the straights.

CORY. Yessir. [*Pause.*] Can I ask you a question?

TROY. What the hell you wanna ask me? Mr. Stawicki the one you got the questions for.

CORY. How come you ain't never liked me?

TROY. Liked you? Who the hell say I got to like you? What law is there say I got to like you? Wanna stand up in my face and ask a damn fool-ass question like that. Talking about liking somebody. Come here, boy, when I talk to you.

CORY *comes over to where* TROY *is working. He stands slouched over and* TROY *shoves him on his shoulder.*

Straighten up, goddammit! I asked you a question…what law is there say I got to like you?

CORY. None.

TROY. Well, all right then! Don't you eat every day? [*Pause.*] Answer me when I talk to you! Don't you eat every day?

CORY. Yeah.

TROY. Nigger, as long as you in my house, you put that sir on the end of it when you talk to me.

CORY. Yes...sir.

TROY. You eat every day.

CORY. Yessir!

TROY. Got a roof over your head.

CORY. Yessir!

TROY. Got clothes on your back.

CORY. Yessir.

TROY. Why you think that is?

CORY. 'Cause of you.

TROY. Ah, hell I know it's 'cause of me...but why do you think that is?

CORY [*hesitant*]. 'Cause you like me.

TROY. Like you? I go out of here every morning...bust my butt...putting up with them crackers every day...'cause I like you? You are the biggest fool I ever saw. [*Pause.*] It's my job. It's my responsibility! You understand that? A man got to take care of his family. You live in my house...sleep you behind on my bedclothes...fill you belly up with my food...cause you my son. You my flesh and blood. Not 'cause I like you! 'Cause it's my duty to take care of you. I owe a responsibility to you! Let's get this straight right here...before it go along any further...I ain't got to like you. Mr. Rand don't give me my money come payday 'cause he likes me. He gives me 'cause he owe me. I done give you everything I had to give you. I gave you your life! Me and your mama worked that out between us. And liking your black ass wasn't part of the bargain. Don't you try and go through life worrying about if somebody like you or not. You best be making sure they doing right by you. You understand what I'm saying boy?

CORY. Yessir.

TROY. Then get the hell out of my face, and get on down to that A&P.

> ROSE *has been standing behind the screen door for much of the scene. She enters as* CORY *exits.*

ROSE. Why don't you let the boy go ahead and play football, Troy? Ain't no harm in that. He's just trying to be like you with the sports.

TROY. I don't want him to be like me! I want him to move as far away from my life as he can get. You the only decent thing that ever happened to me. I wish him that. But I don't wish him a thing else from my life. I decided seventeen years ago that boy wasn't getting involved in no sports. Not after what they did to me in the sports.

ROSE. Troy, why don't you admit you was too old to play in the major leagues? For once...why don't you admit that?

TROY. What do you mean too old? Don't come telling me I was too old. I just wasn't the right color. Hell, I'm fifty-three years old and can do better than Selkirk's .269 right now!

ROSE. How's was you gonna play ball when you were over forty? Sometimes I can't get no sense out of you.

TROY. I got good sense, woman. I got sense enough not to let my boy get hurt over playing no sports. You been mothering that boy too much. Worried about if people like him.

ROSE. Everything that boy do...he do for you. He wants you to say "Good job, son." That's all.

TROY. Rose, I ain't got time for that. He's alive. He's healthy. He's got to make his own way. I made mine. Ain't nobody gonna hold his hand when he get out there in that world.

ROSE. Times have changed from when you was young, Troy. People change. The world's changing around you and you can't even see it.

TROY [*slow, methodical*]. Woman...I do the best I can do. I come in here every Friday. I carry a sack of potatoes and a bucket of lard. You all line up at the door with your hands out. I give you the lint from my pockets. I give you my sweat and my blood. I ain't got no tears. I done spent them. We go upstairs in that room at night...and I fall down on you and try to blast a hole into forever. I get up Monday morning...find my lunch on the table. I go out. Make my way. Find my strength to carry me through to the next Friday. [*Pause.*] That's all I got, Rose. That's all I got to give. I can't give nothing else.

> TROY *exits into the house. The lights go down to black.*

SCENE 4

It is Friday. Two weeks later. CORY *starts out of the house with his football equipment. The phone rings.*

CORY [*calling*]. I got it! [*He answers the phone and stands in the screen door talking.*] Hello? Hey, Jesse. Naw...I was just getting ready to leave now.

ROSE [*calling*]. Cory!

CORY. I told you, man, them spikes is all tore up. You can use them if you want, but they ain't no good. Earl got some spikes.

ROSE [*calling*]. Cory!

CORY [*calling to* ROSE]. Mam? I'm talking to Jesse. [*Into phone.*] When she say that? [*Pause.*] Aw, you lying, man. I'm gonna tell her you said that.

ROSE [*calling*]. Cory, don't you go nowhere!

CORY. I got to go to the game, Ma! [*Into the phone.*] Yeah, hey, look, I'll talk to you later. Yeah, I'll meet you over Earl's house. Later. Bye, Ma.

> CORY *exits the house and starts out the yard.*

ROSE. Cory, where you going off to? You got that stuff all pulled out and thrown all over your room.

CORY [*in the yard*]. I was looking for my spikes. Jesse wanted to borrow my spikes.

ROSE. Get up there and get that cleaned up before your daddy get back in here.

CORY. I got to go to the game! I'll clean it up *when I get back*.

> CORY *exits.*

ROSE. That's all he need to do is see that room all messed up.

> ROSE *exits into the house.* TROY *and* BONO *enter the yard.* TROY *is dressed in clothes other than his work clothes.*

BONO. He told him the same thing he told you. Take it to the union.

TROY. Brownie ain't got that much sense. Man wasn't thinking about nothing. He wait until I confront them on it...then he wanna come crying seniority. [*Calls.*] Hey, Rose!

BONO. I wish I could have seen Mr. Rand's face when he told you.

TROY. He couldn't get it out of his mouth! Liked to bit his tongue! When they called me down there to the Commissioner's office...he thought they was gonna fire me. Like everybody else.

BONO. I didn't think they was gonna fire you. I thought they was gonna put you on the warning paper.

TROY. Hey, Rose! [*To* BONO.] Yeah, Mr. Rand like to bit his tongue.

TROY *breaks the seal on the bottle, takes a drink, and hands it to* BONO.

BONO. I see you run right down to Taylors' and told that Alberta gal.

TROY [*calling*]. Hey Rose! [*To* BONO.] I told everybody. Hey, Rose! I went down there to cash my check.

ROSE [*entering from the house*]. Hush all that hollering, man! I know you out here. What they say down there at the Commissioner's office?

TROY. You supposed to come when I call you, woman. Bono'll tell you that. [*To* BONO.] Don't Lucille come when you call her?

ROSE. Man, hush your mouth. I ain't no dog…talk about "come when you call me."

TROY [*puts his arm around* ROSE]. You hear this, Bono? I had me an old dog used to get uppity like that. You say, "C'mere, Blue!"…and he just lay there and look at you. End up getting a stick and chasing him away trying to make him come.

ROSE. I ain't studying you and your dog. I remember you used to sing that old song.

TROY [*he sings*].

> Hear it ring! Hear it ring!
> I had a dog his name was Blue.

ROSE. Don't nobody wanna hear you sing that old song.

TROY [*sings*]. You know Blue was mighty true.

ROSE. Used to have Cory running around here singing that song.

BONO. Hell, I remember that song myself.

TROY [*sings*].

> You know Blue was a good old dog.
> Blue treed a possum in a hollow log.

That was my daddy's song. My daddy made up that song.

ROSE. I don't care who made it up. Don't nobody wanna hear you sing it.

TROY [*makes a song like calling a dog*]. Come here, woman.

ROSE. You come in here carrying on, I reckon they ain't fired you. What they say down there at the Commissioner's office?

TROY. Look here, Rose…Mr. Rand called me into his office today when I got back from talking to them people down there…it come from up top…he called me in and told me they was making me a driver.

ROSE. Troy, you kidding!

TROY. No I ain't. Ask Bono.

ROSE. Well, that's great, Troy. Now you don't have to hassle them people no more.

LYONS *enters from the street.*

TROY. Aw hell, I wasn't looking to see you today. I thought you was in jail. Got it all over the front page of the *Courier* about them raiding Sefus's place…where you be hanging out with all them thugs.

LYONS. Hey, Pop…that ain't got nothing to do with me. I don't go down there gambling. I go down there to sit in with the band. I ain't got nothing to do with the gambling part. They got some good music down there.

TROY. They got some rogues...is what they got.

LYONS. How you been, Mr. Bono? Hi, Rose.

BONO. I see where you playing down at the Crawford Grill tonight.

ROSE. How come you ain't brought Bonnie like I told you? You should have brought Bonnie with you, she ain't been over in a month of Sundays.

LYONS. I was just in the neighborhood...thought I'd stop by.

TROY. Here he come...

BONO. Your daddy got a promotion on the rubbish. He's gonna be the first colored driver. Ain't got to do nothing but sit up there and read the paper like them white fellows.

LYONS. Hey, Pop...if you knew how to read you'd be all right.

BONO. Naw...naw...you mean if the nigger knew how to drive he'd be all right. Been fighting with them people about driving and ain't even got a license. Mr. Rand know you ain't got no driver's license?

TROY. Driving ain't nothing. All you do is point the truck where you want it to go. Driving ain't nothing.

BONO. Do Mr. Rand know you ain't got no driver's license? That's what I'm talking about. I ain't asked if driving was easy. I asked if Mr. Rand know you ain't got no driver's license.

TROY. He ain't got to know. The man ain't got to know my business. Time he find out, I have two or three driver's licenses.

LYONS [*going into his pocket*]. Say, look here, Pop...

TROY. I knew it was coming. Didn't I tell you, Bono? I know what kind of "Look here, Pop" that was. The nigger fixing to ask me for some money. It's Friday night. It's my payday. All them rogues down there on the avenue...the ones that ain't in jail...and Lyons is hopping in his shoes to get down there with them.

LYONS. See, Pop...if you give somebody else a chance to talk sometimes, you'd see that I was fixing to pay you back your ten dollars like I told you. Here...I told you I'd pay you when Bonnie got paid.

TROY. Naw...you go ahead and keep that ten dollars. Put it in the bank. The next time you feel like you wanna come by here and ask me for something...you go on down there and get that.

LYONS. Here's your ten dollars, Pop. I told you I don't want you to give me nothing. I just wanted to borrow ten dollars.

TROY. Naw...you go on and keep that for the next time you want to ask me.

LYONS. Come on, Pop...here go your ten dollars.

ROSE. Why don't you go on and let the boy pay you back, Troy?

LYONS. Here you go, Rose. If you don't take it I'm gonna have to hear about it for the next six months. [*He hands her the money.*]

ROSE. You can hand yours over here too, Troy.

TROY. You see this, Bono. You see how they do me.

BONO. Yeah, Lucille do me the same way.

GABRIEL *is heard singing off stage. He enters.*

GABRIEL. Better get ready for the Judgment! Better get ready for...Hey!... Hey!...There's Troy's boy!

LYONS. How are you doing, Uncle Gabe?

GABRIEL. Lyons...The King of the Jungle! Rose...hey, Rose. Got a flower for you. [*He takes a rose from his pocket.*] Picked it myself. That's the same rose like you is!

ROSE. That's right nice of you, Gabe.

LYONS. What you been doing, Uncle Gabe?

GABRIEL. Oh, I been chasing hellhounds and waiting on the time to tell St. Peter to open the gates.

LYONS. You been chasing hellhounds, huh? Well...you doing the right thing, Uncle Gabe. Somebody got to chase them.

GABRIEL. Oh, yeah...I know it. The devil's strong. The devil ain't no pushover. Hellhounds snipping at everybody's heels. But I got my trumpet waiting on the Judgment time.

LYONS. Waiting on the Battle of Armageddon, huh?

GABRIEL. Ain't gonna be too much of a battle when God get to waving that Judgment sword. But the people's gonna have a hell of a time trying to get into heaven if them gates ain't open.

LYONS [*putting his arm around* GABRIEL]. You hear this, Pop. Uncle Gabe, you all right!

GABRIEL [*laughing with* LYONS]. Lyons! King of the Jungle.

ROSE. You gonna stay for suppper, Gabe? Want me to fix you a plate?

GABRIEL. I'll take a sandwich, Rose. Don't want no plate. Just wanna eat with my hands. I'll take a sandwich.

ROSE. How about you, Lyons? You staying? Got some short ribs cooking.

LYONS. Naw, I won't eat nothing till after we finished playing. [*Pause.*] You ought to come down and listen to me play, Pop.

TROY. I don't like that Chinese music. All that noise.

ROSE. Go on in the house and wash up, Gabe...I'll fix you a sandwich.

GABRIEL [*to* LYONS, *as he exits*]. Troy's mad at me.

LYONS. What you mad at Uncle Gabe for, Pop?

ROSE. He thinks Troy's mad at him 'cause he moved over to Miss Pearl's.

TROY. I ain't mad at the man. He can live where he want to live at.

LYONS. What he move over there for? Miss Pearl don't like nobody.

ROSE. She don't mind him none. She treats him real nice. She just don't allow all that singing.

TROY. She don't mind that rent he be paying...That's what she don't mind.

ROSE. Troy, I ain't going through that with you no more. He's over there cause he want to have his own place. He can come and go as he please.

TROY. Hell, he could come and go as he please here. I wasn't stopping him. I ain't put no rules on him.

ROSE. It ain't the same thing, Troy. And you know it.

> GABRIEL *comes to the door.*

Now, that's the last I wanna hear about that. I don't wanna hear nothing else about Gabe and Miss Pearl. And next week...

GABRIEL. I'm ready for my sandwich, Rose.

ROSE. And next week...when that recruiter come from that school...I want you to sign that paper and go on and let Cory play football. Then that'll be the last I have to hear about that.

TROY [*to* ROSE *as she exits into the house*]. I ain't thinking about Cory nothing.

LYONS. What...Cory got recruited? What school he going to?

TROY. That boy walking around here smelling his piss...thinking he's grown. Thinking he's gonna do what he want, irrespective of what I say. Look here, Bono...I left the Commissioner's office and went down to the A&P...that

boy ain't working down there. He lying to me. Telling me he got his job back…telling me he working weekends…telling me he working after school…Mr. Stawicki tell me he ain't working down there at all!

LYONS. Cory just growing up. He's just busting at the seams trying to fill out your shoes.

TROY. I don't care what he's doing. When he get to the point where he wanna disobey me…then it's time for him to move on. Bono'll tell you that. I bet he ain't never disobeyed his daddy without paying the consequences.

BONO. I ain't never had a chance. My daddy came on through…but I ain't never knew him to see him…or what he had on his mind or where he went. Just moving on through. Searching out the New Land. That's what the old folks used to call it. See a fellow moving around from place to place…woman to woman…called it searching out the New Land. I can't say if he ever found it. I come along, didn't want no kids. Didn't know if I was gonna be in one place long enough to fix on them right as their daddy. I figured I was going searching too. As it turned out I been hooked up with Lucille near about as long as your daddy been with Rose. Going on sixteen years.

TROY. Sometimes I wish I hadn't known my daddy. He ain't cared nothing about no kids. A kid to him wasn't nothing. All he wanted was for you to learn how to walk so he could start you to working. When it come time for eating…he ate first. If there was anything left over, that's what you got. Man would sit down and eat two chickens and give you the wing.

LYONS. You ought to stop that, Pop. Everybody feed their kids. No matter how hard times is…everybody care about their kids. Make sure they have something to eat.

TROY. The only thing my daddy cared about was getting them bales of cotton in to Mr. Lubin. That's the only thing that mattered to him. Sometimes I used to wonder why he was living. Wonder why the devil hadn't come and got him. "Get them bales of cotton in to Mr. Lubin" and find out he owe him money…

LYONS. He should have just went on and left when he saw he couldn't get nowhere. That's what I would have done.

TROY. How he gonna leave with eleven kids? And where he gonna go? He ain't knew how to do nothing but farm. No, he was trapped and I think he knew it. But I'll say this for him…he felt a responsibility toward us. Maybe he ain't treated us the way I felt he should have…but without that responsibility he could have walked off and left us…made his own way.

BONO. A lot of them did. Back in those days what you talking about…they walk out their front door and just take on down one road or another and keep on walking.

LYONS. There you go! That's what I'm talking about.

BONO. Just keep on walking till you come to something else. Ain't you never heard of nobody having the walking blues? Well, that's what you call it when you just take off like that.

TROY. My daddy ain't had them walking blues! What you talking about? He stayed right there with his family. But he was just as evil as he could be. My mama couldn't stand him. Couldn't stand that evilness. She run off when I was about eight. She sneaked off one night after he had gone to sleep. Told me she was coming back for me. I ain't never seen her no more. All his women run off and left him. He wasn't good for nobody.

When my turn come to head out, I was fourteen and got to sniffing around Joe Canewell's daughter. Had us an old mule we called Greyboy. My daddy sent me out to do some plowing and I tied up Greyboy and went to fooling around with Joe Canewell's daughter. We done found us a nice little spot, got real cozy with each other. She about thirteen and we done figured we was grown anyway...so we down there enjoying ourselves...ain't thinking about nothing. We didn't know Greyboy had got loose and wandered back to the house and my daddy was looking for me. We down there by the creek enjoying ourselves when my daddy come up on us. Surprised us. He had them leather straps off the mule and commenced to whupping me like there was no tomorrow. I jumped up, mad and embarrassed. I was scared of my daddy. When he commenced to whupping on me...quite naturally I run to get out of the way. [*Pause.*] Now I thought he was mad 'cause I ain't done my work. But I see where he was chasing me off so he could have the gal for himself. When I see what the matter of it was, I lost all fear of my daddy. Right there is where I become a man...at fourteen years of age. [*Pause.*] Now it was my turn to run him off. I picked up them same reins that he had used on me. I picked up them reins and commenced to whupping on him. The gal jumped up and run him off...and when my daddy turned to face me, I could see why the devil had never come to get him...'cause he was the devil himself. I don't know what happened. When I woke up, I was laying right there by the creek, and Blue...this old dog we had...was licking my face. I thought I was blind. I couldn't see nothing. Both my eyes were swollen shut. I laid there and cried. I didn't know what I was gonna do. The only thing I knew was the time had come for me to leave my daddy's house. And right there the world suddenly got big. And it was a long time before I could cut it down to where I could handle it.

Part of that cutting down was when I got to the place where I could feel him kicking in my blood and knew that the only thing that separated us was the matter of a few years.

GABRIEL *enters from the house with a sandwich.*

LYONS. What you got there, Uncle Gabe?

GABRIEL. Got me a ham sandwich. Rose gave me a ham sandwich.

TROY. I don't know what happened to him. I done lost touch with everybody except Gabriel. But I hope he's dead. I hope he found some peace.

LYONS. That's a heavy story, Pop. I didn't know you left home when you was fourteen.

TROY. And didn't know nothing. The only part of the world I knew was the forty-two acres of Mr. Lubin's land. That's all I knew about life.

LYONS. Fourteen's kinda young to be out on your own. [*Phone rings.*] I don't even think I was ready to be out on my own at fourteen. I don't know what I would have done.

TROY. I got up from the creek and walked on down to Mobile. I was through with farming. Figured I could do better in the city. So I walked the two hundred miles to Mobile.

LYONS. Wait a minute...you ain't walked no two hundred miles, Pop. Ain't nobody gonna walk no two hundred miles. You talking about some walking there.

BONO. That's the only way you got anywhere back in them days.

LYONS. Shhh. Damn if I wouldn't have hitched a ride with somebody!

TROY. Who you gonna hitch it with? They ain't had no cars and things like they got now. We talking about 1918.

ROSE [*entering*]. What you all out here getting into?

TROY [*to* ROSE]. I'm telling Lyons how good he got it. He don't know nothing about this I'm talking.

ROSE. Lyons, that was Bonnie on the phone. She say you supposed to pick her up.

LYONS. Yeah, okay Rose.

TROY. I walked on down to Mobile and hitched up with some of them fellows that was heading this way. Got up here and found out...not only couldn't you get a job...you couldn't find no place to live. I thought I was in freedom. Shhh. Colored folks living down there on the river banks in whatever kind of shelter they could find for themselves. Right down there under the Brady Street Bridge. Living in shacks made of sticks and tarpaper. Messed around there and went from bad to worse. Started stealing. First it was food. Then I figured, hell, if I steal money I can buy me some food. Buy me some shoes too! One thing led to another. Met your mama. I was young and anxious to be a man. Met your mama and had you. What I do that for? Now I got to worry about feeding you and her. Got to steal three times as much. Went out one day looking for somebody to rob...that's what I was, a robber. I'll tell you the truth. I'm ashamed of it today. But it's the truth. Went to rob this fellow...pulled out my knife...and he pulled out a gun. Shot me in the chest. I felt just like somebody had taken a hot branding iron and laid it on me. When he shot me I jumped at him with my knife. They told me I killed him and they put me in the penitentiary and locked me up for fifteen years. That's where I met Bono. That's where I learned how to play baseball. Got out that place and your mama had taken you and went on to make life without me. Fifteen years was a long time for her to wait. But that fifteen years cured me of that robbing stuff. Rose'll tell you. She asked me when I met her if I had gotten all that foolishness out of my system. And I told her, "Baby, it's you and baseball all what count with me." You hear me, Bono? I meant it too. She say, "Which one comes first?" I told her, "Baby, ain't no doubt it's baseball...but you stick and get old with me and we'll both outlive this baseball." Am I right, Rose? And it's true.

ROSE. Man, hush your mouth. You ain't said no such thing. Talking about, "Baby you know you'll always be number one with me." That's what you was talking.

TROY. You hear that, Bono. That's why I love her.

BONO. Rose'll keep you straight. You get off the track, she'll straighten you up.

ROSE. Lyons, you better get on up and get Bonnie. She waiting on you.

LYONS [*gets up to go*]. Hey, Pop, why don't you come on down to the Grill and hear me play?

TROY. I ain't going down there. I'm too old to be sitting around in them clubs.

BONO. You got to be good to play down at the Grill.

LYONS. Come on, Pop...

TROY. I got to get up in the morning.

LYONS. You ain't got to stay long.

TROY. Naw, I'm gonna get my supper and go on to bed.

LYONS. Well, I got to go. I'll see you again.

TROY. Don't you come around my house on my payday.

ROSE. Pick up the phone and let somebody know you coming. And bring Bonnie with you. You know I'm always glad to see her.

LYONS. Yeah, I'll do that, Rose. You take care now. See you, Pop. See you, Mr. Bono. See you, Uncle Gabe.

GABRIEL. Lyons! King of the Jungle!

LYONS exits

TROY. Is supper ready, woman? Me and you got some business to take care of. I'm gonna tear it up too.

ROSE. Troy, I done told you now!

TROY [*puts his arm around* BONO]. Aw hell, woman...this is Bono. Bono like family. I done known this nigger since...how long I done know you?

BONO. It's been a long time.

TROY. I done know this nigger since Skippy was a pup. Me and him done been through some times.

BONO. You sure right about that.

TROY. Hell, I done know him longer than I known you. And we still standing shoulder to shoulder. Hey look here, Bono...a man can't ask for no more than that. [*Drinks to him.*] I love you, nigger.

BONO. Hell, I love you too...I got to get home see my woman. You got yours in hand. I got to get mine.

> BONO *starts to exit as* CORY *enters the yard, dressed in his football uniform. He gives* TROY *a hard, uncompromising look.*

CORY. What you do that for, Pop?

> *He throws his helmet down in the direction of* TROY.

ROSE. What's the matter? Cory...What's the matter?

CORY. Papa done went up to the school and told Coach Zellman I can't play football no more. Wouldn't even let me play the game. Told him to tell the recruiter not to come.

ROSE. Troy...

TROY. What you Troying me for. Yeah, I did it. And the boy know why I did it.

CORY. Why you wanna do that to me? That was the one chance I had.

ROSE. Ain't nothing wrong with Cory playing football, Troy.

TROY. The boy lied to me. I told the nigger if he wanna play football...to keep up his chores and hold down that job at the A&P. That was the conditions. Stopped down there to see Mr. Stawicki...

CORY. I can't work after school during the football season, Pop! I tried to tell you that Mr. Stawicki's holding my job for me. You don't never want to listen to nobody. And then you wanna go and do this to me!

TROY. I ain't done nothing to you. You done it to yourself.

CORY. Just cause you didn't have a chance! You just scared I'm gonna be better than you, that's all.

TROY. Come here.

ROSE. Troy...

> CORY *reluctantly crosses over to* TROY.

TROY. All right! See. You done made a mistake.

CORY. I didn't even do nothing!

TROY. I'm gonna tell you what your mistake was. See...you swung at the ball and didn't hit it. That's strike one. See, you in the batter's box now. You swung and you missed. That's strike one. Don't you strike out!

Lights fade to black.

ACT 2

SCENE 1

The following morning. CORY *is at the tree hitting the ball with the bat. He tries to mimic* TROY, *but his swing is awkward, less sure.* ROSE *enters from the house.*

ROSE. Cory, I want you to help me with this cupboard.
CORY. I ain't quitting the team. I don't care what Poppa say.
ROSE. I'll talk to him when he gets back. He had to go see about your Uncle Gabe. The police done arrested him. Say he was disturbing the peace. He 'll be back directly. Come on in here and help me clean out the top of this cupboard.

CORY *exits into the house.* ROSE *sees* TROY *and* BONO *coming down the alley.*

Troy...what they say down there?
TROY. Ain't said nothing. I give them fifty dollars and they let him go. I'll talk to you about it. Where's Cory?
ROSE. He's in there helping me clean out these cupboards.
TROY. Tell him to get his butt out here.

TROY *and* BONO *go over to the pile of wood.* BONO *picks up the saw and begins sawing.*

TROY [*to* BONO]. All they want is the money. That makes six or seven times I done went down there and got him. See me coming they stick out their hands.
BONO. Yeah. I know what you mean. That's all they care about...that money. They don't care about what's right. [*Pause.*] Nigger, why you got to go and get some hard wood? You ain't doing nothing but building a little old fence. Get you some soft pine wood. That's all you need.
TROY. I know what I'm doing. This is outside wood. You put pine wood inside the house. Pine wood is inside wood. This here is outside wood. Now you tell me where the fence is gonna be?
BONO. You don't need this wood. You can put it up with pine wood and it'll stand as long as you gonna be here looking at it.
TROY. How you know how long I'm gonna be here, nigger? Hell, I might just live forever. Live longer than old man Horsely.
BONO. That's what Magee used to say.
TROY. Magee's damn fool. Now you tell me who you ever heard of gonna pull their own teeth with a pair of rusty pliers.
BONO. The old folks...my granddaddy used to pull his teeth with pliers. They ain't had no dentists for the colored folks back then.
TROY. Get clean pliers! You understand? Clean pliers! Sterilize them! Besides we ain't living back then. All Magee had to do was walk over to Doc Goldblum's.
BONO. I see where you and that Tallahassee gal...that Alberta...I see where you all done got tight.

TROY. What you mean "got tight"?

BONO. I see where you be laughing and joking with her all the time.

TROY. I laughs and jokes with all of them, Bono. You know me.

BONO. That ain't the kind of laughing and joking I'm talking about.

> CORY *enters from the house.*

CORY. How you doing, Mr. Bono?

TROY. Cory? Get that saw from Bono and cut some wood. He talking about the wood's too hard to cut. Stand back there, Jim, and let that young boy show you how it's done.

BONO. He's sure welcome to it.

> CORY *takes the saw and begins to cut the wood.*

Whew-e-e! Look at that. Big old strong boy. Look like Joe Louis. Hell, must be getting old the way I'm watching that boy whip through that wood.

CORY. I don't see why Mama want a fence around the yard noways.

TROY. Damn if I know either. What the hell she keeping out with it? She ain't got nothing nobody want.

BONO. Some people build fences to keep people out...and other people build fences to keep people in. Rose wants to hold on to you all. She loves you.

TROY. Hell, nigger, I don't need nobody to tell me my wife loves me. Cory...go on in the house and see if you can find that other saw.

CORY. Where's it at?

TROY. I said find it! Look for it till you find it!

> CORY *exits into the house.*

What's that supposed to mean? Wanna keep us in?

BONO. Troy...I done known you seem like damn near my whole life. You and Rose both. I done know both of you all for a long time. I remember when you met Rose. When you was hitting them baseball out the park. A lot of them old gals was after you then. You had the pick of the litter. When you picked Rose, I was happy for you. That was the first time I knew you had any sense. I said...My man Troy knows what he's doing...I'm gonna follow this nigger...he might take me somewhere. I been following you too. I done learned a whole heap of things about life watching you. I done learned how to tell where the shit lies. How to tell it from the alfalfa. You done learned me a lot of things. You showed me how to not make the same mistakes...to take life as it comes along and keep putting one foot in front of the other. [*Pause.*] Rose a good woman, Troy.

TROY. Hell, nigger, I know she a good woman. I been married to her for eighteen years. What you got on your mind, Bono?

BONO. I just say she a good woman. Just like I say anything. I ain't got to have nothing on my mind.

TROY. You just gonna say she a good woman and leave it hanging out there like that? Why you telling me she a good woman?

BONO. She loves you, Troy. Rose loves you.

TROY. You saying I don't measure up. That's what you trying to say. I don't measure up cause I'm seeing this other gal. I know what you trying to say.

BONO. I know what Rose means to you, Troy. I'm just trying to say I don't want to see you mess up.

TROY. Yeah, I appreciate that, Bono. If you was messing around on Lucille I'd be telling you the same thing.

BONO. Well, that's all I got to say. I just say that because I love you both.

TROY. Hell, you know me...I wasn't out there looking for nothing. You can't find a better woman than Rose. I know that. But seems like this woman just stuck onto me where I can't shake her loose. I done wrestled with it, tried to throw her off me...but she just stuck on tighter. Now she's stuck on for good.

BONO. You's in control...that's what you tell me all the time. You responsible for what you do.

TROY. I ain't ducking the responsibility of it. As long as it sets right in my heart...then I'm okay. 'Cause that's all I listen to. It'll tell me right from wrong every time. And I ain't talking about doing Rose no bad turn. I love Rose. She done carried me a long ways and I love and respect her for that.

BONO. I know you do. That's why I don't want to see you hurt her. But what you gonna do when she find out? What you got then? If you try and juggle both of them...sooner or later you gonna drop one of them. That's common sense.

TROY. Yeah, I hear what you saying, Bono. I been trying to figure a way to work it out.

BONO. Work it out right, Troy. I don't want to be getting all up between you and Rose's business...but work it so it come out right.

TROY. Ah hell, I get all up between you and Lucille's business. When you gonna get that woman that refrigerator she been wanting? Don't tell me you ain't got no money now. I know who your banker is. Mellon don't need that money bad as Lucille want that refrigerator. I'll tell you that.

BONO. Tell you what I'll do...when you finish building this fence for Rose...I'll buy Lucille that refrigerator.

TROY. You done stuck your foot in your mouth now!

TROY *grabs up a board and begins to saw.* BONO *starts to walk out the yard.*

Hey, nigger...where you going?

BONO. I'm going home. I know you don't expect me to help you now. I'm protecting my money. I wanna see you put that fence up by yourself. That's what I want to see. You'll be here another six months without me.

TROY. Nigger, you ain't right.

BONO. When it comes to my money...I'm right as fireworks on the Fourth of July.

TROY. All right, we gonna see now. You better get out your bankbook.

BONO *exits, and* TROY *continues to work.* ROSE *enters from the house.*

ROSE. What they say down there? What's happening with Gabe?

TROY. I went down there and got him out. Cost me fifty dollars. Say he was disturbing the peace. Judge set up a hearing for him in three weeks. Say to show cause why he shouldn't be recommitted.

ROSE. What was he doing that cause them to arrest him?

TROY. Some kids was teasing him and he run them off home. Say he was howling and carrying on. Some folks seen him and called the police. That's all it was.

ROSE. Well, what's you say? What'd you tell the judge?

TROY. Told him I'd look after him. It didn't make no sense to recommit the man. He stuck out his big greasy palm and told me to give him fifty dollars and take him on home.

ROSE. Where's he at now? Where'd he go off to?

TROY. He's gone about his business. He don't need nobody to hold his hand.

ROSE. Well, I don't know. Seem like that would be the best place for him if they did put him into the hospital. I know what you're gonna say. But that's what I think would be best.

TROY. The man done had his life ruined fighting for what? And they wanna take and lock him up. Let him be free. He don't bother nobody.

ROSE. Well, everybody got their own way of looking at it I guess. Come on and get your lunch. I got a bowl of lima beans and some cornbread in the oven. Come and get something to eat. Ain't no sense you fretting over Gabe.

> ROSE *turns to go into the house.*

TROY. Rose...got something to tell you.

ROSE. Well, come on...wait till I get this food on the table.

TROY. Rose!

> *She stops and turns around.*

I don't know how to say this. [*Pause.*] I can't explain it none. It just sort of grows on you till it gets out of hand. It starts out like a little bush...and the next thing you know it's a whole forest.

ROSE. Troy...what is you talking about?

TROY. I'm talking, woman, let me talk. I'm trying to find a way to tell you...I'm gonna be a daddy. I'm gonna be somebody's daddy.

ROSE. Troy...you're not telling me this? You're gonna be...what?

TROY. Rose...now...see...

ROSE. You telling me you gonna be somebody's daddy? You telling your *wife* this?

> GABRIEL *enters from the street. He carries a rose in his hand.*

GABRIEL. Hey, Troy! Hey, Rose!

ROSE. I have to wait eighteen years to hear something like this.

GABRIEL. Hey, Rose...I got a flower for you. [*He hands it to her.*] That's a rose. Same rose like you is.

ROSE. Thanks, Gabe.

GABRIEL. Troy, you ain't mad at me is you? Them bad mens come and put me away. You ain't mad at me is you?

TROY. Naw, Gabe, I ain't mad at you.

ROSE. Eighteen years and you wanna come with this.

GABRIEL [*takes a quarter out of his pocket*]. See what I got? Got a brand new quarter.

TROY. Rose...it's just...

ROSE. Ain't nothing you can say, Troy. Ain't no way of explaining that.

GABRIEL. Fellow that give me this quarter had a whole mess of them. I'm gonna keep this quarter till it stop shining.

ROSE. Gabe, go on in the house there. I got some watermelon in the Frigidaire. Go on and get you a piece.

GABRIEL. Say, Rose...you know I was chasing hellhounds and them bad mens come and get me and take me away. Troy helped me. He come down there and told them they better let me go before he beat them up. Yeah, he did!

ROSE. You go on and get you a piece of watermelon, Gabe. Them bad mens is gone now.

GABRIEL. Okay, Rose…gonna get me some watermelon. The kind with the stripes on it.

GABRIEL *exits into the house.*

ROSE. Why, Troy? Why? After all these years to come dragging this in to me now. It don't make no sense at your age. I could have expected this ten or fifteen years ago, but not now.

TROY. Age ain't got nothing to do with it, Rose.

ROSE. I done tried to be everything a wife should be. Everything a wife could be. Been married eighteen years and I got to live to see the day you tell me you been seeing another woman and done fathered a child by her. And you know I ain't never wanted no half nothing in my family. My whole family is half. Everybody got different fathers and mothers…my two sisters and my brother. Can't hardly tell who's who. Can't never sit down and talk about Papa and Mama. It's your papa and your mama and my papa and my mama…

TROY. Rose…stop it now.

ROSE. I ain't never wanted that for none of my children. And now you wanna drag your behind in here and tell me something like this.

TROY. You ought to know. It's time for you to know.

ROSE. Well, I don't want to know, goddamn it!

TROY. I can't just make it go away. It's done now. I can't wish the circumstance of the thing away.

ROSE. And you don't want to either. Maybe you want to wish me and my boy away. Maybe that's what you want? Well, you can't wish us away. I've got eighteen years of my life invested in you. You ought to have stayed upstairs in my bed where you belong.

TROY. Rose…now listen to me…we can get a handle on this thing. We can talk this out…come to an understanding.

ROSE. All of a sudden it's "we." Where was "we" at when you was down there rolling around with some godforsaken woman? "We" should have come to an understanding before you started making a damn fool of yourself. You're a day late and a dollar short when it comes to an understanding with me.

TROY. It's just…She gives me a different idea…a different understanding about myself. I can step out of this house and get away from the pressures and problems…be a different man. I ain't got to wonder how I'm gonna pay the bills or get the roof fixed. I can just be a part of myself that I ain't never been.

ROSE. What I want to know…is do you plan to continue seeing her? That's all you can say to me.

TROY. I can sit up in her house and laugh. Do you understand what I'm saying? I can laugh out loud…and it feels goods. It reaches all the way down to the bottom of my shoes. [*Pause.*] Rose, I can't give that up.

ROSE. Maybe you ought to go on and stay down there with her…if she's a better woman than me.

TROY. It ain't about nobody being a better woman or nothing. Rose, you ain't the blame. A man couldn't ask for no woman to be a better wife than you've been. I'm responsible for it. I done locked myself into a pattern trying to take care of you all that I forgot about myself.

ROSE. What the hell was I there for? That was my job, not somebody else's.

TROY. Rose, I done tried all my life to live decent…to live a clean…hard…useful life. I tried to be a good husband to you. In every way I knew how. Maybe I come into the world backwards, I don't know. But...you born with two strikes on you before you come to the plate. You got to guard it closely...always looking for the curve ball on the inside corner. You can't afford to let none get past you. You can't afford a call strike. If you going down...you going down swinging. Everything lined up against you. What you gonna do. I fooled them, Rose. I bunted. When I found you and Cory and a halfway decent job...I was safe. Couldn't nothing touch me. I wasn't gonna strike out no more. I wasn't going back to the penitentiary. I wasn't gonna lay in the streets with a bottle of wine. I was safe. I had me a family. A job. I wasn't gonna get that last strike. I was on first looking for one of them boys to knock me in. To get me home.

ROSE. You should have stayed in my bed, Troy.

TROY. Then when I saw that gal...she firmed up my backbone. And I got to thinking that if I tried...I just might be able to steal second. Do you understand after eighteen years I wanted to steal second.

ROSE. You should have held me tight. You should have grabbed me and held on.

TROY. I stood on first base for eighteen years and I thought...well, goddamn it...go on for it!

ROSE. We're not talking about baseball! We're talking about you going off to lay in bed with another woman...and then bring it home to me. That's what we're talking about. We ain't talking about no baseball.

TROY. Rose, you're not listening to me. I'm trying the best I can to explain it to you. It's not easy for me to admit that I been standing in the same place for eighteen years.

ROSE. I been standing with you! I been right here with you, Troy. I got a life too. I gave eighteen years of my life to stand in the same spot with you. Don't you think I ever wanted other things? Don't you think I had dreams and hopes? What about my life? What about me? Don't you think it ever crossed my mind to want to know other men? That I wanted to lay up somewhere and forget about my responsibilities? That I wanted someone to make me laugh so I could feel good? You not the only one who's got wants and needs. But I held on to you, Troy. I took all my feelings, my wants and needs, my dreams...and I buried them inside you. I planted a seed and watched and prayed over it. I planted myself inside you and waited to bloom. And it didn't take me no eighteen years to find out the soil was hard and rocky and it wasn't never gonna bloom.

But I held on to you, Troy. I held you tighter. You was my husband. I owed you everything I had. Every part of me I could find to give you. And upstairs in that room...with the darkness falling in on me...I gave everything I had to try and erase the doubt that you wasn't the finest man in the world. And wherever you was going...I wanted to be there with you. 'Cause you was my husband. 'Cause that's the only way I was gonna survive as your wife. You always talking about what you give...and what you don't have to give. But you take too. You take...and don't even know nobody's giving!

ROSE *turns to exit into the house;* TROY *grabs her arm.*

TROY. You say I take and don't give!

ROSE. Troy! You're hurting me!

TROY. You say I take and don't give!

ROSE. Troy...you're hurting my arm! Let go!

TROY. I done give you everything I got. Don't you tell that lie on me.

ROSE. Troy!
TROY. Don't you tell that lie on me!

>   CORY *enters from the house.*

CORY. Mama!
ROSE. Troy. You're hurting me.
TROY. Don't you tell me about no taking and giving.

>   CORY *comes up behind* TROY *and grabs him.* TROY, *surprised, is thrown off balance just as* CORY *throws a glancing blow that catches him on the chest and knocks him down.* TROY *is stunned, as is* CORY.

ROSE. Troy. Troy. No!

>   TROY *gets to his feet and starts at* CORY.

Troy...no. Please! Troy!

>   ROSE *pulls on* TROY *to hold him back.* TROY *stops himself.*

TROY [*to* CORY]. All right. That's strike two. You stay away from around me, boy. Don't you strike out. You living with a full count. Don't you strike out.

>   TROY *exits out the yard as the lights go down.*

SCENE 2

It is six months later, early afternoon. TROY *enters from the house and starts to exit the yard.* ROSE *enters from the house.*

ROSE. Troy, I want to talk to you.
TROY. All of a sudden, after all this time, you want to talk to me, huh? You ain't wanted to talk to me for months. You ain't wanted to talk to me last night. You ain't wanted no part of me then. What you wanna talk to me about now?
ROSE. Tomorrow's Friday.
TROY. I know what day tomorrow is. You think I don't know tomorrow's Friday? My whole life I ain't done nothing but look to see Friday coming and you got to tell me it's Friday.
ROSE. I want to know if you're coming home.
TROY. I always come home, Rose. You know that. There ain't never been a night I ain't come home.
ROSE. That ain't what I mean...and you know it. I want to know if you're coming straight home after work.
TROY. I figure I'd cash my check...hang out at Taylors' with the boys...maybe play a game of checkers...
ROSE. Troy, I can't live like this. I won't live like this. You livin' on borrowed time with me. It's been going on six months now you ain't been coming home.
TROY. I be here every night. Every night of the year. That's 365 days.
ROSE. I want you to come home tomorrow after work.
TROY. Rose...I don't mess up my pay. You know that now. I take my pay and I give it to you. I don't have no money but what you give me back. I just want to have little time to myself...a little time to enjoy life.
ROSE. What about me? When's my time to enjoy life?
TROY. I don't know what to tell you, Rose. I'm doing the best I can.

ROSE. You ain't been home from work but time enough to change your clothes and run out...and you wanna call that the best you can do?

TROY. I'm going over to the hospital to see Alberta. She went into the hospital this afternoon. Look like she might have the baby early. I won't be gone long.

ROSE. Well, you ought to know. They went over to Miss Pearl's and got Gabe today. She said you told them to go ahead and lock him up.

TROY. I ain't said no such thing. Whoever told you that is telling a lie. Pearl ain't doing nothing but telling a big fat lie.

ROSE. She ain't had to tell me. I read it on the papers.

TROY. I ain't told them nothing of the kind.

ROSE. I saw it right there on the papers.

TROY. What it say, huh?

ROSE. It said you told them to take him.

TROY. Then they screwed that up, just the way they screw up everything. I ain't worried about what they got on the paper.

ROSE. Say the government sent part of his check to the hospital and the other part to you.

TROY. I ain't got nothing to do with that if that's the way it works. I ain't made up the rules about how it work.

ROSE. You did Gabe just like you did Cory. You wouldn't sign the paper for Cory...but you signed for Gabe. You signed that paper.

The telephone is heard ringing inside the house.

TROY. I told you I ain't signed nothing, woman! The only thing I signed was the release form. Hell, I can't read, I don't know what they had on that paper! I ain't signed nothing about sending Gabe away.

ROSE. I said send him to the hospital...you said let him be free...now you done went down there and signed him to the hospital for half his money. You went back on yourself, Troy. You gonna have to answer for that.

TROY. See now...you been over there talking to Miss Pearl. She done got mad 'cause she ain't getting Gabe's rent money. That's all it is. She's liable to say anything.

ROSE. Troy, I seen where you signed the paper.

TROY. You ain't seen nothing I signed. What she doing got papers on my brother anyway? Miss Pearl telling a big fat lie. And I'm gonna tell her about it too! You ain't seen nothing I signed. Say...you ain't seen nothing I signed.

> ROSE *exits into the house to answer the*
> *telephone. Presently she returns.*

ROSE. Troy...that was the hospital. Alberta had the baby.

TROY. What she have? What is it?

ROSE. It's a girl.

TROY. I better get on down to the hospital to see her.

ROSE. Troy...

TROY. Rose...I got to go see her now. That's only right...what's the matter...the baby's all right, ain't it?

ROSE. Alberta died having the baby.

TROY. Died...you say she's dead? Alberta's dead?

ROSE. They said they done all they could. They couldn't do nothing for her.

TROY. The baby? How's the baby?

ROSE. They say it's healthy. I wonder who's gonna bury her.

TROY. She had family, Rose. She wasn't living in the world by herself.

ROSE. I know she wasn't living in the world by herself.

TROY. Next thing you gonna want to know if she had any insurance.

ROSE. Troy, you ain't got to talk like that.

TROY. That's the first thing that jumped out your mouth. "Who's gonna bury her?" Like I'm fixing to take on that task for myself.

ROSE. I am your wife. Don't push me away.

TROY. I ain't pushing nobody away. Just give me some space. That's all. Just give me some room to breathe.

> ROSE *exits into the house.* TROY *walks about the yard.*

TROY [*with a quiet rage that threatens to consume him*]. All right...Mr. Death. See now...I'm gonna tell you what I'm gonna do. I'm gonna take and build me a fence around this yard. See? I'm gonna build me a fence around what belongs to me. And then I want you to stay on the other side. See? You stay over there until you're ready for me. Then you come on. Bring your army. Bring your sickle. Bring your wrestling clothes. I ain't gonna fall down on my vigilance this time. You ain't gonna sneak up on me no more. When you ready for me...when the top of your list say Troy Maxson...that's when you come around here. You come up and knock on the front door. Ain't nobody else got nothing to do with this. This is between you and me. Man to man. You stay on the other side of that fence until you ready for me. Then you come up and knock on the front door. Anytime you want. I'll be ready for you.

> *The lights go down to black.*

SCENE 3

The lights come up on the porch. It is late evening three days later. ROSE *sits listening to the ball game waiting for* TROY. *The final out of the game is made and* ROSE *switches off the radio.* TROY *enters the yard carrying an infant wrapped in blankets. He stands back from the house and calls.*

> ROSE *enters and stands on the porch. There is a long, awkward silence, the weight of which grows heavier with each passing second.*

TROY. Rose...I'm standing here with my daughter in my arms. She ain't but a wee bittie little old thing. She don't know nothing about grownups' business. She innocent...and she ain't got no mama.

ROSE. What you telling me for, Troy?

> *She turns and exits into the house.*

TROY. Well...I guess we'll just sit out here on the porch.

> *He sits down on the porch. There is an awkward indelicateness about the way he handles the baby. His largeness engulfs and seems to swallow it. He speaks loud enough for* ROSE *to hear.*

A man's got to do what's right for him. I ain't sorry for nothing I done. It felt right in my heart. [*To the baby.*] What you smiling at? Your daddy's a big man. Got these great big old hands. But sometimes he's scared. And right now your daddy's scared cause we sitting out here and ain't got no home. Oh, I been homeless before. I ain't had no little baby with me. But I been homeless. You just be out on the road by your lonesome and you see one of them trains coming and you just kinda go like this...

He sings as a lullaby.

> Please, Mr. Engineer let a man ride the line
> Please, Mr. Engineer let a man ride the line
> I ain't got no ticket please let me ride the blinds.

ROSE *enters from the house.* TROY, *hearing her steps behind him, stands and faces her.*

She's my daughter, Rose. My own flesh and blood. I can't deny her no more than I can deny them boys. [*Pause.*] You and them boys is my family. You and them and this child is all I got in the world. So I guess what I'm saying is...I'd appreciate it if you'd help me take care of her.

ROSE. Okay, Troy...you're right. I'll take care of your baby for you... 'cause...like you say...she's innocent...and you can't visit the sins of the father upon the child. A motherless child has got a hard time. [*She takes the baby from him.*] From right now...this child got a mother. But you a woman-less man.

ROSE *turns and exits into the house with the baby. Lights go down to black.*

SCENE 4

It is two months later. LYONS *enters the street. He knocks on the door and calls.*

LYONS. Hey, Rose! [*Pause.*] Rose!

ROSE [*from inside the house*]. Stop that yelling. You gonna wake up Raynell. I just got her to sleep.

LYONS. I just stopped by to pay Papa this twenty dollars I owe him. Where's Papa at?

ROSE. He should be here in a minute. I'm getting ready to go down to the church. Sit down and wait on him.

LYONS. I got to go pick up Bonnie over her mother's house.

ROSE. Well, sit it down there on the table. He'll get it.

LYONS [*enters the house and sets the money on the table*]. Tell Papa I said thanks. I'll see you again.

ROSE. All right, Lyons. We'll see you.

LYONS *starts to exit as* CORY *enters.*

CORY. Hey, Lyons.

LYONS. What's happening, Cory? Say man, I'm sorry I missed your graduation. You know I had a gig and couldn't get away. Otherwise, I would have been there, man. So what you doing?

CORY. I'm trying to find a job.

LYONS. Yeah I know how that go, man. It's rough out here. Jobs are scarce.

CORY. Yeah, I know.

LYONS. Look here, I got to run. Talk to Papa...he know some people. He'll be able to help get you a job. Talk to him...see what he say.

CORY. Yeah...all right, Lyons.

LYONS. You take care. I'll talk to you soon. We'll find some time to talk.

LYONS *exits the yard.*

CORY *wanders over to the tree, picks up the bat, and assumes a batting stance. He studies an imaginary pitcher and swings. Dissatisfied with the result, he tries again. TROY enters. They eye each other for a beat. CORY puts the bat down and exits the yard. TROY starts into the house as ROSE exits with RAYNELL. She is carrying a cake.*

TROY. I'm coming in and everybody's going out.

ROSE. I'm taking this cake down to the church for the bake sale. Lyons was by to see you. He stopped by to pay you your twenty dollars. It's laying in there on the table.

TROY [*going into his pocket*]. Well...here go this money.

ROSE. Put it in there on the table, Troy. I'll get it.

TROY. What time you coming back?

ROSE. Ain't no use in you studying me. It don't matter what time I come back.

TROY. I just asked you a question, woman. What's the matter...can't I ask you a question?

ROSE. Troy, I don't want to go into it. Your dinner's in there on the stove. All you got to do is heat it up. And don't you be eating the rest of them cakes in there. I'm coming back for them. We having a bake sale at the church tomorrow.

ROSE *exits the yard.* TROY *sits down on the steps, takes a pint bottle from his pocket, opens it, and drinks. He begins to sing.*

TROY.

> Hear it ring! Hear it ring!
> Had an old dog his name was Blue
> You know Blue was mighty true
> You know Blue as a good old dog
> Blue trees a possum in a hollow log
> You know from that he was a good old dog.

BONO *enters the yard.*

BONO. Hey, Troy.

TROY. Hey, what's happening, Bono?

BONO. I just thought I'd stop by to see you.

TROY. What you stop by and see me for? You ain't stopped by in a month of Sundays. Hell, I must owe you money or something.

BONO. Since you got your promotion I can't keep up with you. Used to see you every day. Now I don't even know what route you working.

TROY. They keep switching me around. Got me out in Greentree now...hauling white folks' garbage.

BONO. Greentree, huh? You lucky, at least you ain't got to be lifting them barrels. Damn if they ain't getting heavier. I'm gonna put in my two years and call it quits.

TROY. I'm thinking about retiring myself.

BONO. You got it easy. You can drive for another five years.

TROY. It ain't the same, Bono. It ain't like working the back of the truck. Ain't got nobody to talk to...feel like you working by yourself. Naw, I'm thinking about retiring. How's Lucille?

BONO. She all right. Her arthritis get to acting up on her sometime. Saw Rose on my way in. She going down to the church, huh?

TROY. Yeah, she took up going down there. All them preachers looking for some-body to fatten their pockets. [*Pause.*] Got some gin here.

BONO. Naw, thanks. I just stopped by to say hello.

TROY. Hell, nigger...you can take a drink. I ain't never known you to say no to a drink. You ain't got to work tomorrow.

BONO. I just stopped by. I'm fixing to go over to Skinner's. We got us a domino game going over his house every Friday.

TROY. Nigger, you can't play no dominoes. I used to whup you four games out of five.

BONO. Well, that learned me. I'm getting better.

TROY. Yeah? Well, that's all right.

BONO. Look here...I got to be getting on. Stop by sometime, huh?

TROY. Yeah, I'll do that, Bono. Lucille told Rose you bought her a new refrigerator.

BONO. Yeah, Rose told Lucille you had finally built your fence...so I figured we'd call it even.

TROY. I knew you would.

BONO. Yeah...okay. I'll be talking to you.

TROY. Yeah, take care, Bono. Good to see you. I'm gonna stop over.

BONO. Yeah. Okay, Troy.

BONO *exits.* TROY *drinks from the bottle.*

TROY.

> Old Blue died and I dig his grave
> Let him down with a golden chain
> Every night when I hear old Blue bark
> I know Blue treed a possum in Noah's Ark
> Hear it ring! Hear it ring!

CORY *enters the yard. They eye each other for a beat.* TROY *is sitting in the middle of the steps.* CORY *walks over.*

CORY. I got to get by.

TROY. Say what? What's you say?

CORY. You in my way. I got to get by.

TROY. You got to get by where? This is my house. Bought and paid for. In full. Took me fifteen years. And if you wanna go in my house and I'm sitting on the steps...you say excuse me. Like your mama taught you.

CORY. Come on, Pop...I got to get by.

CORY *starts to maneuver his way past* TROY. TROY *grabs his leg and shoves him back.*

TROY. You just gonna walk over top of me?

CORY. I live here too!

TROY [*advancing toward him*]. You just gonna walk over top of me in my own house?

CORY. I ain't scared of you.

TROY. I ain't asked if you was scared of me. I asked you if you was fixing to walk over top of me in my own house? That's the question. You ain't gonna say excuse me? You just gonna walk over top of me?

CORY. If you wanna put it like that.

TROY. How else am I gonna put it?

CORY. I was walking by you to go into the house cause you sitting on the steps drunk, singing to yourself. You can put it like that.

TROY. Without saying excuse me???

CORY *doesn't respond.*

I asked you a question. Without saying excuse me???

CORY. I ain't got to say excuse me to you. You don't count around here no more.

TROY. Oh, I see...I don't count around here no more. You ain't got to say excuse me to your daddy. All of a sudden you done got so grown that your daddy don't count around here no more...Around here in his own house and yard that he done paid for with the sweat of his brow. You done got so grown to where you gonna take over. You gonna take over my house. Is that right? You gonna wear my pants. You gonna go in there and stretch out on my bed. You ain't got to say excuse me cause I don't count around here no more. Is that right?

CORY. That's right. You always talking this dumb stuff. Now, why don't you just get out my way?

TROY. I guess you got someplace to sleep and something to put in your belly. You got that, huh? You got that? That's what you need. You got that, huh?

CORY. You don't know what I got. You ain't got to worry about what I got.

TROY. You right! You one hundred percent right! I done spent the last seventeen years worrying about what you got. Now it's your turn, see? I'll tell you what to do. You grown...we done established that. You a man. Now, let's see you act like one. Turn your behind around and walk out this yard. And when you get out there in the alley...you can forget about this house. See? 'Cause this is my house. You go on and be a man and get your own house. You can forget about this. 'Cause this is mine. You go on and get yours cause I'm through with doing for you.

CORY. You talking about what you did for me...what'd you ever give me?

TROY. Them feet and bones! That pumping heart, nigger! I give you more than anybody else is ever gonna give you.

CORY. You ain't never gave me nothing! You ain't never done nothing but hold me back. Afraid I was gonna be better than you. All you ever did was try and make me scared of you. I used to tremble every time you called my name. Every time I heard your footsteps in the house. Wondering all the time...what's Papa gonna say if I do this?...What's he gonna say if I do that?...What's Papa gonna say if I turn on the radio? And mama, too...she tries...but she's scared of you.

TROY. You leave your mama out of this. She ain't got nothing to do with this.

CORY. I don't know how she stand you...after what you did to her.

TROY. I told you to leave your mama out of this!

He advances toward CORY.

CORY. What you gonna do...give me a whupping? You can't whup me no more. You're too old. You just an old man.

TROY [*shoves him on his shoulder*]. Nigger! That's what you are. You just another nigger on the street to me!

CORY. You crazy! You know that?

TROY. Go on now! You got the devil in you. Get on away from me!

CORY. You just a crazy old man...talking about I got the devil in me.

TROY. Yeah, I'm crazy! If you don't get on the other side of that yard...I'm gonna show you how crazy I am! Go on...get the hell out of my yard!

CORY. It ain't your yard. You took Uncle Gabe's money he got from the army to buy this house and then you put him out.

TROY [*advances on* CORY]. Get your black ass out of my yard!

TROY's advance backs CORY *up against the tree.* CORY *grabs up the bat.*

CORY. I ain't going nowhere! Come on...put me out! I ain't scared of you.

TROY. That's my bat!

CORY. Come on!
TROY. Put my bat down!
CORY. Come on, put me out.

> CORY *swings at* TROY, *who backs across the yard.*

What's the matter? You so bad...put me out!

> TROY *advances toward* CORY.

CORY [*backing up*]. Come on! Come on!
TROY. You're gonna have to use it! You wanna draw that bat back on me...you're gonna have to use it.
CORY. Come on!...Come on!

> CORY *swings the bat at* TROY *a second time. He misses.* TROY *continues to advance toward him.*

TROY. You're gonna have to kill me! You wanna draw that bat back on me. You're gonna have to kill me.

> CORY, *backed up against the tree, can go no farther.* TROY *taunts him. He sticks out his head and offers him a target.*

Come on! Come on!

> CORY *is unable to swing the bat.* TROY *grabs it.*

TROY. Then I'll show you.

> CORY *and* TROY *struggle over the bat. The struggle is fierce and fully engaged.* TROY *ultimately is the stronger and takes the bat from* CORY *and stands over him ready to swing. He stops himself.*

Go on and get away from around my house.

> CORY, *stung by his defeat, picks himself up, walks slowly out of the yard and up the alley.*

CORY. Tell Mama I'll be back for my things.
TROY. They'll be on the other side of that fence.

> CORY *exits.*

I can't taste nothing. Helluljah! I can't taste nothing no more. [TROY *assumes a batting posture and begins to taunt Death, the fastball on the outside corner.*] Come on! It's between you and me now! Come on! Anytime you want! Come on! I be ready for you...but I ain't gonna be easy.

> *The lights go down on the scene.*

SCENE 5

The time is 1965. The lights come up in the yard. It is the morning of TROY'S *funeral. A funeral plaque with a light hangs beside the door. There is a small garden plot off to the side. There is noise and activity in the house as* ROSE, LYONS, *and* BONO *have gathered. The door opens and* RAYNELL, *seven years old, enters dressed in a flannel nightgown. She crosses to the garden and pokes around with a stick.* ROSE *calls from the house.*

ROSE. Raynell!
RAYNELL. Mam?

ROSE. What you doing out there?

RAYNELL. Nothing.

> ROSE *comes to the door.*

ROSE. Girl, get in here and get dressed. What you doing?

RAYNELL. Seeing if my garden growed.

ROSE. I told you it ain't gonna grow overnight. You got to wait.

RAYNELL. It don't look like it never gonna grow. Dag!

ROSE. I told you a watched pot never boils. Get in here and get dressed.

RAYNELL. This ain't even no pot, Mama.

ROSE. You just have to give it a chance. It'll grow. Now you come on and do what I told you. We got to be getting ready. This ain't no morning to be playing around. You hear me?

RAYNELL. Yes, mam.

> ROSE *exits into the house.* RAYNELL *continues to poke at her garden with a stick.* CORY *enters. He is dressed in a Marine corporal's uniform, and carries a duffelbag. His posture is that of a military man, and his speech has a clipped sternness.*

CORY [*to* RAYNELL]. Hi. [*Pause.*] I bet your name is Raynell.

RAYNELL. Uh huh.

CORY. Is your mama home?

> RAYNELL *runs up on the porch and calls through the screen door.*

RAYNELL. Mama...there's some man out here. Mama?

> ROSE *comes to the door.*

ROSE. Cory? Lord have mercy! Look here, you all!

> ROSE *and* CORY *embrace in a tearful reunion as* BONO *and* LYONS *enter from the house dressed in funeral clothes.*

BONO. Aw, looka here...

ROSE. Done got all grown up!

CORY. Don't cry, Mama. What you crying about?

ROSE. I'm just so glad you made it.

CORY. Hey Lyons. How you doing, Mr. Bono.

> LYONS *goes to embrace* CORY.

LYONS. Look at you, man. Look at you. Don't he look good, Rose. Got them Corporal stripes.

ROSE. What took you so long?

CORY. You know how the Marines are, Mama. They got to get all their paperwork straight before they let you do anything.

ROSE. Well, I'm sure glad you made it. They let Lyons come. Your Uncle Gabe's still in the hospital. They don't know if they gonna let him out or not. I just talked to them a little while ago.

LYONS. A Corporal in the United States Marines.

BONO. Your daddy knew you had it in you. He used to tell me all the time.

LYONS. Don't he look good, Mr. Bono?

BONO. Yeah, he remind me of Troy when I first met him. [*Pause.*] Say, Rose, Lucille's down at the church with the choir. I'm gonna go down and get the pallbearers lined up. I'll be back to get you all.

ROSE. Thanks, Jim.

CORY. See you, Mr. Bono.

LYONS [*with his arm around* RAYNELL]. Cory…look at Raynell. Ain't she precious? She gonna break a whole lot of hearts.

ROSE. Raynell, come and say hello to your brother. This is your brother, Cory. You remember Cory.

RAYNELL. No, Mam.

CORY. She don't remember me, Mama.

ROSE. Well, we talk about you. She heard us talk about you. [*To* RAYNELL.] This is your brother, Cory. Come on and say hello.

RAYNELL. Hi.

CORY. Hi. So you're Raynell. Mama told me a lot about you.

ROSE. You all come on into the house and let me fix you some breakfast. Keep up your strength.

CORY. I ain't hungry, Mama.

LYONS. You can fix me something, Rose. I'll be in there in a minute.

ROSE. Cory, you sure you don't want nothing? I know they ain't feeding you right.

CORY. No, Mama…thanks. I don't feel like eating. I'll get something later.

ROSE. Raynell…get on upstairs and get that dress on like I told you.

> ROSE *and* RAYNELL *exit into the house.*

LYONS. So…I hear you thinking about getting married.

CORY. Yeah, I done found the right one, Lyons. It's about time.

LYONS. Me and Bonnie been split up about four years now. About the time Papa retired. I guess she just got tired of all them changes I was putting her through. [*Pause.*] I always knew you was gonna make something out yourself. Your head was always in the right direction. So…you gonna stay in…make it a career…put in your twenty years?

CORY. I don't know. I got six already, I think that's enough.

LYONS. Stick with Uncle Sam and retire early. Ain't nothing out here. I guess Rose told you what happened with me. They got me down the workhouse. I thought I was being slick cashing other people's checks.

CORY. How much time you doing?

LYONS. They give me three years. I got that beat now. I ain't got but nine more months. It ain't so bad. You learn to deal with it like anything else. You got to take the crookeds with the straights. That's what Papa used to say. He used to say that when he struck out. I seen him strike out three times in a row…and the next time up he hit the ball over the grandstand. Right out there in Homestead Field. He wasn't satisfied hitting in the seats…he want to hit it over everything! After the game he had two hundred people standing around waiting to shake his hand. You got to take the crookeds with the straights. Yeah, Papa was something else.

CORY. You still playing?

LYONS. Cory…you know I'm gonna do that. There's some fellows down there we got us a band…we gonna try and stay together when we get out…but yeah, I'm still playing. It still helps me to get out of bed in the morning. As long as it do that I'm gonna be right there playing and trying to make some sense out of it.

ROSE [*calling*]. Lyons, I got these eggs in the pan.

LYONS. Let me go on and get these eggs, man. Get ready to go bury Papa. [*Pause.*] How you doing? You doing all right?

CORY *nods.* LYONS *touches him on the shoulder and they share a moment of silent grief.* LYONS *exits into the house.* CORY *wanders about the yard.* RAYNELL *enters.*

RAYNELL. Hi.
CORY. Hi.
RAYNELL. Did you used to sleep in my room?
CORY. Yeah...that used to be my room.
RAYNELL. That's what Papa call it. "Cory's room." It got your football in the closet.

ROSE *comes to the door.*

ROSE. Raynell, get in there and get them good shoes on.
RAYNELL. Mama, can't I wear these? Them other one hurt my feet.
ROSE. Well, they just gonna have to hurt your feet for a while. You ain't said they hurt your feet when you went down to the store and got them.
RAYNELL. They didn't hurt then. My feet done got bigger.
ROSE. Don't you give me no backtalk now. You get in there and get them shoes on.

RAYNELL *exits into the house.*

Ain't too much changed. He still got that piece of rag tied to that tree. He was out here swinging that bat. I was just ready to go back in the house. He swung that bat and then he just fell over. Seem like he swung it and stood there with this grin on his face...and then he just fell over. They carried him on down to the hospital, but I knew there wasn't no need...why don't you come on in the house?
CORY. Mama...I got something to tell you. I don't know how to tell you this...but I've got to tell you...I'm not going to Papa's funeral.
ROSE. Boy, hush your month. That's your daddy you talking about. I don't want hear that kind of talk this morning. I done raised you to come to this? You standing there all healthy and grown talking about you ain't going to your daddy's funeral?
CORY. Mama...listen...
ROSE. I don't want to hear it, Cory. You just get that thought out of your head.
CORY. I can't drag Papa with me everywhere I go. I've got to say no to him. One time in my life I've got to say no.
ROSE. Don't nobody have to listen to nothing like that. I know you and your daddy ain't seen eye to eye, but I ain't got to listen to that kind of talk this morning. Whatever was between you and your daddy...the time has come to put it aside. Just take it and set it over there on the shelf and forget about it. Disrespecting your daddy ain't gonna make you a man, Cory. You got to find a way to come to that on your own. Not going to your daddy's funeral ain't gonna make you a man.
CORY. The whole time I was growing up...living in his house...Papa was like a shadow that followed you everywhere. It weighed on you and sunk into your flesh. It would wrap around you and lay there until you couldn't tell which one was you anymore. That shadow digging in your flesh. Trying to crawl in. Trying to live through you. Everywhere I looked, Troy Maxson was staring back at me...hiding under the bed...in the closet. I'm just saying I've got to find a way to get rid of that shadow, Mama.
ROSE. You just like him. You got him in you good.

CORY. Don't tell me that, Mama.

ROSE. You Troy Maxson all over again.

CORY. I don't want to be Troy Maxson. I want to be me.

ROSE. You can't be nobody but who you are, Cory. That shadow wasn't nothing but you growing into yourself. You either got to grow into it or cut it down to fit you. But that's all you got to make life with. That's all you got to measure yourself against that world out there. Your daddy wanted you to be everything he wasn't...and at the same time he tried to make you into everything he was. I don't know if he was right or wrong...but I do know he meant to do more good than he meant to do harm. He wasn't always right. Sometimes when he touched he bruised. And sometimes when he took me in his arms he cut.

When I first met your daddy I thought...Here is a man I can lay down with and make a baby. That's the first thing I thought when I seen him. I was thirty years old and had done seen my share of men. But when he walked up to me and said, "I can dance a waltz that'll make you dizzy," I thought, Rose Lee, here is a man that you can open yourself up to and be filled to bursting. Here is a man that can fill all them empty spaces you been tipping around the edges of. One of them empty spaces was being somebody's mother.

I married your daddy and settled down to cooking his supper and keeping clean sheets on the bed. When your daddy walked through the house he was so big he filled it up. That was my first mistake. Not to make him leave some room for me. For my part in the matter. But at that time I wanted that. I wanted a house that I could sing in. And that's what your daddy gave me. I didn't know to keep up his strength I had to give up little pieces of mine. I did that. I took on his life as mine and mixed up the pieces so that you couldn't hardly tell which was which anymore. It was my choice. It was my life and I didn't have to live it like that. But that's what life offered me in the way of being a woman and I took it. I grabbed hold of it with both hands.

By the time Raynell came into the house, me and your daddy had done lost touch with one another. I didn't want to make my blessing off of nobody's misfortune...but I took on to Raynell like she was all them babies I had wanted and never had.

The phone rings.

Like I'd been blessed to relive a part of my life. And if the Lord see fit to keep up my strength...I'm gonna do her just like your daddy did you...I'm gonna give her the best of what's in me.

RAYNELL [*entering, still with her old shoes*]. Mama...Reverend Tollivier on the phone.

ROSE *exits into the house.*

RAYNELL. Hi.

CORY. Hi.

RAYNELL. You in the Army or the Marines?

CORY. Marines.

RAYNELL. Papa said it was the Army. Did you know Blue?

CORY. Blue? Who's Blue?

RAYNELL. Papa's dog what he sing about all the time.

CORY [*singing*].

> Hear it ring! Hear it ring!
> I had a dog his name was Blue
> You know Blue was mighty true
> You know Blue was a good old dog
> Blue treed a possum in a hollow log
> You know from that he was a good old dog.
> Hear it ring! Hear it ring!

RAYNELL *joins in singing.*

CORY AND RAYNELL.

> Blue treed a possum out on a limb
> Blue looked at me and I looked at him
> Grabbed that possum and put him in a sack
> Blue stayed there till I came back
> Old Blue's feets was big and round
> Never allowed a possum to touch the ground.
>
> Old Blue died and I dug his grave
> I dug his grave with a silver spade
> Let him down with a golden chain
> Any every night I call his name
> Go on Blue, you good dog you
> Go on Blue, you good dog you.

RAYNELL.

> Blue laid down and died like a man
> Blue laid down and died...

BOTH.

> Blue laid down and died like a man
> Now he's treeing possums in the Promised Land
> I'm gonna tell you this to let you know
> Blue's gone where the good dogs go
> When I hear old Blue bark
> When I hear old Blue bark
> Blue treed a possum in Noah's Ark
> Blue treed a possum in Noah's Ark.

ROSE *comes to the screen door.*

ROSE. Cory, we gonna be ready to go in a minute.

CORY [*to* RAYNELL]. You go on in the house and change them shoes like Mama told you so we can go to Papa's funeral.

RAYNELL. Okay, I'll be back.

RAYNELL *exits into the house.* CORY *gets up and crosses over to the tree.* ROSE *stands in the screen door watching him.* GABRIEL *enters from the alley.*

GABRIEL [*calling*]. Hey, Rose!

ROSE. Gabe?

GABRIEL. I'm here, Rose. Hey Rose, I'm here!

ROSE *enters from the house.*

ROSE. Lord...Look here, Lyons!

LYONS. See, I told you, Rose...I told you they'd let him come.

CORY. How you doing, Uncle Gabe?

LYONS. How you doing, Uncle Gabe?

GABRIEL. Hey, Rose. It's time. It's time to tell St. Peter to open the gates. Troy, you ready? You ready, Troy. I'm gonna tell St. Peter to open the gates. You get ready now.

> GABRIEL, *with great fanfare, braces himself to blow. The trumpet is without a mouthpiece. He puts the end of it into his mouth and blows with great force, like a man who has been waiting some twenty-odd years for this single moment. No sound comes out of the trumpet. He braces himself and blows again with the same results. A third time he blows. There is a weight of impossible description that falls away and leaves him bare and exposed to a frightful realization. It is a trauma that a sane and normal mind would be unable to withstand. He begins to dance. A slow, strange dance, eerie and life-giving. A dance of atavistic signature and ritual.* LYONS *attempts to embrace him.* GABRIEL *pushes* LYONS *away. He begins to howl in what is an attempt at song, or perhaps a song turning back into itself in an attempt at speech. He finishes his dance and the gates of heaven stand open as wide as God's closet.*

That's the way that go!

(Blackout)

[1987]

PREWRITING

Begin your study of *Fences* by writing about and discussing the following ideas.

Analyzing the Characters

1. One way to look at this play is as a story of deceptions. List five or six deceptions that occur in the play. Compare your list with those of others in your class. Discuss how you would rank the seriousness or harmlessness of the deceptions you have identified. Be sure to consider possible self-deceptions for each character.

2. Reread the opening scene involving Troy, Rose, and Bono (pp. 536–40). With two other people, prepare an oral reading of the scene, choosing one quality to emphasize in each of the characters. Present the scene to your class, asking them to identify the qualities you chose. Listen to the other students' interpretations of the scene.

3. In Act 1, scene 4, Rose tells Troy, "Times have changed from when you was young, Troy. People change. The world's changing around you and you can't even see it." How does this statement fit in with

Arthur Miller's concept of tragic heroism? Find statements by other characters that imply being out of step with the times. How is the idea important to understanding the characters?

4. Follow the prominent money motif through the play: losing it, winning it, saving it, spending it, gambling it, lending it, paying it back, and so forth. What does money mean to the characters? Does it mean different things to different characters?

5. Reread Rose's closing speech, Act 2, scene 5 (page 577). Does this monolog encourage a hopeful or a pessimistic reading of the play as a whole?

6. Choose a character from *Fences* and argue that he or she is the hero. Can you argue for more than one character as a hero?

WRITING

In your prewriting, you gathered a list of deceptions that you found in *Fences*. Looking at that list, you may come up with a thesis for an essay on the play. "Deception is an important element in *Fences*" is not enough, even though that may be your first reaction to such a long list. You must say *why* deception is important. Here are some possible thesis ideas:

Troy's ideal roles for himself will never be enacted in the real world, and he maintains a staggering level of illusion to avoid this fact.

The line between outright lies and self-deceptions is not always clear in *Fences* (and even the audience is left without knowing which is which in some cases), suggesting that truth is less clear-cut than it sometimes seems.

Though Troy is presented as a person with both good and bad traits, his betrayal of Rose precludes his being acceptable as a tragic hero.

Choosing a Structure

Your choice of thesis should determine how you organize your raw material—in this case, your list of examples from the prewriting activity. Perhaps your list looks something like this:

Deception and Lies

- Cory not working at the A&P
- Signing papers to put Gabe away in an institution
- Watching the game at Taylors'
- How Troy courted Rose
- Lyons's talent as a musician
- Troy's talent as a baseball player
- Walking 200 miles to Mobile
- The wholesale animosity of whites
- Troy's fantasy self-image when he's with Alberta

- Troy's betrayal of Rose with Alberta
- Gabe's identity
- Playing the numbers
- Troy's encounter with Death
- Rose tries to erase her doubts about Troy
- Other people's beliefs that Gabe either needs or doesn't need to be put away
- Why Gabe moved out
- Troy pretends no anger toward Gabe

This unorganized jumble can be structured in several ways. For the first thesis we mentioned, you would probably pull from the list all of Troy's illusions and lies, concentrating on their relation to his real situation and history. For the second thesis, you would separate items that are outright, conscious lies from those that are self-deceptions, and then make a category of matters whose truth the characters and audience never can be sure about. For the last thesis, you would focus on the illusions embraced by Troy and Rose about their relationship, intending to show that Troy's secret affair with Alberta casts him as a scoundrel, not a hero.

IDEAS FOR WRITING

Ideas for Responsive Writing

1. Cory asserts that he will not attend his father's funeral, but then does go in the end. Consider what he is thinking and feeling about Troy at the end of the play. Write a speech for him to deliver explaining his change of mind.

2. One character, Alberta, never appears on the stage. What do you think is her side of the story about her affair and the conception of Raynell? Write a plausible account of the play's events from her point of view.

3. Take the stance of the director of this play. Explain how you would direct the actor playing Gabriel. In addition, how should the other actors on stage react to Gabriel when they're in a scene with him? Write an explanation of your handling of Gabriel's role, aimed at your entire cast of actors.

Ideas for Critical Writing

1. Devise and support a major claim about the role of imagination and fantasy in each character's life.

2. Expand on Rose's statement about Troy in Act 2, scene 5: "I don't know if he was right or wrong...but I do know he meant to do more good than he meant to do harm." Is the statement true, a lie to appease Cory, or a self-protective illusion?

3. Trace the idea of father-son legacies through the play. Are these legacies positive? negative? unavoidable? superstitious?

4. CRITICAL APPROACHES: Review the discussion of mythological and archetypal approaches to interpreting literature (page 750). Then argue that the character of Rose is a mythic or archetypal figure, using other sources about such figures to support your claims.

5. CRITICAL APPROACHES: Read about cultural criticism in the Critical Approaches to Literature (page 749). In your paper, explain how the dynamics of *Fences* are understandable in terms of its time: the late 1950s.

6. Write an essay explaining why Troy's one real triumph, desegregating the job assignments at work, means little to him.

Ideas for Researched Writing

1. Consider the influence of the African traditions and myth in *Fences*. Two sources on the topic are *The Past as Present in the Drama of August Wilson* (2004) by Harry J. Elam, Jr., and *August Wilson and the African-American Odyssey* (1995) by Kim Pereira. These books will lead you to other reference materials on the topic.

2. CRITICAL APPROACHES: Read about cultural criticism in the Critical Approaches to Literature (page 749). Write a paper explaining how the history of baseball is significant in understanding the play.

REWRITING

The more specifically you support your claims about the work, the more credible you will be to your readers. Another crucial advantage of forcing yourself to be specific is that you will prevent yourself from straying from the printed page into the fields of your own mind, which may be rich and green but not relevant.

Developing Paragraphs Specifically

The following paragraph makes several good observations but lacks specifics:

> Each family member pursues a life's work that is alien to his or her chosen self-image. They each make choices that preclude the fulfillment of their dreams, and they live in an environment that frustrates their attempts to pursue their ideals.

Although these statements are true, the writer has given the reader no particular cause to believe them. The paragraph should have additional details from the play. Compare the following:

> In several ways, the Maxson family fits Arthur Miller's characterization of modern tragedy. Each family member pursues a life's work that is alien to his or her chosen self-image. Troy envisions his potential as a major league

baseball player, while laboring as a garbage man. The poignant contrast between his dreams and his real possibilities makes him an object of pity. Cory, instead of gaining a college education through a football scholarship, becomes a Marine Corporal with a marked lack of enthusiasm, thinking he'll get out in six years. Lyons, who idealized an exciting musical career for himself, turned to robbery and ends up with a sentence in the workhouse. Gabe, the war hero, is delusional from his injuries and lives on government disability funds. Even Rose, who seems to embody feminine domestic virtues so naturally, reveals her derailment as she berates the unfaithful Troy: "Don't you think I ever wanted other things? Don't you think I had dreams and hopes? What about my life?...You not the only one who's got wants and needs. But I held on to you, Troy. I took all my feelings, my wants and needs, my dreams...and I buried them inside you" (803).

The references to the text of the play specifically support the writer's contentions. The exercise that follows will give you practice in finding such support.

Exercise on Providing Quotations

For each general statement, provide appropriate quotations from the play. Some of these generalizations may give you further ideas for papers.

1. Throughout the play, Rose confronts Troy only on minor flaws, while supporting his self-image as a good, strong, capable man.
2. Though they are affected by an inhospitable environment, the characters also worsen their situations through their own questionable choices.
3. Troy's strategies to make Rose agree to mother his illegitimate child consist of crass manipulation and self-serving sentimentality.
4. The fence has several symbolic meanings in the play.
5. Evidence from the play suggests that Raynell is destined for a life of misery and self-deception.

ANTHOLOGY
of Drama

William Shakespeare   1564–1616

William Shakespeare is the most widely known author in all English literature. He was born in Stratford-on-Avon, probably attended grammar school there, and at eighteen married Anne Hathaway, who bore him three children. In 1585 or shortly thereafter, he went to London and began his apprenticeship as an actor. By 1594 he had won recognition as a poet, but it was in the theater that he made his strongest reputation. Shakespeare produced perhaps thirty-five plays in twenty-five years, including historical dramas, comedies, romances, and the great tragedies: *Hamlet* (1602), *Othello* (1604), *King Lear* (1605), and *Macbeth* (1606). His 154 sonnets are supreme examples of the form.

Othello, the Moor of Venice

THE NAMES OF THE ACTORS

OTHELLO, *the Moor.*
BRABANTIO, *a senator, father to Desdemona.*
CASSIO, *an honourable lieutenant to Othello.*
IAGO, *Othello's ancient, a villain.*
RODERIGO, *a gulled gentleman.*
DUKE OF VENICE.
SENATORS *of Venice.*
MONTANO, *governor of Cyprus.*
LODOVICO *and* GRATIANO,
kinsmen to Brabantio, two noble Venetians.
SAILORS.
CLOWN.
DESDEMONA, *daughter to Brabantio and wife to Othello.*
EMILIA, *wife to Iago.*
BIANCA, *a courtezan and mistress to Cassio.*
MESSENGER, HERALD, OFFICERS, GENTLEMEN, MUSICIANS, *and* ATTENDANTS.

[SCENE: VENICE; A SEA-PORT IN CYPRUS]

ACT I

SCENE I

Venice. A street.

[*Enter* RODERIGO *and* IAGO.]

RODERIGO. Tush! never tell me; I take it much unkindly
    That thou, Iago, who hast had my purse
    As if the strings were thine, shouldst know of this.
IAGO. 'Sblood,[1] but you'll not hear me:
    If ever I did dream of such a matter,
    Abhor me.
RODERIGO. Thou told'st me thou didst hold him in thy hate.
IAGO. Despise me, if I do not. Three great ones of the city,[2]
    In personal suit to make me his lieutenant,
    Off-capp'd to him:[3] and, by the faith of man,   10
    I know my price, I am worth no worse a place:
    But he, as loving his own pride and purposes,
    Evades them, with a bombast circumstance
    Horribly stuff'd with epithets of war;
    And, in conclusion,
    Nonsuits[4] my mediators; for, "Certes," says he,
    "I have already chose my officer."
    And what was he?
    Forsooth, a great arithmetician,[5]
    One Michael Cassio, a Florentine,   20
    A fellow almost damn'd in a fair wife;[6]
    That never set a squadron in the field,
    Nor the division[7] of a battle knows
    More than a spinster; unless the bookish theoric,[8]
    Wherein the toged[9] consuls can propose[10]
    As masterly as he: mere prattle, without practice,
    Is all his soldiership. But he, sir, had th' election:
    And I, of whom his eyes had seen the proof

---

[1] **'Sblood** an oath, "by God's blood."

[2] **great ones of the city** Iago means to indicate his importance in the community; this is suggested also by his use of the word *worth* in line 11.

[3] **him** Othello.

[4] **Nonsuits** rejects.

[5] **arithmetician** a man whose military knowledge was merely theoretical, based on books of tactics.

[6] **A...wife** Cassio does not seem to be married, but his counterpart in Shakespeare's source did have a wife.

[7] **division** disposition of a battle line.

[8] **theoric** theory.

[9] **toged** wearing the toga.

[10] **propose** discuss.

James Earl Jones as Othello and Irene Jacob as Desdemona in the 1995 film of *Othello*, directed by Oliver Parker. (Martha Swope/Getty Images/Time Life Pictures.)

At Rhodes, at Cyprus[11] and on other grounds
Christian and heathen, must be be-lee'd and calm'd   30
By debitor and creditor: this counter-caster,[12]
He, in good time,[13] must his lieutenant be,
And I—God bless the mark![14] —Moorship's ancient.[15]
RODERIGO. By heaven, I rather would have been his hangman.
IAGO. Why, there's no remedy; 'tis the curse of service,
Preferment goes by letter and affection,
And not by old gradation,[16] where each second
Stood heir to th' first. Now, sir, be judge yourself,
Whether I in any just term am affin'd[17]
To love the Moor.
RODERIGO.   I would not follow then.   40
IAGO. O, sir, content you;
I follow him to serve my turn upon him:
We cannot all be masters, nor all masters
Cannot be truly follow'd. You shall mark

---

[11]**Rhodes, Cyprus** islands in the Mediterranean south of Asia Minor, long subject to contention between the Venetians and the Turks.
[12]**counter-caster** a sort of bookkeeper; contemptuous term.
[13]**in good time** opportunely.
[14]**God bless the mark** anciently, a pious interjection to avert evil omens.
[15]**ancient** standardbearer, ensign.
[16]**old gradation** seniority; Iago here expresses a characteristic prejudice of professional soldiers.
[17]**affin'd** bound.

Many a duteous and knee-crooking knave,
That, doting on his own obsequious bondage,
Wears out his time, much like his master's ass,
For nought but provender, and when he's old, cashier'd:
Whip me such honest knaves. Others there are
Who, trimm'd in forms and visages of duty,   50
Keep yet their hearts attending on themselves,
And, throwing but shows of service on their lords,
Do well thrive by them and when they have lin'd their coats
Do themselves homage: these fellows have some soul;
And such a one do I profess myself. For, sir,
It is as sure as you are Roderigo,
Were I the Moor, I would not be Iago:[18]
In following him, I follow but myself;
Heaven is my judge, not I for love and duty,
But seeming so, for my peculiar end: 60
For when my outward action doth demonstrate
The native act and figure of my heart
In compliment extern,[19] 'tis not long after
But I will wear my heart upon my sleeve
For daws to peck at: I am not what I am.
RODERIGO. What a full fortune does the thick-lips[20] owe,
    If he can carry 't thus!
IAGO.   Call up her father,
    Rouse him: make after him, poison his delight,
    Proclaim him in the streets, incense her kinsmen,
    And, though he in a fertile climate dwell,   70
    Plague him with flies: though that his joy be joy,
    Yet throw such changes of vexation on 't,
    As it may lose some colour.
RODERIGO. Here is her father's house; I'll call aloud.
IAGO. Do, with like timorous[21] accent and dire yell
    As when, by night and negligence, the fire
    Is spied in populous cities.
RODERIGO. What, ho, Brabantio! Signior Brabantio, ho!
IAGO. Awake! what, ho, Brabantio! thieves! thieves! thieves!
    Look to your house, your daughter and your bags!   80
    Thieves! thieves!

[BRABANTIO *appears above at a window.*]

BRABANTIO. What is the reason of this terrible summons?
    What is the matter there?
RODERIGO. Signior, is all your family within?
IAGO. Are your doors lock'd?
BRABANTIO.   Why, wherefore ask you this?

---

[18]**Were...Iago** Were I in the position of the Moor, I should not feel as Iago feels.
[19]**compliment extern** outward civility.
[20]**thick-lips** Elizabethans often applied the term Moor to Negroes.
[21]**timorous** frightening.

IAGO. 'Zounds, sir, y' are robb'd; for shame, put on your gown;
    Your heart is burst, you have lost half your soul;
    Even now, now, very now, an old black ram
    Is tupping your white ewe. Arise, arise:
    Awake the snorting[22] citizens with the bell,   90
    Or else the devil will make a grandsire of you:
    Arise, I say.
BRABANTIO.   What, have you lost your wits?
RODERIGO. Most reverend signior, do you know my voice?
BRABANTIO. Not I: what are you?
RODERIGO. My name is Roderigo.
BRABANTIO.   The worser welcome:
    I have charg'd thee not to haunt about my doors:
    In honest plainness thou has heard me say
    My daughter is not for thee; and now, in madness,
    Being full of supper and distemp'ring draughts,
    Upon malicious bravery,[23] doest thou come   100
    To start[24] my quiet.
RODERIGO. Sir, sir, sir,—
BRABANTIO.   But thou must needs be sure
    My spirit and my place have in them power
    To make this bitter to thee.
RODERIGO.   Patience, good sir.
BRABANTIO. What tell'st thou me of robbing? this is Venice;
    My house is not a grange.[25]
RODERIGO.   Most grave Brabantio,
    In simple and pure soul I come to you.
IAGO. 'Zounds, sir, you are one of those that will not serve God, if the
    devil bid you. Because we come to do you service and you think we are
    ruffians, you'll have your daughter covered with a Barbary horse; you'll   110
    have your nephews[26] neigh to you; you'll have coursers for cousins and
    gennets[27] for germans.[28]
BRABANTIO. What profane wretch are thou?
IAGO. I am one, sir, that comes to tell you your daughter and the
    Moor are now making the beast with two backs.
BRABANTIO. Thou art a villain.
IAGO.   You are—a senator.
BRABANTIO. This thou shalt answer; I know thee, Roderigo.
RODERIGO. Sir, I will answer any thing. But, I beseech you,
    If 't be your pleasure and most wise consent,
    As partly I find it is, that your fair daughter,   120
    At this odd-even[29] and dull watch o' th' night,

---

[22]**snorting** snoring.
[23]**bravery** defiance, bravado.
[24]**start** disrupt.
[25]**grange** isolated farmhouse.
[26]**nephews** grandsons.
[27]**gennets** small Spanish horses.
[28]**germans** near relatives.
[29]**odd-even** between night and morning.

Transported, with no worse nor better guard
But with a knave of common hire, a gondolier,
To the gross clasps of a lascivious Moor,—
If this be known to you and your allowance,[30]
We then have done you bold and saucy wrongs;
But if you know not this, my manners tell me
We have your wrong rebuke. Do not believe
That, from[31] the sense of all civility,
I thus would play and trifle with your reverence: 130
Your daughter, if you have not given her leave,
I say again, hath made a gross revolt;
Tying her duty, beauty, wit and fortunes
In an extravagant[32] and wheeling[33] stranger
Of here and every where. Straight satisfy yourself:
If she be in her chamber or your house,
Let loose on me the justice of the state
For thus deluding you.

BRABANTIO.   Strike on the tinder,[34] ho!
Give me a taper! call up all my people!
This accident[35] is not unlike my dream: 140
Belief of it oppresses me already.
Light, I say! light!

                                   [Exit above.]

IAGO.   Farewell; for I must leave you:
It seems not meet, nor wholesome to my place,
To be produc'd—as, if I stay, I shall—
Against the Moor: for, I do know, the state,
However this may gall him with some check,[36]
Cannot with safety cast[37] him, for he's embark'd
With such loud reason to the Cyprus wars,
Which even now stand in act,[38] that, for their souls,
Another of his fathom[39] they have none,   150
To lead their business: in which regard,
Though I do hate him as I do hell-pains,
Yet, for necessity of present life,
I must show out a flag and sign of love,
Which is indeed but sign. That you shall surely find him,
Lead to the Sagittary[40] the raised search:
And there will I be with him. So, farewell.

                                     [Exit.]

---

[30]**allowance** permission.
[31]**from** contrary to.
[32]**extravagant** wandering.
[33]**wheeling** vagabond.
[34]**tinder** charred linen kept in a metal box, and ignited by a spark from flint and steel.
[35]**accident** occurrence, event.
[36]**check** rebuke.
[37]**cast** dismiss.
[38]**stand in act** are going on.
[39]**fathom** ability.
[40]**Sagitarry** probably an inn.

[*Enter below* BRABANTIO, *with* SERVANTS *and torches*.]

BRABANTIO. It is too true an evil: gone she is;
    And what's to come of my despised time
    Is nought but bitterness. Now, Roderigo,   160
    Where didst thou see her? O unhappy girl!
    With the Moor, say'st thou? Who would be a father!
    How didst thou know 'twas she? O, she deceives me
    Past thought! What said she to you? Get moe[41] tapers:
    Raise all my kindred. Are they married, think you?
RODERIGO. Truly, I think they are.
BRABANTIO. O heaven! How got she out? O treason of the blood!
    Fathers, from hence trust not your daughters' minds
    By what you see them act. Is[42] there not charms
    By which the property[43] of youth and maidhood   170
    May be abus'd? Have you not read, Roderigo,
    Of some such thing?
RODERIGO.   Yes, sir, I have indeed.
BRABANTIO. Call up my brother. O, would you[44] had had her!
    Some one way, some another. Do you know
    Where we may apprehend her and the Moor?
RODERIGO. I think I can discover him, if you please
    To get good guard and go along with me.
BRABANTIO. Pray you, lead on. At every house I'll call;
    I may command at most. Get weapons, ho!
    And raise some special officers of night.[45]   180
    On, good Roderigo: I will deserve your pains.

                         [*Exeunt.*]

SCENE II

Another street.

[*Enter* OTHELLO, IAGO, ATTENDANTS *with torches*.]

IAGO. Though in the trade of war I have slain men,
    Yet do I hold it very stuff o' th' conscience
    To do no contriv'd murder: I lack iniquity
    Sometime to do me service: nine or ten times
    I had thought t' have yerk'd[46] him here under the ribs.
OTHELLO. 'Tis better as it is.
IAGO.   Nay, but he prated,
    And spoke such scurvy and provoking terms
    Against your honour

---

[41]**moe** more.
[42]**Is** are.
[43]**property** special quality.
[44]**you** Roderigo.
[45]**officers of night** police.
[46]**yerk'd** stabbed.

That, with the little godliness I have,
I did full hard forbear him. But, I pray you, sir,   10
Are you fast married? Be assur'd of this,
That the magnifico[47] is much belov'd,
And hath in his effect[48] a voice potential[49]
As double[50] as the duke's: he will divorce you;
Or put upon you what restraint and grievance
The law, with all his might to enforce it on,
Will give him cable.

OTHELLO.   Let him do his spite;
My services, which I have done the signiory[51]
Shall out-tongue his complaints. 'Tis yet to know—
Which, when I know that boasting is an honour,   20
I shall promulgate—I fetch my life and being
From men of royal siege,[52] and my demerits[53]
May speak unbonneted[54] to as proud a fortune
As this that I have reach'd: for know, Iago,
But that I love the gentle Desdemona,
I would not my unhoused free condition
Put into circumscription and confine
For the sea's worth. But, look! what lights come yond?

IAGO. Those are the raised father and his friends:
You were best go in.   30

OTHELLO.   Not I; I must be found:
My parts, my title and my perfect soul[55]
Shall manifest me rightly. Is it they?

IAGO. By Janus, I think no.

[*Enter* CASSIO *and certain* OFFICERS *with torches.*]

OTHELLO. The servants of the duke, and my lieutenant.
The goodness of the night upon you, friends!
What is the news?

CASSIO.   The duke does greet you, general,
And he requires your haste-post-haste appearance,
Even on the instant.

OTHELLO.   What is the matter, think you?

CASSIO. Something from Cyprus, as I may divine:
It is a business of some heat: the galleys   40
Have sent a dozen sequent[56] messengers
This very night at one another's heels,

---

[47]**magnifico** Venetian grandee (i.e., Brabantio).
[48]**effect** influence.
[49]**potential** powerful.
[50]**double** twice as influential as most men's.
[51]**signiory** Venetian government.
[52]**siege** rank.
[53]**demerits** deserts.
[54]**unbonneted** on equal terms.
[55]**perfect soul** unflawed conscience.
[56]**sequent** successive.

And many of the consuls,[57] rais'd and met,
Are at the duke's already: you have been hotly call'd for;
When, being not at your lodging to be found,
The senate hath sent about three several[58] quests
To search you out.
OTHELLO.   'Tis well I am found by you.
    I will but spend a word here in the house,
    And go with you.

                                                            [Exit.]

CASSIO.   Ancient, what makes he here?
IAGO. 'Faith, he to-night hath boarded a land carack:[59]   50
    If it prove lawful prize, he's made for ever.
CASSIO. I do not understand.
IAGO.   He's married.
CASSIO.   To who?

    [Enter OTHELLO.]

IAGO. Marry, to—Come, captain will you?
OTHELLO.   Have with you.
CASSIO. Here comes another troop to seek for you.

    [Enter BRABANTIO, RODERIGO, with OFFICERS and torches.]

IAGO. It is Brabantio. General, be advis'd;
    He comes to bad intent.
OTHELLO.   Holla! stand there!
RODERIGO. Signoir, it is the Moor.
BRABANTIO.   Down with him, thief!

    [They draw on both sides.]

IAGO. You, Roderigo! come, sir, I am for you.
OTHELLO. Keep up your bright swords, for the dew will rust them.
    Good Signior, you shall more command with years   60
    Than with your weapons.
BRABANTIO. O thou foul thief, where hast thou stow'd my daughter?
    Damn'd as thou art, thou has enchanted her;
    For I'll refer me to all things of sense,[60]
    If she in chains of magic were not bound,
    Whether a maid so tender, fair and happy,
    So opposite to marriage that she shunn'd
    The wealthy curled darlings of our nation,
    Would ever have, t' incur a general mock,
    Run from her guardage[61] to the sooty bosom   70
    Of such a thing as thou, to fear, not to delight.

---

[57]**consuls** senators.
[58]**several** separate.
[59]**carack** large merchant ship.
[60]**things of sense** commonsense understandings of the natural order.
[61]**guardage** guardianship.

Judge me the world, if 'tis not gross in sense[62]
That thou has practis'd on her with foul charms,
Abus'd her delicate youth with drugs or minerals[63]
That weaken motion:[64] I'll have't disputed on;[65]
'Tis probable and palpable to thinking.
I therefore apprehend and do attach thee
For an abuser of the world,[66] a practiser
Of arts inhibited[67] and out of warrant.
Lay hold upon him: if he do resist,   80
Subdue him at his peril.

OTHELLO.   Hold your hands,
Both you of my inclining,[68] and the rest:
Were it my cue to fight, I should have known it
Without a prompter. Whither will you that I go
To answer this charge?

BRABANTIO.   To prison, till fit time
Of law and course of direct session[69]
Call thee to answer.

OTHELLO.   What if I do obey?
How may the duke be therewith satisfied,
Whose messengers are here about my side,
Upon some present business of the state   90
To bring me to him?

FIRST OFFICER.   'Tis true, most worthy signior;
The duke's in council, and your noble self,
I am sure, is sent for.

BRABANTIO.   How! the duke in council!
In this time of night! Bring him away:
Mine's not an idle cause: the duke himself,
Or any of my brothers of the state,
Cannot but feel this wrong as 'twere their own;
For if such actions may have passage free,
Bond-slaves and pagans[70] shall our statesmen be.

                                 [Exeunt.]

SCENE III

A council-chamber

[Enter DUKE, SENATORS *and* OFFICERS *set at a table, with lights and* ATTENDANTS.*]*

DUKE. There is no composition in these news
    That gives them credit.

---

[62]**gross in sense** easily discernible in apprehension or perception.
[63]**minerals** medicine, poison.
[64]**motion** thought, reason.
[65]**disputed on** argued in court by professional counsel.
[66]**abuser of the world** corrupter of society.
[67]**inhibited** prohibited.
[68]**inclining** following, party.
[69]**course of direct session** regular legal proceedings.
[70]**Bond-slaves and pagans** contemptuous reference to Othello's past history.

FIRST SENATOR.   Indeed, they are disproportion'd;[71]
    My letters say a hundred and seven galleys.
DUKE. And mine, a hundred forty.
SECOND SENATOR.   And mine, two hundred:
    But though they jump[72] not on a just account,—
    As in these cases, where the aim[73] reports,
    'Tis oft with difference—yet do they all confirm
    A Turkish fleet, and bearing up to Cyprus.
DUKE. Nay, it is possible enough to judgment:
    I do not so secure me[74] in the error,   10
    But the main article[75] I do approve
    In fearful sense.
SAILOR.   [*Within*] What, ho! what, ho! what, ho!
FIRST OFFICE. A messenger from the galleys.

    [*Enter* SAILOR.]

DUKE.   Now, what's the business?
SAIL. The Turkish preparation makes for Rhodes;
    So was I bid report here to the state
    By Signior Angelo.
DUKE. How say you by this change?
FIRST SENATOR.   This cannot be,
    By no assay[76] of reason: 'tis a pageant,
    To keep us in false gaze. When we consider
    Th' importancy of Cyprus to the Turk,   20
    And let ourselves again but understand,
    That as it more concerns the Turk than Rhodes,
    So may he with more facile question[77] bear it,
    For that it stands not in such warlike brace,[78]
    But altogether lacks th' abilities
    That Rhodes is dress'd in: if we make thought of this,
    We must not think the Turk is so unskilful
    To leave that latest which concerns him first,
    Neglecting an attempt of ease and gain,
    To wake and wage a danger profitless.   30
DUKE. Nay, in all confidence, he's not for Rhodes.
FIRST OFFICE. Here is more news.

    [*Enter a* MESSENGER.]

MESSENGER. The Ottomites, reverend and gracious,
    Steering with due course toward the isle of Rhodes,
    Have there injointed them with an after fleet.

---

[71]**disproportion'd** inconsistent.
[72]**jump** agree.
[73]**aim** conjecture.
[74]**secure me** feel myself secure.
[75]**main article** i.e., that the Turkish fleet is threatening.
[76]**assay** test.
[77]**more facile question** greater facility of effort.
[78]**brace** state of defense.

FIRST SENATOR. Ay, so I thought. How many, as you guess?
MESSENGER. Of thirty sail: and now they do re-stem[79]
      Their backward course, bearing with frank appearance
      Their purposes toward Cyprus. Signior Montano,
      Your trusty and most valiant servitor,   40
      With his free duty recommends you thus,
      And prays you to believe him.
DUKE. 'Tis certain, then, for Cyprus.
      Marcus Luccicos, is not he in town?
FIRST SENATOR. He's now in Florence.
DUKE. Write from us to him; post-post-haste dispatch.
FIRST SENATOR. Here comes Brabantio and the valiant Moor.

[*Enter* BRABANTIO, OTHELLO, CASSIO, IAGO, RODERIGO, *and* OFFICERS.]

DUKE. Valiant Othello, we must straight employ you
      Against the general enemy Ottoman.
      [*To* BRABANTIO.] I did not see you; welcome, gentle signior;   50
      We lack'd your counsel and your help to-night.
BRABANTIO. So did I yours. Good your grace, pardon me;
      Neither my place nor aught I heard of business
      Hath rais'd me from my bed, nor doth the general care
      Take hold on me, for my particular grief
      Is of so flood-gate and o'erbearing nature
      That it engluts[80] and swallows other sorrows
      And it is still itself.
DUKE.   Why, what's the matter?
BRABANTIO. My daughter! O, my daughter!
DUKE *and* SENATOR.   Dead?
BRABANTIO.   Ay, to me;
      She is abus'd, stol'n from me, and corrupted   60
      By spells and medicines bought of mountebanks;
      For nature so preposterously to err,
      Being not deficient, blind, or lame of sense,
      Sans witchcraft could not.
DUKE. Whoe'er he be that in this foul proceeding
      Hath thus beguil'd your daughter of herself
      And you of her, the bloody book of law
      You shall yourself read in the bitter letter
      After your own sense, yea, though our proper son
      Stood in your action.[81]
BRABANTIO.   Humbly I thank your grace.   70
      Here is the man, this Moor, whom now, it seems,
      Your special mandate for the state-affairs
      Hath hither brought.

---

[79] **re-stem** steer again.
[80] **engluts** engulfs.
[81] **Stood . . . action** was under your accusation.

DUKE *and* SENATOR.   We are very sorry for 't.
DUKE [*To Othello.*] What, in your own part, can you say to this?
BRABANTIO. Nothing, but this is so.
OTHELLO. Most potent, grave, and reverend signiors,
    My very noble and approv'd good masters,
    That I have ta'en away this old man's daughter,
    It is most true; true, I have married her:
    The very head and front of my offending   80
    Hath this extent, no more. Rude am I in my speech,
    And little bless'd with the soft phrase of peace;
    For since these arms of mine had seven years' pith,[82]
    Till now some nine moons wasted, they have us'd
    Their dearest action in the tented field,
    And little of this great world can I speak,
    More than pertains to feats of broil and battle,
    And therefore little shall I grace my cause
    In speaking for myself. Yet, by your gracious patience,[83]
    I will a round unvarnish'd tale deliver   90
    Of my whole course of love; what drugs, what charms,
    What conjuration and what mighty magic,
    For such proceeding I am charg'd withal,
    I won his daughter.
BRABANTIO.   A maiden never bold;
    Of spirit so still and quiet, that her motion
    Blush'd at herself,[84] and she, in spite of nature,
    Of years, of country, credit, every thing,
    To fall in love with what she fear'd to look on!
    It is a judgement maim'd and most imperfect
    That will confess perfection so could err   100
    Against all rules of nature, and must be driven
    To find out practices of cunning hell,
    Why this should be. I therefore vouch[85] again
    That with some mixtures pow'rful o'er the blood,
    Or with some dram conjur'd to this effect,
    He wrought upon her.
DUKE.   To vouch this is no proof,
    Without more wider and more overt test
    Than these thin habits and poor likelihoods
    Of modern seeming do prefer against him.
FIRST SENATOR. But, Othello, speak: 110
    Did you by indirect and forced courses
    Subdue and poison this young maid's affections?
    Or came it by request and such fair question
    As soul to soul affordeth?

---

[82]**pith** strength, vigor.
[83]**patience** suffering, permission.
[84]**motion...herself** inward impulses blushed at themselves.
[85]**vouch** assert.

OTHELLO.   I do beseech you,
   Send for the lady to the Sagittary,
   And let her speak of me before her father:
   If you do find me foul in her report,
   The trust, the office I do hold of you,
   Not only take away, but let your sentence
   Even fall upon my life.
DUKE.   Fetch Desdemona hither.   120
OTHELLO. Ancient, conduct them; you best know the place.

                              [*Exeunt* IAGO *and* ATTENDANTS.]

   And, till she come, as truly as to heaven
   I do confess the vices of my blood,
   So justly to your grave ear I'll present
   How I did thrive in this fair lady's love,
   And she in mine.
DUKE. Say it, Othello.
OTHELLO. Her father lov'd me; oft invited me;
   Still question'd me the story of my life,
   From year to year, the battles, sieges, fortunes,   130
   That I have pass'd.
   I ran it through, even from my boyish days,
   To th' very moment that he bade me tell it;
   Wherein I spake of most disastrous chances,
   Of moving accidents by flood and field,
   Of hair-breadth scapes i' th' imminent[86] deadly breach,
   Of being taken by the insolent foe
   And sold to slavery, of my redemption thence
   And portance[87] in my travels' history:
   Wherein of antres[88] vast and deserts idle,[89]   140
   Rough quarries, rocks and hills whose heads touch heaven,
   It was my hint[90] to speak,—such was the process;
   And of the Cannibals that each other eat,[91]
   The Anthropophagi[92] and men whose heads
   Do grow beneath their shoulders. This to hear
   Would Desdemona seriously incline:
   But still the house-affairs would draw her thence:
   Which ever as she could with haste dispatch,
   She 'd come again, and with a greedy ear
   Devour up my discourse: which I observing,   150
   Took once a pliant hour, and found good means
   To draw from her a prayer of earnest heart

---

[86]**imminent** i.e., impending parts when a gap has been made in a fortification.
[87]**portance** conduct.
[88]**antres** caverns.
[89]**idle** barren, unprofitable.
[90]**hint** occasion.
[91]**eat** ate.
[92]**Anthropophagi** man-eaters.

That I would all my pilgrimage dilate,[93]
Whereof by parcels she had something heard,
But not intentively:[94] I did consent,
And often did beguile her of her tears,
When I did speak of some distressful stroke
That my youth suffer'd. My story being done,
She gave me for my pains a world of sighs:
She swore, in faith, 'twas strange, 'twas passing strange,   160
'Twas pitiful, 'twas wondrous pitiful:
She wish'd she had not heard it, yet she wish'd
That heaven had made her such a man: she thank'd me,
And bade me, if I had a friend that lov'd her,
I should but teach him how to tell my story,
And that would woo her. Upon this hint I spake:
She lov'd me for the dangers I had pass'd,
And I lov'd her that she did pity them.
This only is the witchcraft I have us'd:
Here comes the lady; let her witness it.   170

[*Enter* DESDEMONA, IAGO, *and* ATTENDANTS.]

DUKE. I think this tale would win my daughter too.
    Good Brabantio,
    Take up this mangled matter at the best:
    Men do their broken weapons rather use
    Than their bare hands.
BRABANTIO.   I pray you, hear her speak:
    If she confess that she was half the wooer,
    Destruction on my head, if my bad blame
    Light on the man! Come hither, gentle mistress:
    Do you perceive in all this noble company
    Where most you owe obedience?
DESDEMONA.   My noble father,   180
    I do perceive here a divided duty:[95]
    To you I am bound for life and education;
    My life and education both do learn me
    How to respect you; you are the lord of duty;
    I am hitherto your daughter: but here's my husband,
    And so much duty as my mother show'd
    To you, preferring you before her father,
    So much I challenge that I may profess
    Due to the Moor my lord.
BRABANTIO.   God be with you! I have done.
    Please it your grace, on to[96] the state-affairs: 190
    I had rather to adopt a child than get[97] it.
    Come hither, Moor:

---

[93]**dilate** relate in detail.
[94]**intentively** with full attention.
[95]**divided duty** Desdemona recognizes that she still owes a duty to her father even after marriage.
[96]**on to** i.e., proceed with.
[97]**get** beget.

I here do give thee that with all my heart
Which, but thou hast already, with all my heart
I would keep from thee. For your sake,[98] jewel,
I am glad at soul I have no other child;
For thy escape would teach me tyranny,
To hang clogs on them. I have done, my lord.
DUKE. Let me speak like yourself,[99] and lay a sentence,[100]
    Which, as a grise[101] or step, may help these lovers   200
    Into your favour.
    When remedies are past, the griefs are ended
    By seeing the worst, which late on hopes depended.
    To mourn a mischief that is past and gone
    Is the next[102] way to draw new mischief on.
    What cannot be preserv'd when fortune takes,
    Patience her injury a mock'ry makes.
    The robb'd that smiles steals something from the thief;
    He robs himself that spends a bootless grief.
BRABANTIO. So let the Turk of Cyprus us beguile;   210
    We lost it not, so long as we can smile.
    He bears the sentence well that nothing bears
    But the free comfort[103] which from thence he hears,
    But he bears both the sentence and the sorrow
    That, to pay grief, must of poor patience borrow.
    These sentences, to sugar, or to gall,
    Being strong on both sides, are equivocal:
    But words are words; I never yet did hear
    That the bruis'd heart was pierced through the ear.
    I humbly beseech you, proceed to th' affairs of state.   220
DUKE. The Turk with a most mighty preparation makes for Cyprus. Othello, the fortitude[104] of the place is best known to you; and though we have there a substitute of most allowed[105] sufficiency, yet opinion, a sovereign mistress of effects, throws a more safer voice on you:[106] you must therefore be content to slubber[107] the gloss of your new fortunes with this more stubborn and boisterous expedition.
OTHELLO. The tyrant custom, most grave senators,
    Hath made the flinty and steel couch of war
    My thrice-driven[108] bed of down: I do agnize[109]

---

[98]**For your sake** on your account.
[99]**like yourself** i.e., as you would, in your proper temper.
[100]**sentence** maxim.
[101]**grise** step.
[102]**next** nearest.
[103]**comfort** i.e., the consolation that it may be borne with patience.
[104]**fortitude** strength.
[105]**allowed** acknowledged.
[106]**opinion...on you** public opinion, an important determiner of affairs, chooses you as the best man.
[107]**slubber** soil, sully.
[108]**thrice-driven** thrice sifted.
[109]**agnize** know in myself.

A natural and prompt alacrity   230
I find in hardness[110] and do undertake
These present wars against the Ottomites.
Most humbly therefore bending to your state,
I crave fit disposition for my wife,
Due reference of place and exhibition,[111]
With such accommodation and besort[112]
As levels with her breeding.

DUKE.   If you please,
Be 't at her father's.

BRABANTIO.   I'll not have it so.

OTHELLO. Nor I.

DESDEMONA. Nor I; I would not there reside,   240
To put my father in impatient thoughts
By being in his eye. Most gracious duke,
To my unfolding lend your prosperous[113] ear;
And let me find a charter[114] in your voice,
T' assist my simpleness.[115]

DUKE. What would you, Desdemona?

DESDEMONA. That I did love the Moor to live with him,
My downright violence and storm of fortunes,
May trumpet to the world: my heart's subdu'd
Even to the very quality of my lord: 250
I saw Othello's visage in his mind,
And to his honours and his valiant parts
Did I my soul and fortunes consecrate.
So that, dear lords, if I be left behind,
A moth of peace, and he go to the war,
The rites for why I love him are bereft me,
And I a heavy interim shall support
By his dear absence. Let me go with him.

OTHELLO. Let her have your voices.
Vouch with me, heaven, I therefore beg it not,   260
To please the palate of my appetite,
Nor to comply with heat—the young affects[116]
In me defunct—and proper satisfaction,
But to be free and bounteous to her mind:
And heaven defend your good souls, that you think
I will your serious and great business scant
When she is with me. No, when light-wing'd toys
Of feather'd Cupid seel[117] with wanton dullness

---

[110]**hardness** hardship.
[111]**exhibition** allowance.
[112]**besort** suitable company.
[113]**prosperous** propitious.
[114]**charter** privilege.
[115]**simpleness** simplicity.
[116]**affects** inclinations, desires.
[117]**seel** in falconry, to make blind by sewing up the eyes of the hawk in training.

My speculative and offic'd instruments,[118]
That[119] my disports[120] corrupt and taint[121] my business,   270
Let housewives make a skillet of my helm,
And all indign[122] and base adversities
Make head against my estimation![123]

DUKE. Be it as you shall privately determine,
    Either for her stay or going: th' affair cries haste,
    And speed must answer it.

FIRST SENATOR. You must away to-night.

OTHELLO.   With all my heart.

DUKE. At nine i' th' morning here we'll meet again.
    Othello, leave some officer behind,
    And he shall our commission bring to you;   280
    With such things else of quality and respect
    As doth import[124] you.

OTHELLO.   So please your grace, my ancient;
    A man he is of honesty and trust:
    To his conveyance I assign my wife,
    With what else needful your good grace shall think
    To be sent after me.

DUKE.   Let it be so.
    Good night to every one. [*To* BRABANTIO.] And, noble signior,
    If virtue no delighted[125] beauty lack,
    Your son-in-law is far more fair than black.

FIRST SENATOR. Adieu, brave Moor; use Desdemona well.   290

BRABANTIO. Look to her, Moor, if thou hast eyes to see;
    She has deceiv'd her father, and may thee.

              [*Exeunt* DUKE, SENATORS, OFFICERS, *etc.*]

OTHELLO. My life upon her faith! Honest Iago,[126]
    My Desdemona must I leave to thee:
    I prithee, let thy wife attend on her;
    And bring them after in the best advantage.
    Come, Desdemona; I have but an hour
    Of love, of wordly matters and direction,
    To spend with thee: we must obey the time.

              [*Exit with* DESDEMONA.]

RODERIGO. Iago—   300

IAGO. What say'st thou, noble heart?

RODERIGO. What will I do, thinkest thou?

IAGO. Why, go to bed, and sleep.

RODERIGO. I will incontinently[127] drown myself.

---

[118]**speculative...instruments** ability to see and reason clearly.
[119]**That** so that.
[120]**disports** pastimes.
[121]**taint** impair.
[122]**indign** unworthy, shameful.
[123]**estimation** reputation.
[124]**import** concern.
[125]**delighted** delightful.
[126]**Honest Iago** an evidence of Iago's carefully built reputation.
[127]**incontinently** immediately.

IAGO. If thou dost, I shall never love thee after. Why, thou silly gentleman!

RODERIGO. It is silliness to live when to live is torment; and then have we a
prescription to die when death is our physician.

IAGO. O villainous! I have looked upon the world for four times seven
years; and since I could distinguish betwixt a benefit and an injury,
I never found man that knew how to love himself. Ere I would say, 310
I would drown myself for the love of a guinea-hen, I would change
my humanity with a baboon.

RODERIGO. What should I do? I confess it is my shame to be so fond; but it
is not in my virtue[128] to amend it.

IAGO. Virtue! a fig! 'tis in ourselves that we are thus or thus. Our bodies are
our gardens, to the which our wills are gardeners; so that if we will
plant nettles, or sow lettuce, set hyssop[129] and weed up thyme,
supply it with one gender[130] of herbs, or distract it with many, either
to have it sterile with idleness,[131] or manured with industry, why, the
power and corrigible authority[132] of this lies in our wills. If the 320
balance of our lives had not one scale of reason to poise another of
sensuality, the blood and baseness of our natures would conduct us to
most preposterous conclusions:[133] but we have reason to cool our
raging motions,[134] our carnal stings, our unbitted[135] lusts, whereof
I take this that you call love to be a sect[136] or scion.

RODERIGO. It cannot be.

IAGO. It is merely a lust of the blood and a permission of the will. Come, be a
man. Drown thyself! Drown cats and blind puppies. I have professed
me thy friend and I confess me knit to thy deserving with cables of
perdurable[137] toughness; I could never better stead thee than now. Put 330
money in thy purse; follow thou the wars; defeat thy favour[138] with an
usurped beard; I say, put money in thy purse. It cannot be that
Desdemona should long continue her love to the Moor,—put money
in thy purse,—nor he his to her: it was a violent commencement in
her, and thou shalt see an answerable sequestration:[139]—put but
money in thy purse. These Moors are changeable in their wills:—fill
thy purse with money:—the food that to him now is as luscious as
locusts,[140] shall be to him shortly as bitter as coloquintida.[141] She must
change for youth: when she is sated with his body, she will find the

---

[128]**virtue** strength.

[129]**hyssop** an herb of the mint family.

[130]**gender** kind.

[131]**idleness** want of cultivation.

[132]**corrigible authority** the power to correct.

[133]**reason…conclusions** Iago understands the warfare between reason and sensuality, but his
ethics are totally inverted; reason works in him not good, as it should according to natural law, but
evil, which he has chosen for his good.

[134]**motions** appetites.

[135]**unbitted** uncontrolled.

[136]**sect** cutting.

[137]**perdurable** very durable.

[138]**defeat thy favour** disguise and disfigure thy face.

[139]**answerable sequestration** a corresponding separation or estrangement.

[140]**locusts** of doubtful meaning; defined as fruit of the carob tree, as honeysuckle, and as lol-
lipops or sugar sticks.

[141]**coloquintida** colocynth, or bitter apple, a purgative.

error of her choice: she must have change, she must: therefore put   340
money in thy purse. If thou wilt needs damn thyself, do it a more
delicate way than drowning. Make all the money thou canst: if
sanctimony and a frail vow betwixt an erring[142] barbarian and a super-
subtle Venetian be not too hard for my wits and all the tribe of hell,
thou shalt enjoy her; therefore make money. A pox of drowning
thyself! it is clean out of the way: seek thou rather to be hanged in
compassing the joy than to be drowned and go without her.

RODERIGO. Wilt thou be fast to my hopes, if I depend on the issue?

IAGO. Thou art sure of me: —go, make money:—I have told thee often,
and I re-tell thee again and again, I hate the Moor: my cause is   350
hearted;[143] thine hath no less reason. Let us be conjunctive[144] in our
revenge against him; if thou canst cuckold him, thou dost thyself a
pleasure, me a sport. There are many events in the womb of time
which will be delivered. Traverse![145] go, provide thy money. We will
have more of this to-morrow. Adieu.

RODERIGO. Where shall we meet i' the morning?

IAGO. At my lodging.

RODERIGO. I'll be with thee betimes.

IAGO. Go to; farewell. Do you hear, Roderigo?

RODERIGO. What say you?   360

IAGO. No more of drowning, do you hear?

RODERIGO. I am changed. I'll go sell all my land.   *[Exit.]*

IAGO. Thus do I ever make my fool my purse;
    For I mine own gain'd knowledge should profane,
    If I would time expend with such a snipe,[146]
    But for my sport and profit. I hate the Moor;
    And it is thought abroad, that 'twixt my sheets
    H' as done my office: I know not if 't be true;
    But I, for mere suspicion in that kind,
    Will do as if for surety. He holds me well;   370
    The better shall my purpose work on him.
    Cassio's a proper man: let me see now:
    To get his place and to plume up[147] my will
    In double knavery—How, how?—Let's see:—
    After some time, to abuse Othello's ears
    That he[148] is too familiar with his wife.
    He hath a person and a smooth dispose[149]
    To be suspected, fram'd to make women false.
    The Moor is of a free[150] and open nature,

---

[142]**erring** wandering.

[143]**hearted** fixed in the heart.

[144]**conjunctive** united.

[145]**Traverse** go (military term).

[146]**snipe** gull, fool.

[147]**plume up** glorify, gratify.

[148]**he** i.e., Cassio.

[149]**dispose** external manner.

[150]**free** frank.

That thinks men honest that but seem to be so,   380
And will as tenderly be led by th' nose
As asses are.
I have 't. It is engend'red. Hell and night
Must bring this monstrous birth to the world's light.

                                                                 [*Exit.*]

ACT II

SCENE I

A Sea-port in Cyprus. An open place near the quay.

[*Enter* MONTANO *and two* GENTLEMEN.]

MONTANO. What from the cape can you discern at sea?
FIRST GENTLEMAN. Nothing at all: it is a high-wrought flood;
          I cannot, 'twixt the heaven and the main,
          Descry a sail.
MONTANO. Methinks the wind hath spoke aloud at land;
          A fuller blast ne'er shook our battlements:
          If it hath ruffian'd[1] so upon the sea,
          What ribs of oak, when mountains melt on them,
          Can hold the mortise?[2] What shall we hear of this?
SECOND GENTLEMAN. A segregation[3] of the Turkish fleet: 10
          For do but stand upon the foaming shore,
          The chidden billow seems to pelt the clouds:
          The wind-shak'd surge, with high and monstrous mane,
          Seems to cast water on the burning bear,[4]
          And quench the guards[5] of th' ever-fixed pole:
          I never did like molestation view
          On the enchafed[6] flood.
MONTANO.   If that the Turkish fleet
          Be not enshelter'd and embay'd, they are drown'd;
          It is impossible they bear it out.

          [*Enter a third* GENTLEMAN.]

THIRD GENTLEMAN. News, lads! our wars are done.   20
          The desperate tempest hath so bang'd the Turks,
          That their designment[7] halts: a noble ship of Venice
          Hath seen a grievous wrack and sufferance[8]
          On most part of their fleet.
MONTANO. How! is this true?

---

[1]**ruffian'd** raged.
[2]**mortise** the socket hollowed out in fitting timbers.
[3]**segregation** dispersion.
[4]**bear** a constellation.
[5]**quench the guards** overwhelm the stars near the polestar.
[6]**enchafed** angry.
[7]**designment** enterprise.
[8]**sufferance** disaster.

THIRD GENTLEMAN.   The ship is here put in,
  A Veronesa; Michael Cassio,
  Lieutenant to the warlike Moor Othello,
  Is come on shore: the Moor himself at sea,
  And is in full commission here for Cyprus.
MONTANO. I am glad on 't; 'tis a worthy governor.   30
THIRD GENTLEMAN. But this same Cassio, though he speak of comfort
  Touching the Turkish loss, yet he looks sadly,
  And prays the Moor be safe; for they were parted
  With foul and violent tempest.
MONTANO.   Pray heavens he be;
  For I have serv'd him, and the man commands
  Like a full^9 soldier. Let's to the seaside, ho!
  As well to see the vessel that's come in
  As to throw out our eyes for brave Othello,
  Even till we make the main and th' aerial blue
  An indistinct regard.^{10}
THIRD GENTLEMAN.   Come, let's do so;   40
  For every minute is expectancy
  Of more arrivance.^{11}

  [*Enter* CASSIO.]

CASSIO. Thanks, you the valiant of this warlike isle,
  That so approve the Moor! O, let the heavens
  Give him defence against the elements,
  For I have lost him on a dangerous sea.
MONTANO. Is he well shipp'd?
CASSIO. His bark is stoutly timber'd, and his pilot
  Of very expert and approv'd allowance;^{12}
  Therefore my hopes, not surfeited to death,   50
  Stand in bold cure. [*A cry within.*] "A sail, a sail, a sail!"

  [*Enter a fourth* GENTLEMAN.]

CASSIO. What noise?

FOURTH GENTLEMAN. The town is empty; on the brow o' th' sea
  Stand ranks of people, and they cry "A sail!"
CASSIO. My hopes do shape him for the governor.   [*Guns heard.*]
SECOND GENTLEMAN. They do discharge their shot of courtesy:
  Our friends at least.
CASSIO.   I pray you, sir, go forth,
  And give us truth who 'tis that is arriv'd.
SECOND GENTLEMAN. I shall.

                                             [*Exit.*]

MONTANO. But, good lieutenant, is your general wiv'd?   60
CASSIO. Most fortunately: he hath achiev'd a maid

---

^{9}**full** perfect.
^{10}**make...regard** cause the blue of the sea and the air to grow indistinguishable in our view.
^{11}**arrivance** arrival.
^{12}**allowance** reputation.

That paragons[13] description and wild fame;
One that excels the quirks[14] of blazoning[15] pens,
And in th' essential vesture of creation[16]
Does tire the ingener.[17]

[*Enter second* GENTLEMAN.]

                    How now! who has put in?
SECOND GENTLEMAN. 'Tis one Iago, ancient to the general.
CASSIO. Has had most favourable and happy speed:
    Tempests themselves, high seas and howling winds,
    The gutter'd[18] rocks and congregated sands,—
    Traitors ensteep'd[19] to clog the guiltless keel,—   70
    As having sense of beauty, do omit
    Their mortal[20] natures, letting go safely by
    The divine Desdemona.
MONTANO.   What is she?
CASSIO. She that I spake of, our great captain's captain,
    Left in the conduct of the bold Iago,
    Whose footing here anticipates our thoughts
    A se'nnight's[21] speed. Great Jove, Othello guard,
    And swell his sail with thine own powr'ful breath,
    That he may bless this bay with his tall ship,
    Make love's quick pants in Desdemona's arms,   80
    Give renew'd fire to our extinct spirits,
    And bring all Cyprus comfort!

[*Enter* DESDEMONA, IAGO, RODERIGO, *and* EMILIA *with* ATTENDANTS.]

                    O, behold,
The riches of the ship is come on shore!
You men of Cyprus, let her have your knees.
Hail to thee, lady! and the grace of heaven,
Before, behind thee and on every hand,
Enwheel thee round!
DESDEMONA.   I thank you, valiant Cassio.
    What tidings can you tell me of my lord?
CASSIO. He is not yet arriv'd: nor know I aught
    But that he's well and will be shortly here.   90
DESDEMONA. O, but I fear—How lost you company?
CASSIO. The great contention of the sea and skies

---

[13]**paragons** surpasses.
[14]**quirks** witty conceits.
[15]**blazoning** setting forth honorably in words.
[16]**vesture of creation** the real qualities with which creation has invested her.
[17]**ingener** inventor, praiser.
[18]**gutter'd** jagged, trenched.
[19]**ensteep'd** lying under water.
[20]**mortal** deadly.
[21]**se'nnight's** week's.

Parted our fellowship—But, hark! a sail.
[*Within*] "A sail, a sail!" [*Guns heard.*]
SECOND GENTLEMAN. They give their greeting to the citadel:
This likewise is a friend.
CASSIO.   See for the news.

[*Exit* GENTLEMAN.]

Good ancient, you are welcome. [*To* EMILIA.] Welcome, mistress:
Let it not gall your patience, good Iago,
That I extend my manners; 'tis my breeding
That gives me this bold show of courtesy.   [*Kissing her.*]   100
IAGO. Sir, would she give you so much of her lips
As of her tongue she oft bestows on me,
You would have enough.
DESDEMONA.   Alas, she has no speech.
IAGO. In faith, too much;
I find it still, when I have list to sleep:
Marry, before your ladyship, I grant,
She puts her tongue a little in her heart,
And chides with thinking.
EMILIA. You have little cause to say so.
IAGO. Come on, come on; you are pictures out of doors,   110
Bells in your parlours, wild-cats in your kitchens,
Saints in your injuries, devils being offended,
Players in your housewifery, and housewives[22] in your beds.
DESDEMONA. O, fie upon thee, slanderer!
IAGO. Nay, it is true, or else I am a Turk:
You rise to play and go to bed to work.
EMILIA. You shall not write my praise.
IAGO.   No, let me not.
DESDEMONA. What wouldst thou write of me, if thou shouldst praise me?
IAGO. O gentle lady, do not put me to 't;
For I am nothing, if not critical.[23]   120
DESDEMONA. Come on, assay. There's one gone to the harbour?
IAGO. Ay, madam.
DESDEMONA. I am not merry; but I do beguile
The thing I am, by seeming otherwise.
Come, how wouldst thou praise me?
IAGO. I am about it; but indeed my invention
Comes from my pate as birdlime[24] does from frieze;[25]
It plucks out brains and all: but my Muse labours,
And thus she is deliver'd.
If she be fair and wise, fairness and wit,   130
The one's for use, the other useth it.
DESDEMONA. Well praised! How if she be black and witty?
IAGO. If she be black, and thereto have a wit,

---

[22]**housewives** hussies.
[23]**critical** censorious.
[24]**birdlime** sticky substance smeared on twigs to catch small birds.
[25]**frieze** coarse woolen cloth.

She'll find a white[26] that shall her blackness fit.

DESDEMONA. Worse and worse.

EMILIA. How if fair and foolish?

IAGO. She never yet was foolish that was fair;
For even her folly help'd her to an heir.

DESDEMONA. These are old fond[27] paradoxes to make fools laugh i' the alehouse. What miserable praise hast Thou for her that's foul and foolish?   140

IAGO. There's none so foul and foolish thereunto,
But does foul pranks which fair and wise ones do.

DESDEMONA. O heavy ignorance! thou praisest the worst best. But what praise couldst thou bestow on a deserving woman indeed, one that, in the authority of her merit, did justly put on the vouch[28] of her malice itself?

IAGO. She that was ever fair and never proud,
Had tongue at will and yet was never loud,
Never lack'd gold and yet went never gay,
Fled from her wish and yet said "Now I may,"
She that being ang'red, her revenge being nigh,   150
Bade her wrong stay and her displeasure fly,
She that in wisdom never was so frail
To change the cod's head for the salmon's tail,[29]
She that could think and ne'er disclose her mind,
See suitors following and not look behind,
She was a wight, if ever such wight were,—

DESDEMONA. To do what?

IAGO. To suckle fools and chronicle small beer.[30]

DESDEMONA. O most lame and impotent conclusion! Do not learn of him, Emilia, though he be thy husband. How say you, Cassio? Is he not a most   160
profane and liberal[31] counsellor?

CASSIO. He speaks home,[32] madam: you may relish him more in the soldier than in the scholar.

IAGO [*Aside*]. He takes her by the palm: ay, well said, whisper: with as little a web as this will I ensnare as great a fly as Cassio. Ay, smile upon her, do; I will gyve[33] thee in thine own courtship.[34] You say true; 'tis so, indeed: if such tricks as these strip you out of your lieutenantry, it had been better you had not kissed your three fingers[35] so oft, which now again you are most apt to play the sir[36] in. Very good; well kissed! an excellent courtesy! 'tis so, indeed. Yet again your fingers to your lips? would they were clyster-pipes[37] for your sake. [*Trumpet*   170
within.] The Moor! I know his trumpet.

---

[26]**white** a fair person, with a wordplay on *wight*.
[27]**fond** foolish.
[28]**put on the vouch** compel the approval.
[29]**To change...tail** to exchange a delicacy for mere refuse.
[30]**chronicle small beer** keep petty household accounts.
[31]**liberal** licentious.
[32]**speaks home** i.e., without reserve.
[33]**gyve** fetter, shackle.
[34]**courtship** courtesy.
[35]**kissed your three fingers** he kisses his own hand as a token of reverence.
[36]**the sir** i.e., the fine gentleman.
[37]**clyster-pipes** tubes used for enemas.

CASSIO. 'Tis truly so.

DESDEMONA. Let's meet him and receive him.

CASSIO. Lo, where he comes!

[*Enter* OTHELLO *and* ATTENDANTS.]

OTHELLO. O my fair warrior!

DESDEMONA.   My dear Othello!

OTHELLO. It gives me wonder great as my content
    To see you here before me. O my soul's joy!
    If after every tempest comes such calms,
    May the winds blow till they have waken'd death!
    And let the labouring bark climb hills of seas   180
    Olympus-high and duck again as low
    As hell 's from heaven! If it were now to die,
    'Twere now to be most happy; for, I fear,
    My soul hath her content so absolute
    That not another comfort like to this
    Succeeds in unknown fate.

DESDEMONA.   The heavens forbid
    But that our loves and comforts should increase,
    Even as our days do grow!

OTHELLO.   Amen to that, sweet powers!
    I cannot speak enough of this content;
    It stops me here; it is too much of joy: 190
    And this, and this, the greatest discords be [*Kissing her.*]
    That e'er our hearts shall make!

IAGO.   [*Aside.*] O, you are well tun'd now!
    But I'll set down the pegs[38] that make this music,
    As honest as I am.

OTHELLO.   Come, let us to the castle.
    News, friends; our wars are done, the Turks are drowned.
    How does my old acquaintance of this isle?
    Honey, you shall be well desir'd in Cyprus;
    I have found great love amongst them. O my sweet,
    I prattle out of fashion, and I dote
    In mine own comforts. I prithee, good Iago,   200
    Go to the bay and disembark my coffers:
    Bring thou the master to the citadel;
    He is a good one, and his worthiness
    Does challenge much respect. Come, Desdemona,
    Once more, well met at Cyprus.

                [*Exeunt* OTHELLO *and* DESDEMONA
                and all but IAGO *and* RODERIGO.]

IAGO [*To an* ATTENDANT]. Do thou meet me presently at the harbour. [*To* RODERIGO]. Come hither. If thou be'st valiant,—as, they say, base men being in love have then a nobility in their natures more than is native to them,—list me. The lieutenant tonight watches on the court of guard.[39] I must tell thee this—Desdemona is directly in love with him.   210

---

[38]**set down the pegs** lower the pitch of the strings, i.e., disturb the harmony.
[39]**court of guard** guardhouse.

RODERIGO. With him! why 'tis not possible.

IAGO. Lay thy finger thus, and let thy soul be instructed. Mark me with what violence she first loved the Moor, but for bragging and telling her fantastical lies: and will she love him still for prating? Let not thy discreet heart think it. Her eye must be fed; and what delight shall she have to look on the devil? When the blood is made dull with the act of sport, there should be, again to inflame it and to give satiety a fresh appetite, loveliness in favour, sympathy in years, manners and beauties; all which the Moor is defective in: now, for want of these required conveniences, her delicate tenderness will find itself abused, begin to heave the gorge, disrelish and abhor the Moor; very nature will 220 instruct her in it and compel her to some second choice. Now, sir, this granted,—as it is a most pregnant and unforced position—who stands so eminent in the degree of this fortune as Cassio does? a knave very voluble; no further conscionable[40] than in putting on the mere form of civil and humane seeming, for the better compassing of his salt[41] and most hidden loose affection? why, none; why, none: a slipper[42] and subtle knave, a finder of occasions, that has an eye can stamp and counterfeit advantages, though true advantage never present itself; a devilish knave. Besides, the knave is handsome, young, and hath all those requisites in him that folly and green minds look after: a pestilent complete knave; and the woman hath found 230 him already.

RODERIGO. I cannot believe that in her; she's full of most blessed condition.

IAGO. Blessed fig's-end! the wine she drinks is made of grapes: if she had been blessed, she would never have loved the Moor. Blessed pudding! Didst thou not see her paddle with the palm of his hand? didst not mark that?

RODERIGO. Yes, that I did; but that was but courtesy.

IAGO. Lechery, by his hand; an index and obscure prologue to the history of lust and foul thoughts. They met so near with their lips that their breaths embraced together. Villainous thoughts, Roderigo! when these mutualities so marshall the way, hard at hand comes the master and main exercise, the incorporate 240 conclusion. Pish! But, sir, be you ruled by me: I have brought you from Venice. Watch you to-night; for the command, I'll lay't upon you. Cassio knows you not. I'll not be far from you: do you find some occasion to anger Cassio, either by speaking too loud, or tainting[43] his discipline; or from what other course you please, which the time shall more favourably minister.

RODERIGO. Well.

IAGO. Sir, he is rash and very sudden in choler, and haply may strike at you: provoke him, that he may; for even out of that will I cause these of Cyprus to mutiny; whose qualification[44] shall come into no true taste again but by the displanting of Cassio. So shall you have a shorter journey to your desires by 250 the means I shall then have to prefer them; and the impediment most profitably removed, without the which there were no expectation of our prosperity.

RODERIGO. I will do this, if I can bring it to any opportunity.

---

[40]**conscionable** conscientious.
[41]**salt** licentious.
[42]**slipper** slippery.
[43]**tainting** disparaging.
[44]**qualification** appeasement.

IAGO. I warrant thee. Meet me by and by[45] at the citadel: I must fetch his
    necessaries ashore. Farewell.
RODERIGO. Adieu.

                                                        [Exit.]

IAGO. That Cassio loves her, I do well believe 't;
    That she loves him, 'tis apt[46] and of great credit:[47]
    The Moor, howbeit that I endure him not,   260
    Is of a constant, loving, noble nature,
    And I dare think he'll prove to Desdemona
    A most dear husband. Now, I do love her too;
    Not out of absolute lust, though peradventure
    I stand accountant for as great a sin,
    But partly led to diet my revenge,
    For that I do suspect the lusty Moor
    Hath leap'd into my seat; the thought whereof
    Doth, like a poisonous mineral, gnaw my inards;
    And nothing can or shall content my soul   270
    Till I am even'd with him, wife for wife,
    Or failing so, yet that I put the Moor
    At least into a jealousy so strong
    That judgement cannot cure. Which thing to do,
    If this poor trash[48] of Venice, whom I trash[49]
    For his quick hunting, stand the putting on,[50]
    I'll have our Michael Cassio on the hip,[51]
    Abuse him to the Moor in the rank garb—
    For I fear Cassio with my night-cap too—
    Make the Moor thank me, love me and reward me,   280
    For making him egregiously an ass
    And practicing upon his peace and quiet
    Even to madness. 'Tis here, but yet confus'd:
    Knavery's plain face is never seen till us'd.

                                                         [Exit.]

SCENE II

A street.

[Enter Othello's HERALD *with a proclamation.]*

HERALD. It is Othello's pleasure, our noble and valiant general, that, upon certain
    tidings now arrived, importing the mere perdition[52] of the Turkish fleet,
    every man put himself into triumph; some to dance, some to make
    bonfires, each man to what sport and revels his addiction leads him: for,

---

[45]**by and by** immediately.
[46]**apt** probable.
[47]**credit** credibility.
[48]**trash** worthless thing (Roderigo).
[49]**trash** hold in check.
[50]**putting on** incitement to quarrel.
[51]**on the hip** at my mercy (wrestling term).
[52]**mere perdition** complete destruction.

besides these beneficial news, it is the celebration of his nuptial. So much was his pleasure should be proclaimed. All offices[53] are open, and there is full liberty of feasting from this present hour of five till the bell have told eleven. Heaven bless the isle of Cyprus and our general Othello!

[Exit.]

SCENE III

A hall in the castle.

[*Enter* OTHELLO, DESDEMONA, CASSIO, *and* ATTENDANTS.]

OTHELLO. Good Michael, look you to the guard to-night:
    Let's teach ourselves that honourable stop,[54]
    Not to outsport discretion.
CASSIO. Iago hath direction what to do;
    But, notwithstanding, with my personal eye
    Will I look to 't.
OTHELLO.   Iago is most honest.
    Michael, goodnight: to-morrow with your earliest
    Let me have speech with you. [*To* DESDEMONA.] Come, my dear love,
    The purchase made, the fruits are to ensue;
    That profit's yet to come 'tween me and you.   10
    Good night.

[Exit OTHELLO, with DESDEMONA and
ATTENDANTS.]

[*Enter* IAGO.]

CASSIO. Welcome, Iago; we must to the watch.
IAGO. Not this hour, lieutenant; 'tis not yet ten o' the clock. Our general cast[55] us thus early for the love of his Desdemona; who let us not therefore blame: he hath not yet made wanton the night with her; and she is sport for Jove.
CASSIO. She's a most exquisite lady.
IAGO. And, I'll warrant her, full of game.
CASSIO. Indeed, she's a most fresh and delicate creature.
IAGO. What an eye she has! Methinks it sounds a parley of provocation.   20
CASSIO. An inviting eye; and yet methinks right modest.
IAGO. And when she speaks, is it not an alarum to love?
CASSIO. She is indeed perfection.
IAGO. Well, happiness to their sheets! Come, lieutenant, I have a stoup[56] of wine; and here without are a brace of Cyprus gallants that would fain have a measure to the health of black Othello.
CASSIO. Not to-night, good Iago: I have very poor and unhappy brains for drinking: I could well wish courtesy would invent some other custom of entertainment.
IAGO. O, they are our friends, but one cup: I'll drink for you.   30

---

[53]**offices** rooms where food and drink were kept.
[54]**stop** restraint.
[55]**cast** dismissed.
[56]**stoup** measure of liquor, two quarts.

CASSIO. I have drunk but one cup tonight, and that was craftily qualified[57] too, and, behold, what innovation[58] it makes here:[59] I am unfortunate in the infirmity, and dare not task my weakness with any more.

IAGO. What, man! 'tis a night of revels: the gallants desire it.

CASSIO. Where are they?

IAGO. Here at the door; I pray you, call them in.

CASSIO. I'll do 't; but it dislikes me.   [*Exit.*]

IAGO. If I can fasten but one cup upon him,
    With that which he hath drunk to-night already,
    He'll be as full of quarrel and offence   40
    As my young mistress' dog. Now, my sick fool Roderigo,
    Whom love hath turn'd almost the wrong side out,
    To Desdemona hath to-night carous'd
    Potations pottle-deep;[60] and he's to watch:
    Three lads of Cyprus, noble swelling spirits,
    That hold their honours in a wary distance,[61]
    The very elements[62] of this warlike isle,
    Have I to-night fluster'd with flowing cups,
    And they watch[63] too. Now, 'mongst this flock of drunkards,
    Am I to put our Cassio in some action   50
    That may offend the isle.—But here they come:

[*Enter* CASSIO, MONTANO, *and* GENTLEMEN; SERVANTS *following with wine.*]

    If consequence do but approve[64] my dream,
    My boat sails freely, both with wind and stream.

CASSIO. 'Fore God, they have given me a rouse[65] already.

MONTANO. Good faith, a little one; not past a pint, as I am a soldier.

IAGO. Some wine, ho!
    [*Sings.*] And let me the canakin[66] clink, clink;
      And let me the canakin clink
        A soldier's a man;
        A life's but a span;   60
      Why, then, let a soldier drink.
    Some wine, boys!

CASSIO. 'Fore God, an excellent song.

IAGO. I learned it in England, where, indeed, they are most potent in potting your Dane, your German, and your swag-bellied Hollander—Drink, ho!—are nothing to your English.

CASSIO. Is your Englishman so expert in his drinking?

---

[57]**qualified** diluted.
[58]**innovation** disturbance.
[59]**here** i.e., in Cassio's head.
[60]**pottle-deep** to the bottom of the tankard.
[61]**hold...distance** i.e., are extremely sensitive of their honor.
[62]**very elements** true representatives.
[63]**watch** are members of the guard.
[64]**approve** confirm.
[65]**rouse** full draft of liquor.
[66]**canakin** small drinking vessel.

IAGO. Why, he drinks you, with facility, your Dane dead drunk; he sweats not to overthrow your Almain;[67] he gives your Hollander a vomit, ere the next pottle can be filled. 70

CASSIO. To the health of our general!

MONTANO. I am for it, lieutenant; and I'll do you justice.[68]

IAGO. O sweet England! [*Sings.*]

> King Stephen was a worthy peer,
>> His breeches cost him but a crown;
> He held them sixpence all too dear,
> With that he call'd the tailor lown.[69]
>
> He was a wight of high renown,
>> And thou art but of low degree:
> 'Tis pride that pulls the country down; 80
>> Then take thine auld cloak about thee.
>> Some wine, ho!

CASSIO. Why, this is a more exquisite song than the other.

IAGO. Will you hear 't again?

CASSIO. No; for I hold him to be unworthy of his place that does those things. Well, God's above all; and there be souls must be saved, and there be souls must not be saved.

IAGO. It's true, good lieutenant.

CASSIO. For mine own part,—no offence to the general, nor any man of quality,—I hope to be saved. 90

IAGO. And so do I too, lieutenant.

CASSIO. Ay, but, by your leave, not before me; the lieutenant is to be saved before the ancient. Let 's have no more of this; let 's to our affairs.— God forgive us our sins!—Gentlemen, let 's look to our business. Do not think, gentlemen, I am drunk: this is my ancient; this is my right hand, and this is my left: I am not drunk now: I can stand well enough, and speak well enough.

ALL. Excellent well.

CASSIO. Why, very well then; you must not think then that I am drunk. [*Exit.*]

MONTANO. To th' platform, masters; come, let's set the watch. 100

IAGO. You see this fellow that is gone before;

> He's soldier fit to stand by Caesar
> And give direction and do but see his vice;
> 'Tis to his virtue a just equinox,[70]
> The one as long as th' other 'tis pity of him.
> I fear the trust Othello puts him in,
> On some odd time of his infirmity,
> Will shake this island.

MONTANO.   But is he often thus?

IAGO. 'Tis evermore the prologue to his sleep:

---

[67]**Almain** German.

[68]**I'll...justice** i.e., drink as much as you.

[69]**lown** lout, loon.

[70]**equinox** equal length of days and nights; used figuratively to mean "counterpart."

He'll watch the horologe[71] a double set,[72]   110
    If drink rock not his cradle.

MONTANO.   It were well
    The general were put in mind of it.
    Perhaps he sees it not; or his good nature
    Prizes the virtue that appears in Cassio,
    And looks not on his evils: is not this true?

[*Enter* RODERIGO.]

IAGO [*Aside to him*]. How now, Roderigo!
    I pray you, after the lieutenant; go.

                            [*Exit* RODERIGO.]

MONTANO. And 'tis great pity that the noble Moor
    Should hazard such a place as his own second
    With one of an ingraft[73] infirmity: 120
    It were an honest action to say
    So to the Moor.

IAGO.   Not I, for this fair island:
    I do love Cassio well; and would do much
    To cure him of this evil—But, hark! what noise?
    [*Cry within:* "Help! help!"]

[*Enter* CASSIO, *pursing* RODERIGO.]

CASSIO. 'Zounds, you rogue! you rascal!

MONTANO.   What's the matter, lieutenant?

CASSIO. A knave teach me my duty!
    I'll beat the knave into a twiggen[74] bottle.

RODERIGO. Beat me!

CASSIO.   Dost thou prate, rogue?   [*Striking* RODERIGO.]

MONTANO.   Nay, good lieutenant; [*Staying him.*]
    I pray you, sir, hold your hand.   130

CASSIO.   Let me go, sir,
    Or I'll knock you o'er the mazzard.[75]

MONTANO.   Come, come, you're drunk.

CASSIO. Drunk!   [*They fight.*]

IAGO [*aside to* RODERIGO]. Away, I say; go out, and cry a mutiny.

                          [*Exit* RODERIGO.]

    Nay, good lieutenant,—God's will, gentlemen;—
    Help, ho!—Lieutenant,—sir,—Montano,—sir,—
    Help, masters!—Here's a goodly watch indeed!   [*Bell rings.*]
    Who's that which rings the bell?—Diablo,[76] ho!
    The town will rise:[77] God's will, lieutenant, hold!
    You'll be asham'd for ever.

[*Enter* OTHELLO *and* ATTENDANTS.]

---

[71]**horologe** clock.
[72]**double set** twice around.
[73]**ingraft** ingrafted, inveterate.
[74]**twiggen** covered with woven twigs.
[75]**mazzard** head.
[76]**Diablo** the devil.
[77]**rise** grow riotous.

OTHELLO.   What is the matter here?   140
MONTANO. 'Zounds, I bleed still; I am hurt to th' death.
    He dies!   [*Thrusts at* CASSIO.]
OTHELLO. Hold, for your lives!
IAGO. Hold, ho! Lieutenant,—sir,—Montano,—gentlemen,—
    Have you forgot all sense of place and duty?
    Hold! the general speaks to you; hold, for shame!
OTHELLO. Why, how now, ho! from whence ariseth this?
    Are we turn'd Turks[78] and to ourselves do that
    Which heaven hath forbid the Ottomites?
    For Christian shame, put by this barbarous brawl:
    He that stirs next to carve for[79] his own rage   150
    Holds his soul light; he dies upon his motion.
    Silence that dreadful bell: it frights the isle
    From her propriety.[80] What is the matter, masters?
    Honest Iago, that looks dead with grieving,
    Speak, who began this? on thy love, I charge thee.
IAGO. I do not know: friends all but now, even now,
    In quarter,[81] and in terms like bride and groom
    Devesting them for bed; and then, but now—
    As if some planet had unwitted men—
    Swords out, and tilting one at other's breast,   160
    In opposition bloody. I cannot speak
    Any beginning to this peevish odds;[82]
    And would in action glorious I had lost
    Those legs that brought me to a part of it!
OTHELLO. How comes it, Michael, you are thus forgot?
CASSIO. I pray you, pardon me; I cannot speak.
OTHELLO. Worthy Montano, you were wont be civil;
    The gravity and stillness of your youth
    The world hath noted, and your name is great
    In mouths of wisest censure.[83] What's the matter,   170
    That you unlace[84] your reputation thus
    And spend your rich opinion for the name
    Of a night-brawler? Give me answer to it.
MONTANO. Worthy Othello, I am hurt to danger:
    Your officer, Iago, can inform you,—
    While I spare speech, which something now offends me,—
    Of all that I do know: nor know I aught
    By me that's said or done amiss this night;
    Unless self-charity be sometimes a vice,
    And to defend ourselves it be a sin   180
    When violence assails us.
OTHELLO.   Now, by heaven,

---

[78]**turn'd Turks** changed completely for the worse; proverbial.
[79]**carve for** indulge.
[80]**propriety** proper state or condition.
[81]**In quarter** on terms.
[82]**peevish odds** childish quarrel.
[83]**censure** judgment.
[84]**unlace** degrade.

My blood begins my safer guides to rule;
And passion, having my best judgment collied,[85]
Assays to lead the way: if I once stir,
Or do but lift this arm, the best of you
Shall sink in my rebuke. Give me to know
How this foul rout began, who set it on;
And he that is approv'd in[86] this offence,
Though he had twinn'd with me, both at a birth,
Shall lose me. What! in a town of war,   190
Yet wild, the people's hearts brimful of fear,
To manage private and domestic quarrel,
In night, and on the court and guard[87] of safety!
'Tis monstrous. Iago, who began 't?

MONTANO [*to* IAGO]. If partially affin'd,[88] or leagu'd in office,
Thou dost deliver more or less than truth,
Thou art no soldier.

IAGO.   Touch me not so near:
I had rather have this tongue cut from my mouth
Than it should do offense to Michael Cassio;
Yet, I persuade myself, to speak the truth   200
Shall nothing wrong him. Thus it is, general.
Montano and myself being in speech,
There comes a fellow crying out for help;
And Cassio following him with determin'd sword,
To execute[89] upon him. Sir, this gentleman
Steps in to Cassio, and entreats his pause:
Myself the crying fellow did pursue,
Lest by his clamour—as it so fell out—
The town might fall in fright: he, swift of foot,
Outran my purpose; and I return'd the rather   210
For that I heard the clink and fall of swords,
And Cassio high in oath; which till to-night
I ne'er might say before. When I came back—
For this was brief—I found them close together,
At blow and thrust; even as again they were
When you yourself did part them.
More of this matter cannot I report:
But men are men; the best sometimes forget:
Though Cassio did some little wrong to him,
As men in rage strike those that wish them best,   220
Yet surely, Cassio, I believe, receiv'd
From him that fled some strange indignity,
Which patience could not pass.

OTHELLO.   I know, Iago,

---

[85]**collied** darkened.
[86]**approv'd in** found guilty of.
[87]**court and guard** spot and guarding place, i.e., the main guardhouse.
[88]**affin'd** bound by a tie.
[89]**execute** give effect to (his anger).

Thy honesty and love doth mince this matter,
Making it light to Cassio. Cassio, I love thee;
But never more be officer of mine.

[*Enter* DESDEMONA, *attended.*]

Look, if my gentle love be not rais'd up!
I'll make thee an example.

DESDEMONA.   What's the matter?
OTHELLO. All's well now, sweeting; come away to bed.
Sir, for your hurts, myself will be your surgeon: 230
Lead him off.   [*To* MONTANO, *who is led off.*]
Iago, look with care about the town,
And silence those whom this vile brawl distracted.
Come, Desdemona: 'tis the soldiers' life
To have their balmy slumbers wak'd with strife.

[*Exit with all but* IAGO *and* CASSIO.]

IAGO. What, are you hurt, lieutenant?
CASSIO. Ay, past all surgery.
IAGO. Marry, God forbid!
CASSIO. Reputation, reputation, reputation! O, I have lost my reputation! I have
        lost the immortal part of myself, and what remains is bestial. My   240
        reputation, Iago, my reputation!
IAGO. As I am an honest man, I thought you had received some bodily wound;
        there is more sense in that than in reputation. Reputation is an idle and
        most false imposition; oft got without merit, and lost without deserving:
        you have lost no reputation at all, unless you repute yourself such a loser.
        What, man! there are ways to recover the general again: you are but now
        cast in his mood, a punishment more in policy than in malice; even so as
        one would beat his offenseless dog to affright an imperious lion: sue to
        him again, and he 's yours.
CASSIO. I will rather sue to be despised than to deceive so good a commander   250
        with so slight, so drunken, and so indiscreet an officer. Drunk? and speak
        parrot?[90] and squabble? swagger? swear? and discourse fustian[91] with one's
        own shadow? O thou invisible spirit of wine, if thou hast no name to be
        known by, let us call thee devil!
IAGO. What was he that you followed with your sword? What had he done to
        you?
CASSIO. I know not.
IAGO. Is 't possible?
CASSIO. I remember a mass of things, but nothing distinctly; a quarrel, but
        nothing wherefore. O God, that men should put an enemy in their mouths 260
        to steal away their brains! that we should, with joy, pleasance, revel and
        applause, transform ourselves into beasts!
IAGO. Why, but you are now well enough. How came you thus recovered?
CASSIO. It hath pleased the devil drunkenness to give place to the devil wrath: one
        unperfectness[92] shows me another, to make me frankly despise myself.

---

[90]**speak parrot** talk nonsense.
[91]**discourse fustian** talk nonsense.
[92]**unperfectness** imperfection.

IAGO. Come, you are too severe a moraler: as the time, the place, and the condition of this country stands, I could heartily wish this had not befallen; but, since it is as it is, mend it for your own good.

CASSIO. I will ask him for my place again; he shall tell me I am a drunkard! Had I as many mouths as Hydra,[93] such an answer would stop them all. To be now 270 a sensible man, by and by a fool, and presently a beast! O strange! Every inordinate cup is unblessed and the ingredient is a devil.

IAGO. Come, come, good wine is a good familiar creature, if it be well used: exclaim no more against it. And, good lieutenant, I think you think I love you.

CASSIO. I have well approved[94] it, sir. I drunk!

IAGO. You or any man living may be a drunk at a time, man. I'll tell you what you shall do. Our general's wife is now the general: I may say so in this respect, for that he hath devoted and given up himself to the contemplation, mark, and denotement[95] of her parts and graces: confess yourself freely to her; importune her help to put you in your place again: she is of so free, so kind, 280 so apt, so blessed a disposition, she holds it a vice in her goodness not to do more than she is requested: this broken joint between you and her husband entreat her to splinter;[96] and, my fortunes against any lay[97] worth naming, this crack of your love shall grow stronger than it was before.

CASSIO. You advise me well.

IAGO. I protest, in the sincerity of love and honest kindness.

CASSIO. I think it freely; and betimes in the morning I will beseech the virtuous Desdemona to undertake for me. I am desperate of my fortunes if they check[98] me here.

IAGO. You are in the right. Good night, lieutenant; I must to the watch. 290

CASSIO. Good night, honest Iago. [*Exit* CASSIO.]

IAGO. And what 's he then that says I play the villain?
When this advice is free I give and honest,
Probal[99] to thinking and indeed the course
To win the Moor again? For 'tis most easy
Th' inclining[100] Desdemona to subdue[101]
In any honest suit: she 's fram'd as fruitful
As the free elements. And then for her
To win the Moor—were 't to renounce his baptism,
All seals and symbols of redeemed sin, 300
His soul is so enfetter'd to her love,
That she may make, unmake, do what she list,
Even as her appetite shall play the god
With his weak function. How am I then a villain
To counsel Cassio to this parallel[102] course,

---

[93]**Hydra** a monster with many heads, slain by Hercules as the second of his twelve labors.
[94]**approved** proved.
[95]**denotement** observation.
[96]**splinter** bind with splints.
[97]**lay** stake, wager.
[98]**check** repulse.
[99]**Probal** probable.
[100]**inclining** favorably disposed.
[101]**subdue** persuade.
[102]**parallel** corresponding to his best interest.

Directly to his good? Divinity of hell!
When devils will the blackest sins put on,[103]
They do suggest[104] at first with heavenly shows,
As I do now: for whiles this honest fool
Plies Desdemona to repair his fortunes   310
And she for him pleads strongly to the Moor,
I'll pour this pestilence into his ear,
That she repeals him[105] for her body's lust;
And by how much she strives to do him good,
She shall undo her credit with the Moor.
So will I turn her virtue into pitch,
And out of her own goodness make the net
That shall enmesh them all.

[*Enter* RODERIGO.]

How now, Roderigo!

RODERIGO. I do not follow here in the chase, not like a hound that hunts, but one
that fills up the cry.[106] My money is almost spent; I have been tonight   320
exceedingly well cudgellèd; and I think the issue will be, I shall have so
much experience for my pains, and so, with no money at all and a little
more wit, return again to Venice.

IAGO. How poor are they that have not patience!
What wound did ever heal but by degrees?
Thou know'st we work by wit, and not by witchcraft;
And wit depends on dilatory time.
Does 't not go well? Cassio hath beaten thee,
And thou, by that small hurt, hast cashier'd[107] Cassio.
Though other things grow fair against the sun,   330
Yet fruits that blossom first will first be ripe.
Content thyself awhile. By th' mass, 'tis morning;
Pleasure and action make the hours seem short.
Retire thee; go where thou art billeted.
Away, I say; thou shalt know more hereafter:
Nay, get thee gone.   [*Exit* RODERIGO.]
            Two things are to be done:
My wife must move for Cassio to her mistress;
I'll set her on;
Myself the while to draw the Moor apart,
And bring him jump[108] when he may Cassio find   340
Soliciting his wife: ay, that's the way:
Dull not device by coldness and delay.

                                                            [*Exit.*]

---

[103]**put on** further.
[104]**suggest** tempt.
[105]**repeals him** i.e., attempts to get him restored.
[106]**cry** pack.
[107]**cashier'd** dismissed from service.
[108]**jump** precisely.

ACT III

SCENE I

Before the castle.

[*Enter* CASSIO *and* MUSICIANS.]

CASSIO. Masters, play here; I will content[1] your pains;
    Something that 's brief; and bid "Good morrow, general."   [*They play.*]

[*Enter* CLOWN.]

CLOWN. Why, masters, have your instruments been in Naples, that they speak i'
    the nose[2] thus?
FIRST MUSICIAN. How, sir, how!
CLOWN. Are these, I pray you, wind-instruments?
FIRST MUSICIAN. Ay, marry, are they, sir.
CLOWN. O, thereby hangs a tail.
FIRST MUSICIAN. Whereby hangs a tale,[3] sir?
CLOWN. Marry, sir, by many a wind-instrument that I know. But, masters, here's   10
    money for you: and the general so likes your music, that he desires you, for
    love's sake, to make no more noise with it.
FIRST MUSICIAN. Well, sir, we will not.
CLOWN. If you have any music that may not be heard, to 't again: but, as they say,
    to hear music the general does not greatly care.
FIRST MUSICIAN. We have none such, sir.
CLOWN. Then put up your pipes in your bag, for I'll away: go; vanish into
    air; away!   [*Exeunt* MUSICIANS.]
CASSIO. Dost thou hear, my honest friend?
CLOWN. No, I hear not your honest friend; I hear you.   20
CASSIO. Prithee, keep up thy quillets. There 's a poor piece of gold for thee: if the
    gentlewoman that attends the general's wife be stirring, tell her there 's one
    Cassio entreats her a little favour of speech; wilt thou do this?
CLOWN. She is stirring, sir: if she will stir hither, I shall seem to notify unto
    her.
CASSIO. Do, good my friend.   [*Exit* CLOWN.]

[*Enter* IAGO.]

                    In happy time, Iago.
IAGO. You have not been a-bed, then?
CASSIO. Why, no; the day had broke
    Before we parted. I have made bold, Iago,
    To send in to your wife: my suit to her   30
    Is, that she will to virtuous Desdemona
    Procure me some access.
IAGO.   I'll send her to you presently;

---

[1]**content** reward.
[2]**speak i' the nose** i.e., like Neapolitans, who spoke a nasal dialect (with a joke on syphilis, which attacks the nose).
[3]**tale** pun on *tail*, a wind instrument of sorts.

And I'll devise a means to draw the Moor
Out of the way, that your converse and business
May be more free.
CASSIO. I humbly thank you for 't.   [*Exit* IAGO.]
                    I never knew
A Florentine more kind and honest.

[*Enter* EMILIA.]

EMILIA. Good morrow, good lieutenant. I am sorry
For your displeasure; but all will sure be well.   40
The general and his wife are talking of it;
And she speaks for you stoutly: the Moor replies,
That he you hurt is of great fame in Cyprus
And great affinity[4] and that in wholesome wisdom
He might not but refuse you, but he protests he loves you
And needs no other suitor but his likings
To take the safest occasion by the front[5]
To bring you in again.
CASSIO.   Yet, I beseech you,
If you think fit, or that it may be done,
Give me advantage of some brief discourse   50
With Desdemona alone.
EMILIA.   Pray you, come in:
I will bestow you where you shall have time
To speak your bosom freely.
CASSIO. I am much bound to you.   [*Exeunt.*]

SCENE II

A room in the castle.

[*Enter* OTHELLO, IAGO, *and* GENTLEMEN.]

OTHELLO. These letters give, Iago, to the pilot;
And by him do my duties to the senate.
That done, I will be walking on the works.[6]
Repair there to me.
IAGO.   Well, my good lord, I'll do 't.
OTHELLO. This fortification, gentlemen, shall we see 't?
GENTLEMEN. We'll wait upon your lordship.   [*Exeunt.*]

SCENE III

The garden of the castle.

[*Enter* DESDEMONA, CASSIO, *and* EMILIA.]

DESDEMONA. Be thou assur'd, good Cassio, I will do
All my abilities in thy behalf.

---

[4]**affinity** kindred, family connection.
[5]**by the front** i.e., by the forelock.
[6]**works** earthworks, fortifications.

EMILIA. Good madam, do. I warrant it grieves my husband,
    As if the case were his.
DESDEMONA. O, that's an honest fellow. Do not doubt, Cassio,
    But I will have my lord and you again
    As friendly as you were.
CASSIO.   Bounteous madam,
    Whatever shall become of Michael Cassio,
    He's never any thing but your true servant.
DESDEMONA. I know 't; I thank you. You do love my lord: 10
    You have known him long; and be you well assur'd
    He shall in strangeness[7] stand no farther off
    Than in a politic distance.
CASSIO.   Ay, but lady,
    That policy may either last so long
    Or feed upon such nice and waterish diet,
    Or breed itself so out of circumstance,[8]
    That, I being absent and my place supplied,
    My general will forget my love and service.
DESDEMONA. Do not doubt[9] that; before Emilia here
    I give thee warrant of thy place: assure thee,   20
    If I do vow a friendship, I'll perform it
    To the last article: my lord shall never rest;
    I'll watch him tame[10] and talk him out of patience;
    His bed shall seem a school, his board a shrift;[11]
    I'll intermingle every thing he does
    With Cassio's suit: therefore be merry, Cassio;
    For thy solicitor shall rather die
    Than give thy cause away.[12]

    [*Enter* OTHELLO *and* IAGO *at a distance.*]

EMILIA. Madam, here comes my lord.
CASSIO. Madam, I'll take my leave.   30
DESDEMONA. Why, stay, and hear me speak.
CASSIO. Madam, not now. I am very ill at ease,
    Unfit for mine own purposes.
DESDEMONA. Well, do your discretion.   [*Exit* CASSIO.]

IAGO. Ha! I like not that.
OTHELLO.   What dost thou say?
IAGO. Nothing, my lord or if—I know not what.
OTHELLO. Was not that Cassio parted from my wife?
IAGO. Cassio, my lord! No, sure, I cannot think it,
    That he would steal away so guilty-like,
    Seeing you coming.   40

---

[7]**strangeness** distant behavior.
[8]**breed...circumstance** increase itself so on account of accidents.
[9]**doubt** fear.
[10]**watch him tame** tame him by keeping him from sleeping (a term from falconry).
[11]**shrift** confessional.
[12]**away** up.

OTHELLO.   I do believe 'twas he.
DESDEMONA. How now, my lord!
    I have been talking with a suitor here,
    A man that languishes in your displeasure.
OTHELLO. Who is 't you mean?
DESDEMONA. Why, your lieutenant, Cassio. Good my lord,
    If I have any grace or power to move you,
    His present reconciliation take;
    For if he be not one that truly loves you,
    That errs in ignorance and not in cunning,
    I have no judgment in an honest face: 50
    I prithee, call him back.
OTHELLO.   Went he hence now?
DESDEMONA. Ay, sooth; so humbled
    That he hath left part of his grief with me,
    To suffer with him. Good love, call him back.
OTHELLO. Not now, sweet Desdemona; some other time.
DESDEMONA. But shall 't be shortly?
OTHELLO.   The sooner, sweet, for you.
DESDEMONA. Shall 't be to-night at supper?
OTHELLO.   No, not to-night.
DESDEMONA. To-morrow dinner, then?
OTHELLO.   I shall not dine at home;
    I meet the captain at the citadel.
DESDEMONA. Why, then, to-morrow night; or Tuesday morn;   60
    On Tuesday noon, or night; on Wednesday morn:
    I prithee, name the time, but let it not
    Exceed three days: in faith, he's penitent;
    And yet his trespass, in our common reason[13]—
    Save that, they say, the wars must make examples
    Out of their best—is not almost a fault
    T' incur a private check. When shall he come?
    Tell me, Othello. I wonder in my soul,
    What you would ask me, that I should deny,
    Or stand so mamm'ring on.[14] What! Michael Cassio,   70
    That came a-wooing with you, and so many a time,
    When I have spoke of you dispraisingly,
    Hath ta'en your part; to have so much to do
    To bring him in! Trust me, I could do much,—
OTHELLO. Prithee, no more: let him come when he will;
    I will deny thee nothing.
DESDEMONA.   Why, this is not a boon;
    'Tis as I should entreat you wear your gloves,
    Or feed on nourishing dishes, or keep you warm,
    Or sue to you to do a peculiar profit
    To your own person: nay, when I have a suit   80

---

[13]**common reason** everyday judgments.
[14]**mamm'ring on** wavering.

Wherein I mean to touch your love indeed,
It shall be full of poise[15] and difficult weight
And fearful to be granted.
OTHELLO.   I will deny thee nothing:
Whereon, I do beseech thee, grant me this,
To leave me but a little to myself.
DESDEMONA. Shall I deny you? No: farewell, my lord.
OTHELLO. Farewell, my Desdemona. I'll come to thee straight.
DESDEMONA. Emilia, come. Be as your fancies teach you;
Whate'er you be, I am obedient.   [*Exit with* EMILIA.]
OTHELLO. Excellent wretch![16] Perdition catch my soul,   90
But I do love thee! And when I love thee not,
Chaos is come again.
IAGO. My noble lord—
OTHELLO.   What dost thou say, Iago?
IAGO. Did Michael Cassio, when you woo'd my lady,
Know of your love?
OTHELLO. He did, from first to last: why dost thou ask?
IAGO. But for a satisfaction of my thought;
No further harm.
OTHELLO.   Why of thy thought, Iago?
IAGO. I did not think he had been acquainted with her.
OTHELLO. O, yes; and went between us very oft.   100
IAGO. Indeed!
OTHELLO. Indeed! Ay, indeed: discern'st thou aught in that?
Is he not honest?
IAGO.   Honest, my lord!
OTHELLO.   Honest! ay, honest.
IAGO. My lord, for aught I know.
OTHELLO. What dost thou think?
IAGO.   Think, my lord!
OTHELLO.   Think, my lord!
By heaven, he echoes me,
As if there were some monster in his thought
Too hideous to be shown. Thou dost mean something.
I heard thee say even now, thou lik'st not that,
When Cassio left my wife: what didst not like?   110
And when I told thee he was of my counsel
In my whole course of wooing, thou criedst "Indeed!"
And didst contract and purse thy brow together,
As if thou then hadst shut up in thy brain
Some horrible conceit: if thou dost love me,
Show me thy thought.
IAGO. My lord, you know I love you.
OTHELLO.   I think thou dost;
And, for I know thou 'rt full of love and honesty,

[15]**poise** heaviness.
[16]**wretch** term of affectionate endearment with a connotation of pity.

And weigh'st thy words before thou giv'st them breath,
Therefore these stops of thine fright me the more: 120
For such things in a false disloyal knave
Are tricks of custom, but in a man that's just
They 're close delations,[17] working from the heart
That passion cannot rule.
IAGO.   For Michael Cassio,
   I dare be sworn I think that he is honest.
OTHELLO. I think so too.
IAGO.   Men should be what they seem;
   Or those that be not, would they might seem none!
OTHELLO. Certain, men should be what they seem.
IAGO. Why, then, I think Cassio 's an honest man.
OTHELLO. Nay, yet there 's more in this.   130
   I prithee, speak to me as to thy thinkings,
   As thou dost ruminate, and give thy worst of thoughts
   The worst of words.
IAGO.   Good my lord, pardon me:
   Though I am bound to every act of duty,
   I am not bound to that all slaves are free to.
   Utter my thoughts? Why, say they are vile and false;
   As where 's that palace whereinto foul things
   Sometimes intrude not? Who has a breast so pure,
   But some uncleanly apprehensions
   Keep leets[18] and law-days[19] and in sessions sit   140
   With meditations lawful?
OTHELLO. Thou dost conspire against thy friend, Iago,
   If thou but think'st him wrong'd and mak'st his ear
   A stranger to thy thoughts.
IAGO.   I do beseech you—
   Though I perchance am vicious[20] in my guess,
   As, I confess, it is my nature's plague
   To spy into abuses, and oft my jealousy[21]
   Shapes faults that are not—that your wisdom yet,
   From one that so imperfectly conceits,[22]
   Would take no notice, nor build yourself a trouble   150
   Out of his scattering and unsure observance.
   It were not for your quiet nor your good,
   Nor for my manhood, honesty, or wisdom,
   To let you know my thoughts.
OTHELLO.   What dost thou mean?
IAGO. Good name in man and woman, dear my lord,

---

[17]**close delations** secret or involuntary accusations.
[18]**Keep leets** hold courts.
[19]**law-days** court days.
[20]**vicious** wrong.
[21]**jealousy** suspicion of evil.
[22]**conceits** judges.

Is the immediate jewel of their souls.
Who steals my purse steals trash: 'tis something, nothing;
'Twas mine, 'tis his, and has been slave to thousands;
But he that filches from me my good name
Robs me of that which not enriches him   160
And makes me poor indeed.
OTHELLO. By heaven, I'll know thy thoughts.
IAGO. You cannot, if my heart were in your hand;
   Nor shall not, whilst 'tis in my custody.
OTHELLO. Ha!
IAGO.   Oh, beware, my lord, of jealousy;
   It is the green-ey'd monster which doth mock
   The meat it feeds on: that cuckold lives in bliss
   Who, certain of his fate, loves not his wronger;
   But, O, what damned minutes tells he o'er
   Who dotes, yet doubts, suspects, yet strongly loves!   170
OTHELLO. O misery!
IAGO. Poor and content is rich and rich enough,
   But riches fineless[23] is as poor as winter
   To him that ever fears he shall be poor.
   Good God, the souls of all my tribe defend
   From jealousy!
OTHELLO.   Why, why is this?
   Think'st thou I'd make a life of jealousy,
   To follow still the changes of the moon
   With fresh suspicions? No; to be once in doubt
   Is once to be resolv'd: exchange me for a goat,   180
   When I shall turn the business of my soul
   To such exsufflicate and blown[24] surmises,
   Matching thy inference. 'Tis not to make me jealous
   To say my wife is fair, feeds well, loves company,
   Is free of speech, sings, plays and dances well;
   Where virtue is, these are more virtuous;
   Nor from mine own weak merits will I draw
   The smallest fear or doubt of her revolt:
   For she had eyes, and chose me. No, Iago;
   I'll see before I doubt; when I doubt, prove;   190
   And on the proof, there is no more but this,—
   Away at once with love or jealousy!
IAGO. I am glad of this; for now I shall have reason
   To show the love and duty that I bear you
   With franker spirit: therefore, as I am bound,
   Receive it from me. I speak not yet of proof.
   Look to your wife; observe her well with Cassio;
   Wear your eye thus, not jealous nor secure:[25]

---

[23]**fineless** boundless.
[24]**exsufflicate and blown** unsubstantial and inflated, flyblown.
[25]**secure** free from uneasiness.

I would not have your free and noble nature,
Out of self-bounty,[26] be abus'd; look to 't.   200
I know our country disposition well;
In Venice they do let heaven see the pranks
They dare not show their husbands; their best conscience
Is not to leave 't undone, but keep 't unknown.

OTHELLO. Dost thou say so?

IAGO. She did deceive her father, marrying you;
And when she seem'd to shake and fear your looks,
She lov'd them most.

OTHELLO.   And so she did.

IAGO.   Why, go to then;
She that, so young, could give out such a seeming,[27]
To seel[28] her father's eyes up close as oak—   210
He thought 'twas witchcraft—but I am much to blame;
I humbly do beseech you of your pardon
For too much loving you.

OTHELLO.   I am bound to thee for ever.

IAGO. I see this hath a little dash'd your spirits.

OTHELLO. Not a jot, not a jot.

IAGO.   I' faith, I fear it has.
I hope you will consider what is spoke
Comes from my love. But I do see y' are mov'd.
I am to pray you not to strain my speech
To grosser issues nor to larger reach[29]
Than to suspicion.   220

OTHELLO. I will not.

IAGO.   Should you do so, my lord,
My speech should fall into such vile success
As my thoughts aim not at. Cassio 's my worthy friend—
My lord, I see y' are mov'd.

OTHELLO.   No, not much mov'd.
I do not think but Desdemona's honest.

IAGO. Long live she so! and long live you to think so!

OTHELLO. And yet, how nature erring from itself,—

IAGO. Ay, there's the point: as—to be bold with you—
Not to affect many proposed matches
Of her own clime, complexion, and degree,   230
Whereto we see in all things nature tends—
Foh! one may smell in such a will[30] most rank,
Foul disproportion,[31] thoughts unnatural.
But pardon me; I do not in position[32]

---

[26]**self-bounty** inherent or natural goodness.
[27]**seeming** false appearance.
[28]**seel** blind (a term from falconry).
[29]**reach** meaning.
[30]**will** sensuality.
[31]**disproportion** abnormality.
[32]**position** general argument.

Distinctly speak of her; though I may fear
Her will, recoiling to[33] her better judgment,
May fall to match you with her country forms[34]
And happily repent.[35]

OTHELLO.   Farewell, farewell:
If more thou dost perceive, let me know more;
Set on thy wife to observe. Leave me, Iago.   240

IAGO [*going*]. My lord, I take my leave.

OTHELLO. Why did I marry? This honest creature doubtless
Sees and knows more, much more, than he unfolds.

IAGO [*returning*]. My Lord, I would I might entreat your honour
To scan this thing no farther; leave it to time:
Although 'tis fit that Cassio have his place,
For, sure, he fills it up with great ability,
Yet, if you please to hold him off awhile,
You shall by that perceive him and his means:
Note, if your lady strain his entertainment[36]   250
With any strong or vehement importunity;
Much will be seen in that. In the mean time,
Let me be thought too busy in my fears—
As worthy cause I have to fear I am—
And hold her free,[37] I do beseech your honour.

OTHELLO. Fear not my government.[38]

IAGO. I once more take my leave.   [*Exit.*]

OTHELLO. This fellow 's of exceeding honesty,
And knows all qualities; with a learned spirit,
Of human dealings. If I do prove her haggard,[39]   260
Though that her jesses[40] were my dear heartstrings,
I'd whistle her off and let her down the wind,
To prey at fortune.[41] Haply, for I am black
And have not those soft parts of conversation
That chamberers[42] have, or for I am declin'd
Into the vale of years,—yet that 's not much—
She 's gone. I am abus'd, and my relief
Must be to loathe her. O curse of marriage,
That we can call these delicate creatures ours,
And not their appetites! I had rather be a toad,   270
And live upon the vapour of a dungeon,
Than keep a corner in the thing I love

---

[33]**recoiling to** falling back upon, or recoiling against.
[34]**fall...forms** happen to compare you with Venetian norms of handsomeness.
[35]**repent** i.e., of her marriage.
[36]**strain his entertainment** urge his reinstatement.
[37]**hold her free** regard her as innocent.
[38]**government** self-control.
[39]**haggard** a wild female duck.
[40]**jesses** straps fastened around the legs of a trained hawk.
[41]**at fortune** at random.
[42]**chamberers** gallants.

For others' uses. Yet, 'tis the plague of great ones;
Prerogativ'd[43] are they less than the base;
'Tis destiny unshunnable, like death:
Even then this forked[44] plague is fated to us
When we do quicken.[45] Look where she comes:

[*Enter* DESDEMONA *and* EMILIA.]

If she be false, O, then heaven mocks itself!
I'll not believe 't.

DESDEMONA.   How now, my dear Othello!
Your dinner, and the generous[46] islanders   280
By you invited, do attend your presence.

OTHELLO. I am to blame.

DESDEMONA.   Why do you speak so faintly?
Are you not well?

OTHELLO. I have a pain upon my forehead here.

DESDEMONA. 'Faith, that 's with watching;[47] 'twill away again.
Let me but bind it hard, within this hour
It will be well.

OTHELLO.   Your napkin is too little

[*He puts the handkerchief from him; and it drops.*]

Let it alone. Come, I'll go in with you.

DESDEMONA. I am very sorry that you are not well.   [*Exit with* OTHELLO.]

EMILIA. I am glad I have found this napkin.   290
This was her first remembrance from the Moor.
My wayward husband hath a hundred times
Woo'd me to steal it; but she so loves the token,
For he conjur'd her she should ever keep it,
That she reserves it evermore about her
To kiss and talk to. I'll have the work ta'en out,[48]
And give 't Iago: what he will do with it
Heaven knows, not I;
I nothing but to please his fantasy.

[*Enter* IAGO.]

IAGO. How now! what do you here alone?

EMILIA. Do not you chide; I have a thing for you.   300

IAGO. A thing for me? it is a common thing[49]—

EMILIA. Ha!

IAGO. To have a foolish wife.

EMILIA. O, is that all? What will you give me now

---

[43]**Prerogativ'd** privileged.
[44]**forked** an allusion to the horns of the cuckold.
[45]**quicken** receive life.
[46]**generous** noble.
[47]**watching** working late.
[48]**work ta'en out** design copied.
[49]**common thing** *common* suggests coarseness and availability to all, and *thing* is slang for female sexual organs.

For that same handkerchief?
IAGO.   What handkerchief?
EMILIA. What handkerchief!
    Why, that the Moor first gave to Desdemona;
    That which so often you did bid me steal.
IAGO. Hast stol'n it from her?
EMILIA. No, 'faith; she let it drop by negligence,   310
    And, to th' advantage, I, being here, took 't up.
    Look, here it is.
IAGO.   A good wench; give it me.
EMILIA. What will you do with 't, that you have been so earnest
    To have me filch it?
IAGO.   [*Snatching it.*] Why, what is that to you?
EMILIA. If it be not for some purpose of import,
    Give 't me again: poor lady, she'll run mad
    When she shall lack it.
IAGO. Be not acknown on 't;[50] I have use for it.
    Go, leave me.   [*Exit* EMILIA.]
    I will in Cassio's lodging lose this napkin,   320
    And let him find it. Trifles light as air
    Are to the jealous confirmations strong
    As proofs of holy writ: this may do something.
    The Moor already changes with my poison:
    Dangerous conceits are, in their natures, poisons,
    Which at the first are scarce found to distaste,
    But with a little act[51] upon the blood,
    Burn like the mines of sulphur. I did say so.

[*Enter* OTHELLO.]

    Look, where he comes! Not poppy, nor mandragora,
    Nor all the drowsy syrups of the world,   330
    Shall ever medicine thee to that sweet sleep
    Which thou owedst yesterday.
OTHELLO.   Ha! ha! false to me?
IAGO. Why, how now, general! no more of that.
OTHELLO. Avaunt! be gone! thou has set me on the rack;
    I swear 'tis better to be much abus'd
    Than but to know 't a little.
IAGO.   How now, my lord!
OTHELLO. What sense had I of her stol'n hours of lust?
    I saw 't not, thought it not, it harm'd not me:
    I slept the next night well, fed well, was free and merry;
    I found not Cassio's kisses on her lips.   340
    He that is robb'd, not wanting what is stol'n,
    Let him not know 't, and he 's not robb'd at all.
IAGO. I am sorry to hear this.
OTHELLO. I had been happy, if the general camp,

---

[50]**Be…on't** do not confess knowledge of it.
[51]**act** action, working.

Pioners[52] and all, had tasted her sweet body,
So I had nothing known. O, now, for ever
Farewell the tranquil mind! farewell content!
Farewell the plumed troop, and the big wars,
That make ambition virtue! O, farewell!
Farewell the neighing steed, and the shrill trump,   350
The spirit-stirring drum, th' ear-piercing fife,
The royal banner, and all quality,
Pride, pomp and circumstance[53] of glorious war!
And, O you mortal engines,[54] whose rude throats
Th' immortal Jove's dread clamours counterfeit,
Farewell! Othello's occupation 's gone!

IAGO. Is 't possible, my lord?

OTHELLO. Villain, be sure thou prove my love a whore,
Be sure of it; give me the ocular proof;
Or, by the worth of mine eternal soul,   360
Thou hadst been better have been born a dog
Than answer my wak'd wrath!

IAGO.   Is 't come to this?

OTHELLO. Make me see 't; or, at the least, so prove it,
That the probation bear no hinge nor loop
To hang a doubt on; or woe upon thy life!

IAGO. My noble lord,—

OTHELLO. If thou dost slander her and torture me,
Never pray more; abandon all remorse;
On horror's head horrors[55] accumulate;
Do deeds to make heaven weep, all earth amaz'd;   370
For nothing canst thou to damnation add
Greater than that.

IAGO.   O grace! O heaven forgive me!
Are you a man? Have you a soul or sense?
God be wi' you; take mine office. O wretched fool,
That liv'st to make thine honesty a vice!
O monstrous world! Take note, take note, O world,
To be direct and honest is not safe.
I thank you for this profit; and from hence
I'll love no friend, sith love breeds such offense.

OTHELLO. Nay, stay: thou shouldst be honest.   380

IAGO. I should be wise, for honesty 's a fool
And loses that it works for.

OTHELLO.   By the world,
I think my wife be honest and think she is not;
I think that thou are just and think thou art not.
I'll have some proof. Her name, that was as fresh
As Dian's visage, is now begrim'd and black

---

[52]**Pioners** sappers, a low grade of soldiers.
[53]**circumstance** attendant fact; here, formal display.
[54]**mortal engines** i.e., cannon.
[55]**horrors** object of *accumulate*.

As mine own face. If there be cords, or knives,
Poison, or fire, or suffocating streams,
I'll not endure it. Would I were satisfied!

IAGO. I see, sir, you are eaten up with passion: 390
I do repent me that I put it to you.
You would be satisfied?

OTHELLO.   Would! nay, I will.

IAGO. And may: but, how? how satisfied, my lord?
Would you, the supervisor, grossly gape on—
Behold her topp'd?

OTHELLO.   Death and damnation! O!

IAGO. It were a tedious difficulty, I think,
To bring them to that prospect: damn them then,
If ever mortal eyes do see them bolster[56]
More than their own! What then? how then?
What shall I say? Where 's satisfaction?   400
It is impossible you should see this,
Were they as prime as goats, as hot as monkeys,
As salt[57] as wolves in pride, and fools as gross
As ignorance made drunk. But yet, I say,
If imputation[58] and strong circumstances,
Which lead directly to the door of truth,
Will give you satisfaction, you may have 't.

OTHELLO. Give me a living reason she 's disloyal.

IAGO. I do not like the office.
But, sith I am ent'red in this cause so far,   410
Prick'd to 't by foolish honesty and love,
I will go on. I lay with Cassio lately;
And, being troubled with a raging tooth,
I could not sleep.
There are a kind of men so loose of soul,
That in their sleeps will mutter their affairs.
One of this kind is Cassio.
In sleep I heard him say "Sweet Desdemona,
Let us be wary, let us hide our loves";
And then, sir, would he grip and wring my hand,   420
Cry "O sweet creature!" and then kiss me hard,
As if he pluck'd up kisses by the roots
That grew upon my lips: then laid his leg
Over my thigh, and sigh'd and kiss'd; and then
Cried "Cursed fate that gave thee to the Moor!"

OTHELLO. O monstrous! monstrous!

IAGO.   Nay, this was but his dream.

OTHELLO. But this denoted a foregone conclusion.[59]

---

[56]**bolster** lie together.

[57]**salt** wanton, sensual.

[58]**imputation** i.e., opinion founded on strong circumstantial evidence.

[59]**foregone conclusion** previous trial or experience (not used in our sense).

'Tis a shrewd doubt, though it be but a dream.
IAGO. And this may help to thicken other proofs
    That do demonstrate thinly.   430
OTHELLO.   I'll tear her all to pieces.
IAGO. Nay, but be wise: yet we see nothing done;
    She may be honest yet. Tell me but this,
    Have you not sometimes seen a handkerchief
    Spotted with strawberries in your wife's hand?
OTHELLO. I gave her such a one; 'twas my first gift.
IAGO. I know not that: but such a handkerchief—
    I am sure it was your wife's—did I to-day
    See Cassio wipe his beard with.
OTHELLO.   If it be that,—
IAGO. If it be that, or any that was hers,
    It speaks against her with the other proofs.   440
OTHELLO. O, that the slave had forty thousand lives!
    One is too poor, too weak for my revenge.
    Now do I see 'tis true. Look here, Iago;
    All my fond love thus do I blow to heaven.
    'Tis gone.
    Arise, black vengeance, from the hollow hell!
    Yield up, O love, thy crown and hearted[60] throne
    To tyrannous hate! Swell, bosom, with thy fraught,[61]
    For 'tis of aspics'[62] tongues!
IAGO.   Yet be content.
OTHELLO. O, blood, blood, blood!   450
IAGO. Patience, I say; your mind perhaps may change.
OTHELLO. Never, Iago. Like to the Pontic sea,
    Whose icy current and compulsive course
    Ne'er feels retiring ebb, but keeps due on
    To the Propontic and the Hellespont,
    Even so my bloody thoughts, with violent pace,
    Shall ne'er look back, ne'er ebb to humble love,
    Till that a capable and wide revenge
    Swallow them up. Now, by yond marble[63] heaven,
    [*Kneels*] In the due reverence of a sacred vow   460
    I here engage my words.
IAGO.   Do not rise yet.
    [*Kneels.*] Witness, you ever-burning lights above,
    You elements that clip us round about,
    Witness that here Iago doth give up
    The execution[64] of his wit, hands, heart,
    To wrong'd Othello's service! Let him command,

---

[60]**hearted** fixed in the heart.
[61]**fraught** freight, burden.
[62]**aspics'** venemous serpents'.
[63]**marble** i.e., gleaming like marble.
[64]**execution** exercise.

And to obey shall be in me remorse,[65]
What bloody business ever. [*They rise.*]
OTHELLO.   I greet thy love,
  Not with vain thanks, but with acceptance bounteous,
  And will upon the instant put thee to 't.   470
  Within these three days let me hear thee say
  That Cassio 's not alive.
IAGO. My friend is dead; 'tis done at your request:
  But let her live.
OTHELLO. Damn her, lewd minx! O, damn her! damn her!
  Come, go with me apart; I will withdraw,
  To furnish me with some swift means of death
  For the fair devil. Now art thou my lieutenant.
IAGO. I am your own for ever.   [*Exeunt.*]   480

SCENE IV

Before the castle.

[*Enter* DESDEMONA, EMILIA, *and* CLOWN.]

DESDEMONA. Do you know, sirrah, where Lieutenant Cassio lies?
CLOWN. I dare not say he lies any where.
DESDEMONA. Why, man?
CLOWN. He's a soldier, and for one to say a soldier lies, is stabbing.
DESDEMONA. Go to: where lodges he?
CLOWN. To tell you where he lodges, is to tell you where I lie.
DESDEMONA. Can any thing be made of this?
CLOWN. I know not where he lodges, and for me to devise a lodging and say he
  lies here or he lies there, were to lie in mine own throat.
DESDEMONA. Can you inquire him out, and be edified by report?   10
CLOWN. I will catechize the world for him; that is, make questions, and by them
  answer.
DESDEMONA. Seek him, bid him come hither: tell him I have moved my lord on
  his behalf, and hope all will be well.
  CLOWN. To do this is within the compass of man's wit; and therefore I will
  attempt the doing it.   [*Exit* CLOWN.]

DESDEMONA. Where should I lose that handkerchief, Emilia?
EMILIA. I know not, madam.
DESDEMONA. Believe me, I had rather have lost my purse
  Full of crusadoes[66] and but my noble Moor
  Is true of mind and made of no such baseness   20
  As jealous creatures are, it were enough
  To put him to ill thinking.
EMILIA.   Is he not jealous?

---

[65]**remorse** pity for Othello's wrongs.
[66]**crusadoes** Portuguese gold coins.

DESDEMONA. Who, he? I think the sun where he was born
    Drew all such humours from him.
EMILIA.   Look, where he comes.

   [*Enter* OTHELLO.]

DESDEMONA. I will not leave him now till Cassio
    Be call'd to him.—How is 't with you, my lord?
OTHELLO. Well, my good lady. [*Aside*] O, hardness to dissemble!—
    How do you, Desdemona?
DESDEMONA.   Well, my good lord.
OTHELLO. Give me your hand. This hand is moist, my lady.   30
DESDEMONA. It yet hath felt no age nor known no sorrow.
OTHELLO. This argues fruitfulness and liberal heart.
    Hot, hot, and moist this hand of yours requires
    A sequester[67] from liberty, fasting and prayer,
    Much castigation, exercise devout;
    For here 's a young and sweating devil here,
    That commonly rebels. 'Tis a good hand,
    A frank one.
DESDEMONA.   You may, indeed, say so,
    For 'twas that hand that gave away my heart.
OTHELLO. A liberal hand: the hearts of old gave hands;   40
    But our new heraldry is hands, not hearts.[68]
DESDEMONA. I cannot speak of this. Come now, your promise.
OTHELLO. What promise, chuck?
DESDEMONA. I have sent to bid Cassio come speak with you.
OTHELLO. I have a salt and sorry rheum[69] offends me;
    Lend me thy handkerchief.
DESDEMONA.   Here, my lord.
OTHELLO. That which I gave you.
DESDEMONA.   I have it not about me.
OTHELLO. Not?
DESDEMONA. No, indeed, my lord.
OTHELLO.   That 's a fault.
    That handkerchief   50
    Did an Egyptian[70] to my mother give;
    She was a charmer, and could almost read
    The thoughts of people. She told her, while she kept it,
    'Twould make her amiable and subdue my father
    Entirely to her love, but if she lost it
    Or made a gift of it, my father's eye
    Should hold her loathed and his spirits should hunt
    After new fancies: she, dying, gave it me;
    And bid me, when my fate would have me wive,
    To give it her. I did so: and take heed on 't;   60

---

[67] **sequester** separation, sequestration.
[68] **new...hearts** a current expression referring to marriages in which there is a joining of hands without the giving of hearts.
[69] **sorry rheum** distressful head cold.
[70] **Egyptian** gypsy.

Make it a darling like your precious eye;
To lose 't or give 't away were such perdition
As nothing else could match.
DESDEMONA.   Is 't possible?
OTHELLO. 'Tis true. There 's magic in the web of it:
    A sibyl, that had numb'red in the world
    The sun to course two hundred compasses,
    In her prophetic fury sew'd the work;
    The worms were hallow'd that did breed the silk;
    And it was dy'd in mummy[71] which the skilful
    Conserv'd of[72] maidens' hearts.   70
DESDEMONA.   Indeed! is 't true?
OTHELLO. Most veritable; therefore look to 't well.
DESDEMONA. Then would to God that I had never seen 't!
OTHELLO. Ha! wherefore?
DESDEMONA. Why do you speak so startingly and rash?
OTHELLO. Is 't lost? is 't gone? speak, is it out o' th' way?
DESDEMONA. Heaven bless us!
OTHELLO. Say you?
DESDEMONA. It is not lost; but what an if it were?
OTHELLO. How!
DESDEMONA. I say, it is not lost.   80
OTHELLO.   Fetch 't, let me see 't.
DESDEMONA. Why, so I can, sir, but I will not now.
    This is a trick to put me from my suit:
    Pray you, let Cassio be receiv'd again.
OTHELLO. Fetch me the handkerchief: my mind misgives.
DESDEMONA. Come, come;
    You'll never meet a more sufficient man.
OTHELLO. The handkerchief!
DESDEMONA.   I pray, talk me of Cassio.
OTHELLO. The handkerchief!
DESDEMONA.   A man that all his time
    Hath founded his good fortunes on your love,
    Shar'd dangers with you,—   90
OTHELLO. The handkerchief!
DESDEMONA. In sooth, you are to blame.
OTHELLO. Away!   [*Exit* OTHELLO.]

EMILIA. Is not this man jealous?
DESDEMONA. I ne'er saw this before.
    Sure, there 's some wonder in this handkerchief:
    I am most unhappy in the loss of it.
EMILIA. 'Tis not a year or two shows us a man:
    They are all but stomachs, and we all but food;
    They eat us hungerly, and when they are full,   100
    They belch us.

---

[71]**mummy** medicinal or magical preparation drained from the flesh of mummified bodies.
[72]**Conserv'd of** preserved out of.

[*Enter* IAGO *and* CASSIO.]

> Look you, Cassio and my husband!

IAGO. There is no other way; 'tis she must do 't:
> And, lo, the happiness! go, and importune her.

DESDEMONA. How now, good Cassio! what 's the news with you?

CASSIO. Madam, my former suit. I do beseech you
> That by your virtuous means I may again
> Exist, and be a member of his love
> Whom I with all the office of my heart
> Entirely honour. I would not be delay'd.
> If my offense be of such mortal kind   110
> That nor my service past, nor present sorrows,
> Nor purpos'd merit in futurity,
> Can ransom me into his love again,
> But to know so much be my benefit;[73]
> So shall I clothe me in a forc'd content,
> And shut myself up in some other course,
> To fortune's alms.

DESDEMONA.   Alas, thrice-gentle Cassio!
> My advocation[74] is not now in tune;
> My lord is not my lord; nor should I know him,
> Were he in favour as in humour alter'd.   120
> So help me every spirit sanctified
> As I have spoken for you all my best
> And stood within the blank[75] of his displeasure
> For my free speech! You must awhile be patient.
> What I can do I will; and more I will
> Than for myself I dare: let that suffice you.

IAGO. Is my lord angry?

EMILIA.   He went hence but now,
> And certainly in strange unquietness.

IAGO. Can he be angry? I have seen the cannon,
> When it hath blown his ranks into the air,   130
> And, like the devil, from his very arm
> Puff'd his own brother:—and can he be angry?
> Something of moment then. I will go meet him:
> There 's matter in 't indeed, if he be angry.

DESDEMONA. I prithee, do so.   [*Exit* IAGO.]

> Something, sure, of state,
> Either from Venice, or some unhatch'd practice
> Made demonstrable here in Cyprus to him,
> Hath puddled[76] his clear spirit; and in such cases
> Men's natures wrangle with inferior things,
> Though great ones are their object. 'Tis even so;   140

---

[73]**to know...benefit** to know that my case is hopeless will end my vain endeavor.
[74]**advocation** advocacy.
[75]**blank** white spot in the center of a target; here, range.
[76]**puddled** sullied the purity of.

For let our finger ache, and it indues[77]
Our other healthful members even to a sense
Of pain. Nay, we must think men are not gods,
Nor of them look for such observancy
As fits the bridal. Beshrew me much, Emilia,
I was, unhandsome[78] warrior as I am,
Arraigning his unkindness with my soul;
But now I find I had suborn'd the witness,
And he 's indicted falsely.

EMILIA. Pray heaven it be state-matters, as you think,   150
    And no conception[79] nor no jealous toy
    Concerning you.

DESDEMONA. Alas the day! I never gave him cause.

EMILIA. But jealous souls will not be answer'd so;
    They are not ever jealous for the cause,
    But jealous for they are jealous: 'tis a monster
    Begot upon itself, born on itself.

DESDEMONA. Heaven keep that monster from Othello's mind!

EMILIA. Lady, amen.

DESDEMONA. I will go seek him. Cassio, walk here about: 160
    If I do find him fit, I'll move your suit
    And seek to effect it to my uttermost.

CASSIO. I humbly thank your ladyship.   [*Exit* DESDEMONA *with* EMILIA.]

[*Enter* BIANCA.]

BIANCA. Save you, friend Cassio!

CASSIO.   What make you from home?
    How is 't with you, my most fair Bianca?
    I' faith, sweet love, I was coming to your house.

BIANCA. And I was going to your lodging, Cassio.
    What, keep a week away? seven days and nights?
    Eight score eight hours? and lovers' absent hours,
    More tedious than the dial eight score times?   170
    O weary reck'ning!

CASSIO.   Pardon me, Bianca.
    I have this while with leaden thoughts been press'd;
    But I shall, in a more continuate[80] time,
    Strike off this score of absence. Sweet Bianca,

[*Giving her* DESDEMONA'S *handkerchief.*]

Take me this work out.[81]

BIANCA.   O Cassio, whence came this?
    This is some token from a newer friend:
    To the felt absence now I feel a cause:

---

[77]**indues** brings to the same condition.
[78]**unhandsome** unfair.
[79]**conception** mere fancy.
[80]**continuate** uninterrupted.
[81]**Take...out** i.e., copy this embroidery for me.

Is 't come to this? Well, well.

CASSIO.   Go to, woman!
  Throw your vile guesses in the devil's teeth,
  From whence you have them. You are jealous now   180
  That this is from some mistress, some remembrance:
  No, in good troth, Bianca.

BIANCA.   Why, whose is it?

CASSIO. I know not, sweet. I found it in my chamber.
  I like the work well. Ere it be demanded—
  As like enough it will—I would have it copied:
  Take it, and do 't; and leave me for this time.

BIANCA. Leave you! wherefore?

CASSIO. I do attend here on the general;
  And think it no addition, nor my wish,
  To have him see me woman'd.   190

BIANCA.   Why, I pray you?

CASSIO. Not that I love you not.

BIANCA.   But that you do not love me.
  I pray you, bring me on the way a little,
  And say if I shall see you soon at night.

CASSIO. 'Tis but a little way that I can bring you;
  For I attend here, but I'll see you soon.

BIANCA. 'Tis very good; I must be circumstance'd.[82]   [*Exeunt omnes.*]

ACT IV

SCENE I

Cyprus. Before the castle.

[*Enter* OTHELLO *and* IAGO.]

IAGO. Will you think so?

OTHELLO.   Think so, Iago!

IAGO.   What,
  To kiss in private?

OTHELLO.   An unauthoriz'd kiss.

IAGO. Or to be naked with her friend in bed
  An hour or more, not meaning any harm?

OTHELLO. Naked in bed, Iago, and not mean harm!
  It is hypocrisy against the devil:
  They that mean virtuously, and yet do so,
  The devil their virtue tempts, and they tempt heaven.

IAGO. So[1] they do nothing, 'tis a venial slip:
  But if I give my wife a handkerchief,—   10

OTHELLO. What then?

IAGO. Why, then, 'tis hers, my lord: and, being hers,

---

[82]**circumstance'd** governed by circumstances.

[1]**So** so long as.

She may, I think, bestow 't on any man.

OTHELLO. She is protectress of her honour too:
May she give that?

IAGO. Her honour is an essence that 's not seen;
They have it very oft that have it not:
But, for the handkerchief,—

OTHELLO. By heaven, I would most gladly have forgot it.
Thou said'st—O, it comes o'er my memory,   20
As doth the raven o'er the infected house,[2]
Boding to all—he had my handkerchief.

IAGO. Ay, what of that?

OTHELLO.   That 's not so good now.

IAGO.   What,
If I had said I had seen him do you wrong?
Or heard him say,—as knaves be such abroad,
Who having, by their own importunate suit,
Or voluntary dotage of some mistress,
Convinced or supplied[3] them, cannot choose
But they must blab—

OTHELLO.   Hath he said any thing?

IAGO. He hath, my lord; but be you well assur'd,   30
No more than he'll unswear.

OTHELLO.   What hath he said?

IAGO. 'Faith, that he did—I know not what he did.

OTHELLO. What? what?

IAGO. Lie—

OTHELLO. With her?

IAGO.   With her, on her; what you will.

OTHELLO. Lie with her! lie on her! We say lie on her, when they belie her. Lie with her! that's fulsome.—Handkerchief—confessions—handkerchief—To confess, and be hanged for his labour;—first, to be hanged, and then to confess.—I tremble at it. Nature would not invest herself in such shadowing passion without some instruction.[4] It is not words that shakes me thus. Pish! Noses,   40
ears, and lips.—Is 't possible? Confess—handkerchief—O devil!

                                        [*Falls in a trance.*]

IAGO. Work on,
My medicine, work! Thus credulous fools are caught;
And many worthy and chaste dames even thus,
All guiltless, meet reproach. What, ho! my lord!
My lord, I say! Othello!

[*Enter* CASSIO.]

                                        How now, Cassio!

CASSIO. What 's the matter?

IAGO. My lord is fall'n into an epilepsy:

---

[2]**raven...house** allusion to the belief that the raven hovered over a house of sickness or infection.

[3]**Convinced or supplied** i.e., mistresses gained by importunity and those who doted voluntarily.

[4]**Nature...instruction** i.e., my jealousy cannot be merely the result of natural imagination, but must have some foundation in fact.

This is his second fit; he had one yesterday.

CASSIO. Rub him about the temples.   50

IAGO.   No, forbear;
    The lethargy[5] must have his quiet course:
    If not, he foams at mouth and by and by
    Breaks out to savage madness. Look, he stirs:
    Do you withdraw yourself a little while,
    He will recover straight. When he is gone,
    I would on great occasion speak with you.

                                      [*Exit* CASSIO.]

    How is it, general? Have you not hurt your head?

OTHELLO. Dost thou mock me?

IAGO.   I mock you! no, by heaven.
    Would you would bear your fortune like a man!

OTHELLO. A horned man's a monster and a beast.   60

IAGO. There's many a beast then in a populous city,
    And many a civil[6] monster.

OTHELLO. Did he confess it?

IAGO.   Good sir, be a man;
    Think every bearded fellow that's but yok'd
    May draw with you.[7] There's millions now alive
    That nightly lie in those unproper[8] beds
    Which they dare swear peculiar:[9] your case is better.
    O, 'tis the spite of hell, the fiend's arch-mock,
    To lip a wanton in a secure couch,
    And to suppose her chaste! No, let me know;   70
    And knowing what I am, I know what she shall be.

OTHELLO. O, thou are wise; 'tis certain.

IAGO.   Stand you awhile apart;
    Confine yourself but in a patient list.[10]
    Whilst you were here o'erwhelmed with your grief—
    A passion most unsuiting such a man—
    Cassio came hither. I shifted him away,
    And laid good 'scuse upon your ecstasy,
    Bade him anon return and here speak with me;
    The which he promis'd. Do but encave[11] yourself,
    And mark the fleers,[12] the gibes, and notable scorns,   80
    That dwell in every region of his face;
    For I will make him tell the tale anew,
    Where, how, how oft, how long ago, and when
    He hath, and is again to cope your wife:
    I say, but mark his gesture. Marry, patience;

---

[5]**lethargy** unconscious condition.
[6]**civil** i.e., in civilized society.
[7]**draw with you** i.e, share your fate as cuckold.
[8]**unproper** not belonging exclusively to an individual.
[9]**peculiar** private, one's own.
[10]**patient list** within the bounds of patience.
[11]**encave** conceal.
[12]**fleers** sneers.

Or I shall say y' are all in all in spleen,
And nothing of a man.
OTHELLO.   Dost thou hear, Iago?
I will be found most cunning in my patience;
But—dost thou hear?—most bloody.
IAGO.   That 's not amiss;
But yet keep time[13] in all. Will you withdraw?   90

> [OTHELLO *retires*.]

Now will I question Cassio of Bianca,
A housewife that by selling her desires
Buys herself bread and clothes: it is a creature
That dotes on Cassio; as 'tis the strumpet's plague
To beguile many and be beguil'd by one:
He, when he hears of her, cannot refrain
From the excess of laughter. Here he comes:

[*Enter* CASSIO.]

As he shall smile, Othello shall go mad;
And his unbookish[14] jealousy must conster[15]
Poor Cassio's smiles, gestures and light behaviour,   100
Quite in the wrong. How do you know, lieutenant?
CASSIO. The worser that you give me the addition[16]
Whose want even kills me.
IAGO. Ply Desdemona well, and you are sure on 't.
[*Speaking lower*] Now, if this suit lay in Bianca's power,
How quickly should you speed!
CASSIO.   Alas, poor caitiff!
OTHELLO. Look, how he laughs already!
IAGO. I never knew woman love man so.
CASSIO. Alas, poor rogue! I think, i' faith, she loves me.
OTHELLO. Now he denies it faintly, and laughs it out.   110
IAGO. Do you hear, Cassio?
OTHELLO.   Now he importunes him
To tell o'er: go to; well said, well said.
IAGO. She gives it out that you shall marry her:
Do you intend it?
CASSIO. Ha, ha, ha!
OTHELLO. Do you triumph, Roman?[17] do you triumph?
CASSIO. I marry her! what? a customer![18] Prithee, bear some charity to my wit;
do not think it so unwholesome. Ha, ha, ha!
OTHELLO. So, so, so, so they laugh that win.
IAGO. 'Faith, the cry goes that you shall marry her.   120
CASSIO. Prithee, say true.

---

[13]**keep time** use judgment and order.
[14]**unbookish** uninstructed.
[15]**conster** construe.
[16]**addition** title.
[17]**Roman** epithet arising from the association of the Romans with the idea of triumph.
[18]**customer** prostitute.

IAGO. I am a very villain else.

OTHELLO. Have you scored me?[19] Well.

CASSIO. This is the monkey's own giving out: she is persuaded I will marry her, out of her own love and flattery, not out of my promise.

OTHELLO. Iago beckons me; now he begins the story.

CASSIO. She was here even now; she haunts me in every place. I was the other day talking on the seabank with certain Venetians; and thither comes the bauble,[20] and, by this hand, she falls me thus about my neck—

OTHELLO. Crying, 'O dear Cassio!' as it were: his gesture imports it.   130

CASSIO. So hangs, and lolls, and weeps upon me; so shakes, and pulls me ha, ha, ha!

OTHELLO. Now he tells how she plucked him to my chamber. O, I see that nose of yours, but not that dog I shall throw it to.

CASSIO. Well, I must leave her company.

IAGO. Before me![21] look, where she comes.

[*Enter* BIANCA.]

CASSIO. 'Tis such another fitchew![22] marry, a perfumed one.—What do you mean by this haunting of me?

BIANCA. Let the devil and his dam haunt you! What did you mean by that same handkerchief you gave me even now? I was a fine fool to take it. I must take   140 out the work?—A likely piece of work, that you should find it in your chamber, and not know who left it there! This is some minx's token, and I must take out the work? There; give it your hobby-horse.[23] Wheresoever you had it, I'll take out no work on 't.

CASSIO. How now, my sweet Bianca! how now! how now!

OTHELLO. By heaven, that should be my handkerchief!

BIANCA. If you'll come to supper to-night, you may; if you will not, come when you are next prepared for.   [*Exit.*]

IAGO. After her, after her.

CASSIO. 'Faith, I must; she'll rail in the street else.   150

IAGO. Will you sup there?

CASSIO. Yes, I intend so.

IAGO. Well, I may chance to see you; for I would very fain speak with you.

CASSIO. Prithee, come; will you?

IAGO. Go to; say no more.   [*Exit* CASSIO.]

OTHELLO [*Advancing*]. How shall I murder him, Iago?

IAGO. Did you perceive how he laughed at his vice?

OTHELLO. O Iago!

IAGO. And did you see the handkerchief?

OTHELLO. Was that mine?   160

IAGO. Yours, by this hand: and to see how he prizes the foolish woman your wife! She gave it him, and he hath given it his whore.

---

[19]**scored me** made up my reckoning, or branded me.
[20]**bauble** plaything.
[21]**Before me!** On my soul!
[22]**fitchew** polecat (because of her strong perfume; also, slang word for a prostitute).
[23]**hobby-horse** harlot.

OTHELLO. I would have him nine years a-killing. A fine woman! a fair woman! a sweet woman!

IAGO. Nay, you must forget that.

OTHELLO. Ay, let her rot, and perish, and be damned to-night; for she shall not live: no, my heart is turned to stone; I strike it, and it hurts my hand. O, the world hath not a sweeter creature: she might lie by an emperor's side and command him tasks.

IAGO. Nay, that 's not your way.[24]   170

OTHELLO. Hang her! I do but say what she is: so delicate with her needle: an admirable musician: O! she will sing the savageness out of a bear: of so high and plenteous wit and invention:—

IAGO. She 's the worse for all this.

OTHELLO. O, a thousand thousand times: and then, of so gentle a condition!

IAGO. Ay, too gentle.

OTHELLO. Nay, that 's certain: but yet the pity of it, Iago! O Iago, the pity of it, Iago!

IAGO. If you are so fond over her iniquity, give her patent[25] to offend; for, if it touch not you, it comes near nobody.

OTHELLO. I will chop her into messes;[26] cuckold me!   180

IAGO. O, 'tis foul in her.

OTHELLO. With mine officer!

IAGO. That 's fouler.

OTHELLO. Get me some poison, Iago; this night I'll not expostulate with her, lest her body and beauty unprovide[27] my mind again: this night, Iago.

IAGO. Do it not with poison, strangle her in her bed, even the bed she hath contaminated.

OTHELLO. Good, good: the justice of it pleases: very good.

IAGO. And for Cassio, let me be his undertaker.[28] You shall hear more by midnight.   190

OTHELLO. Excellent good. [*A trumpet within.*] What trumpet is that same?

IAGO. I warrant something from Venice.

[*Enter* LODOVICO, DESDEMONA, *and* ATTENDANTS.]

                    'Tis Lodovico.
    This comes from the duke: and, see, your wife's with him.

LODOVICO. God save you, worthy general!

OTHELLO.   With all my heart, sir.

LODOVICO. The duke and the senators of Venice greet you. [*Gives him a letter.*]

OTHELLO. I kiss the instrument of their pleasures.   [*Opens the letter, and reads.*]

DESDEMONA. And what's the news, good cousin Lodovico?

IAGO. I am very glad to see you, signior;
    Welcome to Cyprus.

LODOVICO. I thank you. How does Lieutenant Cassio?   200

IAGO. Lives, sir.

DESDEMONA. Cousin, there's fall'n between him and my lord
    An unkind breach, but you shall make all well.

---

[24]**your way** i.e., the way you should think of her.
[25]**patent** license.
[26]**messes** dishes of food.
[27]**unprovide** weaken, unfit.
[28]**let...undertaker** i.e., let me settle with him.

OTHELLO. Are you sure of that?
DESDEMONA. My lord?
OTHELLO [*Reads*]. "This fail you not to do, as you will—"
LODOVICO. He did not call; he's busy in the paper.
    Is there division 'twixt my lord and Cassio?
DESDEMONA. A most unhappy one. I would do much
    T' atone them, for the love I bear to Cassio.   210
OTHELLO. Fire and brimstone!
DESDEMONA.   My lord?
OTHELLO.   Are you wise?
DESDEMONA. What, is he angry?
LODOVICO.   May be the letter mov'd him:
    For, as I think, they do command him home,
    Deputing Cassio in his government.[29]
DESDEMONA. Trust me, I am glad on 't.
OTHELLO.   Indeed!
DESDEMONA.   My lord?
OTHELLO. I am glad to see you mad.
DESDEMONA.   Why, sweet Othello,—
OTHELLO [*Striking her*]. Devil!
DESDEMONA. I have not deserv'd this.
LODOVICO. My lord, this would not be believ'd in Venice,
    Though I should swear I saw 't; 'tis very much.   220
    Make her amends; she weeps.
OTHELLO.   O devil, devil!
    If that the earth could teem with woman's tears,
    Each drop she falls would prove a crocodile.[30]
    Out of my sight!
DESDEMONA.   I will not stay to offend you.   [*Going.*]
LODOVICO. Truly, an obedient lady.
    I do beseech your lordship, call her back.
OTHELLO. Mistress!
DESDEMONA.   My lord?
OTHELLO.   What would you with her, sir?
LODOVICO. Who, I, my lord?
OTHELLO. Ay; you did wish that I would make her turn:
    Sir, she can turn, and turn, and yet go on,   230
    And turn again; and she can weep, sir, weep;
    And she 's obedient, as you say, obedient,
    Very obedient. Proceed you in your tears.
    Concerning this, sir,—O well-painted passion!—[31]
    I am commanded home. Get you away;
    I'll send for you anon. Sir, I obey the mandate,
    And will return to Venice. Hence, avaunt!

                              [*Exit* DESDEMONA.]

---

[29]**government** office.
[30]**prove a crocodile** i.e., by weeping crocodile tears; it was believed the crocodile shed tears over the body of the person it was eating.
[31]**well-painted passion** well-simulated emotion.

Cassio shall have my place. And, sir, to-night,
I do entreat that we may sup together.
You are welcome, sir, to Cyprus.—Goats and monkeys! *[Exit.]* 240
LODOVICO. Is this the noble Moor whom our full senate
Call all in all sufficient? Is this the nature
Whom passion could not shake? whose solid virtue
The shot of accident, nor dart of chance,
Could neither graze nor pierce?
IAGO.   He is much chang'd.
LODOVICO. Are his wits safe? Is he not light of brain?
IAGO. He's that he is. I may not breathe my censure
What he might be: if what he might he is not,
I would to heaven he were!
LODOVICO.   What, strike his wife!
IAGO. 'Faith, that was not so well; yet would I knew 250
That stroke would prove the worst!
LODOVICO.   Is it his use?
Or did the letters work upon his blood,
And new-create this fault?
IAGO.   Alas, alas!
It is not honesty in me to speak
What I have seen and known. You shall observe him,
And his own courses will denote him so
That I may save my speech: do but go after,
And mark how he continues.
LODOVICO. I am sorry that I am deceiv'd in him. *[Exeunt.]*

SCENE II

A room in the castle.

[Enter OTHELLO *and* EMILIA.*]*

OTHELLO. You have seen nothing then?
EMILIA. Nor ever heard, nor ever did suspect.
OTHELLO. Yes, you have seen Cassio and she together.
EMILIA. But then I saw no harm, and then I heard
Each syllable that breath made up between them.
OTHELLO. What, did they never whisper?
EMILIA.   Never, my lord.
OTHELLO. Nor send you out 'o th' way?
EMILIA. Never.
OTHELLO. To fetch her fan, her gloves, her mask, nor nothing?
EMILIA. Never, my lord. 10
OTHELLO. That 's strange.
EMILIA. I durst, my lord, to wager she is honest,
Lay down my soul at stake: if you think other,
Remove your thought; it doth abuse your bosom.
If any wretch have put this in your head,
Let heaven requite it with the serpent's curse!

For, if she be not honest, chaste, and true,
There's no man happy; the purest of their wives
Is foul as slander.
OTHELLO.   Bid her come hither: go.   [*Exit* EMILIA.]   20

She says enough; yet she's a simple bawd
That cannot say as much. This is a subtle whore,
A closet lock and key[32] of villainous secrets:
And yet she'll kneel and pray; I have seen her do't.

[*Enter* DESDEMONA *and* EMILIA.]

DESDEMONA. My lord, what is your will?
OTHELLO.   Pray, chuck, come hither.
DESDEMONA. What is your pleasure?
OTHELLO.   Let me see your eyes;
    Look in my face.
DESDEMONA.   What horrible fancy 's this?
OTHELLO [*to* Emilia]. Some of your function,[33] mistress;
    Leave procreants[34] alone and shut the door;
    Cough, or cry "hem," if any body come.
    Your mystery, your mystery:[35] nay, dispatch.   [*Exit* Emilia.]   30
DESDEMONA. Upon my knees, what doth your speech import?
    I understand a fury in your words,
    But not the words.
OTHELLO. Why, what art thou?
DESDEMONA.   Your wife, my lord; your true
    And loyal wife.
OTHELLO.   Come, swear it, damn thyself;
    Lest, being like one of heaven, the devils themselves
    Should fear to seize thee: therefore be double damn'd:
    Swear thou are honest.
DESDEMONA.   Heaven doth truly know it.
OTHELLO. Heaven truly knows that thou are false as hell.
DESDEMONA. To whom, my lord? with whom? how am I false?   40
OTHELLO. O Desdemon! away! away! away!
DESDEMONA. Alas the heavy day! Why do you weep?
    Am I the motive of these tears, my lord?
    If haply you my father do suspect
    An instrument of this your calling back,
    Lay not your blame on me: if you have lost him,
    Why, I have lost him too.
OTHELLO.   Had it pleas'd heaven
    To try me with affliction; had they[36] rain'd
    All kinds of sores and shames on my bare head,   50

---

[32]**closet lock and key** complete storeroom.
[33]**Some...function** i.e., set to work in your chosen profession, that of bawd.
[34]**procreants** mating couples.
[35]**mystery** trade, occupation.
[36]**they** heavenly powers.

Steep'd me in poverty to the very lips,
Given to captivity me and my utmost hopes,
I should have found in some place of my soul
A drop of patience: but, alas, to make me
A fixed figure for the time of scorn
To point his slow unmoving finger at![37]
Yet could I bear that too; well, very well.
But there, where I have garner'd up my heart,
Where either I must live, or bear no life;
The fountain from the which my current runs,   60
Or else dries up; to be discarded thence!
Or keep it as a cistern for foul toads
To knot and gender[38] in! Turn thy complexion[39] there,
Patience, thou young and rose-lipp'd cherubin,—
Ay, there, look grim as hell!
DESDEMONA. I hope my noble lord esteems me honest.
OTHELLO. O, ay; as summer flies are in the shambles,[40]
    That quicken[41] even with blowing. O thou weed,
    Who are so lovely fair and smell'st so sweet
    That the sense aches at thee, would thou hads't ne'er been born!   70
DESDEMONA. Alas, what ignorant sin have I committed?
OTHELLO. Was this fair paper, this most goodly book,
    Made to write "whore" upon? What committed!
    Committed! O thou public commoner![42]
    I should make very forges of my cheeks,
    That would to cinders burn up modesty,
    Did I but speak thy deeds. What committed!
    Heaven stops the nose at it and the moon winks,
    The bawdy wind that kisses all it meets
    Is hush'd within the hollow mine of earth,   80
    And will not hear it. What committed!
    Impudent strumpet!
DESDEMONA.   By heaven, you do me wrong.
OTHELLO. Are not you a strumpet?
DESDEMONA.   No, as I am a Christian.
    If to preserve this vessel[43] for my lord
    From any other foul unlawful touch
    Be not to be a strumpet, I am none.
OTHELLO. What, not a whore?
DESDEMONA.   No, as I shall be sav'd.
OTHELLO. Is't possible?

---

[37]**A...at** Othello possibly thinks of himself as a man set in a pillory at whom the scornful world points in mockery. There seems to be a comparison with the sundial, whose gnomon, or indicator, becomes the finger of scornful time.
[38]**gender** engender.
[39]**Turn thy complexion** grow pale.
[40]**shambles** slaughterhouse.
[41]**quicken** come to life.
[42]**commoner** prostitute.
[43]**vessel** body.

DESDEMONA. O, heaven forgive us!
OTHELLO.   I cry you mercy, then.   90
    I took you for the cunning whore of Venice
    That married with Othello. [*Raising his voice*] You, mistress,
    That have the office opposite to Saint Peter,
    And keep the gate of hell!

    [*Enter* EMILIA.]

                     You, you, ay, you!
    We have done our course; there's money for your pains.
    I pray you, turn the key and keep our counsel.   [*Exit.*]

EMILIA. Alas, what does this gentleman conceive?
    How do you, madam? how do you, my good lady?
DESDEMONA. 'Faith, half asleep.
EMILIA. Good madam, what 's the matter with my lord?   100
DESDEMONA. With who?
EMILIA. Why, with my lord, madam.
DESDEMONA. Who is thy lord?
EMILIA.   He that is yours, sweet lady.
DESDEMONA. I have none: do not talk to me, Emilia;
    I cannot weep; nor answers have I none,
    But what should go by water.[44] Prithee, tonight
    Lay on my bed my wedding sheets, remember;
    And call thy husband hither.
EMILIA.   Here 's a change indeed!   [*Exit.*]
DESDEMONA. 'Tis meet I should be us'd so, very meet.
    How have I been behav'd, that he might stick   110
    The small'st opinion on my least misuse?[45]

    [*Enter* IAGO *and* EMILIA.]

IAGO. What is your pleasure, madam? How is 't with you?
DESDEMONA. I cannot tell. Those that do teach young babes
    Do it with gentle means and easy tasks:
    He might have chid me so; for, in good faith,
    I am a child to chiding.
IAGO.   What is the matter, lady?
EMILIA. Alas, Iago, my lord hath so bewhor'd her,
    Thrown such despite[46] and heavy terms upon her,
    As true hearts cannot bear.
DESDEMONA. Am I that name, Iago?
IAGO.   What name, fair lady?   120
DESDEMONA. Such as she said my lord did say I was.
EMILIA. He call'd her whore: a beggar in his drink
    Could not have laid such terms upon his callet.[47]
IAGO. Why did he so?
DESDEMONA. I do not know; I am sure I am none such.

---

[44]**go by water** be expressed by tears.
[45]**misuse** evil conduct.
[46]**despite** contempt, scorn.
[47]**callet** lewd woman.

IAGO. Do not weep, do not weep. Alas the day!
EMILIA. Hath she forsook so many noble matches,
    Her father and her country and her friends,
    To be call'd whore? Would it not make one weep?
DESDEMONA. It is my wretched fortune.
IAGO.   Beshrew him for 't!   130
    How comes this trick upon him?
DESDEMONA.   Nay, heaven doth know.
EMILIA. I will be hang'd, if some eternal villain,
    Some busy and insinuating rogue,
    Some cogging,[48] cozening slave, to get some office,
    Have not devis'd this slander; I will be hang'd else.
IAGO. Fie, there is no such man; it is impossible.
DESDEMONA. If any such there be, heaven pardon him!
EMILIA. A halter pardon him! and hell gnaw his bones!
    Why should he call her whore? who keeps her company?
    What place? what time? what form? what likelihood?   140
    The Moor's abus'd by some most villainous knave,
    Some base notorious knave, some scurvy fellow.
    O heaven, that such companions thou 'dst unfold,
    And put in every honest hand a whip
    To lash the rascals naked through the world
    Even from the east to th' west!
IAGO.   Speak within door.[49]
EMILIA. O, fie upon them! Some such squire he was
    That turn'd your wit the seamy side without,
    And made you to suspect me with the Moor.
IAGO. You are a fool; go to.
DESDEMONA.   Alas, Iago.   150
    What shall I do to win my lord again?
    Good friend, go to him; for, by this light of heaven,
    I know not how I lost him. Here I kneel:
    If e'er my will did trespass 'gainst his love,
    Either in discourse of thought or actual deed,
    Or that mine eyes, mine ears, or any sense,
    Delighted them in any other form;
    Or that I do not yet, and ever did,
    And ever will—though he do shake me off
    To beggarly divorcement—love him dearly,   160
    Comfort forswear me! Unkindness may do much;
    And his unkindness may defeat my life,
    But never taint my love. I cannot say "whore":
    It doth abhor me now I speak the word;
    To do the act that might the addition[50] earn
    Not the world's mass of vanity could make me.
IAGO. I pray you, be content; 'tis but his humour:

---

[48]**cogging** cheating.
[49]**Speak…door** i.e., not so loud.
[50]**addition** title.

The business of the state does him offense,
And he does chide with you.

DESDEMONA. If 'twere no other,—   170

IAGO.   'Tis but so, I warrant.   [*Trumpets within.*]

Hark, how these instruments summon to supper!
The messengers of Venice stay the meat;[51]
Go in, and weep not; all things shall be well.

                          [*Exeunt* DESDEMONA *and* EMILIA.]

[*Enter* RODERIGO.]

How now, Roderigo!

RODERIGO. I do not find that thou dealest justly with me.

IAGO. What in the contrary?

RODERIGO. Every day thou daffest me[52] with some device, Iago; and rather, as it
   seems to me now, keepest from me all conveniency[53] than suppliest me
   with the least advantage of hope. I will indeed no longer endure it, nor am
   I yet persuaded to put up[54] in peace what already I have foolishly suffered.

IAGO. Will you hear me, Roderigo?   180

RODERIGO. 'Faith, I have heard too much, for your words and performances are
   no kin together.

IAGO. You charge me most unjustly.

RODERIGO. With nought but truth. I have wasted myself out of my means. The jewels
   you have had from me to deliver to Desdemona would half have corrupted a
   votarist.[55] You have told me she hath received them and returned me
   expectations and comforts of sudden respect and acquaintance, but I find none.

IAGO. Well; go to; very well.

RODERIGO. Very well! go to! I cannot go to, man; nor 'tis not very well: nay, I
   think it is scurvy, and begin to find myself fopped[56] in it.   190

IAGO. Very well.

RODERIGO. I tell you 'tis not very well. I will make myself known to Desdemona:
   if she will return me my jewels, I will give over my suit and repent my
   unlawful solicitation; if not, assure yourself I will seek satisfaction of you.

IAGO. You have said now.[57]

RODERIGO. Ay, and said nothing but what I protest intendment[58] of doing.

IAGO. Why, now I see there 's mettle in thee, and even from this instance do build
   on thee a better opinion than ever before. Give my thy hand, Roderigo.
   Thou hast taken against me a most just exception; but yet, I protest, I have
   dealt most directly in thy affair.   200

RODERIGO. It hath not appeared.

IAGO. I grant indeed it hath not appeared, and your suspicion is not without wit
   and judgment. But, Roderigo, if thou hast that in thee indeed, which I have

---

[51]**stay the meat** are waiting for supper.
[52]**daffest me** put me off with an excuse.
[53]**conveniency** advantage, opportunity.
[54]**put up** submit to.
[55]**votarist** nun.
[56]**fopped** fooled.
[57]**You...now** well said, quite right.
[58]**intendment** purpose, intention.

greater reason to believe now than ever, I mean purpose, courage and valour, this night show it; if thou the next night following enjoy not Desdemona, take me from this world with treachery and devise engines for[59] my life.

RODERIGO. Well, what is it? Is it within reason and compass?

IAGO. Sir, there is especial commission come from Venice to depute Cassio in Othello's place.

RODERIGO. Is that true? Why, then Othello and Desdemona return again to Venice.　　210

IAGO. O, no; he goes into Mauritania[60] and takes away with him the fair Desdemona, unless his abode be lingered here by some accident: wherein none can be so determinate[61] as the removing of Cassio.

RODERIGO. How do you mean, removing of him?

IAGO. Why, by making him uncapable of Othello's place; knocking out his brains.

RODERIGO. And that you would have me to do?

IAGO. Ay, if you dare do yourself a profit and a right. He sups to-night with a harlotry,[62] and thither will I go to him: he knows not yet of his honourable fortune. If you will watch his going thence, which I will fashion to fall out between twelve and one, you may take him at your pleasure: I will be near　　220 to second your attempt, and he shall fall between us. Come, stand not amazed at it, but go along with me; I will show you such a necessity in his death that you shall think yourself bound to put it on him. It is now high[63] suppertime, and the night grows to waste: about it.

RODERIGO. I will hear further reason for this.

IAGO. And you shall be satisfied.

[*Exeunt.*]

SCENE III

Another room in the castle.

[*Enter* OTHELLO, LODOVICO, DESDEMONA, EMILIA, *and* ATTENDANTS.]

LODOVICO. I do beseech you, sir, trouble yourself no further.

OTHELLO. O, pardon me; 'twill do me good to walk.

LODOVICO. Madam, good night. I humbly thank your ladyship.

DESDEMONA. Your honour is most welcome.

OTHELLO.　　　　　　　　　　　　　　　Will you walk, sir?
　　O,—Desdemona,—

DESDEMONA. My lord?

OTHELLO. Get you to bed on th' instant; I will be returned forthwith. Dismiss your attendant there: look 't be done.

DESDEMONA. I will, my lord.

[*Exit* OTHELLO, *with* LODOVICO *and* ATTENDANTS.]

EMILIA. How goes it now? He looks gentler than he did.　　10

DESDEMONA. He says he will return incontinent.[64]

---

[59]**engines for** plots against.
[60]**Mauritania** Roman name of northwest Africa, supposed land of the Moors.
[61]**determinate** decisive.
[62]**harlotry** courtesan.
[63]**high** quite.
[64]**incontinent** immediately.

He hath commanded me to go to bed,
And bade me to dismiss you.
EMILIA.   Dismiss me!
DESDEMONA. It was his bidding; therefore, good Emilia,
Give me my nightly wearing, and adieu.
We must not now displease him.
EMILIA. I would you had never seen him!
DESDEMONA. So would not I. My love doth so approve him,
That even his stubbornness,[65] his checks,[66] his frowns,—
Prithee, unpin me,—have grace and favour in them.   20
EMILIA. I have laid those sheets you bade me on the bed.
DESDEMONA. All's one. Good faith, how foolish are our minds!
If I do die before thee, prithee, shroud me
In one of those same sheets.
EMILIA.   Come, come, you talk.
DESDEMONA. My mother had a maid call'd Barbary.
She was in love, and he she lov'd prov'd mad
And did forsake her. She had a song of 'willow';
An old thing 'twas, but it express'd her fortune,
And she died singing it. That song to-night
Will not go from my mind; I have much to do,   30
But to[67] go hang my head all at one side,
And sing it like poor Barbary. Prithee, dispatch.
EMILIA. Shall I go fetch your night-gown?[68]
DESDEMONA.   No, unpin me here.
This Lodovico is a proper man.
EMILIA. A very handsome man.
DESDEMONA. He speaks well.
EMILIA. I know a lady in Venice would have walked barefoot to
Palestine for a touch of his nether lip.
DESDEMONA [*Singing*]. "The poor soul sat sighing by a sycamore tree,
Sing all a green willow;   40
Her hand on her bosom, her head on her knee,
Sing willow, willow, willow.
The fresh streams ran by her, and murmur'd her moans;
Sing willow, willow, willow;
Her salt tears fell from her, and soft'ned the stones;—"
Lay by these —
[*Singing*]. "Sing willow, willow, willow"
Prithee, hie thee; he'll come anon —
[*Singing*]. "Sing all a green willow must be my garland.
Let nobody blame him; his scorn I approve,—"   50
Nay, that's not next.—Hark! who is 't that knocks?
EMILIA. It 's the wind.

———————

[65]**stubbornness** harshness.
[66]**checks** rebukes.
[67]**But to** not to.
[68]**night-gown** dressing gown.

DESDEMONA [*Singing*]. "I call'd my love false love; but what said he then?
      Sing willow, willow, willow:
      If I court moe women, you'll couch with moe men.—"
  So, get thee gone; good night. Mine eyes do itch;
  Doth that bode weeping?
EMILIA.   'Tis neither here nor there.
DESDEMONA. I have heard it said so. O, these men, these men!
  Dost thou in conscience think,—tell me, Emilia,—
  That there be women do abuse their husbands   60
  In such gross kind?
EMILIA.   There be some such, no question.
DESDEMONA. Wouldst thou do such a deed for all the world?
EMILIA. Why, would not you?
DESDEMONA.   No, by this heavenly light!
EMILIA. Nor I neither by this heavenly light; I might do 't as well i' the dark.
DESDEMONA. Wouldst thou do such a deed for all the world?
EMILIA. The world 's a huge thing: it is a great price
  For a small vice.
DESDEMONA. In troth, I think thou wouldst not.
EMILIA. In troth, I think I should; and undo 't when I had done. Marry, I would
  not do such a thing for a joint-ring,[69] nor for measures of lawn, nor for   70
  gowns, petticoats, nor caps, nor any petty exhibition;[70] for all the whole
  world,—why, who would not make her husband a cuckold to make him a
  monarch? I should venture purgatory for 't.
DESDEMONA. Beshrew me, if I would do such a wrong
  For the whole world.
EMILIA. Why, the wrong is but a wrong i' the world; and having the world for
  your labour, 'tis a wrong in your own world, and you might quickly make
  it right.
DESDEMONA. I do not think there is any such woman.
EMILIA. Yes, a dozen; and as many   80
  To the vantage[71] as would store the world they played for.
  But I do think it is their husband's faults
  If wives do fall. Say that they slack their duties,
  And pour our treasures into foreign laps,[72]
  Or else break out in peevish jealousies,
  Throwing restraint upon us; or say they strike us,
  Or scant our former having in despite;[73]
  Why, we have galls,[74] and though we have some grace,[75]
  Yet have we some revenge. Let husbands know
  Their wives have sense like them: they see and smell   90
  And have their palates both for sweet and sour,

---

[69]**joint-ring** a ring made in separable halves as a lover's token.
[70]**exhibition** gift, present.
[71]**to the vantage** in addition.
[72]**pour...laps** i.e., are unfaithful.
[73]**scant...despite** reduce our allowance to spite us.
[74]**have galls** are capable of resenting injury and insult.
[75]**grace** i.e., to forgive.

As husbands have. What is it that they do
When they change us for others? Is it sport?
I think it is. And doth affection breed it?
I think it doth. Is 't frailty that thus errs?
It is so too. And have not we affections,
Desires for sport, and frailty, as men have?
Then let them use us well: else let them know,
The ills we do, their ills instruct us so.

DESDEMONA. Good night, good night: heaven me such uses send,   100
    Not to pick bad from bad, but by bad mend!   [*Exeunt.*]

ACT V

SCENE I

Cyprus. A street

[*Enter* IAGO *and* RODERIGO.]

IAGO. Here stand behind this bulk;[1] straight will he come:
    Wear thy good rapier bare, and put it home:
    Quick, quick; fear nothing; I'll be at thy elbow:
    It makes us, or it mars us; think on that,
    And fix most firm thy resolution.
RODERIGO. Be near at hand; I may miscarry in 't.
IAGO. Here, at thy hand: be bold, and take thy stand.   [*Retires.*]

RODERIGO. I have no great devotion to the deed;
    And yet he hath given me satisfying reasons:
    'Tis but a man gone. Forth, my sword: he dies.   10
IAGO. I have rubb'd this young quat[2] almost to the sense,[3]
    And he grows angry. Now, whether he kill Cassio,
    Or Cassio him, or each do kill the other,
    Every way makes my gain. Live Roderigo,
    He calls me to a restitution large
    Of gold and jewels that I bobb'd[4] from him,
    As gifts to Desdemona;
    It must not be. If Cassio do remain,
    He hath a daily beauty in his life
    That makes me ugly; and, besides, the Moor   20
    May unfold me to him; there stand I in much peril:
    No, he must die. But so: I hear him coming.

[*Enter* CASSIO.]

RODERIGO. I know his gait, 'tis he.—Villain, thou diest!

                [*Makes a pass at* CASSIO.]

CASSIO. That thrust had been mine enemy indeed,

---

[1]**bulk** framework projecting from the front of a shop.
[2]**quat** pimple, pustule; used contemptuously.
[3]**to the sense** to the quick.
[4]**bobb'd** filched cunningly.

But that my coat[5] is better than thou know'st.
  I will make proof of thine.   [*Draws, and wounds* RODERIGO.]
RODERIGO.   O, I am slain!
            [IAGO *from behind wounds* CASSIO *in the leg, and exits.*]
CASSIO. I am maim'd for ever. Help, ho! murder! murder!   [*Falls.*]

  [*Enter* OTHELLO.]

OTHELLO. The voice of Cassio. Iago keeps his word.
RODERIGO. O, villain that I am!
OTHELLO.   It is even so.   30
CASSIO. O, help, ho! light! a surgeon!
OTHELLO. 'Tis he: —O brave Iago, honest and just,
      That hast such noble sense of thy friend's wrong!
      Thou teachest me. Minion, your dear lies dead,
      And your unblest fate hies: strumpet, I come.
      Forth of my heart those charms, thine eyes, are blotted;
      Thy bed, lust-stain'd, shall with lust's blood be spotted.
                                              [*Exit* OTHELLO.]

  [*Enter* LODOVICO *and* GRATIANO.]

CASSIO. What, ho! no watch? no passage?[6] murder! murder!
GRATIANO. 'Tis some mischance; the cry is very direful.
CASSIO. O, help!   40
LODOVICO. Hark!
RODERIGO. O wretched villain!
LODOVICO. Two or three groan. It is a heavy[7] night;
      These may be counterfeits. Let 's think 't unsafe
      To come in to the cry without more help.
RODERIGO. Nobody come? Then shall I bleed to death.
LODOVICO. Hark!

  [*Enter* IAGO *with a light.*]

GRATIANO. Here's one comes in his shirt, with light and weapons.
IAGO. Who's there? Whose noise is this that cries on[8] murder?
LODOVICO. We do not know.   50
IAGO.   Did not you hear a cry?
CASSIO. Here, here! for heaven's sake, help me!
IAGO.   What's the matter?
GRATIANO. This is Othello's ancient, as I take it.
LODOVICO. The same indeed; a very valiant fellow.
IAGO. What are you here that cry so grievously?
CASSIO. Iago? O, I am spoil'd, undone by villains!
      Give me some help.
IAGO. O me, lieutenant! what villains have done this?
CASSIO. I think that one of them is hereabout,
      And cannot make away.   60

---

[5]**coat** coat of mail.
[6]**passage** people passing.
[7]**heavy** thick, cloudy.
[8]**cries on** cries out.

IAGO.   O treacherous villains!
  What are you there? Come in, and give some help.
                                    [*To* LODOVICO *and* GRATIANO.]
RODERIGO. O, help me here!
CASSIO. That's one of them.
IAGO.   O murd'rous slave! O villain!
                                    [*Stabs* RODERIGO.]
RODERIGO. O damn'd Iago! O inhuman dog!
IAGO. Kill men i' th' dark!—Where be these bloody thieves?—
  How silent in this town!—Ho! murder! murder!—
  What⁹ you be? Are you of good or evil?
LODOVICO. As you shall prove us, praise us.
IAGO. Signior Lodovico?   70
LODOVICO. He, sir.
IAGO. I cry you mercy. Here's Cassio hurt by villains.
GRATIANO. Cassio!
IAGO. How is 't, brother!
CASSIO. My leg is cut in two.
IAGO.   Marry, heaven forbid!
  Light, gentlemen. I'll bind it with my shirt.

  [*Enter* BIANCA.]

BIANCA. What is the matter, ho? Who is 't that cried?
IAGO. Who is 't that cried?
BIANCA. O my dear Cassio! my sweet Cassio!
  O Cassio, Cassio, Cassio!   80
IAGO. O notable strumpet! Cassio, may you suspect
  Who they should be that have thus mangled you?
CASSIO. No.
GRATIANO. I am sorry to find you thus: I have been to seek you.
IAGO. Lend me a garter. So. O, for a chair,¹⁰
  To bear him easily hence!
BIANCA. Alas, he faints! O Cassio, Cassio, Cassio!
IAGO. Gentlemen all, I do suspect this trash¹¹
  To be a party in this injury.
  Patience awhile, good Cassio. Come, come;   90
  Lend me a light. Know we this face or no?
  Alas, my friend and my dear countryman
  Roderigo! no:—yes, sure:—O heaven! Roderigo.
GRATIANO. What, of Venice?
IAGO. Even he, sir: did you know him?
GRATIANO.   Know him! ay.
IAGO. Signior Gratiano? I cry your gentle pardon;
  These bloody accidents must excuse my manners,
  That so neglected you.
GRATIANO.   I am so glad to see you.
IAGO. How do you, Cassio? O, a chair, a chair!

---

⁹**What** who.
¹⁰**chair** sedan chair.
¹¹**trash** worthless thing—i.e., Bianca.

GRATIANO. Roderigo! 100
IAGO. He, he, 'tis he. [*A chair brought in.*] O, that's well said; the chair.
    Some good man bear him carefully from hence;
    I'll fetch the general's surgeon. [*To* BIANCA] For you, mistress,
    Save you your labour. He that lies slain here, Cassio,
    Was my dear friend: what malice was between you?
CASSIO. None in the world; nor do I know the man.
IAGO [*To* BIANCA]. What, look you pale? O, bear him out o' th' air.
                              [CASSIO *and* RODERIGO *are borne off.*]
    Stay you, good gentlemen. Look you pale, mistress?
    Do you perceive the gastness[12] of her eye?
    Nay, if you stare, we shall hear more anon. 110
    Behold her well; I pray you, look upon her:
    Do you see, gentlemen? Nay, guiltiness will speak,
    Though tongues were out of use.

    [*Enter* EMILIA.]

EMILIA. 'Las, what's the matter? what's the matter, husband?
IAGO. Cassio hath here been set on in the dark
    By Roderigo and fellows that are scap'd:
    He's almost slain, and Roderigo dead.
EMILIA. Alas, good gentlemen! alas, good Cassio!
IAGO. This is the fruit of whoring. Prithee, Emilia,
    Go know of Cassio where he supp'd to-night. 120
    [*To* BIANCA] What, do you shake at that?
BIANCA. He supp'd at my house; but I therefore shake not.
IAGO. O, did he so? I charge you, go with me.
EMILIA. Fie, fie upon thee, strumpet!
BIANCA. I am no strumpet; but of life as honest
    As you that thus abuse me.
EMILIA.   As I! foh! fie upon thee!
IAGO. Kind gentlemen, let's go see poor Cassio dress'd.
    Come, mistress, you must tell's another tale.
    Emilia, run you to the citadel,
    And tell my lord and lady what hath happ'd.
    Will you go on afore? [*Aside*] This is the night
    That either makes me or fordoes[13] me quite.   [*Exeunt.*]

SCENE II

A bedchamber in the castle.

[*Enter* OTHELLO *with a light;* DESDEMONA *in her bed.*]

OTHELLO. It is the cause, it is the cause,[14] my soul,—
    Let me not name it to you, you chaste stars!—

---

[12]**gastness** terror, ghastliness.
[13]**fordoes** undoes, ruins.
[14]**It is the cause** i.e., the cause of justice on which Othello must act, Desdemona's deed, which is too unmentionable to be named to the chaste stars.

It is the cause. Yet I'll not shed her blood;
Nor scar that whiter skin of hers than snow,
And smooth as monumental alabaster.
Yet she must die, else she'll betray more men.
Put out the light, and then put out the light:
If I quench thee, thou flaming minister,
I can again thy former light restore,
Should I repent me: but once put out thy light,   10
Thou cunning'st pattern of excelling nature,
I know not where is that Promethean heat[15]
That can thy light relume.[16] When I have pluck'd the rose,
I cannot give it vital growth again,
It needs must wither: I'll smell thee on the tree.   [*Kissing her.*]
O balmy breath, that dost almost persuade
Justice to break her sword! One more, one more.
Be thus when thou art dead, and I will kill thee,
And love thee after. One more, and that's the last:
So sweet was ne'er so fatal. I must weep,   20
But they are cruel tears: this sorrow's heavenly;[17]
It strikes where it doth love. She wakes.
DESDEMONA. Who's there? Othello?
OTHELLO.   Ay, Desdemona.
DESDEMONA. Will you come to bed, my lord?
OTHELLO. Have you pray'd to-night, Desdemon?
DESDEMONA.   Ay, my lord.
OTHELLO. If you bethink yourself of any crime
     Unreconcil'd as yet to heaven and grace,
     Solicit for it straight.
DESDEMONA. Alack, my lord, what may you mean by that?
OTHELLO. Well, do it, and be brief; I will walk by: 30
     I would not kill thy unprepared spirit;
     No; heaven forfend! I would not kill thy soul.
DESDEMONA. Talk you of killing?
OTHELLO.   Ay, I do.
DESDEMONA.   Then heaven
     Have mercy on me!
OTHELLO.   Amen, with all my heart!
DESDEMONA. If you say so, I hope you will not kill me.
OTHELLO. Hum!
DESDEMONA. And yet I fear you; for you're fatal then
     When your eyes roll so: why I should fear I know not,
     Since guiltiness I know not; but yet I feel I fear.
OTHELLO. Think on thy sins.
DESDEMONA.   They are loves I bear to you.   40

---

[15]**Promethean heat** divine fire; allusion to the theft of fire from heaven by Prometheus.
[16]**relume** rekindle.
[17]**this...heavenly** this tenderness, with which I lament the punishment which justice compels
me to inflict, is a holy passion.

OTHELLO. Ay, and for that thou diest.

DESDEMONA. That death's unnatural that kills for loving.
Alas, why gnaw you so your nether lip?
Some bloody passion shakes your very frame:
These are portents; but yet I hope, I hope,
They do not point on me.

OTHELLO.   Peace, and be still!

DESDEMONA. I will so. What's the matter?

OTHELLO. That handkerchief which I so lov'd and gave thee
Thou gav'st to Cassio.

DESDEMONA.   No, by my life and soul!
Send for the man, and ask him.

OTHELLO.   Sweet soul, take heed,   50
Take heed of perjury; thou are on thy deathbed.

DESDEMONA. Ay, but not yet to die.

OTHELLO.   Yes, presently:
Therefore confess thee freely of thy sin;
For to deny each article with oath
Cannot remove nor choke the strong conception[18]
That I do groan withal. Thou art to die.

DESDEMONA. Then Lord have mercy on me!

OTHELLO.   I say, amen.

DESDEMONA. And have you mercy too! I never did
Offend you in my life; never lov'd Cassio
But with such general warranty of heaven   60
As I might love; I never gave him token.

OTHELLO. By heaven, I saw my handkerchief in 's hand.
O perjur'd woman! thou dost stone[19] my heart,
And makes me call what I intend to do
A murder, which I thought a sacrifice:
I saw the handkerchief.

DESDEMONA.   He found it then;
I never gave it him: send for him hither;
Let him confess a truth.

OTHELLO.   He hath confess'd.

DESDEMONA. What, my Lord?

OTHELLO. That he hath us'd thee.   70

DESDEMONA.   How? unlawfully?

OTHELLO.   Ay.

DESDEMONA. He will not say so.

OTHELLO.   No, his mouth is stopp'd;
Honest Iago hath ta'en order[20] for 't.

DESDEMONA. O! my fear interprets: what, is he dead?

OTHELLO. Had all his hairs been lives, my great revenge
Had stomach for them all.

---

[18]**conception** plan, intention.
[19]**stone** turn to stone, harden; Othello means that he will be tempted to kill her in sheer anger because of her perjury.
[20]**ta'en order** taken measures.

DESDEMONA. Alas! he is betray'd and I undone.
OTHELLO. Out, strumpet! weep'st thou for him to my face?
DESDEMONA. O, banish me, my lord, but kill me not!
OTHELLO. Down, strumpet!
DESDEMONA. Kill me to-morrow: let me live to-night!   80
OTHELLO. Nay, if you strive,—
DESDEMONA. But half an hour!
OTHELLO.   Being done, there is no pause.[21]
DESDEMONA. But while I say one prayer!
OTHELLO.   It is too late.   [*Smothers her.*]
EMILIA [*at the door*]. My lord, my lord! what, ho! my lord, my lord!
OTHELLO. What noise is this? Not dead? not yet quite dead?
    I that am cruel am yet merciful;
    I would not have thee linger in thy pain:
    So, so.
EMILIA [*within*]. What, ho! my lord, my lord!
OTHELLO.   Who's there?
EMILIA [*within*]. O, good my lord, I would speak a word with you!   90
OTHELLO. Yes: 'tis Emilia. By and by. She 's dead.
    'Tis like she comes to speak of Cassio's death.—
    The noise was here. Ha! no more moving?
    Still as the grave. Shall she come in? were 't good?—
    I think she stirs again:—no. What 's best to do?
    If she come in, she'll sure speak to my wife.
    My wife! my wife! what wife? I have no wife.
    O, insupportable! O heavy hour!
    Methinks it should be now a huge eclipse
    Of sun and moon, and that th' affrighted globe   100
    Should yawn[22] at alteration.[23]
EMILIA.   [*Within*] I do beseech you
    That I may speak with you, O, good my lord!
OTHELLO. I had forgot thee: O, come in, Emilia:
    Soft; by and by. Let me the curtains draw.
    Where art thou?   [*Closes bed-curtains and opens door.*]

[*Enter* EMILIA.]

    What's the matter with thee now?
EMILIA. O, my good lord, yonder's foul murders done!
OTHELLO. What, now?
EMILIA. But now, my lord.
OTHELLO. It is the very error[24] of the moon;
    She comes more nearer earth than she was wont,   110
    And makes men mad.

---

[21]**Being…pause** i.e., when the execution of the deed has once begun, there is no stopping.
[22]**yawn** gape in amazement.
[23]**at alteration** at the change.
[24]**error** irregularity.

EMILIA. Cassio, my lord, hath kill'd a young Venetian
    Call'd Roderigo.
OTHELLO.   Roderigo kill'd!
    And Cassio kill'd!
EMILIA.   No, Cassio is not kill'd.
OTHELLO. Not Cassio kill'd! Then murder 's out of tune,
    And sweet revenge grows harsh.
DESDEMONA. O, falsely, falsely murder'd!
EMILIA.   Alas, what cry is that?
OTHELLO. That! what?
EMILIA. Out, and alas! that was my lady's voice.
    Help, help, ho! help. O lady, speak again!   120
    Sweet Desdemona! O sweet mistress, speak!
DESDEMONA. A guiltless death I die.
EMILIA. O, who hath done this deed?
DESDEMONA. Nobody; I myself. Farewell:
    Commend me to my kind lord: O, farewell!   [*Dies.*]
OTHELLO. Why, how should she be murd'red?
EMILIA.   Alas, who knows?
OTHELLO. You heard her say herself, it was not I.
EMILIA. She said so: I must needs report the truth.
OTHELLO. She's, like a liar, gone to burning hell:
    'Twas I that kill'd her.
EMILIA.   O, the more angel she,   130
    And you the blacker devil!
OTHELLO. She turn'd to folly,[25] and she was a whore.
EMILIA. Thou dost belie her, and thou art a devil.
OTHELLO. She was false as water.
EMILIA.   Thou art rash as fire, to say
    That she was false: O, she was heavenly true!
OTHELLO. Cassio did top her; ask thy husband else.
    O, I were damned beneath all depth in hell,
    But that I did proceed upon just grounds
    To this extremity. Thy husband knew it all.
EMILIA. My husband!   140
OTHELLO. Thy husband.
EMILIA. That she was false to wedlock?
OTHELLO. Ay, with Cassio. Nay, had she been true,
    If heaven would make me such another world
    Of one entire and perfect chrysolite,[26]
    I'ld not have sold her for it.
EMILIA. My husband!
OTHELLO.   Ay, 'twas he that told me first:
    An honest man he is, and hates the slime
    That sticks on filthy deeds.

[25]**folly** unchastity.
[26]**chrysolite** the golden stone; a name given to various precious stones of green color.

EMILIA.   My husband!

OTHELLO. What needs this iterance,[27] woman? I say thy husband.   150

EMILIA. O mistress, villainy hath made mocks with[28] love!
    My husband say that she was false!

OTHELLO.   He, woman;
    I say thy husband: dost understand the word?
    My friend, thy husband, honest, honest Iago.

EMILIA. If he say so, may his pernicious soul
    Rot half a grain a day! He lies to th' heart:
    She was too fond of her most filthy bargain.

OTHELLO. Ha!

EMILIA. Do thy worst:
    This deed of thine is no more worthy heaven   160
    Than thou wast worthy her.

OTHELLO.   Peace, you were best.

EMILIA. Thou hast not half that power to do me harm
    As I have to be hurt.[29] O gull! O dolt!
    As ignorant as dirt! thou has done a deed—
    I care not for thy sword; I'll make thee known,
    Though I lost twenty lives.—Help! help, ho! help!
    The Moor hath kill'd my mistress! Murder! murder!

[*Enter* MONTANO, GRATIANO, *and* IAGO *with others.*]

MONTANO. What is the matter? How now, general!

EMILIA. O, are you come, Iago? You have done well,
    That men must lay their murders on your neck.   170

GRATIANO. What is the matter?

EMILIA. Disprove this villain, if thou be'st a man:
    He says thou told'st him that his wife was false:
    I know thou didst not, thou'rt not such a villain:
    Speak, for my heart is full.

IAGO. I told him what I thought, and told no more
    Than what he found himself was apt[30] and true.

EMILIA. But did you ever tell him she was false?

IAGO. I did.

EMILIA. You told a lie; an odious, damned lie;   180
    Upon my soul, a lie, a wicked lie.
    She false with Cassio!—did you say with Cassio?

IAGO. With Cassio, mistress. Go to, charm[31] your tongue.

EMILIA. I will not charm my tongue; I am bound to speak:
    My mistress here lies murdered in her bed,—

ALL. O heavens forfend!

EMILIA. And your reports have set the murder on.

---

[27]**iterance** iteration, repetition.
[28]**made mocks with** derided, made sport of.
[29]**to be hurt** i.e., to endure hurting.
[30]**apt** natural, likely.
[31]**charm** keep silent.

OTHELLO. Nay, stare not, masters: it is true, indeed.

GRATIANO. 'Tis a strange truth.

MONTANO. O monstrous act!

EMILIA.   Villainy, villainy, villainy!   190
> I think upon't, I think: I smell't: O villainy—
> I thought so then:[32] I'll kill myself for grief:—
> O villainy, villainy!

IAGO. What, are you mad? I charge you, get you home.

EMILIA. Good gentlemen, let me have leave to speak:
> 'Tis proper I obey him, but not now.
> Perchance, Iago, I will ne'er go home.

OTHELLO. O! O! O!   [*He falls on the bed.*]

EMILIA.   Nay, lay thee down and roar;
> For thou hast kill'd the sweetest innocent
> That e'er did lift up eye.

OTHELLO.   [*Rising*] O, she was foul!   200
> I scarce did know you, uncle: there lies your niece,
> Whose breath, indeed, these hands have newly stopp'd:
> I know this act shows horrible and grim.

GRATIANO. Poor Desdemon! I am glad thy father 's dead:
> Thy match was mortal to him, and pure grief
> Shore[33] his old thread in twain: did he live now,
> This sight would make him do a desperate turn,
> Yea, curse his better angel from his side,
> And fall to reprobation.[34]

OTHELLO. 'Tis pitiful; but yet Iago knows   210
> That she with Cassio hath the act of shame
> A thousand times committed; Cassio confess'd it:
> And she did gratify his amorous works
> With that recognizance[35] and pledge of love
> Which I first gave her; I saw it in his hand:
> It was a handkerchief, an antique token
> My father gave my mother.

EMILIA. O heaven! O heavenly pow'rs!

IAGO. Come, hold your peace.

EMILIA. '   Twill out, 'twill out: I peace!
> No, I will speak as liberal as the north:[36]   220
> Let heaven and men and devils, let them all,
> All, all, cry shame against me, yet I'll speak.

IAGO. Be wise, and get you home.

EMILIA.   I will not! [IAGO *offers to stab* EMILIA.]

GRATIANO.   Fie!
> Your sword upon a woman?

EMILIA. O thou dull Moor! that handkerchief thou speak'st of

---

[32]**then** i.e., at some earlier time, probably IV, ii, when she suspected the machinations of *some eternal villain*; she did not, however, know that villain to be Iago until this moment.

[33]**Shore** cut.

[34]**reprobation** damnation, rejection by God.

[35]**recognizance** token.

[36]**liberal as the north** freely as the north wind.

I found by fortune[37] and did give my husband;
For often, with solemn earnestness,
More than indeed belong'd to such a trifle,
He begg'd me to steal it.

IAGO.   Villainous whore!

EMILIA. She give it Cassio! no, alas! I found it,   230
And I did give't my husband.

IAGO.   Filth, thou liest!

EMILIA. By heaven, I do not, I do not, gentlemen.
O murd'rous coxcomb![38] what should such a fool
Do with so good a wife!

OTHELLO.   Are there no stones in heaven[39]
But what serves for the thunder?—Precious villain!

                                     [*He runs at* IAGO; IAGO, *from behind,*
                                           stabs EMILIA, *and exits.*]

GRATIANO. The woman falls; sure, he hath kill'd his wife.

EMILIA. Ay, ay: O, lay me by my mistress' side.

GRATIANO. He's gone, but his wife's kill'd.

MONTANO. 'Tis a notorious villain. Take you this weapon,
Which I have here recover'd from the Moor: 240
Come, guard the door without; let him not pass,
But kill him rather. I'll after that same villain,
For 'tis a damned slave.   [*Exit with all but* OTHELLO *and* EMILIA.]

OTHELLO.   I am not valiant neither,
But every puny whipster[40] gets my sword:
But why should honour outlive honesty?[41]
Let it go all.

EMILIA.   What did thy song bode, lady?
Hark, canst thou hear me? I will play the swan,
And die in music. [*Singing*] "Willow, willow, willow.—"
Moor, she was chaste; she lov'd thee, cruel Moor;
So come my soul to bliss, as I speak true;   250
So speaking as I think, I die, I die.   [*Dies.*]

OTHELLO. I have another weapon in this chamber;
It is a sword of Spain, the ice-brook's temper[42]:—
O, here it is. Uncle, I must come forth.

GRATIANO [*within*]. If thou attempt it, it will cost thee dear:
Thou hast no weapon, and perforce must suffer.

OTHELLO. Look in upon me then and speak with me,
Or, naked[43] as I am, I will assault thee.

[*Enter* GRATIANO.]

---

[37]**fortune** chance.

[38]**coxcomb** fool; addressed to Othello.

[39]**stones in heaven** thunderbolts. It was supposed that real stones fell with the thunder and caused the damage.

[40]**whipster** contemptible fellow.

[41]**honour outlive honesty** Othello realizes that he has done a shameful deed; he asks why his reputation for valor should endure.

[42]**ice-brook's temper** usually defined as "tempered in ice-cold water."

[43]**naked** unarmed.

GRATIANO. What is the matter?

OTHELLO.   Behold, I have a weapon;
    A better never did itself sustain   260
    Upon a soldier's thigh: I have seen the day,
    That, with this little arm and this good sword,
    I have made my way through more impediments
    Than twenty times your stop:[44] but, O vain boast!
    Who can control his fate? 'tis not so now.
    Be not afraid, though you do see me weapon'd;
    Here is my journey's end, here is my butt,[45]
    And very sea-mark[46] of my utmost sail.
    Do you go back dismay'd? 'tis a lost fear;
    Man[47] but a rush[48] against Othello's breast,   270
    And he retires. Where should Othello go?
    Now, how dost thou look now? O ill-starr'd wench!
    Pale as thy smock! when we shall meet at compt,[49]
    This look of thine will hurl my soul from heaven,
    And fiends will snatch at it. Cold, cold, my girl!
    Even like thy chastity. O cursed, cursed slave!
    Whip me, ye devils,
    From the possession of this heavenly sight!
    Blow me about in winds! roast me in sulphur!
    Wash me in steep-down gulfs of liquid fire!   280
    O Desdemona! Dead Desdemona! dead!
    Oh! Oh!

[*Enter* LODOVICO, CASSIO *carried in a chair,* MONTANO, *and* IAGO, *prisoner,*
with OFFICERS.]

LODOVICO. Where is this rash and most unfortunate man?

OTHELLO. That's he that was Othello: here I am.

LODOVICO. Where is that viper? Bring the villain forth.

OTHELLO. I look down towards his feet;[50] but that's a fable.
    If that thou be'st a devil, I cannot kill thee.   [*Wounds* IAGO.]

LODOVICO. Wrench his sword from him.

IAGO.   I bleed sir; but not kill'd.

OTHELLO. I am not sorry neither: I 'd have thee live;
    For, in my sense, 'tis happiness to die.   290

LODOVICO. O thou Othello, that wert once so good,
    Fall'n in the practice of a damned slave,
    What shall be said to thee?

OTHELLO.   Why, any thing:
    An honourable murderer, if you will;
    For nought I did in hate, but all in honour.

---

[44]**stop** power.
[45]**butt** mark for archery, goal, limit.
[46]**sea-mark** beacon (marking his destination or limit).
[47]**Man** provide, as in manning a gun.
[48]**rush** reed.
[49]**compt** account, judgment day.
[50]**towards his feet** i.e., to see if they were cloven like a devil's.

LODOVICO. This wretch hath part confess'd his villainy:
  Did you and he consent in Cassio's death?
OTHELLO. Ay.
CASSIO. Dear general, I never gave you cause. 300
OTHELLO. I do believe it, and I ask your pardon.
  Will you, I pray, demand that demi-devil
  Why he hath thus ensnar'd my soul and body?
IAGO. Demand me nothing: what you know, you know:
  From this time forth I never will speak word.
LODOVICO. What, not to pray?
GRATIANO.   Torments will ope your lips.
OTHELLO. Well, thou dost best.
LODOVICO. Sir, you shall understand what hath befall'n,
  Which, as I think, you know not. Here is a letter
  Found in the pocket of the slain Roderigo;
  And here another: the one of them imports 310
  The death of Cassio to be undertook
  By Roderigo.
OTHELLO. O villain!
CASSIO.   Most heathenish and most gross!
LODOVICO. Now here's another discontented[51] paper,
  Found in his pocket too; and this, it seems,
  Roderigo meant t' have sent this damned villain;
  But that belike Iago in the interim
  Came in and satisfied him.
OTHELLO.   O thou pernicious caitiff[52]—
  How came you, Cassio, by that handkerchief
  That was my wife's?
CASSIO.   I found it in my chamber: 320
  And he himself confess'd but even now
  That there he dropp'd it for a special purpose
  Which wrought to his desire.
OTHELLO.   O fool! O fool! fool!
CASSIO. There is besides in Roderigo's letter,
  How he upbraids Iago, that he made him
  Brave[53] me upon the watch; whereon it came
  That I was cast:[54] and even but now he spake,
  After long seeming dead, Iago hurt him,
  Iago set him on.
LODOVICO. You must forsake this room, and go with us:
  Your power and your command is taken off,[55] 330
  And Cassio rules in Cyprus. For this slave,
  If there be any cunning cruelty
  That can torment him much and hold him long,

---

[51]**discontented** expressing dissatisfaction.
[52]**caitiff** wretch.
[53]**Brave** defy.
[54]**cast** dismissed.
[55]**taken off** taken away.

It shall be his. You shall close prisoner rest,
Till that the nature of your fault be known
To the Venetian state. Come, bring him away.
OTHELLO. Soft you; a word or two before you go.
I have done the state some service, and they know 't.
No more of that. I pray you, in your letters,   340
When you shall these unlucky deeds relate,
Speak of me as I am; nothing extenuate,[56]
Nor set down aught in malice: then must you speak
Of one that lov'd not wisely but too well;
Of one not easily jealous, but being wrought,
Perplex'd[57] in the extreme; of one whose hand,
Like the base Judean,[58] threw a pearl away
Richer than all his tribe; of one whose subdu'd eyes,
Albeit unused to the melting mood,
Drop tears as fast as the Arabian trees   350
Their medicinable gum. Set you down this;
And say besides, that in Aleppo[59] once,
Where a malignant and a turban'd Turk
Beat a Venetian and traduc'd the state,
I took by th' throat the circumcised dog,
And smote him, thus.   [*Stabs himself.*]
LODOVICO. O bloody period![60]
GRATIANO. All that is spoke is marr'd.
OTHELLO. I kiss'd thee ere I kill'd thee: no way but this;
  Killing myself, to die upon a kiss.   [*Falls on the bed, and dies.*]
CASSIO. This did I fear, but thought he had no weapon;   360
  For he was great of heart.
LODOVICO.   [*To* IAGO] O Spartan dog,[61]
  More fell than anguish, hunger, or the sea!
  Look on the tragic loading of this bed;
  This is thy work: the object poisons sight;
  Let it be hid. Gratiano, keep the house,
  And seize upon the fortunes of the Moor,
  For they succeed on you. To you, lord governor,
  Remains the censure of this hellish villain;
  The time, the place, the torture: O, enforce it!
  Myself will straight abroad; and to the state   370
  This heavy act with heavy heart relate.   [*Exeunt.*]

                                                                     (1604)

---

[56]**extenuate** diminish, depreciate; the idea is contrasted with the thought of *malice* in the following line.
[57]**Perplex'd** confounded, distracted.
[58]**Judean** infidel or disbeliever.
[59]**Aleppo** a Turkish city where the Venetians had special trading privileges. It is stated that it was immediate death for a Christian to strike a Turk in Aleppo; Othello risked his life for the honor of Venice.
[60]**period** termination, conclusion.
[61]**Spartan dog** Spartan dogs were noted for their savagery.

Questions for Discussion and Writing

1. How does Shakespeare establish the dignity, nobility, and heroism of Othello early in the play? Does Othello regain any of his lost stature in the end? How?
2. Analyze the relationship between Othello and Desdemona, and explain how tragedy enters their lives.
3. Why is Iago committed, above all else, to destroying Desdemona?
4. Explain Desdemona's behavior in the scene in which Othello accuses her of being a whore (Act IV, Scene II). Why can't Othello perceive her goodness and innocence?
5. How do race and racism contribute to Othello's downfall?
6. Shakespearean scholar M. R. Ridley suggests that the theme of *Othello* centers on the conflict between "reason" and "instinct." Write an essay in which you explore this theme in the play.
7. Professor Carol Neely maintains that "the play's central theme is love— especially marital love; its central conflict is between the men and the women." Write an essay in which you argue for or against these claims.
8. Some people think Othello acts with unjustified haste and violence, that it is inexcusable for him to suspect his wife and unbelievable that he would not suspect Iago. Write an essay in which you answer these charges.

Henrik Ibsen   *1828–1906*

Henrik Ibsen, a Norwegian dramatist, was one of the most influential figures in modern theater. He worked as a stage manager, playwright, and director and is best known for breaking away from the romantic tradition in drama in order to portray life realistically. His social plays, such as *A Doll's House* (1879), *Ghosts* (1881), and *Hedda Gabler* (1890), shocked audiences with subject matter (venereal disease, suicide, women's independence) that was considered unmentionable in public. In these and other plays, Ibsen explored the conflict between social restrictions and the psychological, often unconscious demands of individual freedom.

A Doll's House

Translated by R. Farquharson Sharp

CHARACTERS

TORVALD HELMER, *a lawyer*   IVAR, BOB, *and* EMMY,
   and bank manager   *the Helmers' three young children*
NORA, *his wife*   ANNE, *their nurse*

DOCTOR RANK HELEN, *a housemaid*
MRS. CHRISTINE LINDE A PORTER
NILS KROGSTAD, *a lawyer*
    and bank clerk

The action takes place in HELMERS' *apartment*

ACT 1

SCENE. *A room, furnished comfortably and tastefully, but not extravagantly. At the back, a door to the right leads to the entrance hall, another to the left leads to* HELMER'S *study. Between the doors stands a piano. In the middle of the left-hand wall is a door, and beyond it a window. Near the window are a round table, armchairs and a small sofa. In the right-hand wall, at the farther end, another door; and on the same side, nearer the footlights, a stove, two easy chairs and a rocking-chair; between the stove and the door, a small table. Engravings on the walls; a cabinet with china and other small objects, a small book case with well-bound books. The floors are carpeted, and a fire burns in the stove. It is winter.*

    A bell rings in the hall; shortly afterwards the door is heard to open. Enter NORA, *humming a tune and in high spirits. She is in outdoor dress and carries a number of parcels; these she lays on the table to the right. She leaves the outer door open after her, and through it is seen a* PORTER *who is carrying a Christmas Tree and a basket, which he gives to the* MAID *who has opened the door.*

Anthony Hopkins as Torvald and Claire Bloom as Nora in the 1973 film adaptation of *A Doll's House.*
(Picture Desk, Inc./Kobal Collection)

NORA. Hide the Christmas Tree away carefully, Helen. Be sure the children do not see it till this evening, when it is dressed. [*to the* PORTER, *taking out her purse*] How much?

PORTER. Sixpence.

NORA. There is a shilling. No, keep the change.

[*The* PORTER *thanks her, and goes out.* NORA *shuts the door. She is laughing to herself, as she takes off her hat and coat. She takes a packet of macaroons from her pocket and eats one or two; then goes cautiously to her husband's door and listens.*]

Yes, he is in.

[*Still humming, she goes to the table on the right.*]

HELMER. [*calls out from his room*] Is that my little lark twittering out there?

NORA. [*busy opening some of the parcels*] Yes, it is!

HELMER. Is my little squirrel bustling about?

NORA. Yes!

HELMER. When did my squirrel come home?

NORA. Just now. [*puts the bag of macaroons into her pocket and wipes her mouth*] Come in here, Torvald, and see what I have bought.

HELMER. Don't disturb me. [*A little later, he opens the door and looks into the room, pen in his hand.*] Bought, did you say? All these things? Has my little spend-thrift been wasting money again?

NORA. Yes, but, Torvald, this year we really can let ourselves go a little. This is the first Christmas that we have not needed to economise.

HELMER. Still, you know, we can't spend money recklessly.

NORA. Yes, Torvald, we may be a wee bit more reckless now, mayn't we? Just a tiny wee bit! You are going to have a big salary and earn lots and lots of money.

HELMER. Yes, after the New Year; but then it will be a whole quarter before the salary is due.

NORA. Pooh! We can borrow till then.

HELMER. Nora! [*goes up to her and takes her playfully by the ear*] The same little featherhead! Suppose, now, that I borrowed fifty pounds to-day, and you spent it all in the Christmas week, and then on New Year's Eve a slate fell on my head and killed me, and—

NORA. [*putting her hands over his mouth*] Oh! don't say such horrid things.

HELMER. Still, suppose that happened—what then?

NORA. If that were to happen, I don't suppose I should care whether I owed money or not.

HELMER. Yes, but what about the people who had lent it?

NORA. They? Who would bother about them? I should not know who they were.

HELMER. That is like a woman! But seriously, Nora, you know what I think about that. No debt, no borrowing. There can be no freedom or beauty about a home life that depends on borrowing and debt. We two have kept bravely on the straight road so far, and we will go on the same way for the short time longer that there need be any struggle.

NORA. [*moving towards the stove*] As you please, Torvald.

HELMER. [*following her*] Come, come, my little skylark must not droop her wings. What is this! Is my little squirrel out of temper? [*taking out his purse*] Nora, what do you think I have got here?

NORA. [*turning around quickly*] Money!

HELMER. There you are. [*gives her some money*] Do you think I don't know what a lot is wanted for housekeeping at Christmas-time?

NORA. [*counting*] Ten shillings—a pound—two pounds! Thank you, thank you, Torvald; that will keep me going for a long time.

HELMER. Indeed it must.

NORA. Yes, yes, it will. But come here and let me show you what I have bought. And all so cheap! Look, here is a new suit for Ivar, and a sword; and a horse and a trumpet for Bob; and a doll and dolly's bedstead for Emmy—they are very plain, but anyway she will soon break them in pieces. And here are dress-lengths and handkerchiefs for the maids; old Anne ought really to have something better.

HELMER. And what is in this parcel?

NORA. [*crying out*] No, no! You mustn't see that till this evening.

HELMER. Very well. But now tell me, you extravagant little person, what would you like for yourself?

NORA. For myself? Oh, I am sure I don't want anything.

HELMER. Yes, but you must. Tell me something reasonable that you would particularly like to have.

NORA. No, I really can't think of anything—unless, Torvald—

HELMER. Well?

NORA. [*playing with his coat buttons, and without raising her eyes to his*] If you really want to give me something, you might—you might—

HELMER. Well, out with it!

NORA. [*speaking quickly*] You might give me money, Torvald. Only just as much as you can afford; and then one of these days I will buy something with it.

HELMER. But, Nora—

NORA. Oh, do! dear Torvald; please, please do! Then I will wrap it up in beautiful gilt paper and hang it on the Christmas Tree. Wouldn't that be fun?

HELMER. What are little people called that are always wasting money?

NORA. Spendthrifts—I know. Let us do as you suggest, Torvald, and then I shall have time to think what I am most in want of. That is a very sensible plan, isn't it?

HELMER. [*smiling*] Indeed it is—that is to say, if you were really to save out of the money I give you, and then really buy something for yourself. But if you spend it all on the housekeeping and any number of unnecessary things, then I merely have to pay up again.

NORA. Oh but, Torvald—

HELMER. You can't deny it, my dear little Nora. [*puts his arm round her waist*] It's a sweet little spendthrift, but she uses up a deal of money. One would hardly believe how expensive such little persons are!

NORA. It's a shame to say that. I do really save all I can.

HELMER. [*laughing*] That's very true—all you can. But you can't save anything!

NORA. [*smiling quietly and happily*] You haven't any idea how many expenses we skylarks and squirrels have, Torvald.

HELMER. You are an odd little soul. Very like your father. You always find some new way of wheedling money out of me, and, as soon as you have got it, it seems to melt in your hands. You never know where it has gone. Still, one must take you as you are. It is in the blood; for indeed it is true that you can inherit these things, Nora.

NORA. Ah, I wish I had inherited many of papa's qualities.

HELMER. And I would not wish you to be anything but just what you are, my sweet little skylark. But, do you know, it strikes me that you are looking rather—what shall I say—rather uneasy to-day?

NORA. Do I?

HELMER. You do, really. Look straight at me.

NORA. [*looks at him*] Well?

HELMER. [*wagging his finger at her*] Hasn't Miss Sweet-Tooth been breaking rules in town to-day?

NORA. No; what makes you think that?

HELMER. Hasn't she paid a visit to the confectioner's?

NORA. No, I assure you, Torvald—

HELMER. Not been nibbling sweets?

NORA. No, certainly not.

HELMER. Not even taken a bite at a macaroon or two?

NORA. No, Torvald, I assure you really—

HELMER. There, there, of course I was only joking.

NORA. [*going to the table on the right*] I should not think of going against your wishes.

HELMER. No, I am sure of that! besides, you gave me your word—[*going up to her*] Keep your little Christmas secrets to yourself, my darling. They will all be revealed tonight when the Christmas Tree is lit, no doubt.

NORA. Did you remember to invite Doctor Rank?

HELMER. No. But there is no need; as a matter of course he will come to dinner with us. However, I will ask him when he comes in this morning. I have ordered some good wine. Nora, you can't think how I am looking forward to this evening.

NORA. So am I! And how the children will enjoy themselves, Torvald!

HELMER. It is splendid to feel that one has a perfectly safe appointment, and a big enough income. It's delightful to think of, isn't it?

NORA. It's wonderful!

HELMER. Do you remember last Christmas? For a full three weeks beforehand you shut yourself up every evening till long after midnight, making ornaments for the Christmas Tree and all the other fine things that were to be a surprise to us. It was the dullest three weeks I ever spent!

NORA. I didn't find it dull.

HELMER. [*smiling*] But there was precious little result, Nora.

NORA. Oh, you shouldn't tease me about that again. How could I help the cat's going in and tearing everything to pieces?

HELMER. Of course you couldn't, poor little girl. You had the best of intentions to please us all, and that's the main thing. But it is a good thing that our hard times are over.

NORA. Yes, it is really wonderful.

HELMER. This time I needn't sit here and be dull all alone, and you needn't ruin your dear eyes and your pretty little hands—

NORA. [*clapping her hands*] No, Torvald, I needn't any longer, need I! It's wonderfully lovely to hear you say so! [*taking his arm*] Now I will tell you how I have been thinking we ought to arrange things, Torvald. As soon as Christmas is over— [*A bell rings in the hall.*] There's the bell. [*She tidies the room a little.*] There's someone at the door. What a nuisance!

HELMER. If it is a caller, remember I am not at home.

MAID. [*in the doorway*] A lady to see you, ma'am—a stranger.

NORA. Ask her to come in.

MAID. [*to* HELMER] The doctor came at the same time, sir.

HELMER. Did he go straight into my room?

MAID. Yes sir.

[HELMER *goes into his room. The* MAID *ushers in* MRS. LINDE, *who is in travelling dress, and shuts the door.*]

MRS. LINDE. [*in a dejected and timid voice*] How do you do, Nora?

NORA. [*doubtfully*] How do you do—

MRS. LINDE. You don't recognize me, I suppose.

NORA. No, I don't know—yes, to be sure, I seem to—[*suddenly*] Yes! Christine! Is it really you?

MRS. LINDE. Yes, it is I.

NORA. Christine! To think of my not recognising you! And yet how could I—[*in a gentle voice*] How you have altered, Christine!

MRS. LINDE. Yes, I have indeed. In nine, ten long years—

NORA. Is it so long since we met? I suppose it is. The last eight years have been a happy time for me, I can tell you. And so now you have come into the town, and have taken this long journey in winter—that was plucky of you.

MRS. LINDE. I arrived by steamer this morning.

NORA. To have some fun at Christmas-time, of course. How delightful! We will have such fun together! But take off your things. You are not cold, I hope. [*helps her*] Now we will sit down by the stove, and be cosy. No, take this arm-chair; I will sit here in the rocking-chair. [*takes her hands*] Now you look like your old self again; it was only the first moment—You are a little paler, Christine, and perhaps a little thinner.

MRS. LINDE. And much, much older, Nora.

NORA. Perhaps a little older; very, very little; certainly not much. [*stops suddenly and speaks seriously*] What a thoughtless creature I am, chattering away like this. My poor, dear Christine, do forgive me.

MRS. LINDE. What do you mean, Nora?

NORA. [*gently*] Poor Christine, you are a widow.

MRS. LINDE. Yes; it is three years ago now.

NORA. Yes, I knew; I saw it in the papers. I assure you, Christine, I meant ever so often to write to you at the time, but I always put it off and something always prevented me.

MRS. LINDE. I quite understand, dear.

NORA. It was very bad of me, Christine. Poor thing, how you must have suffered. And he left you nothing?

MRS. LINDE. No.

NORA. And no children?

MRS. LINDE. No.

NORA. Nothing at all, then?

MRS. LINDE. Not even any sorrow or grief to live upon.

NORA. [*looking incredulously at her*] But, Christine, is that possible?

MRS. LINDE. [*smiles sadly and strokes her hair*] It sometimes happens, Nora.

NORA. So you are quite alone. How dreadfully sad that must be. I have three lovely children. You can't see them just now, for they are out with their nurse. But now you must tell me all about it.

MRS. LINDE. No, no; I want to hear you.

NORA. No, you must begin. I mustn't be selfish to-day; to-day I must only think of your affairs. But there is one thing I must tell you. Do you know we have just had a great piece of good luck?

MRS. LINDE. No, what is it?

NORA. Just fancy, my husband has been made manager of the Bank!

MRS. LINDE. Your husband? What good luck!

NORA. Yes, tremendous! A barrister's profession is such an uncertain thing, especially if he won't undertake unsavoury cases; and naturally Torvald has never been willing to do that, and I quite agree with him. You may imagine how pleased we are! He is to take up his work in the Bank at the New Year, and then he will have a big salary and lots of commissions. For the future we can live quite differently—we can do just as we like. I feel so relieved and so happy, Christine! It will be splendid to have heaps of money and not need to have any anxiety, won't it?

MRS. LINDE. Yes, anyhow I think it would be delightful to have what one needs.

NORA. No, not only what one needs, but heaps and heaps of money.

MRS. LINDE. [*smiling*] Nora, Nora haven't you learnt sense yet? In our schooldays you were a great spendthrift.

NORA. [*laughing*] Yes, that is what Torvald says now. [*wags her finger at her*] But "Nora, Nora" is not so silly as you think. We have not been in a position for me to waste money. We have both had to work.

MRS. LINDE. You too?

NORA. Yes; odds and ends, needlework, crochet-work, embroidery, and that kind of thing. [*dropping her voice*] And other things as well. You know Torvald left his office when we were married? There was no prospect of promotion there, and he had to try and earn more than before. But during the first year he overworked himself dreadfully. You see, he had to make money every way he could, and he worked early and late; but he couldn't stand it, and fell dreadfully ill, and the doctors said it was necessary for him to go south.

MRS. LINDE. You spent a whole year in Italy didn't you?

NORA. Yes. It was no easy matter to get away, I can tell you. It was just as Ivar was born; but naturally we had to go. It was a wonderfully beautiful journey, and it saved Torvald's life. But it cost a tremendous lot of money, Christine.

MRS. LINDE. So I should think.

NORA. It cost about two hundred and fifty pounds. That's a lot, isn't it?

MRS. LINDE. Yes, and in emergencies like that it is lucky to have the money.

NORA. I ought to tell you that we had it from papa.

MRS. LINDE. Oh, I see. It was just about that time that he died, wasn't it?

NORA. Yes; and, just think of it, I couldn't go and nurse him. I was expecting little Ivar's birth every day and I had my poor sick Torvald to look after. My dear, kind father—I never saw him again, Christine. That was the saddest time I have known since our marriage.

MRS. LINDE. I know how fond you were of him. And then you went off to Italy?

NORA. Yes; you see we had money then, and the doctors insisted on our going, so we started a month later.

MRS. LINDE. And your husband came back quite well?

NORA. As sound as a bell!

MRS. LINDE. But—the doctor?

NORA. What doctor?

MRS. LINDE. I thought your maid said the gentleman who arrived here just as I did was the doctor?

NORA. Yes, that was Doctor Rank, but he doesn't come here professionally. He is our greatest friend, and comes in at least once every day. No, Torvald has not had an hour's illness since then, and our children are strong and healthy and so am I. [*jumps up and claps her hands*] Christine! Christine! it's good to be alive and happy!—But how horrid of me; I am talking of nothing but my own affairs. [*sits on a stool near her, and rests her arms on her knees*] You mustn't be angry with me. Tell me, is it really true that you did not love your husband? Why did you marry him?

MRS. LINDE. My mother was alive then, and was bedridden and helpless, and I had to provide for my two younger brothers; so I did not think I was justified in refusing his offer.

NORA. No, perhaps you were quite right. He was rich at that time, then?

MRS. LINDE. I believe he was quite well off. But his business was a precarious one; and, when he died, it all went to pieces and there was nothing left.

NORA. And then?—

MRS. LINDE. Well, I had to turn my hand to anything I could find—first a small shop, then a small school, and so on. The last three years have seemed like one long working-day, with no rest. Now it is at an end, Nora. My poor mother needs me no more, for she is gone; and the boys do not need me either; they have got situations and can shift for themselves.

NORA. What a relief you must feel it—

MRS. LINDE. No, indeed; I only feel my life unspeakably empty. No one to live for any more. [*gets up restlessly*] That was why I could not stand the life in my little backwater any longer. I hope it may be easier here to find something which will busy me and occupy my thoughts. If only I could have the good luck to get some regular work—office work of some kind—

NORA. But, Christine, that is so frightfully tiring, and you look tired out now. You had far better go away to some watering-place.

MRS. LINDE. [*walking to the window*] I have no father to give me money for a journey, Nora.

NORA. [*rising*] Oh, don't be angry with me.

MRS. LINDE. [*going up to her*] It is you that must not be angry with me, dear. The worst of a position like mine is that it makes one so bitter. No one to work for, and yet obliged to be always on the look-out for chances. One must live, and so one becomes selfish. When you told me of the happy turn your fortunes have taken—you will hardly believe it—I was delighted not so much on your account as on my own.

NORA. How do you mean?—Oh, I understand. You mean that perhaps Torvald could get you something to do.

MRS. LINDE. Yes, that was what I was thinking of.

NORA. He must, Christine. Just leave it to me; I will broach the subject very cleverly—I will think of something that will please him very much. It will make me so happy to be of some use to you.

MRS. LINDE. How kind you are, Nora, to be so anxious to help me! It is doubly kind in you, for you know so little of the burdens and troubles of life.

NORA. I—? I know so little of them?

MRS. LINDE. [*smiling*] My dear! Small household cares and that sort of thing!—You are a child, Nora.

NORA. [*tosses her head and crosses the stage*] You ought not to be so superior.

MRS. LINDE. No?

NORA. You are just like the others. They all think that I am incapable of anything really serious—

MRS. LINDE. Come, come—

NORA. —that I have gone through nothing in this world of cares.

MRS. LINDE. But, my dear Nora, you have just told me all your troubles.

NORA. Pooh!—those were trifles. [*lowering her voice*] I have not told you the important thing.

MRS. LINDE. The important thing? What do you mean?

NORA. You look down upon me altogether, Christine—but you ought not to. You are proud, aren't you, of having worked so hard and so long for your mother?

MRS. LINDE. Indeed, I don't look down on any one. But it is true that I am both proud and glad to think that I was privileged to make the end of my mother's life almost free from care.

NORA. And you are proud to think of what you have done for your brothers.

MRS. LINDE. I think I have the right to be.

NORA. I think so, too. But now, listen to this; I too have something to be proud of and glad of.

MRS. LINDE. I have no doubt you have. But what do you refer to?

NORA. Speak low. Suppose Torvald were to hear! He mustn't on any account—no one in the world must know, Christine, except you.

MRS. LINDE. But what is it?

NORA. Come here. [*pulls her down on the sofa beside her*] Now I will show you that I too have something to be proud and glad of. It was I who saved Torvald's life.

MRS. LINDE. "Saved"? How?

NORA. I told you about our trip to Italy. Torvald would never have recovered if he had not gone there—

MRS. LINDE. Yes, but your father gave you the necessary funds.

NORA. [*smiling*] Yes, that is what Torvald and all the others think, but—

MRS. LINDE. But—

NORA. Papa didn't give us a shilling. It was I who procured the money.

MRS. LINDE. You? All that large sum?

NORA. Two hundred and fifty pounds. What do you think of that?

MRS. LINDE. But, Nora, how could you possibly do it? Did you win a prize in the Lottery?

NORA. [*contemptuously*] In the Lottery? There would have been no credit in that.

MRS. LINDE. But where did you get it from, then?

NORA. [*humming and smiling with an air of mystery*] Hm, hm! Aha!

MRS. LINDE. Because you couldn't have borrowed it.

NORA. Couldn't I? Why not?

MRS. LINDE. No, a wife cannot borrow without her husband's consent.

NORA. [*tossing her head*] Oh, if it is a wife who has any head for business—a wife who has the wit to be a little bit clever—

MRS. LINDE. I don't understand it at all, Nora.

NORA. There is no need you should. I never said I had borrowed the money. I may have got it some other way. [*lies back on the sofa*] Perhaps I got it from some other admirer. When anyone is as attractive as I am—

MRS. LINDE. You are a mad creature.

NORA. Now, you know you're full of curiosity, Christine.

MRS. LINDE. Listen to me, Nora dear. Haven't you been a little bit imprudent?

NORA. [*sits up straight*] Is it imprudent to save your husband's life?

MRS. LINDE. It seems to me imprudent, without his knowledge, to—

NORA. But it was absolutely necessary that he should not know! My goodness, can't you understand that? It was necessary he should have no idea what a dangerous condition he was in. It was to me that the doctors came and said that his life was in danger, and that the only thing to save him was to live in the south. Do you suppose I didn't try, first of all, to get what I wanted as if it were for myself? I told him how much I should love to travel abroad like other young wives; I tried tears and entreaties with him; I told him that he ought to remember the condition I was in, and that he ought to be kind and indulgent to me; I even hinted that he might raise a loan. That nearly made him angry, Christine. He said I was thoughtless, and that it was his duty as my husband not to indulge me in my whims and caprices—as I believe he called them. Very well I thought, you must be saved—and that was how I came to devise a way out of the difficulty—

MRS. LINDE. And did your husband never get to know from your father that the money had not come from him?

NORA. No, never. Papa died just at that time. I had meant to let him into the secret and beg him never to reveal it. But he was so ill then—alas, there never was any need to tell him.

MRS. LINDE. And since then have you never told your secret to your husband?

NORA. Good Heavens, no! How could you think so? A man who has such strong opinions about these things! And besides, how painful and humiliating it would be for Torvald, with his manly independence, to know that he owed me anything! It would upset our mutual relations altogether; our beautiful happy home would no longer be what it is now.

MRS. LINDE. Do you mean never to tell him about it?

NORA. [*meditatively, and with a half smile*] Yes—some day, perhaps, after many years, when I am no longer as nice-looking as I am now. Don't laugh at me! I mean of course, when Torvald is no longer as devoted to me as he is now; when my dancing and dressing-up and reciting have palled on him; then it may be a good thing to have something in reserve—[*breaking off*] What nonsense! That time will never come. Now, what do you think of my great secret, Christine? Do you still think I am of no use? I can tell you, too, that this affair has caused me a lot of worry. It has been by no means easy for me to meet my engagements punctually. I may tell you that there is something that is called, in business, quarterly interest, and another thing called payment in instalments, and it is always so dreadfully difficult to manage them. I have had to save a little here and there, where I could, you understand. I have not been able to put aside much from my housekeeping money, for Torvald must have a good table. I couldn't let my children be shabbily dressed; I have felt obliged to use up all he gave me for them, the sweet little darlings!

MRS. LINDE. So it has all had to come out of your own necessaries of life, poor Nora?

NORA. Of course. Besides, I was the one responsible for it. Whenever Torvald has given me the money for new dresses and such things, I have never spent more than half of it; I have always bought the simplest and cheapest things. Thank Heaven, any clothes look well on me, and so Torvald has never noticed it. But it was often very hard on me, Christine—because it is delightful to be really well dressed, isn't it?

MRS. LINDE. Quite so.

NORA. Well, then I have found other ways of earning money. Last winter I was lucky enough to get a lot of copying to do; so I locked myself up and sat writing every evening until quite late at night. Many a time I was desperately tired; but all the same it was a tremendous pleasure to sit there working and earning money. It was like being a man.

MRS. LINDE. How much have you been able to pay off in that way?

NORA. I can't tell you exactly. You see, it is very difficult to keep an account of a business matter of that kind. I only know that I have paid every penny that I could scrape together. Many a time I was at my wit's end. [*smiles*] Then I used to sit here and imagine that a rich old gentleman had fallen in love with me—

MRS. LINDE. What! Who was it?

NORA. Be quiet!—that he had died; and that when his will was opened it contained, written in big letters, the instruction "The lovely Mrs. Nora Helmer is to have all I possess paid over to her at once in cash."

MRS. LINDE. But, my dear Nora—who could the man be?

NORA. Good gracious, can't you understand? There was no old gentleman at all; it was only something that I used to sit here and imagine, when I couldn't think of any way of procuring money. But it's all the same now; the tiresome old person can stay where he is, as far as I am concerned; I don't care about him or his will either, for I am free from care now. [*jumps up*] My goodness, it's delightful to think of, Christine! Free from care! To be able to be free from care, quite free from care; to be able to play and romp with the children; to be able to keep the house beautifully and have everything just as Torvald likes it! And, think of it, soon the spring will come and the big blue sky! Perhaps we shall be able to take a little trip—perhaps I shall see the sea again! Oh, it's a wonderful thing to be alive and be happy. [*A bell is heard in the hall.*]

MRS. LINDE. [*rising*] There is the bell; perhaps I had better go.

NORA. No, don't go; no one will come in here; it is sure to be for Torvald.

SERVANT. [*at the hall door*] Excuse me, ma'am—there is a gentleman to see the master, and as the doctor is with him—

NORA. Who is it?

KROGSTAD. [*at the door*] It is I, Mrs. Helmer. [MRS. LINDE *starts, trembles, and turns to the window.*]

NORA. [*takes a step towards him, and speaks in a strained, low voice*] You? What is it? What do you want to see my husband about?

KROGSTAD. Bank business—in a way. I have a small post in the Bank, and I hear your husband is to be our chief now—

NORA. Then it is—

KROGSTAD. Nothing but dry business matters, Mrs. Helmer; absolutely nothing else.

NORA. Be so good as to go into the study, then. [*She bows indifferently to him and shuts the door into the hall; then comes back and makes up the fire in the stove.*]

MRS. LINDE. Nora—who was that man?

NORA. A lawyer, of the name of Krogstad.

MRS. LINDE. Then it really was he.

NORA. Do you know the man?

MRS. LINDE. I used to—many years ago. At one time he was a solicitor's clerk in our town.

NORA. Yes, he was.

MRS. LINDE. He is greatly altered.

NORA. He made a very unhappy marriage.

MRS. LINDE. He is a widower now, isn't he?

NORA. With several children. There now, it is burning up.

[*Shuts the door of the stove and moves the rocking-chair aside.*]

MRS. LINDE. They say he carries on various kinds of business.

NORA. Really! Perhaps he does; I don't know anything about it. But don't let us think of business; it is so tiresome.

DOCTOR RANK. [*comes out of* HELMER'*s study. Before he shuts the door he calls to him.*] No, my dear fellow, I won't disturb you; I would rather go in to your wife for a little while. [*shuts the door and sees* MRS. LINDE] I beg your pardon; I am afraid I am disturbing you too.

NORA. No, not at all. [*introducing him*] Doctor Rank, Mrs. Linde.

RANK. I have often heard Mrs. Linde's name mentioned here. I think I passed you on the stairs when I arrived, Mrs. Linde?

MRS. LINDE. Yes, I go up very slowly; I can't manage stairs well.

RANK. Ah! some slight internal weakness?

MRS. LINDE. No, the fact is I have been overworking myself.

RANK. Nothing more than that? Then I suppose you have come to town to amuse yourself with our entertainments?

MRS. LINDE. I have come to look for work.

RANK. Is that a good cure for overwork?

MRS. LINDE. One must live, Doctor Rank.

RANK. Yes, the general opinion seems to be that it is necessary.

NORA. Look here, Doctor Rank—you know you want to live.

RANK. Certainly. However wretched I may feel, I want to prolong the agony as long as possible. All my patients are like that. And so are those who are morally diseased; one of them, and a bad case too, is at this very moment with Helmer—

MRS. LINDE. [*sadly*] Ah!

NORA. Whom do you mean?

RANK. A lawyer of the name of Krogstad, a fellow you don't know at all. He suffers from a diseased moral character, Mrs. Helmer; but even he began talking of its being highly important that he should live.

NORA. Did he? What did he want to speak to Torvald about?

RANK. I have no idea; I only heard that it was something about the Bank.

NORA. I didn't know this—what's his name—Krogstad had anything to do with the Bank.

RANK. Yes, he has some sort of appointment there. [*to* MRS. LINDE] I don't know whether you find also in your part of the world that there are certain people who go zealously snuffing about to smell out moral corruption, and, as soon as they have found some, put the person concerned into some lucrative position where they can keep their eye on him. Healthy natures are left out in the cold.

MRS. LINDE. Still I think the sick are those who most need taking care of.

RANK. [*shrugging his shoulders*] Yes, there you are. That is the sentiment that is turning Society into a sickhouse.

[NORA, *who has been absorbed in her thoughts, breaks out into smothered laughter and claps her hands.*]

RANK. Why do you laugh at that? Have you any notion what Society really is?

NORA. What do I care about tiresome Society? I am laughing at something quite different, something extremely amusing. Tell me, Doctor Rank, are all the people who are employed in the Bank dependent on Torvald now?

RANK. Is that what you find so extremely amusing?

NORA. [*smiling and humming*] That's my affair! [*walking about the room*] It's perfectly glorious to think that we have—that Torvald has so much power over so many people. [*takes the packet from her pocket*] Doctor Rank, what do you say to a macaroon?

RANK. What, macaroons? I thought they were forbidden here.

NORA. Yes, but these are some Christine gave me.

MRS. LINDE. What! I?—

NORA. Oh, well, don't be alarmed! You couldn't know that Torvald had forbidden them. I must tell you that he is afraid they will spoil my teeth. But, bah!—once in a while—That's so, isn't it, Doctor Rank? By your leave? [*puts a macaroon into his mouth*] You must have one too, Christine. And I shall have one, just a little one—or at most two. [*walking about*] I am tremendously happy. There is just one thing in the world now that I should dearly love to do.

RANK. Well, what is that?

NORA. It's something I should dearly love to say, if Torvald could hear me.

RANK. Well, why can't you say it?

NORA. No, I daren't; it's so shocking.

MRS. LINDE. Shocking?

RANK. Well, I should not advise you to say it. Still, with us you might. What is it you would so much like to say if Torvald could hear you?

NORA. I should just love to say—Well, I'm damned!

RANK. Are you mad?

MRS. LINDE. Nora, dear—

RANK. Say it, here he is!

NORA. [*hiding the packet*] Hush! Hush! Hush!

[HELMER *comes out of his room, with his coat over his arm and his hat in his hands.*]

NORA. Well, Torvald dear, have you got rid of him?

HELMER. Yes, he has just gone.

NORA. Let me introduce you—this is Christine, who has come to town.

HELMER. Christine—? Excuse me, but I don't know—

NORA. Mrs. Linde, dear; Christine Linde.

HELMER. Of course. A school friend of my wife's, I presume?

MRS. LINDE. Yes, we have known each other since then.

NORA. And just think, she has taken a long journey in order to see you.

HELMER. What do you mean?

MRS. LINDE. No, really, I—

NORA. Christine is tremendously clever at book-keeping, and she is frightfully anxious to work under some clever man, so as to perfect herself—

HELMER. Very sensible, Mrs. Linde.

NORA. And when she heard you had been appointed manager of the Bank—the news was telegraphed, you know—she travelled here as quick as she could. Torvald, I am sure you will be able to do something for Christine, for my sake, won't you?

HELMER. Well, it is not altogether impossible. I presume you are a widow, Mrs. Linde?

MRS. LINDE. Yes.

HELMER. And have had some experience of book-keeping?

MRS. LINDE. Yes, a fair amount.

HELMER. Ah! well, it's very likely I may be able to find something for you—

NORA. [*clapping her hands*] What did I tell you? What did I tell you?

HELMER. You have just come at a fortunate moment, Mrs. Linde.

MRS. LINDE. How am I to thank you?

HELMER. There is no need. [*puts on his coat*] But to-day you must excuse me—

RANK. Wait a minute; I will come with you.

[*Brings his fur coat from the hall and warms it at the fire.*]

NORA. Don't be long away, Torvald dear.

HELMER. About an hour, not more.

NORA. Are you going too, Christine?

MRS. LINDE. [*putting on her cloak*] Yes, I must go and look for a room.

HELMER. Oh, well then, we can walk down the street together.

NORA. [*helping her*] What a pity it is we are so short of space here: I am afraid it is impossible for us—

MRS. LINDE. Please don't think of it! Good-bye, Nora dear, and many thanks.

NORA. Good-bye for the present. Of course you will come back this evening. And you too, Dr. Rank. What do you say? If you are well enough? Oh, you must be! Wrap yourself up well.

[*They go to the door all talking together. Children's voices are heard on the staircase.*]

NORA. There they are. There they are! [*She runs to open the door: The Nurse comes in with the children.*] Come in! Come in! [*stoops and kisses them*] Oh, you sweet blessings! Look at them, Christine! Aren't they darlings?

RANK. Don't let us stand here in the draught.

HELMER. Come along, Mrs. Linde; the place will only be bearable for a mother now!

[RANK, HELMER *and* MRS. LINDE *go downstairs. The* NURSE *comes forward with the children;* NORA *shuts the hall door.*]

NORA. How fresh and well you look! Such red cheeks!—like apples and roses. [*The children all talk at once while she speaks to them.*] Have you had great fun? That's splendid! What, you pulled both Emmy and Bob along on the sledge?—both at once?—that *was* good. You are a clever boy, Ivar. Let me take her for a little, Anne. My sweet little baby doll! [*takes the baby from the* MAID *and dances it up and down*] Yes, yes, mother will dance with Bob too. What! Have you been snowballing? I wish I had been there too! No, no, I will take their things off, Anne; please let me do it, it is such fun. Go in now, you look half frozen. There is some coffee for you on the stove.

[*The* NURSE *goes into the room on the left.* NORA *takes off the children's things and throws them about, while they all talk to her at once.*]

NORA. Really! Did a big dog run after you? But it didn't bite you? No, dogs don't bite nice little dolly children. You mustn't look at the parcels, Ivar. What are they? Ah, I daresay you would like to know. No, no—it's something nasty! Come, let us have a game! What shall we play at? Hide and Seek? Yes, we'll play Hide and Seek. Bob shall hide first. Must I hide? Very well, I'll hide first.

[*She and the children laugh and shout, and romp in and out of the room; at last* NORA *hides under the table, the children rush in and look for her, but do not see her; they hear her smothered laughter, run to the table, lift up the cloth and find her. Shouts of laughter. She crawls forward and pretends to frighten them. Fresh laughter. Meanwhile there has been a knock at the hall door, but none of them has noticed it. The door is half opened, and Krogstad appears. He waits a little; the game goes on.*]

KROGSTAD. Excuse me, Mrs. Helmer.

NORA. [*with a stifled cry, turns round and gets up on to her knees*] Ah! what do you want?

KROGSTAD. Excuse me, the outer door was ajar; I suppose someone forgot to shut it.

NORA. [*rising*] My husband is out, Mr. Krogstad.

KROGSTAD. I know that.

NORA. What do you want here, then?

KROGSTAD. A word with you.

NORA. With me?—[*to the children, gently*] Go in to nurse. What? No, the strange man won't do mother any harm. When he has gone we will have another game. [*She takes the children into the room on the left, and shuts the door after them.*] You want to speak to me?

KROGSTAD. Yes, I do.

NORA. To-day? It is not the first of the month yet.

KROGSTAD. No, it is Christmas Eve, and it will depend on yourself what sort of a Christmas you will spend.

NORA. What do you want? To-day it is absolutely impossible for me—

KROGSTAD. We won't talk about that till later on. This is something different. I presume you can give me a moment?

NORA. Yes—yes, I can—although—

KROGSTAD. Good. I was in Olsen's Restaurant and saw your husband going down the street—

NORA. Yes?

KROGSTAD. With a lady.

NORA. What then?

KROGSTAD. May I make so bold as to ask if it was a Mrs. Linde?

NORA. It was.

KROGSTAD. Just arrived in town?

NORA. Yes, to-day.

KROGSTAD. She is a great friend of yours, isn't she?

NORA. She is. But I don't see—

KROGSTAD. I knew her too, once upon a time.

NORA. I am aware of that.

KROGSTAD. Are you? So you know all about it; I thought as much. Then I can ask you, without beating about the bush—is Mrs. Linde to have an appointment in the Bank?

NORA. What right have you to question me, Mr. Krogstad?—You, one of my husband's subordinates! But since you ask, you shall know. Yes, Mrs. Linde *is* to have an appointment. And it was I who pleaded her cause, Mr. Krogstad, let me tell you that.

KROGSTAD. I was right in what I thought, then.

NORA. [*walking up and down the stage*] Sometimes one has a tiny little bit of influence, I should hope. Because one is a woman, it does not necessarily follow that—. When anyone is in a subordinate position, Mr. Krogstad, they should really be careful to avoid offending anyone who—who—

KROGSTAD. Who has influence?

NORA. Exactly.

KROGSTAD. [*changing his tone*] Mrs. Helmer, you will be so good as to use your influence on my behalf.

NORA. What? What do you mean?

KROGSTAD. You will be so kind as to see that I am allowed to keep my subordinate position in the Bank.

NORA. What do you mean by that? Who proposes to take your post away from you?

KROGSTAD. Oh, there is no necessity to keep up the pretence of ignorance. I can quite understand that your friend is not very anxious to expose herself to the chance of rubbing shoulders with me; and I quite understand, too, whom I have to thank for being turned out.

NORA. But I assure you—

KROGSTAD. Very likely; but, to come to the point, the time has come when I should advise you to use your influence to prevent that.

NORA. But, Mr. Krogstad, I *have* no influence.

KROGSTAD. Haven't you? I thought you said yourself just now—

NORA. Naturally I did not mean you to put that construction on it. I! What should make you think I have any influence of that kind with my husband?

KROGSTAD. Oh, I have known your husband from our student days. I don't suppose he is any more unassailable than other husbands.

NORA. If you speak slightingly of my husband, I shall turn you out of the house.

KROGSTAD. You are bold, Mrs. Helmer.

NORA. I am not afraid of you any longer. As soon as the New Year comes, I shall in a very short time be free of the whole thing.

KROGSTAD. [*controlling himself*] Listen to me, Mrs. Helmer. If necessary, I am prepared to fight for my small post in the Bank as if I were fighting for my life.

NORA. So it seems.

KROGSTAD. It is not only for the sake of the money; indeed, that weighs least with me in the matter. There is another reason—well, I may as well tell you. My position is this. I daresay you know, like everybody else, that once, many years ago, I was guilty of an indiscretion.

NORA. I think I have heard something of the kind.

KROGSTAD. The matter never came into court; but every way seemed to be closed to me after that. So I took to the business that you know of. I had to do something; and, honestly, I don't think I've been one of the worst. But now I must cut myself free from all that. My sons are growing up; for their sake I must try and win back as much respect as I can in the town. This post in the Bank was like the first step up for me—and now your husband is going to kick me downstairs again into the mud.

NORA. But you must believe me, Mr. Krogstad; it is not in my power to help you at all.

KROGSTAD. Then it is because you haven't the will; but I have means to compel you.

NORA. You don't mean that you will tell my husband that I owe you money?

KROGSTAD. Hm!—suppose I were to tell him?

NORA. It would be perfectly infamous of you. [*sobbing*] To think of his learning my secret, which has been my joy and pride, in such an ugly, clumsy way— that he should learn it from you! And it would put me in a horribly disagreeable position—

KROGSTAD. Only disagreeable?

NORA. [*impetuously*] Well, do it, then!—and it will be the worse for you. My husband will see for himself what a blackguard you are, and you certainly won't keep your post then.

KROGSTAD. I asked you if it was only a disagreeable scene at home that you were afraid of?

NORA. If my husband does get to know of it, of course he will at once pay you what is still owing, and we shall have nothing more to do with you.

KROGSTAD. [*coming a step nearer*] Listen to me, Mrs. Helmer. Either you have a very bad memory or you know very little of business. I shall be obliged to remind you of a few details.

NORA. What do you mean?

KROGSTAD. When your husband was ill, you came to me to borrow two hundred and fifty pounds.

NORA. I didn't know any one else to go to.

KROGSTAD. I promised to get you that amount—

NORA. Yes, and you did so.

KROGSTAD. I promised to get you that amount, on certain conditions. Your mind was so taken up with your husband's illness, and you were so anxious to get the money for your journey, that you seem to have paid no attention to the conditions of our bargain. Therefore it will not be amiss if I remind you of them. Now, I promised to get the money on the security of a bond which I drew up.

NORA. Yes, and which I signed.

KROGSTAD. Good. But below your signature there were a few lines constituting your father a surety for the money; those lines your father should have signed.

NORA. Should? He did sign them.

KROGSTAD. I had left the date blank; that is to say your father should himself have inserted the date on which he signed the paper. Do you remember that?

NORA. Yes, I think I remember—

KROGSTAD. Then I gave you the bond to send by post to your father. Is that not so?

NORA. Yes.

KROGSTAD. And you naturally did so at once, because five or six days afterwards you brought me the bond with your father's signature. And then I gave you the money.

NORA. Well, haven't I been paying it off regularly?

KROGSTAD. Fairly so, yes. But—to come back to the matter in hand—that must have been a very trying time for you, Mrs. Helmer?

NORA. It was, indeed.

KROGSTAD. Your father was very ill, wasn't he?

NORA. He was very near his end.

KROGSTAD. And died soon afterwards?

NORA. Yes.

KROGSTAD. Tell me, Mrs. Helmer, can you by any chance remember what day your father died?—on what day of the month, I mean.

NORA. Papa died on the 29th of September.

KROGSTAD. That is correct; I have ascertained it for myself. And, as that is so, there is a discrepancy [*taking a paper from his pocket*] which I cannot account for.

NORA. What discrepancy? I don't know—

KROGSTAD. The discrepancy consists, Mrs. Helmer, in the fact that your father signed this bond three days after his death.

NORA. What do you mean? I don't understand—

KROGSTAD. Your father died on the 29th of September. But, look here; your father has dated his signature the 2nd of October. It is a discrepancy, isn't it? [NORA *is silent.*] Can you explain it to me? [NORA *is still silent.*] It is a remarkable thing, too, that the words "2nd of October," as well as the year, are not written in your father's handwriting but in one that I think I know. Well, of course it can be explained; your father may have forgotten to date his signature, and someone else may have dated it haphazard before they knew of his death. There is no harm in that. It all depends on the signature of the name; and that is genuine, I suppose, Mrs. Helmer? It was your father himself who signed his name here?

NORA. [*after a short pause, throws her head up and looks defiantly at him*] No, it was not. It was I that wrote papa's name.

KROGSTAD. Are you aware that is a dangerous confession?

NORA. In what way? You shall have your money soon.

KROGSTAD. Let me ask you a question; why did you not send the paper to your father?

NORA. It was impossible; papa was so ill. If I had asked him for his signature, I should have had to tell him what the money was to be used for; and when he was so ill himself I couldn't tell him that my husband's life was in danger—it was impossible.

KROGSTAD. It would have been better for you if you had given up your trip abroad.

NORA. No, that was impossible. That trip was to save my husband's life; I couldn't give that up.

KROGSTAD. But did it never occur to you that you were committing a fraud on me?

NORA. I couldn't take that into account; I didn't trouble myself about you at all. I couldn't bear you, because you put so many heartless difficulties in my way, although you knew what a dangerous condition my husband was in.

KROGSTAD. Mrs. Helmer, you evidently do not realise clearly what it is that you have been guilty of. But I can assure you that my one false step, which lost me all my reputation, was nothing more or nothing worse than what you have done.

NORA. You? Do you ask me to believe that you were brave enough to run a risk to save your wife's life?

KROGSTAD. The law cares nothing about motives.

NORA. Then it must be a very foolish law.

KROGSTAD. Foolish or not, it is the law by which you will be judged, if I produce this paper in court.

NORA. I don't believe it. Is a daughter not to be allowed to spare her dying father anxiety and care? Is a wife not to be allowed to save her husband's life? I don't know much about law; but I am certain that there must be laws permitting such things as that. Have you no knowledge of such laws—you who are a lawyer? You must be a very poor lawyer, Mr. Krogstad.

KROGSTAD. Maybe. But matters of business—such business as you and I have had together—do you think I don't understand that? Very well. Do as you please. But let me tell you this—if I lose my position a second time, you shall lose yours with me.

[*He bows, and goes out through the hall.*]

NORA. [*appears buried in thought for a short time, then tosses her head*] Nonsense! Trying to frighten me like that!—I am not so silly as he thinks. [*begins to busy herself putting the children's things in order*] And yet—? No, it's impossible! I did it for love's sake.

THE CHILDREN. [*in the doorway on the left*] Mother, the stranger man has gone out through the gate.

NORA. Yes, dears, I know. But, don't tell anyone about the stranger man. Do you hear? Not even papa.

CHILDREN. No, mother; but will you come and play again?

NORA. No, no—not now.

CHILDREN. But, mother, you promised us.

NORA. Yes, but I can't now. Run away in; I have such a lot to do. Run away in, my sweet little darlings. [*She gets them into the room by degrees and shuts the door on them; then sits down on the sofa, takes up a piece of needlework and sews a few stitches, but soon stops.*] No! [*throws down the work, gets up, goes to the hall door and calls out*] Helen! bring the Tree in. [*goes to the table on the left, opens a drawer, and stops again*] No, no! it is quite impossible!

MAID. [*coming in with the Tree*] Where shall I put it, ma'am?

NORA. Here, in the middle of the floor.

MAID. Shall I get you anything else?

NORA. No, thank you. I have all I want.

[*Exit Maid.*]

NORA. [*begins dressing the tree*] A candle here—and flowers here—. The horrible man! It's all nonsense—there's nothing wrong. The Tree shall be splendid! I will do everything I can think of to please you, Torvald!—I will sing for you, dance for you—[HELMER *comes in with some papers under his arm*] Oh! are you back already?

HELMER. Yes. Has anyone been here?

NORA. Here? No.

HELMER. That is strange. I saw Krogstad going out of the gate.

NORA. Did you? Oh yes, I forgot, Krogstad was here for a moment.

HELMER. Nora, I can see from your manner that he has been here begging you to say a good word for him.

NORA. Yes.

HELMER. And you were to appear to do it of your own accord; you were to conceal from me the fact of his having been here; didn't he beg that of you too?

NORA. Yes, Torvald, but—

HELMER. Nora, Nora, and you would be a party to that sort of thing? To have any talk with a man like that, and give him any sort of promise? And to tell me a lie into the bargain?

NORA. A lie—?

HELMER. Didn't you tell me no one had been here? [*shakes his finger at her*] My little song-bird must never do that again. A song-bird must have a clean beak to chirp with—no false notes! [*puts his arm round her waist*] That is so, isn't it? Yes, I am sure it is. [*lets her go*] We will say no more about it. [*sits down by the stove*] How warm and snug it is here!

[*Turns over his papers.*]

NORA. [*after a short pause, during which she busies herself with the Christmas Tree*] Torvald!

HELMER. Yes.

NORA. I am looking forward tremendously to the fancy dress ball at the Stenborgs' the day after to-morrow.

HELMER. And I am tremendously curious to see what you are going to surprise me with.

NORA. It was very silly of me to want to do that.

HELMER. What do you mean?

NORA. I can't hit upon anything that will do; everything I think of seems so silly and insignificant.

HELMER. Does my little Nora acknowledge that at last?

NORA. [*standing behind his chair with her arms on the back of it*] Are you very busy, Torvald?

HELMER. Well—

NORA. What are all those papers?

HELMER. Bank business.

NORA. Already?

HELMER. I have got authority from the retiring manager to undertake the necessary changes in the staff and in the rearrangement of the work; and I must make use of the Christmas week for that, so as to have everything in order for the new year.

NORA. Then that was why this poor Krogstad—

HELMER. Hm!

NORA. [*leans against the back of his chair and strokes his hair*] If you hadn't been so busy I should have asked you a tremendously big favour, Torvald.

HELMER. What is that? Tell me.

NORA. There is no one has such good taste as you. And I do so want to look nice at the fancy-dress ball. Torvald, couldn't you take me in hand and decide what I shall go as, and what sort of a dress I shall wear?

HELMER. Aha! so my obstinate little woman is obliged to get someone to come to her rescue?

NORA. Yes, Torvald, I can't get along a bit without your help.

HELMER. Very well, I will think it over, we shall manage to hit upon something.

NORA. That is nice of you. [*Goes to the Christmas Tree. A short pause.*] How pretty the red flowers look—. But, tell me, was it really something very bad that this Krogstad was guilty of?

HELMER. He forged someone's name. Have you any idea what that means?

NORA. Isn't it possible that he was driven to do it by necessity?

HELMER. Yes; or, as in so many cases, by imprudence. I am not so heartless as to condemn a man altogether because of a single false step of that kind.

NORA. No you wouldn't, would you, Torvald?

HELMER. Many a man has been able to retrieve his character, if he has openly confessed his fault and taken his punishment.

NORA. Punishment—?

HELMER. But Krogstad did nothing of that sort; he got himself out of it by a cunning trick, and that is why he has gone under altogether.

NORA. But do you think it would—?

HELMER. Just think how a guilty man like that has to lie and play the hypocrite with everyone, how he has to wear a mask in the presence of those near and dear to him, even before his own wife and children. And about the children—that is the most terrible part of it all, Nora.

NORA. How?

HELMER. Because such an atmosphere of lies infects and poisons the whole life of a home. Each breath the children take in such a house is full of the germs of evil.

NORA. [*coming nearer him*] Are you sure of that?

HELMER. My dear, I have often seen it in the course of my life as a lawyer. Almost everyone who has gone to the bad early in life has had a deceitful mother.

NORA. Why do you only say—mother?

HELMER. It seems most commonly to be the mother's influence, though naturally a bad father's would have the same result. Every lawyer is familiar with the fact. This Krogstad, now, has been persistently poisoning his own children with lies and dissimulation; that is why I say he has lost all moral character. [*holds out his hands to her*] That is why my sweet little Nora must promise me not to plead his cause. Give me your hand on it. Come, come, what is this? Give me your hand. There now, that's settled. I assure you it would be quite impossible for me to work with him; I literally feel physically ill when I am in the company of such people.

NORA. [*takes her hand out of his and goes to the opposite side of the Christmas Tree*] How hot it is in here; and I have such a lot to do.

HELMER. [*getting up and putting his papers in order*] Yes, and I must try and read through some of these before dinner; and I must think about your costume, too. And it is just possible I may have something ready in gold paper to hang up on the Tree. [*Puts his hand on her head.*] My precious little singing-bird!

[*He goes into his room and shuts the door after him.*]

NORA. [*after a pause, whispers*] No, no—it isn't true. It's impossible; it must be impossible.

[*The NURSE opens the door on the left.*]

NURSE. The little ones are begging so hard to be allowed to come in to mamma.

NORA. No, no, no! Don't let them come in to me! You stay with them, Anne.

NURSE. Very well, ma'am.

[*Shuts the door.*]

NORA. [*pale with terror*] Deprave my little children? Poison my home? [*a short pause. Then she tosses her head.*] It's not true. It can't possibly be true.

ACT 2

THE SAME SCENE. *The Christmas Tree is in the corner by the piano, stripped of its ornaments and with burnt-down candle-ends on its dishevelled branches.* NORA'S *cloak and hat are lying on the sofa. She is alone in the room, walking about uneasily. She stops by the sofa and takes up her cloak.*

NORA. [*drops the cloak*] Someone is coming now! [*goes to the door and listens*] No— it is no one. Of course, no one will come to-day, Christmas Day—nor tomorrow either. But, perhaps—[*opens the door and looks out*] No, nothing in the letter-box; it is quite empty. [*comes forward*] What rubbish! of course he can't be in earnest about it. Such a thing couldn't happen; it is impossible—I have three little children.

[*Enter the* NURSE *from the room on the left, carrying a big cardboard box.*]

NURSE. At last I have found the box with the fancy dress.
NORA. Thanks; put it on the table.
NURSE. [*doing so*] But it is very much in want of mending.
NORA. I should like to tear it into a hundred thousand pieces.
NURSE. What an idea! It can easily be put in order—just a little patience.
NORA. Yes, I will go and get Mrs. Linde to come and help me with it.
NURSE. What, out again? In this horrible weather? You will catch cold, ma'am, and make yourself ill.
NORA. Well, worse than that might happen. How are the children?
NURSE. The poor little souls are playing with their Christmas presents, but—
NORA. Do they ask much for me?
NURSE. You see, they are so accustomed to have their mamma with them.
NORA. Yes, but, nurse, I shall not be able to be so much with them now as I was before.
NURSE. Oh well, young children easily get accustomed to anything.
NORA. Do you think so? Do you think they would forget their mother if she went away altogether?
NURSE. Good heavens!—went away altogether?
NORA. Nurse, I want you to tell me something I have often wondered about— how could you have the heart to put your own child out among strangers?
NURSE. I was obliged to, if I wanted to be little Nora's nurse.
NORA. Yes, but how could you be willing to do it?
NURSE. What, when I was going to get such a good place by it? A poor girl who has got into trouble should be glad to. Besides, that wicked man didn't do a single thing for me.
NORA. But I suppose your daughter has quite forgotten you.
NURSE. No, indeed she hasn't. She wrote to me when she was confirmed, and when she was married.
NORA. [*putting her arms round her neck*] Dear old Anne, you were a good mother to me when I was little.
NURSE. Little Nora, poor dear, had no other mother but me.
NORA. And if my little ones had no other mother, I am sure you would—What nonsense I am talking! [*opens the box*] Go in to them. Now I must—. You will see tomorrow how charming I shall look.
NURSE. I am sure there will be no one at the ball so charming as you, ma'am.

[*Goes into the room on the left.*]

Nora. [*begins to unpack the box, but soon pushes it away from her*] If only I dared go out. If only no one would come. If only I could be sure nothing would happen here in the meantime. Stuff and nonsense! No one will come. Only I mustn't think about it. I will brush my muff. What lovely gloves! Out of my thoughts, out of my thoughts! One, two, three, four, five, six—[*Screams.*] Ah! there is someone coming—

[*Makes a movement towards the door, but stands irresolute.*]

[*Enter* Mrs. Linde *from the hall, where she has taken off her cloak and hat.*]

Nora. Oh, it's you, Christine. There is no one else out there, is there? How good of you to come!

Mrs. Linde. I heard you were up asking for me.

Nora. Yes, I was passing by. As a matter of fact, it is something you could help me with. Let us sit down here on the sofa. Look here. To-morrow evening there is to be a fancy-dress ball at the Stenborgs', who live above us; and Torvald wants me to go as a Neapolitan fisher-girl, and dance the Tarantella that I learnt at Capri.

Mrs. Linde. I see; you are going to keep up the character.

Nora. Yes, Torvald wants me to. Look, here is the dress; Torvald had it made for me there, but now it is all so torn, and I haven't any idea—

Mrs. Linde. We will easily put that right. It is only some of the trimming come unsewn here and there. Needle and thread? Now then, that's all we want.

Nora. It *is* nice of you.

Mrs. Linde. [*sewing*] So you are going to be dressed up to-morrow, Nora. I will tell you what—I shall come in for a moment and see you in your fine feathers. But I have completely forgotten to thank you for a delightful evening yesterday.

Nora. [*gets up, and crosses the stage*] Well I don't think yesterday was as pleasant as usual. You ought to have come to town a little earlier, Christine. Certainly Torvald does understand how to make a house dainty and attractive.

Mrs. Linde. And so do you, it seems to me; you are not your father's daughter for nothing. But tell me, is Doctor Rank always as depressed as he was yesterday?

Nora. No; yesterday it was very noticeable. I must tell you that he suffers from a very dangerous disease. He has consumption of the spine, poor creature. His father was a horrible man who committed all sorts of excesses; and that is why his son was sickly from childhood, do you understand?

Mrs. Linde. [*dropping her sewing*] But, my dearest Nora, how do you know anything about such things?

Nora. [*walking about*] Pooh! When you have three children, you get visits now and then from—from married women, who know something of medical matters, and they talk about one thing and another.

Mrs. Linde. [*goes on sewing. A short silence*] Does Doctor Rank come here every day?

Nora. Every day regularly. He is Torvald's most intimate friend, and a great friend of mine too. He is just like one of the family.

Mrs. Linde. But tell me this—is he perfectly sincere? I mean, isn't he the kind of man that is very anxious to make himself agreeable?

Nora. Not in the least. What makes you think that?

MRS. LINDE. When you introduced him to me yesterday, he declared he had often heard my name mentioned in this house; but afterwards I noticed that your husband hadn't the slightest idea who I was. So how could Doctor Rank—?

NORA. That is quite right, Christine. Torvald is so absurdly fond of me that he wants me absolutely to himself, as he says. At first he used to seem almost jealous if I mentioned any of the dear folk at home, so naturally I gave up doing so. But I often talk about such things with Doctor Rank, because he likes hearing about them.

MRS. LINDE. Listen to me, Nora. You are still very like a child in many things, and I am older than you in many ways and have a little more experience. Let me tell you this—you ought to make an end of it with Doctor Rank.

NORA. What ought I to make an end of?

MRS. LINDE. Of two things, I think. Yesterday you talked some nonsense about a rich admirer who was to leave you money—

NORA. An admirer who doesn't exist, unfortunately! But what then?

MRS. LINDE. Is Doctor Rank a man of means?

NORA. Yes, he is.

MRS. LINDE. And has no one to provide for?

NORA. No, no one; but—

MRS. LINDE. And comes here every day?

NORA. Yes, I told you so.

MRS. LINDE. But how can this well-bred man be so tactless?

NORA. I don't understand you at all.

MRS. LINDE. Don't prevaricate, Nora. Do you suppose I don't guess who lent you the two hundred and fifty pounds?

NORA. Are you out of your senses? How can you think of such a thing! A friend of ours, who comes here every day! Do you realise what a horribly painful position that would be?

MRS. LINDE. Then it really isn't he?

NORA. No, certainly not. It would never have entered into my head for a moment. Besides, he had no money to lend then; he came into his money afterwards.

MRS. LINDE. Well, I think that was lucky for you, my dear Nora.

NORA. No, it would never have come into my head to ask Doctor Rank. Although I am quite sure that if I had asked him—

MRS. LINDE. But of course you won't.

NORA. Of course not. I have no reason to think it could possibly be necessary. But I am quite sure that if I told Doctor Rank—

MRS. LINDE. Behind your husband's back?

NORA. I *must* make an end of it with the other one, and that will be behind his back too. I *must* make an end of it with him.

MRS. LINDE. Yes, that is what I told you yesterday, but—

NORA. [*walking up and down*] A man can put a thing like that straight much easier than a woman—

MRS. LINDE. One's husband, yes.

NORA. Nonsense! [*standing still*] When you pay off a debt you get your bond back, don't you?

MRS. LINDE. Yes, as a matter of course.

NORA. And can tear it into a hundred thousand pieces, and burn it up—the nasty dirty paper!

MRS. LINDE. [*looks hard at her, lays down her sewing and gets up slowly*] Nora, you are concealing something from me.

NORA. Do I look as if I were?

MRS. LINDE. Something has happened to you since yesterday morning. Nora, what is it?

NORA. [*going nearer to her*] Christine! [*listens*] Hush! there's Torvald come home. Do you mind going in to the children for the present? Torvald can't bear to see dressmaking going on. Let Anne help you.

MRS. LINDE. [*gathering some of the things together*] Certainly—but I am not going away from here till we have had it out with one another.

[*She goes into the room on the left, as* HELMER *comes in from the hall.*]

NORA. [*going up to* HELMER] I have wanted you so much, Torvald dear.

HELMER. Was that the dressmaker?

NORA. No, it was Christine; she is helping me to put my dress in order. You will see I shall look quite smart.

HELMER. Wasn't that a happy thought of mine, now?

NORA. Splendid! But don't you think it is nice of me, too, to do as you wish?

HELMER. Nice?—because you do as your husband wishes? Well, well, you little rogue, I am sure you did not mean it in that way. But I am not going to disturb you; you will want to be trying on your dress, I expect.

NORA. I suppose you are going to work.

HELMER. Yes. [*shows her a bundle of papers*] Look at that. I have just been into the bank. [*Turns to go into his room.*]

NORA. Torvald.

HELMER. Yes.

NORA. If your little squirrel were to ask you for something very, very prettily—?

HELMER. What then?

NORA. Would you do it?

HELMER. I should like to hear what it is, first.

NORA. Your squirrel would run about and do all her tricks if you would be nice, and do what she wants.

HELMER. Speak plainly.

NORA. Your skylark would chirp about in every room, with her song rising and falling—

HELMER. Well, my skylark does that anyhow.

NORA. I would play the fairy and dance for you in the moonlight, Torvald.

HELMER. Nora—you surely don't mean that request you made of me this morning?

NORA. [*going near him*] Yes, Torvald, I beg you so earnestly—

HELMER. Have you really the courage to open up that question again?

NORA. Yes, dear, you *must* do as I ask; you *must* let Krogstad keep his post in the Bank.

HELMER. My dear Nora, it is his post that I have arranged Mrs. Linde shall have.

NORA. Yes, you have been awfully kind about that; but you could just as well dismiss some other clerk instead of Krogstad.

HELMER. This is simply incredible obstinacy! Because you chose to give him a thoughtless promise that you would speak for him, I am expected to—

NORA. That isn't the reason, Torvald. It is for your own sake. This fellow writes in the most scurrilous newspapers; you have told me so yourself. He can do you an unspeakable amount of harm. I am frightened to death of him—

HELMER. Ah, I understand; it is recollections of the past that scare you.

NORA. What do you mean?

HELMER. Naturally you are thinking of your father.

NORA. Yes—yes, of course. Just recall to your mind what these malicious creatures wrote in the papers about papa, and how horribly they slandered him. I believe they would have procured his dismissal if the Department had not sent you over to inquire into it, and if you had not been so kindly disposed and helpful to him.

HELMER. My little Nora, there is an important difference between your father and me. Your father's reputation as a public official was not above suspicion. Mine is, and I hope it will continue to be so, as long as I hold my office.

NORA. You never can tell what mischief these men may contrive. We ought to be so well off, so snug and happy here in our peaceful home, and have no cares— you and I and the children. Torvald! That is why I beg you so earnestly—

HELMER. And it is just by interceding for him that you make it impossible for me to keep him. It is already known at the Bank that I mean to dismiss Krogstad. Is it to get about now that the new manager has changed his mind at his wife's bidding—

NORA. And what if it did?

HELMER. Of course!—if only this obstinate little person can get her way! Do you suppose I am going to make myself ridiculous before my whole staff, to let people think that I am a man to be swayed by all sorts of outside influence? I should very soon feel the consequences of it, I can tell you! And besides, there is one thing that makes it quite impossible for me to have Krogstad in the Bank as long as I am manager.

NORA. Whatever is that?

HELMER. His moral failings I might perhaps have overlooked, if necessary—

NORA. Yes, you could—couldn't you?

HELMER. And I hear he is a good worker, too. But I knew him when we were boys. It was one of those rash friendships that so often prove an incubus in after life. I may as well tell you plainly, we were once on very intimate terms with one another. But this tactless fellow lays no restraint on himself when other people are present. On the contrary, he thinks it gives him the right to adopt a familiar tone with me, and every minute it is "I say, Helmer, old fellow!" and that sort of thing. I assure you it is extremely painful for me. He would make my position in the Bank intolerable.

NORA. Torvald, I don't believe you mean that.

HELMER. Don't you? Why not?

NORA. Because it is such a narrow-minded way of looking at things.

HELMER. What are you saying? Narrow-minded? Do you think I am narrow-minded?

NORA. No, just the opposite, dear—and it is exactly for that reason.

HELMER. It's the same thing. You say my point of view is narrow-minded, so I must be so too. Narrow-minded! Very well—I must put an end to this. [*Goes to the hall-door and calls.*] Helen!

NORA. What are you going to do?

HELMER. [*looking among his papers*] Settle it. [*Enter* MAID.] Look here; take this letter and go downstairs with it at once. Find a messenger and tell him to deliver it, and be quick. The address is on it, and here is the money.

MAID. Very well, sir.

[*Exits with the letter.*]

HELMER. [*putting his papers together*] Now then, little Miss Obstinate.

NORA. [*breathlessly*] Torvald—what was that letter?

HELMER. Krogstad's dismissal.

NORA. Call her back, Torvald! There is still time. Oh Torvald, call her back! Do it for my sake—for your own sake—for the children's sake! Do you hear me, Torvald? Call her back!! You don't know what that letter can bring upon us.

HELMER. It's too late.

NORA. Yes, it's too late.

HELMER. My dear Nora, I can forgive the anxiety you are in, although really it is an insult to me. It is, indeed. Isn't it an insult to think that I should be afraid of a starving quill-driver's vengeance? But I forgive you nevertheless, because it is such eloquent witness to your great love for me. [*takes her in his arms*] And that is as it should be, my own darling Nora. Come what will, you may be sure I shall have both courage and strength if they be needed. You will see I am man enough to take everything upon myself.

NORA. [*in a horror-stricken voice*] What do you mean by that?

HELMER. Everything, I say—

NORA. [*recovering herself*] You will never have to do that.

HELMER. That's right. Well, we will share it, Nora, as man and wife should. That is how it shall be. [*caressing her*] Are you content now? There! there!—not these frightened dove's eyes! The whole thing is only the wildest fancy!— Now, you must go and play through the Tarantella and practise with your tambourine. I shall go into the inner office and shut the door, and I shall hear nothing; you can make as much noise as you please. [*turns back at the door*] And when Rank comes, tell him where he will find me.

[*Nods to her, takes his papers and goes into his room, and shuts the door after him.*]

NORA. [*bewildered with anxiety, stands as if rooted to the spot, and whispers*] He is capable of doing it. He will do it. He will do it in spite of everything.—No, not that! Never, never! Anything rather than that! Oh, for some help, some way out of it! [*The door-bell rings.*] Doctor Rank! Anything rather than that— anything, whatever it is!

[*She puts her hands over her face, pulls herself together, goes to the door and opens it. RANK is standing without, hanging up his coat. During the following dialogue it begins to grow dark.*]

NORA. Good-day, Doctor Rank. I knew your ring. But you mustn't go in to Torvald now; I think he is busy with something.

RANK. And you?

NORA. [*brings him in and shuts the door after him*] Oh, you know very well I always have time for you.

RANK. Thank you. I shall make use of as much of it as I can.

NORA. What do you mean by that? As much of it as you can?

RANK. Well, does that alarm you?

NORA. It was such a strange way of putting it. Is anything likely to happen?

RANK. Nothing but what I have long been prepared for. But I certainly didn't expect it to happen so soon.

NORA. [*gripping him by the arm*] What have you found out? Doctor Rank, you must tell me.

RANK. [*sitting down by the stove*] It is all up with me. And it can't be helped.

NORA. [*with a sigh of relief*] Is it about yourself?

RANK. Who else? It is no use lying to one's self. I am the most wretched of all my patients, Mrs. Helmer. Lately I have been taking stock of my internal economy. Bankrupt! Probably within a month I shall lie rotting in the churchyard.

NORA. What an ugly thing to say!

RANK. The thing itself is cursedly ugly, and the worst of it is that I shall have to face so much more that is ugly before that. I shall only make one more examination of myself; when I have done that, I shall know pretty certainly when it will be that the horrors of dissolution will begin. There is something I want to tell you. Helmer's refined nature gives him an unconquerable disgust at everything that is ugly; I won't have him in my sick-room.

NORA. Oh, but, Doctor Rank—

RANK. I won't have him there. Not on any account. I bar my door to him. As soon as I am quite certain that the worst has come, I shall send you my card with a black cross on it, and then you will know that the loathsome end has begun.

NORA. You are quite absurd to-day. And I wanted you so much to be in a really good humour.

RANK. With death stalking beside me?—To have to pay this penalty for another man's sin! Is there any justice in that? And in every single family, in one way or another, some such inexorable retribution is being exacted—

NORA. [*putting her hands over her ears*] Rubbish! Do talk of something cheerful.

RANK. Oh, it's a mere laughing matter, the whole thing. My poor innocent spine has to suffer for my father's youthful amusements.

NORA. [*sitting at the table on the left*] I suppose you mean that he was too partial to asparagus and pâté de foie gras, don't you.

RANK. Yes, and to truffles.

NORA. Truffles, yes. And oysters too, I suppose?

RANK. Oysters, of course, that goes without saying.

NORA. And heaps of port and champagne. It is sad that all these nice things should take their revenge on our bones.

RANK. Especially that they should revenge themselves on the unlucky bones of those who have not had the satisfaction of enjoying them.

NORA. Yes, that's the saddest part of it all.

RANK. [*with a searching look at her*] Hm!—

NORA. [*after a short pause*] Why did you smile?

RANK. No, it was you that laughed.

NORA. No, it was you that smiled, Doctor Rank!

RANK. [*rising*] You are a greater rascal than I thought.

NORA. I am in a silly mood to-day.

RANK. So it seems.

NORA. [*putting her hands on his shoulders*] Dear, dear Doctor Rank, death mustn't take you away from Torvald and me.

RANK. It is a loss you would easily recover from. Those who are gone are soon forgotten.

NORA. [*looking at him anxiously*] Do you believe that?

RANK. People form new ties, and then—

NORA. Who will form new ties?

RANK. Both you and Helmer, when I am gone. You yourself are already on the high road to it, I think. What did that Mrs. Linde want here last night?

NORA. Oho!—you don't mean to say you are jealous of poor Christine?

RANK. Yes, I am. She will be my successor in this house. When I am done for, this woman will—

NORA. Hush! don't speak so loud. She is in that room.

RANK. To-day again. There, you see.

NORA. She has only come to sew my dress for me. Bless my soul, how unreasonable you are! [*sits down on the sofa*] Be nice now, Doctor Rank, and tomorrow you will see how beautifully I shall dance, and you can imagine I am doing it all for you—and for Torvald too, of course. [*takes various things out of the box*] Doctor Rank, come and sit down here, and I will show you something.

RANK. [*sitting down*] What is it?

NORA. Just look at those!

RANK. Silk stockings.

NORA. Flesh-coloured. Aren't they lovely? It is so dark here now, but to-morrow—. No, no, no! you must only look at the feet. Oh well, you may have leave to look at the legs too.

RANK. Hm!—

NORA. Why are you looking so critical? Don't you think they will fit me?

RANK. I have no means of forming an opinion about that.

NORA. [*looks at him for a moment*] For shame! [*hits him lightly on the ear with the stockings*] That's to punish you. [*folds them up again*]

RANK. And what other nice things am I to be allowed to see?

NORA. Not a single thing more, for being so naughty. [*She looks among the things, humming to herself.*]

RANK. [*after a short silence*] When I am sitting here, talking to you as intimately as this, I cannot imagine for a moment what would have become of me if I had never come into this house.

NORA. [*smiling*] I believe you do feel thoroughly at home with us.

RANK. [*in a lower voice, looking straight in front of him*] And to be obliged to leave it all—

NORA. Nonsense, you are not going to leave it.

RANK. [*as before*] And not be able to leave behind one the slightest token of one's gratitude, scarcely even a fleeting regret—nothing but an empty place which the first comer can fill as well as any other.

NORA. And if I asked you now for a—? No!

RANK. For what?

NORA. For a big proof of your friendship—

RANK. Yes, yes!

NORA. I mean a tremendously big favour—

RANK. Would you really make me so happy for once?

NORA. Ah, but you don't know what it is yet.

RANK. No—but tell me.

NORA. I really can't, Doctor Rank. It is something out of all reason; it means advice, and help, and a favour—

RANK. The bigger a thing is, the better. I can't conceive what it is you mean. Do tell me. Haven't I your confidence?

NORA. More than anyone else. I know you are my truest and best friend, and so I will tell you what it is. Well, Doctor Rank, it is something you must help me to prevent. You know how devotedly, how inexpressibly deeply Torvald loves me; he would never for a moment hesitate to give his life for me.

RANK. [*leaning towards her*] Nora—do you think he is the only one—?

NORA. [*with a slight start*] The only one—?

RANK. The only one who would gladly give his life for your sake.

NORA. [*sadly*] Is that it?

RANK. I was determined you should know it before I went away, and there will never be a better opportunity than this. Now you know it, Nora. And now you know, too, that you can trust me as you would trust no one else.

NORA. [*rises, deliberately and quietly*] Let me pass.

RANK. [*makes room for her to pass him, but sits still*] Nora!

NORA. [*at the hall door*] Helen, bring in the lamp. [*goes over to the stove*] Dear Doctor Rank, that was really horrid of you.

RANK. To have loved you as much as anyone else does? Was that horrid?

NORA. No, but to go and tell me so. There was really no need—

RANK. What do you mean? Did you know—? [MAID *enters with lamp, puts it down on the table, and goes out.*] Nora—Mrs. Helmer—tell me, had you any idea of this?

NORA. Oh, how do I know whether I had or whether I hadn't? I really can't tell you—To think you could be so clumsy, Doctor Rank! We were getting on so nicely.

RANK. Well, at all events you know now that you can command me, body and soul. So won't you speak out?

NORA. [*looking at him*] After what happened?

RANK. I beg you to let me know what it is.

NORA. I can't tell you anything now.

RANK. Yes, yes. You mustn't punish me in that way. Let me have permission to do for you whatever a man may do.

NORA. You can do nothing for me now. Besides, I really don't need any help at all. You will find that the whole thing is merely fancy on my part. It really is so—of course it is! [*Sits down in the rocking-chair, and looks at him with a smile.*] You are a nice sort of man, Doctor Rank!—don't you feel ashamed of yourself, now the lamp has come?

RANK. Not a bit. But perhaps I had better go—for ever?

NORA. No, indeed, you shall not. Of course you must come here just as before. You know very well Torvald can't do without you.

RANK. Yes, but you?

NORA. Oh, I am always tremendously pleased when you come.

RANK. It is just that, that put me on the wrong track. You are a riddle to me. I have often thought that you would almost as soon be in my company as in Helmer's.

NORA. Yes—you see there are some people one loves best, and others whom one would almost rather have as companions.

RANK. Yes, there is something in that.

NORA. When I was at home, of course I loved papa best. But I always thought it tremendous fun if I could steal down into the maid's room, because they never moralised at all, and talked to each other about such entertaining things.

RANK. I see—it is *their* place I have taken.

NORA. [*jumping up and going to him*] Oh, dear, nice Doctor Rank, I never meant that at all. But surely you can understand that being with Torvald is a little like being with papa—

[*Enter* MAID *from the hall.*]

MAID. If you please, ma'am. [*whispers and hands her a card*]

NORA. [*glancing at the card*] Oh! [*puts it in her pocket*]

RANK. Is there anything wrong?

NORA. No, no, not in the least. It is only something—it is my new dress—

RANK. What? Your dress is lying there.

NORA. Oh, yes, that one; but this is another. I ordered it. Torvald mustn't know about it—

RANK. Oho! Then that was the great secret.

NORA. Of course. Just go in to him; he is sitting in the inner room. Keep him as long as—

RANK. Make your mind easy; I won't let him escape. [*goes into* HELMER'*s room.*]

NORA. [*to the* MAID] And he is standing waiting in the kitchen?

MAID. Yes; he came up the back stairs.

NORA. But didn't you tell him no one was in?

MAID. Yes, but it was no good.

NORA. He won't go away?

MAID. No; he says he won't until he has seen you, ma'am.

NORA. Well, let him come in—but quietly. Helen, you mustn't say anything about it to anyone. It is a surprise for my husband.

MAID. Yes, ma'am, I quite understand.

NORA. This dreadful thing is going to happen! It will happen in spite of me! No, no, no, it can't happen—it shan't happen!

[*She bolts the door of* HELMER'*s room. The* MAID *opens the hall door for* KROGSTAD *and shuts it after him. He is wearing a fur coat, high boots and a fur cap.*]

NORA. [*advancing towards him*] Speak low—my husband is at home.

KROGSTAD. No matter about that.

NORA. What do you want of me?

KROGSTAD. An explanation of something.

NORA. Make haste then. What is it?

KROGSTAD. You know, I suppose, that I have got my dismissal.

NORA. I couldn't prevent it, Mr. Krogstad. I fought as hard as I could on your side, but it was no good.

KROGSTAD. Does your husband love you so little, then? He knows that what I can expose you to, and yet he ventures—

NORA. How can you suppose that he has any knowledge of the sort?

KROGSTAD. I didn't suppose so at all. It would not be the least like our dear Torvald Helmer to show so much courage—

NORA. Mr. Krogstad, a little respect for my husband, please.

KROGSTAD. Certainly—all the respect he deserves. But since you have kept the matter so carefully to yourself, I make bold to suppose that you have a little clearer idea, than you had yesterday, of what it actually is that you have done?

NORA. More than you could ever teach me.

KROGSTAD. Yes, such a bad lawyer as I am.

NORA. What is it you want of me?

KROGSTAD. Only to see how you were, Mrs. Helmer. I have been thinking about you all day long. A mere cashier, a quill-driver, a—well, a man like me—even he has a little of what is called feeling, you know.

NORA. Show it, then; think of my little children.

KROGSTAD. Have you and your husband thought of mine? But never mind about that. I only wanted to tell you that you need not take this matter too seriously. In the first place there will be no accusation made on my part.

NORA. No, of course not; I was sure of that.

KROGSTAD. The whole thing can be arranged amicably; there is no reason why anyone should know anything about it. It will remain a secret between us three.

NORA. My husband must never get to know anything about it.

KROGSTAD. How will you be able to prevent it? Am I to understand that you can pay the balance that is owing?

NORA. No, not just at present.

KROGSTAD. Or perhaps that you have some expedient for raising the money soon?

NORA. No expedient that I mean to make use of.

KROGSTAD. Well, in any case, it would have been of no use to you now. If you stood there with ever so much money in your hand, I would never part with your bond.

NORA. Tell me what purpose you mean to put it to.

KROGSTAD. I shall only preserve it—keep it in my possession. No one who is not concerned in the matter shall have the slightest hint of it. So that if the thought of it has driven you to any desperate resolution—

NORA. It has.

KROGSTAD. If you had it in your mind to run away from your home—

NORA. I had.

KROGSTAD. Or even something worse—

NORA. How could you know that?

KROGSTAD. Give up the idea.

NORA. How did you know I had thought of *that*?

KROGSTAD. Most of us think of that at first. I did, too—but I hadn't the courage.

NORA. [*faintly*] No more had I.

KROGSTAD. [*in a tone of relief*] No, that's it, isn't it—you hadn't the courage either?

NORA. No, I haven't—I haven't.

KROGSTAD. Besides, it would have been a great piece of folly. Once the first storm at home is over—. I have a letter for your husband in my pocket.

NORA. Telling him everything?

KROGSTAD. In as lenient a manner as I possibly could.

NORA. [*quickly*] He mustn't get the letter. Tear it up. I will find some means of getting money.

KROGSTAD. Excuse me, Mrs. Helmer, but I think I told you just now—

NORA. I am not speaking of what I owe you. Tell me what sum you are asking my husband for, and I will get the money.

KROGSTAD. I am not asking your husband for a penny.

NORA. What do you want, then?

KROGSTAD. I will tell you. I want to rehabilitate myself, Mrs. Helmer; I want to get on; and in that your husband must help me. For the last year and a half I have not had a hand in anything dishonourable, and all that time I have been struggling in most restricted circumstances. I was content to work my way up step by step. Now I am turned out, and I am not going to be satisfied with merely being taken into favour again. I want to get on, I tell you. I want to get into the Bank again, in a higher position. Your husband must make a place for me—

NORA. That he will never do!

KROGSTAD. He will; I know him; he dare not protest. And as soon as I am in there again with him, then you will see! Within a year I shall be the manager's right hand. It will be Nils Krogstad and not Torvald Helmer who manages the Bank.

NORA. That's a thing you will never see!

KROGSTAD. Do you mean that you will—?

NORA. I have courage enough for it now.

KROGSTAD. Oh, you can't frighten me. A fine, spoilt lady like you—

NORA. You will see, you will see.

KROGSTAD. Under the ice, perhaps? Down into the cold, coal-black water? And then, in the spring, to float up to the surface, all horrible and unrecognisable, with your hair fallen out—

NORA. You can't frighten me.

KROGSTAD. Nor you me. People don't do such things, Mrs. Helmer. Besides, what use would it be? I should have him completely in my power all the same.

NORA. Afterwards? When I am no longer—

KROGSTAD. Have you forgotten that it is I who have the keeping of your reputation? [NORA *stands speechlessly looking at him.*] Well, now, I have warned you. Do not do anything foolish. When Helmer has had my letter, I shall expect a message from him. And be sure you remember that it is your husband himself who has forced me into such ways as this again. I will never forgive him for that. Good-bye, Mrs. Helmer.

[*Exit through the hall.*]

NORA. [*goes to the hall door, opens it slightly and listens*] He is going. He is not putting the letter in the box. Oh no, no! that's impossible! [*opens the door by degrees*] What is that? He is standing outside. He is not going downstairs. Is he hesitating? Can he—

[*A letter drops into the box; then* KROGSTAD'*s footsteps are heard, till they die away as he goes downstairs.* NORA *utters a stifled cry and runs across the room to the table by the sofa. A short pause.*]

NORA. In the letter-box. [*steals across to the hall door*] There it lies—Torvald, Torvald, there is no hope for us now!

[MRS. LINDE *comes in from the room on the left, carrying the dress.*]

MRS. LINDE. There, I can't see anything more to mend now. Would you like to try it on—?

NORA. [*in a hoarse whisper*] Christine, come here.

MRS. LINDE. [*throwing the dress down on the sofa*] What is the matter with you? You look so agitated!

NORA. Come here. Do you see that letter? There, look—you can see it through the glass in the letter-box.

MRS. LINDE. Yes, I see it.

NORA. That letter is from Krogstad.

MRS. LINDE. Nora—it was Krogstad who lent you the money!

NORA. Yes, and now Torvald will know all about it.

MRS. LINDE. Believe me, Nora, that's the best thing for both of you.

NORA. You don't know all. I forged a name.

MRS. LINDE. Good heavens—!

NORA. I only want to say this to you, Christine—you must be my witness.

MRS. LINDE. Your witness? What do you mean? What am I to—?

NORA. If I should go out of my mind—and it might easily happen—

MRS. LINDE. Nora!

NORA. Or if anything else should happen to me—anything, for instance, that might prevent my being here—

MRS. LINDE. Nora! Nora! you are quite out of your mind.

NORA. And if it should happen that there were someone who wanted to take all the responsibility, all the blame, you understand—

MRS. LINDE. Yes, yes—but how can you suppose—?

NORA. Then you must be my witness, that it is not true, Christine. I am not out of my mind at all; I am in my right senses now, and I tell you no one else has known anything about it; I, and I alone, did the whole thing. Remember that.

MRS. LINDE. I will, indeed. But I don't understand all this.

NORA. How should you understand it? A wonderful thing is going to happen.

MRS. LINDE. A wonderful thing?

NORA. Yes a wonderful thing!—But it is so terrible, Christine; it *mustn't* happen, not for all the world.

MRS. LINDE. I will go at once and see Krogstad.

NORA. Don't go to him; he will do you some harm.

MRS. LINDE. There was a time when he would gladly do anything for my sake.

NORA. He?

MRS. LINDE. Where does he live?

NORA. How should I know—? Yes [*feeling in her pocket*] here is his card. But the letter, the letter—!

HELMER. [*calls from his room, knocking at the door*] Nora!

NORA. [*cries out anxiously*] Oh, what's that? What do you want?

HELMER. Don't be so frightened. We are not coming in; you have locked the door. Are you trying on your dress?

NORA. Yes, that's it. I look so nice, Torvald.

MRS. LINDE. [*who has read the card*] I see he lives at the corner here.

NORA. Yes but it's no use. It is hopeless. The letter is lying there in the box.

MRS. LINDE. And your husband keeps the key?

NORA. Yes, always.

MRS. LINDE. Krogstad must ask for his letter back unread, he must find some pretence—

NORA. But it is just at this time that Torvald generally—

MRS. LINDE. You must delay him. Go in to him in the meantime. I will come back as soon as I can.

[*She goes out hurriedly through the hall door.*]

NORA. [*goes to* HELMER'*s door, opens it and peeps in*] Torvald!

HELMER. [*from the inner room*] Well? May I venture at last to come into my own room again? Come along, Rank, now you will see—[*halting in the doorway*] But what is this?

NORA. What is what, dear?

HELMER. Rank led me to expect a splendid transformation.

RANK. [*in the doorway*] I understood so, but evidently I was mistaken.

NORA. Yes, nobody is to have the chance of admiring me in my dress until tomorrow.

HELMER. But, my dear Nora, you look so worn out. Have you been practising too much?

NORA. No, I have not practised at all.

HELMER. But you will need to—

NORA. Yes, indeed I shall, Torvald. But I can't get on a bit without you to help me; I have absolutely forgotten the whole thing.

HELMER. Oh, we will soon work it up again.

NORA. Yes, help me, Torvald. Promise that you will! I am so nervous about it— all the people—. You must give yourself up to me entirely this evening. Not the tiniest bit of business—you mustn't even take a pen in your hand. Will you promise, Torvald dear?

HELMER. I promise. This evening I will be wholly and absolutely at your service, you helpless little mortal. Ah, by the way, first of all I will just—

[*Goes towards the hall door.*]

NORA. What are you going to do there?

HELMER. Only see if any letters have come.

NORA. No, no! don't do that, Torvald!

HELMER. Why not?

NORA. Torvald, please don't. There is nothing there.

HELMER. Well, let me look. [*Turns to go to the letter-box.* NORA, *at the piano, plays the first bars of the Tarantella.* HELMER *stops in the doorway.*] Aha!

NORA. I can't dance to-morrow if I don't practise with you.

HELMER. [*going up to her*] Are you really so afraid of it, dear.

NORA. Yes, so dreadfully afraid of it. Let me practise at once; there is time now, before we go to dinner. Sit down and play for me, Torvald dear; criticise me, and correct me as you play.

HELMER. With great pleasure, if you wish me to.

of a piece fit together, deconstructionists look for the way these elements contradict each other and undermine coherence. Their point of view is rooted in a philosophy of language which says that words are incapable of accurately expressing meaning, that every utterance contains a lie by omitting all other possible utterances at the moment. Other critical stances reject interpretations that cannot be supported by evidence within the work, but deconstructionists delight in bizarre and contradictory claims. For example, while most people view J. Alfred Prufrock as a timid, self-effacing, and fearful fellow, deconstructionists might ask why a timid person would present such a lengthy, detailed, self-absorbed introspection (the poem itself). They could argue that J. Alfred is a braggart and narcissist, enchanted with his own superhuman sensitivity.

Intertextual Approaches

The meaning of literature is frequently enriched by each work's interdependence with other texts and the way they cast light on each other. Thus, critics use an *intertextual approach* in interpreting meaning. Sometimes intertextuality is right there on the surface, as it is in Susan Ludvigson's "Inventing My Parents." The author imagines her parents in lively intellectual chat about modernist writers Ernest Hemingway, Sinclair Lewis, Kay Boyle, and F. Scott Fitzgerald, and her father quotes by heart from the seventeenth-century poet John Donne. If you investigate these writers and their devotees, you will understand much about why Ludvigson wrote a charming, lighthearted response to the painting *Nighthawks*, which usually evokes feelings of isolation and hopelessness in its viewers (see page 441). You can create an intertextual approach even when it is not explicit, by noticing relationships among literary pieces. For example, the subject of *work* is common to the poems "What I Wouldn't Do," "Digging," "Richard Cory," and "My Mother Sews Blouses." Through comparing and contrasting what *work* means in each poem, you could write an essay of intertextual criticism.

Where Do You Stand?

As you read our brief summaries of critical approaches, you probably recognized the ones that you most regularly use when you think and write about literature. You may find it illuminating to try out some different approaches, especially when your usual tools are not working. You may also find it mind-expanding to look up work by other critics who share your favorite stance, learning from them how to use it more consciously and effectively.

[*Sits down at the piano.*]

NORA. [*takes out of the box a tambourine and a long variegated shawl. She hastily drapes the shawl round her. Then she springs to the front of the stage and calls out.*] Now play for me! I am going to dance!

[HELMER *plays and* NORA *dances.* RANK *stands by the piano behind* HELMER *and looks on.*]

HELMER. [*as he plays*] Slower, slower!

NORA. I can't do it any other way.

HELMER. Not so violently, Nora!

NORA. This is the way.

HELMER. [*stops playing*] No, no—that is not a bit right.

NORA. [*laughing and swinging the tambourine*] Didn't I tell you so?

RANK. Let me play for her.

HELMER. [*getting up*] Yes, do. I can correct her better then.

[RANK *sits down at the piano and plays.* NORA *dances more and more wildly.* HELMER *has taken up a position beside the stove, and during her dance gives her frequent instructions. She does not seem to hear him; her hair comes down and falls over her shoulders; she pays no attention to it, but goes on dancing. Enter* MRS. LINDE.]

MRS. LINDE. [*standing as if spell-bound in the doorway*] Oh!—

NORA. [*as she dances*] Such fun, Christine!

HELMER. My dear darling Nora, you are dancing as if your life depended on it.

NORA. So it does.

HELMER. Stop, Rank; this is sheer madness. Stop, I tell you! [RANK *stops playing, and* NORA *suddenly stands still.* HELMER *goes up to her.*] I could never have believed it. You have forgotten everything I taught you.

NORA. [*throwing away the tambourine*] There, you see.

HELMER. You will want a lot of coaching.

NORA. Yes, you see how much I need it. You must coach me up to the last minute. Promise me that, Torvald!

HELMER. You can depend on me.

NORA. You must not think of anything but me, either to-day or to-morrow; you mustn't open a single letter—not even open the letter-box—

HELMER. Ah, you are still afraid of that fellow—

NORA. Yes, indeed I am.

HELMER. Nora, I can tell from your looks that there is a letter from him lying there.

NORA. I don't know; I think there is; but you must not read anything of that kind now. Nothing horrid must come between us till this is all over.

RANK. [*whispers to Helmer*] You mustn't contradict her.

HELMER. [*taking her in his arms*] The child shall have her way. But to-morrow night, after you have danced—

NORA. Then you will be free.

[*Maid appears in the doorway to the right.*]

MAID. Dinner is served, ma'am.

NORA. We will have champagne, Helen.

MAID. Very good, ma'am.

[*Exit.*]

HELMER. Hullo!—are we going to have a banquet?

NORA. Yes a champagne banquet till the small hours. [*calls out*] And a few maca-roons, Helen—lots, just for once!

HELMER. Come, come, don't be so wild and nervous. Be my own little skylark, as you used.

NORA. Yes, dear, I will. But go in now and you too, Doctor Rank. Christine, you must help me to do up my hair.

RANK. [*whispers to* HELMER *as they go out*] I suppose there is nothing—she is not expecting anything?

HELMER. Far from it, my dear fellow; it is simply nothing more than this childish nervousness I was telling you of.

[*They go into the right-hand room.*]

NORA. Well!

MRS. LINDE. Gone out of town.

NORA. I could tell from your face.

MRS. LINDE. He is coming home to-morrow evening. I wrote a note for him.

NORA. You should have let it alone; you must prevent nothing. After all, it is splendid to be waiting for a wonderful thing to happen.

MRS. LINDE. What is it that you are waiting for?

NORA. Oh you wouldn't understand. Go in to them, I will come in a moment. [MRS. LINDE *goes into the dining-room.* NORA *stands still for a little while, as if to compose herself. Then she looks at her watch.*] Five o'clock. Seven hours till midnight; and then four-and-twenty hours till the next midnight. Then the Tarantella will be over. Twenty-four and seven? Thirty-one hours to live.

HELMER. [*from the doorway on the right*] Where's my little skylark?

NORA. [*going to him with her arms outstretched*] Here she is!

ACT 3

THE SAME SCENE. *The table has been placed in the middle of the stage, with chairs round it. A lamp is burning on the table. The door into the hall stands open. Dance music is heard in the room above.* MRS. LINDE *is sitting at the table idly turning over the leaves of a book; she tries to read, but does not seem able to collect her thoughts. Every now and then she listens intently for a sound at the outer door.*

MRS. LINDE. [*looking at her watch*] Not yet—and the time is nearly up. If only he does not—. [*listens again*] Ah, there he is. [*Goes into the hall and opens the outer door carefully. Light footsteps are heard on the stairs. She whispers.*] Come in. There is no one here.

KROGSTAD. [*in the doorway*] I found a note from you at home. What does this mean?

MRS. LINDE . It is absolutely necessary that I should have a talk with you.

KROGSTAD. Really? And is it absolutely necessary that it should be here?

MRS. LINDE . It is impossible where I live; there is no private entrance to my rooms. Come in; we are quite alone. The maid is asleep, and the Helmers are at the dance upstairs.

KROGSTAD. [*coming into the room*] Are the Helmers really at a dance to-night?

MRS. LINDE . Yes, why not?

KROGSTAD. Certainly—Why not?

MRS. LINDE . Now, Nils, let us have a talk.

KROGSTAD. Can we two have anything to talk about?

MRS. LINDE . We have a great deal to talk about.

KROGSTAD. I shouldn't have thought so.

MRS. LINDE. No, you have never properly understood me.

KROGSTAD. Was there anything else to understand except what was obvious to all the world—a heartless woman jilts a man when a more lucrative chance turns up?

MRS. LINDE. Do you believe I am as absolutely heartless as all that? And do you believe that I did it with a light heart?

KROGSTAD. Didn't you?

MRS. LINDE. Nils, did you really think that?

KROGSTAD. If it were as you say, why did you write to me as you did at the time?

MRS. LINDE. I could do nothing else. As I had to break with you, it was my duty also to put an end to all that you felt for me.

KROGSTAD. [*wringing his hands*] So that was it, and all this—only for the sake of money!

MRS. LINDE. You must not forget that I had a helpless mother and two little brothers. We couldn't wait for you, Nils; your prospects seemed hopeless then.

KROGSTAD. That may be so, but you had no right to throw me over for any one else's sake.

MRS. LINDE. Indeed I don't know. Many a time did I ask myself if I had the right to do it.

KROGSTAD. [*more gently*] When I lost you, it was as if all the solid ground went from under my feet. Look at me now—I am a shipwrecked man clinging to a bit of wreckage.

MRS. LINDE. But help may be near.

KROGSTAD. It *was* near; but then you came and stood in my way.

MRS. LINDE. Unintentionally, Nils. It was only to-day that I learnt it was your place I was going to take in the Bank.

KROGSTAD. I believe you, if you say so. But now that you know it, are you not going to give it up to me?

MRS. LINDE. No, because that would not benefit you in the least.

KROGSTAD. Oh, benefit, benefit—I would have done it whether or no.

MRS. LINDE. I have learnt to act prudently. Life, and hard, bitter necessity have taught me that.

KROGSTAD. And life has taught me not to believe in fine speeches.

MRS. LINDE. Then life has taught you something very reasonable. But deeds you must believe in.

KROGSTAD. What do you mean by that?

MRS. LINDE. You said you were like a shipwrecked man clinging to some wreckage.

KROGSTAD. I had good reason to say so.

MRS. LINDE. Well, I am like a shipwrecked woman clinging to some wreckage—no one to mourn for, no one to care for.

KROGSTAD. It was your own choice.

MRS. LINDE. There was no other choice—then.

Krogstad. Well, what now?

Mrs. Linde. Nils, how would it be if we two shipwrecked people could join forces?

Krogstad. What are you saying?

Mrs. Linde. Two on the same piece of wreckage would stand a better chance than each on their own.

Krogstad. Christine!

Mrs. Linde. What do you suppose brought me to town?

Krogstad. Do you mean that you gave me a thought?

Mrs. Linde. I could not endure life without work. All my life, as long as I can remember, I have worked, and it has been my greatest and only pleasure. But now I am quite alone in the world—my life is so dreadfully empty and I feel so forsaken. There is not the least pleasure in working for one's self. Nils, give me someone and something to work for.

Krogstad. I don't trust that. It is nothing but a woman's overstrained sense of generosity that prompts you to make such an offer of yourself.

Mrs. Linde. Have you ever noticed anything of the sort in me?

Krogstad. Could you really do it? Tell me—do you know all about my past life?

Mrs. Linde. Yes.

Krogstad. And do you know what they think of me here?

Mrs. Linde. You seemed to me to imply that with me you might have been quite another man.

Krogstad. I am certain of it.

Mrs. Linde. Is it too late now?

Krogstad. Christine, are you saying this deliberately? Yes, I am sure you are. I see it in your face. Have you really the courage, then—?

Mrs. Linde. I want to be a mother to someone, and your children need a mother. We two need each other. Nils, I have faith in your real character—I can dare anything together with you.

Krogstad. [*grasps her hands*] Thanks, thanks, Christine! Now I shall find a way to clear myself in the eyes of the world. Ah, but I forgot—

Mrs. Linde. [*listening*] Hush! The Tarantella! Go, go!

Krogstad. Why? What is it?

Mrs. Linde. Do you hear them up there? When that is over, we may expect them back.

Krogstad. Yes, yes—I will go. But it is all no use. Of course you are not aware what steps I have taken in the matter of the Helmers.

Mrs. Linde. Yes, I know all about that.

Krogstad. And in spite of that have you the courage to—?

Mrs. Linde. I understand very well to what lengths a man like you might be driven by despair.

Krogstad. If I could only undo what I have done!

Mrs. Linde. You can. Your letter is lying in the letter-box now.

Krogstad. Are you sure of that?

Mrs. Linde. Quite sure, but—

Krogstad. [*with a searching look at her*] Is that what it all means?—that you want to save your friend at any cost? Tell me frankly. Is that it?

Mrs. Linde. Nils, a woman who has once sold herself for another's sake, doesn't do it a second time.

Krogstad. I will ask for my letter back.

MRS. LINDE. No, no.

KROGSTAD. Yes, of course I will. I will wait here till Helmer comes; I will tell him he must give me my letter back—that it only concerns my dismissal—that he is not to read it—

MRS. LINDE. No, Nils, you must not recall your letter.

KROGSTAD. But, tell me, wasn't it for that very purpose that you asked me to meet you here?

MRS. LINDE. In my first moment of fright, it was. But twenty-four hours have elapsed since then, and in that time I have witnessed incredible things in this house. Helmer must know all about it. This unhappy secret must be disclosed; they must have a complete understanding between them, which is impossible with all this concealment and falsehood going on.

KROGSTAD. Very well, if you will take the responsibility. But there is one thing I can do in any case, and I shall do it at once.

MRS. LINDE. [*listening*] You must be quick and go! The dance is over; we are not safe a moment longer.

KROGSTAD. I will wait for you below.

MRS. LINDE. Yes, do. You must see me back to my door.

KROGSTAD. I have never had such an amazing piece of good fortune in my life.

[*Goes out through the outer door. The door between the room and the hall remains open.*]

MRS. LINDE. [*tidying up the room and laying her hat and cloak ready*] What a difference! what a difference! Someone to work for and live for—a home to bring comfort into. That I will do, indeed. I wish they would be quick and come— [*listens*] Ah, there they are now. I must put on my things.

[*Takes up her hat and cloak.* HELMER's *and* NORA's *voices are heard outside; a key is turned, and* HELMER *brings* NORA *almost by force into the hall. She is in an Italian costume with a large black shawl round her; he is in evening dress and a black domino which is flying open.*]

NORA. [*hanging back in the doorway, and struggling with him*] No, no, no!—don't take me in. I want to go upstairs again; I don't want to leave so early.

HELMER. But, my dearest Nora—

NORA. Please, Torvald dear—please, *please*—only an hour more.

HELMER. Not a single minute, my sweet Nora. You know that was our agreement. Come along into the room; you are catching cold standing there.

[*He brings her gently into the room, in spite of her resistance.*]

MRS. LINDE. Good evening.

NORA. Christine!

HELMER. You here, so late, Mrs. Linde?

MRS. LINDE. Yes, you must excuse me; I was so anxious to see Nora in her dress.

NORA. Have you been sitting here waiting for me?

MRS. LINDE. Yes, unfortunately I came too late, you had already gone upstairs; and I thought I couldn't go away without having seen you.

HELMER. [*taking off Nora's shawl*] Yes, take a good look at her. I think she is worth looking at. Isn't she charming, Mrs. Linde?

MRS. LINDE. Yes, indeed she is.

HELMER. Doesn't she look remarkably pretty? Everyone thought so at the dance. But she is terribly self-willed, this sweet little person. What are we to do with her? You will hardly believe that I had almost to bring her away by force.

NORA. Torvald, you will repent not having let me stay, even if it were only for half an hour.

HELMER. Listen to her, Mrs. Linde! She had danced her Tarantella, and it had been a tremendous success, as it deserved—although possibly the performance was a trifle too realistic—a little more so, I mean, than was strictly compatible with the limitations of art. But never mind about that! The chief thing is, she had made a success—she had made a tremendous success. Do you think I was going to let her remain there after that, and spoil the effect? No indeed! I took my charming little Capri maiden—my capricious little Capri maiden, I should say—on my arm; took one quick turn round the room; a curtsey on either side, and, as they say in novels, the beautiful apparition disappeared. An exit ought always to be effective, Mrs. Linde; but that is what I cannot make Nora understand. Pooh! this room is hot. [*throws his domino on a chair and opens the door of his room*] Hullo! it's all dark in here. Oh, of course—excuse me—.

[*He goes in and lights some candles.*]

NORA. [*in a hurried and breathless whisper*] Well?

MRS. LINDE. [*in a low voice*] I have had a talk with him.

NORA. Yes, and—

MRS. LINDE. Nora, you must tell your husband all about it.

NORA. [*in an expressionless voice*] I knew it.

MRS. LINDE. You have nothing to be afraid of as far as Krogstad is concerned; but you must tell him.

NORA. I won't tell him.

MRS. LINDE. Then the letter will.

NORA. Thank you, Christine. Now I know what I must do. Hush—!

HELMER. [*coming in again*] Well, Mrs. Linde, have you admired her?

MRS. LINDE. Yes, and now I will say good-night.

HELMER. What already? Is this yours, this knitting?

MRS. LINDE. [*taking it*] Yes, thank you, I had very nearly forgotten it.

HELMER. So you knit?

MRS. LINDE. Of course.

HELMER. Do you know, you ought to embroider.

MRS. LINDE. Really? Why?

HELMER. Yes, it's far more becoming. Let me show you. You hold the embroidery thus in your left hand, and use the needle with the right—like this—with a long, easy sweep. Do you see?

MRS. LINDE. Yes, perhaps—

HELMER. But in the case of knitting—that can never be anything but ungraceful; look here—the arms close together, the knitting-needles going up and down—it has a sort of Chinese effect—. That was really excellent champagne they gave us.

MRS. LINDE. Well,—good-night, Nora, and don't be self-willed any more.

HELMER. That's right, Mrs. Linde.

MRS. LINDE. Good-night, Mr. Helmer.

HELMER. [*accompanying her to the door*] Good-night, good-night. I hope you will get home all right. I should be very happy to—but you haven't any great distance to go. Good-night, good-night. [*She goes out; he shuts the door after her, and comes in again.*] Ah!—at last we have got rid of her. She is a frightful bore, that woman.

NORA. Aren't you very tired, Torvald?

HELMER. No, not in the least.

NORA. Nor sleepy?

HELMER. Not a bit. On the contrary, I feel extraordinarily lively. And you?—you really look both tired and sleepy.

NORA. Yes, I am very tired. I want to go to sleep at once.

HELMER. There, you see it was quite right of me not to let you stay there any longer.

NORA. Everything you do is quite right, Torvald.

HELMER. [*kissing her on the forehead*] Now my little skylark is speaking reasonably. Did you notice what good spirits Rank was in this evening?

NORA. Really? Was he? I didn't speak to him at all.

HELMER. And I very little, but I have not for a long time seen him in such good form. [*looks for a while at her and then goes nearer to her*] It is delightful to be at home by ourselves again, to be all alone with you—you fascinating, charming little darling!

NORA. Don't look at me like that, Torvald.

HELMER. Why shouldn't I look at my dearest treasure?—at all the beauty that is mine, all my very own?

NORA. [*going to the other side of the table*] You mustn't say things like that to me tonight.

HELMER. [*following her*] You have still got the Tarantella in your blood, I see. And it makes you more captivating than ever. Listen—the guests are beginning to go now. [*in a lower voice*] Nora—soon the whole house will be quiet.

NORA. Yes, I hope so.

HELMER. Yes, my own darling Nora. Do you know, when I am out at a party with you like this, why I speak so little to you, keep away from you, and only send a stolen glance in your direction now and then?—do you know why I do that? It is because I make believe to myself that we are secretly in love, and you are my secretly promised bride, and that no one suspects there is anything between us.

NORA. Yes, yes—I know very well your thoughts are with me all the time.

HELMER. And when we are leaving, and I am putting the shawl over your beautiful young shoulders—on your lovely neck—then I imagine that you are my young bride and that we have just come from the wedding, and I am bringing you for the first time into our home—to be alone with you for the first time—quite alone with my shy little darling! All this evening I have longed for nothing but you. When I watched the seductive figures of the Tarantella, my blood was on fire; I could endure it no longer, and that was why I brought you down so early—

NORA. Go away, Torvald! You must let me go. I won't—

HELMER. What's that? You're joking, my little, Nora! You won't? Am I not your husband—?

[*A knock is heard at the outer door.*]

NORA. [*starting*] Did you hear—?

HELMER. [*going into the hall*] Who is it?

RANK. [*outside*] It is I. May I come in for a moment?

HELMER. [*in a fretful whisper*] Oh, what does he want now? [*aloud*] Wait a minute!
[*unlocks the door*] Come, that's kind of you not to pass by our door.

RANK. I thought I heard your voice, and felt as if I should like to look in. [*with a
swift glance round*] Ah, yes!—these dear familiar rooms. You are very happy
and cosy in here, you two.

HELMER. It seems to me that you looked after yourself pretty well upstairs too.

RANK. Excellently. Why shouldn't I? Why shouldn't one enjoy everything in this
world?—at any rate as much as one can, and as long as one can. The wine was
capital—

HELMER. Especially the champagne.

RANK. So you noticed that too? It is almost incredible how much I managed to
put away!

NORA. Torvald drank a great deal of champagne tonight, too.

RANK. Did he?

NORA. Yes, and he is always in such good spirits afterwards.

RANK. Well, why should one not enjoy a merry evening after a well-spent day?

HELMER. Well spent? I am afraid I can't take credit for that.

RANK. [*clapping him on the back*] But I can, you know!

NORA. Doctor Rank, you must have been occupied with some scientific investigation to-day.

RANK. Exactly.

HELMER. Just listen!—little Nora talking about scientific investigations!

NORA. And may I congratulate you on the result?

RANK. Indeed you may.

NORA. Was it favourable, then?

RANK. The best possible, for both doctor and patient—certainty.

NORA. [*quickly and searchingly*] Certainty?

RANK. Absolute certainty. So wasn't I entitled to make a merry evening of it after
that?

NORA. Yes, you certainly were, Doctor Rank.

HELMER. I think so too, so long as you don't have to pay for it in the morning.

RANK. Oh well, one can't have anything in this life without paying for it.

NORA. Doctor Rank—are you fond of fancy-dress balls?

RANK. Yes, if there is a fine lot of pretty costumes.

NORA. Tell me—what shall we two wear at the next?

HELMER. Little featherbrain!—are you thinking of the next already?

RANK. We two? Yes, I can tell you. You shall go as a good fairy—

HELMER. Yes, but what do you suggest as an appropriate costume for that?

RANK. Let your wife go dressed just as she is in everyday life.

HELMER. That was really very prettily turned. But can't you tell us what you
will be?

RANK. Yes, my dear friend, I have quite made up my mind about that.

HELMER. Well?

RANK. At the next fancy dress ball I shall be invisible.

HELMER. That's a good joke!

RANK. There is a big black hat—have you never heard of hats that make you
invisible? If you put one on, no one can see you.

HELMER. [*suppressing a smile*] Yes, you are quite right.

RANK. But I am clean forgetting what I came for. Helmer, give me a cigar—one of the dark Havanas.

HELMER. With the greatest pleasure. [*offers him his case*]

RANK. [*takes a cigar and cuts off the end*] Thanks.

NORA. [*striking a match*] Let me give you a light.

RANK. Thank you. [*she holds the match for him to light his cigar.*] And now good-bye!

HELMER. Good-bye, good-bye, dear old man!

NORA. Sleep well, Doctor Rank.

RANK. Thank you for that wish.

NORA. Wish me the same.

RANK. You? Well, if you want me to sleep well! And thanks for the light.

> [*He nods to them both and goes out.*]

HELMER. [*in a subdued voice*] He has drunk more than he ought.

NORA. [*absently*] Maybe. [HELMER *takes a bunch of keys out of his pocket and goes into the hall.*] Torvald! what are you going to do there?

HELMER. Empty the letter-box; it is quite full; there will be no room to put the newspaper in to-morrow morning.

NORA. Are you going to work to-night?

HELMER. You know quite well I'm not. What is this? Some one has been at the lock.

NORA. At the lock—

HELMER. Yes, someone has. What can it mean? I should never have thought the maid—. Here is a broken hairpin. Nora, it is one of yours.

NORA. [*quickly*] Then it must have been the children—

HELMER. Then you must get them out of those ways. There, at last I have got it open. [*Takes out the contents of the letter-box, and calls to the kitchen.*] Helen!— Helen, put out the light over the front door. [*Goes back into the room and shuts the door into the hall. He holds out his hand full of letters.*] Look at that—look what a heap of them there are. [*turning them over*] What on earth is that?

NORA. [*at the window*] The letter—No! Torvald, no!

HELMER. Two cards—of Rank's.

NORA. Of Doctor Rank's?

HELMER. [*looking at them*] Doctor Rank. They were on the top. He must have put them in when he went out.

NORA. Is there anything written on them?

HELMER. There is a black cross over the name. Look there—what an uncomfortable idea! It looks as if he were announcing his own death.

NORA. It is just what he is doing.

HELMER. What? Do you know anything about it? Has he said anything to you?

NORA. Yes. He told me that when the cards came it would be his leave-taking from us. He means to shut himself up and die.

HELMER. My poor old friend. Certainly I knew we should not have him very long with us. But so soon! And so he hides himself away like a wounded animal.

NORA. If it has to happen, it is best it should be without a word—don't you think so, Torvald?

HELMER. [*walking up and down*] He had so grown into our lives. I can't think of him as having gone out of them. He, with his sufferings and his loneliness, was like a cloudy background to our sunlit happiness. Well, perhaps it is best so. For him, anyway. [*standing still*] And perhaps for us too, Nora. We two are thrown quite upon each other now. [*puts his arms round her*] My darling wife, I don't feel as if I could hold you tight enough. Do you know, Nora, I have often wished that you might be threatened by some great danger, so that I might risk my life's blood, and everything, for your sake.

NORA. [*disengages herself, and says firmly and decidedly*] Now you must read your letters Torvald.

HELMER. No, no; not to-night. I want to be with you, my darling wife.

NORA. With the thought of your friend's death—

HELMER. You are right, it has affected us both. Something ugly has come between us—the thought of the horrors of death. We must try and rid our minds of that. Until then—we will each go to our own room.

NORA. [*hanging on his neck*] Good-night, Torvald—Good-night!

HELMER. [*kissing her on the forehead.*] Good-night, my little singing-bird. Sleep sound, Nora. Now I will read my letters through.

> [*He takes his letters and goes into his room,*
> *shutting the door after him.*]

NORA. [*gropes distractedly about, seizes* HELMER'*s domino, throws it round her, while she says in quick, hoarse, spasmodic whispers*] Never to see him again. Never! Never! [*puts her shawl over her head*] Never to see my children again either— never again. Never! Never!—Ah! the icy, black water—the unfathomable depths—If only it were over! He has got it now—now he is reading it. Good-bye, Torvald and my children!

> [*She is about to rush out through the hall, when* HELMER *opens his door hurriedly and stands with an open letter in his hand.*]

HELMER. Nora!

NORA. Ah!—

HELMER. What is this? Do you know what is in this letter?

NORA. Yes, I know. Let me go! Let me get out!

HELMER. [*holding her back*] Where are you going?

NORA. [*trying to get free*] You shan't save me, Torvald!

HELMER. [*reeling*] True? Is this true, that I read here? Horrible! No, no—it is impossible that it can be true.

NORA. It is true. I have loved you above everything else in the world.

HELMER. Oh, don't let us have any silly excuses.

NORA. [*taking a step towards him*] Torvald—!

HELMER. Miserable creature—what have you done?

NORA. Let me go. You shall not suffer for my sake. You shall not take it upon yourself.

HELMER. No tragedy airs, please. [*locks the hall door*] Here you shall stay and give me an explanation. Do you understand what you have done? Answer me? Do you understand what you have done?

NORA. [*looks steadily at him and says with a growing look of coldness in her face*] Yes, now I am beginning to understand thoroughly.

HELMER. [*walking about the room*] What a horrible awakening! All these eight years—she who was my joy and pride—a hypocrite, a liar—worse, worse—a criminal! The unutterable ugliness of it all! For shame! For shame! [NORA *is silent and looks steadily at him. He stops in front of her.*] I ought to have suspected that something of the sort would happen. I ought to have foreseen it. All your father's want of principle—be silent!—all your father's want of principle has come out in you. No religion, no morality, no sense of duty—. How I am punished for having winked at what he did! I did it for your sake, and this is how you repay me.

NORA. Yes, that's just it.

HELMER. Now you have destroyed all my happiness. You have ruined all my future. It is horrible to think of! I am in the power of an unscrupulous man; he can do what he likes with me, ask anything he likes of me, give me any orders he pleases—I dare not refuse. And I must sink to such miserable depths because of a thoughtless woman!

NORA. When I am out of the way, you will be free.

HELMER. No fine speeches, please. Your father had always plenty of those ready, too. What good would it be to me if you were out of the way, as you say? Not the slightest. He can make the affair known everywhere; and if he does, I may be falsely suspected of having been a party to your criminal action. Very likely people will think I was behind it all—that it was I who prompted you! And I have to thank you for all this—you whom I have cherished during the whole of our married life. Do you understand now what it is you have done for me?

NORA. [*coldly and quietly*] Yes.

HELMER. It is so incredible that I can't take it in. But we must come to some understanding. Take off that shawl. Take it off, I tell you. I must try and appease him some way or another. The matter must be hushed up at any cost. And as for you and me, it must appear as if everything between us were just as before—but naturally only in the eyes of the world. You will still remain in my house, that is a matter of course. But I shall not allow you to bring up the children; I dare not trust them to you. To think that I should be obliged to say so to one whom I have loved so dearly, and whom I still—. No, that is all over. From this moment happiness is not the question; all that concerns us is to save the remains, the fragments, the appearance—

[*A ring is heard at the front-door bell.*]

HELMER. [*with a start*] What is that? So late! Can the worst—? Can he—? Hide yourself, Nora. Say you are ill.

[NORA *stands motionless.* HELMER *goes and unlocks the hall door.*]

MAID. [*half-dressed, comes to the door*] A letter for the mistress.

HELMER. Give it to me. [*takes the letter, and shuts the door*] Yes, it is from him. You shall not have it; I will read it myself.

NORA. Yes, read it.

HELMER. [*standing by the lamp*] I scarcely have the courage to do it. It may mean ruin for both of us. No, I must know. [*tears open the letter, runs his eye over a few lines, looks at a paper enclosed and gives a shout of joy*] Nora! [*she looks at him questioningly.*] Nora!—No, I must read it once again—. Yes, it is true! I am saved! Nora, I am saved!

NORA. And I?

HELMER. You too, of course; we are both saved, both you and I. Look, he sends you your bond back. He says he regrets and repents—that a happy change in his life—never mind what he says! We are saved, Nora! No one can do anything to you. Oh, Nora, Nora!—no, first I must destroy these hateful things. Let me see—[*takes a look at the bond*] No, no, I won't look at it. The whole thing shall be nothing but a bad dream to me. [*tears up the bond and both letters, throws them all into the stove, and watches them burn*] There—now it doesn't exist any longer. He says that since Christmas Eve you—. These must have been three dreadful days for you, Nora.

NORA. I have fought a hard fight these three days.

HELMER. And suffered agonies, and seen no way out but—. No, we won't call any of the horrors to mind. We will only shout with joy, and keep saying "It's all over! It's all over!" Listen to me, Nora. You don't seem to realise that it is all over. What is this?—such a cold, set face! My poor little Nora, I quite understand; you don't feel as if you could believe that I have forgiven you. But it is true, Nora, I swear it; I have forgiven you everything. I know that what you did, you did out of love for me.

NORA. That is true.

HELMER. You have loved me as a wife ought to love her husband. Only you had not sufficient knowledge to judge of the means you used. But do you suppose you are any the less dear to me, because you don't understand how to act on your own responsibility? No, no; only lean on me; I will advise you and direct you. I should not be a man if this womanly helplessness did not just give you a double attractiveness in my eyes. You must not think any more about the hard things I said in my first moment of consternation, when I thought everything was going to overwhelm me. I have forgiven you, Nora; I swear to you I have forgiven you.

NORA. Thank you for your forgiveness.

[She goes out through the door to the right.]

HELMER. No, don't go—. [*looks in*] What are you doing in there?

NORA. [*from within*] Taking off my fancy dress.

HELMER. [*standing at the open door*] Yes, do. Try and calm yourself, and make your mind easy again, my frightened little singing-bird. Be at rest, and feel secure; I have broad wings to shelter you under. [*walks up and down by the door*] How warm and cosy our home is, Nora. Here is shelter for you; here I will protect you like a hunted dove that I have saved from a hawk's claws. I will bring peace to your poor beating heart. It will come, little by little, Nora, believe me. Tomorrow morning you will look upon it all quite differently; soon everything will be just as it was before. Very soon you won't need me to assure you that I have forgiven you; you will yourself feel the certainty that I have done so. Can you suppose I should ever think of such a thing as repudiating you, or even reproaching you? You have no idea what a true man's heart is like, Nora. There is something so indescribably sweet and satisfying, to a man, in the knowledge that he has forgiven his wife—forgiven her freely, and with all his heart. It seems as if that had made her, as it were, doubly his own; he has given her a new life, so to speak; and she has in a way become both wife and child to him. So you shall be for me after this, my little scared, helpless darling. Have no anxiety about anything, Nora; only be frank and open with me, and I will serve as will and conscience both to you—. What is this? Not gone to bed? Have you changed your things?

NORA. [*in everyday dress*] Yes, Torvald, I have changed my things now.

HELMER. But what for?—so late as this.

NORA. I shall not sleep to-night.

HELMER. But, my dear Nora—

NORA. [*looking at her watch*] It is not so very late. Sit down here, Torvald. You and I have much to say to one another.

[*She sits down at one side of the table.*]

HELMER. Nora—what is this?—this cold, set face?

NORA. Sit down, it will take some time; I have a lot to talk over with you.

HELMER. [*sits down at the opposite side of the table*] You alarm me, Nora!—and I don't understand you.

NORA. No, that is just it. You don't understand me, and I have never understood you either—before to-night. No, you mustn't interrupt me. You must simply listen to what I say. Torvald, this is a settling of accounts.

HELMER. What do you mean by that?

NORA. [*after a short silence*] Isn't there one thing that strikes you as strange in our sitting here like this?

HELMER. What is that?

NORA. We have been married now eight years. Does it not occur to you that this is the first time we two, you and I, husband and wife, have had a serious conversation?

HELMER. What do you mean by serious?

NORA. In all these eight years—longer than that—from the very beginning of our acquaintance, we have never exchanged a word on any serious subject.

HELMER. Was it likely that I would be continually and forever telling you about worries that you could not help me to bear?

NORA. I am not speaking about business matters. I say that we have never sat down in earnest together to try and get at the bottom of anything.

HELMER. But, dearest Nora, would it have been any good to you?

NORA. That is just it; you have never understood me. I have been greatly wronged, Torvald—first by papa and then by you.

HELMER. What! By us two—by us two, who have loved you better than anyone else in the world?

NORA. [*shaking her head*] You have never loved me. You have only thought it pleasant to be in love with me.

HELMER. Nora, what do I hear you saying?

NORA. It is perfectly true, Torvald. When I was at home with papa, he told me his opinion about everything, and so I had the same opinions; and if I differed from him I concealed the fact, because he would not have liked it. He called me his doll-child, and he played with me just as I used to play with my dolls. And when I came to live with you—

HELMER. What sort of an expression is that to use about our marriage?

NORA. [*undisturbed*] I mean that I was simply transferred from papa's hands into yours. You arranged everything according to your own taste, and so I got the same tastes as you—or else I pretended to, I am really not quite sure which— I think sometimes the one and sometimes the other. When I look back on it, it seems to me as if I had been living here like a poor woman—just from hand to mouth. I have existed merely to perform tricks for you, Torvald. But you would have it so. You and papa have committed a great sin against me. It is your fault that I have made nothing of my life.

HELMER. How unreasonable and how ungrateful you are, Nora! Have you not been happy here?

NORA. No, I have never been happy. I thought I was, but it has never really been so.

HELMER. Not—not happy!

NORA. No, only merry. And you have always been so kind to me. But our home has been nothing but a playroom. I have been your doll-wife, just as at home I was papa's doll-child; and here the children have been my dolls. I thought it great fun when you played with me, just as they thought it great fun when I played with them. That is what our marriage has been, Torvald.

HELMER. There is some truth in what you say—exaggerated and strained as your view of it is. But for the future it shall be different. Playtime shall be over, and lesson-time shall begin.

NORA. Whose lessons? Mine, or the children's?

HELMER. Both yours and the children's, my darling Nora.

NORA. Alas, Torvald, you are not the man to educate me into being a proper wife for you.

HELMER. And you can say that!

NORA. And I—how am I fitted to bring up the children?

HELMER. Nora!

Torvald Helmer (Sam Waterston) begs Nora (Liv Ullmann) to reconsider her decision to leave home in the Joseph Papp New York Shakespeare Festival production (1995) of *A Doll's House* (director, Tormod Skagestad).

NORA. Didn't you say so yourself a little while ago—that you dare not trust me to bring them up?

HELMER. In a moment of anger! Why do you pay any heed to that?

NORA. Indeed, you were perfectly right. I am not fit for the task. There is another task I must undertake first. I must try and educate myself—you are not the man to help me in that. I must do that for myself. And that is why I am going to leave you now.

HELMER. [*springing up*] What do you say?

NORA. I must stand quite alone, if I am to understand myself and everything about me. It is for that reason that I cannot remain with you any longer.

HELMER. Nora! Nora!

NORA. I am going away from here now, at once. I am sure Christine will take me in for the night—

HELMER. You are out of your mind! I won't allow it! I forbid you!

NORA. It is no use forbidding me anything any longer. I will take with me what belongs to myself. I will take nothing from you, either now or later.

HELMER. What sort of madness is this!

NORA. To-morrow I shall go home—I mean, to my old home. It will be easiest for me to find something to do there.

HELMER. You blind, foolish woman!

NORA. I must try and get some sense, Torvald.

HELMER. To desert your home, your husband and your children! And you don't consider what people will say!

NORA. I cannot consider that at all. I only know that it is necessary for me.

HELMER. It's shocking. This is how you would neglect your most sacred duties.

NORA. What do you consider my most sacred duties?

HELMER. Do I need to tell you that? Are they not your duties to your husband and your children?

NORA. I have other duties just as sacred.

HELMER. That you have not. What duties could those be?

NORA. Duties to myself.

HELMER. Before all else, you are a wife and a mother.

NORA. I don't believe that any longer. I believe that before all else I am a reasonable human being, just as you are—or, at all events, that I must try and become one. I know quite well, Torvald, that most people would think you right, and that views of that kind are to be found in books; but I can no longer content myself with what most people say, or with what is found in books. I must think over things for myself and get to understand them.

HELMER. Can you not understand your place in your own home? Have you not a reliable guide in such matters as that?—have you no religion?

NORA. I am afraid, Torvald, I do not exactly know what religion is.

HELMER. What are you saying?

NORA. I know nothing but what the clergyman said when I went to be confirmed. He told us that religion was this, and that, and the other. When I am away from all this, and am alone, I will look into that matter too. I will see if what the clergyman said is true, or at all events if it is true for me.

HELMER. This is unheard of in a girl of your age! But if religion cannot lead you aright, let me try and awaken your conscience. I suppose you have some moral sense? Or—answer me—am I to think you have none?

Nora. I assure you, Torvald, that is not an easy question to answer. I really don't know. The thing perplexes me altogether. I only know that you and I look at it in quite a different light. I am learning, too, that the law is quite another thing from what I supposed; but I find it impossible to convince myself that the law is right. According to it a woman has no right to spare her old dying father, or to save her husband's life. I can't believe that.

Helmer. You talk like a child. You don't understand the conditions of the world in which you live.

Nora. No, I don't. But now I am going to try. I am going to see if I can make out who is right, the world or I.

Helmer. You are ill, Nora; you are delirious; I almost think you are out of your mind.

Nora. I have never felt my mind so clear and certain as to-night.

Helmer. And is it with a clear and certain mind that you forsake your husband and your children?

Nora. Yes, it is.

Helmer. Then there is only one possible explanation.

Nora. What is that?

Helmer. You do not love me any more.

Nora. No, that is just it.

Helmer. Nora!—and you can say that?

Nora. It gives me great pain, Torvald, for you have always been so kind to me, but I cannot help it. I do not love you any more.

Helmer. [*regaining his composure*] Is that a clear and certain conviction too?

Nora. Yes, absolutely clear and certain. That is the reason why I will not stay here any longer.

Helmer. And can you tell me what I have done to forfeit your love?

Nora. Yes, indeed I can. It was to-night, when the wonderful thing did not happen; then I saw you were not the man I had thought you.

Helmer. Explain yourself better—I don't understand you.

Nora. I have waited so patiently for eight years; for, goodness knows, I knew very well that wonderful things don't happen every day. Then this horrible misfortune came upon me; and then I felt quite certain that the wonderful thing was going to happen at last. When Krogstad's letter was lying out there, never for a moment did I imagine that you would consent to accept this man's conditions. I was so absolutely certain that you would say to him: Publish the thing to the whole world. And when that was done—

Helmer. Yes, what then?—when I had exposed my wife to shame and disgrace?

Nora. When that was done, I was so absolutely certain, you would come forward and take everything upon yourself, and say I am the guilty one.

Helmer. Nora—!

Nora. You mean that I would never have accepted such a sacrifice on your part? No, of course not. But what would my assurances have been worth against yours? That was the wonderful thing which I hoped for and feared; and it was to prevent that, that I wanted to kill myself.

Helmer. I would gladly work night and day for you, Nora—bear sorrow and want for your sake. But no man would sacrifice his honour for the one he loves.

Nora. It is a thing hundreds of thousands of women have done.

Helmer. Oh, you think and talk like a heedless child.

NORA. Maybe. But you neither think nor talk like the man I could bind myself to. As soon as your fear was over—and it was not fear for what threatened me, but for what might happen to you—when the whole thing was past, as far as you were concerned it was exactly as if nothing at all had happened. Exactly as before, I was your little skylark, your doll, which you would in future treat with doubly gentle care, because it was so brittle and fragile. [*getting up*] Torvald—it was then it dawned upon me that for eight years I had been living here with a strange man, and had borne him three children—. Oh, I can't bear to think of it! I could tear myself into little bits!

HELMER. [*sadly*] I see, I see. An abyss has opened between us—there is no denying it. But, Nora, would it not be possible to fill it up?

NORA. As I am now, I am no wife for you.

HELMER. I have it in me to become a different man.

NORA. Perhaps—if your doll is taken away from you.

HELMER. But to part!—to part from you! No, no, Nora, I can't understand that idea.

NORA. [*going out to the right*] That makes it all the more certain that it must be done.

[*She comes back with her cloak and hat and a small bag which she puts on a chair by the table.*]

HELMER. Nora, Nora, not now! Wait till to-morrow.

NORA. [*putting on her cloak*] I cannot spend the night in a strange man's room.

HELMER. But can't we live here like brother and sister—?

NORA. [*putting on her hat*] You know very well that would not last long. [*puts the shawl round her*] Good-bye, Torvald. I won't see the little ones. I know they are in better hands than mine. As I am now, I can be of no use to them.

HELMER. But some day, Nora—some day?

NORA. How can I tell? I have no idea what is going to become of me.

HELMER. But you are my wife, whatever becomes of you.

NORA. Listen, Torvald. I have heard that when a wife deserts her husband's house, as I am doing now, he is legally freed from all obligations towards her. In any case I set you free from all your obligations. You are not to feel yourself bound in the slightest way, any more than I shall. There must be perfect freedom on both sides. See here is your ring back. Give me mine.

HELMER. That too?

NORA. That too.

HELMER. Here it is.

NORA. That's right. Now it is all over. I have put the keys here. The maids know all about everything in the house—better than I do. To-morrow, after I have left her, Christine will come here and pack up my own things that I brought with me from home. I will have them sent after me.

HELMER. All over! All over!—Nora, shall you never think of me again?

NORA. I know I shall often think of you and the children and this house.

HELMER. May I write to you, Nora?

NORA. No—never. You must not do that.

HELMER. But at least let me send you—

NORA. Nothing—nothing—

HELMER. Let me help you if you are in want.

NORA. No. I can receive nothing from a stranger.

HELMER. Nora—can I never be anything more than a stranger to you?

NORA. [*taking her bag*] Ah, Torvald, the most wonderful thing of all would have to happen.

HELMER. Tell me what that would be!

NORA. Both you and I would have to be so changed that—. Oh, Torvald, I don't believe any longer in wonderful things happening.

HELMER. But I will believe in it. Tell me? So changed that—?

NORA. That our life together would be a real wedlock. Good-bye.

[*She goes out through the hall.*]

HELMER. [*sinks down on a chair at the door and buries his face in his hands*] Nora! Nora! [*looks round, and rises*] Empty. She is gone. [*A hope flashes across his mind.*] The most wonderful thing of all—?

[*The sound of a door slamming is heard from below.*]

(1879)

Questions for Discussion and Writing

1. What do the early conversations between Nora and Torvald tell us about their relationship?
2. At what point did you realize that Nora was going to leave her husband?
3. What or who is the main antagonist? Is it a person, an environment, or a social force? Is there more than one?
4. This play follows traditional dramatic structure rather closely. What point would you identify as the climax?
5. Why do Torvald's arguments against Nora's leaving fail?
6. Is Ibsen attacking marriage? What else may he be attacking?
7. What will become of Nora? Will she find happiness and fulfillment? Write an essay about Nora's future.
8. Write an essay in which you support this claim: "*A Doll's House* concerns the trouble caused by clinging to illusions."

Susan Glaspell *1882–1948*

Born in Davenport, Iowa, Susan Glaspell took a degree in philosophy from Drake University before becoming a newspaper reporter in Des Moines. She turned her play *Trifles*, based on a murder case she covered on the job, into a widely anthologized short story, "A Jury of Her Peers." She married a freethinker who also believed in free love and unfettered drinking, making her life with him difficult. The couple moved to the East Coast, where they founded the Provincetown Players, an experimental theater group. Glaspell won the 1931 Pulitzer Prize for her play *Alison's House*, which depicted the life of Emily Dickinson. She said she promoted "all progressive movements, whether feminist, social, or economic."

🖎 Trifles

CHARACTERS

COUNTY ATTORNEY	HALE
MRS. PETERS	MRS. HALE
SHERIFF	

SCENE

The kitchen in the now abandoned farmhouse of JOHN WRIGHT, *a gloomy kitchen, and left without having been put in order—the walls covered with a faded wallpaper. Down right is a door leading to the parlor. On the right wall above this door is a built-in kitchen cupboard with shelves in the upper portion and drawers below. In the rear wall at right, up two steps is a door opening onto stairs leading to the second floor. In the rear wall at left is a door to the shed and from there to the outside. Between these two doors is an old-fashioned black iron stove. Running along the left wall from the shed door is an old iron sink and sink shelf, in which is set a hand pump. Downstage of the sink is an uncurtained window. Near the window is an old wooden rocker. Center stage is an unpainted wooden kitchen table with straight chairs on either side. There is a small chair down right. Unwashed pans under the sink, a loaf of bread outside the breadbox, a dish towel on the table—other signs of incompleted work. At the rear the shed door opens and the* SHERIFF *comes in followed by the* COUNTY ATTORNEY *and* HALE. *The* SHERIFF *and* HALE *are men in middle life, the* COUNTY ATTORNEY *is a young man; all are much bundled up and go at once to the stove. They are followed by the two women—the* SHERIFF's *wife,* MRS. PETERS, *first; she is a slight wiry woman, a thin nervous face.* MRS. HALE *is larger and would ordinarily be called more comfortable looking, but she is disturbed now and looks fearfully about as she enters. The women have come in slowly, and stand close together near the door.*

COUNTY ATTORNEY [*at the stove rubbing his hands*]. This feels good. Come up to the fire, ladies.

MRS. PETERS [*after taking a step forward*]. I'm not—cold.

SHERIFF [*unbuttoning his overcoat and stepping away from the stove to right of the table as if to mark the beginning of official business*]. Now, Mr. Hale, before we move things about, you explain to Mr. Henderson just what you saw when you came here yesterday morning.

COUNTY ATTORNEY [*crossing down to left of the table*]. By the way, has anything been moved? Are things just as you left them yesterday?

SHERIFF [*looking about*]. It's just the same. When it dropped below zero last night I thought I'd better send Frank out this morning to make a fire for us—[*sits right of center table*] no use getting pneumonia with a big case on, but I told him not to touch anything except the stove—and you know Frank.

COUNTY ATTORNEY. Somebody should have been left here yesterday.

SHERIFF. Oh—yesterday. When I had to send Frank to Morris Center for that man who went crazy—I want you to know I had my hands full yesterday. I knew you could get back from Omaha by today and as long as I went over everything here myself—

COUNTY ATTORNEY. Well, Mr. Hale, tell just what happened when you came here yesterday morning.

A photo of the original 1916 production of *Trifles*. (The New York Public Library for the performing Arts/Art Resource, Billy Rose Theatre Collection, The New York Public Library for the Performing Arts. Astor, Lenox and Tilden Foundations)

HALE [*crossing down to above table*]. Harry and I had started to town with a load of potatoes. We came along the road from my place and as I got here I said, "I'm going to see if I can't get John Wright to go in with me on a party telephone." I spoke to Wright about it once before and he put me off, saying folks talked too much anyway, and all he asked was peace and quiet—I guess you know about how much he talked himself; but I thought maybe if I went to the house and talked about it before his wife, though I said to Harry that I didn't know as what his wife wanted made much difference to John—

COUNTY ATTORNEY. Let's talk about that later, Mr. Hale. I do want to talk about that, but tell now just what happened when you got to the house.

HALE. I didn't hear or see anything; I knocked at the door, and still it was all quiet inside. I knew they must be up, it was past eight o'clock. So I knocked again, and I thought I heard somebody say, "Come in." I wasn't sure, I'm not sure yet, but I opened the door—this door [*indicating the door by which the two women are still standing*] and there in that rocker—[*pointing to it*] sat Mrs. Wright. [*They all look at the rocker down left.*]

COUNTY ATTORNEY. What—what was she doing?

HALE. She was rockin' back and forth. She had her apron in her hand and was kind of—pleating it.

COUNTY ATTORNEY. And how did she—look?

HALE. Well, she looked queer.

COUNTY ATTORNEY. How do you mean—queer?

HALE. Well, as if she didn't know what she was going to do next. And kind of done up.

COUNTY ATTORNEY [*takes out notebook and pencil and sits left of center table*]. How did she seem to feel about your coming?

HALE. Why, I don't think she minded—one way or other. She didn't pay much attention. I said, "How do, Mrs. Wright, it's cold, ain't it?" And she said, "Is it?"—and went on kind of pleating at her apron. Well, I was surprised; she didn't ask me to come up to the stove, or to set down, but just sat there, not even looking at me, so I said, "I want to see John." And then she—laughed. I guess you would call it a laugh. I thought of Harry and the team outside, so I said a little sharp: "Can't I see John?" "No," she says, kind o' dull like. "Ain't he home?" says I. "Yes," says she, "he's home." "Then why can't I see him?" I asked her, out of patience. "'Cause he's dead," says she. "*Dead?*" says I. She just nodded her head, not getting a bit excited, but rockin' back and forth. "Why—where is he?" says I, not knowing what to say. She just pointed upstairs—like that. [*Himself pointing to the room above.*] I started for the stairs, with the idea of going up there. I walked from there to here—then I says, "Why, what did he die of?" "He died of a rope round his neck," says she, and just went on pleatin' at her apron. Well, I went out and called Harry. I thought I might—need help. We went upstairs and there he was lyin'—

COUNTY ATTORNEY. I think I'd rather have you go into that upstairs, where you can point it all out. Just go on now with the rest of the story.

HALE. Well, my first thought was to get that rope off. It looked... [*stops, his face twitches*]...but Harry, he went up to him, and he said, "No, he's dead all right, and we'd better not touch anything." So we went back downstairs. She was still sitting that same way. "Has anybody been notified?" I asked. "No," says she, unconcerned. "Who did this, Mrs. Wright?" said Harry. He said it business-like—and she stopped pleatin' on her apron. "I don't know," she says. "You don't *know?*" says Harry. "No," says she. "Weren't you sleepin' in the bed with him?" says Harry. "Yes," says she, "but I was on the inside." "Somebody slipped a rope round his neck and strangled him and you didn't wake up?" says Harry. "I didn't wake up," she said after him. We musta looked as if we didn't see how that could be, for after a minute she said, "I sleep sound." Harry was going to ask her more questions but I said maybe we ought to let her tell her story first to the coroner, or the sheriff, so Harry went fast as he could to Rivers' place, where there's a telephone.

COUNTY ATTORNEY. And what did Mrs. Wright do when she knew that you had gone for the coroner?

HALE. She moved from the rocker to that chair over there [*pointing to a small chair in the down right corner*] and just sat there with her hands held together and looking down. I got a feeling that I ought to make some conversation, so I said I had come in to see if John wanted to put in a telephone, and at that she started to laugh, and then she stopped and looked at me—scared. [*The* COUNTY ATTORNEY, *who has had his notebook out, makes a note.*] I dunno, maybe it wasn't scared. I wouldn't like to say it was. Soon Harry got back, and then Dr. Lloyd came, and you, Mr. Peters, and so I guess that's all I know that you don't.

COUNTY ATTORNEY [*rising and looking around*]. I guess we'll go upstairs first—and then out to the barn and around there. [*To the* SHERIFF.] You're convinced that there was nothing important here—nothing that would point to any motive?

SHERIFF. Nothing here but kitchen things. [*The* COUNTY ATTORNEY, *after again looking around the kitchen, opens the door of a cupboard closet in right wall. He brings a small chair from right—gets up on it and looks on a shelf. Pulls his hand away, sticky.*]

COUNTY ATTORNEY. Here's a nice mess. [*The women draw nearer up center.*]

MRS. PETERS [*to the other woman*]. Oh, her fruit; it did freeze. [*To the* LAWYER.] She worried about that when it turned so cold. She said the fire'd go out and her jars would break.

SHERIFF [*rises*]. Well, can you beat the women! Held for murder and worryin' about her preserves.

COUNTY ATTORNEY [*getting down from chair*]. I guess before we're through she may have something more serious than preserves to worry about. [*Crosses down right center.*]

HALE. Well, women are used to worrying over trifles. [*The two women move a little closer together.*]

COUNTY ATTORNEY [*with the gallantry of a young politician*]. And yet, for all their worries, what would we do without the ladies? [*The women do not unbend. He goes below the center table to the sink, takes a dipperful of water from the pail and pouring it into a basin, washes his hands. While he is doing this the* SHERIFF *and* HALE *cross to cupboard, which they inspect. The* COUNTY ATTORNEY *starts to wipe his hands on the roller towel, turns it for a cleaner place.*] Dirty towels! [*Kicks his foot against the pans under the sink.*] Not much of a housekeeper, would you say, ladies?

MRS. HALE [*stiffly*]. There's a great deal of work to be done on a farm.

COUNTY ATTORNEY. To be sure. And yet [*with a little bow to her*] I know there are some Dickson County farmhouses which do not have such roller towels. [*He gives it a pull to expose its full length again.*]

MRS. HALE. Those towels get dirty awful quick. Men's hands aren't always as clean as they might be.

COUNTY ATTORNEY. Ah, loyal to your sex, I see. But you and Mrs. Wright were neighbors. I suppose you were friends, too.

MRS. HALE [*shaking her head*]. I've not seen much of her of late years. I've not been in this house—it's more than a year.

COUNTY ATTORNEY [*crossing to women up center*]. And why was that? You didn't like her?

MRS. HALE. I liked her all well enough. Farmers' wives have their hands full, Mr. Henderson. And then—

COUNTY ATTORNEY. Yes———?

MRS. HALE [*looking about*]. It never seemed a very cheerful place.

COUNTY ATTORNEY. No—it's not cheerful. I shouldn't say she had the homemaking instinct.

MRS. HALE. Well, I don't know as Wright had, either.

COUNTY ATTORNEY. You mean that they didn't get on very well?

MRS. HALE. No, I don't mean anything. But I don't think a place'd be any cheerfuller for John Wright's being in it.

COUNTY ATTORNEY. I'd like to talk more of that a little later. I want to get the lay of things upstairs now. [*He goes past the women to up right where steps lead to a stair door.*]

SHERIFF. I suppose anything Mrs. Peters does'll be all right. She was to take in some clothes for her, you know, and a few little things. We left in such a hurry yesterday.

COUNTY ATTORNEY. Yes, but I would like to see what you take, Mrs. Peters, and keep an eye out for anything that might be of use to us.

MRS. PETERS. Yes, Mr. Henderson.

[*The men leave by up right door to stairs. The women listen to the men's steps on the stairs, then look about the kitchen.*]

MRS. HALE [*crossing left to sink*]. I'd hate to have men coming into my kitchen, snooping around and criticizing. [*She arranges the pans under sink which the Lawyer had shoved out of place.*]

MRS. PETERS. Of course it's no more than their duty. [*Crosses to cupboard up right.*]

MRS. HALE. Duty's all right, but I guess that deputy sheriff that came out to make the fire might have got a little of this on. [*Gives the roller towel a pull.*] Wish I'd thought of that sooner. Seems mean to talk about her for not having things slicked up when she had to come away in such a hurry. [*Crosses right to Mrs. Peters at cupboard.*]

MRS. PETERS [*who has been looking through the cupboard, lifts one end of a towel that covers a pan*]. She had bread set. [*Stands still.*]

MRS. HALE [*eyes fixed on a loaf of bread beside the breadbox, which is on a low shelf of the cupboard*]. She was going to put this in there. [*Picks up loaf, then abruptly drops it. In a manner of returning to familiar things.*] It's a shame about her fruit. I wonder if it's all gone. [*Gets up on the chair and looks.*] I think there's some here that's all right, Mrs. Peters. Yes—here; [*holding it toward the window*] this is cherries, too. [*Looking again.*] I declare I believe that's the only one. [*Gets down, jar in her hand. Goes to the sink and wipes it off on the outside.*] She'll feel awful bad after all her hard work in the hot weather. I remember the afternoon I put up my cherries last summer. [*She puts the jar on the big kitchen table, center of the room. With a sigh, is about to sit down in the rocking chair. Before she is seated realizes what chair it is; with a slow look at it, steps back. The chair which she has touched rocks back and forth.* MRS. PETERS *moves to center table and they both watch the chair rock for a moment or two.*]

MRS. PETERS [*shaking off the mood which the empty rocking chair has evoked. Now in a businesslike manner she speaks*]. Well, I must get those things from the front room closet. [*She goes to the door at the right, but, after looking into the other room, steps back.*] You coming with me, Mrs. Hale? You could help me carry them. [*They go in the other room; reappear,* MRS. PETERS *carrying a dress, petticoat and skirt,* MRS. HALE *following with a pair of shoes.*] My, it's cold in there. [*She puts the clothes on the big table, and hurries to the stove.*]

MRS. HALE [*right of center table examining the skirt*]. Wright was close. I think maybe that's why she kept so much to herself. She didn't even belong to the Ladies' Aid. I suppose she felt she couldn't do her part, and then you don't enjoy things when you feel shabby. I heard she used to wear pretty clothes and be lively, when she was Minnie Foster, one of the town girls singing in the choir. But that—oh, that was thirty years ago. This all you was to take in?

MRS. PETERS. She said she wanted an apron. Funny thing to want, for there isn't much to get you dirty in jail, goodness knows. But I suppose just to make her feel more natural. [*Crosses to cupboard.*] She said they was in the top drawer of this cupboard. Yes, here. And then her little shawl that always hung behind the door. [*Opens stair door and looks.*] Yes, here it is. [*Quickly shuts door leading upstairs.*]

MRS. HALE [*abruptly moving toward her*]. Mrs. Peters?

MRS. PETERS. Yes, Mrs. Hale? [*At up right door.*]

MRS. HALE. Do you think she did it?

MRS. PETERS [*in a frightened voice*]. Oh, I don't know.

MRS. HALE. Well, I don't think she did. Asking for an apron and her little shawl. Worrying about her fruit.

MRS. PETERS [*starts to speak, glances up, where footsteps are heard in the room above. In a low voice*]. Mr. Peters says it looks bad for her. Mr. Henderson is awful sarcastic in a speech and he'll make fun of her sayin' she didn't wake up.

MRS. HALE. Well, I guess John Wright didn't wake when they was slipping that rope under his neck.

MRS. PETERS [*crossing slowly to table and placing shawl and apron on table with other clothing*]. No, it's strange. It must have been done awful crafty and still. They say it was such a—funny way to kill a man, rigging it all up like that.

MRS. HALE [*crossing to left of* MRS. PETERS *at table*]. That's just what Mr. Hale said. There was a gun in the house. He says that's what he can't understand.

MRS. PETERS. Mr. Henderson said coming out that what was needed for the case was a motive; something to show anger, or—sudden feeling.

MRS. HALE [*who is standing by the table*]. Well, I don't see any signs of anger around here. [*She puts her hand on the dish towel which lies on the table, stands looking down at table, one-half of which is clean, the other half messy.*] It's wiped to here. [*Makes a move as if to finish work, then turns and looks at loaf of bread outside the breadbox. Drops towel. In that voice of coming back to familiar things.*] Wonder how they are finding things upstairs. [*Crossing below table to down right.*] I hope she had it a little more red-up[1] up there. You know, it seems kind of *sneaking.* Locking her up in town and then coming out here and trying to get her own house to turn against her!

MRS. PETERS. But, Mrs. Hale, the law is the law.

MRS. HALE. I s'pose 'tis. [*Unbuttoning her coat.*] Better loosen up your things, Mrs. Peters. You won't feel them when you go out. [MRS. PETERS *takes off her fur tippet,[2] goes to hang it on chair back left of table, stands looking at the work basket on floor near down left window.*]

MRS. PETERS. She was piecing a quilt. [*She brings the large sewing basket to the center table and they look at the bright pieces,* MRS. HALE *above the table and* MRS. PETERS *left of it.*]

MRS. HALE. It's a log cabin pattern. Pretty, isn't it? I wonder if she was goin' to quilt it or just knot it? [*Footsteps have been heard coming down the stairs. The* SHERIFF *enters followed by* HALE *and the* COUNTY ATTORNEY.]

SHERIFF. They wonder if she was going to quilt it or just knot it! [*The men laugh, the women look abashed.*]

COUNTY ATTORNEY [*rubbing his hands over the stove*]. Frank's fire didn't do much up there, did it? Well, let's go out to the barn and get that cleared up.

[*The men go outside by up left door.*]

MRS. HALE [*resentfully*]. I don't know as there's anything so strange, our takin' up our time with little things while we're waiting for them to get the evidence. [*She sits in chair right of table smoothing out a block with decision.*] I don't see as it's anything to laugh about.

MRS. PETERS [*apologetically*]. Of course they've got awful important things on their minds. [*Pulls up a chair and joins* MRS. HALE *at the left of the table.*]

---

[1] **red-up** cleaned up, neat.
[2] **tippet** a scarf-like wrap.

MRS. HALE. [*examining another block*]. Mrs. Peters, look at this one. Here, this is the one she was working on, and look at the sewing! All the rest of it has been so nice and even. And look at this! It's all over the place! Why, it looks as if she didn't know what she was about! [*After she has said this they look at each other, then start to glance back at the door. After an instant* MRS. HALE *has pulled at a knot and ripped the sewing.*]

MRS. PETERS. Oh, what are you doing, Mrs. Hale?

MRS. HALE. [*mildly*]. Just pulling out a stitch or two that's not sewed very good. [*Threading a needle.*] Bad sewing always made me fidgety.

MRS. PETERS [*with a glance at door, nervously*]. I don't think we ought to touch things.

MRS. HALE. I'll just finish up this end. [*Suddenly stopping and leaning forward.*] Mrs. Peters?

MRS. PETERS. Yes, Mrs. Hale?

MRS. HALE. What do you suppose she was so nervous about?

MRS. PETERS. Oh—I don't know. I don't know as she was nervous. I sometimes sew awful queer when I'm just tired. [MRS. HALE *starts to say something, looks at* MRS. PETERS, *then goes on sewing.*] Well, I must get these things wrapped up. They may be through sooner than we think. [*Putting apron and other things together.*] I wonder where I can find a piece of paper, and string. [*Rises.*]

MRS. HALE. In that cupboard, maybe.

MRS. PETERS [*crosses right looking in cupboard*]. Why, here's a bird-cage. [*Holds it up.*] Did she have a bird, Mrs. Hale?

MRS. HALE. Why, I don't know whether she did or not—I've not been here for so long. There was a man around last year selling canaries cheap, but I don't know as she took one; maybe she did. She used to sing real pretty herself.

MRS. PETERS [*glancing around*]. Seems funny to think of a bird here. But she must have had one, or why would she have a cage? I wonder what happened to it?

MRS. HALE. I s'pose maybe the cat got it.

MRS. PETERS. No, she didn't have a cat. She's got that feeling some people have about cats—being afraid of them. My cat got in her room and she was real upset and asked me to take it out.

MRS. HALE. My sister Bessie was like that. Queer, ain't it?

MRS. PETERS [*examining the cage*]. Why, look at this door. It's broke. One hinge is pulled apart. [*Takes a step down to* MRS. HALE'*s right.*]

MRS. HALE. [*looking too*]. Looks as if someone must have been rough with it.

MRS. PETERS. Why, yes. [*She brings the cage forward and puts it on the table.*]

MRS. HALE. [*glancing toward up left door*]. I wish if they're going to find any evidence they'd be about it. I don't like this place.

MRS. PETERS. But I'm awful glad you came with me, Mrs. Hale. It would be lonesome for me setting here alone.

MRS. HALE. It would, wouldn't it? [*Dropping her sewing.*] But I tell you what I do wish, Mrs. Peters. I wish I had come over sometimes when *she* was here. I—[*looking around the room*]—wish I had.

MRS. PETERS. But of course you were awful busy, Mrs. Hale—your house and your children.

MRS. HALE [*rises and crosses left*]. I could've come. I stayed away because it weren't cheerful—and that's why I ought to have come. I—[*looking out left window*]—I've never liked this place. Maybe because it's down in a hollow and you don't see the road. I dunno what it is, but it's a lonesome place and always was. I wish I had come over to see Minnie Foster sometimes. I can see now—[*Shakes her head.*]

MRS. PETERS [*left of table and above it*]. Well, you mustn't reproach yourself, Mrs. Hale. Somehow we just don't see how it is with other folks until—something turns up.

MRS. HALE. Not having children makes less work—but it makes a quiet house, and Wright out to work all day, and no company when he did come in. [*Turning from window.*] Did you know John Wright, Mrs. Peters?

MRS. PETERS. Not to know him; I've seen him in town. They say he was a good man.

MRS. HALE. Yes—good; he didn't drink, and kept his word as well as most, I guess, and paid his debts. But he was a hard man, Mrs. Peters. Just to pass the time of day with him—[*Shivers.*] Like a raw wind that gets to the bone. [*Pauses, her eye falling on the cage.*] I should think she woulda wanted a bird. But what do you suppose went wrong with it?

MRS. PETERS. I don't know, unless it got sick and died. [*She reaches over and swings the broken door, swings it again; both women watch it.*]

MRS. HALE. You weren't raised round here, were you? [MRS. PETERS *shakes her head.*] You didn't know—her?

MRS. PETERS. Not till they brought her yesterday.

MRS. HALE. She—come to think of it, she was kind of like a bird herself—real sweet and pretty, but kind of timid and—fluttery. How—she—did—change. [*Silence; then as if struck by a happy thought and relieved to get back to everyday things. Crosses right above* MRS. PETERS *to cupboard, replaces small chair used to stand on to its original place down right.*] Tell you what, Mrs. Peters, why don't you take the quilt in with you? It might take up her mind.

MRS. PETERS. Why, I think that's a real nice idea, Mrs. Hale. There couldn't possibly be any objection to it, could there? Now, just what would I take? I wonder if her patches are in here—and her things. [*They look in the sewing basket.*]

MRS. HALE [*crosses to right of table*]. Here's some red. I expect this has got sewing things in it. [*Brings out a fancy box.*] What a pretty box. Looks like something somebody would give you. Maybe her scissors are in here. [*Opens box. Suddenly puts her hand to her nose.*] Why—[MRS. PETERS *bends nearer, then turns her face away.*] There's something wrapped up in this piece of silk.

MRS. PETERS. Why, this isn't her scissors.

MRS. HALE [*lifting the silk*]. Oh, Mrs. Peters—it's—[MRS. PETERS *bends closer.*]

MRS. PETERS. It's the bird.

MRS. HALE. But, Mrs. Peters—look at it! Its neck! Look at its neck! It's all—other side *to.*

MRS. PETERS. Somebody—wrung—its—neck. [*Their eyes meet. A look of growing comprehension, of horror. Steps are heard outside.* MRS. HALE *slips box under quilt pieces, and sinks into her chair. Enter* SHERIFF *and* COUNTY ATTORNEY. MRS. PETERS *steps down left and stands looking out of window.*]

COUNTY ATTORNEY [*as one turning from serious things to little pleasantries*]. Well, ladies, have you decided whether she was going to quilt it or knot it? [*Crosses to center above table.*]

MRS. PETERS. We think she was going to—knot it. [SHERIFF *crosses to right of stove, lifts stove lid and glances at fire, then stands warming hands at stove.*]

COUNTY ATTORNEY. Well, that's interesting, I'm sure. [*Seeing the bird-cage.*] Has the bird flown?

MRS. HALE [*putting more quilt pieces over the box*]. We think the—cat got it.

COUNTY ATTORNEY [*preoccupied*]. Is there a cat? [*Mrs. Hale glances in a quick covert way at Mrs. Peters.*]

MRS. PETERS [*turning from window takes a step in*]. Well, not now. They're super-stitious, you know. They leave.

COUNTY ATTORNEY [*to* SHERIFF PETERS, *continuing an interrupted conversation*]. No sign at all of anyone having come from the outside. Their own rope. Now let's go up again and go over it piece by piece. [*They start upstairs.*] It would have to have been someone who knew just the—[MRS. PETERS *sits down left of table. The two women sit there not looking at one another, but as if peering into something and at the same time holding back. When they talk now it is in the man-ner of feeling their way over strange ground, as if afraid of what they are saying, but as if they cannot help saying it.*]

MRS. HALE [*hesitatively and in hushed voice*]. She liked the bird. She was going to bury it in that pretty box.

MRS. PETERS [*in a whisper*]. When I was a girl—my kitten—there was a boy took a hatchet, and before my eyes—and before I could get there—[*Covers her face an instant.*] If they hadn't held me back I would have—[*catches herself, looks upstairs where steps are heard, falters weakly*]—hurt him.

MRS. HALE [*with a slow look around her*]. I wonder how it would seem never to have had any children around. [*Pause.*] No, Wright wouldn't like the bird—a thing that sang. She used to sing. He killed that, too.

MRS. PETERS [*moving uneasily*]. We don't know who killed the bird.

MRS. HALE. I knew John Wright.

MRS. PETERS. It was an awful thing done in this house that night, Mrs. Hale. Killing a man while he slept, slipping a rope around his neck that choked the life out of him.

MRS. HALE. His neck. Choked the life out of him. [*Her hand goes out and rests on the bird-cage.*]

MRS. PETERS [*with rising voice*]. We don't know who killed him. We don't *know*.

MRS. HALE [*her own feeling not interrupted*]. If there'd been years and years of nothing, then a bird to sing to you, it would be awful—still, after the bird was still.

MRS. PETERS [*something within her speaking*]. I know what stillness is. When we homesteaded in Dakota, and my first baby died—after he was two years old, and me with no other then—

MRS. HALE [*moving*]. How soon do you suppose they'll be through looking for the evidence?

MRS. PETERS. I know what stillness is. [*Pulling herself back.*] The law has got to punish crime, Mrs. Hale.

MRS. HALE [*not as if answering that*]. I wish you'd seen Minnie Foster when she wore a white dress with blue ribbons and stood up there in the choir and sang. [*A look around the room.*] Oh, I *wish* I'd come over here once in a while! That was a crime! That was a crime! Who's going to punish that?

MRS. PETERS [*looking upstairs*]. We mustn't—take on.

MRS. HALE. I might have known she needed help! I know how things can be—for women. I tell you, it's queer, Mrs. Peters. We live close together and we live far apart. We all go through the same things—it's all just a different kind of the same thing. [*Brushes her eyes, noticing the jar of fruit, reaches out for it.*] If I was you I wouldn't tell her her fruit was gone. Tell her it ain't. Tell her it's all right. Take this in to prove it to her. She—she may never know whether it was broke or not.

MRS. PETERS [*takes the jar, looks about for something to wrap it in; takes petticoat from the clothes brought from the other room, very nervously begins winding this around the jar. In a false voice*]. My, it's a good thing the men couldn't hear us. Wouldn't they just laugh! Getting all stirred up over a little thing like a— dead canary. As if that could have anything to do with—with—wouldn't they *laugh*! [*The men are heard coming downstairs.*]

MRS. HALE [*under her breath*]. Maybe they would—maybe they wouldn't.

COUNTY ATTORNEY. No, Peters, it's all perfectly clear except a reason for doing it. But you know juries when it comes to women. If there was some definite thing. [*Crosses slowly to above table.* SHERIFF *crosses down right.* MRS. HALE *and* MRS. PETERS *remain seated at either side of table.*] Something to show—something to make a story about—a thing that would connect up with this strange way of doing it—[*The women's eyes meet for an instant. Enter* HALE *from outer door.*]

HALE [*remaining up left by door*]. Well, I've got the team around. Pretty cold out there.

COUNTY ATTORNEY. I'm going to stay awhile by myself. [*To the* SHERIFF.] You can send Frank out for me, can't you? I want to go over everything. I'm not satisfied that we can't do better.

SHERIFF. Do you want to see what Mrs. Peters is going to take in? [*The* LAWYER *picks up the apron, laughs.*]

COUNTY ATTORNEY. Oh, I guess they're not very dangerous things the ladies have picked out. [*Moves a few things about, disturbing the quilt pieces which cover the box. Steps back.*] No, Mrs. Peters doesn't need supervising. For that matter a sheriff's wife is married to the law. Ever think of it that way, Mrs. Peters?

MRS. PETERS. Not—just that way.

SHERIFF [*chuckling*]. Married to the law. [*Moves to down right door to the other room.*] I just want you to come in here a minute, George. We ought to take a look at these windows.

COUNTY ATTORNEY [*scoffingly*]. Oh, windows!

SHERIFF. We'll be right out, Mr. Hale. [HALE *goes outside. The* SHERIFF *follows the* COUNTY ATTORNEY *into the other room. Then* MRS. HALE *rises, hands tight together, looking intensely at* MRS. PETERS, *whose eyes make a slow turn, finally meeting* MRS. HALE'S. *A moment* MRS. HALE *holds her, then her own eyes point the way to where the box is concealed. Suddenly* MRS. PETERS *throws back quilt pieces and tries to put the box in the bag she is carrying. It is too big. She opens box, starts to take bird out, cannot touch it, goes to pieces, stands there helpless. Sound of a knob turning in the other room.* MRS. HALE *snatches the box and puts it in the pocket of her big coat. Enter* COUNTY ATTORNEY *and* SHERIFF, *who remains down right.*]

COUNTY ATTORNEY [*crosses to up left door; facetiously*]. Well, Henry, at least we found out that she was not going to quilt it. She was going to—what is it you call it, ladies?

MRS. HALE [*standing center below table facing front, her hand against her pocket*]. We call it—knot it, Mr. Henderson.

CURTAIN.

(1916)

Questions for Discussion and Writing

1. Describe the atmosphere evoked by the play's setting.
2. How would you characterize the men in the play?
3. What is the point of the women's concern about the quilt and whether Mrs. Wright "was going to quilt it or knot it"? What is the significance of the last line of the play and why is it ironic?
4. What sort of person was Minnie Foster before she married? What do you think happened to her?
5. Describe your reaction to the decision made by Mrs. Peters and Mrs. Hale to hide the dead bird from the men. Did they do the right thing? Write an essay in which you explain your answer to this question.

Jane Martin   1938?–

Jane Martin is a woman of mystery. She has never been seen, has given no interviews, and there are no pictures. Theater critics speculate that her spokesperson, Jon Jory, retired artistic director of the Actors Theatre of Louisville, wrote the plays in collaboration with his wife. He firmly denies it, saying simply, "I'm not going to talk about that." But he has been the first to produce all of her plays and has accepted all of her awards for her. When asked whether her identity would be disclosed after her death, Jory responded, "That's a press conference that no one will come to. By the time I die, no one will care anyway." So Jane Martin remains, as one critic attests, "The best-known unknown playwright in America."

Beauty

CHARACTERS

CARLA
BETHANY

An apartment. Minimalist set. A young woman, Carla, on the phone.

CARLA. In love with me? You're in love with me? Could you describe yourself again? Uh-huh. Uh-huh. And you spoke to me? [*A knock at the door.*] Listen, I always hate to interrupt a marriage proposal, but...could you possibly hold that thought? [*Puts phone down and goes to door. Bethany, the same age as Carla and a friend, is there. She carries the sort of Mideastern lamp we know of from Aladdin.*]
BETHANY. Thank God you were home. I mean, you're not going to believe this!
CARLA. Somebody on the phone. [*Goes back to it.*]
BETHANY. I mean, I just had a beach urge, so I told them at work my uncle was dying...

CARLA [*motions to Bethany for quiet*]. And you were the one in the leather jacket with the tattoo? What was the tatoo? [*Carla again asks Bethany, who is gesturing wildly that she should hang up, to cool it.*] Look, a screaming eagle from shoulder to shoulder, maybe. There were a lot of people in the bar.

BETHANY [*gesturing and mouthing*]. I have to get back to work.

CARLA [*on phone*]. See, the thing is, I'm probably not going to marry someone I can't remember ... particularly when I don't drink. Sorry. Sorry. Sorry. [*She hangs up.*] Madness.

BETHANY. So I ran out to the beach ...

CARLA. This was some guy I never met who apparently offered me a beer ...

BETHANY. ... low tide and this ... [*The lamp.*] ... was just sitting there, lying there ...

CARLA. ... and he tracks me down ...

BETHANY. ... on the beach, and I lift this lid thing ...

CARLA. ... and seriously proposes marriage.

BETHANY. ... and a genie comes out.

CARLA. I mean, that's twice in a ... what?

BETHANY. A genie comes out of this thing.

CARLA. A genie?

BETHANY. I'm not kidding, the whole Disney kind of thing, swirling smoke, and then this twenty-foot-high, see-through guy in like an Arabian outfit.

CARLA. Very funny.

BETHANY. Yes, funny, but twenty feet high! I look up and down the beach, I'm alone. I don't have my pepper spray or my hand alarm. You know me, when I'm petrified I joke. I say his voice is too high for Robin Williams, and he says he's a castrati. Naturally. Who else would I meet?

CARLA. What's a castrati?

BETHANY. You know ...

[*The appropriate gesture.*]

CARLA. Bethany, dear one, I have three modeling calls. I am meeting Ralph Lauren!

BETHANY. Okay, good. Ralph Lauren. Look, I am not kidding!

CARLA. You're not kidding what?!

BETHANY. There is a genie in this thingamajig.

CARLA. Uh-huh. I'll be back around eight.

BETHANY. And he offered me *wishes!*

CARLA. Is this some elaborate practical joke because it's my birthday?

BETHANY. No, happy birthday, but I'm like crazed because I'm on this deserted beach with a twenty-foot-high, see-through genie, so like sarcastically ... you know how I need a new car ... I said fine, gimme 25,000 dollars ...

CARLA. On the beach with the genie?

BETHANY. Yeah, right, exactly, and it rains down out of the sky.

CARLA. Oh sure.

BETHANY [*pulling a wad out of her purse*]. Count it, those are thousands. I lost one in the surf.

[*Carla sees the top bill. Looks at Bethany, who nods encouragement. Carla thumbs through them.*]

CARLA. These look real.

BETHANY. Yeah.

CARLA. And they rained down out of the sky?

BETHANY. Yeah.

CARLA. You've been really strange lately, are you dealing?

BETHANY. Dealing what, I've even given up chocolate.

CARLA. Let me see the genie.

BETHANY. Wait, wait.

CARLA. Bethany, I don't have time to screw around. Let me see the genie or let me go on my appointments.

BETHANY. Wait! So I pick up the money…see, there's sand on the money … and I'm like nuts so I say, you know, "Okay, look, ummm, big guy, my uncle is in the hospital" … because as you know when I said to the people at work my uncle was dying, I was on one level telling the truth although it had nothing to do with the beach, but he was in Intensive Care after the accident, and that's on my mind, so I say, okay, Genie, heal my uncle … which is like impossible given he was hit by two trucks, and the genie says, "Yes, Master" … like they're supposed to say, and he goes into this like kind of whirlwind, kicking up sand and stuff, and I'm like, "Oh my God!" and the air clears, and he bows, you know, and says, "It is done, Master," and I say, "Okay, whatever-you-are, I'm calling on my cell phone," and I get it out and I get this doctor who is like dumbstruck who says my uncle came to, walked out of Intensive Care and left the hospital! I'm not kidding, Carla.

CARLA. On your mother's grave?

BETHANY. On my mother's grave.

[*They look at each other.*]

CARLA. Let me see the genie.

BETHANY. No, no, look, that's the whole thing … I was just, like, reacting, you know, responding, and that's already two wishes … although I'm really pleased about my uncle, the $25,000 thing, I could have asked for $10 million, and there is only one wish left.

CARLA. So ask for $10 million.

BETHANY. I don't think so. I don't think so. I mean, I gotta focus in here. Do you have a sparkling water?

CARLA. No. Bethany, I'm missing Ralph Lauren now. Very possibly my one chance to go from catalogue model to the very, very big time, so, if you are joking, stop joking.

BETHANY. Not joking. See, see, the thing is, I know what I want. In my guts. Yes. Underneath my entire bitch of a life is this unspoken, ferocious, all-consuming urge…

CARLA [*trying to get her to move this along*]. Ferocious, all-consuming urge …

BETHANY. I want to be like you.

CARLA. Me?

BETHANY. Yes.

CARLA. Half the time you don't even like me.

BETHANY. Jealous. The ogre of jealousy.

CARLA. You're the one with the $40,000 job straight out of school. You're the one who has published short stories. I'm the one hanging on by her fingernails in modeling. The one who has creeps calling her on the phone. The one who had to have a nose job.

BETHANY. I want to be beautiful.

CARLA. You are beautiful.

BETHANY. Carla, I'm not beautiful.

CARLA. You have charm. You have personality. You know perfectly well you're pretty.

BETHANY. "Pretty," see, that's it. Pretty is the minor leagues of beautiful. Pretty is what people discover about you after they know you. Beautiful is what knocks them out across the room. Pretty, you get called a couple of times a year; *beautiful* is twenty-four hours a day.

CARLA. Yeah? So?

BETHANY. So?! We're talking *beauty* here. Don't say "So?" Beauty is the real deal. You are the center of any moment of your life. People stare. Men flock. I've seen you get offered discounts on makeup for no reason. Parents treat beautiful children better. Studies show your income goes up. You can have sex anytime you want it. Men have to know me. That takes up to a year. I'm continually horny.

CARLA. Bethany, I don't even like sex. I can't have a conversation without men coming on to me. I have no privacy. I get hassled on the street. They start pressuring me from the beginning. Half the time, it never occurs to them to start with a conversation. Smart guys like you. You've had three long-term relationships, and you're only twenty-three. I haven't had one. The good guys, the smart guys are scared to death of me. I'm surrounded by male bimbos who think a preposition is when you go to school away from home. I have no woman friends except you. I don't even want to talk about this!

BETHANY. I knew you'd say something like this. See, you're "in the club" so you can say this. It's the way beauty functions as an elite. You're trying to keep it all for yourself.

CARLA. I'm trying to tell you it's no picnic.

BETHANY. But it's what everybody wants. It's the nasty secret at large in the world. It's the unspoken tidal desire in every room and on every street. It's the unspoken, the soundless whisper...millions upon millions of people longing hopelessly and forever to stop being whatever they are and be beautiful, but the difference between those ardent multitudes and me is that I have a goddamn genie and one more wish!

CARLA. Well, it's not what I want. This is me, Carla. I have never read a whole book. Page six, I can't remember page four. The last thing I read was *The Complete Idiot's Guide to WordPerfect*. I leave dinner parties right after the dessert because I'm out of conversation. You know the dumb blond joke about the application where it says, "Sign here," she put Sagittarius? I've done that. Only beautiful guys approach me, and that's because they want to borrow my eye shadow. I barely exist outside a mirror! You don't want to be me.

BETHANY. None of you tell the truth. That's why you have no friends. We can all see you're just trying to make us feel better because we aren't in your league. This only proves to me it should be my third wish. Money can only buy things. Beauty makes you the center of the universe.

[*Bethany picks up the lamp.*]

CARLA. Don't do it. Bethany, don't wish it! I am telling you you'll regret it.

[*Bethany lifts the lid. There is a tremendous crash, and the lights go out. Then they flicker and come back up, revealing Bethany and Carla on the floor where they have been thrown by the explosion. We don't realize it at first, but they have exchanged places.*]

CARLA/BETHANY. Oh God.

BETHANY/CARLA. Oh God.

CARLA/BETHANY. Am I bleeding? Am I dying?

BETHANY/CARLA. I'm so dizzy. You're not bleeding.

CARLA/BETHANY. Neither are you.

BETHANY/CARLA. I feel so weird.

CARLA/BETHANY. Me too. I feel ... [*Looking at her hands.*] Oh, my God, I'm wearing your jewelry. I'm wearing your nail polish.

BETHANY/CARLA. I know I'm over here, but I can see myself over there.

CARLA/BETHANY. I'm wearing your dress. I have your legs!!

BETHANY/CARLA. These aren't my shoes. I can't meet Ralph Lauren wearing these shoes!

CARLA/BETHANY. I wanted to be beautiful, but I didn't want to be you.

BETHANY/CARLA. Thanks a lot!!

CARLA/BETHANY. I've got to go. I want to pick someone out and get laid.

BETHANY/CARLA. You can't just walk out of here in my body!

CARLA/BETHANY. Wait a minute. Wait a minute. What's eleven eighteenths of 1,726?

BETHANY/CARLA. Why?

CARLA/BETHANY. I'm a public accountant. I want to know if you have my brain.

BETHANY/CARLA. One hundred thirty-two and a half.

CARLA/BETHANY. You have my brain.

BETHANY/CARLA. What shade of Rubenstein lipstick does Cindy Crawford wear with teal blue?

CARLA/BETHANY. Raging Storm.

BETHANY/CARLA. You have my brain. You poor bastard.

CARLA/BETHANY. I don't care. Don't you see?

BETHANY/CARLA. See what?

CARLA/BETHANY. We both have the one thing, the one and only thing everybody wants.

BETHANY/CARLA. What is that?

CARLA/BETHANY. It's better than beauty for me; it's better than brains for you.

BETHANY/CARLA. What? What?!

CARLA/BETHANY. Different problems.

Blackout.

END OF PLAY

(2001)

Questions for Discussion and Writing

1. What values and obsessions does this play satirize?

2. What stereotype does each character represent? Are they both objects of derision? Do you think one of them gets a better deal in the end?

3. Why does Bethany not believe Carla when she (Carla) tries to explain the downside of beauty?

4. Does this play have to be about females? Write an essay explaining how you would adapt the play to satirize two young men.

David Ives　1950–

Born and raised on Chicago's south side, David Ives began his career in Hollywood writing scripts for TV movies. After moving to New York, he did humorous pieces for the *New York Times Magazine* and the *New Yorker* before turning to playwriting. He describes one of his short plays featuring a cross-dressing corporate executive as being about "the ontological problem of lingerie" and says that he's grateful for the shortness of his plays because "when the lights go down, at least the audience isn't thinking, 'Oh, God, two more hours of this.'" Asked by a reporter, "If you weren't a writer, what would you be?" he responded, "I'd be a hawk. Or maybe a seal in the waters off Alaska. Preferably with my wife Martha as my fellow hawk or fellow seal."

Sure Thing

CHARACTERS

BILL, *in his late twenties*　　　BETTY, *in her late twenties*

SETTING

A café table, with a couple of chairs.

SCENE

[BETTY, *reading at the table. An empty chair opposite her.* BILL *enters.*]

BILL. Excuse me. Is this chair taken?
BETTY. Excuse me?
BILL. Is this taken?
BETTY. Yes, it is.
BILL. Oh. Sorry.
BETTY. Sure thing.

　　[*A bell rings softly*]

BILL. Excuse me. Is this chair taken?
BETTY. Excuse me?
BILL. Is this taken?
BETTY. No, but I'm expecting somebody in a minute.
BILL. Oh. Thanks anyway.
BETTY. Sure thing.

　　[*A bell rings softly*]

BILL. Excuse me. Is this chair taken?
BETTY. No, but I'm expecting somebody very shortly.
BILL. Would you mind if I sit here till he or she or it comes?
BETTY [*Glances at her watch*]. They seem to be pretty late ...
BILL. You never know who you might be turning down.
BETTY. Sorry. Nice try, though.

BILL. Sure thing.

[*Bell*]

BILL. Is this seat taken?
BETTY. No, it's not.
BILL. Would you mind if I sit here?
BETTY. Yes, I would.
BILL. Oh.

[*Bell*]

BILL. Is this chair taken?
BETTY. No, it's not.
BILL. Would you mind if I sit here?
BETTY. No. Go ahead.
BILL. Thanks. [*He sits. She continues reading*] Everyplace else seems to be taken.
BETTY. Mm-hm.
BILL. Great place.
BETTY. Mm-hm.
BILL. What's the book?
BETTY. I just wanted to read in quiet, if you don't mind.
BILL. No. Sure thing.

[*Bell*]

BILL. Everyplace else seems to be taken.
BETTY. Mm-hm.
BILL. Great place for reading.
BETTY. Yes, I like it.
BILL. What's the book?
BETTY. *The Sound and the Fury.*
BILL. Oh. Hemingway.

[*Bell*]

BILL. What's the book?
BETTY. *The Sound and the Fury.*
BILL. Oh. Faulkner.
BETTY. Have you read it?
BILL. Not ... actually. I've read *about* it, though. It's supposed to be great.
BETTY. It is great.
BILL. I hear it's great. [*Small pause*] Waiter?

[*Bell*]

BILL. What's the book?
BETTY. *The Sound and the Fury.*
BILL. Oh. Faulkner.
BETTY. Have you read it?
BILL. I'm a Mets fan, myself.

[*Bell*]

BETTY. Have you read it?
BILL. Yeah, I read it in college.
BETTY. Where was college?
BILL. I went to Oral Roberts University.

[*Bell*]

BETTY. Where was college?
BILL. I was lying. I never really went to college. I just like to party.

> [*Bell*]

BETTY. Where was college?
BILL. Harvard.
BETTY. Do you like Faulkner?
BILL. I love Faulkner. I spent a whole winter reading him once.
BETTY. I've just started.
BILL. I was so excited after ten pages that I went out and bought everything else
he wrote. One of the greatest reading experiences of my life. I mean, all that
incredible psychological understanding. Page after page of gorgeous prose.
His profound grasp of the mystery of time and human existence. The smells
of the earth... What do you think?
BETTY. I think it's pretty boring.

> [*Bell*]

BILL. What's the book?
BETTY. *The Sound and the Fury.*
BILL. Oh! Faulkner!
BETTY. Do you like Faulkner?
BILL. I love Faulkner.
BETTY. He's incredible.
BILL. I spent a whole winter reading him once.
BETTY. I was so excited after ten pages that I went out and bought everything else
he wrote.
BILL. All that incredible psychological understanding.
BETTY. And the prose is so gorgeous.
BILL. And the way he's grasped the mystery of time—
BETTY. —and human existence. I can't believe I've waited this long to read him.
BILL. You never know. You might not have liked him before.
BETTY. That's true.
BILL. You might not have been ready for him. You have to hit these things at the
right moment or it's no good.
BETTY. That's happened to me.
BILL. It's all in the timing. [*Small pause*] My name's Bill, by the way.
BETTY. I'm Betty.
BILL. Hi.
BETTY. Hi.

> [*Small pause*]

BILL. Yes, I thought reading Faulkner was ... a great experience.
BETTY. Yes.

> [*Small pause*]

BILL. *The Sound and the Fury* ...

> [*Another small pause*]

BETTY. Well. Onwards and upwards. [*She goes back to her book*]
BILL. Waiter—?

> [*Bell*]

BILL. You have to hit these things at the right moment or it's no good.

BETTY. That's happened to me.

BILL. It's all in the timing. My name's Bill, by the way.

BETTY. I'm Betty.

BILL. Hi.

BETTY. Hi.

BILL. Do you come in here a lot?

BETTY. Actually I'm just in town for two days from Pakistan.

BILL. Oh. Pakistan.

[*Bell*]

BILL. My name's Bill, by the way.

BETTY. I'm Betty.

BILL. Hi.

BETTY. Hi.

BILL. Do you come in here a lot?

BETTY. Every once in a while. Do you?

BILL. Not much anymore. Not as much as I used to. Before my nervous breakdown.

[*Bell*]

BILL. Do you come in here a lot?

BETTY. Why are you asking?

BILL. Just interested.

BETTY. Are you really interested, or do you just want to pick me up?

BILL. No, I'm really interested.

BETTY. Why would you be interested in whether I come in here a lot?

BILL. Just ... getting acquainted.

BETTY. Maybe you're only interested for the sake of making small talk long enough to ask me back to your place to listen to some music, or because you've just rented some great tape for your VCR, or because you've got some terrific unknown Django Reinhardt record, only all you'll really want to do is fuck—which you won't do very well—after which you'll go into the bathroom and pee very loudly, then pad into the kitchen and get yourself a beer from the refrigerator without asking me whether I'd like anything, and then you'll proceed to lie back down beside me and confess that you've got a girlfriend named Stephanie who's away at medical school in Belgium for a year, and that you've been involved with her—*off and on*—in what you'll call a very intricate relationship, for about *seven* YEARS. None of which *interests* me, mister!

BILL. Okay.

[*Bell*]

BILL. Do you come in here a lot?

BETTY. Every other day, I think.

BILL. I come in here quite a lot and I don't remember seeing you.

BETTY. I guess we must be on different schedules.

BILL. Missed connections.

BETTY. Yes. Different time zones.

BILL. Amazing how you can live right next door to somebody in this town and never even know it.

BETTY. I know.

BILL. City life.

BETTY. It's crazy.

BILL. We probably pass each other in the street every day. Right in front of this place, probably.

BETTY. Yep.

BILL [*Looks around*]. Well, the waiters here sure seem to be in some different time zone. I don't see one anywhere...Waiter! [*He looks back*] So what do you...

[*He sees that she's gone back to her book*]

BETTY. I beg pardon?

BILL. Nothing. Sorry.

[*Bell*]

BETTY. I guess we must be on different schedules.

BILL. Missed connections.

BETTY. Yes. Different time zones.

BILL. Amazing how you can live right next door to somebody in this town and never even know it.

BETTY. I know.

BILL. City life.

BETTY. It's crazy.

BILL. You weren't waiting for somebody when I came in, were you?

BETTY. Actually I was.

BILL. Oh. Boyfriend?

BETTY. Sort of.

BILL. What's a sort-of boyfriend?

BETTY. My husband.

BILL. Ah-ha.

[*Bell*]

BILL. You weren't waiting for somebody when I came in, were you?

BETTY. Actually I was.

BILL. Oh. Boyfriend?

BETTY. Sort of.

BILL. What's a sort-of boyfriend?

BETTY. We were meeting here to break up.

BILL. Mm-hm...

[*Bell*]

BILL. What's a sort-of boyfriend?

BETTY. My lover. Here she comes right now!

[*Bell*]

BILL. You weren't waiting for somebody when I came in, were you?

BETTY. No, just reading.

BILL. Sort of a sad occupation for a Friday night, isn't it? Reading here, all by yourself?

BETTY. Do you think so?

BILL. Well sure. I mean, what's a good-looking woman like you doing out alone on a Friday night?

BETTY. Trying to keep away from lines like that.

BILL. No, listen—

[*Bell*]

BILL. You weren't waiting for somebody when I came in, were you?
BETTY. No, just reading.
BILL. Sort of a sad occupation for a Friday night, isn't it? Reading here all by yourself?
BETTY. I guess it is, in a way.
BILL. What's a good-looking woman like you doing out alone on a Friday night anyway? No offense, but...
BETTY. I'm out alone on a Friday night for the first time in a very long time.
BILL. Oh.
BETTY. You see, I just recently ended a relationship.
BILL. Oh.
BETTY. Of rather long standing.
BILL. I'm sorry—Well listen, since reading by yourself *is* such a sad occupation for a Friday night, would you like to go elsewhere?
BETTY. No...
BILL. Do something else?
BETTY. No thanks.
BILL. I was headed out to the movies in a while anyway.
BETTY. I don't think so.
BILL. Big chance to let Faulkner catch his breath. All those long sentences get him pretty tired.
BETTY. Thanks anyway.
BILL. Okay.
BETTY. I appreciate the invitation.
BILL. Sure thing.

    [Bell]

BILL. You weren't waiting for somebody when I came in, were you?
BETTY. No, just reading.
BILL. Sort of a sad occupation for a Friday night, isn't it? Reading here all by yourself?
BETTY. I guess I was trying to think of it as existentially romantic. You know—capuccino, great literature, rainy night....
BILL. That only works in Paris. We *could* hop the late plane to Paris. Get on a Concorde. Find a café...
BETTY. I'm a little short on plane fare tonight.
BILL. Darn it, so am I.
BETTY. To tell you the truth, I was headed to the movies after I finished this section. Would you like to come along? Since you can't locate a waiter?
BILL. That's a very nice offer, but—I can't.
BETTY. Uh-huh. Girlfriend?
BILL. Two of them, actually. One of them's pregnant, and Stephanie—

    [Bell]

BETTY. Girlfriend?
BILL. No, I don't have a girlfriend. Not if you mean the castrating bitch I dumped last night.

    [Bell]

BETTY. Girlfriend?
BILL. Sort of. Sort of...

BETTY. What's a sort-of girlfriend?
BILL. My mother.

[Bell]

BILL. I just ended a relationship, actually.
BETTY. Oh.
BILL. Of rather long standing.
BETTY. I'm sorry to hear it.
BILL. This is my first night out alone in a long time. I feel a little bit at sea, to tell you the truth.
BETTY. So you didn't stop to talk because you're a Moonie, or you have some weird political affiliation—?
BILL. Nope. Straight-down-the-ticket Republican.

[Bell]

Straight-down-the-ticket Democrat.

[Bell]

Can I tell you something about politics?

[Bell]

I consider myself a citizen of the universe.

[Bell]

I'm unaffiliated.

BETTY. That's a relief. So am I.
BILL. I vote my beliefs.
BETTY. Labels are not important.
BILL. Labels are not important, exactly. Like me, for example. I mean, what does it matter if I had a two-point—

[Bell]

—three-point—

[Bell]

—four-point at college, or if I did come from Pittsburgh—

[Bell]

—Cleveland—

[Bell]

—Westchester County?

BETTY. Sure.
BILL. I believe that a man is what he is.

[Bell]

A person is what he is.

[Bell]

A person is what they are.

BETTY. I think so, too.

BILL. So what if I admire Trotsky?

[*Bell*]

So what if I once had a total body liposuction?

[*Bell*]

So what if I don't have a penis?

[*Bell*]

So what if I spent a year in the Peace Corps? I was acting on my convictions.

BETTY. Convictions are important.

BILL. You just can't hang a sign on a person.

BETTY. Absolutely. I'll bet you're a Scorpio.

[*Many bells ring*]

BETTY. Listen, I was headed to the movies after I finished this section. Would you like to come along?

BILL. That sounds like fun. What's playing?

BETTY. A couple of the really early Woody Allen movies.

BILL. Oh.

BETTY. Don't you like Woody Allen?

BILL. Sure, I like Woody Allen.

BETTY. But you're not crazy about Woody Allen.

BILL. Those early ones kind of get on my nerves.

BETTY. Uh-huh.

[*Bell*]

BILL.	[*Simultaneously*]	BETTY.
Y'know, I was headed to the …		I was thinking about …

BILL. I'm sorry.

BETTY. No, go ahead.

BILL. I was just going to say that I was headed to the movies in a little while, and…

BETTY. So was I.

BILL. The Woody Allen festival?

BETTY. Just up the street.

BILL. Do you like the early ones?

BETTY. I think anybody who doesn't ought to be run off the planet.

BILL. How many times have you seen *Bananas*?

BETTY. Eight times.

BILL. Twelve. So are you still interested?

BETTY. Do you like Entenmann's crumb cake?

BILL. I went out at two o'clock this morning to buy one. Did you have an Etch-a-Sketch as a child?

BETTY. Yes! Do you like brussel sprouts?

BILL. I think they're gross.

BETTY. They *are* gross!

BILL. Do you still believe in marriage in spite of current sentiments against it?

BETTY. Yes.

BILL. And children?

BETTY. Three of them.

BILL. Two girls and a boy.
BETTY. Harvard, Vassar, and Brown.
BILL. And will you love me?
BETTY. Yes.
BILL. And cherish me forever?
BETTY. Yes.
BILL. Do you still want to go to the movies?
BETTY. Sure thing.
BILL *and* BETTY [*Together*]. Waiter!

BLACKOUT

(1988)

Questions for Discussion and Writing

1. The play was originally set at a bus stop. What does its setting in a café say about the characters?
2. At one point Bill says, "You have to hit these things at the right moment or it's no good." Explain how this statement describes the play's basic dramatic premise.
3. What is the purpose of the ringing bell?
4. Describe the play's plot. What is its central conflict and how is it resolved? Where does the climax occur?
5. In 2001 a theater company in Denver put on *Sure Thing* by using three separate couples, each with the names Bill and Betty. The lines shifted from one couple to the next after each ring of the bell. Can you picture how this performance would work? Try reading the play this way out loud in class. You can make it easier to follow if you put numbers in the margin of the script to indicate which couple should read.

Critical Approaches for Interpreting Literature

We are all critics. That is, we find ourselves in conversations about books, movies, and TV shows, conversations in which we express our likes and dislikes, approval and disapproval, often disagreeing with one another. You may devour romance novels in your spare time, while your best friend thinks those same novels are silly and a waste of time. Meanwhile, that friend seeks out the latest in experimental science fiction, which you find confusing and pointless. The two of you are coming from different tastes, for sure, but you are both taking different critical stances about what makes a book good. You value emotional involvement and absorption, as well as a satisfying beginning–middle–happy-ending structure, and that's what you get in romance novels. Your friend doesn't care at all about a predictable structure and an absorbing love story but values mental playfulness, challenge, and the element of surprise in her leisure reading. No one can say that one or the other is right. In using the word *criticism* in relation to the arts, we do not mean faultfinding as in everyday conversation; literary criticism has to do with interpretation of a work. Some literary criticism does evaluate or judge a work as good or bad, but appraisal is not the main point in most cases.

Just as friends can be separated into groups according to what they look for in leisure reading, literary critics can be loosely grouped according to what they look for in written works. They apply a systematic method to the interpretation of a piece and usually have a preferred method or combination of methods. For example, one critic may customarily think about a work in terms of how it reflects the historical period in which it was written, whereas another likes to focus on the images of femininity and masculinity depicted in the work. You can learn the various points of view that people use to interpret and judge literature. Probably some of them are the points of view you already use informally, and seeing them laid out in an orderly way will help you study and write about literature. You will want to be acquainted with all the standard approaches, because you need to match the critical point of view with the specific work you are studying. There is no one-size-fits-all option.

Formalism

A formalist critic looks at a piece of literature as complete within itself. The formalist approach appreciates the way in which all the features of a piece work together in a unified, meaningful whole. These features are, for the most part, what you study in this textbook: structure, imagery, character development, setting, language, and so on. The term *formalist*, instead of being directly related to the idea of formality, is related to the idea of *form*. In this book we encourage you to perceive the form and content of literature as deeply entwined. For example, on page 387, rhythm and rhyme are considered for the way they enhance tone and meaning. A prominent technique of the formalist critic is *close reading*, which we have promoted in this textbook as essential in making a first attempt at interpreting literature.

A strictly formalist reading does not bring in outside sources. The main tools are imagination and skill in analyzing the various features of literature. Support for an interpretation comes from evidence within the poem, story, or play.

Historical Approaches

In contrast with formalism, several approaches emphasize that the writer was leading a life in a certain time in history and that events in personal life and in the world affect the literature produced. Historical critics examine a work in the context of its time. They try to see the work as people in the original audience would. For example, Ibsen's *A Doll's House*, published in 1879, shocked its original nineteenth-century audience with its endorsement of Nora's self-liberation from a stifling marriage to a benevolent patriarch. Such separations are commonplace in our time, so it helps us understand the play to know that in its own day a sympathetic portrayal of Nora was considered outrageous.

Several types of historical approach are possible, focusing on specialized aspects of the past. These aspects may be biographical, cultural, or political.

Biographical

Diaries, letters, journals, biographies, and autobiographies are tools of the critic who investigates how an author's life is reflected in his or her imaginative writing. Emily Dickinson's hermitlike seclusion in real life often serves to help illuminate her difficult poems, because we can speculate on how her unusual solitude gave her an extraordinary point of view on things others take for granted or do not see at all. Similarly, we can appreciate Wilfred Owen's "Dulce et Decorum Est" more fully when we know that he served in World War I, was wounded in 1917 (shortly before the poem was written), and died in action in 1918. The powerful, detailed imagery of the poem is rooted in real-life experience.

Cultural

Cultural critics use materials beyond the standard biographical information and history books to examine literature. They are likely to look at cultural artifacts like the period's advertisements, architecture, journalism, campaign speeches, political tracts, fads, and popular literature such as comic books when they set a work in historical context. May Sarton's 1988 poem "AIDS" lends itself to such an approach, because it was written during the time of the nation's awakening to the horrors of the disease, and the poem draws much from the atmosphere of the era. A cultural critic might use various late-1980s journalistic writings about the epidemic, leaflets from demonstrations, and political speeches in analyzing the poem. A cultural critic would be more likely than a formalist to examine a work of literature in terms of its time. For example, such a critic might argue that Sarton's poem focuses on positive individual growth in the AIDS sphere, without mentioning the larger and uglier political struggle involved. Bharati Mukherjee's story "A Father" must be examined in terms of two cultures at two time periods: Bombay, India, at the time when the Bhowmick family lived there, and Detroit, Michigan, USA, during the time of the story, when the Bhowmicks have immigrated there. The clashes between the cultures illuminate the shocking family violence in the story if you learn about the battling conditions and beliefs in the two settings.

Marxist

Another historical point of view that may include judgment or evaluation of literature is the Marxist approach. Marxist critics take the stance that literature is an artifact of history, which is driven by economic forces and class struggle. They see the fine arts as frequently a reflection of the values of the privileged class, endorsing the status quo rather than challenging it. A Marxist critic would probably point out that Alice Walker's "Everyday Use" demonstrates the shift from a barter-based to a cash-based economy, in which a homemade quilt is detached from its natural purpose and instead elevated as a fetish, a work of folk art never to be used. Many works of literature do lend themselves to a more fruitful Marxist analysis; for example, one professional critic productively analyzes D. H. Lawrence's "The Rocking-Horse Winner" in terms of the parents' relentless, socially driven quest for more money and their exploitation of the child's labor.

Psychological Approaches

"The Rocking-Horse Winner" could also be approached from a psychological point of view. The family in the story shows signs of obsessive-compulsive disorder, in which people have uncontrollable, intrusive thoughts and behaviors that interfere with leading their everyday lives. Because a grasp of human motivation is key to understanding so much literature, psychology comes into play continually, and many critics make a practice of looking at literature through the lenses of psychological theories. It is difficult to discuss a poem like Robert Browning's "My Last Duchess" without psychoanalyzing the speaker, the Duke, who seems narcissistic as well as paranoid. Freud's early twentieth-century theories inform much psychological literary criticism, so explorations of characters' subconscious motivations, defenses, inner conflicts, and symbolic acts are commonplace. Frank O'Connor's "My Oedipus Complex" humorously hinges on the Freudian notion that little boys want to marry their mothers and be rid of their competitors (their dads) but eventually change their loyalty and identify with their fathers. Contemporary psychological research often comes into play as well, because literature so often entails emotional experience and its aftereffects. Louis Erdrich's "The Red Convertible" involves a portrait of post-traumatic stress disorder (PTSD), a common syndrome among soldiers returning from the Vietnam War.

Sometimes psychological critics use their tools not to examine the characters but to analyze the author in their search for meaning in the literary work, and in such cases their pursuit combines the biographical and psychological approaches.

Mythological and Archetypal Approaches

Another approach is related to mass psychology rather than individual idiosyncrasies. Mythological or archetypal critics look at commonalities among dreams, myths, legends, religions, visual arts, and literature, and they see the same threads running through human imaginative work throughout the ages and across cultures. One such thread, for instance, is the quest or journey, during which the main character is challenged sorely (often three times), gaining wisdom and insight along the way to a heroic ending point (or not, having failed the challenge). Another thread is the hero who dies for the salvation of all humankind. Archetypal plots and characters are associated with the theories of the Swiss psychologist Carl Jung, who believed that every person is born equipped with a collective unconscious, a set of images including many universal fictional characters such as the wise old man, the fool, the trickster, the manly rescuer, the earth mother, and the mysterious stranger, as well as others. Our attraction to certain types of stories and characters comes from the way they appeal to our collective unconscious. Arnold Friend, the menacing yet magnetic visitor in Joyce Carol Oates's "Where Are You Going, Where Have You Been?" can be seen as a trickster archetype.

Gender Focus

Drawing from psychological, sociological, and political thought as well as from literary studies, many critics in the twentieth and twenty-first centuries look at art through the lenses of gender. They ponder how sex roles, sexual identity, and relationships between the sexes affect the way that a work is written and read. A gender-based reading of Tillie Olsen's "I Stand Here Ironing" would emphasize that all three main characters are female, with experiences different from those they would have if they were men. Within the fold of gender-focused critics are feminist critics, who would analyze the story in terms of women's strategies to cope with their powerlessness in the male-oriented world. Feminists explain the disparate experiences of the sexes by analyzing the effects of the differences in power, privilege, and expectations. Hisaye Yamamoto's "Seventeen Syllables" is ripe for a feminist approach, especially for understanding the mother's motivations. Feminist critics are interested in the images of women and men as presented in literature, often pointing out negative portrayals of women that might otherwise go unnoticed.

Another gender focus involves the lives and lifestyles of gay and lesbian authors, characters, and readers. As a minority culture, gays and lesbians have a distinctive experience that has often been ignored, despised, or treated as exotic. These attitudes frequently affect the way they write and are written about (or avoided). Sherwood Anderson's "Hands" would be baffling without the allusions to fear-ridden stereotypes of gay men, especially gay teachers.

Reader Response

The critical approaches discussed so far share the idea that a work of literature has a meaning, probably one that is stable and coherent. The last two we will take up do not share this idea but focus on the variety of interpretation that is possible. The reader response approach accepts that each person brings his or her own experiences and points of view to bear while reading. No one reads a work in exactly the same way as anyone else, as you have probably noticed in discussions with classmates and friends. In fact, you may have read the same work differently within your own life as you get older. One of our colleagues claims that no one can possibly understand *Macbeth* before the age of thirty! Although reader response critics will not allow totally far-fetched interpretations of a work, they are interested in individuals' different reactions to ambiguous clues. For example, when J. Alfred Prufrock asks, "Do I dare to eat a peach?" one reader may think that Prufrock is worried about the embarrassing messiness of consuming a ripe peach, another may think that he fears looking greedy, and another may decide that the peach is a feminine symbol and Prufrock fears the sex act. All of these thoughts are defensible using other evidence within the poem, and all are probably projections of the reader's own fears.

Deconstruction

Deconstructionists take a step beyond reader response critics by viewing a work of literature as unstable and therefore vulnerable to being taken apart (de-constructed). Whereas formalists look for the way that all the elements

Credits

Sherwood Anderson, "Hands" from *Winesburg, Ohio*, 1919.

Matthew Arnold, "Dover Beach," 1867.

W. H. Auden, "The Unknown Citizen," copyright 1940 and renewed 1968 by W.H. Auden from *Collected Poems* by W.H. Auden. Used by permission of Random House, Inc.

Jimmy Santiago Baca, "There Are Black" from *Immigrants in Our Own Land*. Copyright © 1977, 1979, 1981, 1982, 1990 by Jimmy Santiago Baca. Reprinted by permission of New Directions Publishing Corp.

Toni Cade Bambara, "The Lesson," copyright © 1972 by Toni Cade Bambara, from *Gorilla, My Love* by Toni Cade Bambara. Used by permission of Random House, Inc.

David Bevington, Notes to "Othello" from *The Complete Works of Shakespeare*, 4th ed., by David Bevington. Copyright © 1992 HarperCollins Publishers. Reprinted by permission of Pearson Education, Inc.

George Bilgere, "Like Riding a Bicycle" from *The Good Kiss*. Copyright © 2002. Reprinted by permission of The University of Akron Press.

Elizabeth Bishop, "One Art" from *The Complete Poems 1927–1979*. Copyright © 1979, 1983 by Alice Helen Methfessel. Reprinted by permission of Farrar, Straus and Giroux, LLC.

Gwendolyn Brooks, "Sadie and Maud," "We Real Cool," and "The Bean Eaters" from *Blacks*. (Third World Press, 1991). Reprinted by permission of the author.

Robert Browning, "My Last Duchess," 1842.

Hayden Carruth, "In the Long Hall" from *Scrambled Eggs & Whiskey: Poems 1991–1995*. Copyright © 1996 by Hayden Carruth. Reprinted with permission of Copper Canyon Press, www.coppercanyonpress.org.

Raymond Carver, "What We Talk About When We Talk About Love" from *What We Talk About When We Talk About Love*. Copyright © 1974, 1976, 1978, 1980, 1981 by Raymond Carver. Used by permission of Alfred A. Knopf, a division of Random House, Inc.

Kate Chopin, "The Story of an Hour," 1894.

Lucille Clifton, "homage to my hips." Copyright © 1980 by Lucille Clifton. First appeared in *Two-Headed Woman*, published by The University of Massachusetts Press. Reprinted by permission of Curtis Brown, Ltd.

Judith Ortiz Cofer, "Latin Women Pray" from *Reaching for the Mainland and Selected New Poems*. Bilingual Press/Editorial Bilingüe, 1995, Tempe, Arizona. Reprinted by permission of the publisher.

Billy Collins, "Introduction to Poetry" from *The Apple That Astonished Paris*. Copyright © 1988, 1996 by Billy Collins. Used by permission of The University of Arkansas Press, www.uapress.com.

Billy Collins, "Sonnet," copyright © 2001 by Billy Collins, from *Sailing Alone Around the Room* by Billy Collins. Used by permission of Random House, Inc.

Stephen Crane, "War Is Kind," 1899.

Countee Cullen, "Incident" as published in *Color*. Copyright 1925 Harper & Bros, NY. Copyright renewed 1952 by Ida M. Cullen. Copyrights held by Amistad Research Center Tulane University. Administered by Thompson and Thompson, Brooklyn, NY. By permission.

E.E. Cummings, "next to of course god america i." Copyright 1926, 1954, © 1991 by the Trustees for the E.E. Cummings Trust. Copyright © 1985 by George James Firmage; "anyone lived in a pretty how town." Copyright 1940, © 1968, 1991 by the Trustees for the E.E. Cummings Trust. From *Complete Poems: 1904–1962* by E.E. Cummings, edited by George J. Firmage. Used by permission of Liveright Publishing Corporation.

Emily Dickinson, "Because I could not stop for death," "Much madness is divinest sense," "Wild nights! Wild nights!" Reprinted by permission of the publishers and the Trustees of Amherst College from *The Poems of Emily Dickinson*, Thomas H. Johnson, ed., Cambridge, MA: The Belknap Press of Harvard University Press, Copyright © 1951, 1955, 1979, 1983 by the President and Fellows of Harvard College.

John Donne, "Death, Be Not Proud" and "A Valediction: Forbidden Mourning," 1633.

Rita Dove, "Daystar" from *Thomas and Beulah*, Carnegie Mellon University Press, © 1986 by Rita Dove. Reprinted by permission of the author.

T.S. Eliot, "The Love Song of J. Alfred Prufrock" from *Collected Poems 1909–1950* by T. S. Eliot. Reprinted by permission of Faber and Faber Ltd.

Louise Erdrich, "The Red Convertible" pp. 1–16, from *The Red Convertible: Selected and New Stories 1978–2008* by Louise Erdrich. Copyright © 2009 by Louise Erdrich. Reprinted by permission of HarperCollins Publishers.

Martin Espada, "Bully" from *Rebellion Is the Circle of a Lover's Hands* by Martin Espada (Curbstone Press, 1990). Reprinted with permission of Curbstone Press. Distributed by Consortium.

William Faulkner, "A Rose for Emily," copyright 1930 and renewed 1958 by William Faulkner, from *Collected Stories of William Faulkner* by William Faulkner. Used by permission of Random House, Inc.

PHOTO CREDITS

Index of Authors, Titles, and First Lines of Poems

Note: First lines are set in roman type; all titles are italicized

Subject Index